MR. SOCIAL SECURITY

MR. SOCIAL SECURITY
THE LIFE OF WILBUR J. COHEN

EDWARD D. BERKOWITZ

Foreword by Joseph A. Califano, Jr.

 UNIVERSITY PRESS OF KANSAS

©1995 by the University Press of Kansas

Published by the University Press of Kansas (Lawrence, Kansas 66049), which was organized by the Kansas Board of Regents and is operated and funded by Emporia State University, Fort Hays State University, Kansas State University, Pittsburg State University, the University of Kansas, and Wichita State University

Library of Congress Cataloging-in-Publication Data

Berkowitz, Edward D.
    Mr. Social Security : the life of Wilbur J. Cohen / Edward D. Berkowitz.
        p. cm.
    Includes index.
    ISBN 0-7006-0707-2
    1. Cohen, Wilbur J. (Wilbur Joseph), 1913–1987. 2. United States. Dept. of Health, Education, and Welfare–Biography. 3. United States. Social Security Administration–History. 4. Social security–United States–History. 5. Insurance, Health–United States–History. I. Cohen, Wilbur J. (Wilbur Joseph), 1913–1987. II. Title. III. Title: Mister Social Security.
    HD7125.C573B47 1995
    368.4'3'0092–dc20
    [B]   94-39964

British Library Cataloguing in Publication Data is available.

Printed in the United States of America

10 9 8 7 6 5 4 3 2 1

The paper used in this publication meets the minimum requirements of the American National Standard for Permanence of Paper for Printed Library Materials Z39.48-1984.

To Robert Wiebe and William Becker: mentors

CONTENTS

ILLUSTRATIONS

FOREWORD

Wilbur Cohen was one of the most effective public servants of the twentieth century. What makes this book so relevant is its perceptive chronicling of the life of a bureaucrat–in the best sense of the term–who made a difference because he was a quintessential Washington insider, a man who not only understood the wicked and wonderful ways of Washington but whose belief that the democratic system could work for all the people who helped make it work.

Wilbur Cohen had the four legs necessary to move the ball down the field in the nation's capital: energy, expertise, commitment, and tenacity. He understood instinctively what too few presidents and politicians appreciate when they move to Washington: it's important–and enough–to move the ball down the field; it's not necessary–or possible–to score a touchdown on every possession.

By the time I met Wilbur Cohen, he was the Johnson administration's expert and a key congressional broker on Medicare, Medicaid, welfare, Social Security, and aid to elementary and secondary education. I was a new arrival on the LBJ staff, moving over from my job as Bob McNamara's assistant at the Pentagon to become the president's (and the nation's) first White House Special Assistant for Domestic Affairs.

Without question, Wilbur was the most knowledgeable domestic department professional (and later, when he became Secretary of Health, Education, and Welfare in 1968, the most knowledgeable cabinet officer) with whom I dealt. What made his expertise so precious was that it encompassed, not only a profound understanding of the fine print of social legislation within his jurisdiction, but also an understanding of political cartography that helped me and the Johnson administration avoid the political mine fields that have taken the legs off so many well-intentioned legislative proposals.

Wilbur Cohen's commitment was to use government to help vulnerable people. He appreciated the difference between the New Deal, in which he had grown up, with its focus on financial security and retirement, and the Great Society, in which he flourished, with its push for opportunity and investment in people. It was the difference between a hand out for those in need who could not help themselves and a hand up for those in need who, with the kind of support most Americans receive from their parents – education, health care, decent housing, for example – could be prepared to stand on their own two feet.

What was so special about Wilbur Cohen's commitment was that it was selfless. He used his talents and expertise to further programs he believed in, not to advance his own career. Because he didn't care who got credit for an administrative success, because he had no ambitions for elective political office, because he sought pragmatic progress, he enjoyed the trust of the president, the White House staff, his cabinet colleagues, members of Congress, and the committed ideologues on all sides of the social issues that consumed Washington in the 1960s.

His energy and tenacity were legendary. In all the many calls I made to him in the middle of the night or at dawn, he was immediately engaged, ready to answer questions, get to work, or argue with me as to why what we wanted to do made no sense. When I thought we had hit a brick wall on one of our proposals, or when I though we had blown it on one of LBJ's bills, Wilbur was ready with some cheer – and most important, with a way around or under or over the wall, or with a compromise that would move us a little closer to our goal.

At the memorial celebration for Wilbur on Capitol Hill after his death, I noted that upon his arrival in heaven, I was certain he would be telling God how to improve Social Security benefits for the older saints and how to set up a better disability program for angels with broken wings.

Wilbur Cohen's life is what government at its best is all about – helping the most vulnerable among us. This book comes at a time when we all need to be reminded of that. It should be given to every young civil servant on the day he or she arrives, fresh out of college, to begin a government career. In a few hours of reading this book, they'll learn more about public service than at any college or school or public administration. More important, they'll learn that each of them can make a difference.

For, when all is said and done that's what makes Wilbur Cohen such a success: he made a difference.

Joseph A. Califano, Jr.

PREFACE

Wilbur Cohen bounded off the plane and down the jetway at Logan Airport. Unlike the other passengers, who were somewhat tentative as they faced the uncertainties of a new city, he did not measure his step. He walked, with determined energy, straight ahead. Later, alone in a Boston hotel room, Cohen took out a document and began to read. It was late at night, but Cohen seldom confined his work to the standard working hours. As always, he was able to concentrate on the material before him even though it was written in the highly technical language that characterized reports associated with Social Security. On this particular evening in 1978, Cohen studied disability benefits, the topic of the moment in Washington.

The next morning Cohen got up early and ate a large breakfast. When a driver came to take him to his speaking engagement at the other end of town, he was ready. He made a fetish of being on time and was, as always, eager to face the task at hand. In Boston on this April morning Cohen spoke to a group of students about President Kennedy's social policy; Eunice Kennedy Shriver, the late president's sister, shared the podium with him. After the talk, the dignitaries, including Cohen, assembled for a luncheon. It soon became apparent that most of the people in the room felt slightly intimidated by Eunice Shriver, in part because one could not look at her without thinking of her family and its tragedies. In contrast to nearly everyone else, Wilbur Cohen felt little self-consciousness with Mrs. Shriver, and in a completely open manner, he introduced a subject that to nearly everyone was taboo. He talked about his father, a Milwaukee grocer, and described him as an intensely competitive person who did not like to lose. "He was like your dad, Eunice," he said, referring to Joseph P. Kennedy, Sr., whose presence, like that of her three dead brothers, lingered in the air about her, omnipresent but never explicitly mentioned.

This small incident reveals something of Cohen's easy amiability and his skill in putting everyone on an equal footing. He believed his father in Milwaukee to be as worthy of mention as Eunice Shriver's father in Boston. Indeed, Cohen's knack for ingratiating himself with a variety of audiences was a quality he had developed as a young bureaucrat in New Deal Washington, a congressional liaison for the Social Security program, a teacher at the University of Michigan, a high official in the Kennedy and Johnson administrations, and the dean of the School of Education at Michigan.

Wilbur Cohen's career spanned from the New Deal era to the era of Ronald Reagan. In those years, Cohen rose from little more than an office boy to become the Secretary of Health, Education, and Welfare, and he also was a key figure in the development of Social Security, which many people have described as America's most successful social program.[1] Toward the end of his career, Cohen also became an expert in other areas of social policy such as education and health care.

For all his activities and accomplishments, Cohen remains an obscure figure. Historians of Social Security or social policy know of him, but he is hardly a household name. I suspect that many people could place Robert McNamara, Dean Rusk, and Clark Clifford as members of Pres. Lyndon Johnson's cabinet. Far fewer people remember that in 1968, the year of the Tet offensive, the McCarthy moral victory in New Hampshire, the withdrawal of LBJ from the presidential race, the assassinations of Martin Luther King and Robert Kennedy, and the victory of Richard Nixon, Wilbur Cohen served as Secretary of Health, Education, and Welfare. Nor do most people know that with the possible exceptions of Pres. Lyndon Johnson and Congressman Wilbur Mills (D-Ark.), Cohen played the leading role in the passage of Medicare in 1965.

It is not my intention simply to bring Cohen back into the limelight. I think there are more valid intellectual reasons for studying him. In the first place, he represents a distinctive type of post–Progressive Era reformer. To twist the words that Richard Hofstadter made famous, Cohen was born in the city and moved to the suburbs.[2] Unlike many of the reformers of the Progressive Era, he came from a Jewish immigrant family and was the first of his family to go to college. Also unlike many of those reformers, who became interested in social reform through largely voluntary institutions like the settlement house, Cohen's interest in social reform stemmed from his college studies at the University of Wisconsin and from his work in the government. He sought fame and financial security, not through the worlds of business or politics, but through government service. Arriving in Washington in 1934, he eventually became the chief link between the professional economists and social workers who worked for the Social Security program and the politicians who served in Congress. For the twenty years between 1935 and 1955, he was a bureaucrat in what Louis Galambos has called "the new American state." Studying Wilbur Cohen therefore allows us to people the now faceless Social Security bureaucracy and to discover more about how it has operated. Such a study also provides a window on the process of state building.[3]

A second reason to concentrate on Cohen is that the details of his life help illuminate the politics of Social Security and those of the social policies of the Kennedy and Johnson eras. Many people will need a rough map of the development of the Social Security program to make sense of Cohen's career.[4] Suffice it to say that the program began in 1935 when Congress passed an omnibus piece of legislation known as the Social Security Act. This act contained an old-age insurance program that most people refer to as Social Security. Between 1935 and 1950, the old-age insurance program struggled to become established; in those years more elderly people benefited from welfare than from Social Security. In 1950 Congress passed a seminally important law that expanded the percentage of the labor force covered by Social Security and raised Social Security benefits above welfare benefits. That law began a long, incremental process of the expansion of Social Security benefits that lasted at least until 1972. As one indication of the program's growth, we might consider that in 1940 Social Security affected less than 1 percent of the nation's elderly; in 1970, 88.3 percent of the nation's elderly received Social Security benefits.[5] The growth of Social Security has another dimension as well. Over time, the range of benefits offered increased to embrace survivors' benefits (1939), disability benefits (1956), and hospital benefits (1965).

Cohen was little more than an observer of the passage of the Social Security Act in 1935. In 1939 he assisted the head of the program in doing some of the necessary background studies and preparing the necessary congressional testimony that led to the creation of survivors' benefits. In the 1940s he became a leader of a group of young individuals who formed the human elements of the "iron triangle," to use the political science term, that supported the growth of the program in the 1950s.[6] In that decade, Cohen emerged as a major figure in Social Security politics. He helped persuade the head of the Ways and Means Committee to liberalize the program in 1952, and he, as much as anyone, convinced the Eisenhower administration to support it in 1954. Along with organized labor, Cohen mobilized the political backing that led to the creation of disability insurance in 1956, and he worked closely with Wilbur Mills on amendments to the program in 1958 and with Sen. Robert Kerr (D-Okla.) on amendments in 1960. Then, in 1961, Cohen took over the management of Medicare, helping to write the legislation and overseeing its presentation to Congress. As an official in the Department of Health, Education, and Welfare, he also became deeply involved in amendments to the program in 1961, 1962, and 1967.

As this list of legislative enactments makes clear, the history of Social Security does not mesh with most conceptions of domestic reform. After its creation in

1935, the program has become largely invisible to historians, surfacing only in moments of high political drama, such as the passage of Medicare.[7] Through Cohen's life one can get close to the subterranean politics of Social Security, which although disciplined by the president and by partisan forces, has proceeded largely on its own. The imperatives of program development and the forces of continuity within the bureaucracy and the Congress have mattered far more than conventional political factors. At the same time, the process of program expansion has not been automatic.[8] People in Congress have needed people in the bureaucracy to give them a sense of the possible (how much can Social Security benefits be expanded this year without bankrupting the system now and in the future?) and to help implement difficult social projects. Through Cohen's life we can understand better the decisions that have shaped the Social Security program.[9]

Cohen's life thus permits an inside look not only at the politics of Social Security but also at other aspects of social policy in the Kennedy and Johnson administrations. Because Cohen began in the New Deal and came to full power in the Kennedy administration, he serves as an ideal figure through whom to study changes in social policy between the New Deal and the Great Society. In the 1950s, briefly out of the government and working as a professor in the social work school at the University of Michigan, Cohen had an opportunity to rethink some of the basic intellectual assumptions that he had inherited from the founders of Social Security, which led him to change his views on the function of welfare. Originally looking upon it as a monetary pension, he began to view it as a source of rehabilitation and renewal. Just as Cohen's outlook on welfare changed, so the basic focus of social policy changed between the New Deal and the Great Society. The former emphasized security and retirement; the programs of the latter stressed investment and opportunity. Cohen's experiences shed light on these changes that he helped to carry out as a member of the Kennedy and Johnson administrations. In particular, he took a leading part in the convoluted political dealings that led to the passage of the Elementary and Secondary Education Act in 1965.

Through Cohen one gets an impression of the 1960s different from the perception one receives from most historians who have written on the period.[10] In the first place, Cohen worked on domestic legislation, not foreign policy. He tried to pass programs that included broad entitlements for the middle class and that did not consciously differentiate people on the basis of race and gender. In his work, he put the passage of Medicare and federal aid to education in the foreground and civil rights legislation and the War on Poverty in the background, thereby reminding us that much of the 1960s social policy agenda was formulated before civil rights and antipoverty measures became major preoccupations. Indeed, Cohen's life serves as a case study of the ways in which the familiar events of the 1960s, such as the shifting of the civil rights movement from the South to the North and the escalation of the Vietnam War, complicated the politics of the programs first proposed by Kennedy and later enacted under Johnson.

A third and final reason for studying Cohen is that he illustrates a generational style that is an important element of postwar liberal reform. In common with many members of his age cohort, Cohen, born in 1913, possessed a sense of optimism that led him to believe that social problems could be solved, just as the New Deal had conquered the depression and the nation had won World War II. Like many Americans of his generation, Cohen had a deep respect for Congress: he viewed the political system as slow, imperfect, but ultimately benevolent. This fundamental approval of Congress made Cohen eager to join in the haggling between policy entrepreneur and legislator. He regarded congressional lobbying as ennobling, not sordid, work. It helped, also, that he entertained few doubts about the programs he advocated. As a longtime associate noted, Wilbur Cohen believed in Social Security deeply, "so he wasn't going through this business that many people do of searching their souls about whether they should be getting into something that is more useful or more exciting. He found it very exciting."[11] Unlike younger or older men, Cohen lived in a world marked by long-run growth and progress. Although reform moved in cycles, its general direction was forward. As Cohen put it, "A cycle governs society's affairs that limits how much can be done at any one time and leaves important things for the next generation to do."[12]

In this book, I seek to link the life of Wilbur Cohen and the pattern of American social reform. To be sure, the process has already begun since Cohen appears in many accounts of modern social policy. He represents the policy insider, one of the Washington-based circle of legislative strategists and technicians, to use James Sundquist's phrase, who fashioned the programs of the Great Society. Researchers interested in those programs discover that Cohen shows up in the archives, if not always in the newspapers. By putting Cohen into their accounts of particular policy, they demonstrate an understanding of the importance of staff work and of the fact that public utterances represent only the tip of the policy iceberg.[13]

The list of books in which Cohen has made an appearance is accordingly long and distinguished. In *Struggle against Poverty*, James Patterson tells us that Cohen, "informed, pragmatic, and persuasive," was "a key formulator and implementer of legislation under both Kennedy and Johnson." In an account of education legislation, Hugh Graham, describing Cohen as "the self-proclaimed 'salami-slicer' whose relentless incrementalism in social legislation was appropriately reflected in that metaphor," makes frequent use of him to explain the educational laws of the 1960s. Stephen Bailey and Edith Mosher portray Cohen "as one of Washington's most creative policy innovators," who played a vital role in the passage of the Elementary and Secondary Education Act of 1965. Martha Derthick, perhaps our leading policy historian, explains an important 1967 welfare law as a product of " 'the dynamic of the two Wilburs.' . . . Mills for the legislative branch and Cohen for the executive – pragmatists both."[14]

The fact that so many historians feel compelled to mention Cohen in their works on specific policies encourages me to write an account of the full sweep of his life. What follows is a sympathetic biography. I have tried to guard against uncritical admiration by relying on primary evidence to shape the narrative. In some cases, such as on the history of federal aid to education, I have had to use secondary sources to make sense of the primary documents.[15] To some degree, I have interviewed Cohen's family, friends, and professional colleagues, some of whom were very helpful in pointing out Cohen's weaknesses. For the most part, however, I have written this book almost entirely from Cohen's papers, from his published writing, and from his oral and written reminiscences.[16] In so doing, I have attempted not to put him at the center of the policy universe or to insist that he was the principal player in every important event. At the same time, I feel his story is worth telling, if only to add data to the extraordinary reconsideration of the welfare state that is taking place among historians, sociologists, and political scientists.[17]

At base, this book blends a portrait of Wilbur Cohen with a series of vignettes from what the *New Yorker* might call the "annals of legislation." I have tried to show not only the final moments of enactment but also the many dress rehearsals. The reader follows Cohen from his birthplace in Milwaukee, to his college years in Madison between 1930 and 1934, to his years in Washington between 1934 and 1955 working for the Social Security program, to his brief stint as an academic in Michigan, to his return to Washington in 1961 and his key role in the passage of education legislation and Medicare, and finally to his career as an academic at the University of Michigan and the University of Texas between 1969 and his death in 1987. Through the eyes of an influential individual, the reader can see the details of the development of key American social welfare programs by following the path of first New Deal and later Great Society programs from their ascendancy in the period between 1935 and 1967 through their often painful decline in subsequent decades.

ACKNOWLEDGMENTS

Ever since I first met Wilbur Cohen as a young graduate student in 1975, I have entertained the notion of writing a book about him. As this book has taken shape, I have acquired innumerable debts. These begin with the members of Cohen's family, including Eloise Cohen, Chris, Bruce, and Stuart Cohen, and Darwin Huxley, each of whom has taken the time to discuss the project with me. Darwin sent me many valuable letters and other family memorabilia. Bruce kept me supplied not only with letters but with photographs as well. Others of Cohen's associates to whom I am particularly indebted are Elizabeth Wickenden, who shared her personal letters and talked with me at length, and Robert Ball, who granted me a lengthy interview. Robert Frase, Merlyn Pitzele, and Julius Edelstein also contributed many useful ideas and materials, as did Dean Coston and Sid Johnson. I appreciate, also, the kindness of John Gardner, who corresponded with me about Cohen and granted me access to his interview in the Oral History Collection at the LBJ Library.

Without the active assistance of archivists and research assistants, I could never have completed this book. My primary debt is to Cindy Knight at the Wisconsin State Historical Society, who catalogued Cohen's papers in Madison and then graciously guided me through them. Her sparkling personality, combined with her professional competence and common sense, make her a wonderful person with whom to work. I cannot thank her enough for her help in Madison and for her subsequent help in sending me materials and checking the notes. As much as anyone else, she made this project possible. I would also like to thank Harry Miller at the Wisconsin State Historical Society, Mary Knill at the LBJ Library, and Thomas Rosenbaum at the Rockefeller Archives Center for extraordinary archival assistance. William Wheeler culled materials on Medicare from the Washington National Records Center; Kelli Keenan investigated archival sources at the Library of Congress; Christine Bogdanovich researched the background of the Experimental College; and John Sherwood made a heroic trip to Boston to gather materials at the JFK Library. All have my thanks.

I also received timely financial assistance from George Washington University, which granted me both a sabbatical and summer research money, and from the Lyndon Baines Johnson Foundation and the Rockefeller Archives Center. I hope the book in some measure repays the faith that these organizations have shown in me.

My fellow academics have also come to my aid. W. Andrew Achenbaum, who shares my interest in Wilbur Cohen and in Social Security, gave an earlier version of this book a particularly close reading. I am grateful for his sensitivity and insight and for his friendship over the years. Daniel Fox, the president of the Milbank Fund and a person who has combined the study of history and the conduct of public policy as successfully as anyone, also read the manuscript and offered valuable criticism. Odin Anderson shared ideas with me as together we worked on the life and times of Wilbur Cohen. Hugh Graham read the sections on education in a helpful and responsible manner. Mark Perlman read drafts of the early chapters with particular care. Chester Pach provided me with a scholarly forum in which to present the chapters related to the Eisenhower years, and at this session, Mark Leff offered perceptive and caring comments. James Patterson and Morton Keller commented on another paper, taken from the work in progress, and gave me considerable encouragement as did the group of historians associated with James Banner's Washington Seminar on History and American Civilization. The comments of Cynthia Harrison were particularly helpful. My friends Kim McQuaid, Leo Ribuffo, Blanche Coll, and Eric Kingson kept my scholarly morale high enough to allow me to finish the book. The interest of Mike Brown, Brian Balogh, Howell Baum, Frank Hubbard (who installed at least two of the computers that I used), Mark Graber, and Julia Frank (who provided me with hospitality in Austin) was also appreciated. None of these individuals should be blamed for any errors or infelicities that remain.

At George Washington University, I owe a considerable debt of gratitude to Dean Linda Salamon, Vice-President Roderick French, and President Stephen Trachtenberg, each of whom has demonstrated considerable interest in facilitating the research activities of the faculty. Michael Weeks of the history department staff ran off countless versions of the manuscript and performed other feats with humor and grace; he has my profound thanks. I want also to thank Mike Briggs of the University Press of Kansas. He is that rarest of creatures: an editor who can maintain his interest in a project over a long period of time and who knows just how to encourage his authors.

Finally, I would like to thank Emily Frank, who knows how to live with an academic, and to mention Sarah and Rebecca in print since they can now read their names. I think it particularly appropriate to dedicate this book to two of my mentors. Robert Wiebe got me started, and William Becker kept me on track. I owe both a tremendous debt of gratitude that I will never be able to repay.

1
THE EDUCATION OF
WILBUR COHEN

Wilbur Cohen respected history, but he romanticized his own past.[1] Growing up in Milwaukee, he regarded it as a place from which to escape. As he aged, his attitudes toward his hometown softened until eventually he came to regard Milwaukee as a launching pad of opportunity. This transformation in attitude coincided with Cohen's ascendance on the professional ladder: the more successful he became, the more he grew to like his childhood. Like many children of Jewish immigrants, Cohen achieved liberation from the world of his fathers by obtaining a college degree. During the depression years between 1930 and 1934, he met three professors in the economics department at the University of Wisconsin who transformed his life; John R. Commons, Selig Perlman, and Edwin Witte became mentors who provided him with a passport to travel from Milwaukee to Washington, D.C. Instead of becoming a grocer like his father, Wilbur Cohen became a government bureaucrat and a social insurance expert.

EASTERN EUROPEAN JEWS

Wilbur Cohen possessed an inner confidence that the details of his life would be the stuff of history, yet little in his family background differed from those of millions of other Eastern European Jews who came to America in the late nineteenth century.[2] The Cohen and Rubenstein families, like so many others, eventually settled in an American city and made a life in the retail trade. The Rubensteins, Cohen's mother's family, came from Russia, the Cohen family from Poland.

David (sometimes spelled as Davis) Mendel Rubenstein, Cohen's maternal grandfather, was born in Minsk, Russia, on March 3, 1858. Perhaps because of the pogroms in Minsk and throughout the Pale of Settlement in the 1880s,

Rubenstein emigrated to America. The exact date and circumstances of his emigration were unknown to Cohen. By 1891, however, David lived on the lower East Side of New York, working as a Hebrew teacher when he could and as a peddler at other times.[3] By this time David had met Sara Lifschitz (or Lifchiz), who had come from a small settlement near Kapulia, seventy miles from Minsk. Born around 1870, Sara was David's second wife. She bore him three children, including Bessie Rubenstein, Wilbur's mother, in 1891.[4] Sometime between 1893 and 1897, David moved his family to Milwaukee where he taught Hebrew at a school associated with a local temple and pursued his studies of Jewish history.[5] In 1897 he published a pamphlet, written in English, on the star of David, because, as he explained, "most of our brethren don't know its origin or its source."[6] David died in 1917, and his wife Sarah died the next year.

Abraham Cohen, Wilbur's paternal grandfather, was born in 1845 near Poznan, Poland, in the town of Steszew.[7] In 1871 he married Henrietta Hamburger in the mayor's office, and together they embarked on a long journey that took them first to Great Britain and ultimately to America. Following the available jobs for tailors, Abraham made his way to London and then to Glasgow, Dublin, and Edinburgh. Abraham and Henrietta Cohen had children at each of their stops. Caroline, who became a favorite aunt of Wilbur's, was born in Dublin. Aaron, Wilbur's father, was born in Edinburgh in the summer of 1887.

When Aaron Cohen was five, he traveled with his nine living siblings (he was the tenth child by birth order) on the ship *Furnesia* from Glasgow to New York.[8] The family spent only a little time there before Abraham Cohen took them to Indianapolis, where he joined a relative. His large family soon proved difficult to accommodate in small quarters, particularly since his wife was pregnant with yet another child. This child, who died as an infant, was born in Milwaukee, which proved to be the family's ultimate destination. The family went there for the same reason it had gone to Indianapolis: the promise of a job and the security that came from knowing that a relative was already there. In Milwaukee, Abraham Cohen worked first as a tailor and later as the proprietor of a small grocery store. Wilbur remembered him as small "with a beautiful white beard." In the manner of many Jewish patriarchs, Abraham conducted himself with impeccable dignity as his wife scrambled to do all the hard work associated with running the house and managing the family.

Aaron Cohen, Wilbur's father, grew up in Milwaukee, helping at his parents' store and attending the local schools. He finished high school before opening up a succession of grocery and variety stores. In the summer of 1912, at the age of twenty-five, Aaron Cohen married Bessie Rubenstein.[9] The couple had two boys: Wilbur Joseph, the first, was born on June 10, 1913, in an apartment over the family's current business, Coyne's Grocery Store, at 1674 Hopkins Street; six years later, Darwin Mendel arrived, also on Hopkins Street.

Aaron and Bessie Cohen spent their lives running small stores and moving their family to be near them. The first stores were located just to the north of the downtown district in an area traversed by the Milwaukee River and populated by Greeks, Italians, Poles, and Jews. In later years Aaron moved his businesses slightly to the west of the downtown, but all his enterprises were well within the city limits. In 1923 Aaron established the ABC Market at 2101 West Wells Street, which he continued to run until 1944. Named for Aaron and Bessie Cohen, the market advertised itself as providing quality meats, poultry, fruits, and vegetables and noted that hotel and restaurant supplying was a specialty. Aaron's sister Caroline and her husband Edward Goldberg ran a dry-goods store next door. With the establishment of the ABC Market, the family moved to the west of the city center although not more than a mile from the central business district. In 1929 the Cohens settled at 751 North Twenty-first Street, where Aaron continued to live until he died. Three years later, Bessie Cohen started the Wells Variety Store, a five-and-dime that was quite successful during the depression. This store remained in the family until Aaron died in 1977 at the age of eighty-nine.[10]

Wilbur loved his mother and feared his father. Bessie Rubenstein Cohen, the second of three children and the second girl, had the conciliatory qualities of a middle child. People who knew her invariably described her as easy to get along with and as patient, gentle, and sensitive. One of Wilbur's childhood friends remembered her as "benign and soft."[11] Cohen later credited his ability to work with a wide variety of people, many of whom could not stand one another, to attributes he had inherited from his quiet and perceptive mother.[12] Aaron Cohen was short and stocky, with a hairline that quickly receded to baldness. He possessed inordinate physical strength and stamina, and he admired those traits in others, becoming a devoted fan of the sport of boxing. He worked the punishing hours and performed the hard labor that owning a small service-oriented business demanded. He routinely got up before dawn and drove a carriage to the wholesale market to stock up on fresh fruits and vegetables; he thought nothing of lifting a heavy barrel of pickles. His domineering physical presence, combined with his tendency to be sparing in his words of praise, added to the uneasy sense of awe with which his family regarded him. When he did say something, he spoke in a loud and commanding voice that tended to embarrass his nonimmigrant children. His sharp temper created a frightening sense of unpredictability. As Wilbur remembered, "When he spoke he gave the impression that he felt very strongly about what he was saying. As a result, he was usually taken seriously, obeyed and even feared when he was angry."[13]

Over time Cohen revised the events of his childhood. As a sophomore in college, he wrote a paper that described the meaner sides of his life in Milwaukee. His father's desire to live close to his place of business, for example, meant that the family lived next door to a "prostitute in a cheap, dirty apartment house." In another family apartment on the east side of the Milwaukee River, Wilbur "watched the rats and the cockroaches which propagated so rapidly because of the sausage factory on the left of his home and the beer plant on the right."[14] By 1981, when he sat down to write his autobiography, Cohen noted that although the family lived "plainly," there was always enough to eat and they never regarded themselves as poor. Even though his father left the house very early, adding to his remoteness, according to Cohen, he inhabited a world that was not without its own sense of intrigue. The wholesale market had a "romantic character . . . lots of boxes and crates piled high and men milling around, so early in the morning when most men were asleep."[15] Even Aaron's passion for boxing acquired a retrospective charm for Wilbur Cohen. What some saw as a brutal sport, Cohen, who began to accompany his father to the fights when he was ten, claimed to enjoy as "one-to-one encounters of strategy and ability." To be sure, Cohen preferred the team-oriented American sport of football to the individually oriented and more European sport of boxing, yet he had overcome his aversion to it.[16]

By the time Cohen adopted such a benign view of his past, he knew he had successfully escaped it. In college, it was far less clear that he would ever leave the world of his extended family; indeed, until he went to college, he had never strayed too far from his family members. His grandmother Henrietta and his Aunt Caroline were constant presences in his life; in high school, for example, he often stopped off for lunch at his aunt's store. When he was about eleven, Wilbur began to spend a few weeks each summer with his mother's brother Harry in Minneapolis. He marveled at the sophistication of his uncle's household, in which, to his amazement, the members went out to restaurants.[17]

The Cohen/Rubenstein family in Minneapolis and Milwaukee was unabashedly Jewish, the family names immediately identifying them as such. As Cohen later told his children, "With a name like Cohen, people will ask you about being Jewish, and you should think about what to say about it."[18] Being Jewish, he noted, was something inescapable.[19] In Cohen's case, he and his family were not only identified as Jewish but they were also observant. His parents, according to what he could remember, went to temple on high holy days, if not daily or weekly. He himself went to religious school on Sundays and, beginning at age eleven, took special lessons in Hebrew from a rabbi, which served as preparation for his bar mitzvah in 1926.[20] Cohen said that at certain moments he even entertained ambitions of being a rabbi, perhaps stirred by stories his mother and grandmother told about the rabbis in their families, perhaps motivated by a genuine spiritual feeling. "I prayed to God as a boy," he later recalled. In what would be a common association for members of his generation, he equated his desire to be a rabbi with his interest in reading books. Becoming a rabbi was a culturally sanctioned form of scholarly pursuit, long before it became a common ambition of Jewish boys to get a Ph.D. and enter academia. In Cohen's case, there was the additional association between his name and the priesthood. With the name of Cohen, he wrote, "you are automatically accepted among Jews as one of the high priests of Israel."[21]

Despite these early leanings, Cohen's involvement with the formal aspects of Judaism did not outlast his childhood, and he eventually married outside the faith. His own children, products of a mixed marriage, felt that their father did not go far enough in explaining to them just how they should react to being born with the name Cohen.[22] In part, Cohen had no solid guidance for them because of his sense of himself primarily as a member of a profession rather than as a Jew.[23] As Cohen and his friends became more successful at their jobs and mixed professionally and socially with many non-Jews, they tended to downplay the Jewish content of their childhoods. In a revealing memory, one of Cohen's childhood friends recalled that the Cohen family was not overtly religious; their only major religious observance came during Passover, he believed. Wilbur had a bar mitzvah, he thought, only because of the insistence of his mother's family in Minneapolis. Indeed, the friend envied the fact that Wilbur's parents, unlike his, spoke with little or no Yiddish accent since they were both born in English-speaking countries.[24]

Neither Cohen nor many of his Jewish friends completely transcended their Jewish identities, however. In the highly acculturated words of one of Cohen's politically sophisticated college friends, "I am sensitive to philo- and anti-Semitism when I am exposed to it."[25] Cohen, like his college friend, had a keen sense of what he perceived to be anti-Semitism in the workplace, often attributing attacks on his work or the work of his colleagues as veiled forms of it.[26] He had little doubt, for example, that criticisms of him as an advocate of socialized medicine carried a strong anti-Semitic component, particularly when a critic lumped him with another Jewish bureaucrat and argued that a cabal was plotting to destroy the integrity of American medicine.[27]

For all his sensitivity, however, Cohen marveled not so much at the anti-Semitism he encountered as at the lack of it. Like other Jews who arrived at positions of influence within professional circles, he could excuse the slights he had received along the way because events had turned out so well. By the time he got around to composing his memoirs, he had come to believe that he had never felt discriminated against in growing up. Being Jewish, initially a disadvantage, became an advantage: "I was always accepted as being smart because I was a Jew," Cohen wrote. Even when people accused him of being a Communist, "it was assumed I was a very smart one!"[28] Cohen wrote these upbeat, ironically self-deprecating sentiments knowing that his own brother had had a very different religious experience. Darwin, who remained in Milwaukee, married a Jewish girl, and went into the meat business like his father, encountered overt and intolerable anti-Semitism during military service in the marines. He reacted with his own sense of irony and changed his last name from Cohen to Huxley, transforming his full name, Darwin Mendel Huxley, into a list of scientific geniuses. Even with his new non-Jewish name, Darwin remained far more identified with Jewish causes than did his brother Wilbur.[29] Darwin was quick to talk about anti-Semitism even though Wilbur never saw himself as a victim. On the contrary, Wilbur Cohen regarded himself as a twentieth-century version of a self-made American man who did not allow Old World labels to hamper him.

Whatever the place of Judaism in Cohen's life, his parents ran a recognizably Jewish home. Mel Pitzele, whom Cohen met in college, described a visit to Cohen's home in traditional and bountiful terms: "You come to Milwaukee and the first thing that you had to do was to eat. I mean a real Jewish kind of hospitality—every kind of food." Aaron Cohen would invite Pitzele to take some food home, and he would depart groaning under a load of sardines, rye bread, pickles.[30]

Furthermore, Julius Edelstein, Cohen's first close friend, was Jewish. Edelstein's parents had come to America from Russia and Lithuania between 1906 and 1908. In the early 1920s, Edelstein's father ran a tailor shop near Aaron's grocery, and the two families lived in the same apartment. A great one for making lists, ranging from his favorite high school teachers to the ten most important Supreme Court justices, Cohen ranked Edelstein as his top childhood friend, and according to Edelstein, the two were inseparable during their preteen years. A year older than Cohen, Edelstein assumed the role of leader, although in their childhood gang of two he took the rank of general to Cohen's admiral.[31]

MILWAUKEE LIFE

Wilbur and Julius went through the usual succession of public elementary schools, with their bucolic and patriotic names of Prairie and Jefferson, until Wilbur entered Lincoln High School in 1926. By then school had become the focal point of Cohen's life, dispelling any thought that he would spend his life in exclusive service to the Jewish community. Indeed, Cohen had never lived in a predominantly Jewish neighborhood, and in school he encountered a world dominated by Slavs, Germans, Greeks, and Italians. In the seventh grade, Italians constituted nearly 30 percent of the student body in Wilbur's Jefferson Street School. Although this percentage lessened through the high school years, the student body remained 20 percent Italian by the time he graduated in 1930. The second largest group were students of German descent. In all, thirty nationalities were represented at the Lincoln High School. As Cohen wrote, the very mention of the school sickened those of pilgrim descent because it suggested the "repulsive air of the European foreigner."[32]

Like so many other thoughts about his past, Cohen's recollections of the ethnic composition of his school changed over the years as his own sense of being an American changed. In 1965 he could sit at his desk and suddenly remember himself as a high school junior standing outside the windows of the *Milwaukee Sentinel,* watching the 1928 election returns. As the count revealed a Hoover landslide, Cohen recalled that he cried because he realized that Smith owed his defeat to his being a Catholic. That, said Cohen, was not fair. "I always thought it unfair to dislike people as a whole because of their religion or race or nationality," he wrote, at a time when much of his professional life was concerned with the passage of civil rights laws.[33] A few years later, Cohen spoke movingly of how Lincoln High School prepared him for the outside world, how it "reinforced the deep sense of friendship and gemütlichkeit my family found here when they came in 1892."[34] It was the oldest and roughest school in the city, according to one of Cohen's high school friends, where the football team called signals in Italian, but it was also a place where people of different nationalities overcame their differences.[35]

Wilbur's senior yearbook captured the sentimental aspirations that in later years he and his successful classmates remembered as the reality. The yearbook, which he edited, described the school as a "crucible" that forged the "frank clear-eyed American youth" from the raw material of European immigration, including "the artistry of the Italian, the adaptability of the Hebrew, the practicality of the German, the deliberation of the Anglo-Saxon, the industry of the Greek, the poetry of the Negro, the spontaneity of the Irish, and the mysticism of the Slav."[36]

When Cohen lived in Milwaukee, he had more than his share of doubts about the vision of this American youth, as his 1932 college paper demonstrated. Written in the scientific spirit of the pioneering urban sociologists such as Park and Burgess, the study featured a negative, even hostile portrait of the Italians whom Cohen met in high school: "Congestion, filth, dirt, ignorance, uncleanliness, vice, poverty – these describe the Italian and the communities in which he lives."[37] The Italians who lived in the city's Third Ward, near Lincoln High School, inhabited "crowded, unpainted, half-tottering bungalows fit for condemnation."[38] The air reeked from "the stench of garlic in salami sausage and the smoke of big, long black Italian 'rope' cigars."[39] The children ran around in rags and played with the goats who roamed the streets.[40] According to Cohen, Italian children posed serious educational and social problems for the school system. Parents, who were unschooled and ignorant in the ways of democracy, contributed to the delinquency of the children by lying to the truant officer. Such parents were "unfit for the industrial life of Democratic America" because they revolted against state-sponsored education, bred large families as a result of a passion that "knew no bounds or reason," and allowed their children to settle for any job that was available, no matter how unpromising or menial.[41] If the Italians were the urban underclass of the early twentieth century, the young Wilbur Cohen felt little optimism about their assimilation into the American mainstream. When the older Wilbur Cohen had a chance to contribute to the policy discussion about urban blacks in northern ghettos, he had long forgotten his earlier feelings about Italians.

By all accounts, Wilbur associated with few Italians during high school. By age twelve, he had a new close friend, whom he most likely met in school rather than in his immediate neighborhood. Hugo Autz was a gentile. His Austrian family lived in what Cohen remembered as a big house that was located on Prospect Street, a pleasant location near Juneau Park and the lake front.[42] Hugo, like Wilbur, was an achiever in high school, who became the president of Wilbur's senior class. Like Wilbur, he was short in stature: "We were little guys, both about five feet two or three," Autz later recalled.[43] The little guys formed a partnership that included managing the football team and selling stamps and coins.[44]

Neither rough football players nor handsome socialites, Cohen and Autz nonetheless achieved considerable popularity and influence in high school. Cohen was president of the student council, serving on that body during his four high school years. He also edited the yearbook, acted as master of ceremonies at the farewell banquet, and served as president of the literary society and as treasurer of the German Club. On the side, he joined a debating club, the Philomathians, who met once a week in the Lapham Park Social Center, for what Cohen remembered as extemporaneous speaking and discussions of current issues.[45]

On the margins of Cohen's high school yearbook, the girls wrote that he was short but cute, a good student but funny. Above all, he was, in high school parlance, a "brain." As one of his admirers wrote in his yearbook, "You may be small in stature but what you have in your upper extremity balances the rest."[46]

At a time when grades were, on average, much lower than today, Cohen seldom received less than a 90, and he excelled in civics, history, and English. He graduated eighth in a class of 112, and his principal told admissions officials at the University of Wisconsin that he judged him to be at the "top in everything, an honors student."[47]

Cohen's success in high school increased his self-confidence and gave him a sense of control over his destiny. His high school years began a process of separation from his father's authority and of disengagement from his father's business. He began to believe that if he could not match his father's physical intensity, he could nonetheless master the world with his mind. Graduating in 1930, Cohen presented the class gift in a speech at commencement and then spent the summer clerking in his father's store. Already, however, he found the routines of the grocery "dull" and claimed to "despise" the business world.[48]

Somewhere during his education, Cohen had discovered the special powers conferred upon people who gain control over words. Two years after graduation from high school, he found an opportunity to celebrate himself in his exuberant sophomore essay, extravagantly boasting of how his intelligence made him special. He may have been short, but "he towered intellectually over his companions." He may have been young, but "it would not be long and then he would be a genius. He thought he had the makings of an intellectual superman who would someday be the greatest figure in the world. He would be president of the United States; . . . he would be the outstanding individual in whatever he undertook. He was superior; he could do anything as well as anyone else and many things even better."[49]

The words were intended to be tongue-in-cheek, a self-portrait of an arrogant young man, and they were the words of a college sophomore. Yet they expressed the real feeling that Cohen, an oldest son making his own way in the new world, possessed the self-confidence to embark on an ambitious path of education. Not surprisingly, Henry Adams's *Education* captured Cohen's attention and influenced him. Like Cohen, Adams was on a journey between two worlds, traversing the path between the eighteenth and twentieth centuries.[50] If Adams, a scion of America, tended to believe that his life was a failure, Cohen, an offshoot of the new immigration, believed that he had an inner light within him, as he put it, the "germ from which leaders, intelligent men, even geniuses are made."[51]

In the spring of 1930 the egoist made plans to realize his destiny by attending college. He won the Harvard Book Award, a prize that the always self-conscious Cohen thought important enough to list as one of his three major high school achievements more than fifty years later. When Harvard showed no interest in recruiting him, he took a competitive examination at the University of Chicago and earned a scholarship to study history there.[52] Then, by chance, he heard about the Experimental College that Alexander Meiklejohn, the former president of Amherst and dean of Brown University, had started at the University of Wisconsin (he later claimed to have read about the college in a June 1930 *Milwaukee Sentinel* article). He sent away for more information; as he put it, in his best Henry Adams style, "In July by some good fortune an early mail brought news of an Experimental College and he set to thinking."[53] Perusing the catalog, he decided to go to Madison and talk with the people in charge.

He told the Experimental College official who interviewed him that he liked history and civics and disliked Latin and German. He said that he was most interested in studying economics and political science and hoped someday to teach political science, presumably at the college level. As befit someone so keenly interested in his special destiny, Cohen said that he enjoyed reading biographies and engaging in the process of debate.[54]

In September 1930, Wilbur Joseph Cohen, the son of an immigrant grocer and grandson of an itinerant tailor, left Milwaukee for Madison, and except for the briefest of vacations, he never returned. An important link in the chain of his life was forged. His brother, his father, and his mother remained behind, pursuing the commercial enterprises that had defined the Cohen family for generations; Wilbur J. Cohen moved along a track that would take him to Washington and to prominence in a professional, policy-oriented world. Milwaukee receded until it became a pleasant and instructive object in the collection of materials that composed Cohen's life; the world of Italians smoking smelly cigars and playing with goats became a city of "friendship and Gemütlichkeit."

THE EXPERIMENTAL COLLEGE

When Cohen came to Madison he felt uneasy. In his more insecure moments, he considered himself to be "uneducated," and, in the presence of so many people from New York and the East, unsophisticated as well.[55] Cohen was entering a scene that for him was almost completely new. He had never spent much time in the suburbs, let alone the bucolic stretches of a college campus along the shores of Lake Mendota.[56] Julius Edelstein was already there, one class ahead of him, but Cohen knew few others.[57] In time, however, he learned how to fit into college life. At a time when jobs were scarce, he developed contacts among his professors that enabled him to find work after his graduation in 1934.

The Experimental College was, in many respects, an isolated place. University of Wisconsin president Glenn Frank had brought Meiklejohn, who had served as president of Amherst from 1912 to 1924, to Madison in 1926 to start the Experimental College. Cohen's class was the fourth and, due to exigencies of state politics and national economics, also the last; it contained only seventy-three people, making it a tiny part of the university community. For this small group, the Ex-College, as the students referred to it, functioned as something of an honors college, and Meiklejohn's reputation attracted students from across the country. Cohen's class contained, in addition to the twenty-one people from Wisconsin, eleven students from New York City and ten from Chicago.[58]

The Experimental College became one of the permanent reference points in Cohen's life. He retained many of his friends from this period, including Herman Somers, who, like Wilbur Cohen, would eventually become an expert in social insurance. On a list of fellow students compiled years later, Cohen also jotted down the names of Ken Decker and Harold November, both of whom would be roommates in Washington, as well as Robert W. Frase, who later joined Cohen as a staff member of the Social Security Board.[59] Cohen also became an enthusiastic supporter of Alexander Meiklejohn, with whom he kept in touch for the remainder of Meiklejohn's life. Six years after graduation, Cohen still got together with his fellow alumni of the college when Meiklejohn came to Washington, D.C.[60] Experimental College reunions lasted throughout Cohen's life and continue to the present. Cohen invariably described his exposure to the school as the source of his interest in education and as one of the justifications for his later service as a dean of education; "The ex coll was a tremendous influence in my life," Cohen wrote his former mentor in 1962.[61]

For Cohen and many of his classmates, the Experimental College became an all-consuming experience by virtue of its intense communal nature. Students and faculty lived together in Adams House, a stone dormitory located on the lake shore. It was a beautiful setting, then and now, and it had a feeling of remove from the industrial and commercial sections of Madison and even from the main section of the campus. Students shared not only living quarters but also a common curriculum. Everyone studied the same basic texts and enjoyed a great deal of freedom to interpret them in a creative manner. The idea was to provide a common core in the students' education and to drill each of them in the processes of logical argument. Meiklejohn wanted to make the college "fundamentally a place of the mind" and to limit the students' ability "to wander about the college curriculum." He compared the practice of taking courses at random to "intellectual agnosticism, a kind of intellectual bankruptcy."[62]

The college curriculum lasted only two years, after which its members became regular college juniors. In the first year, the students studied fifth-century Athens, the golden age of Pericles. The students examined this civilization in all its aspects, working with a tutor who assigned them regular essays. In the second year, they turned to the study of contemporary America. Major first-year texts included Plato and histories of ancient Greece; in the second year, the students read such books as Lincoln Steffens, *The Shame of the Cities*, and Henry Adams's *Education*. Cohen later claimed that the integrated nature of the Experimental College was one of its greatest virtues. "As I look back upon it," he wrote in 1937, "one of the real contributions of the Ex College was that it gave the student a feeling for the interrelationships between the many problems of human living through the study of particular civilizations."[63]

The Experimental College week began at nine on Monday morning with the students climbing the hill from Adams Hall to the agricultural college building, which housed the college's only formal classroom. Each week in this formal assembly, Meiklejohn or another faculty member lectured on an aspect of liberal education. It was, according to Cohen, the "big event," the one most eagerly anticipated by the students.[64] Then, according to a contemporary description, the class heard a separate lecture, either on Greece or contemporary America, and participated in a group discussion. By eleven, the students were free to go to the library or, for that matter, to wander down the lakeside path and contemplate nature.[65] Tutorial sessions took place in Adams Hall with instructors who were rotated every six weeks.

Superimposed on this regular schedule were special events, such as lectures from other University of Wisconsin professors, including, in Cohen's tenure, sociologist Edward Ross and philosopher Max Otto. Special trips allowed the students to experience the shock of the modern even as they were contemplating the verities of ancient Greece. Harold November, one of Cohen's fellow students at the college, recalled a trip to look at a Frank Lloyd Wright house.[66] Cohen himself remembered a trip down State Street to the state capitol in December 1931, where he and his classmates listened to the Wisconsin Assembly debate an unemployment compensation bill. Both the bill and Paul Raushenbush, the field-trip leader, were to play lasting roles in Cohen's life.[67]

If one were to judge from the reports prepared by Raushenbush and Cohen's other tutors, Cohen did well at the Experimental College. A report, submitted early in Cohen's second semester, noted his tremendous energy "in the direction of collecting and cataloguing." He filled a paper on art history, for example, with an abundance of illustrations, and he began to collect files of current newspaper stories. The danger, according to the adviser, was that this "purely mechanical energy may swamp any reflecting quality he possesses." At the same time, Cohen, despite his fondness for the "grand and the pompous," took criticism well and wanted earnestly to improve. The adviser concluded that Cohen needed a more reflective, less kinetic existence: "He must be made to sit and think."[68] At the end of Cohen's first year in college, he received a laudatory report that emphasized his energy and vitality even though his advisers noted that his work was sometimes superficial.[69] At times he allowed his desire for external approval to overcome his efforts to engage in what his advisers called "fullest reflection"; he needed to think more deeply, they believed.[70]

In his sophomore year, he continued to draw cautious accolades from his advisers as he pursued his studies of nineteenth- and twentieth-century America. As in his freshman year, he persisted in compensating for his intellectual insecurities through sheer industry. John Powell, one of the instructors at the college, called him a "firecracker" who viewed the world in highly personal terms. In stereotypical language, Powell portrayed Cohen as a self-absorbed, self-made man: "It's what the world does to, and for, its Willy Cohens that excites him." As a self-made student, Cohen had many characteristics of the type, including "self-consciousness, pride in his rise out of the pack." According to Powell, Cohen was "terribly eager," as "bright and inquisitive as a happy little terrier."[71] Others were more reserved in their judgments, blaming Cohen for confusing motion with substance. R. J. Havighurst, another of Cohen's instructors (who later became a prominent sociologist at the University of Chicago), said that his writing was wordy and lacking in clarity. Havighurst attributed some of Cohen's bad habits to his penchant for activities, which left little time for reading.[72] In Cohen's advisers' final report at the end of his second year, they concluded that he was above average, a B student, but criticized his writing and thinking as disorganized. They believed, however, that with his "vigor and enthusiasm," he would have a "good career as a student." No doubt his "strong sense of the urgency of social problems" would help him in this regard.[73]

He was, in other words, someone who experienced ideas personally and who sometimes allowed passion to overshadow analysis. The papers that he submitted revealed these qualities. Skipping easily from ancient Greece to modern America in an early paper, "Conflicts about Wealth," Cohen argued that conflicts over wealth were inevitable and that the "rich class" was "practically dictating the course of life" in America and Europe. Only Russia offered hope, since "there are no rich in Russia that can use their wealth to obtain political control as well as social preeminence over the masses." Cohen claimed to be ambivalent about whether the rich should dictate to the masses.[74] A month later, Cohen wrote a paper on the theme of democracy, and once again, he transformed a discussion of ancient Greece into a position paper on the politics of contemporary America. Here he sought the same sort of balance that informed his views on economics: "I do not feel that what the world needs is a revolution. I feel that what this world needs is more careful considerations of its present situations and an attempt to better them."[75]

Cohen filled his second-year papers, written explicitly on contemporary American problems, with expressions of indignation over America's inability to come to grips with the depression. In the past, he wrote, he had been "wishy-washy" and overly conciliatory; now he wished to align himself with definite beliefs and political positions. It would not do to remain indifferent to the nation's problems just because his parents had enough money to send him to school and to feed his brother. Instead, "logic and a development of principles must take the place of laissez-faire."[76] For, as Cohen noted, "everyone knows we are in a depression. Everyone knows that there are close to ten million unemployed at present, that women and children are hungry, miners cold and homeless, and panhandlers walking the streets."[77]

During his sophomore year, as his papers indicated, Cohen became more self-consciously radical, perhaps in response to the way in which the depression worsened in 1931 and 1932, perhaps as a result of exposure to classmates with decidedly radical views. Julius Edelstein, a committed Socialist at the time who had helped to found the Student Socialist Club at Madison, claimed that Wilbur underwent "a transformation toward the left" at Madison.[78] As a student journalist, for example, Cohen wrote an editorial favorable to Soviet Russia. In prose that mirrored the essays he was writing in the Experimental College, he noted that "America is watching Russia, and Americans are interested in the Russians . . . even Wisconsin is interested in these newcomers. Russia presents a new situation to a conservative, slowly-changing world. It demands immediate action for social progress, instead of laissez-faire procrastination." The United States, in contrast, had "no plan, nor device to administer [social] knowledge for the benefit of the populace."[79]

Despite this dramatic rhetoric, Cohen, unlike many of his friends, could never quite bring himself to become a Socialist. For example, Harold November, with whom he roomed his junior year, helped Julius Edelstein run the Socialist Club.[80] Mel Pitzele, Cohen's closest college friend who lived in an adjoining room in Adams Hall during Cohen's second year, devoted much of his time to radical activities. So did Ken Decker, a close friend of both Cohen and Pitzele, who later lived with Cohen in Washington.[81]

Cohen, for his part, continued to support melioristic legislation, such as the 1932 unemployment compensation bill, known as the Groves bill, that allowed laid-off workers to collect unemployment benefits from their employers. In a sense, Cohen never got beyond the politics of the Groves bill, and for the rest of his career he attempted to keep the "machine working without any serious noises from within."[82] His feelings reflected not only an innate caution but also the practical circumstances of his life. During the summers, for example, the young Pitzele worked in the mills, just as his father had, and became involved in union activities. Cohen worked in the grocery store as the son of a small merchant; there was no union for him to join.

Although Cohen tended to shy away from direct action, he nonetheless showed considerable sympathy toward radical causes in his college years and even, on occasion, turned passive support into action. His main extracurricular activities at Madison were conventional enough. He participated in a limited way in student government and enthusiastically on the staff of the *Daily Cardinal,* the student newspaper.[83] In his second year of school, he was elected to the Experimental College's student council, and he managed his friend Pitzele's unsuccessful bid to become president of the sophomore class, running on a platform promising to abolish fraternities.[84] At the same time, he occasionally indulged in actions that took him beyond his tight circle of Madison friends. One such adventure involved an attempt to come to the aid of strikers in a southern Illinois wildcat coal strike called by the Progressive Mine Workers of America. In Madison, Cohen collected a truckload of food from stores and raised money to rent a truck; Pitzele, who was at the University of Chicago, did the same thing in Chicago. The two drove to Verdun, Illinois, where they were met by the sheriff, who refused to let them into the county.[85]

It was sex, as much as politics, that animated Cohen during his college years. His friend and fellow Experimental College member Herman Somers, who later became a prominent political scientist and social insurance expert, remembered him as a "very popular guy . . . a cupie doll type. One thought of him as being particularly cute. . . . He was always playing it for humor."[86] The Experimental College contained only men, but Cohen and his friends constantly sought the social attention of women. According to Pitzele, reflecting many years after the fact, he and Cohen enjoyed a "rich social life." Because they lived in single rooms, they enjoyed a degree of privacy and resolved that they would bring girls to their rooms on Saturdays. Girls were forbidden to enter dormitory rooms on weekdays, and all social encounters that took place on weekends were expected to be social rather than sexual. The strict university parietal rules applied to the Experimental College dorms, and Meiklejohn, not wishing to attract scandal and exacerbate his already growing problems with the university administration and the state legislature, did his best to cooperate with the administration. Pitzele and Cohen did their best to thwart the enforcement of the rules. Although the two friends seldom discussed their sex lives, Pitzele knew that Cohen had lost his virginity by his second year of college.[87]

Just as Cohen found a niche for himself in high school, so he became a consummate member of the Experimental College, unconsciously absorbing its attitudes and prejudices. He professed great admiration for Meiklejohn's book on the liberal college, writing in his major second-year paper that "I have willfully acquiesced in the philosophy which this great educational and spiritual leader has tried to experiment with." Cohen described Meiklejohn as "another Socrates" and repeated an important article of Experimental College faith.[88] Good teaching, of the sort that required a student to think, depended on a personal relationship between student and teacher.[89] Cohen's hero worship of Meiklejohn became the first in a series of intellectual and personal attachments that would guide his life. It is tempting to see this aspect of Cohen's character in Freudian terms. His father, by all accounts, was a remote and sometimes forbidding presence. Perhaps in reaction, Wilbur sought and found substitutes whose moral precepts and intellectual skills he could admire.

THE ECONOMICS DEPARTMENT

When the Experimental College ended for Cohen in the spring of 1932, he needed to decide on a major. Through his choice of the economics department, he fell into another distinctive subculture of the University of Wisconsin, one that also played a major role in his life. He decided to concentrate on the study of labor economics, a field in which Wisconsin had a deep and rich history.

Wisconsin's reputation owed much to the work of John R. Commons, who was well established as a campus legend by the time Cohen got to Madison. Within academic and reform circles, Commons achieved national fame for his work with the Wisconsin state legislature in the design and implementation of labor laws, for his academic studies in what he called institutional economics, and for his collective scholarly projects on the history of labor. A fragile and often mentally distracted man, Commons had arrived in Madison in 1904, having failed to secure a niche at Syracuse, Wesleyan, and the University of Indiana. At Madison, he enjoyed a productive career that lasted until his retirement in 1932.[90]

By then Commons had collected more information about organized labor in America than any other person in the country, which he published in the *Documentary History of American Industrial Society* and *History of Labour in the United States*. Because he was so busy and because he was often disorganized and unable to cope with the mundane details of research and writing, Commons turned each of these multivolume endeavors into collaborative projects. He edited and guided; his students and associates did much of the research and writing. In this manner Commons forged close relationships with his graduate and advanced undergraduate students, who not only got to work on important research but also assisted their professor in practical studies designed to produce labor legislation or to assist in its administration.

Regular Friday night dinners, held first in restaurants and later in Commons's home overlooking Lake Mendota, helped to cement the bonds between the professor and his students. Through these dinners, students got to know one another socially and to observe their professor in an informal setting as he ruminated about economic theory, labor relations, and the issues of the day. One observer described the events as a "sort of regular family picnic," in which Commons talked and the students reported on their research.[91] Commons himself described the experience as a "lap supper" and two hours of talk, which graduate students and senior economics majors and their spouses attended; as many as sixty people showed up on these occasions.[92] Students proudly wore the badge of a "Friday nighter" for the rest of their lives, some feeling, in the words of Commons's successor and one of his most prominent students, as though he were "a second father, unselfishly interested in our welfare, in and out of the classroom."[93]

In his senior year, Cohen took Commons's course on Institutional Economics and became a Friday nighter. "Becoming a student of Professor Commons opened up a comradeship with many people the remainder of my life," he later wrote.[94] For Cohen, the experience with Commons was "electrifying" even though he was an old man when Cohen came to study with him.[95] Retired from the university, Commons held the rank of professor emeritus, teaching an occasional class such as the one that Cohen took.[96] Even Commons's most extravagant admirers conceded that he was not a brilliant lecturer, nor were his classes well organized.[97] His fame as a teacher rested largely on his ability to inspire his graduate students and to create an esprit de corps among them. Many of his students left Madison with expertise in particular areas of labor law administration and with specific knowledge about a particular area of labor history. The Friday nighters formed the nucleus of a group from which many future leaders in Social Security, including Wilbur Cohen, and in the academic field of labor relations emerged.[98]

When Cohen was studying economics at Wisconsin, the work that Commons initiated continued through his students, two of whom, Selig Perlman and Edwin Witte, became Cohen's mentors. They worked on the third floor of the university's Sterling Hall, described by Cohen as a "dismal place, very unartistic." In this unpromising setting sat some of the nation's leading institutional economists, instilled by Commons with what Cohen called "a remarkable sense of competence and integrity about their performance."[99]

During Cohen's involvement in activities at Sterling Hall, the professors associated with Commons concentrated on implementing the nation's first unemployment compensation law. Their activities were typical of the interchange that Commons encouraged between the state government and the state university. Cohen, by virtue of taking classes from these professors, gained a privileged view of the proceedings. In 1932 the state legislature had passed the Groves unemployment compensation law. Cohen had written on the bill when he was at the Experimental College and had gone with Paul Raushenbush, one of its principal authors, to watch the state legislature debate the measure. Both Harold Groves and Paul Raushenbush were Commons's students, as was Elizabeth Brandeis, the daughter of the Supreme Court justice and Raushenbush's wife (not the first such partnership forged among the Friday nighters). Through Commons, Cohen got to know them all.

For Cohen the opportunity to observe social welfare policy in the process of formation mattered less than the opportunity to study the development of the American labor movement. Selig Perlman, a vigorous man of forty-four in Cohen's junior year, became Cohen's major professor. Beginning in his junior year, Cohen took courses in labor economics with Perlman and watched with fascination the performance of a man who shared many of the mannerisms of Cohen's grandfather. Like Cohen's grandparents, Selig Perlman was a Jewish refugee from Eastern Europe.[100] Born in Bialystock, Russia, in 1888, Perlman studied in Russian schools and then made his way to Italy, where he became deeply involved in the study of Marxism. Then he went to America, where he was told that he should go to Wisconsin and study with Commons and Richard Ely, one of the founders of the American Economics Association. He arrived in Madison in 1908, a small and rather ungainly man. In Madison, he studied with historian Frederick Jackson Turner and graduated with a B.A. in 1910. He then became a graduate student with Commons and, among other projects, worked on the *History of Labour in the United States*.

For the rest of his life, Cohen retained vivid memories of Perlman's classroom manner: Perlman closed his eyes when he lectured; his stutter called attention to his speech as did his "Russian, Yiddish accent." Perlman was in the tradition of the Jewish scholar who offered his commentary on the great texts, in this case secular rather than religious, and on the issues of the day. As Cohen recalled, "He walked in the classroom and started commenting on what he had just read in the *New York Times* on Mussolini, Stalin, or the American labor movement."[101]

In his senior year, Cohen resolved to write an honors thesis on an aspect of labor history with Perlman. At first, he thought he would concentrate on the women's garment trades, the labor end of his Aunt Caroline's dry-goods business.[102] Within a few months, he shifted his topic to the machinist's union during World War I.[103] Devoting long hours to reading documents at the Wisconsin State Historical Society Library, Cohen produced "A History of the International Association of Machinists, 1911–1926." Just as his second year paper at the Experimental College acknowledged an intellectual debt to Alexander Meiklejohn, so his senior thesis began with an explicit homage to Selig Perlman. Cohen described his acquaintance with Perlman as an "unusual stroke of good luck." In the thesis, Cohen explained, he "merely adapted Professor Perlman's point of view to the concrete developments in the history of the Machinists' union."[104] Perlman, for his part, liked Cohen's thesis enough to award it the John Landrum Mitchell Memorial Gold Medal for the Outstanding Thesis in Industrial Relations. In the best Commons collaborative tradition, Cohen's thesis also became a footnote in volume four of the *History of Labour* that Perlman and Philip Taft, later a distinguished academic at Brown, wrote.[105]

Not surprisingly, Cohen began to think of emulating Perlman and Commons and becoming an institutional economist or an economic historian. As an upperclassman, he became increasingly preoccupied with what he would do with his college education. In the fall of his senior year, he wrote his parents that the professors in the economics department kept discussing Roosevelt's National Recovery Administration (NRA) and wondering if it would bring America out of the depression. Opinions varied. Some observers emphasized the need for monetary reforms, others spoke of a permanent depression, and still others cited the inevitability of a revolution. Cohen worried far more about finding and keeping a job than about the revolution. He told his parents that among the options that he discussed with his fellow students were "civil service examinations for parole officers; teachers in the state prison; teaching positions in Alaska, the Philippines and the Indian Reservations; scholarships at Tufts College in Massachusetts."[106]

Cohen had already seen what the depression could do to people. He later cited three specific instances that underscored the brutality of economic conditions in the 1930s. Early in his college career, he witnessed a protest staged by farmers on the steps of the state capitol. Even yeoman farmers, it seemed, could not escape the dictates of the market. Closer to home, Cohen observed one of his uncles as he "lost everything. Wiped out . . . impersonal forces engulfed [him] to render [him] virtually penniless." Finally, and most vividly, Cohen watched as his father invested $600 in a bank only to see it go broke; by the rules of double indemnity, his father ended up owing $1,200. Cohen recalled his father "paying something like $5 a week, scrimping and saving because he didn't want to be a bankruptcy case."[107]

Cohen knew how hard it would be to find a job in the middle of the Great Depression, pointing to the fact that there were 460,000 college graduates and that after his class graduated, the ranks would bulge to 580,000. There were simply not enough jobs to absorb the supply. The NRA, Cohen concluded, offered little help. Unless it did more to increase employment and boost purchasing power, "we will be at the 1932–1933 level of 'prosperity' for a long time to come."[108]

Aware of the economic realities, Cohen nonetheless deeply wanted to engage in the academic life and to free himself from financial dependence on his parents' businesses. He simply refused to sacrifice the bookish habits he had acquired in college in favor of devoting himself exclusively to business opportunities. During his senior year, as he struggled to maintain the discipline necessary to finish his thesis, he spent at least an hour a day reading the *New York Times*. A form of relaxation, away from the pressing realities of relentless research files in the State Historical Society, his reading enabled him to keep abreast of current events of the early Roosevelt era – the elections in Germany, FDR's gold policies, and the latest chicanery at Tammany Hall. In the manner of his learned professors, he tried to analyze these events and, like John R. Commons himself, to apply his intelligence toward the solution of social problems. Cohen concluded that the nation might think its way out of the depression. He argued that "some principle, some institutions got us into this mess" and therefore some institutional changes would be necessary to get the country out of it.[109]

Engaged in this sort of intellectual pursuit, Cohen exhibited a marked impatience with his family. He told his brother Darwin that young people must come to understand the changes in society and "must make intelligent analyses of the causes of these changes." In language that mirrored the Commons approach to the solution of social problems, Cohen exhorted his brother to "study history to find out what conditioned the institutions that we have today, and how we can change them to better satisfy human needs." But when Darwin set out to study history in a critical manner, he would find, according to Wilbur, that his teachers would be of no help since the local authorities took the attitude that "America is the best country in the world, and you must not find fault with it." Yet the most important thing for every young man to do was "read, discuss, appreciate – to understand critically."[110] When Darwin tried to do exactly that, he received a close critique of his efforts that could only have discouraged him. Commenting on one of Darwin's letters, Cohen wrote his parents that it "was exceptionally well written from the interest point of view but Dar is a bit weak on sentence construction, apostrophes, agreement with the verb, and legible writing. . . . I hope he will make every serious effort to improve his writing and the expression of his thoughts."[111] In these and other ways, Cohen reminded his family members that he was educated and they were not.

Not only had Cohen been educated, he had also, although he did not know it in June 1934, made contacts that proved essential to his career. These contacts were near misses. If Cohen had been a year younger, he could not have gone to the Experimental College. In 1934 John R. Commons endured a car accident in which his sister was killed, and he left for Florida. Consequently, Cohen met both Meiklejohn and Commons at the last possible moment, at the end of their Wisconsin careers. Under the influence of these two individuals, Cohen took a series of courses, at a time when the economy could not have been worse, and laid the foundation for a successful career. Although he graduated with the notion that he would do graduate work with Perlman, another of his college contacts provided him with the basis for his first job, one that proved so absorbing and so rewarding that he never went to graduate school. Cohen's next academic appointment would, in fact, be at the level of full professor at a prestigious university, after a twenty-one-year period of on-the-job training.

WITTE AND WASHINGTON

Edwin Witte was the man who came through for Cohen. Forty-seven years old in 1934, he had performed a variety of jobs.[112] He was born on a farm in a rural, German-speaking area of Wisconsin in 1887, making him almost an exact contemporary of Selig Perlman. Like Perlman, Witte studied at the University of Wisconsin, with the famous historian Frederick Jackson Turner, graduating with a history degree in 1909. He then decided to do graduate work in history, but after Turner left Wisconsin in 1911, Witte switched directions and, again like Perlman, became a Commons student. In 1912 he put his graduate work aside to work as a secretary to a Wisconsin congressman although he eventually earned his doctorate in 1927. There followed a variety of public-service jobs, most of them in Wisconsin state government. Between 1922 and 1933, Witte served as chief of the Wisconsin Legislative Reference Library, taking over from the legendary Charles McCarthy in the task of supplying information and lending technical assistance to Wisconsin legislators. In this post, Witte worked on the Groves bill among many pieces of legislation. On the side, he taught classes in the economics department. Cohen later described him as a professor with "encyclopedic knowledge and with a perpetual scissors and indelible pencil in his hands and mouth."[113] Cohen claimed to have learned his system for filing information from Witte, whom Cohen described as "avid for information, absolutely unrelenting." Like Cohen, Witte also enjoyed a reputation as an exceptionally open and unpretentious man, the sort who took an interest in his students and went out of his way to help them. "You would think of him as an ordinary fellow who was working in a filling station," Cohen said.[114]

When Commons retired in 1933 he announced that Edwin Witte would be his successor, and in fall of that year Witte left government to work full time at the university.[115] There Witte found Wilbur J. Cohen among his students in a first semester course on government and business and in a spring 1934 seminar, Wisconsin Economic Problems.[116] Cohen impressed Witte, who later called Cohen one of the two best students in his classes that year, and "I have never had two such students since."[117]

After graduation, Cohen headed back to Milwaukee, and Witte went back to state government, called in to serve as acting director of Wisconsin's unemployment compensation program. On July 24, 1934, Witte received a long-distance call from Arthur Altmeyer, an assistant secretary of labor in Washington, who asked Witte to become the executive director of the Committee on Economic Security. Witte immediately cleared his calendar. Requesting and receiving leaves of absences from both the university and the Unemployment Compensation Division of the Industrial Commission of Wisconsin, Witte arrived in Washington on the morning of July 26, 1934.[118]

Arthur Altmeyer, the Washington bureaucrat who had placed the call to Witte, knew the route. He, like Witte and Perlman, had studied as an undergraduate at the University of Wisconsin. He was forty-three years old in the summer of 1934, a member of the class of 1914 in Madison. Like the others in Common's orbit, he made his way back to the university for graduate study in economics, becoming Commons's research assistant in 1918 at a time when his attention was centered on health insurance. In 1920 Altmeyer, like Witte, entered the Wisconsin state government, first as chief statistician of the Wisconsin Industrial Commission and then in 1922 as secretary of the commission. In the spring of 1933, Labor Secretary Frances Perkins sought to use Altmeyer's expertise in the implementation of FDR's National Industrial Recovery Act (NIRA), the centerpiece of the administration's efforts at industrial recovery. By May 1934 Altmeyer was back in Madison, ready to resume his duties at the Wisconsin Industrial Commission.[119] He had barely unpacked his bags when he learned that Perkins was trying to reach him, this time to offer him the job of assistant secretary of labor.

Within a month, Altmeyer received the responsibility of chairing a technical board to assist the President's Cabinet Committee on Economic Security; Roosevelt created this committee through an Executive Order on June 29, 1934, that Altmeyer himself had drafted.[120] Three weeks earlier, Roosevelt had sent a message to Congress in which he announced that he was looking "for a sound means which I can recommend to provide at once security against several of the great disturbing factors in life – especially those that relate to unemployment and old age."[121] Altmeyer set out to staff this effort, looking for an executive director who was to be in charge of making the studies that would lead to policy recommendations by December 1, 1934. The executive director had the power to "appoint such additional staff as may be necessary."[122] After considering an authority on health policy and an expert on industrial pension plans, Altmeyer, Perkins, and Harry Hopkins agreed to appoint Edwin Witte.[123]

Wilbur Cohen, a June graduate of the University of Wisconsin with a bachelor of philosophy in economics, was tired from the work he had done on his thesis and distracted by the question of what he should do next. He decided to follow his usual summer pattern of going to visit his mother's brother Harry and his wife Bert in Minneapolis. In late July, still uncertain about whether he should try to find research work with a union, or perhaps seek employment in a lawyer's office working on labor injunctions, or maybe begin a formal course of graduate study with Selig Perlman, Cohen returned to Madison. By then Witte had already left for Washington.[124]

"Where have you been?" Perlman asked. "Professor Witte has been looking for you." Cohen immediately got in touch with Florence Witte (Edwin's wife) and sent Witte a telegram in Washington on July 31. Witte replied on August 4, apologizing for the delay. He told Cohen that the committee's main need was for specialists in social insurance, actuaries, and lawyers. "It is probable," Witte noted, "that we have places for a small number of staff people to assist our specialists in any research they may wish to undertake." But the staff people had to be agreeable to the specialists. "I have a very high opinion of your ability and think you could do a great deal of work for us in the next months which would be very useful," Witte noted. He warned, however, that Cohen could not rate as a specialist and that Wilbur's Wisconsin background created an additional difficulty. So many people from Wisconsin already worked for the committee, wrote Witte, "that we have to be careful in employing many more people from our state. Frankly, however, I hope that I will be able to find a place for you."[125]

That was good enough for Cohen. Selig Perlman, Florence Witte, and Herman Somers encouraged him to go to Washington to talk directly with

Witte. Somers told Cohen, "You've got nothing to lose. If you went down and appeared on the doorstep, it might make quite a difference compared to writing a letter from Madison."[126] So Cohen appeared on Witte's doorstep. Cohen, who had never been east, hitched a ride to Richmond from Walker H. Hill, a friend from the Experimental College. The two drove through the Blue Ridge Mountains at night, Hill at the wheel and Cohen in the "cold rumble seat." They arrived at Hill's big white house in the morning, and Cohen sat down to his first southern breakfast of grits and other exotic foods, served by black domestics. Then Cohen boarded a bus for Washington and arrived on what he remembered as a "warm humid day in early August."[127] He quickly rented a room on Twenty-fifth Street, off Pennsylvania Avenue in the rundown Foggy Bottom neighborhood, for five dollars a week and went to see Edwin Witte. Although Witte was not very encouraging, he told Cohen to come back later.[128]

Then on Saturday, August 11, 1934, Witte called Cohen and told him to report for work on Monday. Witte felt confident that he could offer Cohen a job for $1,800 a year, nearly $35 a week, provided that Cohen receive political approval and the assent of the specialists. Witte expected the job to last only three months, however. Undaunted, Cohen applied for jobs elsewhere, including the National Labor Relations Board (NLRB), and, as he told his parents, "perhaps I could find something else later depending on my experience and contacts."[129]

Cohen resolved to go to the Library of Congress on Sunday and "begin reading up on social insurance to be capable of holding down my job." He wanted to know more about old-age pensions, unemployment insurance, and maternity insurance. "A broad reading all day tomorrow will familiarize me with the leading experts and plans in the field, a representative bibliography and terminology," he wrote his parents.[130]

When Cohen left for Washington, his brother Darwin had cried, aware that Wilbur's departure marked a point of permanent change in the family.[131] Even though Wilbur's job with the Committee on Economic Security (CES) was temporary, he had no plans to return to Milwaukee or Madison. He now wished to live in what he described as the "Roosevelt aura" and to contribute to the New Deal.[132] Besides, he knew from experience that there were few jobs at home, and he instinctively realized that he would receive more valuable training in Washington than he would in graduate school.

Once again, Wilbur J. Cohen had seized the moment. He graduated from college just when Edwin Witte, his professor, and Arthur Altmeyer, his future boss, had been called from Madison to Washington, D.C. "I was given the opportunity to participate in . . . the New Deal not simply because of my experience as a state official but more importantly because this experience had been acquired in a state noted for its progressive social legislation," Altmeyer later wrote.[133] By substituting the word "student" for "state official," one had Cohen's situation exactly. Along with his former professors, Cohen would bring Wisconsin's experience in social insurance to a national forum. As one of the last of Commons's students, he would be one of the first to make his career in Washington rather than in Madison or Albany or Columbus or any of a host of other state capitals. A few months after receiving his diploma, Cohen had already received a substantial return on the money invested in his education. His Wisconsin degree was his ticket from Milwaukee to Washington and to the very heart of the New Deal.

FORGING A CAREER
IN NEW DEAL
WASHINGTON

When Wilbur Cohen arrived in Washington, he knew a limited number of people—friends and professional acquaintances from Madison. Within five years, his range of contacts broadened, and he became an expert in the new field of Social Security. In a sense, he had intellectual property rights in this area, which was invented in 1934 and 1935 right before his eyes. After a crash course in Social Security that included intimate involvement with writing the legislation and shepherding it through Congress, Cohen remained in Washington as a member of the bureaucracy in charge of implementing the Social Security Act. As an employee of the Social Security Board (SSB), he was someone to whom politicians could turn for advice, secure in the knowledge that the adviser was not out for personal political gain. Cohen also took a significant step in his personal life: he found romance and married a Baptist woman from Texas. By decade's end, thoroughly established as a New Deal bureaucrat and Washington resident, he gave no thought to returning to Milwaukee.

THE COMMITTEE ON ECONOMIC SECURITY

In the summer of 1934 President Roosevelt asked the Committee on Economic Security to assist in preparing the first national social insurance law and put Secretary of Labor Frances Perkins in charge.[1] The committee submitted a report to the president in January 1935 that formed the basis for the Social Security Act, which Roosevelt signed into law in August of that year. This comprehensive law began the modern Social Security and unemployment compensation programs and initiated permanent federal grants to the states for welfare, public health, vocational rehabilitation, and infant and children's health and welfare.[2]

In the summer of 1934 Wilbur Cohen had just turned twenty-one, and his knowledge about these complex matters of social policy consisted only of what his Wisconsin professors had told him. When he heard that he would have a job with the Committee on Economic Security, he felt it necessary to go to the Library of Congress and read as much as he could about social insurance in a day, a desperate crash course that could not compensate for a basic lack of knowledge. Still, no one knew a great deal about social insurance in America because with very few exceptions it had never been tried in this country. In some ways, Cohen's lack of experience worked to his advantage; it enabled him to approach his work with an open mind.

Cohen was free to learn, constrained only by the need to remain alert for the next job opportunity. Washington, he realized, offered at least as much opportunity as did the cities of the Midwest; indeed, D.C. became a mecca for college graduates who wanted to establish themselves as government officials. Washington job aspirants in the high days of the New Deal in fact could arrange their social lives according to their alma maters. By Cohen's second day on the job, he had already met five acquaintances from Madison, some of whom worked in the same building. It eased the problems of transition, as did the reassuring presence of Edwin Witte who, like Cohen, was away from home and family. Early in Cohen's tenure, Witte invited him out to dinner and confided in him about the work with the Committee on Economic Security.[3]

Despite Cohen's ease in transition, he found himself close to the center of national power, and, combined with the strange surroundings, his new situation must have created a sense of disorientation. On Cohen's second day in the office, for example, he and Witte bumped into Rexford Tugwell, an assistant secretary of the treasury and an important member of the president's brain trust.[4] Harry Hopkins, the federal relief administrator and a key New Deal figure, was on vacation, and Witte and Cohen occupied his private office in the Federal Emergency Relief Agency Building on New York Avenue, only a block from the White House and connected to the president's office by a direct phone line. On Cohen's first day on the job, he accidentally picked up the phone and found himself instantly connected to the White House.[5]

Cohen worked for a kindly boss in an exciting place.[6] It was, as Cohen later recalled, a "heady atmosphere," and it brought back some of the sense of insecurity that he had felt during his first days in Madison.[7] Once again, he compensated for a perceived lack of preparation by working hard. He marveled at the fact that the official workweek lasted only thirty-nine hours. Government employees worked from nine to five on weekdays, with an hour off for lunch, and from nine until one on Saturdays. Cohen immediately began to put in extra hours in an effort, as he put it, "to get acquainted."[8] In later recollections, Cohen stressed the amount of work that he and his coworkers did. As he recalled, Washington "was filled with eager-beaver young people who worked ten to twelve hours a day, some days sixteen hours, and then four hours on Saturday and sometimes on Sunday to try to repair the damage resulting from the depression."[9]

Cohen was in an ideal position to work hard. He had no family and few social responsibilities. When he knew that he would have a semipermanent job, he moved to a boarding house in a nice section of town, just off Dupont Circle. For $3.50 a week, including linens, he secured what he described as an "exceptionally, clean, quiet, cozy room" that was only a fifteen-minute walk from the office. He still had much of his laundry done at home, shipping a laundry case between Washington and Milwaukee.[10]

Neither Witte nor Cohen expected the job to last very long. Since the president wanted a completed social insurance bill to present to Congress in January 1935, Cohen operated on the assumption that his job would end by Christmas 1934. Technically, he was employed by the Federal Emergency Relief Administration (FERA), the major New Deal relief agency. The FERA had enough money in its budget to bankroll the Committee on Economic Security staff, which at its height in November 1934 numbered as many as one hundred people.[11]

Cohen's actual job, besides running errands for Witte, entailed doing specific research assignments such as preparing reports on social insurance programs in foreign countries, and he began by writing reports on those systems in Italy, Switzerland, and Russia. As he later recalled, he would spend about a week on each assignment and produce what he described as "short, snappy memos."[12] Witte preferred simple facts to complex analysis; should anyone question him about the Italian approach to retirement pensions, he would have the information at hand. Cohen in turn regarded these tasks as opportunities to do pleasant reading and to gather information that might advance his career. "The reading is fine, and I enjoy it," he told his parents.[13]

Cohen described Witte as the "amanuensis" of the president's and secretary of labor's preferences. In this role, Witte frequently mediated disputes between different parts of the complicated Committee on Economic Security's apparatus. At the top level, the committee consisted of the secretaries of labor, treasury, and agriculture, the attorney general, and the federal emergency relief administrator. At a secondary level, the committee functioned through an elaborate series of outside advisory groups, including an advisory council, a technical board of government employees, four actuarial consultants, four advisory committees, and a committee on child welfare. At a tertiary level, the committee operated through its own staff, filled with people on temporary assignment such as Witte and Cohen. This committee staff, in turn, contained largely independent substaffs working on unemployment compensation, old-age security, unemployment relief, and health insurance. Friction between Witte and the substaffs developed almost immediately. Barbara Nachtrieb Armstrong, a lawyer from the University of California at Berkeley who headed the group investigating old-age security, considered herself to be completely independent of Witte, the committee's executive director, and had little respect for him.[14]

Working in this confusing milieu, Edwin Witte frequently found himself called upon to prepare basic memorandums on the fundamental questions before the committee. Witte and nearly everyone else put unemployment insurance at the head of the committee's agenda.[15] Thus, within a few days of Cohen's arrival, Witte asked Cohen to summarize the arguments in favor of an unemployment compensation bill that had been debated in the last Congress.[16] Witte found he could rely on Cohen for unbiased information, in part because Cohen was assigned to him directly rather than to one of the other parts of the Committee on Economic Security.[17] "Invariably," Witte later said, when he wanted some information, Cohen found it, "although very often I had no idea where he might be able to get the data wanted."[18]

Cohen also helped Witte field public inquiries about the committee's work. Like most experts, the professional staff members of the committee were not inclined to take popular advice. The popular demand, if a country so disparate as America could be said to speak in a single voice, was for relief in the form of immediate monetary payments to the elderly and unemployed. But the staff, many of whom were devoted to the principles of social insurance, wanted to create a sustainable social policy not geared to an emergency like the depression. They commonly differentiated contributory social insurance, a prepaid form of protection, from noncontributory relief, a stop-gap form of the dole.[19] In this regard, nothing so offended the professional sensibilities of the staff as did the Townsend Plan, and it was this plan that generated most of the letters to the committee.[20]

In August 1934 Witte asked Cohen to prepare an analysis of the Townsend Old Age Revolving Pension Plan. Unlike the arcania of unemployment compensation, which was accessible only to specialists, the Townsend Plan attracted intense national interest. Like many other Americans in the summer of 1934, Cohen had had personal experience with it. Once, when Wilbur was helping out in his father's store, a man came to sell crackers; the salesman brought with him a pamphlet explaining the Townsend Plan, a proposal to pay $200 to every

American over sixty with the requirement that the elderly person spend all the money each month. By the time Cohen got to Washington, the letters to the president about the Townsend Plan averaged 1,500 a day; every day, Cohen found dozens of these letters, many from the West Coast, sent over from the White House.[21] It was his job, as he explained to his parents, to analyze the plan so as to expose its "economic and social absurdities." Cohen believed that the measure could never clear Congress, would be declared unconstitutional even if it did, and could never be implemented because there simply was not money on hand to pay the fantastic benefits. This sort of work drilled him, as he put it, "in the fundamentals of economics and law."[22]

By the fall of 1934 Cohen felt as if he belonged on the committee staff, and he realized how extraordinarily lucky he was to have such an interesting job. His letters home detailed his delight. He wrote his brother with wonder about all the things he and his coworkers talked about, including "unemployment insurance, old age pensions, unemployment estimates, strikes, unionism, labor injunctions etc, etc. It's a grand time and a grand place—and to get paid for doing and seeing and hearing it all is like feeding a baby candy."[23]

At Madison, Cohen had taken on the identities first of an Experimental College member and then of a Friday nighter. His Washington experience remade him yet again, this time into a social insurance staff member. This change, however, was less abrupt, the need for a transformation less complete. Edwin Witte was himself a veteran Friday nighter. Cohen's social friends, furthermore, tended to be people like himself, transplanted Wisconsin students who saw the New Deal as an opportunity to learn about social policy and to launch a career. Even during his first weeks in Washington, he managed to make contact with fellow graduates of the Experimental College, attending a meeting with eight former students and two faculty members.[24] Harold November, a friend from the college, soon joined Cohen at the rooming house on P Street near Dupont Circle. In January 1935 they wrote Ken Decker, another Ex-College graduate, and invited him to join them as well. The three, living on different floors of the same building, often stayed up late into the night, reminiscing about the college and contemplating their futures.[25]

Cohen remained in close touch with his parents and brother. As during his college days, he felt free to offer his family unsolicited advice. He reacted with concern to reports of the family's inability to rent a restaurant that was attached to the ABC Market. Nonetheless, he advised his father to hold onto his various properties since he suspected the country was about to enter a period of inflation. "Money," he noted, "is the worst thing to have in such an era. Property is the best."[26] He also continually advised his parents not to work so hard and to better themselves culturally: "You must go out and meet people and enjoy yourself," he wrote, almost as soon as he had arrived in Washington. "Sixteen hours a day, seven days a week, 365 days a year in the grocery store won't widen your knowledge or give you enjoyment. I hope you will break away from the routine and dullness of the fruit business and give yourself a bit of personal enjoyment while you can get it."[27]

At other times he criticized his parents and his brother for being so unschooled. He ended one letter by chastising his mother for making seventeen errors in her last letter, mostly in spelling, capitalization, and punctuation. "Illiteracy is most obvious through correspondence," wrote the college-educated son.[28] Writing, he advised his brother, "is an excellent way to clarify one's thoughts and stimulate new ideas."[29] Cohen claimed that his brother did not write carefully enough or proofread his letters. Indeed, Cohen's instructions and exhortations gushed like water from a fountain: "Express your *own* ideas, paragraphing, and developing one idea after another as clearly and fully as you can."[30]

Cohen himself faced an educational dilemma. He had always thought that he would go back to school, but he found his job so absorbing and time-consuming that he began to postpone his graduate education. "No," he told his parents in November, "I haven't been going to school because I felt I could learn more putting the time in on my work. And I found that the additional time spent on my work was well spent. I've been learning a lot of new things—that one can't learn in school."[31]

On one November day, for example, Cohen rushed back from a union meeting to write a letter to his parents and have dinner. He had joined the American Federation of Government Employees, affiliated with the American Federation of Labor, and become active in its activities. After dinner, he returned to the Committee on Economic Security, where he continued his work of the moment, in this case compiling charts and tables on the older worker in American industry. Manipulating data, he gained practical experience in the use of statistical techniques, and he found this experience more compelling than learning statistical theory from a book.

Even as Cohen postponed graduate school, he never abandoned his educational plans. He became an auditor of courses in law and economics, and he continued to save money in the hope of someday spending it on his graduate studies.[32] "I hope to stay here until I build up enough experience and prestige (and civil service standing) to go back to school—on the money I save," he told his parents in the fall of 1935. "I now have saved $1,000 since I have been here and if I keep going at the rate I have been I will be able to go back to school and do my graduate work very comfortably by 1939."[33]

Wilbur Cohen thought of education as a way of gaining control over his life, and that idea explained his reluctance to abandon the thought of graduate school. When he envisioned the world, he saw a highly competitive place, in which, because of his religion and social class, he was at a disadvantage. He wanted to survive in this world and, at the same time, to contribute to it. In a letter to his brother, Cohen succinctly stated the resulting technocratic credo: "Our times are hectic times and we must be trained technicians if we are not to fall by the wayside. This is not only our personal responsibility to ourselves and to our family but our responsibility to society." By a trained technician, Cohen meant someone who worked with his mind rather than with his hands. The proper academic training was essential. When Cohen's brother proposed the idea of going to vocational school rather than completing the academic high school course, Wilbur reacted viscerally. It was a matter of status; the vocational school lacked prestige, and nothing could be gained "from a cultural point of view" by Darwin's attending it. For the Cohen family, heavily motivated by the goal of upward social mobility, a vocational degree brought nothing and accounted for nothing. Wilbur explained to Darwin that "college degrees, civil service qualifications, etc. etc. all recognize the value of *generally accepted* degrees and institutions."[34]

Even as Cohen urged his brother to join the white-collar mainstream, he instinctively realized that the role of a technician–someone who fixed things for others–suited a Jewish person better than did that of a frontline politician or bureaucratic manager. Voters did not want to see Jewish people as public officials, as Cohen learned from the example of his own father. Aaron Cohen, who had begun to take an interest in local Democratic politics, ran for the Milwaukee School Board in 1934 and met with resounding defeat. Wilbur J. Cohen said that his father's loss illustrated the power of anti-Semitism in politics, even in a state and a city noted for their political radicalism. "One must think very clearly on the issue of Jews in politics. There is no need to have illusions about what is possible. I have always felt that the less desires I had for power and prestige the better I would be. . . . With a name like Cohen there are certain definite limitations to activity."[35]

Stated this way, the problem for Cohen became how best to become a trained technician, and his assignment as a research assistant, in effect, solved it. He would learn what he could from his Washington experience and when the temporary assignment ended go back to school. Yet as the work ended, Cohen kept looking for ways to extend it, always rationalizing that he was learning too much on the job to quit. "Supposedly our jobs end December 1. But perhaps we will be kept on if the President decides he needs more information. . . . I'll probably stick around here anyway for awhile," Cohen wrote to his parents toward the end of November.[36] He realized that many of the key decisions, such as the type of unemployment plan to recommend to the president, had not yet been made. He also began to sense that some of the committee staff members might be kept on even after the committee's report was drafted, the background studies completed, and the legislation drafted.

LEGISLATIVE ANALYST

Cohen was kept on, remaining on the Committee on Economic Security's payroll through the winter and spring of 1935. His job shifted from that of helping to write the committee's report to assisting the Congress in its deliberations over the Social Security Act. The choice to keep Cohen reflected both his skill and his situation. Nearly all the experts on the committee staff, including Edwin Witte himself, had academic or other research-related jobs to which they needed to return. Cohen was available and, because of the work he had done for Witte, knowledgeable about the committee's report and the Social Security legislation. So he stayed, even though his job remained on a temporary and highly insecure basis. "There are very few people left on our staff and things are very rapidly dwindling," he wrote in March 1935. "I can hardly judge what will happen next."[37]

It did not add to Cohen's already fragile sense of security that in the spring of 1935 the Supreme Court invalidated key pieces of New Deal legislation. Not only did the decisions throw many New Dealers out of work, they also added to the fears that the Social Security Act might be passed by Congress only to be invalidated by the Supreme Court. Writing to his parents on Memorial Day, after the Schecter Poultry decision closed the NRA, Cohen estimated that 4,000 former NRA employees were looking for jobs, making his life "much more difficult."[38]

Even before the Schecter decision, Cohen reported being fatigued as the result of the flurry of activity that surrounded completing the Committee on Economic Security's report and presenting a draft of the Social Security Act to Congress. By March 1935 he told his parents that he definitely needed a vacation. In this respect, he manifested behavior that would be characteristic throughout his career. Although outsiders invariably commented on Cohen's constant energy, he actually worked in what he called "spasms," bursts marked by frenetic activity to meet a deadline that were followed by a down period of nearly total exhaustion. The spring of 1935 marked the end of the first great "spasm" of his working life.[39]

Even as Cohen expressed concerns about what to do next and claimed to be exhausted, he was already launched on the next leg of his career. As had proved to be the pattern, he did not recognize the importance of what was happening to him at the time it occurred. In the transition from research assistant to legislative analyst, Cohen had found another of the talents that he would translate into a successful career. In retrospect, he described the experience of observing Congress at work with a sense of awe: "Witte says, 'Go up and monitor the legislation,' and I'm 21 years old and all of a sudden I'm sitting in these rooms watching these heroic figures try to struggle with this thing for six or eight months. And I became a great advocate of the legislative process."[40] Just as Cohen met many of FDR's advisers in his work on the drafting of the committee report, he began in 1935 to meet and occasionally to interact with important congressmen on Capitol Hill.

The Social Security bill, or Economic Security Act as it was first called, traveled on a legislative route that would soon become familiar to Cohen. The measure went first to the House Committee on Ways and Means and then to the Senate Committee on Finance. Each of these important committees contained their share of senior representatives, many of whom, including the chairmen, came from the South. In the House, Cohen got to know Congressman Robert L. "Muley" Doughton (D-N.C.), who was famous among other things for his inability to hear; as the years passed, witnesses before his committee had to yell louder and louder to make themselves understood. At one point in the spring of 1935, Cohen delivered draft copies of model state unemployment compensation bills to Doughton, who looked at them and asked Cohen if they had White House approval; without hesitating, Cohen said that they did. It was the first instance that he could remember of serving as liaison between the executive and legislative branches of government.[41]

For the most part, Cohen sat and listened as others debated the details of a difficult and politically sensitive piece of legislation. He was in no way central to the process. Still, by May 1935 Cohen had made a significant contact with Congressman Henry Ellenbogen (D-Pa.), who asked him to help with a piece of legislation unrelated to the Social Security Act. Cohen began to spend evenings with a New York lawyer drafting a bill to create a rent-regulation commission in the District of Columbia. Ellenbogen then told him to write the committee report to accompany the bill. Although the report would appear under the congressman's name, the words would be Cohen's. Cohen, in fact, was writing legislation, work that he found engaging and worthwhile: "It gives one the opportunity to see just how the legislative process starts," he told his parents. Furthermore, he found that his stint on the Committee on Economic Security had prepared him well for this sort of work. Already, in the spring of 1935, he was settling into the role of Washington staff man.[42]

Whatever his level of skill, he still needed a permanent job, and logic dictated that he try to secure a position with the organization that would administer the new act. On Memorial Day, Cohen predicted that the Social Security Act would pass around July 1, the very day that his job with the Committee on Economic Security expired. The act itself called for the creation of a Social Security Board, whose three members would be appointed by the president. Cohen, in an ideal position to listen to the rumors of impending personnel appointments, heard that Edwin Witte might be selected to fill one of the positions. If so, Cohen believed that "I shall very probably get in somehow," and at a handsome salary of $2,600 a year, the level of an FERA research assistant.[43]

To Cohen's chagrin, the Social Security Act stalled in Congress, so he prepared to complete his assignment on June 16 and then take two weeks of paid vacation before going off the payroll. He told his brother that it would be impossible for him to come home because of his uncertain employment situation: "I hope to be able to rest up and seek some new work around here and await the passage of the Social Security Act from which there may be some work that I will be able to do."

Although battered by the unsettled job market, Cohen still had high hopes for success. His vacation, he solemnly told his brother, would give him a chance to trek through the Virginia mountains and take a self-inventory. In the pompous language that he often used in addressing Darwin, Cohen wrote that "much water has flowed under the bridge for me and I feel it is both fitting and proper that I should sit down to objectively evaluate my experiences at this time." He urged his sixteen-year-old brother to do the same thing, to "plot your sense of direction and be constantly aware of yourself as an individual – a personality in a world of masses of people." In the manner of Polonius, Wilbur dispensed advice freely, explaining to Darwin how to handle women – treat them with "fairness, frankness, honesty, and sincerity" – and how to appreciate the importance of family. Darwin should live with his family, "cooperatively, and sympathetically, as if engaged in a common enterprise." Even after offering so much of this advice, Wilbur felt the need to teach Darwin a lesson; because his brother did not properly appreciate his family, Wilbur refused to send him a birthday present.[44] The worldly Wilbur celebrated his own twenty-second birthday in style. He double-dated with Ken Decker, his friend and roommate, and the foursome went out for dinner and dancing. During a hilarious evening, they exchanged drinks with a merry group of visiting Shriners, dressed in funny Egyptian hats. Cohen, unwilling to give himself completely over to frivolity, saw the date not only as commemorating his birthday but also as marking the first anniversary of his graduation from college.

As the July deadline approached, Cohen negotiated with his Washington contacts over a suitable job. Edwin Witte recommended Cohen for a post with the International Labor Office in Geneva. Cohen himself thought he might receive an offer from the Federal Emergency Relief Agency, which, more than two years into the New Deal, continued to dispense aid to a far-from-recovered work force.[45] As it turned out, he did not need to pursue either of these opportunities since he received a grant from the Social Science Research Council that enabled him to continue his work with the Committee on Economic Security. According to Witte, the council had been anxious to undertake research in social insurance and in the summer of 1935 created a special committee for this purpose. Cohen, who was to perform research for this committee, went on its payroll on August 1, 1935.[46]

Actual passage of the Social Security Act dragged on through the summer. A filibuster by Sen. Huey Long (D-La.) meant that the Senate did not even take up the bill until June 14. A stalemate in conference over the right of private employers with their own pension plans to opt out of old-age insurance created further delays, and the president did not sign the legislation until August 14, 1935. By then it was too late to pass the appropriations necessary to fund the new Social Security Board. The board operated under makeshift arrangements, with office equipment and personnel from the National Recovery Administration and with a special grant from the Federal Emergency Relief Administration. The fact that Cohen was paid by the Social Science Research Council eased some of the financial burden.[47]

As the Social Security bill neared passage, Cohen felt a mounting sense of excitement. On August 10, just four days before passage, he told his parents that he was "on my toes for whatever happens here. . . . I am like a busybody who wants to know everything that is going on."[48] Soon after the bill's passage, Cohen naturally began to speculate on just what sort of assignment he would receive. On August 23 Cohen was working in his office in the Municipal Auditorium at Nineteenth and E Streets. One of less than fifteen people still associated in some manner with the Committee on Economic Security, he knew that the Senate had confirmed the three members of the Social Security Board. The phone rang. Leona MacKinnon, Arthur Altmeyer's secretary, called to say that Altmeyer, one of the three members of the board, wanted Cohen to come to the Department of Labor. Along with Martha Ring, who had also worked with Witte on the Committee on Economic Security, Cohen, carrying a typewriter, papers, and charts, got into a taxicab and rode to the Department of Labor, where MacKinnon told Cohen to start working in a

Arthur Altmeyer, head of the Social Security program from 1937 to 1953, became almost like a father to Cohen. As Altmeyer's assistant, Cohen learned the intricacies of the program and perfected his skills as a legislative liaison. (Courtesy of the Social Security Administration)

room on the third floor. Although paid by the Social Science Research Council, he now belonged to the instantly created Social Security Board.[49]

ALTMEYER AND THE SOCIAL SECURITY BOARD

By September 1935 Cohen received assurances that he would become a permanent employee of the Social Security Board. He hoped to receive the necessary

Civil Service rating to qualify for $3,200 a year, and he expected to concentrate his energies on unemployment compensation.[50] Although he would report to Merrill G. Murray, acting director of the Bureau of Unemployment Compensation, he continued to do odd jobs for Arthur Altmeyer, which, he explained, "keeps me close to the inside workings."[51] In fact, he ended up working more for Altmeyer than for Murray. Under Altmeyer's supervision, he studied state unemployment compensation laws and prepared estimates of the amounts Congress should appropriate for the various welfare programs.[52]

Cohen sat in a large room on the same floor of the Department of Labor as Secretary Frances Perkins. On Saturday afternoons and at other odd times, he would often be the only one in the office, and occasionally he would field an important inquiry from a leading state official. In one instance, for example, he took a call from the governor of Utah who asked a technical question about welfare that Cohen was able to answer.[53]

In his new job, Cohen experienced the sense of insecurity that attended the beginning of each of his new projects, but in this case it quickly evaporated. "Until I feel secure enough, I will stick around here," he told his parents in September. "I want always to be ready for the occasion. When other people are out of town, sick, or absent, I am called upon to fill their shoes and this gives me my chance to show myself. You know how true it is that when you're on the spot you are very likely to get the breaks."[54] Many years after the fact, his friend Merlyn Pitzele observed that when Cohen came to Washington, "there was something Sammy Glickish about him." Then he realized that he had something to offer the Social Security Board, and he underwent what Pitzele regarded as an "abrupt" personality change.[55] No longer quite so uptight and eager to please, he reverted to the easy and outgoing personality his friends had known in Madison. "He was a very gay boy," according to Herman Somers.[56]

Even as he slipped into his new life, Cohen resolutely refused to make long-term plans. His parents sent him information about buying an annuity from an insurance company, and he told them that he was not interested. Instead, he talked about spending money to travel and to buy books and of his need for freedom. He said that he did not want to evade his responsibilities, yet neither did he want to be burdened by the annual payments. His "entire plans," he stressed, "were as yet unformulated."[57]

Although Cohen could not have known it in the fall of 1935, his entire plans for the next twenty years were nearly complete. He had found a niche as a staff member of the Social Security Board. His attachment to Milwaukee and his family loosened. He ate his 1935 Thanksgiving dinner not with his family but with friends at a farm in the Virginia countryside, and then he and his roommate Harold November took the train to New York City. Cohen described it as

A young Wilbur Cohen confers with Maurine Mulliner in the offices of the Social Security Board. Mulliner became a lifelong friend who hosted parties for Cohen after each of his three swearing-in ceremonies in the 1960s. (Courtesy of Bruce Cohen)

"a continent unto itself . . . alive with issues, struggles, people." It was impossible to appreciate the simplicity of the Midwest without first experiencing the bustle of New York: "It is part of everyone's education to see and get to know it."[58]

Even though Cohen constantly dropped these sorts of hints in his letters home, his parents remained resolutely uneducated, and their attitudes began to grate on him. When his mother wrote that one of his friends would find work because God was merciful, Cohen snapped, "One cannot put one's hope in the Lord nor can one just hope on nothing. . . . There is no God that is not made by man. There is no hope that is not made by man." The religion of New Deal social engineering must replace the false pieties of traditional religion: "We must have faith in *men* that they will so reorganize the social system that all of us can live intelligent, significant lives," he preached.[59] At the same time, he appreciated reminders of home, such as the cakes and baskets of fruit from the store, and when it came time for rest and relaxation, he headed home. By the end of

1935, however, he no longer took his place in the store; instead he had earned the right, as he put it, "just to lounge around." He was a visitor.[60]

Throughout 1936 Cohen concentrated his work on unemployment compensation and, to a limited degree, on old-age insurance. Free to travel, he went on assignment to North Carolina to explain the complexities of unemployment compensation to state officials. As the legislature passed the state's unemployment compensation law, Cohen played the role of technical adviser, describing how other states handled the technical details of unemployment compensation and how federal officials would view the various parts of the state's law.[61] He also helped to sort out the thousands of details that attended the beginnings of payroll tax collections for old-age insurance from employees in January 1937. He explored the possibility, for example, of giving workers a passbook in which they could paste stamps to signify their contributions to the Social Security fund.[62]

Emerging as an important figure in the organization, Cohen still had his doubts about the direction of his career. In the summer of 1936, turning twenty-three, he subjected himself to intense self-scrutiny. As usual, his thoughts turned to the prospect of beginning graduate studies in the fall; as usual, he found his work more of a draw than the notion of returning to school.

Part of Washington's attraction that summer was the prospect of being close to the presidential campaign. Cohen's father, in his role as minor politician, was selected as an alternate to the Democratic convention in Philadelphia, and Cohen, as always, offered advice freely to his neophyte political dad. The convention, he said, would have to defer to James Farley and the president on the platform. Still, the delegates had an obligation to exert pressure for "a progressive, liberal and socially-minded platform." In Cohen's mind, such a platform should include "*adequate* Federal relief and social security. Higher income and inheritance taxes. A constitutional amendment to give us State *and* Federal legislation of a social and economic character." He also stressed the need to "curtail the huge expenditures for military and naval purposes and give more relief to the unemployed."[63] As these sentiments revealed, he identified himself as an enthusiastic, liberal New Dealer.

As it turned out, Social Security played a part in the 1936 campaign, and the issue settled itself in such a way that Cohen resolved any remaining doubts about his career. Late in September, Republican candidate Alfred Landon attacked Social Security as "unjust, unworkable, stupidly drafted, and wastefully financed."[64] Landon's attacks prompted the resignation of John Winant as chairman of the Social Security Board, who then offered his services to the Roosevelt campaign in order to defend the Social Security program.[65] A few days before the election, Cohen went to New York where he and Social Security actuary Robert Myers met in a hotel room with Winant. Murray Latimer, director of the board's Bureau of Old-Age Benefits, and presidential adviser Benjamin Cohen also attended the meeting. According to Wilbur Cohen, this group wrote speeches and supplied information about Social Security that the Democrats could use. It was not the last time that the nonpartisan Social Security administration shaded into partisan politics.[66]

With the resignation of Winant, the president appointed Arthur Altmeyer as acting chairman of the Social Security Board. From that date forward, Altmeyer chaired the three-member board that served as a quasi-judicial policymaking body, establishing the rules governing Social Security, unemployment, and welfare programs. Each of the operating and service bureaus reported to Altmeyer and the board.[67] Cohen, with his Wisconsin connections, had already developed a working relationship with Altmeyer and as early as June 1936 described himself as a special assistant to him.[68] When Winant resigned, Cohen moved into an office that connected with Altmeyer's and immediately set out to make himself indispensable. After the campaign, in February 1937, Altmeyer became the board's second permanent chairman. Cohen, who had once been a staff assistant to Edwin Witte, formally joined Altmeyer's staff. From the position of associate economic analyst, Cohen became the technical adviser to the chairman and also acquired an important organizational identity as Chairman Altmeyer's right-hand man; his career as a Social Security bureaucrat was firmly launched.

Wilbur J. Cohen had much to offer Arthur J. Altmeyer. Where Altmeyer was somewhat dour, Cohen was exuberant; where Altmeyer was somewhat impatient with the reassurances demanded by politicians, Cohen learned how to flatter them. Although Altmeyer's institutional knowledge undoubtedly exceeded Cohen's, Cohen also knew a great deal about the Social Security program. By the end of 1936, he could, for example, write to Congressman Ellenbogen on how to spend the reserves in the Social Security account, draft a reply to Sen. Hugo Black (D-Ala.) detailing the board's position on a bill for the education of handicapped children, and inform Altmeyer on how much of a worker's income went for Social Security in Britain.[69] He wrote easily, and he also had a feel for statistics and could make sense of the complexities in actuarial reports and budget estimates. Having observed the program as it came into existence, he was in an ideal position to interpret it to a variety of audiences inside and outside the Social Security Board.

Twenty-two years separated Altmeyer from Cohen, as did major differences in ethnic background – Altmeyer attended the Unitarian church – and in temperament. Altmeyer had his doctorate; Cohen had only a bachelor's degree. Altmeyer had worked as secretary of the Wisconsin Industrial Commission, and Cohen had only studied about it. Cohen had debated the efficacy of the National Recovery Administration in college bull sessions, and Altmeyer had helped to administer it. Still, the two had grown up in Wisconsin and studied at the University of Wisconsin with John R. Commons, had moved from academic work into government administration, and had served on the Committee on Economic Security staff. Altmeyer had headed the technical board of government workers that advised the committee and had hired Witte who hired Cohen. Both monitored the Social Security legislation as it moved through Congress, and both had moved from the Committee on Economic Security to the Social Security Board.[70]

In the larger scheme of the history of American social policy, Altmeyer and Cohen represented a new breed of reformer. The comparison with other self-conscious crusaders for social justice, such as Jane Addams and the residents of Chicago's Hull House in the late nineteenth and early twentieth centuries, is instructive. Whereas Jane Addams and the residents of Hull House concentrated their energies on passing legislation in Illinois, Altmeyer and Cohen administered laws that affected the entire nation. Altmeyer had served what amounted to an apprenticeship in Wisconsin; Cohen went directly to Washington and moved immediately into a responsible position. Jane Addams represented a voluntary tradition of social action, in which few residents of Hull House were paid for their labor, but Altmeyer and Cohen depended on their salaries to make ends meet. Social reform was for them a living as much as it was a calling. Consequently, Altmeyer and Cohen operated in a world that resembled the rest of the labor force: it was dominated by men. Jane Addams, despite her efforts to make social work a professional undertaking, concentrated her energies on what one feminist historian describes as "female-dominated networks of private charity."[71]

Unlike previous generations of social reformers, Altmeyer and Cohen were neither social workers nor modern versions of friendly visitors who aided the poor in their homes. The two men managed large systems of social welfare that paid benefits as a matter of entitlement: a person received unemployment compensation because he was unemployed, not because he was poor. Although Cohen and Altmeyer worked with social workers who administered welfare programs, both preferred to be called economists.[72] They viewed social problems from the vantage point of the entire economy rather than as intervention at the family or community levels.[73]

Working with Altmeyer, Cohen found another of the significant mentors who guided his life. Like Cohen's father, Altmeyer was somewhat remote. In Altmeyer's case, however, his formal and austere manner masked a warm personality, often given to sentimental expressions of affection, and a quick, dry sense of humor. Although it took some time, he and Wilbur formed a relationship that resembled that of a father and son. Altmeyer and his wife never had any children, and Cohen became their surrogate son, Cohen's children their surrogate grandchildren.[74]

By Thanksgiving 1936, Altmeyer and Cohen knew one another well enough for Altmeyer to invite his junior associate for Thanksgiving dinner. Cohen took a fruit cake from Milwaukee to Altmeyer's house in Virginia, where he ate a large turkey dinner. The day passed with a splendid sense of ease, marred only by the behavior of one of the guests. Recently returned from Germany, a young man reported on how well that country appeared to be doing under Hitler's leadership. Cohen reacted with anger, criticizing the Nazi government.[75]

LOVE AND MARRIAGE

For Cohen, the moment marked a transition between Roosevelt's first term, dominated by the New Deal, and the second term, in which international affairs began to distract people from domestic reform, but it also demarcated a change in his social life. Initially, Cohen's social life in Washington had been an extension of his life in Madison. He lived with friends from the Experimental College, and he went to parties with them or with acquaintances from the Committee on Economic Security. Herman Somers recalled that whenever he visited Washington, Cohen and his friends took him out "to visit similar groups of girls who lived together."[76] Cohen told his parents that Saturday was the biggest day of his week as he worked until one o'clock, shopped and visited friends in the afternoon, and went on a date or to a dance or party in the evening.[77]

His social life did not amount to much, even though by the spring of 1935 Cohen began to see Dora Hershkovitz, who worked as a secretary at the Department of Agriculture, on a steady basis. Ken Decker remembered her as an "auburn-haired, genteel girl from Boston," who wore dark dresses and white gloves. Wilbur and Dora hiked along the Chesapeake Canal, saw Katherine Cornell in *Romeo and Juliet,* attended Sunday afternoon concerts at the Library of Congress, and occasionally went out for dinner or dancing. They even shared Thanksgiving dinner. Still, as Cohen noted, "it never dawned on me to consider marriage."[78]

Cohen met Eloise Bittel at a union meeting in 1936 when Dan Goldie, a Wisconsin classmate, drifted over to say hello and introduced Wilbur to her. Eloise, as it turned out, worked for the Social Security Board and aspired to be a social worker; she was Cohen's age and lived nearby. A few days later, Cohen was rushing to a meeting on the ninth floor of his office on 1712 G Street, NW. As he came around the corner, Eloise came out of her office to go to the water cooler; seizing the moment, he invited her to lunch. Cohen said that the meal "changed everything in my life. I found Eloise fascinating." Although she came from a different background, "we found a remarkable correspondence of our views on politics, people, and events." New Deal cosmopolitanism triumphed over American provincialism, and a romance was launched.[79]

Eloise and Wilbur shared a generational outlook, yet their backgrounds could not have been more different.[80] Born in 1913, Eloise grew up in the tiny town of Ingram, Texas, located in the hill country not too far from Lyndon B. Johnson's birthplace, with her parents and five siblings. Her father raised goats for their mohair. The family controlled over 300 acres—an enormous amount of land by eastern standards. But much of this land was only semiarid, with a rocky, limy soil, and the topography was hilly. The ranch supported goats, hardy animals that could climb on the mountains, and produced vegetables for the family but provided little else. Land rich, the solidly Baptist family lived a hardscrabble existence with no car, no electricity, and no plumbing.

Eloise enjoyed a reputation as a quick-witted, intelligent child, almost a prodigy. Her father, barely educated himself, served on the local school board and believed in the importance of education. In this respect, the German Bittels mirrored the Jewish Cohens: Wilbur's father had run for the Milwaukee School Board and lost. When it came time for high school, Eloise, her mother, and one of her sisters moved to Kerrville, the county seat and the site of the area's only high school. She graduated at fifteen and earned a scholarship to the women's branch of Baylor, in Belden, Texas, where she became student body president.

Just as a Wisconsin network moved Wilbur along from school to job, so Eloise benefited by going to Baylor. After a brief time back in Kerrville, she took a job in Austin, working for the state program in infant and maternal health. Her supervisor urged her to study at Chicago's School of Social Service Administration. She went to Chicago, took courses, and worked for Sophonisba Breckinridge, the petite great-granddaughter of Sen. John Breckinridge (D-Ky.).[81] Soon, however, Eloise received a call from her Austin benefactor who had been put in charge of a statewide dental survey and needed a deputy. Back in Austin and once again working for the state government, she began to grow restless and wrote to the federal government inquiring about jobs. She wanted to work for the National Labor Relations Board, but when the chance came to work as a secretary for the Bureau of Public Assistance, she took it. At the bureau, she met Wilbur and the two spent more and more time together, riding horses in Rock Creek Park and talking about their futures.[82]

Working as a secretary, Eloise grew more interested in finishing her graduate work, and in the fall of 1937 she enrolled at the New York School of Social Work, living in a settlement house run by the Methodist church. Two days a week she went to classes, and the other three she worked at the Institute of Family Service. Her school was about a mile from the settlement house, but, as she wrote her parents, "I just get on the subway, which is a train underneath the street and am up there in about five minutes. It only costs a nickel." Striving to be a social worker, she wanted to learn about foreign cultures and took her meals in ethnic restaurants. "One night this week I ate shashlik at a Russian place and for lunch had potato blintzes one day and kashe varnishkes another time at a Jewish restaurant," she reported to her parents, who felt as though she had gone to the other end of the earth.[83]

Washington was much closer to New York than Texas, and Eloise and Wilbur continued to see one another. She told her parents that "her new friend" was a "Jewish boy," a "very smart and darling person. . . . All of you would like him, I know." Besides eating in Jewish restaurants, she practiced social work and learned more about the world that Wilbur had left behind in Milwaukee.[84] Early in 1938 he began to mention Eloise in letters home, reporting that the two planned to drive together to Mexico during the summer, stopping in Texas. By March Wilbur had told his parents that he and Eloise planned to marry "very shortly" and then to travel either to Europe or Mexico. Eloise favored Mexico because she wanted to visit her folks on the way; Wilbur wanted to visit Europe because "it may disappear by next year."[85]

Formally engaged, Wilbur and Eloise made plans for their wedding, but there were complications.[86] After much searching, he located a Jewish justice of the peace in Arlington. Aaron and Bessie came in from Milwaukee; Eloise's parents remained in Texas. Even after his parents arrived in town, Wilbur could not find the time to get over to Arlington for the ceremony, but on April 8, 1938, he told Eloise that he could make it. Everyone trooped over to Arlington for the nondenominational service, which nonetheless contained some Jewish touches: Aaron said a blessing, and Wilbur stepped on a glass. Wilbur then announced that he was needed back at the office and left Eloise alone with Aaron and Bessie; Eloise took them to a diner for hamburgers. In the emotionally charged atmosphere, ethnic bargaining promptly ensued. Bessie asked Eloise to agree to Wilbur's being buried in the family plot. Eloise hedged.[87] In Ingram, meanwhile, Eloise's marriage to Wilbur was the talk of that Texas town. At first, Jenny, Eloise's mother, claimed not to know what Jews were. Relationships between Jews and Germans were becoming increasingly tenuous.

Eloise's dad tried to reassure her mother by pointing out that Mr. Herzog in Kerrville was Jewish and that he was a fine, upstanding, and, not coincidentally, wealthy man.

Eloise and Wilbur set up temporary lodging in an apartment in a structure known as the Rossdhu Castle in Chevy Chase, Maryland, and described their first spring together in idyllic terms. One April morning they received Ken Decker and another guest for breakfast, hiked for several hours in the woods, and collected flowers and pine cones. They celebrated their first month together by "staying home and having a swell time around the castle. . . . We ate breakfast late – took a walk in the woods – gathered firewood and made a fire in our fireplace. We read the papers and now we are preparing to go out somewhere." Meanwhile, they sent out wedding announcements to their somewhat stunned friends and family in Milwaukee and Texas. Wilbur specifically asked that an announcement be sent to the family's rabbi.[88]

Eloise took a temporary social work assignment in the District of Columbia's public relief office, but she concentrated her energies on preparing for their delayed honeymoon. They had decided on Europe rather than Mexico. On May 18, they departed on a whirlwind tour of England, France, Switzerland, Czechoslovakia, Holland, and Belgium. By the end of May, the Cohens had been to Paris and seen Notre Dame, the Sorbonne, the Latin Quarter, the Seine, the Cluny Museum, and the Eiffel Tower. "The more I am with Wilbur the more I treasure him," Eloise told her parents; "the fun of it all is in experiencing these joys together – with someone you love," wrote Wilbur to his.[89]

As the Cohens traveled in the summer of 1938, they realized that Europe stood on the brink of war. Wilbur spent much of his time collecting information for the Social Science Research Council and in this way defrayed some of the costs of trip. He also tried to observe the effect of international tensions on the countries he visited. He reported that he could detect nothing on the faces of the Parisians that betrayed a fear of war, and Eloise wrote from Prague that "the [Czechs] do not want war but they are willing and prepared to defend their country in case the Germans invade it. Hitler has found this out and it has slowed him down."[90] Still, as the trip wound down, Wilbur and Eloise realized that they might never have another opportunity to visit Europe. Friends they had met there told them of refugees coming to Belgium and Holland from Germany and Austria, many without money but all glad to be alive. It was a sobering experience that led to a certain sense of fatalism. "So we say it is better that we enjoy ourselves while we can. Who knows when and where the next blow may fall," Wilbur told his parents at the end of the trip.[91]

THE 1939 AMENDMENTS

Returning home at the end of June Cohen had little time to write up his data. Instead, he became swept up in the events that led to the Social Security Act amendments of 1939 and that cemented the working relationship between him and Altmeyer. The 1939 amendments, crucial to the future of the Social Security program, originated with a report from a Social Security Advisory Council. This report, which appeared in December 1938, contained a blueprint for expanding Social Security from a retirement to a life insurance program. When a breadwinner died, the program would pay benefits to his widow and children; in the parlance of Social Security, such payments were known as survivors' benefits. Congress adopted the advisory council's suggestions, and President Roosevelt signed the 1939 Social Security amendments into law on August 10, 1939.[92]

Although Cohen remained in the background throughout the long process that culminated in the 1939 amendments, this process nonetheless marked a personal breakthrough. By his own reckoning, he played a leadership role within the organization for the first time in 1939. He was a young man, only twenty-six at the time, yet he performed at least four demanding functions. First, he did much of the staff work that went into the preparation of discussion papers and draft proposals for the advisory council members to consider. It was Cohen, for example, who met with the Social Security actuaries in order to get them to agree on cost figures for disability coverage.[93] Second, he served as intermediary between the members of the advisory council and the members of the Social Security Board. In particular, he remained close to Edwin Witte, who had been appointed by the Senate Finance Committee to the advisory council.[94] Third, Cohen worked closely with Altmeyer in presenting the Social Security proposals to Congress, and Altmeyer took Cohen with him when he went to the Hill to testify. Fourth, Cohen attended all the executive (closed) sessions of the Senate Finance Committee, the House Committee on Ways and Means, and the conference committee as they "marked up" the legislation.[95]

To be sure, he was still learning how to do each of these jobs. Although well-schooled in congressional behavior, Cohen still received a few surprises in 1939. At one point during the conference committee deliberations, Sen. Tom Connally (D-Tex.) asked him how much a particular proposal, probably a welfare proposal for the elderly, would cost. Cohen estimated it would cost between $80 and $120 million, depending on how the states reacted to the measure. Connally became annoyed and asked for a definite figure. At the next meeting, Cohen replied that the cost would be $100 million, and Connally appeared to be perfectly satisfied. Cohen realized, if he had not already done so, that closed congressional deliberations were not the place for academic niceties.[96]

Although Cohen might have still been learning about Congress, he had moved beyond the educational phase of his career that he had begun in the fall of 1930 as a freshman in Madison. At the end of the decade, he lived in Washington, D.C., and gave no thought to returning to Milwaukee. He was married to a woman whose ethnic background was far different from his own. He had been to New York and to Paris and to Prague and had acquired a cosmopolitan air that neither his parents nor his brother could match. More important, he was established as an expert in social insurance and as an authority on the Social Security program. He was a trained technician, just as he desired to be. His identification with the Social Security program was nearly complete; the ideology of social melioration that underlay the program had become Cohen's ideology as well. Cut off from the world of his fathers by his location, profession, and marriage, Cohen's faith in manmade social progress came as close to a religious belief as anything he had.

3

THE 1940S, SOCIAL SECURITY APPARATUS, AND TRIUMPH OF 1950

Wilbur Cohen spent the entire decade of the 1940s working on the Social Security program in the federal bureaucracy. Little about his job changed. It was, in many respects, a dreary time of many legislative defeats, and Cohen twice sought to escape from the daily routine. On one occasion, he took extended leave to work on a presidential commission; on another, he devoted many hours to an independent writing project. In other respects, however, these years were a crucial time for Cohen's professional growth and for the development of the Social Security program. In the 1940s a group consisting of Cohen, Elizabeth Wickenden, Nelson Cruikshank, and Robert Ball formed in support of Social Security and provided the impetus for the expansion of the program, including 1950 legislation that guaranteed its survival.

The decade also marked a time of generational change and renewal for Cohen's family. In 1939, Albert Bittel, Eloise's father, climbed up a cliff on his ranch to gather a sheep that had strayed from the herd. The cliff gave way underneath him, and he suffered a fall that killed him.[1] Bessie Cohen, Wilbur's mother, died the day after Pearl Harbor of a heart attack. Christopher Bittel Cohen was born in July 1942; a second son, Bruce, arrived in June 1944; and a third son, Stuart, made the family complete in October 1946.[2] By that time Eloise's mother had died, and only Aaron Cohen, vigorous and destined to live another thirty years, survived as a link to his generation.[3]

SOCIAL SECURITY, THE NEW EMPHASIS, AND THE HEALTH PROPOSALS

After the passage of the Social Security amendments of 1939, Cohen became Altmeyer's principal assistant and the program's chief legislative liaison. It was

49

Cohen's job to sell the Social Security program to Congress, but this task was harder than it had been in 1935 and even in 1939. Unlike those years that were dominated by America's response to the depression, attention after 1939 shifted to preparing America for possible war. The new emphasis, euphemistically known as defense, changed the nature of the Social Security Board's responsibilities. The board's most important activities had centered on compensating unemployment, but Altmeyer and Cohen now had to concentrate on promoting employment. As they worked on a national defense program, they also spent considerable time discussing the expansion of the Social Security program and the problems of meshing their legislative objectives with changing economic conditions.[4] In the 1930s it had been easy: American workers needed security in difficult economic times; in the 1940s it was much harder to define the proper federal role in a resurgent economy.

Both Altmeyer and Cohen realized that improving economic conditions meant a change in the rationale for Social Security. A policy that in the 1930s had been a program for social spending would have to become a vehicle for social saving. Altmeyer had received considerable criticism in the 1930s from Keynesians who questioned the point of an old-age insurance program that impounded money in the form of compulsory payroll taxes as the economy slipped into a recession.[5] But in 1941 Altmeyer and Cohen turned the tables on their critics by proposing to link the Social Security program with the government's efforts to manage the wartime economy. "If a national savings plan were inaugurated," they suggested, "its effectiveness would be greatly enhanced by the expanded social insurance system recommended."[6]

According to Altmeyer and Cohen's new wisdom, the Social Security program should tax workers' wages in a time of prosperity and become a vehicle for social spending in a time of depression. The law already contained a provision to raise payroll taxes to pay for old-age and survivors' insurance. To this tax Altmeyer and Cohen proposed to add further taxes and to create federal programs for unemployment, disability, sick leave, and compensation for hospital bills. Moreover, Altmeyer and Cohen advocated covering farmers and independent businessmen under Social Security. If Congress adopted these suggestions, the newly expanded Social Security program could produce a $7.4 billion surplus and, in the short run, make an additional $1.7 billion available for the treasury to spend on defense. Should depression conditions return after the war, the new social program would supply a sustained purchasing power of at least $6 billion per year.[7] The Treasury Department, long opposed to the Social Security Board's plans, agreed with this analysis, calling it a "happy coincidence that the improvement of the insurance plan harmonizes almost perfectly with fiscal considerations."[8]

In November 1942 U.S. Social Security bureaucrats received a boost from the wide publicity that attended the release of the Beveridge report in Great Britain. In "Social Insurance and Allied Services," William L. Beveridge, a British public servant and labor market expert, made a case for a social insurance that covered citizens from the cradle to the grave.[9] Hoping to use a somewhat similar report to advance the U.S. legislative program, the Advisory Committee on Long-Range Relief and Social Security Policies of the National Resources Planning Board (NRPB) submitted "Security, Work and Relief Policies" just three days before Pearl Harbor. On the one hand, the report, written with the research assistance of the Social Security Board, was out of step with current affairs: its notions that the states should put more people on welfare had little currency in the wartime economy.[10] On the other hand, the proposals to expand Social Security meshed with the Social Security Board's plans. For this reason, Altmeyer urged the president to submit the report to Congress as a precursor to endorsing the board's legislative program. "The report," he wrote in a memo that Cohen helped to prepare, "is an impressive document and would furnish a fine background for the specific recommendations contained in [the Social Security Board's] report."[11]

President Roosevelt, concerned about his slim congressional margins and worried about his ability to raise enough money and manpower to fight the war, ignored Altmeyer's suggestions.[12] With a war to pursue and a conservative Congress to contend with, Roosevelt hesitated to put the Social Security proposals at the top of his agenda. Social Security officials pushed him hard but failed to achieve substantive results. Cohen gained only an augmented title for his wartime work, spent at home as an essential government employee. In 1941 in addition to being the technical adviser to the chairman of the Social Security Board, he became the assistant director of the Bureau of Research and Statistics.[13]

Since Roosevelt backed away from so many of the board's legislative proposals, Altmeyer and Cohen learned to operate in a freelance style. In December 1942, just at the time the president refused to release "Security, Work and Relief Policies" or to introduce new Social Security legislation, Cohen and fellow SSB employee I. S. Falk went to Sen. Robert F. Wagner's (D-N.Y.) office and asked him if he would introduce a bill they had prepared.[14] The incident formed the basis for one of Cohen's favorite legislative anecdotes. Cohen had spent hours drafting a speech for Wagner, which he modestly imagined as "a bold and innovative combination of creative ideas which came second only to Thomas Jefferson's imaginative proposals incorporated in the Declaration of Independence." Wagner was underwhelmed. After sharing pleasantries, Cohen, unable to contain himself any longer, asked the senator if he wanted

to look at the bill or the speech. "No," replied Wagner; he saw his role as limited to introducing the measure, which, if it ever passed, would be redrafted many times.[15]

On June 3, 1943, Wagner, acting on his own rather than on the administration's initiative, introduced the Wagner-Murray-Dingell bill, which became a celebrated cause of the era with its elaborate list of medical services that the federal government would fund.[16] A second Wagner-Murray-Dingell bill appeared on May 24, 1945, and in November the sponsors introduced still another version that reflected President Truman's November 19, 1945, message to Congress on health policy. Samuel Rosenman, a New York judge and an adviser to Roosevelt, wrote the message for Truman, which meant he took suggestions from Cohen, Falk, and Altmeyer and weaved them with suggestions from other agencies.[17]

Cohen became involved in the production of Wagner-Murray-Dingell and its successor bills. When a Congress of Industrial Organizations (CIO) official requested a factual summary of the bill, Cohen obliged by composing a short pamphlet, which the CIO decided to print, and the Social Security Board promptly ordered 600 copies. When Robert J. Watt, a union official, needed help with an article for a Connecticut state medical journal, "My Reasons for Favoring the Wagner-Murray-Dingell Bill," Cohen assisted in the drafting. When journalists, such as Albert Deutsch of the left-leaning tabloid *PM*, required background for their stories on the bill, Cohen again tried to help. In this manner Cohen shaded the boundary between policy technician and policy advocate.[18]

Cohen's work on national health insurance made him an expert in the scripting of public policy. Whenever political figures introduced laws, made speeches, and held hearings, they required a script to follow. Responding to that need, Cohen wrote many of the words spoken in the debate over national health insurance. In the spring of 1946, for example, he told Senator Wagner that he was preparing a draft of the senator's statement to present before the Senate Committee on Education and Labor and he hoped Wagner would be able to read it on a train trip from Florida to New York. As Wagner read the draft and made suggestions, Cohen planned to revise it "from the point of view of getting good publicity" and stressed the importance of having the statement mimeographed so that it could be presented to the press at the time Wagner testified.[19] In another instance, Cohen and other health insurance advocates assembled in Sen. James Murray's (D-Mont.) office on April 30, 1947, to discuss who would write a joint statement for Senate sponsors, who would prepare a series of questions and answers explaining the legislation, and who would write a radio talk for the senator.[20]

WICKENDEN AND CRUIKSHANK

Cohen and his fellow health insurance advocates failed to sway a majority of congressmen to pass health or disability insurance, and after the Republican victory in the 1946 congressional elections, passage of national health insurance became even more unlikely.[21] In the middle of adversity and frustration, however, Cohen made contacts that would prove invaluable for the rest of his career. One was Elizabeth Wickenden, whom nearly everyone called Wicky. In the 1940s, she emerged as a key member of a network of individuals inside and outside government who advanced the items in a liberal reform agenda, a group Cohen sometimes referred to as "the apparatus."[22] Within this apparatus, Wickenden became the expert on public assistance and welfare reform. Wicky's husband, Tex, referred to her association with Cohen as a bedroom relationship; she and Wilbur talked constantly on the phone, often in bed late at night, and developed a rapport they could translate into effective political action.

Born in 1909, Elizabeth Wickenden graduated from Vassar in 1931. Her engineer father worked for universities and for American Telephone and Telegraph, and she spent her childhood in Madison, Boston, and the New Jersey suburbs of New York City. After college, she went abroad for a year and then took a job in New York with the Emergency Exchange Association, which was organized to provide barter and exchange among the unemployed. There she met and married Tex Goldschmidt, from Fredericksburg, Texas, near Lyndon Johnson's birthplace. In 1933, Tex's work took him to Washington, and Wicky reluctantly went along. She slipped into the life of the New Deal, serving as acting director of the Transient Program of the Federal Emergency Relief Administration and later becoming part of a social crowd that also included Abe Fortas and Lyndon Johnson. Eventually, she became an assistant to Aubrey Williams, deputy administrator of the Works Progress Administration (WPA), and worked for the National Youth Administration. In 1940, as the character of the New Deal public works programs shifted from social work to defense preparedness, she quit the government, did odd jobs, and emerged as a halftime Washington representative for the American Public Welfare Association (APWA) in Washington in addition to raising two children.[23]

Wickenden first met Cohen late in 1934, as she put it, "through the accident of propinquity," when she still worked for FERA and he worked for the Committee on Economic Security (she sat on one side of a row of filing cabinets in the Municipal Auditorium and Wilbur on the other). She handled the emergencies that came from assisting people on the margins of starvation; he took part in "cerebrally planning" the Social Security Act. At the time, she dismissed him as a theorist, inventing "pie-in-the-sky" schemes.[24] But in the course of their jobs, in the 1940s, they took one another's measure and discovered that they had much in common. The interplay of politics and policy fascinated them, and both enjoyed the special sense of power that comes from the ability to set down appropriate words quickly on a page. Like Cohen, Wickenden wrote easily and did not mind that others often took credit for her words. Also like Cohen, she had experienced the collaboration that is the nature of government and learned to put the advancement of her political proposals above her personal gain. She trusted that her own competence ultimately would be enough to earn her influence over the legislative process.

Perhaps more important, Wickenden grasped the grand design that Altmeyer and Cohen sought to promote. She envisioned a social welfare system that paid monetary benefits as a matter of right through the Social Security system and that used the public assistance system as a means of aiding families and making them function effectively at home and in the labor force.[25] In other words, the "need for public assistance" should "be reduced to a minimum through strengthening the social insurance programs." In 1945 Wickenden put together a statement of objectives for the American Public Welfare Association that embodied this basic approach.[26]

Wickenden acted as a convener of the Social Security crowd during the 1940s. In this role, she helped bring together representatives of a splintered labor movement, divided between the industrial approach of the CIO and the craft approach of the American Federation of Labor (AFL), and united them in support of the Wagner-Murray-Dingell bills and the other social welfare legislation of the era. In particular, she facilitated communication between Nelson Cruikshank, who represented the Social Security interests of the AFL, and Katherine Ellickson, who performed the same function for the CIO. Since the two organizations refused to enter each other's turf, Wickenden provided a neutral spot for them to meet. In this way, she furthered the collaboration between the Social Security Administration and the central offices of the organized labor movement, just as she brought the representatives of the more than fifty state and territorial public welfare programs into a closer working relationship with the Social Security Administration (SSA). Like Cohen, she kept a national Social Security agenda alive during the 1940s.

Of the labor union officials interested in Social Security, Cruikshank became a key member of the postwar liberal apparatus. Born in 1902, the son of a Ohio grain merchant, Nelson Cruikshank attended Ohio Wesleyan and then Union Theological Seminary, starting his career as a Methodist minister and as a labor organizer. In the 1930s he worked for the WPA and then for the Farm Security Administration (FSA) before moving during the war years to the War Manpower Commission (WMC). He came to the American Federation of Labor in

1944, innocent, as Martha Derthick puts it, "of experience with social insurance or acquaintance with the SSA's staff." He soon remedied that. "I guess if there was one, there were fifty people who told me that the thing I should do was get acquainted with Wilbur Cohen," he said. Cruikshank combined competence, honesty, and commitment. His ironic sense of humor enabled him to temper his fervor for social action with a tolerance for the morally ambiguous ways in which Washington worked. Further, Cruikshank, like Wickenden, grasped the grand design that Cohen and Altmeyer intended for social policy. Cohen and Cruikshank soon became collaborators on the Wagner-Murray-Dingell bill and its successors.[27]

In Cruikshank's work with labor unions, he faced challenges that were similar to those that Wickenden encountered in her dealings with social workers and public welfare administrators. Just as Wickenden's group regarded social insurance with indifference, so Cruikshank represented a political interest that had never seen Social Security as central to its basic mission of organizing the American labor force. And just as Wickenden worked with a group that responded to the widely divergent needs of many different localities, so Cruikshank had to find common ground among unions who were concerned about many local issues. It was difficult for Cruikshank to distract labor unions from their local concerns and interest them in a national health insurance law, for example, or an expanded social insurance law. Adding to his difficulties, he faced the disadvantage of working for the AFL and having always to negotiate a common position with the CIO.

INTERLUDE: UNIVERSAL TRAINING

In the days of the Republican Eightieth Congress, the members of the Social Security apparatus, despite their congenital optimism, sought occasional relief from their regular routines. Cohen received a special assignment that provided some diversion from proposing and failing to pass the agency's legislation: in January 1947 Harry Truman requested that Cohen become director of research for the President's Advisory Commission on Universal Training.[28] The president had appointed this commission after the 1946 elections, putting Karl T. Compton, president of MIT, in charge and selecting eight other distinguished individuals to serve. When Truman met with this group, he told its members that he wanted them to produce a program that helped young people stay physically fit and that enforced the social democracy of military life. Given the growing tension between Russia and the United States and with the domestic discord evidenced by a record number of labor strikes, the president wanted to adopt a stance of constant alertness. Further, the emphasis on military training reflected a more general postwar interest in making investments in the nation's future through the development of healthy, motivated, and productive individuals.[29]

Cohen's experience with military life and training was nearly zero; his entire focus had been on domestic legislation, with little reference to foreign affairs.[30] That did not stop him from taking an active part in the commission's work, however. In his usual role as anonymous staff man, Cohen wrote background reports for "Labor Market Aspects of Universal Training of Males" and helped write chapters of the report itself. Through these assignments, he did what he could to make the commission's recommendations consistent with liberal policy proposals. In this regard, the report provided an early exercise in meshing social reform and the cold war. One of the commission's recommendations, for example, consisted of a call for federal support of health and physical education programs, psychiatric services, and vocational guidance in the public schools.[31] Cohen also stressed the theme of universal training as a source of opportunity and as a means of eroding class and racial barriers in the labor force. "The intermingling of individuals of diverse origins and characteristics can have a constructive effect," he wrote.[32]

REPUBLICAN POLITICS AND THE COLD WAR

Valuable as the experience was for appreciating the connections between the warfare and welfare states and for participating in a realm removed from Social Security, Cohen's assignment was only temporary. By May 1947 the commission had completed most of its work, and its report was in circulation by January. Even in the atmosphere of the cold war, the report did little to change the American antipathy toward conscription and standing armies. Cohen, rather than pursuing the topic of universal training, turned his attention back to Social Security. He told Merrill Murray, his former boss, that although his universal training assignment had exposed him to "a lot of matters relative to national security," he looked forward to returning "full time to my social security interests." At the same time, he advised Murray that he did not "expect any important legislation" in 1947. He and his fellow employees were "waiting until next year to concentrate all our energies to obtaining extension of coverage, permanent disability insurance, and liberalization of benefits."[33]

Congress proved Cohen right. The first session of the Eightieth Congress did little except to keep Social Security payroll taxes at the rate of 1 percent for employers and 1 percent for employees. Because Altmeyer was away on a temporary assignment, Cohen did almost all his agency's liaison work with Congress. As he explained in July 1947 to Douglas Brown, the Princeton economist and former staff member of the Committee on Economic Security, "I have been extremely busy in Arthur's absence in connection with the [Social Security] contribution rates. . . . We are getting very little out of this year's legislation but it was awfully hard work to keep what we now have."[34]

In the summer of 1947 an exhausted Cohen took a long vacation and prepared for a difficult legislative season ahead. In a direct rebuke to the Social Security Administration, Congress held hearings on excluding newspaper and magazine vendors from coverage, and when the measure eventually passed, Truman vetoed it. Cohen expressed satisfaction over the veto. Even though only a few people were involved, he thought that the bill set an undesirable precedent.[35] Congress passed the measure over Truman's veto the next spring, providing the president with an important issue to use against the Eightieth Congress: he wanted to expand Social Security, and Congress had voted to make it smaller.[36]

The Republican Congress followed the strategy of expanding the public assistance programs and trying to contain the social insurance programs. In the summer of 1948 Congress passed another bill over the president's veto that altered the definition of the word "employee" in the legislation, thus reducing Social Security coverage for at least .5 million people; the same measure increased federal grants to the states for public assistance. Cohen noted that it had been a "hard and somewhat discouraging legislative session," as Congress "continues to liberalize the assistance programs without doing anything substantial for the insurance programs."[37]

It was an irony of the late 1940s that even though the Social Security Administration made little headway in selling its proposals in America, foreign governments eagerly sought its advice about how the victorious Americans handled social welfare policy. It was a time in which people from Cohen's agency embarked on a series of special assignments abroad. Merrill G. Murray, Cohen's old boss in the unemployment compensation bureau, was in Germany, helping to provide social services to that ravaged country. In March 1947 Arthur Altmeyer departed for five months in Geneva to work with the International Refugee Organization. That same year American officials even contemplated establishing national health insurance in occupied Japan although they admitted they understood little about the Japanese institutional setting. One of Cohen's correspondents, on the scene in Japan, told him, "I have tried to understand the existing programs in Japan. I think it is fair to say that no American here understands them."[38]

For a moment it even looked as though Cohen and Altmeyer might go on a mission to Japan.[39] On July 17, 1947, a teleconference took place between Cohen and other officials in Washington and War Department officials in Tokyo as the Supreme Commander of Allied Powers requested more technical people to assist in handling Japanese health problems. Altmeyer and Cohen considered making the trip but found themselves overwhelmed with the task of holding the Eightieth Congress at bay.[40]

Although Cohen did not go to Japan, he did fly to Rio in November 1947 where, along with Clara Beyer of the Department of Labor and Arthur Altmeyer, he attended an international Social Security meeting.[41] Cohen and Altmeyer's involvement in this sort of international activity was probably unwise. As the facts about the agency's foreign aid missions emerged, they were presented in such a way as to make the agency leaders appear to be sympathetic to Communist aims and cooperative with fellow travelers. Marjorie Shearon, a public health researcher who had worked for I. S. Falk in the research section at the Social Security Administration before she "recanted," led the critics. She issued news releases and bulletins that purported to inform the medical profession of the conspiracy to socialize it. For a time, Shearon even worked for Sen. Robert Taft (R-Ohio) and tried to help him advance his welfare-oriented alternative to national health insurance.[42] Her views played particularly well with politicians who feared the consequences of America's loss of its isolationist stance.

During the beleaguered days of the Eightieth Congress, Shearon, who had written a forty-one page pamphlet, "Blueprint for the Nationalization of Medicine," watched over the Social Security Administration. When the Senate Labor and Public Welfare Committee met to consider the health care proposals of Senators Murray and Taft, she told the committee about the proposed trip to Japan, claiming that Altmeyer, Cohen, and Maurine Mulliner wanted to "foist a WMD bill on the defenseless Japanese" and calling it a "brazen scheme." Falk did the planning; Altmeyer gave the mission official sanction and accepted leadership for it; Cohen and Mulliner executed the plan; and the public paid "the freight."[43]

Choosing Cohen, Falk, and Mulliner as conspirators was particularly shrewd. Cohen and Falk were Jewish, and both had made trips to Europe to gather data on health insurance. Both Cohen and Falk had attended what Shearon maintained was a secret meeting in Montreal in 1943 to develop an international Social Security charter. At this meeting and at many others, America, according to Shearon, had played the part of the patsy, "a novice among a group of experienced left-wing actors," and had agreed to advance proposals "mapped out by representatives of foreign countries whose ideologies are repugnant to

Robert Ball, with whom Cohen began to work in the 1940s, was a key member of the Social Security apparatus that helped to sustain the program through hard times in the 1940s and that helped to engineer the expansion of the program in the 1950s. From 1962 to 1973, Ball served as commissioner of Social Security and worked closely with Cohen on Medicare. (Courtesy of the National Academy of Social Insurance)

us."[44] Maurine Mulliner was a Mormon from Utah, but in Shearon's view she too had been seduced by left-wing influences.[45]

ROBERT BALL AND THE ADVISORY COUNCIL

Despite this assault on the legitimacy of Social Security Administration personnel and their legislative goals, Cohen and Altmeyer persevered in their efforts to expand the Social Security program. Just as at the end of the 1930s, they hoped to progress through the vehicle of an Advisory Council that the Senate Finance Committee authorized in the summer of 1947.[46] Altmeyer and Cohen realized that they would have far more control over an advisory council than they had over Congress. Cohen assumed his usual position as point man between the council and the Social Security Administration, and by October 1947 he and his coworkers were preparing material for the council's use, a process that Cohen himself described as pouring old wine into new bottles.[47] He worked closely with Robert Ball, the staff director of the Advisory Council, on this task.

Three members of the apparatus: Robert Ball *(left)*, William Haber, and Nelson Cruikshank. Ball and Cruikshank were particularly important to the advancement of Social Security. Haber, Cohen's coeditor for the book of Social Security readings, became his closest friend on the faculty at the University of Michigan. (Courtesy of Bruce Cohen)

Like Elizabeth Wickenden and Nelson Cruikshank, Ball (almost always referred to somewhat formally as "Mr. Ball" within Social Security circles) became an important part of the liberal apparatus in the postwar era. A year younger than Cohen and the son of a Methodist minister, Ball grew up in northern New Jersey and attended Wesleyan, where he received an undergraduate degree in English (1935) and a graduate degree in economics (1936). Like Cohen, Ball studied about the labor movement during college and wrote a thesis on it, a comparison of the craft and industrial approach to union organization. Indeed, Ball had attended the famous labor convention in Atlantic City in 1935 in which John L. Lewis challenged the conservative union leadership by punching one of its champions in the mouth.

Unlike Cohen, Ball joined a fraternity that was noted chiefly for its social activities. The very fact that he went to a private rather than to a state school in the middle of the depression indicated his relative affluence, compared to Cohen. As he later explained, Methodist ministers did not make much money, but they enjoyed a degree of security since the Methodists did not admit more people into their ministry than they needed to fill the available openings. Ball came from solidly American stock. Standing over six feet tall and wearing black rimmed glasses, he projected a serious image as though he were a business executive rather than a social reformer. Despite his air of gravity, he managed always to be affable, quick to smile at other people's jokes. He seldom fumbled in his social interactions, being endowed with what a later generation would call interpersonal skills. He appeared always to be prepared, to know what he wanted from a situation, and yet he seldom gave the impression of dictating to others.[48]

Robert Ball also had the talent to rise rapidly through the Social Security ranks. After a brief stint as a minor financial functionary at a New York department store, he accepted a job with Social Security, having turned down a job as a fingerprint technician at the FBI. In 1939 he entered the Social Security Board, not in the central administration as Cohen had done but as a field representative in Newark, New Jersey. He worked in a variety of field positions in the northern New Jersey area before he moved to the central Social Security office in downtown Baltimore. He eventually settled in the training office, where he instructed new employees on the principles of social insurance. In 1945 Ball made a wrenching decision to leave government and to go to work with Karl de Schweinitz at the University Government Center on Social Security, a new organization that held short-term training seminars in which academics and state administrators learned about social insurance.[49] In this job Ball met many of the leaders in the field, who would come to lecture on various topics related to Social Security. After two years there, he accepted an assignment from Sen. Eugene Milliken (R-Mich.) of the Senate Finance Committee to serve as staff director of the Advisory Council. When the senator had requested an expert on Social Security who was not an employee of the Social Security Administration, Douglas Brown, on the board of de Schweinitz's center, had suggested Ball.[50]

Although Ball tried to restrict the number of Social Security employees who attended the Advisory Council's meetings and to maintain his distance from Altmeyer, he knew how to work with Cohen in order to get information. Their work on the council in 1947 and 1948 provided the first opportunity for the two of them to collaborate on a social policy project. As council staff director, Ball held his first important independent position, and his work, judged by nearly everyone to be of extraordinarily high quality, marked his emergence as an important leader in the Social Security field. In 1949 he returned to government and became an assistant director of the Bureau of Old-Age and Survivors' Insurance, in the 1950s serving as deputy director and de facto head of the bureau. The Advisory Council was the start of an exceptionally effective partnership between him and Cohen.

The Advisory Council, relying heavily upon data generated by the SSA and upon Ball's ability to tutor the members on the fundamentals of Social Security without appearing to dictate to them, issued a series of reports between April and December 1948. Many of the members, such as Douglas Brown, kept in close touch with Cohen, who advised Brown that "a number of the other members have not had the close contact with the operation of the program that you have, and I know will look to you for help and guidance."[51] The key report on old-age and survivors' insurance arrived in April. The council, no doubt with Ball's urging, accepted the SSA's social policy formulation that equated preventing dependency and reducing the need for public assistance; the best way to lower the public assistance rate, according to the council, was to extend social insurance. The council members looked forward to universal coverage under old-age and survivors' insurance.[52]

Wilbur Cohen added his personal endorsement to the report, which, he informed Sumner Slichter, a Harvard economist and an Advisory Council member, provided the place to begin in devising a legislative program for 1949.[53] As Cohen and the other members of the apparatus realized, the council's report supplied one of the few bright spots in the period between 1946 and 1949.

A SECOND INTERLUDE: COHEN AS AUTHOR

By the time the Advisory Council report appeared, Cohen was already launched on a book-length project to interpret the Social Security program to a wider audience. Undertaking this task, Cohen no doubt wanted to distance himself from the immediate congressional scene, and as the father of three, he also began to contemplate ways of supplementing his income. Looking for a means to bridge his considerable administrative accomplishments and his unrealized academic aspirations, he envisioned the project either as a brief monograph or as a collaborative effort. An academic might handle the theoretical end, and Cohen would write about the administrative, technical, and legislative aspects of Social Security. Cohen's friends in academia, such as J. Douglas Brown, told him that he knew so much about Social Security that he owed them and their students a book on the subject.[54]

Cohen realized that he was trampling on the academics' turf. As he investigated the undertaking he learned, for example, that Professors Edwin Witte of Wisconsin and William Haber of the economics department at Michigan, both of whom had served on the 1938 Advisory Council, entertained the notion of doing their own Social Security books.[55] Haber thought he might edit a book of readings in Social Security, and Cohen agreed that the idea of an anthology was an excellent one. "I can say this," he added, "because I have been giving thought to preparing just such an anthology myself." But Cohen, always willing to negotiate in these situations, agreed to "withdraw completely from the field" if someone else decided to pursue it.[56]

The flexible approach paid off in the form of a collaboration between Haber and Cohen, who together edited a book of comprehensive readings on Social Security. Haber, as the academic and senior member of the team, lent his name to the effort, made some suggestions, and then left on a postwar assignment to Germany, where he advised Gen. Lucius Clay on Jewish affairs. Meanwhile, Cohen remained at home, fully occupied with administrative duties, and tried to cope with his editorial responsibilities. "It is a little difficult to negotiate with your co-author so far away," Cohen noted, even as he expressed great enjoyment with the work.[57] In the spring of 1948 Cohen's burden became even heavier: Altmeyer was on special assignment, and Cohen took major responsibility for his agency's presentation to the House Ways and Means Committee as it met in executive session to consider Social Security amendments. "Consequently," he told Witte, "I have not had time to do much work on my book."[58]

In typical style, Cohen managed to make time, however, taking the manuscript home and working on it when he could. He sent it off to the editor at Prentice Hall early in June 1948, "in pretty rough shape." The editor promised to rush it through the production process so that it would be ready by October, still in time to use for the fall semester. Because Cohen pushed so hard to read galleys and to attend to the other details of production, Prentice Hall did have the book out by then.[59]

Haber and Cohen's *Readings in Social Security* represented Cohen's first major book-length publication. Although in this venture, as in his Washington activities, he remained the junior partner and received second billing, as usual he had done most of the staff work in the book's preparation. For Haber, an academic at the University of Michigan, the book amounted to a modest contribution; in the pejorative idiom of academia, it was only an edited volume, not a research monograph, a text, not a theoretical treatise. For Cohen, a bureaucrat in the Social Security Administration, the book marked a major breakthrough.[60] It gave him a semblance of academic credentials to match his considerable administrative ones and put his name into the literature of institutional economics that he had studied with Witte and Commons.[61]

The book presented an overview of the issues in social insurance as Cohen perceived them in the late 1940s. He attempted to balance the selections so that, for example, calls to federalize the unemployment compensation program were matched by arguments to retain state administration. He tried to balance President Truman's arguments for national health insurance with the counterarguments of the medical profession. If one read through to the end of the book, one could learn about the Townsend Plan. In general, however, the book made a case for the expansion of Social Security and the passage of national health insurance, just as the Social Security Administration advocated at the time. In addition, it supplied valuable background reading on other, peripheral topics, such as workers' compensation, the Railroad Retirement Act, and children's allowances. It was indeed a valuable reference book, and it remains so.

In editing the book, Cohen shed some of the anonymity that attended his role as a staff member to Altmeyer. He also had the opportunity to resurrect some of his pieces that had appeared in relatively obscure places, including an article he had written for a labor economics textbook, "Attitude of Organized Groups toward Social Insurance."[62] In a rather sly move, Cohen also included pieces written anonymously by the members of the apparatus. An essay that he had written for Altmeyer on temporary disability insurance appeared in the anthology.[63] A position paper by Elizabeth Wickenden on public assistance also made it into print as did large sections of Robert Ball's Advisory Council report.

With the 1948 election approaching, Cohen perhaps saw this book as capital that he could invest in finding another job. When the book appeared, few people gave Harry Truman much chance to win the election. His defeat would mean the end of a sixteen-year Democratic reign, and Thomas Dewey's victory was certain to bring changes in the administrative ranks at Social Security. Between 1936 and 1948, Altmeyer and Cohen had enjoyed a run of twelve years of continuous administrative supervision of the program. During this long run, which would never be equaled, Altmeyer had established an enduring administrative structure and created a working team whose effectiveness was enhanced by the members' familiarity with one another.

In the summer of 1948 Altmeyer began to consider his employment beyond the Social Security Administration. He thought he might start a consulting firm to advise unions and state governments on health and pension matters and wanted to take Cohen along as a partner, but Cohen remained ambivalent about the move. He enjoyed something like tenure at Social Security because his job had civil service protection, and to start something new at a time when he had so many financial responsibilities involved an element of potentially unacceptable risk. Many of his friends counseled him to stay at Social Security in the Dewey administration. His friend Merlyn Pitzele, once a Communist, now served as a Dewey adviser, writing speeches and offering advice on labor-relations issues; Dewey therefore indirectly received advice on Social Security from Cohen through Pitzele. Dewey, although a Republican, was a liberal and not necessarily averse to the Social Security program. Moreover, someone needed to remain behind to bridge what was certain to be a difficult bureaucratic transition from Democratic to Republican rule. "I would hate to see you leave the federal service," wrote Edwin Witte to Cohen from Wisconsin.[64]

At the end of the 1930s, Cohen was suspended between academic inquiry and public administration, between government service and graduate school, operating as a technocrat who carried out the wishes of others. At the end of the 1940s, he remained suspended between the public and private sectors, between working for Social Security from within the government and working for it as a private consultant to interested parties. He played a major role, although one that was secondary to Arthur Altmeyer's, in shaping Social Security policy and in selling its proposals to Congress. He was still a technocrat but one who was gaining greater individual recognition through his academic and his legislative endeavors. By November 1948 Wilbur Cohen was no longer the kid who did other people's errands. Among the generation of younger Social Security experts such as Elizabeth Wickenden, Nelson Cruikshank, and Robert Ball, Cohen was a leader.

THE 1950 AMENDMENTS

When Dewey lost the election, Wilbur Cohen no longer had to contemplate finding another job. Instead, he and Altmeyer remained and made another attempt to push their program so that Social Security rather than welfare would become America's primary social response to the problems of the elderly. In 1950 their efforts paid off in the form of a handsome piece of new legislation that boosted Social Security benefits and extended coverage. With the passage of the 1950 amendments, the days of deadlock and inactivity ended.

After the 1948 election Altmeyer and Cohen had a plan that was endorsed by a bipartisan Advisory Council and that was the creature of a Republican Congress. It was a relatively simple matter for them to present this plan to the new Democratic Congress, elected along with President Truman in November, and to ask for its passage. Cohen shed his Eightieth Congress pessimism and began to entertain the thought that Social Security would be expanded.[65]

Aware that a long period of work lay ahead, Cohen set aside his extracurricular plans to write a Social Security textbook.[66] Instead, he and Altmeyer spent the first two months of 1949 preparing the Truman administration's new Social Security bill. The House Ways and Means Committee decided to open hearings in February 1949 on welfare rather than on Social Security, but Altmeyer and Cohen advised the president that Social Security should constitute the administration's top priority. They portrayed the situation as a race between those people who advocated a general pension system, such as Dr. Townsend had once proposed, and those who favored contributory social insurance. As matters stood, it was "nip and tuck" as to which side won. If the president wanted social insurance to win, he needed to recommend a "very substantial increase in insurance benefits and broadening of coverage."[67] Hearings in the House stretched from the end of February to the end of April, and executive sessions lasted from the beginning of May to the middle of August.[68] At the committee's request, Cohen attended each of the executive sessions.[69] By July, Cohen, noting that he had put in over twenty weeks with the House committee, characterized the process as a "slow, steady grind."[70]

During the House deliberations, Cohen performed several distinct functions, but above all else he lobbied Congress on behalf of the Social Security Administration. It was his job to see that legislation recommended and largely written by the SSA moved through the House and into the Senate. If a congressman conceived a contrary idea, it was Cohen's task to dissuade him from writing it into the bill. Congressman Doughton, for example, insisted on adding a provision to the bill that allowed optometrists to examine applicants for aid to the blind; if an optometrist declared a person to be blind, that person would be eligible for welfare payments. Cohen and those he represented wanted only ophthalmologists or other doctors skilled in the diseases of the eye to do the examinations. Doughton hoped to help out optometrists by writing them into the legislation; the SSA strived to maintain professional standards in public welfare administration. As was not unusual in such struggles, Doughton, chairman of the committee, got his way, despite Cohen's best efforts to convey the Social Security Administration's views to him and the other committee members.[71]

A second function that Cohen performed was to write Social Security policy into the formal legislative record. In August 1949, for example, he heard from Edwin Witte about attacks on the integrity of the program's trust fund; some people thought the money was being improperly used. At the time, Cohen was working on the Committee on Ways and Means report to accompany the Social Security legislation, and he promptly drafted a statement maintaining that the "investment of these funds is completely proper and safe," gained committee approval of it, and inserted it on pages 36 and 37 of the report. Later he responded to inquiries by asserting that the "House has confirmed the safety of the trust fund investments in its report," conveniently failing to mention that it had done so entirely on Cohen's initiative.[72]

Another function Cohen performed was to try to influence public opinion through the press so as to create a favorable climate for a proposal, such as disability insurance, that the agency favored. Although the 1948 Advisory

Council had endorsed disability insurance and the SSA had favored it since at least 1941, the measure remained highly controversial. Cohen and Altmeyer saw it as a logical extension of the retirement program for those under sixty-five and unable to work, but others perceived it as a nightmare of administrative complexity. As a modest way of adding to the public record in support of disability insurance, Cohen drafted a letter for Mrs. Abraham Epstein, the widow of the noted Social Security authority, to send to the *New York Times*. After the newspaper printed it, he sent the clipping to Julius Edelstein, his childhood friend from Milwaukee and Sen. Herbert Lehman's (D-N.Y.) chief of staff, and prompted Edelstein to have Lehman insert the letter into the *Congressional Record*. In this way, Cohen's words drifted into the public realm.[73]

Finally, as the Social Security lobbyist, Cohen constantly had to be on guard against the proposals of other lobbyists. In 1949, for example, when the House Ways and Means Committee met in executive session, Cohen persuaded Doughton and the other members to make a change in the Aid to Dependent Children (ADC) program. This program, not yet a major congressional concern, allowed the federal government to grant money to the states so that they could pay welfare benefits to needy children in families where a parent was dead, disabled, or absent from the home. Cohen suggested striking out the qualifications so that the states could aid children in poor families even if the father was present. When Father John O'Grady of the National Catholic Welfare Conference heard about the committee's action, he "really hit the ceiling," as Cohen later recalled. O'Grady and a sympathetic Lutheran minister visited the members of the committee, arguing that such a change constituted an invasion of unemployment insurance and that it was the wedge that would allow the federal government into the area of foster care of children. They portrayed the law as a challenge to private charities. Because no one wanted to confront O'Grady, the committee reversed itself.[74]

The long process of trying to influence the committee came to an end on August 22, 1949, when Ways and Means reported out the Social Security bill. Because the House voted under a closed rule, the committee essentially legislated for that body. Despite Cohen's initial pessimism, the votes within the committee went well: it decided to raise Social Security benefits and to extend coverage to new groups such as the nonfarm self-employed.[75] On the question of disability insurance, first the committee and subsequently the House voted to begin a program of permanent and total disability benefits to those workers with a substantial attachment to the labor force. Over all, the SSA won a major victory in the House of Representatives although the agency also made concessions that became apparent in the technical details of the legislation. The committee, for example, did not raise the tax base as much as Altmeyer and

Cohen had wanted. Altmeyer had hoped that the amount of wages on which Social Security taxes were payable would rise from $3,000 to $4,200; the House took it to $3,600.[76]

The legislative process in the House took so long that the Senate did not get to consider the legislation until 1950.[77] Cohen, who realized that congressmen voted with an eye toward how the Senate would handle the measure, tried to stay ahead of the process. Even before the measure passed the House early in October, he alerted his friend Douglas Brown of the need for the Senate Finance Committee to hire a special staff member to help with the legislation and suggested Bob Ball, who had reentered government as an assistant director of the Bureau of Old Age and Survivors' Insurance. He instructed Brown to write economist Sumner Slichter on Ball's behalf and have Slichter write to Sen. Eugene Milliken and Sen. Walter George (D-Ga.).[78]

When the fatigue of tending legislation became too much for Cohen, he entertained the thought of taking a sabbatical. No longer envisioning himself as a graduate student, he saw himself as a professor who taught his own graduate classes. Not content simply to gather data on how foreign countries handled Social Security problems, he regarded himself as an expert who could advise other countries on their programs.[79] As the new decade began, however, Cohen was just too absorbed in the rush of Washington life to get away for more than a few days at a time.

He immersed himself in the Senate's handling of the Social Security legislation, using whatever resources he could summon to influence the outcome. He worked not only on the senators but also on their staff members. Although the House had taken thousands of pages of testimony, the Senate Finance Committee insisted on doing it again. This process did not end until March; executive sessions lasted until May 1950. And in the Senate, unlike in the House, important action always occurred on the floor, even after the Senate Finance Committee had reported out a bill.

Typical of the technical yet vitally important issues that arose in the Senate was the matter of the retirement test. Altmeyer believed that Social Security was a retirement program, not a general pension program for those over sixty-five; hence, he felt that someone should withdraw from the labor force before becoming eligible for benefits. At the same time, it was a constant temptation for senators to ease the retirement test. The law stated that if a retired Social Security beneficiary made more than fifteen dollars in a month, he lost his Social Security benefit for that month. In 1949 the House, in the legislation that the Senate considered in 1950, changed the limit to fifty dollars a month and eliminated it entirely after age seventy-five; on a person's seventy-fifth birthday, he could make $1 million and still get Social Security. When the measure reached the Senate, legislators with many elderly constituents, such as Sen. Claude Pepper (D-Fla.), proposed making the law even more liberal so that a person between the ages of sixty-five and seventy-five could keep more of his income without losing his Social Security. Pepper wanted to double the limit for those under seventy-five, enabling a sixty-nine-year-old to make ninety-nine dollars a month without any reduction in his Social Security check. Cohen tried to dissuade Pepper through one of the senator's staff members. Echoing arguments he had learned from Altmeyer, Cohen said that raising the earning limit would put the non–Social Security beneficiary at a serious disadvantage in competing for jobs in a low-wage industry; employers would use the fact that elderly people were receiving benefits as an excuse to keep wages low. Further, paying Social Security to the working elderly population would be costly and make it harder to provide other benefits such as disability insurance.[80]

Although Cohen's agency fared less well in the Senate than in the House on these and other matters, the Senate for the most part followed the House's lead.[81] When the process finally ended on August 28, 1950, and the bill became law, Altmeyer and Cohen had much of what they wanted: a greatly expanded Social Security program that paid substantially higher benefits. Altmeyer later termed the 1950 law "crucial" to the program's survival; it meant that Social Security had finally attained parity with welfare.[82]

If anyone deserved credit for the 1950 legislation, it was Altmeyer. Cohen functioned as his operative throughout the process and in so doing relied on ideas and strategies that Altmeyer had devised. At the same time, the logistics of the legislative process often made it difficult for Cohen to consult with him. As the person on the scene, in front of the committee as it marked up the bill, Cohen learned how to make spot decisions. He also helped to nurture the political support that enabled the 1950 amendments to be passed. In the late 1940s and early 1950s, the institutional structure that supported Social Security was just being forged. In the hearings leading to the 1950 legislation, Cohen believed that representatives of organized labor, such as Walter Reuther and William Green, made a particularly favorable impression; working through Cruikshank, Cohen helped these labor leaders with their testimony. He also worked closely with the few congressional staff members who specialized in Social Security, such as Fedele Fauri of the Congressional Research Service.[83] On the staff level, Cohen, more than any other single individual, brought together the sides of the "iron triangle" (to use the political science term) and provided the impetus for the passage of the 1950 amendments.

He was still relatively invisible except to those individuals who followed the details of increments in the formula, the level of the taxable wage base, and the hundreds of other pieces of Social Security arcania. Yet by tending to these matters, Cohen helped to ensure institutional continuity, often at the expense of individual recognition. Nor was he highly regarded as a conceptual thinker, in part because he was so tightly linked with Altmeyer, the man who dominated Social Security discourse from within the federal bureaucracy and whose force of personality was such that few within his agency opposed him. As Altmeyer's chief assistant, Cohen had the advantage of being close to the center of the agency's power and the disadvantage of being unable to take positions that separated him from Altmeyer.

The great significance of the 1950 amendments also tended to be overlooked. President Truman set the tone when he signed the measure, calling it an "outstanding achievement" but then highlighting its shortcomings, such as the omission of disability insurance.[84] From that point of view, the amendments became not the climax of the battle between welfare and Social Security, as Cohen and Altmeyer saw it, but another skirmish in the battle for national health insurance. Then again, the amendments became law at the very beginning of the Korean War, which distracted the nation's attention from their importance.

For Cohen and Altmeyer, the 1950 amendments were a source of almost instant satisfaction. In an article that appeared early in 1952, Cohen described 1951 as a milestone year, noting that in February for the first time in the nation's history, more people received old-age insurance than old-age assistance. In August, also for the first time in the nation's history, the total amount of insurance payments exceeded the amount of old-age assistance payments. Social insurance had triumphed over welfare. The 1950s had begun with a legislative victory that in some measure compensated for the frustrations of the 1940s and that foreshadowed the legislative victories of the Eisenhower years.[85]

4

THE NEW POLITICS
OF SOCIAL SECURITY
AND THE IKE AGE

The triumph of Social Security, satisfying as it was, tended to be overshadowed by the outbreak of the Korean War, which delayed the start of a new political regime for the program. In 1952, however, Congress embarked on a program of steady incremental expansion of old-age and survivors' insurance that lasted for the next twenty years and that enjoyed bipartisan support. In the early 1950s, therefore, interest in Social Security increased among members of Congress, and Cohen's job as congressional liaison gained in stature and importance. He learned how to provide members of Congress with bills that aided in the expansion of the program and that fit the members' particular political needs. His skill at congressional liaison, his contacts with the other members of the apparatus, and his ability to explain the program to a wide variety of audiences contributed to its acceptance by the Eisenhower administration in 1953 and 1954.

The era of Social Security's greatest growth began inauspiciously with the outbreak of the Korean War. Cohen found himself pressed into special wartime service as chairman and public member of the Tripartite Panel on Health, Welfare, and Pension Plans.[1] During World War II there had been a ban on wage increases, but employers and employees had undercut it by increasing fringe benefits, such as health care. The question thus arose as to what the policy toward fringe benefits should be during the Korean War. In the panel's report, issued on October 22, 1951, Cohen and labor representatives, at least one of whom was his close personal friend, argued that health and welfare plans should be decontrolled. Management representatives maintained that such plans should be reviewed by the government to see if they were consistent with prudent management of the wartime economy. Truman and his advisers in charge of wage stabilization decided on a policy that permitted the establishment of plans that met "prevailing practice." If a plan exceeded normal limits, its representatives needed to gain the approval of the Tripartite Health and Welfare Committee, which, by the middle of 1952, had received about 6,000 cases. Three-quarters of the cases met the basic criteria and required no further adjudication, but there were still over 1,000 cases in which, for example, the employer paid all the health care costs for a worker's dependents rather than the recommended 40 percent.[2] Cohen sat with representatives of labor and industry and made recommendations for each case. Later, writing a reflective essay on the experience, he called tripartism a "success, partly because the subject matter was in a highly technical and controversial field."[3]

THE 1952 AMENDMENTS

If past experience served as any sort of guide, the Korean War would make the passage of Social Security legislation almost impossible because of what Cohen described as "everyone's preoccupation with international matters and defense costs."[4] Early in 1952 Cohen sensed a slow period ahead and made plans to travel to an International Labor Conference in Rio and to California to talk at a social work conference. He assumed he would not miss much in Washington since it had taken Congress eleven years to amend the Social Security program in a significant way. The 1940s had passed without a single important development in the old-age insurance law. Since Congress had devoted so much time and energy to Social Security in 1949 and 1950 and because the country was fighting a war, one could expect another long hibernation period.

Before Cohen left for Rio in April he gave Arthur Altmeyer a checklist of legislative projects. Oscar Ewing, head of the Federal Security Agency, wanted to be sure that health legislation was ready.[5] Ewing showed particular interest in paying for the hospital bills of Social Security beneficiaries, a measure that would eventually be known as Medicare. Other matters on the short-term agenda involved drafting bills for the program's coverage of state and local government employees and for those in military service. Sen. Hubert Humphrey (D-Minn.) wanted to raise Social Security benefits by an average of five dollars, and Cohen had given Max Kampelman of Humphrey's staff a draft bill.[6]

Cohen showed most interest in a comprehensive bill that would receive the backing of the administration and of the House Committee on Ways and Means. He wanted to include components related to public assistance, old-age and survivors' insurance, and disability. Public assistance grants, Cohen believed, should be increased so as to keep pace with the cost of living.[7] He knew that Sen. Ernest McFarland, the majority leader from Arizona who faced a tough reelection fight in 1952, had already introduced an amendment to a minor revenue bill that would raise welfare benefits by five dollars a month to the aged, blind, and disabled and by three dollars a month to dependent children.[8] Cohen also felt that the comprehensive bill should include an average increase of five dollars in Social Security benefits, similar to the bill that he had prepared for Hubert Humphrey. According to Cohen, the benefits should be increased to keep pace with public assistance benefits and to take advantage of rising wage rates. As a final major feature of the comprehensive bill, he hoped to begin a modest disability program; in particular, he sought to institute the "disability freeze." Under this proposal, government authorities first declared a person as disabled, unable to work. Should that person survive until retirement age, he would receive regular retirement benefits even though he had failed to pay into the Social Security fund for many years.

Reviewing the proposal, Cohen told Altmeyer in April that he had already met with Richard Neustadt and Charlie Davis of President Truman's staff to discuss it. They had agreed that neither the president nor Chairman Doughton would want to introduce such a bill. Cohen and the White House staffers decided to wait to see what Congressman Robert Kean, a liberal Republican from New Jersey, came up with before taking further action; they would use the Republican proposal as a base on which to build. If Kean said to raise Social Security benefits by four dollars, then Doughton or Senators Humphrey and Lehman might want to raise benefits by five dollars. In fact, Cohen had already discussed Kean's bill with the congressmen many times, and together with Robert Ball and Sidney Saperstein, an agency lawyer, had helped to prepare a draft of it. He expected it to contain a four dollar increase in benefits and the disability freeze, coupled with a rehabilitation program for those people declared disabled.[9]

Cohen went to Brazil, at least his fifth trip to Latin America on government business, and then, as planned, he flew to Los Angeles. In the middle of a pleasant stay, he received word that something was happening in Washington and that he should return immediately.[10] Encouraged by Robert Ball, Chairman Doughton had decided to introduce the comprehensive Social Security bill, and it looked as though the measure might make it through the committee. Doughton's bill followed the outline that Cohen had proposed and included an increase in insurance benefits and the disability freeze provision. Doughton, whose committee did not have a major tax bill to consider, sensed an emerging consensus on Social Security; with the presidential election approaching, he thought it a good idea to raise benefits.

The bill moved quickly through the Ways and Means Committee (it had taken a year and a half for Congress to consider the 1950 amendments). In this instance, Ways and Means decided to skip hearings altogether and reported the 1952 bill out in four days. Under a suspension of the rules that allowed Social Security supporters to bypass lengthy proceedings in the Rules Committee, the House voted on the bill on May 19, but it failed to pass by the necessary two-thirds margin. Most people thought that would end the matter. The situation took an even more amazing turn, however. The next day Congressman Daniel Reed, the ranking Republican on the committee, introduced another Social Security bill that included an increase in Social Security benefits. For the first time, Republicans and Democrats agreed on the political desirability of an increase in these benefits, and both parties thought that such a move would be helpful to them in an election year.

As early as May 1952, therefore, a change had occurred in the politics of Social Security. In the 1940s, the program was largely irrelevant to the war effort, and neither party strained to pass Social Security legislation. The 1950s appeared to be different, the change a direct consequence of expanded Social Security coverage that made more politicians interested in the program, higher benefits that allowed Social Security to compete successfully with welfare, and the prosperous economic conditions of the postwar era. The key factor, as Cohen explained, was that prosperity made Social Security expansion politically painless. When Congress passed the 1950 amendments, it had based its assumptions on a steady wage level. Since wages were rising, the system was receiving more money than Congress had anticipated, and members could expect it to do so into the future. In this situation, it became possible to raise the benefit level without raising the tax rate. Cohen referred to this phenomenon as a "miracle" that made it possible to change the system "without changing the contributions of the program or impairing the actuarial soundness of the system."[11]

Congress, under the tutelage of Altmeyer, Cohen, and Ball, seized the moment. Four weeks after the introduction of Reed's bill, the House voted to pass Doughton's original bill. In less than a week, the Senate Finance Committee, racing to conclude the matter before Congress adjourned for the political season, reported out a bill that deleted the provision for a disability freeze but included a Social Security benefit increase. On June 26, 1952, the Senate passed its version of the bill by a voice vote.

The conference committee took place over the Fourth of July weekend, and Cohen, as was his custom, attended each of the closed sessions. It soon became apparent that the committee faced an impasse. The issue concerned not the increase in Social Security benefits but the provision for a disability freeze.[12] The freeze had been a contentious matter in both houses; its inclusion was one of the reasons the bill failed to pass the first time the House had voted on it. When the American Medical Association (AMA) received word about the bill, it had dispatched telegrams to every member of the House saying that the freeze amounted to "socialized medicine" and did not belong in a Social Security bill.[13] Faced with the telegram, many congressmen decided to vote against the bill. Kean, however, continued to back the freeze, and he persuaded Chairman Doughton to retain its provisions, with some administrative adjustments, in the bill. Although the measure passed the House, the Senate, using the convenient argument that there had not been sufficient time to hold hearings on it, refused to back the disability freeze. In this state the matter arrived in the conference committee, which, because it was meeting in an election year, wanted to conclude its business quickly.

As Cohen understood, the issue embraced personalities and presidential politics as well as considerations related to social policy. Conservatives such as Sen. Robert Taft, who was in the midst of a campaign for the Republican nomination, accepted the fact that Social Security benefits could be increased without raising tax rates. They remained skeptical, however, of the desirability of extending the system into new realms, such as disability; hence, powerful figures in the Senate resisted the freeze. In the House, meanwhile, Doughton had embraced the disability freeze as a provision important to him, and the House conferees wanted to do something special for him since he had announced that he would retire from Congress at the end of the session.

The deadlocked conference committee held its meetings in a small room in a hot season. At one point, Congressman Wilbur Mills bounded up from his chair and asked Cohen for suggestions on ways to break the impasse. Cohen suggested that the disability freeze be tried for only a year, but the Senate conferees objected. Mills requested another suggestion from Cohen, who floated the notion of enacting the disability freeze and then repealing it before it went into effect. The freeze would end on June 30, 1953, but no applications could be filed before July 1, 1953; in short, it would end before it began. Doughton could have his tribute; the Senate could forestall the enactment of the disability freeze; Congress could have its increase in Social Security benefits. The conferees agreed to the idea. Both houses accepted this compromise on July 5, and the bill became law on July 18, 1952.[14]

The story of the 1952 conference committee, suitably embellished, entered Washington lore. The very idea of ending something before it began was humorous, yet it was also instructive as an example of getting a program on the record, if not into operation. The 1952 amendments were the first of the famous Cohen compromises: the means by which he left his personal rather than an anonymous imprint on the legislative process. He referred to these amendments so often that they became part of his legacy, and Teddy Kennedy told the story behind them at Cohen's memorial service. When Cohen himself told the story, he always emphasized his independence from Altmeyer, his ability to ad lib on the spot. On the one hand, Cohen owed his reputation to his abilities as a staff worker who honored his commitments and did his homework; on the other, he gloried in the moments when the legislative process was fluid and he could bend it to his will.[15] He liked the sense of freedom his job as congressional liaison sometimes provided, in part because he was so often expected to follow a script written by others. Little oddities like the disability freeze that ended before it began only reinforced Cohen's devotion to the many nuances of the legislative process and to the Social Security cause.

In 1952 the legislative process, so dry, dull, and mysterious to so many, became a garden of delights for Wilbur Cohen. He gloated over a big victory: "I believe that very few people thought we would get any legislation in 1952," he told Elizabeth Wickenden. "But we exploited our advantages. Doughton's last year, the ability to increase OASI without any tax increase, and the political push for the McFarland Amendment." The legislation, according to Cohen, "gets us away from the idea that OASI is a depression phenomenon and that it will be another 10 years before benefits can be increased."[16] He astutely grasped the fact that the 1952 amendments were different, that they were the first of what would be a steady stream of incremental expansions of Social Security, the first bipartisan endorsement of the program, the first real manifestation of Social Security's political popularity. And it was Cohen, the legislative technician, who enabled the process to begin. He found the device that released the amendments from the conference committee and put them into the statute books.

RETREAT FROM WASHINGTON

After President Truman signed the 1952 amendments, Wilbur, Eloise, and the three boys left Washington for a long summer vacation in Texas. Cohen and his sons swam in a local stream and went walking and hunting in the Texas hills; as an urban Jew, he did not take naturally to hunting, but he came to regard it as an excuse for walking. Not a single rabbit or squirrel came his way, sparing him from firing his rifle. He did cross the path of a snake and claimed to have killed it with a rock. The solitude of the Texas hills helped him to relax; he liked to walk there because, as he put it, "you can see so much of the sky—so much more than we see up in Washington."[17]

His Texas sojourn also permitted him a panoramic view of the Washington scene in an uncertain political year. As always, he regarded leisure as a time for self-improvement and for reflecting on his basic goals. It annoyed him that the Democratic platform was so out of step with Altmeyer's views on Social Security. In particular, he lamented the fact that the party endorsed the repeal of the work clause or retirement test, which Altmeyer opposed, and failed to mention disability insurance, which Altmeyer strongly supported. Even on vacation, Cohen received requests to comment on social welfare issues for the presidential campaign. He prepared a lengthy paper on Social Security issues for Adlai Stevenson's advisers in which he proposed larger benefits for those who waited until age seventy to retire than for those who retired at sixty-five. He continued to push for the enactment of disability insurance, and he urged that consideration be given to the coverage of farmers in the Social Security system.[18]

None of Cohen's proposals made a particular impression on Stevenson, and none of these issues figured in the campaign. During a presidential campaign candidates spoke in vague generalities; it was a totally different exercise from the painstaking political work involved in marking up a Social Security bill in the Committee on Ways and Means. Nonetheless, it helped to have people like Cohen on hand since the candidates required interpreters who could translate the technical language of social legislation into English on short notice, and he had an impressive ability to do so.[19]

Immediately after the election, Cohen tried to assess what the first Republican administration in the twenty years that covered his entire professional life would mean, attempting to glean hints from their platform. Since it indicated that the Republicans wanted to study the logistics of a pay-as-you-go Social Security system, Cohen anticipated that there would be some type of advisory council similar to the ones in 1938 and 1948. Those had worked out well, and Cohen recommended that the Social Security Administration should "give our enthusiastic support to a comprehensive study of the program." On most other issues, he believed that it was best to sit tight, with the exception of extending Social Security coverage. "I believe we should use the next year or two to do everything we can to obtain universal coverage," he argued.[20] Once again, he sent out cautious feelers about other jobs and asked Witte to send him his course materials since "I may want to do some teaching next year."[21]

Cohen retreated from the situation by taking a trip around the world. For nearly two months, he traveled with Federal Security Administrator Oscar Ewing on a journey that combined aspects of a research trip and a goodwill mission.[22] First, he went to England and met with the doctors who administered the National Health Service, where he played the traditional role of social welfare pilgrim visiting the shrine of socialized medicine. In Rome, he had an audience with the pope and enjoyed being an American tourist glorying in the wonders of the Old World. Then he left for Asia, no longer a pilgrim but an ambassador of U.S. capitalism to the troubled Third World. As Ewing put it on his return in January 1953, "I went to South Asia and the Far East because the President and the Secretary of State wanted me to counteract . . . communist propaganda." If Americans could still learn from the Europeans, then they were required to teach the Asians about "American life and ideals."[23]

Like Ewing, Cohen worried about whether countries such as India would become Communist. During his trip, he could not avoid noticing the country's pervading poverty. In the southern Indian city of Madras, he saw children on the streets begging for money, yelling, "no papa, no mamma." People urinated in the open sewers. In Calcutta, people slept on the sidewalks outside of Cohen's hotel and implored him for money.

The trip briefly turned his attention away from U.S. Social Security and toward the problems of international development. This field had gained the attention of many of Cohen's fellow liberals in the 1950s and 1960s in part because it provided an outlet for the planning impulses that had blossomed during the New Deal and had then been frustrated by congressional refusal to pass planning legislation on the order of the 1945 Full Employment Act. Ideas such as prepaid group health or manpower planning that were rejected at home could always be dumped abroad, where the governments had at least to listen to the U.S. experts if they expected to get their share of U.S. foreign aid.[24] In India Cohen felt himself seized by the development impulse and dashed off a five-year plan in which he touted such ideas as "modern techniques and know-how" that would result in "substantially increased productivity."[25]

For the most part, Cohen saw the trip not as an important campaign in the cold war but as a political junket taken by two representatives of the Truman administration at a time when their services were not in heavy demand in Washington. Cohen, always eager to sample the new, ate chapatis in Bombay, saw the Taj Mahal in Aggra, attended a Siamese boxing match in Thailand, and observed ancient pagodas covered with gold and shining in the warm sun in Burma.

The highlight of the trip came in Japan, where Japanese Social Security officials took Ewing and Cohen to a geisha house. There he soaked in a warm bath while a geisha girl scrubbed his back until he felt "warm, sleepy, relaxed and very kindly." He put on a large kimono and went into the private dining room. Bowing low and delighted that his actions seemed so amusing to his hosts, Cohen sat down next to Ewing on a big purple pillow and ate from a low table. He marveled at the artistic composition of the many dishes before him—

raw fish, turtle soup with turtle eggs, tempura. He tucked into the food, drank his share of the sake, and watched a geisha in a white kimono do the snow dance. He felt sleepy almost to the point of pleasant exhaustion, and his efforts at feeding himself lagged. The geisha in attendance took that as her cue to begin feeding him: "I just sat back, completely relaxed, while she took the tempura, dipped it in the sauce and fed it to me with chopsticks." Oscar Ewing turned to Cohen and told him that he would no longer be fit to live with at home.[26]

No doubt Cohen permitted himself a moment of satisfaction at the geisha house, indulging himself in what surely approximated a universal fantasy: lying back in a stimulating, opulent, and exotic environment and letting other people take care of things. As he sat in the company of high Japanese officials and America's chief minister for health, education, and welfare, he perhaps thought of the distance between Tokyo and Milwaukee. Yet, as he reflected on his success, he might also have realized that he was in his customary role as staff support to a political principle. The geisha pampered everyone alike; she was paid to spin a web of fantasy around quite ordinary people. And Cohen and Ewing, two ordinary people, were cashing in their last chips before returning home to a country where they were not conquering heroes but just two more New Deal veterans about to face life in the Ike age.

CURTIS, HOBBY, AND LINTON

When Cohen arrived home in mid-January 1953, the battle for the soul of the Eisenhower administration was already well under way. Within another year, one marked by considerable friction between Cohen and his political superiors, the Republicans resolved their internal divisions over Social Security and came out in favor of expanding the program. In 1954 President Eisenhower shepherded a piece of legislation through Congress that extended Social Security coverage and raised benefits. Cohen played a crucial role in bridging the transition between the New Deal and modern Republicanism.

Early in the Eisenhower administration, conservative critics had reason to believe the president might favor them, rather than the members of Cohen's apparatus, in making Social Security policy. One influential conservative was Albert Linton of the Provident Mutual Life Insurance Company, who operated on the inside of Social Security politics, having served on the advisory commissions in 1934, 1938, and 1948. An actuary by training, he possessed the technical skills to comprehend complicated Social Security planning documents, and he criticized the program for what he regarded as its inevitable tendency toward expansion. Although Cohen and his colleagues tried to keep

Social Security in close actuarial balance, the solvency of the program invariably depended on congressional willingness to raise taxes in the future. Whether Congress would do so, however, remained uncertain, even doubtful. The resulting pattern, according to Linton, was to expand the program far beyond the means to fund it in the future.[27]

Around the time that Cohen was abroad with Oscar Ewing, Linton and others in the insurance industry submitted a policy declaration to the chamber of commerce. Beginning on November 15, 1952, the chamber polled its members on the proposal, "Social Security for the Aged," which, influenced by Linton's ideas, suggested that every old person should be covered under Social Security at a minimum payment of twenty-five dollars a month. Welfare for the elderly would be abolished, since everyone, including those who had never paid Social Security taxes, would be covered. The plan would be funded in the traditional manner through payroll taxes, the difference being that taxes would be set at a level to pay only for current benefits with no attempt to build a surplus for the future.[28] In this manner, as the publication accompanying the referendum explained, the chamber hoped to institute "more checks and balances" into the program and inhibit its growth. Under Linton's plan, for example, the surplus in the Social Security trust fund would be reduced to zero; any increase in benefits would then have to come from a rise in taxes or an increase in employment or wages. Whether the members of the chamber of commerce understood the meaning of this proposal is not clear, but the referendum carried overwhelmingly by a margin of sixteen to one and with the highest vote total of any referendum in the chamber's history.[29]

Eisenhower kept his own counsel on the chamber of commerce plan. When the president delivered his State of the Union message on February 2, 1953, he recommended that the "old-age and survivors insurance law should promptly be extended to cover millions of citizens who have been left out of the social security system."[30] Such rhetoric could mean an endorsement of the present program, or it might be perceived as a call to adopt the chamber's proposal.

An employee of the Eisenhower administration, Cohen bided his time. In mid-February, he reported to Elizabeth Wickenden that "nothing much has happened around the office, and I think that the main development is likely to be: stop, look, and listen."[31] Of more immediate interest to Cohen were the president's personnel appointments and his plans for bureaucratic reorganization. For the Social Security field, Eisenhower selected Democrat-turned-Republican Oveta Culp Hobby of the Houston political and newspaper family to head the Federal Security Agency. She proceeded cautiously on Social

Security, neither accepting nor rejecting the chamber's proposal.[32] At the top of her list stood plans to reorganize the FSA and to elevate it into a cabinet-level department to be called the Department of Health, Education, and Welfare (HEW). Mrs. Hobby would be its first secretary, only the second female cabinet officer in the nation's history. Forty-four-year-old Nelson A. Rockefeller supervised the details from his post as chairman of the President's Committee on Reorganization. By March the president presented Congress with a firm plan; by April 1, 1953, the new department opened its doors for business.[33]

Far from seeing this development as a promotion in bureaucratic rank, the people in Cohen's apparatus feared the worst from the new department. Edwin Witte observed that the order of words in its title was significant: the administration, he believed, wanted to emphasize welfare, not Social Security. The administration's placing health ahead of welfare was, according to Witte, "a give away that the AMA will call the shots."[34] The creation of the new department also provided the Eisenhower administration with some additional though unwanted leverage over the Social Security Administration. For example, the reorganization changed the commissioner of Social Security's job into a presidential appointment, subject to the Senate's approval. This meant that Arthur Altmeyer would leave, and Cohen knew that Altmeyer's departure would change his job substantially.

Even before Altmeyer left, Mrs. Hobby sought the advice of some outside experts on the chamber of commerce plan, a group that became known as the "Hobby lobby" that was to function somewhat like the advisory councils that had met in 1938 and 1948. Only this time Mrs. Hobby did not ask for much advice from the Social Security Administration, nor did she feel obligated to balance the parties at interest. Initially, there were no labor members or farmers; instead, the five-person group consisted of three strong advocates of the chamber of commerce plan, one New Hampshire resident apparently selected by presidential assistant Sherman Adams, and only one Social Security advocate – Eveline Burns, the academic expert who had worked on the staffs of the Committee on Economic Security and the National Resources Planning Board.

When Cohen and the other Social Security officials heard of the existence of the Hobby group early in March 1953, they were frightened and worried. The administration appeared to be taking the chamber of commerce plan seriously and might interpret the president's mandate to expand the system as a vote of confidence in the chamber's plan, as Albert Linton would advise. "You can see how fast the CofC boys will work," Cohen pointed out to Wickenden in a letter that he deliberately wrote at home, rather than at the office.[35]

Although Altmeyer remained in office when the Hobby lobby was appointed, he and Cohen decided that they should stay away from the initial meeting and agreed that the best representative would be Robert Ball. As Cohen noted, Ball already knew many of the key players, such as insurance executive Reinie Hohaus, Linton, Treasury Undersecretary Marion Folsom, and Burns, from his work as staff director of the 1948 council and from his earlier work arranging seminars in Social Security at the American Council on Education. Ball was astute, patient, and conciliatory, and his job as a deputy director within the Bureau of Old-Age and Survivors' Insurance was not in immediate danger of being made into a presidential appointment. Ball, said Cohen, also would not antagonize another important participant, Congressman Carl Curtis (R-Nebr.), "as AJA or I would."[36]

At the initial March 5 meeting of the Hobby lobby, Robert Ball quickly established himself as a de facto staff director. Before the meeting, he, Altmeyer, and Cohen prepared a kit of materials and held extensive strategy sessions, and both before and after the meeting, Eveline Burns talked to Cohen and gained his insights about how to proceed. Much of the meeting, Cohen reported to Wickenden, involved explaining to Curtis the need to guarantee benefits; the congressman seemed to think that benefit levels could be set each year.[37]

Carl Curtis was emphatically not one of Cohen's congressional clients; indeed, he had opposed the 1950 amendments and was sympathetic to the chamber of commerce proposal. Worse, Curtis was leading the fight to have Cohen replaced at the Social Security Administration. Reflecting long after the fact, Cohen placed Curtis in the same camp as Alfred Landon. Each of these politicians, who came from prairie states with many farmers and relatively few Social Security beneficiaries, favored a Townsend-style flat pension, financed from general revenues. Curtis was an unreconstructed conservative who chose not to participate in the Social Security consensus.[38]

Cohen eagerly sought the aid of other Republicans who had helped to pass the 1952 amendments. Although the administration had not yet made up its mind on Social Security in the spring of 1953, Cohen continued to lobby Congress, just as he had during the Truman administration. Among the Republicans on the Ways and Means Committee, Cohen made it a special point to stay in touch with Robert Kean, the liberal Republican from New Jersey.[39] In a typical bit of congressional service, Cohen visited Kean in February 1953 to ask if he would like to reintroduce his bill from the previous Congress. Saying that he would, Kean told Cohen to come back in a few days. Cohen confided in his diary that Kean "seemed quite friendly by the time I left."[40] On Wednesday, February 25, Cohen received a call from Kean, who asked for a bill expanding

Social Security coverage, enabling a retired person to earn $100 with no loss of Social Security benefits and restoring the previously passed disability freeze. Kean wanted the bill quickly. On Friday, February 27, Cohen convened a meeting of Social Security officials, including the actuary and legislative drafts-men, to refine the bill for Kean. He took it to the congressman late in the afternoon and then handed him a polished version on Monday, March 2, 1953; Kean introduced the bill that day.[41]

Although Cohen spent a great deal of time with Kean and the Republicans, he did not neglect his other clients. At one point in March 1953, he was working with five Democratic members of the Ways and Means Committee, composing a liberal Lehman-Dingell-Roosevelt bill, advising the Democratic leadership on Social Security, and dissuading Sen. Hubert Humphrey from introducing a bill to repeal the work test. "So you see how my time has been taken up," he wrote to Wickenden. "Yet I believe there is a real job to be done in working up these bills."[42]

In these dealings with Congress, Cohen pursued his agency's agenda rather than the president's. With Democrats, for example, Cohen made no secret that he, too, was a Democrat. He urged Jere Cooper, the ranking Tennessee Democrat on Ways and Means, as he put it, to "take the initiative" and wrote a modest bill for him to introduce, noting in one of his many letters to Elizabeth Wickenden his success in getting Cooper "off dead center." Cohen began to give Cooper suggestions for what he called a "constructive program," which included higher Social Security benefits, a $6,000 wage base, and disability insurance benefits. He resolved to continue talking with Cooper, patiently modifying the proposal "until I get something he will accept."[43] The striking fact about this process was that the Eisenhower administration had not officially accepted any of the items on the list, yet Cohen pushed them anyway.

Lobbying Congress, Cohen worked hard to discredit the chamber of com-merce proposal, in which he and the other members of the apparatus per-ceived many political liabilities. For the package to be appealing, the guaran-teed benefit had to be high, yet the twenty-five dollar level in the chamber plan was below the average old-age assistance payment in all but five states; raising the minimum benefit made the plan more costly and less appealing. Since the entire package depended on payroll taxes, it proposed that the elderly be supported by highly regressive payroll taxes rather than by broad-based general revenues. Not only would the working population support people who had never worked, but poorer workers would bear a far greater bur-den than richer workers: someone earning $100,000 would pay the same amount as someone making $3,600. Hence, liberal and labor groups de-nounced the plan as a form of "fraud" and "stealing."[44] So that Congressmen

Aime Forand (D-R.I.), Hale Boggs (D-La.), and John Dingell (D-Mich.) understood this point, Cohen resolved to explain it to them personally. In March 1953 he was "hurrying, hurrying to see them all because I don't know when the axe will fall."[45]

In addition to discrediting the chamber proposal, Cohen spent a great deal of time and thought counteracting the work of Congressman Curtis, who, in the spring of 1953, headed a special Ways and Means subcommittee to investigate Social Security.[46] Cohen perceived Curtis to be engaging in a witch hunt that could only harm the program. From Curtis's choice of staff director, Cohen knew that the subcommittee would follow a line purporting that Social Security, contrary to the claims of its supporters, was not really insurance. The public, according to this analysis, would be better served by a program similar to the chamber of commerce plan.[47] Since Cohen disagreed so completely with this appraisal, he offered to help the Democrats on the Ways and Means Committee discredit Curtis and his investigation. He worried, however, that the Democrats, in the minority for the first time since 1947, needed more staff support.[48]

In Cohen's efforts to discredit Curtis and the chamber of commerce proposal, he formed a partnership with Elizabeth Wickenden. Unlike Cohen, Wickenden did not have to maintain her civil service status or cooperate with the Eisenhower administration; she could function entirely as a Social Security advocate. Cohen wrote to her so regularly in the early months of the Eisenhower administration that he began one letter, "We have already given up the whiskey in order to save money for stamps." He told her, "You and I are the only ones who have such an intense personal interest in promoting social security"; yet someone needed to uphold the cause "until we are again in an era of progress and advancement." Cohen reminded Wickenden that they were young enough to wait a few years for another "decade of social progress. But we must have people and ideas ready to act in 1956 or 1960 or when the need arises."[49]

In a typical act of partnership, Wickenden asked Cohen if he wanted her to leak the story about the limited range of the Hobby group's membership. As matters stood, the composition of the group was not public knowledge. Cohen advised her to wait until the group had more meetings: "then it can really be exploited." He noted that Hobby had already turned down a chance to meet with the CIO Social Security Committee and, "if she also refuses the AFL, then it will make a terrific story, don't you think? My idea is that they will use enough rope to hang themselves."[50] A few days later, Cohen decided to expose the Hobby lobby and urged Wickenden to publicize Mrs. Hobby's decision not to meet with representatives of organized labor and other liberal groups.[51] Within two days, Cohen told Wickenden that he had begun to get phone calls about the Hobby lobby, and in another ten days, he informed her that criticism of the group had yielded definite results.[52] By now labor leaders such as Walter Reuther had sent telegrams to their senators, and under congressional pressure, Hobby announced that she would meet with labor and farm groups. Although the pressure came through private sources, such as Wickenden and Walter Reuther, it had originated from Cohen, a civil servant and Eisenhower administration employee.

In time, Cohen and the apparatus managed to turn the Hobby lobby completely around and make it an instrument for the expansion of Social Security. Cohen worked particularly closely on this matter with Cruikshank and Ball. On March 25, 1953, for example, Nelson Cruikshank and other officials from the AFL went to see Mrs. Hobby. Cruikshank could not decide whether the AFL should join the group, but Cohen urged him to so that Cruikshank could "ask Bob Ball officially then to prepare certain materials . . . to help them in pressing" the AFL point of view. Having breached the tight hold of Linton and the chamber of commerce sympathizers over the group, Mrs. Hobby also extended an offer to representatives of the CIO and began to consider additional members, such as Fedele Fauri, dean of the Michigan School of Social Work, and Loula Dunn of the American Public Welfare Association.[53] Cruikshank and the others soon agreed to join.

Consequently, when the augmented group met on April 1, 1953, it resembled nothing so much as a conventional Social Security advisory council, right down to the fact that Robert Ball served as the staff director. The group soon agreed to limit its discussions to the extension of Social Security coverage rather than to attempt a radical reworking of the program as suggested in the chamber plan. As Martha Derthick has written in her magisterial and authoritative account of Social Security policy, "The broadening of representation narrowed the potential range of discussion and inhibited conservative innovation. Extending coverage was the one measure on which the forces contending over social security policy could agree."[54]

As the subversion of the Hobby lobby unfolded, Cohen faced a major career crisis. On April 10, 1953, Arthur J. Altmeyer, the only commissioner of Social Security in the program's history, left government service. Cohen, who had worked more closely with Altmeyer than anyone in the agency, staffed his boss's departure. Cohen watched as tearful employees came to say goodbye, and then he spent considerable time sending copies of Altmeyer's handwritten farewell address to people across the country. Altmeyer, accompanied by Ball and Cohen, paid a courtesy call on Treasury Undersecretary Marion Folsom and urged him to reject the chamber plan and to preserve the equities in the system. If people did not perceive a relationship between contributions and benefits, Altmeyer maintained, the system would collapse. Then, at 5:30 P.M., Cohen left Arthur Altmeyer. Later that night, Altmeyer called Cohen at home and thanked him for his years of service. "It was the end of an era," Cohen wrote in his diary; "there was a catch in my throat and a tear in my eye."[55]

Without his mentor, Cohen could not quite decide what to do next. Cohen knew that he, along with I. S. Falk and others, was on a list of people slated to be fired.[56] In May Cohen learned that the administration intended to make the bureau chiefs in the SSA into presidential appointments. Then in July, his job as technical adviser to the commissioner of Social Security was taken out of the civil service and made into a discretionary appointment.[57] Rather than leave immediately, Cohen decided to see who Hobby and Nelson Rockefeller, the new undersecretary of the department, would name to the position of commissioner.[58] Cohen then bargained with Rockefeller to remain in government employment. As was characteristic, he tried to be conciliatory; under the circumstances, he had few other options.[59]

After considerable negotiations with Rockefeller that lasted into fall, Cohen agreed to take I. S. Falk's vacated job and become director of the Division of Research and Statistics in the Office of the Commissioner of the Social Security Administration. It was a demotion in everything but title, and it involved less pay. "It is true that Mrs. Hobby appointed me to a new position with a very fancy title," Cohen wrote his friend Merlyn Pitzele, "although to be quite frank, I did have to take a salary cut to stay on. The main point was that I was taken out of Schedule C. position and placed in a regular Civil Service position such as one I had before."[60]

As head of the research division, the very part of the agency that worked on health and disability proposals that so many Republicans opposed, Cohen led a complicated life. On one level he operated as a conventional bureaucrat for the Republican administration, doing staff work for Oveta Culp Hobby and Nelson Rockefeller; on other levels he functioned as a partisan Democrat and as a Social Security advocate from the Roosevelt and Truman eras. In these capacities, he worked with the Democratic National Committee (DNC) and the Democratic congressional leadership and maneuvered Social Security policy so that the same proposals appeared in the Republican Congress in 1953 as had appeared in the Democratic Congress in 1952. At times he would brief Mrs. Hobby on meetings with Social Security advocates and brief the advocates on the same meetings with Mrs. Hobby. It was a harrowing experience that tested Cohen's capacity for resilience. "There is little in each day's work to make me enthusiastic," wrote a played-out Cohen at the end of one of his activity spasms, exhausted from reconciling so many contrary forces, in the summer of 1953.[61]

Hard as the work was, it paid substantial dividends. Instead of the Eisenhower administration bending the Social Security Administration to its will, the SSA converted it to the Social Security cause. The first domino to fall was the Hobby lobby, which began as a vehicle to advance the chamber of commerce plan and ended with a strong endorsement of the existing program. On June 24 a report from this group appeared that, far from attacking Social Security, simply laid out ways of extending coverage to new groups of current workers, such as farm operators. Astute readers of the report could detect Robert Ball's hand in its composition; once again, he had transformed a major threat to Social Security into an affirmation of the program. As he modestly recalled, the Hobby lobby "proved very helpful in shaping the attitude of the Eisenhower Administration . . . and bringing it toward a much more favorable attitude toward the program."[62]

The next step in the process was the selection of a sympathetic commissioner to replace Altmeyer. In September 1953 the administration named John Tramburg, the director of Wisconsin's Department of Public Welfare, to the post. According to Rockefeller, Tramburg was close to the Republican governor of the state and was well respected in social welfare circles. Tramburg's background indeed resembled Arthur Altmeyer's. Born in Wisconsin (Madison, 1913), he taught public school before attending graduate school at the University of Chicago's School of Social Service Administration and then receiving a degree from the Columbus Law School. Like Altmeyer, he had gone into state government.[63]

To be sure, Tramburg had not been Cohen's first choice. Ever since Cohen had learned, probably through Merlyn Pitzele, that Thomas Dewey had asked Fedele Fauri to prepare memorandums on Social Security for the Eisenhower campaign, he had entertained the idea of Fauri's becoming the next Social Security commissioner. Cohen moved cautiously on Fauri's appointment. As he put it, Mrs. Hobby was "a very smart lady," much smarter than her predecessor Oscar Ewing, and it was important that she feel that she was making the appointment "on her own initiative."[64] Fauri refused to cooperate, however, and Cohen dropped the matter; still, Tramburg proved an acceptable choice to him.[65]

It turned out that Tramburg had some conditions for taking the job, and he had accepted the position only on a trial basis, with every intention of returning to Madison after a year. He also told Altmeyer, over dinner in Madison, that he insisted that Hobby retain Cohen and Ball. According to Altmeyer, Tramburg informed Hobby that "he couldn't get along without you two [Ball and Cohen] when she first broached the subject of his taking the Commissionership. She told him at that time that she had no intention of letting either of you go." "I believe," Altmeyer continued in a letter to Cohen, "he will rely heavily upon you in whatever position you fill."[66]

The administration agreed to Tramburg's demands in part because Hobby and Rockefeller wanted to fill the job before Congress reconvened. It was important for the administration to take what Rockefeller described as a "positive approach" to Social Security in an election year. Besides, the Republicans, as Rockefeller noted in a memorandum to Sherman Adams in the White House, were divided on this subject and "reconciliation of divergent points of view is needed to enable the Administration to secure support of constructive legislation in this field."[67]

In this process of reconciliation, Cohen won another victory. Instead of making Carl Curtis the voice of their party, the Republicans chose a more moderate approach. Due in large part to Cohen's efforts, Curtis became a marginal figure in his party and in Congress on the subject of Social Security. His hearings, which began in the summer of 1953 and concluded in November, proved a complete bust in discrediting the program. As often happened in legislative battles, the chief contests took place in settings far removed from the public eye.

The battle over Arthur Altmeyer's testimony serves as a good example. Curtis wanted Altmeyer, who had moved back to Madison, to be a consultant to his committee, perhaps with the motive of putting his imprimatur on an investigation designed to discredit the program. Before requesting Altmeyer's services, Curtis summoned Cohen to his office on a Friday morning, read the letter to Altmeyer he had drafted, and urged Cohen to persuade Altmeyer to accept. Cohen, who found Curtis to be pompous and curt, made no promises. Moving down the corridor, he talked with Jere Cooper and Wilbur Mills, both prominent Democrats and future chairmen of the Committee on Ways and Means. Mills expressed his disapproval of Curtis, and neither congressman urged that Altmeyer respond favorably to him.[68] A series of phone calls between Cohen and Altmeyer ensued, and Altmeyer decided not to help the committee in any way. Cohen called Curtis on Monday and told him that "Altmeyer was not inclined to undertake the project." That same day Altmeyer wrote to Curtis and, in a letter meant to have wide public circulation, declined his invitation. Altmeyer carefully sent copies of the letter to Democrats Cooper, Mills, and Dingell with accompanying notes; to Dingell he wrote, "You know without my saying so that if at any time I can be of assistance to you as a member of this subcommittee you have only to command." Altmeyer wanted to help the Democrats, not the Republicans, and definitely not Curtis.[69] Curtis waited a few weeks and then sent Altmeyer another letter hoping that "after more deliberate consideration" he would change his mind; Altmeyer again declined.[70] Curtis concluded that Altmeyer could not be persuaded to participate and compelled his testimony by means of a subpoena. Altmeyer then arranged to appear before the subcommittee late in November.[71]

Cohen, meanwhile, paved the way for Altmeyer's testimony. He personally persuaded Jere Cooper, heavily involved in other business, to remain on the subcommittee, advising Altmeyer that Cooper "wants to be helpful but he isn't quite sure of all the technical details and he is so cautious. A little refresher the day before will give him encouragement and confidence." Cohen also wrote a briefing paper for the minority staffer on the subcommittee in which he tried to anticipate the questions Curtis would ask. Sending a copy to Altmeyer, he wrote, "We are expecting to see Sir Arthur kill the dragon."[72]

Altmeyer eventually appeared before the subcommittee on November 27.[73] Through a long day of testimony that lasted until 6:55, he sparred repeatedly with Curtis and the committee counsel over whether Social Security was really insurance. He insisted on reading a long series of legal decisions and reports into the record. In the end, Curtis failed to gain the public advantage for which he had hoped. He later complained about "left-wing partisan opposition" that "didn't want any questions asked about this multi-dollar program," but to no avail. Altmeyer, with Cohen's considerable assistance, had slain or at least paralyzed the dragon.[74]

By the time Altmeyer testified, Curtis was already out of favor with Rockefeller and Hobby. At the end of 1953 Curtis sent Chairman Reed a report that his staff had prepared on the subcommittee's findings, which made the case that Social Security was not insurance and that the right to its assistance was "a conditional, statutory right—subject always to legislative change." After sixteen years of Social Security coverage, 60 percent of the aged remained without benefits, and those who did receive them would get back more than fifty times the amount they had paid into the system. The line between insurance benefits and no insurance benefits is "often a seemingly whimsical one for an insurance program," yet the public continued to believe that Social Security was a universal insurance program. As Curtis understood, it simply was not, yet it appeared as reasonable by the early 1950s to expand Social Security coverage as to create an entirely new system.[75]

Early in 1954 Curtis introduced his own Social Security bill, but like the staff report of his subcommittee, his bill found little support. It called for minimum grants of forty-five dollars to the aged and thirty dollars each to a widow and child. It also contained major political liabilities, such as a new 2 percent tax on unearned income and the elimination of federal grants to poor families where the father had deserted the mother. Even conservatives in the Eisenhower administration opposed the bill.[76]

Once administration officials sorted out the political options available to them, they realized that Social Security was a done deal. In a cabinet discussion, administration members characterized the chamber of commerce plan as "bad math" and a "numbers racket we would always lose." In other words, once the link between contributions and benefits was lost, pensions could be bid higher and higher. Republicans, more reluctant to spend money than the Democrats, would be outbid on the level of pensions by the Democrats. In October 1953 Eisenhower himself wrote a letter to stockbroker E. F. Hutton, who had called Social Security "tyranny." "It would appear logical to build upon the system that has been in effect for almost twenty years," the president argued. The alternative, according to Eisenhower, was "turning it completely upside down and running the very real danger that we would end up with no system at all."[77]

By the fall of 1953 Wilbur Cohen had gained much of what he had sought. He remained in government employment, and Curtis was in retreat. The Hobby lobby endorsed the program in July, and the administration tentatively proposed the extension of coverage, along the lines of the Hobby report, in August. In September, the administration agreed to the appointment of John Tramburg.

During these first months of the Eisenhower administration, Cohen had stepped well over the line that separated civil servants and politicians. The SSA claimed its motto was "Never Advocate – Always Explain."[78] Cohen's service to Congressmen Cooper and Kean might possibly be viewed as "explaining" Social Security policy options; his behind-the-scenes work with Elizabeth Wickenden marked an explicit effort to shape policy. Undoubtedly, Cohen advocated for continuity in the early years of the Eisenhower administration, doing far more than simply explaining the consequences of taking certain actions. He actively intervened in the policy process and in effect took over from Arthur Altmeyer, even after Eisenhower had fired him.

The process of subverting an administration from within left him feeling uncomfortable and often discouraged. In a candid letter to Elizabeth Wickenden early in 1954, Cohen wrote of the "intellectual isolation and despair which haunts those of us trying to ride a donkey and an elephant at the same time." The ride was "hazardous" and required "more forbearance than I have most of the time. . . . How long I will last in the present state of affairs is beyond me. Sometimes I think I can't last through the day. But I try and keep my eye on the main objective – to preserve what we have and pass it on so when the pendulum swings to 'social progress' once again there will be a solid foundation on which to build."[79]

THE 1954 LAW

Cohen's ultimate victory came in the 1954 Social Security legislation. Even after the work of Curtis and the Hobby lobby, officials at HEW still felt the need for a thorough internal review before they submitted their proposals. This forum would be the court of last resort. Thus, beginning in the fall of 1953, Cohen turned his attention to working with the administration. On October 7 he attended what he termed his "most important meeting," which took place in the "chart room" created by HEW undersecretary Nelson Rockefeller. On the table was the subject of noncontributory pensions, such as the chamber of commerce plan. Oveta Culp Hobby presided, in Cohen's words, "as if she were the Prime Minister asking her Cabinet officials for their views before she announced her decision." After Assistant Secretary Roswell Perkins, a Rockefeller family lawyer described by Cohen as a "brilliant, objective chap," summarized the pros and cons of the plan under discussion, Hobby recognized each person in turn. Cohen told her (whom he pictured in his overheated imagination as "Queen Victoria in her younger days") that "OASI was a delicate institution which existed only with the support of employers, unions and the public to make the necessary contributions." He said that it was "easy to make changes which would ultimately lead to a system supported largely or entirely out of general revenues. This would lead to a flat-rate benefit system which would be subject to outright political decisions." He wondered whether employers, unions, and employees would support such a system.[80]

By the fall of 1953 Hobby and Rockefeller needed little additional coaxing on the matter. As Cohen noted in his diary, "Mrs. H. and N. Rockefeller seemed particularly opposed to the CC plan."[81] "After much travail I think the recommendations will be on the constructive side," Cohen advised Altmeyer in November. "We have shed a lot of blood in the process but we are eating lots of red blood to make up for our loss," Cohen noted.[82]

In the end, the administration decided to follow the incremental path established by the 1952 amendments. It opted for a major extension of coverage to farm operators and other groups, for raising the average level of Social Security benefits, and for raising the tax base from $3,600 to $4,200. The problem of blanketing in the elderly was quietly laid aside. Instead, the administration concentrated much of its energy on establishing a disability freeze for Social Security beneficiaries and on improving and augmenting the rehabilitation services available to people with disabilities. Due largely to the tutelage of Cohen and Ball, the administration rejected the chamber of commerce plan as one that would destroy the Social Security system.

Back in Madison, Arthur Altmeyer could not have been more pleased. In public, he complained to reporters that the administration had chosen not to endorse disability insurance and had not recommended higher benefits, but in private, he understood that it had chosen to play by his rules and to accept the principles of Social Security. It was, he told Cohen, "a great tribute to you personally." According to Altmeyer, Cohen made it possible for the administration to understand technical material and practical politics as well. "I shudder to think of what might have happened if you had not been there to facilitate the thinking and bridge the transition," Altmeyer confided to him.[83]

The administration, for its part, took pains not to offend Congressman Curtis or the chamber of commerce and to downplay the influence of Wilbur Cohen. During the 1954 hearings to consider the administration's proposals, its officials made certain that Cohen was out of sight. Cohen briefed Hobby and Perkins on their testimony before the Ways and Means Committee but stayed away from the hearings themselves. He told Witte that Ball would play a key role at the hearings, "but since he was not so closely identified with the past administration they think they can get by with him. But as for me, I will have to stay in the background."[84]

Being in the background did not prevent Cohen from lobbying Congress from behind the scenes. Although he strongly supported the administration bill, his support did not stop him from pushing for more. He continued to serve as an adviser to the Democrats on the Ways and Means Committee and to Congressman Kean, urging him to persuade Chairman Reed to expedite the hearings and not to give much attention to Curtis. He also drafted a statement that Kean could use to rebut Curtis. He pressed the Democrats to preserve their position as being more liberal than the Republicans, in part by advocating disability insurance and by proposing a higher wage base. He realized, however, that the Democrats could not handle anything "very complicated" because they did not have the staff assistance. Cohen advised that the Democrats should also recommend higher welfare grants to "show that they are for the people."[85]

As the legislation worked its way through Congress, the extension of Social Security coverage to farm operators surfaced as the major issue. The Senate Finance Committee eliminated the coverage of farmers and all self-employed persons from the bill, partly on the initiative of Sen. Walter George. Arthur Altmeyer, for one, doubted that Congressman Cooper would stand firm for the House version in the conference committee. At the beginning of August, Altmeyer confided to Cohen his assessment "that the odds aren't better than 50-50."[86]

Despite Altmeyer's doubts, the legislation passed at the end of August 1954, and farm operators entered the Social Security system. "It really is a miracle to get farm coverage. I am still amazed," wrote Altmeyer to Cohen. "The Lord works in mysterious ways his wonders to perform! Of course, you helped the Lord a lot."[87] "We shall strike off a special medal for you when we return to power, for valor, patience, and ingenuity far and above the call of duty," an appreciative Altmeyer told Cohen.[88]

With the 1954 amendments, the Eisenhower administration accepted the Social Security consensus, extended coverage, and raised benefits in an election year. For the first time, a Republican president and a Republican Congress had collaborated on a Social Security bill. The events of 1954 confirmed the bipartisan support for the program that had been present but not wholly evident in 1952. Ultimately, the administration could not resist supporting a program that, as Curtis noted, paid people far more than they contributed and that was enjoying growing popularity.

Social Security, it seemed, could be as appealing to the Republicans as to the Democrats.[89] The vital center, as Arthur Schlesinger called it, could govern. Before this time, the Republicans, in their brief reign during the Eightieth Congress, had chosen to concentrate on public assistance rather than on social insurance. In 1954 they disciplined the laggards in their party, such as Curtis, and seized the moment.

As the Republicans worked on the 1954 amendments, Cohen concluded twenty years of working with Social Security and told Pitzele that the Republican era had brought "trials and tribulations." Those were minor, however, compared to the fact that "Mrs. Hobby and President Eisenhower have reaffirmed the fundamental principles of the social security program which are the key elements which I believed and which I have advocated." Cohen said that an "emotional attachment to the program and to the work has made me want to stay on and finish the full 20 years"; beyond that and earning a minimal pension, however, he made few promises.[90]

Cohen missed the firm guidance of Altmeyer, who, even though absent, provided him with external validation. The new politics of Social Security, marked by incremental growth and bipartisan support, would survive Altmeyer's departure and persist through the Ike age. Despite Cohen's maturing skills as a lobbyist and a legislative analyst, however, he did not enjoy quite the influence he had had as Altmeyer's assistant. He was no longer a fixture at congressional hearings, for example. With the task of bridging the transition accomplished and with twenty years on the job behind him, Cohen was free to explore other possibilities, and he examined new prospects with interest. "Don't be downhearted," Altmeyer told Cohen at the end of 1954. "You have achieved a miracle already, reconciling so many factors not controllable by anything except sheer persistence and merit."[91]

A NEW LIFE: COHEN
IN ACADEMIA, 1956–1961

"As one emigre to another, I salute you!" wrote Arthur Altmeyer in Madison to Wilbur Cohen in Ann Arbor early in 1956.[1] Cohen had decided to leave the government to take a job at the University of Michigan. The move allowed him to acquire a new role in the policy process, that of an action intellectual who helped to shape the nation's perceptions of its social welfare programs. In this new role, Cohen modified some of the New Deal principles he had learned from Altmeyer and helped to transform the Democrats from the party of depression to the party of prosperity. More important, he managed to put some distance between himself and Altmeyer and to change his image from that of a competent bureaucrat to that of an independent authority on social welfare policy. With his newly acquired prestige, Cohen helped to formulate the liberal line that affluence, far from solving all social problems, exposed new problems. Instead of succumbing to self-congratulation, the nation needed to invest its newfound wealth in activities, such as education, that would help it to sustain prosperity and allow it to reach its maximum potential. It needed, in short, to close the gap between performance and potential. As John Kenneth Galbraith, another influential critic of the politics of complacency, wrote in 1958, "The affluent country which conducts its affairs in accordance with the rules of another and poorer age also forgoes opportunities." Cohen, like Galbraith, gained influence over the intellectual discourse of the era precisely because he not only criticized the status quo, giving the Democrats a policy mission, but also suggested that the challenges of the 1950s could be met.[2]

THE DECISION TO LEAVE AND THE RED STIGMA

"We are in the midst of preparing our legislative program for next year," Cohen reported to Altmeyer in October 1954. "We have to do about three times as much staff work as is really necessary in order to consider all sorts of alternatives which are impractical. We prepare all sorts of memos analyzing the pros and cons of various proposals." Unless someone with real knowledge of the program arrived to serve as secretary or assistant secretary, Cohen said that he and his fellow Social Security bureaucrats would be worn out. "We are still waiting for you in 1957," Cohen added.[3]

Between the fall of 1954 and the summer of 1955, three events occurred that convinced Wilbur Cohen to leave Washington. First, the Democrats won the congressional elections in November and prepared to take over the key committees that made Social Security policy, enabling them to pursue an independent agenda for the program's expansion. It also put Cohen in the awkward position of officially dissuading the Democrats from actions that he unofficially endorsed. Although Cohen had seen several variations on the executive-congressional relationship, he had never worked with the combination of a Democratic Congress and a Republican president; the rules for this situation had not yet been written. The years of divided rule in the 1940s had been unpleasant, with the president vetoing at least two Social Security bills produced by the Republican Congress. Since that time, a consensus had developed on the desirability of social expansion, but major disagreements over the pace and direction of that expansion remained. Although one could hide within the bureaucracy and aid the Democrats surreptitiously, it would be difficult for Cohen, a partisan figure identified with Altmeyer, to remain camouflaged.

The second development that motivated Cohen to leave was his realization that the Eisenhower administration would not support disability insurance. If that were the case, then, according to Cohen, "I couldn't possibly stay in the Eisenhower administration."[4] As late as 1954 Cohen thought he might be able to convince Secretary Hobby to sanction the policy: "I believe that Mrs. Hobby might ultimately endorse disability insurance," Cohen told Witte. "So far, she has been careful not to say anything against it."[5] Despite his optimism, Cohen never persuaded Hobby to support disability insurance. In 1955 she resigned, and the administration announced that Marion Folsom, the Eastman Kodak executive and longtime Social Security insider, would be her replacement. Folsom enjoyed a reputation as a forward-looking business executive who in the late 1930s had convinced many of his fellow businessmen to support Social Security and not to regard it as a fundamental threat to free enterprise. This statesmanlike position earned him a place on the Social Security Advisory Councils of 1938 and 1948.[6] Folsom had always been wary of advocating disability insurance, however, speaking against it in both advisory councils and joining Linton in a formal condemnation of it in 1948.[7]

By the time that Folsom was appointed as Secretary of Health, Education, and Welfare, Altmeyer dismissed his accomplishments and told Cohen that "in spite of the great contributions he has made in the past, he will also be a Secretary of not too much Health, Education, and Welfare." Cohen came to see Folsom as a business representative who was only a little ahead of his group. Nelson Cruikshank agreed with this assessment, saying that Folsom was "vastly overrated as a liberal" and that he took a strong position in favor of social welfare programs after, but not before, they were enacted. It did not appear to Cohen in 1955, particularly after he discussed the matter with Nelson Cruikshank, that Folsom would support disability insurance. [8]

The third factor in Cohen's decision to leave was that he had received a good job offer from his friend Fedele Fauri. [9] Ever since Fauri had left the Congressional Research Service and become dean of the school of social work at the University of Michigan in the early 1950s, he had urged Cohen to join him. [10] In the spring of 1955 Fauri invited Cohen, with no advanced degrees, to become a tenured, full professor of public welfare administration at Michigan. Asked years later about how Cohen came to the university, Fauri replied, "Oh, I offered him a job . . . on the basis that I thought he was the kind of person who could stimulate students and stimulate everybody else who was around him." [11] Fauri made the job offer to Cohen at a professional meeting in San Francisco that spring, reiterating the point that Folsom was not likely to support disability insurance. Cohen later wrote that he accepted because "the 2 ½ years under the Eisenhower administration had been a great emotional and intellectual strain for me." [12]

The idea of teaching in a university setting was hardly unfamiliar to Cohen; ever since his student days with Selig Perlman, teaching had appealed to him. He had never acted on his desires because he had become enmeshed in the Social Security program and had never found the time to get a graduate degree. When his children arrived in the 1940s, the security of a civil service job also became a factor in keeping him in the government. On the rare occasions when he lectured in college classrooms, he found the experience enjoyable. He liked the give-and-take with the students, perhaps because it permitted him to assert his own ego and provided a refreshing counterpoint to his button-downed, self-effacing interactions with congressmen. At forty-two, he no longer wanted to be invisible.

As Cohen contemplated returning to academic life, he realized that he was a generation removed from the concerns of the undergraduates who were entering college in the 1950s. Just after Altmeyer left the government, Cohen had traveled to Mount Holyoke and spoken to a political science seminar; he noted that the women asked "hard questions" about whether or not Social Security discouraged thrift. Cohen marveled that the students appeared to believe in "permanent prosperity," which they felt stemmed from an "individual's own initiative." Although Cohen was puzzled by these attitudes and could not help but notice other differences between the Holyoke students and those in Madison twenty years earlier, he recorded in his diary how much he enjoyed being on campus, expressing pleasure "in the green fields, the hills – the young people – and the library."[13]

On July 25, 1955, the University of Michigan's Board of Regents approved Cohen's appointment. Ever cautious, he waited for this final step in the process before he told Commissioner Charles Schottland of his decision to leave the government, effective January 15, 1956. When word of Cohen's decision reached Marion Folsom, he asked him to reconsider and even offered him a two-day-a-week consultantship. Although Cohen was tempted by this offer, Eloise urged him to reject it, not relishing the thought of his being gone for a considerable portion of each week. After he considered the matter, he decided that to stay "would curtail" his "freedom of action"; he wanted to go to the Democrats on the Ways and Means and Finance committees with clean hands. He also probably wanted to leave the Social Security Administration behind and begin a new life.[14] "I think you made the right decision," Altmeyer told Cohen; "it is a 'natural' which might never have occurred again. . . . But for me the life has gone out of social security when you leave."[15]

If Cohen thought he could escape from the pressing political concerns of the era by moving to academia, he soon learned otherwise. In the fall of 1955 Fauri told Cohen that some opposition had developed to his appointment at Michigan. Although he had an offer that had been confirmed by the Board of Regents and need not have worried, he resolved to confront his critics, who turned out to be two physicians who had learned of Cohen's activities on behalf of national health insurance. The two doctors, both important financial donors at the university, had branded Cohen as a Communist and a Socialist. Cohen went to Ann Arbor, arranged an appointment with the president and vice-president of the university, and told them that he was neither.[16] The moment passed, but it carried a reminder that the university was not hermetically sealed; the issue of McCarthyism resonated in academia as much as it did in Washington.

Cohen, like many other New Deal bureaucrats, battled the charge that he was soft on communism throughout the fifties. He had the specific disadvantage of attracting the constant attention of Marjorie Shearon, the disgruntled former Social Security employee who shadowed his actions and reported on them in a newsletter, *Challenge to Socialism*. Using this forum, published more than thirty times a year, Shearon wrote about the efforts to pass health insurance in great detail and frequently found reasons to criticize Cohen. Altmeyer, who received a copy of her newsletter, told Cohen that it was "a crazy way" for Shearon to spend her life, yet for all her eccentricities, she still managed to stir up trouble. In 1958, to cite one example, Altmeyer received a request from Sen. William Proxmire's (D-Wis.) office for information about Shearon's publication. Altmeyer replied, "This is a one-woman sheet written by a former disgruntled employee of the Social Security who was eased out about 15 years ago. In my opinion she is a very emotionally disturbed person who nevertheless has a very good mind. . . . She has advocated for a long time the complete repeal of the Social Security Act, calling it every name she could think of."[17]

In the 1940s Shearon's efforts to expose conspiracies behind efforts to pass a national health insurance bill had amused Cohen, but his amusement yielded to real anxiety in the 1950s. "I am glad to know that you are getting all of the interesting current information from Mrs. Shearon," he wrote, tongue-in-cheek, to Edwin Witte in 1947. In a few years, as Shearon shifted her attention from Falk and Altmeyer, no longer active in government, to Cohen, very much the visible advocate for health insurance for the elderly in the 1950s, he grew more worried about her attacks and her labeling him a Communist. Cohen claimed that Shearon had made him "persona non grata" to many Eisenhower administration officials and that her work among doctors had made it more difficult for him to obtain his job in Ann Arbor.[18]

In the spring of 1960 Cohen decided to respond to Shearon directly. "I know, and you know, that you have tried to ruin my reputation time after time with members of Congress and the Administration, with members of the medical profession, and with the University of Michigan," he charged. It was her right to disagree with his views but not to call him a Communist or a Communist sympathizer: "I want to say to you, categorically, that I am *not* a Communist, or a Communist sympathizer—and I never have been. I abhor Communism and its philosophy."[19]

Cohen was definitely not a Communist, nor had he ever been one, even at Madison in the 1930s when his friends Merlyn Pitzele and Ken Decker took pride in calling themselves Socialists and when Pitzele, as he put it, "bracketed as a communist."[20] Still, Cohen had an FBI file; he had been investigated by departmental loyalty boards, and for Marjorie Shearon that was enough to cast suspicion upon him.[21] Shearon sincerely believed that Cohen was part of a Communist-inspired conspiracy to promote nationalized medicine. She accused him of being a liaison to Senators Wagner and Murray, at a time when their staffs contained Communist agents such as John Abt and Harold Ware, and of trying to dictate policy to the House Committee on Ways and Means and the Senate Finance Committee. According to Shearon, Cohen had devoted his life to "foisting upon the United States a program supported by the USSR, the Communist Party, USA, and the Socialist ILO."[22]

If Shearon had been able to read Cohen's FBI file, she would have found little of interest. In April 1942 he appeared before Special Agent R. F. Ryan of the FBI and denied that he had ever been a member of any organization that advocated the overthrow of the federal government. Agent Ryan asked Cohen about his involvement with such organizations as the Washington Committee for Democratic Action, the American Peace Mobilization, and the American Youth Congress. It turned out that Cohen's dealings with each of these now-forgotten organizations were inconsequential. Five years later, Cohen talked with Agents Dudley Payne and F. M. Fawcett about his efforts on behalf of the Wagner-Murray-Dingell bill and about the Social Security Administration's aborted mission to assist the Japanese in planning their health-care system. In December 1948 he responded to an interrogatory in which he once again reiterated that he had never belonged to the Communist party. He noted that he had attended meetings of the American League for Peace and Democracy and said that in 1936 and 1937 he believed in that organization's objective of preserving peace and democracy. In 1939 he had dropped out of the organization "when it became obvious that we could not avoid war. I was for support for Britain, France, and Finland irrespective of the views of the USSR."[23] Even in the 1930s, that most radical of decades, Cohen was too implicated in the American system of social welfare, too much a celebrant of American democracy, ever to have entertained thoughts of Communist revolution. In the 1950s, the same person who helped design health insurance finance programs funded through the Social Security system, the act that Marjorie Shearon regarded as treason, also worried actively about how to keep India from going Communist. Whatever the facts of the case, Shearon remained an irritant who did not lose interest in Cohen when he left Washington and moved to Ann Arbor.

A NEW LIFE

At the beginning of 1956, after attending three parties in his honor, Cohen left for Ann Arbor in time to teach second semester classes. The first of the parties took place on a rare snowy night in Washington and featured both sentimental tributes, led by William Mitchell, deputy commissioner of Social Security, and the comic antics of Cohen's children. Some politicians, such as Robert Kean, came to the dinner, and others, John F. Kennedy for one, sent telegrams. Kennedy, in a statement probably written by Theodore Sorensen, called

Wilbur Cohen as a professor at the University of Michigan in the 1950s. (Courtesy of Bruce Cohen)

Cohen "Mr. Social Security himself" and predicted that he would return "to Washington and to public service in the kind of high office he deserves."[24]

As speakers paid tribute to Cohen, his children raced around the room. Eloise tried to keep Stuart, nine, occupied by encouraging him to draw pictures on the program while Bruce, eleven, took photographs of the event, often by standing up on chairs to gain a better view. And Chris, reflective at thirteen, tried to absorb what the people were saying about his dad. William Mitchell, in a jovial mood, approached Chris and asked, "What do you think of your father now?" "Well," Christopher replied, "they can't all be lying."[25]

Arthur Altmeyer could not bring himself to speak at Cohen's departure dinner for fear of breaking down and crying. "I can't find words to tell you how much our association through the years has meant to me and still means to me. So I won't try," Altmeyer later wrote to him. Like Senator Kennedy, Altmeyer believed that Cohen's departure from Washington would not be permanent. After establishing himself at Michigan, he would be able to spend progressively longer periods of time away from Ann Arbor, and even sooner he could make quick trips to Washington to intervene in the legislative process at strategic moments.[26]

Just after his last day at Social Security, Cohen received a letter from Elizabeth Wickenden that helped him to make sense of his feelings. He told her that although it was difficult for him to leave, "for my sense of personality and growth, I just had to do it." Cohen said that he had become a fixture at SSA and people doubted he would ever leave; when Fauri approached him, even Altmeyer thought he would say no. "When that happened I knew that I must get out for my own sense of wellbeing," he wrote.[27]

Early in 1956 the family made the hard trip to Michigan, reversing Cohen's 1934 route from the Midwest to the East. Ironically, as Cohen came to Ann Arbor, Fedele Fauri left for a temporary assignment in Washington as an adviser to the Senate Committee on Finance on the pending Social Security bill.[28] Dean Fauri's ability to blend his academic and policy responsibilities so successfully encouraged Cohen, who hoped to follow a similar pattern. Indeed, neither he nor Fauri was a typical social work professor. As a professor of public welfare administration, Cohen had license to concentrate on public programs and on the policy process; the majority of social work professors focused on the individual. They wrote about how individuals adjusted to social environments, such as the family, home, or workplace, rather than about how society could be changed through the political process and taught courses about casework, not legislation. They used psychological theory, not economic analysis, and their realm was the individual psyche, not the body politic.[29]

In 1956 Cohen experienced little of the apprehension that had attended the beginning of his career in 1934. He was older, more experienced, and, above all, tenured. As a consequence, he felt no need to prove himself to his social work colleagues or to hide his lack of academic credentials. He had never gone to social work school and knew nearly nothing about theoretical approaches in the field. "The academic world is very stimulating," he told Max Kampelman of Senator Humphrey's staff shortly after arriving in Ann Arbor; "the telephone doesn't ring as many times, and I don't have as many memos or bills to write."[30]

Cohen envisioned his job at Ann Arbor as a means of teaching students about social welfare policy. He would tell them about his career experiences in Washington, helping Congress pass a law and designing Social Security legislation. He would instruct them in the history of welfare and social insurance, a subject that Commons and his colleagues had largely invented. He would describe current policy dilemmas, just as he had once done for Arthur Altmeyer and many others in Washington.

As that work description implies, Cohen was far from a typical academic. Even in his role as a scholar, he wrote about matters that were close to the surface of political life. Reacting to one of Cohen's publications, Altmeyer told him he had demonstrated "that there is a world of difference between the approach that an academic person . . . takes and the approach of someone who has been an actual participant in the shaping and execution of the policy."[31] Cohen never abandoned the point of view of the participant in his academic writings. He often made analytic comments, but the source for these comments was his own observations rather than the results of testing social science theories.

Immediately after the passage of a major new Social Security law in 1956, for example, Cohen sat down with Fauri and wrote a description and an analysis of it that appeared in the journal of the American Public Welfare Association. If it had been a year earlier, the article would probably have been written with Robert Ball and Robert J. Myers and would have appeared in the *Social Security Bulletin,* the official government publication. But in 1956 Cohen used a different organizational vehicle to create a factual and interpretive record of the events that he and Fauri in effect had done much to influence.[32] He never mentioned his own role in the process; he and Fauri would permit only a short note at the head of the article explaining that the two were writing "from first-hand knowledge."[33]

Aware that he needed to gather publications to justify the university's faith in him, Cohen also wrote a book that described the various retirement policies under Social Security, a tight, dry research monograph with little of Cohen's characteristic humor. Resembling the memorandums he had prepared for Edwin Witte in 1934 as a research assistant at the Committee on Economic Security, it demonstrated Cohen's mental agility and his ability to comprehend the almost impossibly complex details of the Social Security program. The book was laden with institutional detail, for example, particulars about the right of working women and wives to elect to receive actuarially reduced benefits between age sixty-two and sixty-five. The persistent reader learned exactly how Congress set the retirement age, determined the amount of money that a retired person could receive and still receive Social Security benefits, and initiated disability benefits.[34]

The book, Cohen's first full-length academic monograph, demonstrated his ability to produce publishable copy, often written in a beautiful hand, with a minimum of anguish and concern for artistic niceties. In his writing Cohen processed information like a journalist rather than constructing a narrative like a novelist. "If you assigned Wilbur to work on something, it moved fast," recalled Herman Somers. "He had a sort of decisiveness that caused him not to brood over words."[35] Although Cohen wrote the book quickly, he also made a determined effort to interject more analytic sophistication into his writing. In an attempt to imitate the academic tone, he tried to present himself, whenever possible, as an impartial expert who produced a balanced policy brief.[36]

Even as he played the publication game, Cohen never became the consummate academic; he simply did not share the interest of the other social scientists in research methods. One example of his attitude concerned the weekly brown-bag seminars that began in 1956 on the problems of poverty. Economists Kenneth Boulding and James Morgan participated, and the seminar on income maintenance eventually led to a grant from the Ford Foundation and a major research monograph, published in 1962, on income and welfare in the United States.[37] Cohen was listed as the third author of the book, but by the time of its publication he could barely work his way through the complicated econometric details. "I am especially delighted that you were able to go through my book," he told Altmeyer. "I must say that I don't always remember the meaning of all the statistical conceptions and formulas which I had to learn when I got back to the University of Michigan."[38]

If Cohen was not a master researcher, he nonetheless became an acclaimed teacher. "He's really a great teacher," said Fedele Fauri; "students identify with him and just get a terrific feeling of participation in what's going on. He makes legislation, not only the current but the past, live."[39] It was an era in academia when teaching was emphasized as much as research. Everyone, including senior professors, taught at least three courses a term. The only compensating advantage was that courses in the social work school tended to be concentrated on Mondays and Tuesdays since students needed to devote several days a week to their field placements. "I assure you I am putting in full time on my school work," Cohen told Altmeyer.[40]

During a typical fall semester, Cohen taught two large classes in public welfare and a seminar for doctoral students. In his courses he relied heavily on current government documents rather than on standard textbooks. He tried to immerse students simultaneously in the history and in the current discussion of a particular issue. Whether consciously or not, Cohen replicated the instructional pattern he had observed at Meiklejohn's Experimental College: read the classics and study the current debate. In his public welfare courses, for example, he emphasized the historical development of social programs. He wanted, as he explained to Elizabeth Wickenden, to "give the students some feeling for the origins of present day policy," and he therefore assigned explicitly historical works, such as Arthur Schlesinger's *Crisis of the Old Order,* to his classes. In the doctoral seminar, he gave the students case studies of current problems, such as hospitalization for Social Security beneficiaries, as a means of getting them to understand "the elements that go into social welfare policy."[41]

COHEN AS POLITICIAN

Cohen's arrival in Ann Arbor, far from causing him to retreat into research or esoteric regression analyses, brought him closer to the forces of partisan politics. More than ever before, he entered politics through the front rather than the back door. In previous years, for example, he might have hesitated before attending the Democratic National Convention, but he did so quite openly in 1956. As he made more public appearances as an academic rather than as a bureaucrat, he acquired a reputation as an authority in the fields of aging, Social Security, and income maintenance. He was an outside consultant, not an inside staff member, someone who testified rather than someone who wrote testimony for someone else. As Fauri put it, moving to Ann Arbor "took him out of being a public servant, always functioning for Altmeyer or for somebody else, and gave him visibility on his own."[42] To use the sexist cliché, he became his own man.

Cohen's newfound influence manifested itself as early as the 1956 campaign; along with Altmeyer, he helped to draft the sections of the Democratic platform concerned with Social Security and health care. He persuaded Phil Stern, a party official, to delete a plank in favor of catastrophic health insurance and to substitute a proposal to extend health insurance to the aged.[43] He also offered advice freely to Adlai Stevenson's campaign. In a typical letter to a campaign official, he made a pitch for health insurance for the elderly, which he regarded as the logical next major step in Social Security. "No matter how high you raise the social security benefits," he explained, "you can't make them high enough to provide people with adequate health protection."[44] When he heard that Stevenson might come out in favor of a catastrophic health plan of the sort that he and Altmeyer had kept out of the platform, he effectively lobbied against it. Cohen called Nelson Cruikshank, who got in touch with Willard Wirtz and Phil Stern of the Stevenson campaign, and they agreed to delay Stevenson's statement until "Nelson had a chance to comment on it."[45]

As Cohen became more visible, he did not relinquish his role as a technician who functioned behind the scenes, nor did he allow his activities in national electoral politics to diminish his interest in issue-oriented politics. As James Sundquist has perceptively noted, influence over legislation resided in Washington, not in academia. The academic community defined problems and developed data that bore on their solution; the Washington legislative community devised legislative solutions. As Sundquist points out, "Few men live simultaneously in both." Yet it was Cohen's unique role to do so.[46] That he did live in both communities enabled him to see that issue politics and electoral politics could be pursued independently of one another. Cohen wanted Adlai Stevenson to win the 1956 election, but he regarded the maintenance of sympathetic committees in Congress as his primary political goal. He was disappointed, not devastated, by Stevenson's loss. "It's hard to lick a peace loving general," Altmeyer succinctly stated.[47] Cohen knew, however, that the advancement of Social Security did not depend on a Democratic president.

During and after the election, Cohen continued his careful bipartisan cultivation of Congress. Robert Kean, the liberal Republican, remained an important client who did not hesitate to ask Cohen for ideas that he could use in his 1956 reelection campaign. No longer the Social Security point man in the Congress, Cohen did not allow his newfound academic dignity to deter him from helping Kean even though Cohen fully realized that Kean planned to run for the Senate in 1958 against Congressman Harrison Williams (D-N.J.). At the risk of depriving the Democrats of a seat in the Senate, Cohen maintained his loyalty to Kean. It could not be said that Kean was somehow simpatico with Cohen on a personal level; on the contrary, Kean was an aristocratic, Harvard-educated investment banker who had served in Congress since 1938. What was important to Cohen was Kean's status, in Nelson Rockefeller's words, as "the main authority in Congress" on Social Security. He had gained that status under Cohen's tutelage, and that relationship continued when Cohen went to Ann Arbor. He continually sent Kean Social Security bills to sponsor and offered him hot political tips.[48] At one point, for example, Cohen did some work for Sen. Lister Hill's (D-Ala.) Committee on Labor and Public Welfare on the subject of aging.[49] He kept Kean fully informed, offered him copies of all the staff studies, and gave him a chance to see an advanced copy of a bill on aging.[50]

Dealing with both Democrats and Republicans on a wide range of issues, Cohen did not hide his activities from Altmeyer or Ball, his allies in the Social Security policy network, nor did he advise Republicans such as Kean surreptitiously. Still, particularly since he remained in close contact with the Democrats on the House Ways and Means Committee, he had always to perform a balancing act between his advice to the Democrats and his advice to Kean. "You will have to continue to be the honest broker, reconciling your two sets of recommendations," Altmeyer wrote.[51] In general, Cohen tried to orchestrate public policy by taking each politician as far as he wanted to go but in a consistent direction. As he told Altmeyer, his main objective was not to persuade everyone to adopt the same proposals "that you and I might favor but, first, to keep them off the more doubtful ones and to try to move them generally along the lines of the proposals which seem to me to have the highest social priorities."[52] Working actively in this manner, Cohen maintained continuity between his activities as a Social Security employee and his endeavors as a University of Michigan professor.

WELFARE, ELITE DISCOURSE, AND THE POLITICS OF PROSPERITY

During the Ann Arbor years Cohen spent more time on welfare policy, as opposed to Social Security policy, than he ever had before. Welfare was one of the subjects on which Cohen's thinking shifted during the 1950s, and the course of his thoughts revealed the differences between his depression-era and his postwar outlook. As his reluctance to engage in theoretical research indicated, he was not a deep conceptual thinker, in part because he was so pragmatic in outlook and because he accepted a basic framework for social policy developed by others. Social welfare programs were such pressing realities for Wilbur Cohen that he could not easily transform them into flighty metaphors. As his friend Merlyn Pitzele remarked, he was "bright, very bright, but he was not innovative. His brightness moved along established tracks. He had a strong proprietary sense."[53] This sense and his ability to manipulate formulae served him well in the area of Social Security, an area where he could be clever in the manner of an engineer rather than creative in the style of a scientist. In the area of welfare, quite strikingly, Cohen could find no easy formula, and he did not feel comfortable with the advice of his elders, such as Altmeyer. Instead, he struggled to find his own voice and to come to terms with what emerged as a leading policy problem in the second half of the twentieth century. Concerning welfare, Cohen showed his willingness to recast formulae to fit the facts as he perceived them.

He began, as he did on most things, with the views of his mentor Arthur Altmeyer, who regarded welfare in simple terms. In Altmeyer's opinion, people in poverty required financial assistance. As a corollary to this axiom, Altmeyer believed that poor people needed money, not advice; welfare policy should therefore not center on rehabilitating the recipients. Altmeyer feared that intensive efforts to intervene in the lives of welfare recipients to make them more independent would be counterproductive. In the first place, such efforts would lead to "undue interference" in the lives of public-assistance recipients. In the second place, such efforts would be used as excuses for not raising the monetary level of welfare benefits.[54] "I am afraid that in the name of rehabilitation, increased self-help, and provision of constructive social services we will depreciate the need for effective income maintenance programs and weaken such principles as unrestricted money payment and the right of needy persons to assistance," Altmeyer wrote in 1957.[55]

Since he believed so strongly in unrestricted money payments, Altmeyer deplored the practice of "workfare," or requiring welfare recipients, including young mothers, to work in return for receiving state support. Speaking before a group of social workers in 1957, he argued that a "mother had a right to assistance even if she refused to go to work," a view that apparently shocked the audience.[56] He put the needs of children foremost and therefore argued that "a mother making a good home for her children should have a free choice in deciding whether or not it is in their best interests that she stay at home or go to work."[57] In this regard, Altmeyer followed the progressive precepts that he had practiced during the New Deal, untainted by newer considerations related to race or gender. He did not feel that women could participate in the labor force on the same terms as men, in part because they had special obligations as mothers that limited the amount of work they should do. He also realized that the debate over welfare in the 1950s was conditioned, in ways that it had not been before, by the subject of race, yet in his mind, the conjuncture of race and welfare made it even more important to protect the rights of welfare recipients. State laws with specifications such as requiring a person to establish a year's residence before he or she could receive welfare were "aimed of course at the Negroes." So were guidelines such as removing a welfare mother who had an illegitimate child from the rolls. In North Carolina, for example, state authorities made the suspected father a "resource," which thus made the child ineligible, and a mother who was able to work was required to do so. "All of this depresses me no end," Altmeyer declared.[58]

For Cohen, race and gender had not yet become the primary determinants of social policy. His view of the problem differed almost completely from Altmeyer's. Money, far from being the "entire solution," sometimes only served "to perpetuate the problem." The solution lay in the ability of trained social welfare practitioners, the very sort being trained at Ann Arbor, to resolve social problems. "I . . . certainly don't believe in cutting them off the rolls when we don't have a satisfactory substitute," Cohen said. He noted, however, that there were "lots of other elements we must emphasize other than assistance, such as training, research, casework services, medical care, rehabilitation."[59]

His sentiments amounted to a real break between him and Altmeyer, as serious a disagreement as the two of them had ever had. The differences stemmed in part from dissimilar generational outlooks. Altmeyer came from an era when most of the welfare money went to the elderly, not to children in families with no father present. In this era, as Altmeyer simply assumed and Cohen simply accepted, most people were on welfare because they had no other choice; nearly everyone strived to be self-sufficient and turned to government help only as a last resort. Responding to this situation, the 1935 Social Security Act established a system of determining need that protected an individual's dignity. Although he had begun his career in Altmeyer's era and accepted most of his teachings, Cohen, working in an environment dedicated to therapeutic interventions among people with social problems, came to see the 1950s as a different time. In the new era, as Cohen put it, "relatively few families are in need for reasons which can be described as being beyond their control." The typical welfare client was no longer elderly, and in some cases welfare served to maintain a family "which has little or nothing constructive to offer to children." Cohen went on to say that "from an examination of the ADC caseload, it appears that a high proportion of the caseload has multiple problems of a psychological and social nature."[60]

It was only natural that more of the era's optimism would rub off on the forty-something Cohen than on the sixty-something Altmeyer and make Cohen more sanguine than Altmeyer about casework and other forms of rehabilitation. In a reversal of their traditional roles, Cohen explained to Altmeyer how to blend social services and income maintenance: "We need to identify the 'Mrs. Lees' in the caseload, who need no service other than the grant, so that we can stay out of their lives except as called on; and, on the other hand, to identify those who need service, so that we can go to them with active vigorous services of a preventive and rehabilitative nature."[61]

Cohen, unlike Altmeyer, was in a much better position to move from the theory of social dependency to the reality of social work practice. As an academic, he enjoyed the chance to engage in applied social experiments, such as a late 1950s study of the general assistance caseload around Ann Arbor. General assistance was a local program run by the individual counties without federal financial assistance. The program aided poor families, with both parents present, or it helped single individuals who were not disabled and had no dependent children. In other words, the program came to the aid of those people who fell through the cracks of the federal public assistance programs.

One case from this study concerned the H family. After six years on the general assistance rolls, county authorities referred the family to the Special Services Project, run by Cohen and Sid Bernard, his colleague in the social work school. The husband could neither read nor write and at age forty-seven faced the prospect of continuing unemployment. His forty-one-year-old wife had married at sixteen. Six of the eight children remained at home, all had severe problems in school, and two of the daughters had illegitimate children. The parents stayed together only out of apathy and did little to help their children; indeed, the family "had lost its central bonds, becoming a collection of hopeless, miserable, distrustful people." The family members hid from their problems, denying them rather than facing them. The social workers judged that the "family was not fulfilling its basic responsibilities in child rearing" and set as a "treatment goal" to have the parents improve their care of the children. The treatment "method" involved weekly interviews with the parents, "helping them step-by-step to choose family goals and to accomplish them." Slowly, the family gave up their pattern of "drifting apologetically through life, hoping that no one would punish them too harshly and in return accepting impoverished living conditions as their due." Cured of apathy, they began to function better, and they left the welfare rolls.[62]

The case of the H family showed how social workers diagnosed and attempted to cure problems. Arthur Altmeyer gave little credence to this process because it permitted social workers to enter the lives of the poor in intrusive ways and detracted from the basic goal of income maintenance. In striking contrast, Wilbur Cohen became a convert to the cause of intervention, if only in these sorts of problem cases. He did not see the intervention as punitive so much as he viewed it as therapeutic and beneficial.

A certified member of a new cohort of social welfare professionals, Cohen had many opportunities to expand on his ideas. During the Ann Arbor years, as never before, Cohen participated in what might be described as the elite forms of policy discourse, such as the meetings of blue-ribbon panels or reports to foundations. As one example, Cohen's increased visibility and his proximity to Sen. Robert Kerr (D-Okla.) made him a natural selection for the Advisory Council on Public Assistance created by the 1958 Social Security amendments.[63] Senator Kerr himself wired the secretaries of HEW and the Treasury recommending Cohen for membership on the council. "I am not eager for this at all but Kerr wants me to be on it," Cohen told his friend Elizabeth Wickenden. Before Cohen went to Ann Arbor, his name might have come up in connection with staffing the advisory council; he was now one of its members, and no one thought that he was in any way misplaced.[64] Cohen also participated on other blue-ribbon panels created in the second half of the 1950s to consider the national purpose.

In 1956 Nelson Rockefeller, perhaps seeking to demonstrate a thoughtful approach to public policy that would serve him well in later elections, decided, along with his brothers, to launch a special study on the nation's direction. As Rockefeller put it, he wanted to give "perspective to our national purpose."[65] He assembled a group of thirty-two individuals and organized seven panels on various topics ranging from education to foreign affairs.[66] Wilbur Cohen's name was mentioned early in the deliberations. For staff assistance, Rockefeller relied on Henry Kissinger, at the time a young Harvard academic. Kissinger knew Herman Somers and engaged him and his wife to write a paper on social insurance; asked to recommend others for the project, Somers suggested Douglas Brown, Fedele Fauri, Edwin Witte, and Cohen.[67] Cohen worked out an agreement in which he contributed a background paper, "Social Policies and Social Services in an Expanding Economy," which became a source of ideas for a panel report that appeared in April 1958 with the rather grandiose title, "The Challenge to America: Its Economic and Social Aspects."[68]

In the spring of 1957 Cohen had expressed many of his ideas in a talk that he delivered in Madison as part of a special symposium to honor Edwin Witte. He was a bit uncertain about what to say, perhaps because he was aware that he was himself a candidate to replace Witte, who was retiring from full-time teaching. Altmeyer told him that the audience would "lap up" anything on institutional economics and on how the Wisconsin idea became the New Deal. Cohen resisted offering a sentimental tribute to his old professors and decided to talk about the future of Social Security.[69]

Cohen regarded prosperity as the central reality of the decade and exhorted policymakers to adjust to it. For a long time, people's attitudes toward social welfare programs had reflected their "bitter memory of the depression" and their "fear of another depression." But in the 1950s Social Security was not a "poor man's program," and prosperity was not something ephemeral. On the contrary, social insurance and welfare programs were permanent parts of the institutional landscape, governed by a bipartisan consensus. The old-age insurance program, which had covered 60 percent of the labor force in 1937, received contributions from nearly 90 percent in 1957. "Rather than justify changes or improvements in social programs on the basis of a crusade against the threat of unemployment or depression," Cohen urged that changes "be justified on a high level of economic literacy which assumes a continued increase in productivity and wages and the ability of the country to finance improvements in social welfare out of a growing national income."

In this manner Cohen came home to Madison and spoke in a new voice that commanded attention. On the one hand, he paid homage to Edwin Witte and dwelled on the accomplishments of Witte's generation.[70] On the other hand, he suggested that it was time for a change. Simply put, the depression agenda of the New Deal should be replaced with a growth agenda. Cohen argued that growth itself led to social problems, particularly in the suburbs and among children, the aged, the disabled, and the racial minorities. If the government funded necessary public goods, its actions would reap dividends in the form of greater productivity and an increased national product. "We need more schools, more roads, more hospital beds, and more housing. We want more teachers, more doctors, nurses, social workers," he told his 1957 Madison audience, invoking what would become the familiar liberal boilerplate of the era.[71]

In a sense, Cohen's growth agenda marked a natural progression from the depression agenda as the very success of the old one led to the need for the new. For Cohen the transition also marked a form of social progress. "Those of us in social security who were nurtured here in Madison, in the Commons-Perlman-Witte philosophy, believe in the idea of progress," Cohen affirmed. "We believe that there can be a better life for all. We believe that, for all practical purposes, want can be abolished and poverty eradicated. We believe that human problems are capable of solution."[72]

This defining sense of optimism from his Madison speech carried over into the work that Cohen did for the Rockefeller study. He assumed that it was possible for the "American economy to meet generally accepted standards for health, education, and welfare and to provide the income which would enable every person and family to have a minimum level of living." Although the economy generated enough wealth to accomplish this goal, gaps remained in the country's health, educational, and welfare services. As a nation, America needed to fill in these gaps between performance and potential. The nation needed to fund services for children that would strengthen and promote family life, to increase expenditures for the elderly population, and to expand efforts to rehabilitate people with disabilities. The goal of this effort was to encourage every individual to make maximum use of his abilities. Some people needed encouragement and opportunities; others needed exposure to trained personnel in the helping professions; still others were potential beneficiaries of research in social services that the country should fund.[73]

Cohen's report to the Rockefeller project highlighted three themes that characterized liberal social policy discourse of the era. The first concerned the existence of a gap between what the country could do and what it did do. The idea was that the United States, although doing well, could do better, a notion that received considerable play in the period after the launch of *Sputnik* in October 1957. This position served as a way of criticizing the Eisenhower administration for achieving only superficial success and for not doing more to make America stronger, richer, or more secure. The second theme emphasized the need to concentrate more social services on children. Hardly a new concern, the problems of youth received renewed attention at the very height of the postwar baby boom that was itself a response to prosperity. In the depression the Committee on Economic Security had written, "It must not for a moment be forgotten that the core of any social plan must be the child." In the midst of the baby boom, particular anxiety centered on children who exhibited such maladjustment that they became, in the expression of the era, juvenile delinquents. Cohen said that the concern over juvenile delinquency underscored "the needs for additional services to children and youth, their families and communities." Not just delinquents but all children required "many professional services" if they were "to grow up to be healthy personalities in a changing, complex world."[74] Chief among these professional services was education, which many of Cohen's fellow liberals believed could benefit from an infusion of federal funds.

The third theme was that the costs of inaction were high. If, for example, the nation did nothing about such problems as accidents, disability, disease, and mental illness, it would continue to pay a high price in terms of foregone productivity and the cost of custodial care. The solution was for the government to fund research projects that would yield ways of preventing many of these problems, to encourage rehabilitation rather than custodial care, and to foster the integration, rather than the segregation, of those people with mental or physical disabilities.

The formal report of the Rockefeller panel on economic and social problems followed many of the themes identified by Cohen in his background report. And although the panel emphasized national challenges, it exhibited a sense of contentment with many of the nation's social welfare institutions, as in the recommendation that there be "no major change" in the concept of social insurance. Just as Cohen had suggested, however, the panel noted that the country could do better in a prosperous era, such as spending more on medical research or eliminating the waste caused by the misallocation of manpower that stemmed from racial discrimination.[75]

The Rockefeller report showed that Cohen had learned to speak the language of the 1950s. He had escaped from his depression-era roots and latched on to the concerns of a different era. "I was really thrilled by your piece for the Rockefeller Brothers Fund and I really do not thrill easily when it comes to this type of belles lettres," Elizabeth Wickenden told him. "The writing is really fine . . . with a classic directness and simplicity. In fact, I have been noting that your writing gets better and better; it goes to show what lifting the shackles of institutional prose and thinking will do." The move to Ann Arbor had paid off.[76]

Cohen had somehow managed to emerge from Altmeyer's and Witte's shadows without losing the allegiance of either mentor. Even as he veered from some of their teachings, he continued to be the dutiful son. Between the old ethnic world of the inner-city retail business and the new professional world of intellectual pursuits lay a path that many Jewish people of Cohen's generation, the children of immigrants, traveled. Often they emerged from the journey closer to the people of their new world than to their kin who still lived in the old one. And, like Cohen, they developed a special affection for the people who guided them along the professional path. Edwin Witte was an exact contemporary of Cohen's father, and in many ways Cohen learned more from Witte than from Aaron Cohen.[77] Wilbur Cohen lived far more like Edwin Witte, who juggled government service and university teaching, than he did like Aaron

Cohen, who continued to run a variety store and never dreamed of participating in politics beyond Milwaukee.

Yet it was to Cohen's credit that he never turned his back on either his father or his surrogate fathers, even as his professional stock rose and as the reputations of his mentors declined. Whatever his uneasy feelings toward Aaron, Wilbur stressed the importance of family to his sons. One of the clichés that he used most often was that blood was thicker than water; the rituals of family life mattered to Cohen, who remained the good son to the end of Aaron's life.[78] Similarly, he never tried to disassociate himself from Altmeyer or Witte; as with Witte, he stayed in touch with Altmeyer until he died in October 1972.

Maurine Mulliner, a former colleague at the Social Security Administration and a close friend, summed up the feelings of many people in Washington about Cohen's years in Ann Arbor: "It was very good for Wilbur to go away for those few years. I could see a great development in him after he came back. . . . He was so young when he came into the program . . . and I felt was not as open-minded about program proposals or alternate ways of doing things as he should have been for his age. And it was, in my opinion, because he was just too immersed in this."[79]

At the University of Michigan, Cohen had a chance to listen to the policy debates of the era in a fresh setting. He said that the experience "kind of made me rethink my professional goals. I decided I'd rather be a professor, and I have no regret."[80] As matters turned out, becoming a professor proved to be no drawback to gaining influence over social welfare policy. Cohen was no longer someone's surrogate. Instead, he was a figure of intellectual stature who contributed ideas that found their ultimate expression in the 1960 presidential campaign and in the administrations of John F. Kennedy and Lyndon B. Johnson. The Ann Arbor years helped Cohen to build a bridge between the New Deal and the Great Society.

COURTING JFK, EXPANDING SOCIAL SECURITY

In retrospect, Cohen, ever the optimist, came to regard his move to Ann Arbor as part of a great chain of opportunity: "I don't think I would have become a secretary of HEW if I hadn't made that shift. By making that shift I became a professor. By becoming a professor, Kennedy used me. By Kennedy using me, he appointed me assistant secretary."[1] Thus Wilbur J. Cohen, the action intellectual, came to the attention of John F. Kennedy, the action intellectual's politician, and in 1952 added Kennedy to his long list of political clients.

Between 1956 and 1960, as Cohen refined his intellectual analysis of social problems in a way that appealed to Kennedy, he directed the apparatus in support of an expanded Social Security program. The years proved uncommonly productive, with the passage of major new laws that initiated a disability insurance program (1956), expanded Social Security benefits (1958), and created an enlarged welfare-medicine program (1960). Cohen, outside the government when each of the laws was passed, nonetheless remained on the inside of Social Security politics and proved indispensable to the legislative process. Moreover, he also became increasingly involved in the politics of the 1960 Democratic nomination. Hence, during these years, he advised congressional leaders, such as Wilbur Mills and Robert Kerr, on specific pieces of legislation and presidential aspirant John F. Kennedy on broader social welfare policy issues, working hard to reconcile all the interests involved. Cohen accomplished his tasks well enough to allow President Kennedy to put him in charge of getting his administration's ambitious social program through Congress.

KENNEDY AS COHEN'S CLIENT AND DISABILITY INSURANCE IN 1956

Cohen first met John Fitzgerald Kennedy in the late 1940s. Cohen, the staff member in the Social Security commissioner's office, and Kennedy, the second-term congressman from Boston, attended a meeting on wage differentials between the North and the South.[2] Kennedy, despite his storied background as the son of FDR's ambassador to Great Britain, could not have looked too special to Cohen, being just one of many Democratic congressmen. Since Kennedy did not sit on the Ways and Means Committee, he did not rate special attention; Herman Eberharter or Jere Cooper, neither of whom became household names, were far more important to Cohen. As Cohen recalled, "I liked Kennedy from this first meeting but certainly gave no special thought to his potentialities or how this first meeting might affect my future relationship to him."[3]

Kennedy would not have impinged on Cohen's consciousness if Cohen had not known Kennedy's staffer Theodore Sorensen, a young lawyer from Nebraska who had come to work in Washington in the early 1950s just after graduation from the University of Nebraska Law School. Before he started with Kennedy, Sorensen served two brief stints as a general counsel at the Federal Security Agency (the predecessor to the Department of Health, Education, and Welfare) and as a counsel for a congressional committee. While preparing testimony for this committee, Cohen met Sorensen. Over time their relationship became closer, even though, as Cohen noted, their social relationship was "not very extensive."[4] When Sorensen went to work for Kennedy, after Kennedy's impressive victory over Henry Cabot Lodge in the 1952 elections, he sought to use his Washington contacts to strengthen the senator's knowledge of important policy areas. It was natural for Sorensen to associate Cohen with Social Security and to call on him for help on the subject. As Cohen recalled of his dealings with Sorensen in the years between 1955 and 1957, "We had a lot of conversations; I used to go to his house and talk with him in his home." A rapport developed between the two men.[5]

"I had lunch with Senator Kennedy last week," wrote Cohen to Wickenden in February 1954, just when Cohen was working to get the 1954 amendments passed. "He is very willing to make speeches in Massachusetts, New York, or elsewhere on social security." Cohen and the senator reviewed an article that Sorensen had written for Kennedy's signature for the *New Republic*. "I like Kennedy very much," Cohen told Wickenden, "Sorenson (*sic*) knows a great deal about social security so we have someone really good to work with."[6]

In 1956 Kennedy emerged as an important player in national politics, just at the time that Cohen was immersed in the battle to pass disability insurance. Having just left for Ann Arbor, Cohen became the informal leader of a coalition of Social Security supporters, including Nelson Cruikshank and Loula Dunn of the American Public Welfare Association, that pressed for disability insurance. He made frequent trips back to Washington during the winter and spring of

1956, meeting with Congressman Wilbur Mills, Sen. Robert Kerr, and, most important, with Sen. Walter George; Kennedy did not figure in the politics of disability insurance. Instead, the issue was conducted through complicated maneuvers within the Senate Committee on Finance that Cohen, as much as anyone, orchestrated.

For one thing, Cohen coached those individuals who testified in favor of disability insurance. On February 27, 1956, for example, he flew to Washington to talk with John Tramburg, his former boss at Social Security, who was to testify before the Senate Finance Committee on February 28. He told Douglas Brown that Tramburg's testimony would show a "certain affinity to our point of view."[7] Cohen hoped Tramburg's testimony would counter the influence of Sen. Harry Byrd (D-Va.), the conservative chairman of the Senate Finance Committee, who remained firmly opposed to disability insurance even though the House had passed the measure in 1955. To further his goal, Byrd tried to fashion an alliance between himself, the administration, and the Republicans on the committee.[8]

For another thing, Cohen lobbied administration officials who were undecided on the measure. The most important figure in the debate was HEW Secretary Marion Folsom, who decided to withhold his testimony until the very end of the Senate Finance Committee hearings.[9] Cohen worked on Folsom through surrogates, encouraging Douglas Brown to communicate with Folsom, only to learn from Brown that "Marion has certainly gone conservative."[10] Cohen also wrote to insurance executive Reinie Hohaus, "knowing that Reinie and Marion stay in very close touch with each other."[11] Nothing persuaded Folsom, who, even though he had once given lukewarm support to disability insurance for people at age fifty-five, testified against it for people at age fifty in 1956.[12]

Undaunted, Cohen launched a counterstrategy that involved using Sen. Walter George. On the same late February visit in which he coached John Tramburg on his testimony, he and Loula Dunn went to see Elizabeth Springer, the clerk of the Senate Committee on Finance. When Cohen and Dunn talked with Springer, they discovered that she was dispirited over the situation facing Senator George, who was up for reelection and had a tough primary fight with Herman Talmadge on his hands. George was old, had spent considerable time away from Georgia, and was portrayed by Talmadge as being too close to the Coca-Cola Company. As Springer told Cohen and Dunn of George's dejection, it occurred to Cohen that as a former chairman of the Finance Committee, George would be an ideal figure to lead the fight for disability insurance. Springer, who also thought it would be a good idea, brought the senator into the room. After they had exchanged pleasantries,

Cohen put forth his suggestion. He realized that the senator had opposed disability insurance in the past but told him that this proposal, unlike the previous ones, had enough safeguards to protect disability benefits from being abused. George kept puffing on his cigar. "When I finished," Cohen later related, "he did not speak for a few seconds but then said simply 'when could I have the amendment and a little statement?' " Cohen said he could produce it in a few days.[13]

Cohen told Wickenden that this development was "unexpected." In order to meet George's needs, he had "to drop everything else," but the work was "essential because nobody was organizing the fight against Byrd."[14] Cohen returned to George's office on March 2 and gave him a draft bill and a statement; the one that George eventually submitted was "exactly as I had written it," Cohen later recalled with pride.[15]

In May Senator George announced that he would not run for reelection. The Senate Finance Committee, relying upon the staff assistance of Fedele Fauri, finally released its report in June. "I see that the Finance Committee performed as expected," lamented Arthur Altmeyer, disappointed that disability insurance was not included in the committee's bill.[16] As Derthick notes, "The disability measure then became [George's] sentimental parting gift to the nation." Just as the House had passed the disability freeze as a tribute to the retiring Doughton, now the Senate would have an opportunity to pass disability insurance to honor Senator George even though his committee opposed the measure.[17]

Cohen and his allies, such as Nelson Cruikshank, prepared for a difficult floor fight. The administration continued to oppose the measure, as did the American Medical Association. According to the AMA, disability payments would become the entering wedge for socialized medicine.[18] Proponents of the measure included the Democratic leadership—particularly Sen. Lyndon Johnson—Senator George, and the newly merged AFL-CIO. As the battle dragged deeper into summer, the elections drew nearer.

The vote on Senator George's disability insurance amendment came on Tuesday, July 17, 1956. On Monday Cohen had received a call saying that the vote would be close, and "it would probably be best if I came down to help." Arriving in Washington at 1:00 P.M. on Tuesday, he went immediately to the Senate gallery and met with Cruikshank and Robert Kerr, ready to marshal arguments that would convince wavering senators to support disability insurance. Senator George presented his amendment, using material that Cohen had drafted, and Senator Byrd presented his rebuttal, using material that Fedele Fauri had drafted. After a tense roll call vote, Senator George's amendment carried by a final count of 47 to 45.[19]

The passage of disability insurance marked an extension of Social Security into significant new realms and raised the level of Cohen's prestige and his influence over the program's policy. The law was a product of political independence: Congress had defied the administration, and Cohen had operated independently of his former institutional bases. Cruikshank did much of the hard political work in selling disability insurance, but it was Wilbur Cohen who made the crucial contact with Walter George. This law was the first for which Cohen could claim much of the credit. "No one but you," Altmeyer told Cohen, "could have worked so fast and deftly in reconciling, cajoling and improvising."[20]

That same summer, Cohen's first in Ann Arbor, Kennedy charmed the delegates at the Democratic convention and nearly became the party's nominee for vice-president. After Adlai Stevenson's crushing defeat in the 1956 elections, Kennedy emerged as a leading contender for the 1960 nomination. Cohen realized that Kennedy, as a national candidate, could not devote himself as closely to the daily business of Congress as could a "permanent" congressman, such as Wilbur Mills or Senate majority leader Lyndon Johnson of Texas. At the same time, Kennedy required a record on which to run that showed some connection with the legislative business of Congress. In the 1950s it was vital for a candidate who hoped to win the Democratic nomination to demonstrate strong support for Social Security. Someone like Kennedy therefore needed someone like Wilbur Cohen, and even though Kennedy was completely removed from the political bargaining over Social Security that mattered most to Cohen, Cohen offered to help.[21]

In the period between 1956 and 1960, Cohen would visit Kennedy, somewhat like a salesman calling on Cohen's father in Milwaukee, to see what Kennedy wanted to buy. "I frequently stopped in Senator Kennedy's office," he later said. "I was always greeted very friendly and told to sit down and start working and to help us on something and we're glad you're here and what ideas do you have."[22] Cohen, although a tenured academic at a prestigious university, had not abandoned his old identity as a legislative salesman.

In the summer of 1957 Sorensen solicited Cohen's advice in designing a Social Security bill for the senator and in his letter included some of the boilerplate that he had prepared for Kennedy on the subject. The rhetoric said nothing about the depression, which Kennedy seldom considered. He had little reason to do so since he was only fifteen when Roosevelt took office and could not claim to have been one of its victims. The glory years of the New Deal were a political disaster for the Kennedy family that culminated in the bitter dispute between Ambassador Joseph P. Kennedy and President Roosevelt over whether to support Great Britain. Kennedy consequently cast himself as a new-style politician, who based his positions on the hard realities of the 1950s rather than on the sentimental echoes of the 1930s. For such a politician, Social Security benefits needed to be expanded because, as Sorensen put it, "Social Security benefits are falling behind as the economy expands."[23] In other words, old people, not to mention children and other Social Security beneficiaries, should share in America's prosperity. It was a good example of basing social welfare legislation on the expectations of rising productivity and higher wages, just as Cohen had suggested only a few months earlier in his talk honoring Edwin Witte.

Early in 1958 Cohen presented Sorensen with an outline of a Social Security bill for the senator, who faced reelection in the fall and wanted to run up a substantial vote total in order to impress party leaders. Cohen, respectful of the senator's desires not to move too far ahead of public opinion, took as his basic approach that Kennedy should "espouse a proposal which is forward looking and progressive, reasonably comprehensive and imaginative, and while different than what others have introduced, would not be inconsistent with what liberal groups were pushing for."[24] The outline included a phased-in program of hospital insurance for the elderly on Social Security, with benefits starting at age seventy-five in 1959 and reaching all retired beneficiaries in 1965. The outline also contained such standard features as an increase in Social Security benefits, an increase in federal payments for public assistance, and changes in unemployment insurance and the maternal- and child-health programs. The proposal indicated Cohen's willingness to tailor his measures to Kennedy's specific needs while at the same time furthering his own long-range ideological agenda.

Cohen understood Kennedy's desire to benefit from Social Security's popularity but not to be branded as a wild-spending liberal. In order to balance social vision and fiscal prudence, he used the device of making some of his proposals effective in the future. For example, Cohen suggested that every state should pay twenty-four weeks of unemployment compensation in 1959, twenty-six weeks in 1961, and thirty weeks in 1965. As Cohen explained to Sorensen, "By introducing various provisions gradually you can minimize some of the immediate cost effects and place the whole package in a framework of 'confidence in the growth and productivity of our economic system.' "[25] He must have known that this sort of thinking appealed to Sorensen and Kennedy.[26]

In 1958 unemployment compensation emerged as a major issue and became another area of collaboration between Cohen and Kennedy. It was, as Cohen admitted, "a very complicated legislative controversy" that centered on how the federal government could help the state unemployment compensation systems meet their obligations at a time of recession.[27] As Cohen and Sorensen discussed how Senator Kennedy could influence the debate, Cohen suggested changing the ADC program to cover families in which children were needy because the father was unemployed. Under existing law, the states aided single-parent families in which the father had died, become disabled, or deserted his wife and children but gave nothing to "intact" families in which the breadwinner was neither dead nor disabled but simply unemployed. Cohen's idea was not a new one. He had pushed a similar proposal in 1950 and nearly had persuaded Congress to agree. Nonetheless, Sorensen and Kennedy liked Cohen's proposal because, as Cohen later noted, "it met a very practical need and also, I think, because it was a little bit different than what other people were talking about."[28] It was pragmatic, innovative, and already tested in Congress: perfect for an aspiring presidential candidate. It became a way of influencing a debate, firmly in the hands of Senate regulars such as Russell Long (D-La.), at its margins.[29]

Even as Kennedy's efforts to influence unemployment compensation came to nothing, he and his staff launched a new project that involved drafting a speech on public policy toward the aged.[30] On August 19, 1958, toward the end of the congressional session, Kennedy took the Senate floor and announced a program for older citizens. The ten-point plan, with its emphasis on Social Security and the need to decrease the number of elderly people on public assistance, reflected Cohen's influence in its creation. Cohen had once again gently aligned Kennedy with liberal thinking without creating political controversy.[31]

In the summer of 1958, with this and other speeches, Kennedy was in fact developing a consistent critique of the nation's public policies that he would use to great advantage in 1960, one that centered on the concept of the gap. He argued that the role of national leaders was not to rally the country behind great social causes so much as to call attention to gaps that separated the country from excellence. Through better techniques, the gaps could be closed. In domestic policy, for example, the country should encourage the wider use of employees in the older age brackets because the "superiority of America" depended on the "use of all the knowledge, experience, and wisdom of its people."[32] In foreign policy, America suffered from missile gaps, because, as Kennedy put it, "we tailored our strategy and military requirements to fit our budget—instead of fitting our budget to our military requirements and strategy."[33] In both areas of policy, the nation was being complacent about the deployment of its resources and as a consequence creating long-term problems. Short-run economies were not only dangerous, they were also costly. Not using all the productive capacity of the nation's old people or paying for large military projects on a crash basis cost money that could be better spent elsewhere. By invoking these various gaps, Kennedy and his cohort of politicians therefore defined an important presidential mission: the president, by exhorting the people to do better, should energize America and close the gaps that separated the nation from excellence. The United States had the means to solve its problems; it was only a question of finding the right leader who could motivate Americans so that they realized their potential.

In making these political points, neither Kennedy nor Cohen took a broadly ideological approach to policy. Cohen, in an article published in 1958, defined controversial issues as matters on which people disagreed on details or methods. He wrote that it was not an era of "emotional and moral crusades" so much as one of "decisions on specific issues of great complexity."[34] Kennedy's speeches, written by Sorensen and cast in crisper, more direct language, took much the same tone.

Wilbur Cohen did not have Sorensen's rhetorical eloquence; he concerned himself always with the cumbersome details of complicated social programs. Nonetheless, in the late 1950s, Cohen gave speeches containing sentiments that echoed Kennedy's, even if all too often Cohen inundated his audiences with social policy facts. In a typical performance, Cohen announced that "we in the United States can accomplish far more than we are willing to admit. We have the resources, material and intellectual; we have the know-how."[35] By the summer of 1958, he was going swimming with Ted Sorensen and had initiated a friendship with Myer Feldman, a lawyer who served as legislative assistant for Kennedy. Cohen was drawing closer to Kennedy's staff.[36]

CONGRESSIONAL POLITICS: THE 1958 SOCIAL SECURITY AMENDMENTS

In 1958, even as Cohen devoted more time to Kennedy, he continued his role as adviser to the people in Congress who presided over Social Security. The major product of his work that summer was the 1958 Social Security amendments, and interestingly, the lead actors on this measure were Wilbur Mills and Robert Kerr, not John F. Kennedy. It was as if presidential politicians such as Kennedy and congressional politicians such as Mills appealed to different sides of Cohen's personality. Kennedy harmonized with the professor who wanted to analyze policy and to influence the country's mood, despite the overwhelmingly political atmosphere that surrounded the Kennedy operation. Mills was in synch with Cohen as the legislative technician and tactician, despite the often statesmanlike way in which Mills handled his job as head of the Ways and Means Committee.[37] The senator floated above the incidental details of policy to which the congressman paid such close attention. Kennedy, with the help of technicians like Cohen, defined himself in personal terms; Mills, also with such help, defined himself in institutional terms.

The 1958 Social Security amendments were very much a product of closed politics within congressional committees, and in that year the institutional scene in Congress changed. Late in 1957 Jere Cooper, chairman of the House Committee on Ways and Means, died of a heart attack; Wilbur Mills took over as head of the committee.[38]

Mills was a smalltown lawyer from Arkansas who had been in Congress since 1942. Like his two Democratic predecessors as committee chairman, he came from the South and was regarded as both conservative and cautious. In the 1956 fight over disability insurance, for example, Altmeyer told Cohen that he had "no confidence in Mills."[39] In time, however, Wilbur Cohen came to admire Wilbur Mills extravagantly, perceiving him as a lawyerly individual, the sort of person who researched both sides of a question and came away knowing more than anyone on either side. Cohen also saw that Mills was a hard worker in an institution where people in secure seats could coast. Mills became involved in the issues that his committee handled, reading the material that people gave him and talking to experts. He had the sort of mind that could comprehend both complex legal details—he was trained at Harvard Law School—and complex financial details—he was the son of a banker.[40]

In dealing with Mills, Cohen always outlined his arguments in actuarial terms and seldom spoke about people in need, talking about such concepts the taxable wage base and percentage of payrolls on a level premium basis. Mills was a tax man, the head of Congress' tax committee, and Cohen counseled him about tax revenues and expenditures. In 1958 Cohen advised Mills that the administration's lack of initiative would leave "a vacuum which the Democrats can step into if they want to do so." Furthermore, Cohen noted, changes could be made in Social Security "without increasing the tax rate." The idea was not to increase the tax rate but to raise the amount of a person's income on which he paid Social Security taxes.[41] In addition to raising Social Security benefits, Cohen also believed that welfare payments to the needy and the amount of federal grants for maternal and child health to the states should be raised.[42]

At the Committee on Ways and Means hearings in June, HEW Secretary Folsom proposed a new type of selective benefit increase.[43] Someone who retired before 1955 would get a raise of 8 percent; someone who retired before 1957 would get 5; someone who retired in 1957 or 1958 would get 3. Folsom promised nothing to those who retired after 1958. On the surface it did not appear to be bad politics. For one thing, the administration wanted to raise

Wilbur Mills, who became chairman of the House Committee on Ways and Means in 1958, emerged as the single most powerful influence over Social Security policy in the late 1950s. The dynamic of the two Wilburs, as Martha Derthick has called it, was responsible for Medicare and many other important pieces of Social Security legislation. The two became so close that Cohen even offered to staff Mills's retirement. (Courtesy of the Historian's Office, U.S. House of Representatives)

benefits without raising the tax rate, and Folsom's proposal did not create a permanent liability for the Social Security trust fund. Once the last of the dependents of the people who retired in 1958 died, the costs of the increase would disappear from the Social Security accounts. Mills, for his part, rather liked the idea of what came to be called a temporary increase in benefits.[44] He received further encouragement from Nelson Cruikshank and Andy Biemiller of the AFL-CIO, who said they could support a "temporary" increase of 10 percent through 1960, with no tax increase.

Cohen talked with Mills and staff director Leo Irwin by phone on July 7 and told them that, contrary to the feelings of Cruikshank and Biemiller, he was not in favor of a temporary benefit increase. Mills asked Cohen to come to Washington, and by the time he arrived on July 10 he had talked with Altmeyer and Fedele Fauri, who had strengthened his feelings against a temporary increase. Altmeyer had always believed that benefit increases should be funded by tax increases, and Fauri, a frequent consultant to the Senate Finance Committee, told Cohen that Harry Byrd, its chairman, would never accept a benefit increase unless it was soundly financed. Cohen emphasized what he described as "the financial integrity of the system," in part because it was "necessary if we are to obtain any extension of health benefits in OASDI over insurance company and other conservative opposition." His instincts, reinforced by the advice of his friends, told him that he could best protect his long-range interests if he argued against the temporary increase.

Mills seemed unconvinced by Cohen's arguments. As Cohen concluded his visit by walking with Mills to the Ways and Means committee room, the congressman said, "You know more about this than I do. You may be right. See if you can work it out." Cohen, like a salesman given a last minute reprieve, assured Mills that he would work out the details and get back to him that afternoon. Cohen thrived on this sort of deadline. He quickly produced a memorandum for Mills in which he proposed a permanent 10 percent benefit increase that would apply to all present and future retirees, to be financed by raising the taxable wage base to $4,800 and by increasing the tax rate in 1960 from 5.5 to 6 percent of covered payroll (and with a gradually rising tax rate after that until the rate reached 9 percent in 1975). The fact that Cohen could produce this suggestion at such short notice illustrated his dexterity with figures and his familiarity with the intricacies of Social Security legislation.

Cohen went back to see Mills, and after they had talked in a relaxed and informal manner he gave the chairman the memo he had prepared. According to Cohen, Mills "seemed impressed with my point that he shouldn't get tainted by newspaper men with the mantle of 'fiscal irresponsibility.' " He seemed on his way to accepting Cohen's notion of a tax increase.

Cohen flew home, and Mills led his committee into executive session where he stressed to the members the importance of fiscal responsibility.[45] He spoke so fervently on the subject that Congressman John Byrnes (R-Wis.), a conservative, urged that taxes be increased in 1959 rather than in 1960. Mills, in fact, received bipartisan support for his bill, which passed on July 31 by an overwhelming majority. Cohen had succeeded in changing the entire tenor of the House debate from Mills's initial infatuation with a temporary increase with no new taxes to his subsequent conversion to a tax increase. And Cohen was not even a member of an organized staff.

Immediately after the 1958 bill passed the House, Cohen turned his attention to influencing the Senate. Here his point of entry was Robert Kerr, the influential member of the Finance Committee who had emerged as one of Cohen's most important political clients in the mid-1950s. There were few similarities between the rich, cattle-raising Kerr and the middle-class, urban-homesteading Cohen; nonetheless, as one of Kerr's staff members remembered, Kerr "often called on Wilbur for his professional opinion on matters." Even though Kerr positioned himself far to the right of Cohen on social issues, the senator admired him, believing he "had as fine a mind and was as dedicated to his field as any man he'd ever seen."[46]

Before talking with Kerr, Cohen went to see Lloyd Rader, the director of Public Welfare in Oklahoma whom he had first come to know in 1953 when they had consulted about testimony for the Curtis subcommittee.[47] It was a good example of how Cohen cultivated staff members and then through them gained entry to a political principal. Instead of concentrating on Social Security, Cohen highlighted welfare in his dealings with Rader and Kerr. The House, it seemed, had adopted an "equalization" formula for both public assistance and child welfare services, in which the federal government paid a larger share of welfare costs in poorer states (like Oklahoma) than in richer states. Rader explained to Kerr that Oklahoma was feeling the effects of the recession, and if the federal government did not provide more money to his state, then Rader would have no choice but to decrease public assistance payments. Hearing this news, Kerr resolved to do what he could to bring in a bill that benefited Oklahoma.

Senator Kerr took the lead on the legislation as it made its way through the Finance Committee. Procedures would have gone smoothly except for the intervention of Sen. Paul Douglas (D-Ill.). Before the hearings began in the Senate, Cohen had briefed Douglas and his staff and told them that President Eisenhower's Bureau of the Budget opposed the public assistance provision in the House-passed bill because it increased the federal share of welfare payments. At the hearings, Douglas asked Secretary of HEW Arthur Flemming, who had just taken over the post, whether the president would veto the bill in its present form; Flemming said that he would.

Arthur Flemming, always known in Washington conversation as Doctor Flemming, would eventually become one of Wilbur Cohen's closest working associates. In August 1958, however, he had just taken over as Secretary of Health, Education, and Welfare from Marion Folsom.[48] An experienced administrator, Flemming still felt the need to consult closely with the president on Social Security legislation, about which the new secretary understandably knew little or nothing. Reinforced by exposure to Eisenhower's sentiments, Flemming thought he had a clear directive to indicate that the president would veto the bill.

Senator Kerr, anxious to pass the law, asked Cohen for suggestions on how to placate the Eisenhower administration and still benefit Oklahoma. Once again, Rader and Cohen met with the senator, along with Social Security commissioner Charles Schottland. Cohen had two suggestions. First, there should be an advisory council on public assistance that would discuss the whole matter of federal-state responsibilities in public assistance, thus allowing the administration to agree to an increase in the federal share of public assistance without losing face.[49] Second, steps should be taken to meet the administration's objection that the public assistance formula in the House bill was too costly. Kerr agreed to the first suggestion and asked Cohen to come up with some specific ideas on how to cut welfare costs. As usual, Cohen obliged; overnight he produced a memo for Kerr in which he presented a menu of possibilities, such as reducing the maximum average monthly welfare payment by one dollar and reducing the maximum federal matching percentage by three percentage points. When Kerr met with Cohen again, they chose some items on the menu that would preserve the principle of giving the poorer states a higher percentage of aid than the richer states and that would reduce welfare costs from the levels in the House bill but not harm Oklahoma unduly. These suggestions were eventually written into the bill.

The bill moved quickly through committee and then to the floor, where the Senate completed action on August 16, so rapidly that the senators did not even have transcripts of the hearings to read as they voted on the bill. Just as the members relied on Mills in the House, they depended on Kerr in the Senate. He even served as the floor manager for the bill, the first time in Cohen's memory that a chairman of a Senate committee had relinquished control. Although the president complained that the increases in the federal share of public assistance "can lead only to weakening of the responsibility of the states and communities," he signed the bill into law.[50]

In the Senate, as in the House, Wilbur Cohen played an indispensable role in facilitating passage of legislation. The 1958 amendments affirmed his position not just as a central figure in Social Security policy but arguably as the leader among those who advised the Congress.[51]

Cohen's efforts to facilitate passage of the new public assistance financing formula illustrated his penchant for coming up with compromises that preserved the basic principles of a piece of legislation, in this case the equalization formula, but that modified the details to be acceptable to both sides. In time, the Cohen compromise became almost his legislative signature, to the admiration of those people who believed that his efforts saved controversial proposals and to the consternation of those who believed that such measures would have passed anyway. The Cohen compromise worked best in an environment in which there were two well-defined sides that were in substantial agreement on the general design of social policy but that disagreed over an important detail. The Eisenhower years, in which Congress worked with a measure of party discipline and in which consensus prevailed on most social welfare questions, proved a perfect breeding ground for the Cohen compromise.

KERR-MILLS: PRESIDENTIAL AND CONGRESSIONAL POLITICS

After the passage of the 1958 amendments, Cohen juggled time for Kennedy with time for Mills and Kerr on his visits to Washington. In the election year of 1960, Cohen continued to pursue the strategy of assisting the congressional leaders in the passage of specific legislation and of backing Kennedy for president. At times, it became difficult for Cohen to keep the two elements of his strategy from impinging on one another.

As the election year began, Cohen found himself simultaneously involved in nearly all aspects of the effort to pass a Social Security bill. First, he consulted with a subcommittee of the Senate Committee on Labor and Public Welfare concerned with the problems of the aged.[52] In 1959 this subcommittee, under the direction of Sen. Pat McNamara (D-Mich.), had helped to publicize the issue of health insurance for the elderly. McNamara and his staff, which included a Wisconsin classmate of Cohen's, William Reidy, held dramatic hearings at which elderly citizens spoke of their inability to secure adequate health care. These people, delivering details that historian Sherri David describes as "heart-rending," generated enough publicity to make health insurance, in Cohen's words, "the major issue in social security in Congress and in the nation in 1959."[53]

Second, Wilbur Cohen gave advice to John F. Kennedy and Myer Feldman as they attempted to maneuver the senator into the congressional debate. Since a consensus appeared to be forming on national health insurance for the elderly and since the issue had become so prominent, Kennedy wanted to be a player. Among other advantages, it would help to shore up his support with organized labor and with elderly voters. The former had played a large role in the preparation and introduction of the Forand bill in 1957, the first in a series of health insurance bills targeted on the elderly that appeared in the late 1950s. As a member of the Senate Committee on Labor and Public Welfare and as a member of McNamara's subcommittee, Kennedy had plausible credentials to participate in the debate. Cohen felt much more comfortable with Senator Kennedy, with whom he had developed a smooth working relationship, than with Senator McNamara, with whom he had developed an uncharacteristically contentious relationship.

Although Kennedy consulted with Nelson Cruikshank of the AFL in writing a health insurance bill in 1959 and 1960, he remained in close touch with Cohen, who advised him to pare down his bill so as to attract the broadest base of political support. That meant, for example, deleting surgical benefits, a major point of contention with the American Medical Association. Kennedy accepted nearly all of Cohen's suggestions as well as the general strategy that the health insurance advocates bypass the Senate Committee on Labor and Public Welfare and concentrate on the Committee on Finance.[54]

Third, Cohen remained in close touch with congressional leaders such as Mills in the House and Kerr in the Senate. As Cohen tried to push Mills toward acceptance of health insurance for the elderly, he framed his arguments in terms of political compromises and statistical measures of cost. As always, Cohen regarded the notion of health insurance, funded through Social Security contributions and administered by the federal government, as the essential goal. He was willing to compromise in any conceivable direction on any conceivable aspect to win acceptance of the notion. He presented Mills with a set of possibilities, hoping that one of the compromises would appeal to him and inspire him to carry along the rest of his committee.[55]

Cohen made a point of keeping his communications with Mills confidential, never wanting to embarrass him or to force his hand. He always appealed to his political-statesman side, telling him that hospital insurance would be an "important achievement to the credit of the Democratic leadership and take the initiative away from the Republican presidential candidate."[56] He never sought to dictate to Mills; rather, he proposed alternatives. In this case, for example, he suggested raising the eligibility age to seventy-two and increasing the deductible that people would pay out of pocket to as much as fifteen dollars a day.[57] With Mills, as with Kennedy, he always offered to do more if he were asked.[58]

In the matter of health insurance for the aged, Mills preferred that the Senate take the lead. When little support for the measure developed in his committee, he did little to change the situation, despite heavy pressure from organized labor and from the House leadership. On June 3, 1960, the House Ways and Means Committee rejected national health insurance for the elderly by a vote of 17 to 8; as usual, the committee legislated for the House.[59] "Well the Ways and Means Committee labored mightily and brought forth a flea on the back of a mouse. What a spectacle," commented Altmeyer from his armchair in Madison.[60]

"We have had a long and difficult situation in the House, but we look forward to the Senate making some important improvements," Cohen noted in June.[61] Here he found himself dealing simultaneously with Kerr, Johnson, Kennedy, and McNamara and trying to keep his apparatus of Cruikshank, Ball, and others from working at cross-purposes. He worked with Myer Feldman and Senator Kennedy on amendments related to cash benefits under Social Security.[62] At the suggestion of Lyndon Johnson, he toyed with a compromise plan that offered Social Security recipients a choice between a higher cash benefit or health insurance benefits.[63] But it was Kerr who was Cohen's most important client on the Finance Committee and in the Senate itself. Indeed, with Harry Byrd, the nominal chairman, ailing, Kerr served as the de facto head of the committee. Cohen hastened to do what he could for Senator Kerr, who lost little time calling on Cohen for assistance. As William Reynolds of Kerr's staff explained, the senator directed him to "get hold of Mr. Cohen up at the University of Michigan and seek his help." Kerr hired Cohen as a consultant, paying him out of his own pocket because he wanted Cohen's "expertise in the draftsmanship and also his knowledge of the need for a program of some sort."[64]

Kerr had little use for national health insurance or for John F. Kennedy; he supported his friend and fellow rancher Lyndon Johnson for president, realizing that Kennedy had almost no chance of carrying Oklahoma, a solidly Baptist state. Kerr was himself up for reelection in 1960, did not relish the prospect of running on the same ticket as Kennedy, and wanted to make sure that the doctors in the state did not regard him as a friend of socialized medicine. If he backed health insurance under Social Security, he explained, "I'll lose every doctor in the state."[65] Yet he wanted to offer something to the elderly in the field of health insurance, preferably a measure that voters could differentiate from the Kennedy proposal and that benefited the state of Oklahoma.[66] Just as they had worked together on public assistance amendments in 1958, Kerr put Cohen to work producing a new sort of medical assistance bill in 1960.

Cohen designed a measure that concentrated on medical benefits for people unable to pay for them. This idea, like almost all the ideas that he offered in 1960, was not new. Beginning in 1950 the federal government shared some of the costs of providing medical care to welfare recipients with the states. The terms of these payments to hospitals and doctors, known as vendor payments, were complicated. Nonetheless, the idea of limiting medical care payments to those on welfare – people who could prove they were poor – continued to appeal to those individuals who wanted to control the amount of money that the federal government spent on medical care. The idea was also attractive to those who instinctively preferred locally administered programs over programs administered in Washington. Welfare, after all, was a state program that allowed the states a great deal of autonomy; Social Security was a federal program in which the federal government made the rules for the entire nation.[67]

Wilbur Mills had already agreed to an expansion of vendor payments for elderly welfare recipients in the bill passed by the House in June.[68] To this basic provision, Cohen, working for Kerr, added another, more innovative proposal. He called for the establishment of a new category of federal aid to the states, Medical Assistance to the Aged, which would include federal grants to the states to pay doctors and hospitals for services to elderly people deemed "medically indigent." Such people need not be poor enough to qualify for welfare but poor enough to be unable to afford medical care. For example, an eighty-year-old individual, just scraping by on his resources without welfare, might go to the hospital for several weeks and be unable to pay the bill; Cohen designed Medical Assistance to the Aged for just such an individual.[69]

As Kerr and Cohen developed this new plan in private, the Senate Finance Committee held very public hearings late in June and considered a wide array of proposals for health insurance for the elderly.[70] Crucial deliberations occurred in August after the political nominating conventions. With the Finance Committee meeting in executive session, Kerr revealed the plan that he and Cohen had crafted and on August 13 secured committee acceptance of it. Meanwhile, Kennedy's health insurance plan was defeated, but for candidate Kennedy this outcome was unsatisfactory.[71] He wanted an open debate on his measure on the Senate floor so that he could make health insurance for the elderly a campaign issue.

Cohen was scheduled to deliver a talk on August 9 in San Francisco, but Sorensen called him, probably on August 7, and asked him to come back to Washington to help with the floor fight on health insurance. Cohen hopped a plane back to Washington on August 8.[72] He now faced the consequences of maintaining his contacts with both Kennedy and Kerr, with both the presidential candidate and the permanent member of Congress. Cohen had worked on both Kennedy's and Kerr's proposals, even though many people considered the Kerr proposal to be a substitute for Kennedy's. Some observers thought that the Senate Finance Committee's passage of Kerr's proposal increased the odds against passage of Kennedy's. In such a view, Cohen had undercut his own actions, selling the compromise even before the preferred proposal had been defeated.

Cohen responded by keeping his lines of communication open. He did not hide his association with Kerr from Sorensen, nor did he regard his actions as contradictory. "It was my position that you ought to have both of them," he explained. "And I was the only one who believed that." Cohen tried to convince Senators Kennedy, Douglas, McNamara, and Albert Gore (D-Tenn.) that "you've got Kerr and you've got Kennedy. But you don't need to choose between these two. You can be for both." "And that was my way of having an allegiance to both Kerr and Kennedy," Cohen said. "I think Kennedy and Sorensen thought that was a great act of political realism and pragmatism because up to that time, everybody . . . thought they were antagonistic."[73]

By the time the measure came to the Senate floor, no one had to choose between Kerr's and Kennedy's proposals. Instead, the Senate voted on Kennedy's amendment and on the entire bill, which included what came to be called the Kerr-Mills program. When the vote on the Kennedy amendment came on August 23, it failed to pass by a substantial margin. Then, in short order, both the Senate and House accepted the bill, which Eisenhower signed into law on September 13, 1960. The new law contained what became known as the Kerr-Mills program, after the major congressional proprietors of the Social Security program. It expanded the vendor-payments program and initiated a new program of federal grants for medical care to the indigent.[74]

As Cohen and Kennedy had assumed, the votes were not yet there for health insurance for the elderly or for Medicare. Still, the outcome provided each of the protagonists, at least those on the Democratic side of the aisle, with what he wanted. Kennedy had his campaign issue, building on his support for health insurance.[75] Kerr had his alternative, and among conservatives he had the credit for turning back national health insurance. Cohen had his allegiance to his congressional and presidential allies, and he had the beginnings of an improved welfare program.

THE 1960 CAMPAIGN: COHEN AS OFFICE SEEKER

As much time as he spent in Washington, Cohen continued throughout this period to teach in Ann Arbor. In the fall of 1960 he added work on the

Kennedy campaign to his considerable portfolio. By then, he had long been a Kennedy supporter although he also had ties to Humphrey and Johnson.[76] In contrast to his assignments for the other Democratic senators, his work for Kennedy had always been of a personal nature rather than strictly program-oriented. He had designed specific policy proposals for Kennedy, just as he had for Humphrey and Johnson, yet he had also helped to draft speeches that were intended to call attention to Kennedy as a presidential candidate as much as they were a vehicle to advance a specific policy proposal. At some point during 1960 Cohen agreed to serve as vice-chairman of Senior Citizens for Kennedy, even though Cohen was hardly a senior citizen at forty-six.[77] Still, his identity as an expert was bound up with the work that he had done in the design and implementation of such programs as Social Security that were of primary benefit to the elderly. As a well-known advocate of health insurance for the elderly, as a professor at a prestigious university, as a recognizable member of a politically important ethnic group, Cohen's was an attractive name to place on a letterhead.

Cohen fit two sides of the Kennedy image. On the one hand, he represented the senator's efforts to align himself with traditional liberal causes and with America's leading thinkers on social issues; on the other, he understood the nature of practical politics and could be relied upon to help guard Kennedy's political interests. Cohen could go on the letterhead and off into the real world, a rare combination of pedigree and talent.

During the campaign itself, Cohen remained in touch with Sorensen as much as was possible; he never became a member of the inner circle of Kennedy advisers who devoted all their time to the campaign. In the fall of 1960 Cohen taught full time and lived his normal academic life, helping the campaign where he could. At one point he mentioned to Sorensen the need for a director of research who could supply the candidate with timely information on issues as they arose. His suggestion indirectly might have reinforced the idea in Sorensen's mind, an idea that led to the appointment of Archibald Cox, then a Harvard Law School professor, as head of a loosely organized research effort. As Cohen recalled, he met with Cox a number of times in Washington.[78]

As the campaign progressed and Kennedy appeared to be doing well, Cohen turned his attention to whether or not to seek a post in the Kennedy administration. He noted in his diary in October that his efforts on behalf of the Kerr-Mills bill, just as his previous efforts to pass health insurance for the elderly, had made him a controversial figure. Fedele Fauri told him that a state legislative committee had complained that he was a Socialist. Cohen knew that controversy of this sort did not increase his chances of being selected for the Kennedy administration and wondered how he could maintain his ideals and his effectiveness in the face of such attacks. Drawing upon images that Kennedy had made famous, he wrote about the "erosion of courage" and claimed that Fauri wanted him to be "more careful."[79] Cohen indeed was very careful, quick to compromise and reluctant to denigrate his opponents. He did not choose to be a controversial figure; it was just that the logic of Social Security's development drew him into the fight for health insurance. By taking a definite position in favor of health insurance for the elderly, he invited the opposition of the American Medical Association and other foes of what the AMA called socialized medicine.

As Cohen weighed his chances of being selected for a policy post, he observed the final, unsettling weeks of the campaign. Kennedy's lead began to erode, and it became apparent that the election would be very close. On the evening of October 21, Cohen watched Kennedy and Nixon conduct the last of their four televised debates—the "dreariest" of the four, according to Theodore H. White.[80] With the election less than three weeks away, Cohen decided that Kennedy would win. "If so," he recorded in his diary, "I would like to help develop his program. So I am keeping an open mind and an open calendar for the future."[81] On election night itself, Cohen watched television until ten, then went to the local Democratic headquarters, and from there to two rounds of parties. Somewhere in the course of the evening it became clear that John F. Kennedy would win.[82]

The members of Cohen's apparatus wasted no time in making plans for the Kennedy administration. On the day after the election, Robert Ball invited Cohen to lunch with Nelson Cruikshank in Washington. Ball said that people "representing the administration" should establish "formal liaison" with his bureau so that "we could perform various kinds of work for the new Administration right way." Ball, always a cautious and competent individual, nearly bubbled over with ideas that he was eager to share with Cohen.[83] He took it for granted that Cohen would work in the new administration.

In the first weeks after Kennedy's election, Cohen continued to brood about what role he should play in the new administration.[84] Ball articulated the reasons why Cohen should join the administration rather than continuing to influence Social Security legislation from Ann Arbor, explaining that "when the Executive Branch is not pushing the program in which you believe, it is quite correct to reason that your influence outside might well be greater than inside." But when the issue was "how to accomplish the program" and how to manage the program "in detail," then "the real job" was done by "the one officially in charge." Ball said that in Cohen's absence things "could be quite a mess," with the Social Security Administration having to educate an untutored individual on Social Security policy, just as they had once done for Roswell Perkins in

1954. Ball ended his pitch by saying that Cohen should not "miss the fun and excitement of being in charge of the next forward step in social security."[85]

Cohen sat by the telephone and waited for the call from Washington or Palm Beach or New York that would tap him for the new administration. He did not have too long to wait. On November 22, 1960, Myer Feldman telephoned him and asked for the names of people who should serve on a special transition task force concerned with Social Security and health. Cohen suggested Dean Clark and James Dixon, two prominent doctors and public health authorities who were sympathetic to health insurance for the elderly; he also mentioned Herman Somers, his old friend from the Experimental College and a recognized authority on the politics of social insurance. The next day Leonard Lesser of the United Auto Workers (UAW) phoned to ask what position Cohen might want to fill; he replied, with little hesitation, that he wanted to be the assistant secretary for legislation at the Department of Health, Education, and Welfare. That evening Ted Sorensen called from Palm Beach and asked him to chair the Health and Social Security Task Force, and he consented.[86] It was clear that President Kennedy would use Cohen's services, just as Senator Kennedy had.

Cohen appointed Dean Clark, James Dixon, and Herman Somers to the transition task force, as he said he would, and he also asked Elizabeth Wickenden for help. She began as a consultant and then became a full-fledged member. Myer Feldman then requested that two other people be added to the task force. The subsequent appointment of Dr. Robert Cooke, a pediatrician at Johns Hopkins, and Joshua Lederberg, a geneticist at Stanford, reflected the interest of Eunice Shriver and other members of the Kennedy family in passing federal legislation on behalf of the mentally retarded.[87]

The task force operated on a tight deadline and with little staff support. Cohen arranged for the group to meet on December 15 and 19. The members, such as Dixon and Somers, had experience with blue-ribbon panels of this sort, having worked with the Rockefeller project and with the President's Commission on National Goals. The participants compiled little new information; instead, they relied on the wisdom they had already gathered and on their sense of political priorities. Because the group dynamics were already well established, it did not take long for the task force to compose a report. As expected, Cohen put Medical Care for the Aged at the top of the agenda while other members pressed their special concerns. Dr. Dixon expressed interest in increasing the supply of doctors through the construction of medical schools and the provision of scholarship aid to medical school students. Dr. Clark, who worked at Massachusetts General Hospital, concentrated on the expansion of the Hill-Burton hospital construction program so that it could provide more aid to urban hospitals. Dr. Cooke suggested that the Kennedy administration endorse the creation of a children's health institute within the Public Health Service.[88]

Cohen did not have time to organize an elaborate process of consultation, but he did manage to have the group meet with the commissioner of Social Security and with the surgeon general. When Kennedy announced that Abraham Ribicoff, governor of Connecticut and an early Kennedy supporter, would become the Secretary of Health, Education, and Welfare, Cohen made arrangements for the group to meet with both Ribicoff and Sorensen in Hartford. "I think this turned out to be a rather important session," Cohen later said, because the discussions facilitated a "consensus between Ribicoff, Sorensen and myself which stood us in good stead in the ensuing weeks."[89]

At the end of December, Ribicoff discussed Cohen's joining his staff. Cohen later wrote to him that "my particular abilities and interests could best be utilized as Assistant Secretary for legislation in the way in which previous Secretaries used Roswell Perkins and Eliot Richardson. . . . I am reasonably certain that the Senate Committee on Finance would approve my nomination."[90] As he realized, the confirmation process played to one of his strengths; clearly he had cultivated the Senate Finance Committee over the years. Cohen and Chairman Harry Byrd agreed about very little, but when Ribicoff checked with Byrd, he learned that the senator regarded Cohen as an "honest and frank man." Cohen contacted his friend Lloyd Rader and asked him to sound out Robert Kerr on the possible nomination; Rader said that Kerr would back him wholeheartedly.[91]

In the fluid atmosphere at the beginning of the administration, the various presidential appointments were moved back and forth like pieces on a chess board. Ribicoff was Jewish, and it occurred to some observers that one of his assistant secretaries should not be Jewish also. Sorensen, who no doubt was punch-drunk from lists of names and jobs, suggested to Cohen that the particular job he held did not matter and that he should consider becoming director of the census.[92] Cohen himself discouraged talk of his becoming the commissioner of Social Security, because William Mitchell, the present commissioner, was a good friend of his.[93]

As speculation over whom Kennedy would select to the various cabinet positions mounted, Cohen made arrangements to present his task force report to the president-elect. Kennedy's staff decided that Cohen should come to New York and make his presentation on Tuesday, January 10, at the Hotel Carlyle. He spent the night there and on Tuesday morning took the elevator on his way to see Kennedy. Mrs. Roosevelt, also scheduled to see the president that morning, accompanied him in the elevator. Reporters stalked the lobby, waiting for news. The president fell behind in his appointments, giving

Ribicoff and Cohen plenty of time to chat further about Cohen's post in the new administration.[94]

Eventually, Cohen and Ribicoff went in to see the president, Sorensen, and Pierre Salinger, and Cohen handed Kennedy a copy of the report, Kennedy remarking that he did not want the newspapers to play up the cost of implementing the proposals in it. He then thumbed through it and suggested that the last three recommendations be omitted so that the report highlighted health insurance for the elderly and Social Security. Cohen, Sorensen, and Salinger promptly tore off the back pages of it, conveniently forgetting that the deleted recommendations were discussed in the front. Meanwhile, Kennedy continued to thumb through; when he came to the recommendation about paying ADC benefits to the children of unemployed parents, he said, "Let's be sure to do this particular thing as soon as we can." Cohen then went down to the lobby and answered questions. Ribicoff made no commitments about honoring any of the recommendations.[95]

Cohen headed for Washington, traveling on the *Caroline,* the president's special plane, with Sorensen, Kenny O'Donnell, and Ambassador George Kennan, among others. Kennan talked with Cohen about the importance of health insurance for the elderly; Cohen talked with Kennan about the cold war, Russia, and the importance of foreign policy. Perhaps Cohen felt the sense of disbelief that he had experienced on his first day on the job in 1934, when people in the newspapers such as Rexford Tugwell suddenly had materialized before him.[96] At one point during the trip, Cohen turned to Sorensen and asked what the president had meant when he said that he wanted Cohen to work on changes in the ADC law. Sorensen explained that Kennedy wanted him to be a member of his administration and that he would discuss a specific position later. Cohen told Sorensen that he needed to grade his exams and that he had already made arrangements to teach spring semester.[97]

Not too long after this discussion, Cohen accompanied his son Chris to the gymnasium in Ann Arbor. Chris, a freshman at the university, hoped to make the track team as a long distance runner in the spring, but in the dead of winter he ran indoors. Then Cohen heard someone call his name: "Is Professor Cohen here?" Expecting that someone had died, Cohen went to the phone with a sense of trepidation. At the other end was Andrew Hacker, an assistant press secretary for Kennedy, who was preparing a press release and wanted to know the names of Cohen's wife and children; the president, he said, would announce his appointment as assistant secretary the next morning.[98]

Even though Cohen had contemplated working in the Kennedy administration, he left Ann Arbor abruptly. He later told an interviewer of his last long night in Michigan: "My final exams in my course were January 16. . . . The exam was finished about two or three or four in the afternoon. I graded exam papers until 4:45 in the morning. I completed them all, gave them to my wife, told her to take them back that morning, went upstairs and took a shower. I finished showering and shaving about 5:30 or quarter to six, called a taxicab, went to Willow Run, took a seven o'clock plane to Washington on January 17, 1961. I left my office, my papers, my home, and walked out."[99]

Three days later, Wilbur and Eloise sat on the left side of the stands in the twelfth row and watched John F. Kennedy deliver his inaugural address; on their right sat Governor Swanson of Michigan. Cohen thought Kennedy's speech magnificent: "Courageous, crisp, vigorous, forward looking . . . how proud I was to be a member of his administration."[100]

Wilbur Cohen entered the Kennedy administration with his usual sense of optimism. It was an article of faith among Cohen and his fellow liberals that Eisenhower had not done enough for America.[101] As Cohen surely realized, however, the political system did not change in any fundamental way with the election of John F. Kennedy, and he knew that passage of key social legislation such as health insurance for the elderly lay several years in the future. Wilbur Mills and Robert Kerr remained entrenched in Congress. The job of reconciling the differences between congressional and presidential politics would now be Cohen's direct responsibility. It was, nonetheless, with a tremendous sense of exhilaration that Wilbur Cohen returned to Washington, ready to turn his years of academic thought into coherent political action.

THE NEW FRONTIER

Once again Wilbur Cohen traveled from a midwestern university town to Washington, leaving academia to serve in a Democratic administration. Compared with his 1934 journey by car and bus, however, this trip was made in relative style. Having functioned as a New Deal junior research assistant who validated the decisions made by others, in the Kennedy era he would make policy on matters in which the president took a personal interest. In effect, Kennedy wanted Cohen to establish a second generation of social welfare programs, programs that took the explicit forms of federal aid to education, federal investment in medical care, and federal efforts to spark the rehabilitation of welfare beneficiaries. Unlike the elements of the New Deal, the New Frontier initiatives emphasized investment rather than spending and participation rather than retirement. By 1965, after the tumultuous events of Kennedy's assassination, Congress had passed most of the items on the agenda into law. First, however, came a frustrating period in which Congress continually refused to approve federal aid to education or health insurance for the elderly. During this time, as Cohen tried to manage a large and sprawling department, he worked with his old legislative contacts and facilitated the passage of new welfare and mental retardation laws. In the Kennedy years, therefore, Cohen enjoyed some quiet victories in low-profile areas even as he endured loud defeats on Medicare and education.

FIRST DAYS ON THE JOB

During the Kennedy years, Cohen functioned as a member of the president's senior staff, and he knew much more about the legislative process in 1961 than he did in 1935. In the New Deal era, Cohen had carried within him the economic insecurities of the times and the psychological insecurities of youth, working in what were to him unfamiliar realms when he first came to Washington. Despite his institutionally oriented Wisconsin education, he understood little about policy-related research, and he had no experience in partisan politics as practiced at the national level. During the New Frontier, Cohen, although still only forty-eight, had advance knowledge of the territory over which he was expected to travel. He had already worked with Kennedy, Sorensen, and Feldman in the senator's office, and he would continue to work with them in the president's office. He had already collaborated with Wilbur Mills and Robert Kerr, the two most important figures in Social Security policy, and he had more than a casual acquaintance with Sen. Lister Hill and Congressman John Fogarty (D-R.I.), the two most influential figures in determining HEW's budget. Further, Cohen maintained close ties with people in many levels of the HEW bureaucracy.

As the third person ever to be appointed as assistant secretary for legislation at the Department of Health, Education, and Welfare, Cohen came to the job with the most preparation. President Eisenhower had brought in two people with little or no experience in social welfare policy. Roswell Perkins, Eisenhower's first appointment, was a lawyer whose close connections to Undersecretary Nelson Rockefeller netted him the job. Elliot Richardson, the second Eisenhower appointee and a protégé of HEW Secretary Arthur Flemming, specialized not in a specific area of policy so much as in the management of the policy process itself. President Kennedy appointed Cohen, who had a great deal of practical policy experience in the social welfare field.

Third in command at HEW, Wilbur Cohen became the point from which the thin level of political appointees fanned into the thousands of lawyers, economists, and other technicians who ran the department's many programs. Although not without a strong ego, he instinctively saw himself as staff to the politicians rather than as a politician himself. Both of his superiors were politicians who plunged from one job to the other, constantly trading on their futures. Abraham Ribicoff, former governor of Connecticut, used his year-and-a-half at HEW to shore up his political contacts in that state and make a successful run for Prescott Bush's seat in the Senate. Cohen, who seldom criticized anyone, described Ribicoff as a "poor administrator" and as "self-centered and egotistical."[1] Undersecretary Ivan Nestingen, former mayor of Madison who had helped Kennedy in the Wisconsin primary and been rewarded with a Washington job, was by his own admission a man with "a political background and political inclinations."[2] After Ribicoff left in the summer of 1962, Kennedy replaced him with Anthony Celebrezze. A former mayor of Cleveland, Celebrezze, according to Cohen, was not perceived as particularly intelligent or competent by the administration. Like Ribicoff, Celebrezze had his eyes on another political prize, a federal judgeship. Rumors ascribed his appointment to the president's desire to appease Italians and thus boost his brother Ted's candidacy for senator.[3]

Cohen had the daunting task of trying to bring a degree of unity and order to what was in fact an unwieldy collection of semiautonomous agencies. The Office of the Secretary, of which Cohen's operation was a part, functioned on a budget of less than $7.5 million in fiscal 1961. In contrast, the entire Department of Health, Education, and Welfare spent $3.8 billion that year, not including the money used to pay Social Security benefits. As a consequence, the Office of the Secretary operated like a holding company, loosely uniting such major agencies as the Public Health Service, with its budget of over $.5 billion dollars, the Social Security Administration, with its largely independent legislative agenda, and the Office of Education.[4]

When Cohen took office, he was one of only two assistant secretaries, and James Quigley, the other one, concentrated almost entirely on internal management.[5] As the professional in the field, Cohen was expected to take the lead in writing legislative proposals. As one astute observer later told an interviewer, Ribicoff realized that his first objective was to write legislation and bring it up to the Hill; Cohen was "the *only* one around that could do it." Cohen could write bills and produce presidential messages: "He knew the channels . . . to get it up to the Congress and get it to the White House."[6]

Cohen called his first day on the job "strenuous" and did not slacken his pace for the next few months.[7] In one of the most intense activity spasms of his life, he drafted presidential messages relating to Social Security, welfare, health, education, and water pollution.[8] Working with a tiny staff of about five people, including two deputies and two special assistants, he concentrated on many different policy areas at once. In the summer of 1961, for example, he told a friend about how he was coping with "10 different areas going on simultaneously. I have been handling education, health, social security, water pollution and other legislation."[9] He filled his letters with complaints of "sheer exhaustion" that stemmed from the knowledge that President Kennedy expected his appointees to work "15 to 18 hours a day."[10]

Cohen did work long hours, reverting to behavior common to his first days in Washington. Starting any new project, he tried to tame the unfamiliar by devoting an inordinate number of hours to the task at hand. He was in an environment where such behavior was common, where people showed how tough they were in part by how hard they worked. Cohen, whose family remained behind in Ann Arbor until summer, rented a house in Cleveland Park in which he spent little time. As he put it, "I feel that I am more or less locked into my office about 15 hours a day."[11]

The long days produced their share of despair. He told his friends that he found his job to be the "most frustrating, complex job I ever had in my life."[12] He filled his letters with expressions of his longings to go back to Ann Arbor, writing Fauri, in a moment of exhaustion, that he had never worked so hard in all his life: "I have never had as many difficult decisions and frustrations to face. I do not look forward to continuing in this situation." But Cohen could see "no way out" and reluctantly asked Fauri in May 1961 for an extended leave of absence.[13] He confessed to a former colleague in Social Security that, although he enjoyed his job, he felt disappointed about the "long hours and the inadequacy of the staff work I have been able to do under tremendous pressure."[14]

One source of pressure was that many of the areas he covered were new to him, despite his long period of apprenticeship with Altmeyer and Fauri. Within days of getting to Washington, for example, he prepared a presidential message devoted to natural resources that discussed water and air pollution.[15] In the field of food and drug legislation, Cohen found himself dragged into a political dispute between Senator Estes Kefauver (D-Tenn.) and the White House with little time for preparation. On budgetary matters, Cohen had to deal with a set of congressional players who, although not entirely new to him, were different from the ones who earlier had taken the lead on Social Security legislation.

Another source of pressure stemmed from the circumstance that passage of the president's program required extraordinary deference to Congress, and Cohen had to figure out just whom to defer to on what. Nearly all forms of health legislation, for instance, required the assent of Senator Hill and Congressman Fogarty. As Cohen put it, "Senator Hill and Mr. Fogarty gave the definite impression that they were running the health aspects of the department and not Kennedy and Ribicoff." Among the senators, Hill had the most influence over HEW since his committees controlled health and education legislation as well as the department's level of appropriations. Hence, as the administration prepared its program for 1962, Hill needed to be consulted on the administration's bills for higher education, improving the quality of education, increasing the number of health professionals, creating the Institute of Child Health and Human Development, amending the food and drug act, setting the level of appropriations, and reorganizing the bureaus within the department.

Like Hill, Fogarty enjoyed an impressive measure of influence over the department's appropriations and its health-related legislation. He also took a special interest in such subjects as water pollution, aid to the elderly, juvenile delinquency, and vocational rehabilitation and would need to be consulted on each of these matters. In Fogarty's case, Cohen and the other legislative handlers for the administration had constantly to keep in mind that Fogarty, an Irish Catholic from New England, thought that he, rather than Kennedy, should be president. Fogarty once told Cohen that he knew more than Kennedy and was a better politician.[16] Not to reach agreement with these legislative leaders meant almost certain defeat for the president's program, since in effect they held a veto over it.

Understandably, then, Cohen felt harassed by the political difficulties and technical complexities of his job, yet he also experienced his customary elation in working so closely with Congress and helping to advance the cause of reform. He imbued the process with a sense of romance. Negotiations with all the political players were tedious but also exciting. As he commented, the legislative process was "complex and precarious" and demanded considerable negotiating skills. To be involved in the resulting "secret meetings" gave him access to the law when it was in its most malleable state.[17]

At times, too, Cohen, with his sense of history, imagined that he was helping to finish the uncompleted business of the Progressive Era and the New Deal. Food and drug legislation was a good case in point. In college, Cohen had read many of Upton Sinclair's novels, including *The Jungle*. Later he learned about Rexford Tugwell's efforts to amend the Food and Drug Law in 1938 and the battles that he had fought with the drug companies. Since he was one of the first people whom Cohen had seen when he arrived in Washington in 1934, he took a special interest in Tugwell's activities. In 1961 Cohen suddenly found himself in Tugwell's place, responsible for handling food and drug legislation. "The importance of protecting the consumer remained with me from *The Jungle*," Cohen said, "and was a significant driving force in helping to retain my ability to continue the work for some constructive legislation against overwhelming opposition."[18]

CONFIRMATION

Even as Cohen struggled with pure food and drug legislation and other vexing matters in his first days on the job, he also had to worry about being confirmed by the Senate. For three months he was the assistant secretary-designate, and his first sustained project consisted of securing confirmation. Early in February, to begin the process of scripting the confirmation hearings for his supporters, he sent Sen. Philip Hart (D-Mich.) a detailed biographical sketch that, he admitted, looked "a little bit like a laundry list, but it might be just the kind of thing you might use."[19] Because Hart was from Cohen's home state, he would play an important role in the hearings.

As Cohen had predicted, the American Medical Association opposed his nomination. From the AMA's viewpoint, he was the very person who had expanded the Social Security system and impinged on the doctors' freedom. "I am amazed and shocked that you consider Wilbur J. Cohen a candidate for Assistant Secretary of the Department of Health, Education and Welfare for Legislative Matters. . . . This man is not morally fit to hold a job in the American government," an indignant doctor wrote to the president.[20] Dr. Edward Annis, a Miami doctor who later headed the AMA's Speakers Bureau, went to see Sen. George Smathers (D-Fla.) and urged him to lead the fight against Cohen in the Finance Committee. Smathers, a careful politician, explored the possibility of having the president withdraw Cohen's appointment and giving Cohen another, similar position that did not require Senate approval. Sen. Carl Curtis, a long-time adversary of Cohen's dating back to his service on the Ways and Means Committee and his 1953 investigation of the Social Security program, also expressed an interest in opposing his nomination.[21]

Cohen told Sorensen of the problem with Smathers. Sorensen talked with Kennedy, who phoned Smathers, an old friend from his bachelor days, and ordered him in effect to back off. The president wanted Cohen confirmed and went to the trouble of using a small amount of political capital to get what he wanted. Cohen, as always, was appreciative, telling Kennedy that he would do his best "to merit your continued support and confidence."[22] Smathers, covering his tracks, met with Cohen and told him that the doctors in Florida had asked him to vote against his confirmation but that he personally bore him no animosity.[23]

The hearings on Cohen's nomination took place on March 22 and 23, 1961. Senator McNamara, a member of the Finance Committee, introduced Cohen, who then entered his long and elaborate biographical statement into the record. He produced the task force report that he had prepared for Kennedy and asked that it, too, become a part of the record. After he made a short statement about his loyalty to the U.S. government, the committee members began to question him. Senator Kerr noted that "there is far from complete agreement between myself and Mr. Cohen" in philosophical viewpoint, "but I have found him to be very able, very conscientious, very trustworthy, and very reliable."[24] That statement alone was enough to ensure a favorable recommendation from the committee.

Cohen still faced tough questions from the Republicans on the committee, who objected to his relentless incrementalism, his ability to build small proposals into large programs. Curtis charged that Medicare, as health insurance for the elderly was now called, although designed to pay the hospital bills for the elderly, would be followed by a program in which the government paid everyone's hospital bill. In an exchange on Social Security that could have been lifted from Curtis's cross-questioning of Arthur Altmeyer in 1953, Cohen defended the program as a "conservative and intelligent way of doing business." Sen. Wallace Bennett (R-Utah) astutely noted that Congress might permit early retirement at age sixty-two and wondered if Medicare benefits might not be extended to people of that age. Cohen said that he would not recommend Medicare for such people "at this time." "You would save that for a little while later, so there would be another program to bring up here," retorted Bennett.[25]

It was in the middle of such testy exchanges that Sen. Paul Douglas (D-Ill.) decided to break the tension, and his remarks provided Cohen with the quotation that would define him for the rest of his life: "Mr. Cohen is well known as probably the greatest expert on social security that we have. Someone once said that an expert on social security is a person who knows Wilbur Cohen's telephone number. I think that well may be true."[26]

Support from Douglas, the professional economist, provided the perfect counterpoint to the shrill testimony of Marjorie Shearon, who appeared as the major witness to speak against Cohen. Shearon regaled the committee with her tales of Communist conspiracy and her suspicions about him. "Surely," concluded Mrs. Shearon, "the American people have a right to expect that the Senate of the United States will protect them from a man like Professor Cohen. . . . He has spent the major portion of his professional life . . . in a twilight zone peopled by espionage agents."[27] Shearon failed to influence Congress in part because by attacking Cohen she also criticized legislation that bore the names of many of the senators on the Finance Committee. Ignoring Marjorie Shearon, the members of the committee voted to approve Cohen by a vote of 13 to 1; only Curtis voted against him.

Cohen understood enough about Congress to know that the Senate Finance Committee's approval meant that he would be confirmed by the full Senate. The vote came during Easter week, when only a handful of senators were present, however. Senator Curtis spoke against Cohen, and then another senator requested a vote. Hubert Humphrey was the only Democrat on the floor so the clerk of the Senate Finance Committee ran into the Democratic cloakroom and rounded up Smathers, Holland (D-Fla.), and Mansfield (D-Mont.). Cohen was confirmed by a vote of 4 to 3, with Curtis, Williams (R-Del.), and Aiken (R-Vt.) voting against him.[28]

On Friday, April 14 at 4:30 P.M., Wilbur Cohen took the oath of office in the HEW Auditorium and became an assistant secretary of Health, Education, and Welfare. In the years before he moved to Ann Arbor, he had worked on the fifth floor of the HEW building, and he would now move to the secretary's suite of offices on that same floor. The auditorium was located on the ground floor, near the library with its carefully bound volumes recording the legislation that Cohen had done so much to create. On the wall near the auditorium's entrance was a series of murals, painted in the heroic style of Diego Rivera, that reflected the department's roots in the era of the New Deal and the WPA.[29]

WELFARE REFORM

Once confirmed, Cohen proceeded as he had before with the myriad items on the administration's legislative agenda. Some of these items, such as aid to education, were intensely collaborative projects, involving long and highly sensitive negotiations with Congress; others concerned such areas as welfare, in which Cohen enjoyed a high degree of freedom to push his own ideas and proposals. In striking contrast to later years, in the early 1960s welfare reform was a relatively uncontroversial matter, and Cohen enjoyed considerable success in shaping legislation to suit his preferences. He worked on these measures from his arrival in 1961, through the period of legislative development in the fall of that year, to the spring of 1962 when Congress passed legislation, to the creation of a new bureaucratic entity to administer the law in 1963. Almost from the start, welfare reform was left to Cohen. "I will be prepared to say," Cohen noted in a rare public display of his ego, "if it hadn't been for me, there wouldn't have been any 62 amendments. Because neither Kennedy, nor Sorensen, nor Ribicoff, nor Johnson was for it. They would let me do things as long as I took the responsibility."[30]

Just as anyone else in a hectic job, Cohen relied on past intellectual capital to develop welfare reform proposals rather than coming up with new ideas. He approached welfare reform with two main objectives. First, he wanted to broaden the ADC program so that it paid benefits to as many poor children as possible instead of only to those families where the father was absent. Second, he hoped to change the program so that it included services designed to reduce welfare dependency, in addition to the traditional monetary grants or "pensions."

In thinking about the first objective, Cohen tried to incorporate the political lessons from twenty-seven years of working with Congress. He knew that proposals such as General Assistance, federal grants to any poor person, had no political support and should not even be considered.[31] Instead, Cohen contemplated passage of ADC grants for "intact" poor families, those that consisted of a father, a mother, and children but in which the father was unemployed. The idea went back to Senator Kennedy's efforts to amend the unemployment compensation law in 1958 and had the endorsement of the Advisory Council on Public Assistance on which Cohen had served and of the transition task force that he had chaired. The president appeared predisposed to favor the idea, in part because he was familiar with it.

The second objective, adding services to ADC, was a piece of intellectual baggage that Cohen had picked up from his experiences in Ann Arbor. "My idea was to develop a plan for each child," Cohen explained. Many children needed help other than money: "It might be counseling, it might be referral to a job, it might be the mother going back to high school or a job."[32] Cohen wanted to establish a mechanism for uniting problem children with therapeutic social services, similar to the system he had helped to establish in Washtenaw County, Michigan. Elizabeth Wickenden, who remained close to Cohen during his Kennedy and Johnson years, encouraged him in this line of thought.[33]

Cohen started on welfare reform the day he arrived in Washington as assistant secretary of HEW. As always in the development of public policy, he needed to marry his ideas with the events of the moment and with the ways in which the administration wanted to present social policy. The president decided to send Congress a quickly prepared antirecession package that included such items as an increase in the minimum wage level and an extension of unemployment compensation benefits. Cohen tucked the notion of paying ADC benefits to families with unemployed fathers into the package.

He also included a temporary provision in the legislative package to deal with a situation in Louisiana that had attracted national attention. Officials there had decided to suspend ADC payments to children who lived in what local authorities declared to be "unsuitable homes." Houses in which a mother on welfare had a second illegitimate baby or who lived with a man without marrying him were automatically considered to be unsuitable. Eisenhower's HEW secretary Arthur Flemming had hastily ruled that the state could not cut off aid to a household if the children remained in the home. In 1961 Cohen moved to give Flemming's ruling the authority of law: no state could deny aid to a child on the basis that the child's home was unsuitable as long as the child continued to live in the home.[34]

Congress moved quickly on the 1961 ADC proposals. Within a month, the House Ways and Means Committee reported out the bill favorably, with only a few negative comments from the Republicans. Congressman Thomas B. Curtis (R-Mo.) noted, for example, that "apparently not a State in the Union requested this program. . . . This program seems to have been promoted directly by the officials in the Department of Health, Education, and Welfare."[35] Indeed, Curtis was right; the proposal was promoted by only one top official in the department. Later, talking about what came to be known as the unemployed parents segment of the ADC program, Cohen said bluntly, "I persuaded Kennedy and Ribicoff to do that." Ribicoff in particular was not very enthusiastic.[36]

Even though Cohen in a sense engineered the demand for the Public Assistance amendments of 1961, Congress passed the legislation with a minimum of fuss since the key provisions in the law were temporary and could be undone at a later date. It was early in the legislative session, and Congress wanted to give the administration a victory on a matter that was not very controversial.

Cohen saw the 1961 legislation as a building block. By putting the notion of paying welfare to families with unemployed parents into the law, for example, Cohen hoped to pave the way for congressional authorization of training programs for welfare recipients. As Cohen expressed it, "If you had people who were employable [receiving welfare], then you had to have some kind of work and training program."[37] Cohen told Jane Hoey, who had run the welfare programs under Arthur Altmeyer, that he had put in "a lot of sustained work on the bill, especially to save the Flemming 'suitable home' ruling. I think the legislation will serve as a basis for a complete reconsideration for next year."[38]

Sometime after the passage of the 1961 amendments, Secretary Ribicoff decided to give welfare reform visibility as a departmental initiative. His decision perhaps reflected the fact that welfare was making a greater impression on the nation's consciousness as part of a growing discussion of black equality. One highly publicized incident occurred in the Hudson River town of Newburgh, New York. Among other related actions, the city manager asked welfare recipients to pick up their relief checks at the local police station and put severe restrictions on the receipt of welfare payments. The Newburgh incident highlighted the growing suspicion that welfare, once the domain of sturdy elderly people, was becoming a social benefit for blacks and was serving as a prime force in drawing them from southern states, which paid low welfare benefits, to northern states, which prided themselves on maintaining high benefits. Ribicoff promised a thorough review of the programs and enlisted the aid of key professional groups, such as the National Association of Social Workers (NASW), in the process.[39]

Although Ribicoff signed many of the memorandums to prominent people and many of the articles on welfare, Cohen was the prime mover on reform. He coordinated a series of departmental reports and served as the principal author of welfare reform legislation. He worked to create a bill that embodied his notion of providing services for welfare beneficiaries on terms that were generous enough to induce the states to begin such programs.[40] Cohen also coached Ribicoff on five types of administrative actions he could take without having to ask the approval of Congress. Some were merely cosmetic, such as changing the name of the Bureau of Public Assistance to the Bureau of Family Aid and Services. Others dealt with the matter of personnel, such as urging that Ribicoff appoint a person "identified with services and rehabilitation" as head of the Bureau of Public Assistance. Still other suggestions involved federal instructions to the states. For example, Cohen recommended that Ribicoff take steps to force the states to limit the caseloads of each of its caseworkers to ninety per month. He also urged the secretary to force the states to prepare a "plan for each child to see that he receives proper care and services to enable him to achieve health, growth, and independence." Finally, Cohen recommended that Ribicoff explore the creation of an entirely new office in HEW to be headed by a Commissioner of Rehabilitation and Family Services.[41]

By November 1961 Ribicoff was ready to bring welfare reform to the president's direct attention. In a letter meant to have public release, Ribicoff stated, "From the day of my confirmation hearing I have been convinced that the demand for changes in the welfare laws would become a hot issue," noting that the publicity that had attended the events in Newburgh, New York, "confirmed my prediction." He presented welfare reform as a bipartisan measure that could draw support from conservatives and liberals. Conservatives worried about welfare abuses and demanded that something be done about the "AFDC mother with a dozen illegitimate kids, the relief checks that buy liquor instead of food and rent, the able-bodied man who spurns a decent job to stay on relief." Liberals wanted to reorient the "whole approach to welfare from a straight cash-hand-out operation to one in which the emphasis is on rehabilitation of those on relief and prevention ahead of time." Although Ribicoff did not burden the president with too many specifics, he mentioned the authorization of funds to give states an incentive to provide rehabilitation services to people on welfare. He also said that he intended to highlight the issues in the weeks ahead to build momentum for the passage of legislation in 1962.[42]

Ribicoff worked in the foreground and Cohen in the background, consulting with the Bureau of the Budget (BOB) and with the constituent agencies on the specific contents of a welfare reform bill. Ribicoff mentioned to the president that discussions with the BOB were taking place "under the direction of Assistant Secretary Wilbur J. Cohen."[43] In one of those meetings, Cohen told bureau officials of how his department wanted to expand rehabilitation services in the public assistance program. Although specific issues remained to be resolved, the meeting resulted in an agreement "that we should make a big push on rehabilitation services – broadening the character of the services, adding more attractive matching, and perhaps imposing mandatory requirements on the States."[44]

Meanwhile, Ribicoff conducted his highly visible publicity campaign. By December he was ready to take administrative actions that Cohen told Sorensen were "sound and desirable and long over due and I believe will bring great credit to the Administration." The political packaging of the administrative actions probably reflected Ribicoff's influence, but the contents of the proposals were largely Cohen's work. Ribicoff began his ten-point program with measures designed to locate parents who deserted their families and measures intended to reduce and control fraud. Only then did he move on to such suggestions as the improvement of staff training programs and the development of services to families. He also asked to meet with all state welfare directors early in 1962.[45]

Cohen told William Haber on December 19, 1961, that he had just finished spending about six weeks on the ten-point program that Ribicoff had announced.[46] On that same date, the secretary made his plans for new legislation public by writing a series of letters, which Cohen had drafted, to influential figures in public welfare administration and politics. In one of the first, to Eleanor Roosevelt and containing a laudatory reference to her husband, Ribicoff wrote that FDR's 1935 welfare legislation, included in the Social Security Act, met the problems of the time but that "the quarter of a century that has passed has taught us many new things." He noted that he would ask the Congress for more federal money to give the states an incentive to rehabilitate those people on welfare and to prevent others from going on it. As matters stood, the federal government paid half the states' administrative and service costs; Ribicoff proposed having the federal government pay three-quarters of the costs of rehabilitation services. Ribicoff also announced that he wanted more federal funds for child welfare services, including money for day care of children of working mothers. In general, he highlighted the liberal side of the welfare reform agenda, such as providing federal money for community work-training programs "with adequate safeguards to protect the health and safety of the individual."[47]

Ribicoff concluded his appeal to Mrs. Roosevelt by mentioning his hope that his reforms would "reorient the whole approach to welfare from an eligibility operation to one in which the emphasis is on rehabilitation." To effect this change, he stressed that the people who worked in the program would have to become more than caseworkers who processed appeals for aid; they would have to learn how to diagnose problems, coordinate and purchase services, and monitor a person's progress toward independence. All in all, it would amount to a "tremendous improvement in our welfare programs which will greatly help to strengthen family life and prevent continued dependency of many families."[48]

In later years, Cohen regretted the hype that attended the Kennedy welfare-reform proposals, calling the statements in support of the program "over-enthusiastic" although at the time he believed such rhetoric was part of creating a political demand for needed change. Even then, however, he noted that the social work profession was not eager to aid the cause of welfare reform and did not encourage students to work in public assistance programs. "Practically everybody wants to be a psychiatric social worker or a child welfare worker or some other kind of *professional* worker that has prestige, status and deals with clients who are not so difficult to handle," Cohen noted. If the welfare reform were to pass and to succeed in its objectives, it would require more whole-hearted support from the social work community.[49]

Such quibbles aside, the cause of welfare reform moved forward like a juggernaut. In January 1962 the legislative leaders received letters similar to the one that Ribicoff had sent Eleanor Roosevelt. As always, Cohen tailored the merchandise to suit the consumer. Senator Byrd's letter made no mention of Franklin D. Roosevelt, nor were the nine major points in the legislation listed in the same order as in Mrs. Roosevelt's letter. For Byrd, money for day care was item four; for Roosevelt, it was item two. Mrs. Roosevelt learned far more about training social work personnel in her letter than did Senator Byrd or the other conservative congressmen who received letters, and Senator Byrd and Congressman Mills learned far more about encouraging welfare recipients to work than did Mrs. Roosevelt.[50]

It was exactly the appeal of welfare reform to both conservatives and liberals, combined with the optimism that the right sort of professional intervention would solve the problem by lowering the welfare rolls, that facilitated passage of the Public Welfare amendments of 1962. A liberal reform, it would bring more money to the congressmen's home districts and produce results that would be lauded by liberals and conservatives alike. It did not require any state to do anything; it simply offered incentives for such programs as rehabilitation services and for the extension of ADC to cover unemployed parents. Unlike education, welfare was an area that had already been breached by the federal government, and states depended on federal money to make ends meet. When the president himself decided to send Congress an unprecedented special message devoted to public welfare, passage of the new law appeared to be ensured. "We have here," declared the president, "a realistic program which will pay dividends on every dollar invested."[51]

Wilbur Mills agreed to hold prompt hearings on the president's proposals and asked Ribicoff to be the first witness.[52] The secretary told the House Ways and Means Committee on February 7, 1962, that "essentially our task is to wage war on dependency."[53] When the questioning from Mills's committee or from Senate Finance got specific, Ribicoff turned matters over to Assistant Secretary Cohen. In May, for example, Sen. Clinton Anderson (D-N.Mex.) asked Ribicoff a detailed question about vendor medical payments under the Kerr-Mills program, and Cohen, the main author of that legislation, answered it.[54] When Senator Curtis raised questions about the welfare program in the District of Columbia, Cohen again came to the secretary's rescue.

"As you can well imagine," wrote Cohen to one of his Michigan colleagues, "the 'apparent ease' with which this bill moved along concealed a great deal of work."[55] On July 25, President Kennedy signed the bill into law and repeated the thought that it provided "rehabilitation instead of relief," stressing its objectives of preventing or reducing dependency and encouraging self-care and self-support. Cohen himself contributed to the expectations engendered by the new law when he called it "the most extensive improvement and redirection of Federal-State public assistance and child welfare programs since 1935."[56]

The law never produced the results for which Cohen had hoped, largely because the newly authorized social services had little or no effect on the demographic and social forces that contributed to the increases in the welfare rolls. The law itself followed almost exactly the suggestions that Cohen had developed over the entire process. It increased from 50 to 75 percent the federal portion of the cost of rehabilitation services, extended federal authority to pay benefits to both parents when the father was disabled or unemployed, allowed federal funds to be used for community work and training programs, increased federal funds for child welfare services, and met Cohen's basic objectives of increasing welfare services and extending eligibility for ADC.

The politics of welfare reform in the Kennedy administration now shifted from Congress to the Department of Health, Education, and Welfare. Just as Cohen took the lead in maneuvering the bill through Congress, he also supervised the implementation process within his own department. By the time of the law's passage, he had already been in touch with Ellen Winston, the commissioner of Public Welfare for the state of North Carolina, about administering it.[57] He also consulted with important figures in HEW, such as Mary Switzer and Robert Ball, and with the members of his personal network on the welfare issue, such as Elizabeth Wickenden, Arthur Altmeyer, and Fedele Fauri.

Cohen discovered that the new law generated more conflict within HEW than it had in Congress. At issue was the role that Mary Switzer, a departmental veteran, would play in its administration. Secretary Ribicoff urged Cohen to talk with Switzer, the director of the vocational rehabilitation program since 1950, about serving as the head of a new departmental division that would combine welfare, currently being administered by a bureau within the Social

Security Administration, and vocational rehabilitation. Ribicoff knew that Switzer enjoyed a large and enthusiastic following on Capitol Hill, including the strong support of Senator Hill and Congressman Fogarty; the trouble was that neither Cohen nor Arthur Altmeyer favored her for the post. Altmeyer told Cohen that putting vocational rehabilitation and welfare together ran the risk of "destroying rather than promoting family rehabilitation." Switzer would emphasize putting welfare mothers to work and neglect other family-oriented problems. The family, Altmeyer concluded, was a fragile institution and "it would be most unfortunate if the government itself put into effect a policy which accentuated the danger of family breakdown." An instinctive defender of his old bureaucratic turf, Altmeyer also endorsed leaving welfare with the rest of Social Security.[58]

Robert Ball, newly promoted to commissioner of Social Security, disagreed with Altmeyer.[59] "Mr. Ball wanted to get rid of welfare," Cohen recalled. He desired no part of the new welfare law and feared that it would sully his reputation as a competent administrator and spoil the chance to pass new social insurance laws such as Medicare. "So Ball would constantly talk with me and the Secretary about shedding welfare," Cohen said.[60]

As a result of these discussions, Cohen came out against combining vocational rehabilitation and welfare and in favor of creating what would be called the Welfare Administration, an independent agency within HEW. Cohen decided to recommend Ellen Winston for the new job as commissioner of Welfare. To assuage Mary Switzer, he suggested that her program be elevated within the bureaucracy and that she should become the commissioner of Vocational Rehabilitation. As Cohen told Secretary Anthony Celebrezze in November 1962, "There is an urgent need for new blood, new and imaginative thinking, and competent administrative experience in the Federal welfare program."[61] Hence, welfare should be removed from the Social Security Administration and given an agency of its own.

Accepting Cohen's advice, Celebrezze announced the formation of the Welfare Administration on December 20, 1962: "The first major realignment of welfare functions since the Department was established in 1953," he called it. The secretary described Ellen Winston as "one of the outstanding State welfare administrators in the country" and praised the other bureaucratic principles involved. Robert Ball was a man of "exceptional competence and leadership," and Mary Switzer was a woman of "outstanding ability."[62] Wilbur Cohen, who had engineered so many of these bureaucratic changes, remained in the background.

Yet, as Celebrezze knew, Cohen had done most of the work on welfare reform, which is why the 1962 law and the Welfare Administration proved so disappointing to Cohen. Not to put too fine a point on it, Cohen watched the Welfare Administration become mired in failure; it never developed into a strong operating arm of the department as had the Public Health Service or the Social Security Administration. Advocates of social services for children and the elderly strongly resisted having their programs merged with the Welfare Administration, and that agency, so closely tied to an increasingly unpopular program, proved an unglamorous setting for departmental initiatives in fields such as juvenile delinquency.

Ellen Winston was brought down by the program she administered after spending a frustrating four years as its head. At fifty-nine, Winston came to the post with a great deal of experience that, although impressive, failed to prepare her for the job of administering federal welfare programs in the 1960s. A sociologist trained at the University of Chicago, she had worked for various federal agencies in the 1930s, had taught at Meredith College in North Carolina for four years, and then had become the chief of North Carolina's public welfare program in 1944. She was very much a member of Cohen's and Wickenden's policy network, associated with such organizations as the American Public Welfare Association and the Council of Social Work Education. She served on Ribicoff's Ad Hoc Committee on Welfare and testified on behalf of the American Public Welfare Association in support of the administration bill.[63]

Although Cohen remained one of her major boosters, he soon realized that the 1962 amendments would not meet their objectives. "Ellen is certainly doing a very splendid job. Her energy, her enthusiasm, and her knowledge are proving to provide the spark that certainly has been missing in our welfare programs," he told Altmeyer in 1963.[64] Soon, however, hope turned to disappointment, and he quickly began to have second thoughts about the 1962 legislation. In later years, Cohen expressed his frustration quite openly, describing the 1962 legislation as his "greatest disappointment," "a dismal, 100% failure."[65] The law, over which Cohen had so much personal control, ultimately proved ineffectual.

MENTAL RETARDATION

Mental retardation legislation, another self-contained initiative of the Kennedy years, provided more opportunity for Cohen to orchestrate the legislative and implementation processes. In this endeavor, unlike in welfare reform, he operated as the servant of others, working hard because Eunice Kennedy Shriver, an extraordinarily dedicated woman, wanted him to do so. More than any other individual, Mrs. Shriver urged that the Department of Health,

Education, and Welfare pay attention to mental retardation. In this way, she helped to make a personal concern of the Kennedy family into a national cause that was supported by federal funds. Mrs. Shriver and the Kennedy family brought mental retardation to the attention of Congress; Wilbur Cohen translated the demand for action into coherent legislation that meshed with the other ongoing activities of the department.

As early as May 1961, Cohen began meeting with the Shrivers, Dr. Robert Cooke, and Myer Feldman of the White House staff to fashion an administration program in mental retardation. Cohen envisioned a basic package of proposals that would include the establishment of the National Institute of Child Health and Human Services, the authorization of the Children's Bureau to make research grants in the fields of maternal and child health and crippled children's services, and increases in grants for basic maternal health and child welfare services. He also urged an expansion of the Vocational Rehabilitation program so that it would work more closely with people who were mentally retarded. Moreover, he envisioned special survey, planning, and construction grants, similar to the existing grants for hospital construction, that could be used to build residential care facilities for mentally retarded children. Finally, he wanted Congress to enact a program of grants that could be used to train teachers who worked with mentally retarded children.[66]

It took some time for the administration to decide on its approach to this legislation. Instead of simply sending up bills, the president and Mrs. Shriver appointed a special panel to formulate a "comprehensive and concentrated attack on mental retardation." The panel deliberated through the winter, spring, and summer of 1962 and did not release its report until the fall of 1962.[67]

Meanwhile, the National Institute of Child Health and Human Development bill made its way through Congress. This proposal stemmed from a suggestion that Dr. Cooke had made as a member of Cohen's transition task force to create a new governmental organization devoted to pediatric research, and Cohen had arranged for the preparation of a bill to carry out the doctor's wishes.[68] He convinced Senator Kerr, among others, to introduce Cooke's bill and Luther Terry, the surgeon general, to prepare a speech for Kerr to use.[69] The process moved smoothly until the bill ran into the opposition of the Children's Bureau. Cohen explained to Myer Feldman in the White House that although Kerr was "eagerly awaiting co-sponsoring the bill," Congressmen John Fogarty and Melvin Laird (R-Wis.), leaders of health legislation in their respective parties, opposed the measure.[70] Opposition in part grew from a concern that the new institute would overlap and conflict with the work of the Children's Bureau. Fogarty had expressly written in the report of his appropriations committee for fiscal 1962 that "the Committee feels that the Children's Bureau should be given more responsibility for research."[71] Cohen, realizing that he would have to appease the Children's Bureau if there were to be any chance of creating the research institute in pediatrics, ensured that the mental retardation legislation authorized the Children's Bureau to make grants for research projects related to maternal and child health services and crippled children's services.[72] By July 17, 1961, he was able to send Sen. Lister Hill a copy of the National Institute of Child Health and Human Development bill, which ultimately became law.[73]

It was not the first problem with the Children's Bureau that Cohen had encountered. The bureau was one of a number of departmental agencies that maintained an independent power base in Congress and that often resisted reorganization. As assistant secretary, Cohen wanted to diminish the bureau's influence and strip away its various programs because he saw it as old-fashioned, out of step with the realities of modern social problems, and an impediment to their solution. Cohen knew its historical details as well as anyone. Started in 1912 and one of the oldest agencies in the department, the bureau had developed a series of programs relating to child welfare, infant and maternal health, and crippled children's services. These programs responded to the bureau's original broad mandate "to investigate and report upon all matters pertaining to the welfare of children and child life." Inevitably, however, the agency had faced a series of readjustments as the federal government expanded its responsibilities in the areas of health, education, and welfare.[74]

Cohen, encouraged by Elizabeth Wickenden, had wanted to reorganize the Children's Bureau, placing its responsibilities for infant and maternal health in the Public Health Service and its programs for child welfare in the Welfare Administration.[75] Far from diminishing the bureau's influence, he ended up leaving it intact as an agency within the Welfare Administration and mollifying it by giving it a key role in the department's mental retardation program. Years later, Cohen told a congressional appropriations committee, "There is a very, very strong constituency that believes the Children's Bureau should be kept intact." People who proposed reorganization for the bureau soon found themselves portrayed as enemies of children.[76]

As Cohen battled the Children's Bureau and tended to the creation of the National Institute on Child Health and Human Development, the president's panel engaged in acrimonious debates over such subjects as whether environment or heredity held the key to understanding mental retardation. Cohen tried to anticipate the direction its report would take, and he began to see the possibility for a more ambitious legislative program than he had originally envisioned. In particular, he contemplated legislation that could be introduced in 1963 that would provide funds for the construction of facilities devoted to mental retardation research.[77]

Early in 1963 Cohen completed much of the staff work for the introduction of a complete legislative program devoted to mental retardation, one that would be introduced by a special presidential message concerned exclusively with that subject and mental health policy. If the legislation passed and if Congress authorized the administration's requests for increased funds to existing programs, the department would spend more than $200 million on activities related to mental retardation in fiscal 1964. The new legislative proposals included a plethora of grants: project grants to the states for comprehensive planning on mental retardation, grants for the construction of mental retardation research centers, grants for the construction of mental retardation treatment centers, and grants for improving the education of "exceptional children."[78]

Beginning in February 1963, Cohen personally oversaw the preparation of weekly progress reports on mental retardation that went to Mrs. Shriver and to other interested parties in the government. The reports detailed the progress of the legislation through Congress and described departmental efforts to publicize its efforts in the field.[79] The first report followed closely upon the president's message to Congress in which Kennedy spoke of the nation's obligation "to prevent mental retardation, whenever possible, and to ameliorate it when possible."[80]

As Kennedy conducted his high-profile publicity for the program, Cohen began an endless series of meetings to get the legislation enacted. He talked with Wilbur Mills and convinced him to introduce a bill that combined the planning grants and the various proposed changes in the programs run by the Children's Bureau, all of which took the form of amendments to the Social Security Act. Mills told Cohen that he could not begin hearings on the bill before he completed action on the administration's tax bill; still, he agreed to sponsor the legislation. Cohen then sent copies of a second bill, one that contained the various grants to the states for the construction of facilities related to mental retardation, to Senator Hill and Congressman Oren Harris (D-Ark.), who agreed to introduce it.[81]

Cohen negotiated with the major players in Washington and at the same time traveled around the country making speeches in support of the mental retardation program, appealing for the support of the professionals who would be largely responsible for implementing the new legislation. In 1963 people understood mental retardation as a medical problem that should be handled by professionals. Despite the emphasis on integrating mentally retarded people into the community, few people thought of these citizens as an active constituency in their own right. Hence, Cohen spoke to professional groups whose members differed substantially from later groups of advocates for disability rights. The speeches themselves tended to be dull and dutiful recitals of legislative details.[82]

Crucial to the acceptance of the president's program was the assent of Congressmen Mills and Harris, who were in charge of the two key committees in the House. They acquiesced simply because the president favored the program, and it promised to bring substantial federal aid to the state of Arkansas, which ranked high in the receipt of federal funds for social welfare activities. The state, which ranked dead last in per capita income, spent the most per capita on vocational rehabilitation.[83] The mental retardation legislation represented just the sort of small-scale, well-targeted legislation of which the congressmen approved. Although neither supported Medicare or general federal aid to education, they reacted favorably to more limited aid to medicine in the form of planning and facility-construction grants and more limited aid to education in the form of grants for the training of teachers in special education.[84] Mills decided not to hold hearings; instead, he simply solicited written comments that proved sufficiently encouraging, as Cohen put it, "to permit the Committee to move expeditiously."[85]

Mills did hold closed executive sessions on the "Maternal and Child Health and Mental Retardation Planning Amendments of 1963" in July and as was customary invited Cohen to attend and to answer questions about the legislation. The sessions resulted only in minor changes to the bill. By making these, Mills placed his distinctive stamp on a bill of which he largely approved and from which he stood to gain tangible political benefits in his home district.[86] Mrs. Shriver and other administration officials relied on Cohen's judgment as to whether to accept Mills's changes.[87]

The facility construction and education bill, the second of the mental retardation bills, posed more of a political challenge for Cohen. Here a significant dispute developed between the House and the Senate over the amount of money authorized for the three types of mental retardation facilities specified in the legislation. The House wanted to authorize three years of spending, but the Senate preferred to authorize five. The dispute had nothing to do with mental retardation policy; instead, it concerned the desire of Oren Harris to protect the power of his Interstate and Foreign Commerce Committee—an authorizing committee—and not to cede more power to Fogarty and his Appropriations Committee. Hence, Harris wanted the mental retardation advocates to return within a few years for the reauthorization of the bill rather than to let the policy action shift to winning already authorized funds from the Appropriations Committee. It was the sort of byzantine, internal politics that people such as

Cohen understood but that could be comprehended only within its immediate context. Cohen resolved the matter simply by compromising the difference: he asked that four years of funding be included in the bill, and the conferees accepted his suggestion.[88]

Ultimately, the Kennedy administration won approval of both mental retardation bills.[89] Cohen's work on this subject showed his competence in undertaking a project that involved composing, passing, and implementing legislation. He managed to satisfy Eunice Shriver that the department was giving sufficient attention to her area of special interest, to gain departmental support for a coherent program, and to respond to the demands of congressional leaders. It was a particularly adroit performance, especially given Cohen's relative lack of knowledge about the topic and the fact that almost always other projects took precedence over mental retardation.

Cohen's work on this project also demonstrated the inner workings of the legislative process. Even as Congress refused to pass big-ticket items such as federal aid to education or national health insurance, it routinely handled less controversial measures. A measure became routine if it could be linked with previously passed legislation, if a strong professional or bureaucratic interest supported it, and if it was not perceived by southerners as undermining local control over race relations. On these routine measures, congressional leaders, particularly in the House of Representatives, made sure that the legislation contained tangible benefits for their constituents.

CAMELOT

Since John F. Kennedy was the political patron who brought Cohen back into the government, Cohen, perhaps not surprisingly, was devoted to Kennedy. For the rest of Cohen's life, he wore a PT-109 tie clasp as others wore an old school tie.[90] He delighted in his personal association with Kennedy, treasured the occasions on which he saw him, and even compiled a scrapbook of his memories. It was as if Cohen could not quite believe he was so close to the center of the nation's political life; hence, every minute with Kennedy needed to be savored and carefully preserved for the historical record.

On November 9, 1961, Cohen sat next to Arthur Goldberg, only a few feet from Robert Kennedy and Dean Rusk, at a cabinet meeting. He watched the president stride into the room, clutching the *New York Herald Tribune* and joking about the Republicans' poor showing in the 1961 elections. Kennedy asked Robert McNamara about sending additional military equipment to Southeast Asia. As Dean Rusk talked about his trip to Japan, the president exhibited his famous impatience: he talked to Ted Sorensen and Pierre Salinger; he doodled; he pulled his chair aside and chatted with his brother. Then Sorensen led a discussion of the 1962 legislative program, and suddenly Cohen became involved, commenting on the administration's failure to pass an education bill. After the meeting, he walked out by the west entrance, chatting with Goldberg and Robert Kennedy about how much the administration should request in education appropriations. It was heady stuff for Cohen, the sort of moment that frames a lifetime.[91]

In the summer of 1962, Cohen returned to the cabinet room, but this time he sat with other staff members, with his back to the wall. Ribicoff occupied the HEW position between Commerce Secretary Luther Hodges and Labor Secretary Arthur Goldberg at the cabinet table. At this meeting, Cohen noted that the president was quite serious, using little of his famous sense of humor. Then again, Cohen felt slightly uncomfortable because he was the only assistant secretary in attendance. Sorensen told him that he had asked Ribicoff to bring Cohen because so much of the administration's legislative program involved HEW. Indeed, of the top-ten priority items, three involved the department.[92]

All in all, the nature of Cohen's activities between 1961 and 1963 illustrates why historians would have such difficulty assessing Kennedy's accomplishments.[93] Simply put, Kennedy enjoyed legislative successes but not on many of the issues that he chose to highlight. The passage of a welfare reform bill or mental retardation legislation went relatively unheralded; the continued failure to pass Medicare and aid to education attracted a great deal of attention. Further, many of the key Kennedy measures, the controversial ones that involved the expansion of federal power into new areas, were eventually passed into law after Kennedy's death, causing understandable confusion about how much credit he should receive for them. In the Kennedy years, small-scale victories were the order of the day.

8
EDUCATION AND MEDICARE IN THE KENNEDY ADMINISTRATION

Wilbur Cohen, as staff to Kennedy and Johnson, spent so much of his time between 1961 and 1965 working on federal aid to education and Medicare that they became the two major projects of his life. Each of the efforts eventually proved successful and resulted in the Social Security amendments of 1965, which started Medicare and Medicaid, and in the Elementary and Secondary Education Act of 1965, which began large-scale federal aid to local school districts. In the Kennedy years, however, Cohen experienced considerable frustration as he courted Wilbur Mills on Medicare and tried to accommodate southern and religious interests on federal aid to education. By the end of that administration, Cohen's efforts had resulted in only limited measures in education and Social Security policy.

Cohen approached education legislation with a deep sense of conviction. He believed in its healing power and thought it the single most important vehicle in the creation of economic opportunity. He came to this belief instinctively as a direct result of his own experience and cerebrally as a student of social policy. He often expressed his approval of federal aid to education as a desire to replicate his experience on a grander scale. As he explained in 1962, "My own educational experience meant so much to me that I hope every qualified person in the United States who wants to go to college or university can do so."[1]

Cohen demonstrated his faith in education in the book on wealth and income that he coauthored in 1962. According to the analysis in it, a person's level of education reflected his level of earnings and had "a powerful effect on occupational advancement, job security, and income stability as well." Education was nothing less than "the nexus of generational change" because it was the "dynamic mechanism by which economic level is passed on from one generation to the next." This analysis produced two policy corollaries. First, ending poverty or dependency required increasing the level of educational quality. Second, "given the diversity of the ability and willingness of states and local areas to provide adequate public education," federal funds were necessary for "school construction, teachers' salaries, and student scholarships."[2]

Cohen understood the urgency of the task, not just because a college degree had been his ticket out of Milwaukee but also because he was a current consumer of education: Cohen worried about the education of his children.[3] For these reasons and because he regarded it as his duty to follow the president's lead, Cohen worked for legislation designed to improve elementary and secondary schools and to expand the number of people who could attend college. He constantly looked for compromises that would bridge political differences. For Cohen, education policy was a matter of finding the right deal, not the right idea. In the field of education, he was a legislative jockey, hoping to ride one of the president's proposals to victory.

Although Cohen dabbled in many areas of policy, he specialized in Social Security and Medicare. Throughout his career, he pursued the seductive vision of financing medical care on a group basis rather than on an individual one, with Social Security as the mechanism for collecting premiums and reimbursing doctors and hospitals. His experience in this field had begun with the 1934 Committee on Economic Security that discussed and rejected the notion of including health insurance in the original Social Security bill. In the 1940s he had helped to write and publicize the Wagner-Murray-Dingell bills and had participated in President Truman's unsuccessful efforts to pass national health insurance. In the 1950s he had worked with Nelson Cruikshank and other representatives of organized labor on bills that included health insurance for the elderly, and he had collaborated with Senator Kerr on the creation of a program that provided federal aid for the health care of the indigent.[4]

It was therefore not surprising that Kennedy and Sorensen hired Cohen to manage the processes of writing Medicare legislation, getting it through Congress, and then helping to implement it. He was the perfect person to oversee the space where the theoretical concerns of the health policy experts met the political concerns of Wilbur Mills. Cohen knew Mills, had worked closely with him ever since Mills had taken over the Ways and Means Committee in 1958; he was practically the administration's ambassador to Wilbur Mills. Cohen clearly was the right man for the job, but Medicare, like federal aid to education, proved to be hard to sell.

1961: THE FIRST ROUND IN EDUCATION

When John F. Kennedy and Wilbur Cohen arrived in Washington in 1961, they sought to reauthorize and amend existing education legislation, but they also wanted to pass a new general aid to education law. Even in this new endeavor, they hoped to build on previous legislative initiatives, such as those of the late 1950s and 1960, when both houses of Congress had approved a general aid to education law but could not reach agreement with each other.[5] As with the other pieces of the 1961 Kennedy legislative program, Cohen, Sorensen, and Myer Feldman planned to move quickly and gain an early victory for the new administration.

Cohen knew that the Congress that legislated education policy was a different body from the one that presided over Social Security.[6] Although Lister Hill and Wayne Morse (D-Oreg.) kept a reasonably firm grip on education bills in the Senate, authority over that policy lay scattered among several warring subcommittees in the House. Congressman Adam Clayton Powell (D-N.Y.), whose pattern of attendance at committee meetings was erratic, did little to assert discipline over these subcommittees. In contrast, Wilbur Mills maintained a strong hold on the Social Security program. Compared with education, Social Security was a more cohesive policy endeavor since statutory authority over old-age, survivors', and disability insurance came from one law. Several different laws, each with its own bureaucratic and congressional defenders, governed education policy. Old-age insurance had begun as a federal undertaking, administered almost solely by the government so that Social Security could, as a consequence, be governed from the top down. Education had started as a strictly local operation, run almost entirely by local authorities. Policy initiatives in education bubbled up from the local to the federal level, making it difficult to administer education policy from Washington.

Cohen soon discovered that education would be a much harder area of legislative endeavor than Social Security. In a February 1961 conversation with Myer Feldman and a member of Senator Hill's staff, Cohen learned that if the administration chose to follow the costly recommendations of Kennedy's transition task force on education, then Senator Hill would refuse to sponsor the legislation and Senator McNamara would not vote for it.[7] In a session with House leaders, Cohen listened to Roman Pucinski (D-Ill.) of Chicago berate him for not including parochial schools in the administration's plans. Meanwhile, Adam Clayton Powell, the Harlem congressman, continued to press the administration not to aid school districts that discriminated against black students.[8] On the job for only a few weeks, Cohen soon learned that religion and civil rights complicated the matter of providing federal funds to education.

Aware of the difficulties, Cohen nonetheless plunged into the staff work required to produce presidential messages and to write bills. By the end of February he had cleared an elementary and secondary education bill with Ted Sorensen and the Bureau of the Budget and made arrangements to talk with Senator Morse, Congressman Frank Thompson (D-N.J.), and Adam Clayton Powell about it. The same bill also contained titles amending the "impacted-area" law. Early in March Cohen sent an aid to higher education bill to Myer Feldman in the White House, and in April he completed departmental and White House discussions on amendments to the National Defense Education Act (NDEA).[9]

The basic purposes behind each of the three bills were simple to understand even if the bills themselves became the object of baroque political dealings. The administration's proposal on aid to elementary and secondary schools, the first of the three bills, would appropriate more than $800 million (by fiscal 1964) to help the states build elementary and secondary schools and to hire more teachers and raise their salaries.[10] This bill also contained two titles amending the existing law that authorized federal assistance for operating and constructing public schools in "federally affected areas." The idea here was for the federal government to make up tax revenues that were lost to local school districts because a family, which sent its children to public school, lived on a military base and did not pay property taxes. As one of the few viable vehicles for federal aid to education, the law had devolved into a general federal subsidy to perhaps 10 percent of the nation's school districts. Whether these school districts deserved or needed the money was unclear. The Kennedy administration hoped to tighten some of the loopholes that had crept into this law since its initial passage in 1941 and its reenactment in 1950 and thus to build support for general federal aid to education rather than aid limited to these impacted areas.[11]

The aid to higher education proposal, the second of the three bills, authorized money for the construction of academic facilities and funded scholarships for undergraduates. The Kennedy bill permitted federal aid to go to private colleges and universities in addition to the public colleges and universities run by the states. In particular, the Kennedy program called for "long-term, low-interest" loans that could be used to finance the construction or rehabilitation of "classrooms, libraries, administrative and other academic facilities." Each state would also have a state scholarship commission to select scholarship recipients on the basis of need and merit; the winners, in turn, would be able to attend any college that admitted them, whether it was public or private.[12]

Amendments to the National Defense Education Act, the third bill, were the last of the 1961 proposals to be completed. In essence, the administration proposed to extend the provisions of the act, which included a loan program for college and university students that enabled them to pay for their postsecondary education and financial assistance for strengthening science, mathematics, and modern foreign language instruction in elementary and secondary schools. In addition to preserving these features, the administration wanted to extend and expand programs in foreign language development, guidance counseling, and testing. Finally, the administration proposed making physical fitness an area of national concern and hoped to include English in the language development program.[13]

The National Defense Education Act provided an important subsidy to both public and private education, at the elementary/secondary and at the college levels. Like the impacted-area program, it enjoyed considerable congressional support, and Sorensen and Ribicoff realized that the NDEA had considerable strategic value in the education debate. Kennedy felt that he simply could not recommend aid to Catholic schools; the NDEA could, however, be used as a bargaining chip with Catholics to secure general aid to education. If Congress, with the tacit approval of the administration, amended the NDEA proposals to include federal loans for facility construction, Catholics might accept those loans as a substitute for more general aid to Catholic schools and drop their opposition to the administration's elementary and secondary education bill (which excluded Catholic schools from aid).[14]

The results of the three bills that Cohen helped to prepare in 1961 were nothing short of a political disaster as they became pawns in an elaborate political game. Played in the House Rules Committee, the game involved deciding which of the three pieces of education legislation would be sent to the House floor for a vote. Catholics worried that if the general aid to education bill passed, then, as Msgr. Frederick G. Hochwalt put it, "a second measure, which would provide for our schools, wouldn't have much of a chance." Thus Catholics wanted the NDEA amendments, with the possibility that they presented for aid to Catholic schools, to come up first. But if the NDEA amendments came up first, then, according to historian Irving Bernstein, three southern Democrats would team up with the five Republicans on the Rules Committee and kill the NDEA bill. If the administration's aid to elementary and secondary education bill came up first, then three northern Catholic Democrats would join the Republicans in killing it. In the end, the Rules Committee decided to table the three measures.[15]

Cohen often repeated an anecdote about what happened next. Kennedy called Cohen into his office and asked, "Why couldn't you get one more Republican to vote with us?" Cohen replied, "Mr. President, why couldn't you get one more Catholic?" According to Cohen, the president "threw up his hands in frustration and we went on to discuss other alternatives." The picture that Cohen painted portrayed two men of the world caught up in the ironies of the political process but determined to salvage something from the situation.[16]

In the summer of 1961 the Kennedy administration made one last effort. Cohen prepared material for what came to be called the Emergency Education Act of 1961. In a draft of a letter from the president to the Speaker of the House, Cohen wrote, "It is a source of deep regret that the House of Representatives has as yet not had an opportunity to debate and vote upon the [education] measures." Still, the need for educational legislation, the letter stated, was urgent. International tensions required that the nation summon its sources of strength, and "one great source of strength which can never be neglected is the education and training of our young people." In this cold war spirit, the president endorsed temporary emergency legislation. Ted Sorensen told him that "this is the one program needed to make this session a complete success."[17] The administration proposed a five-point program, four of which came from the three pieces of legislation that the president had already submitted: a one-year extension of the impacted-area legislation, a program of grants and loans to institutions of higher education to build academic facilities, a scholarship program for high school students, and a one-year extension of the NDEA student loan program. The fifth point, the only new one, involved changing the impacted-area law so that the federal government helped on a temporary basis to pay for the construction of classrooms "in certain school districts which have a serious and substantial classroom shortage." Through this measure the administration hoped to alleviate, at least for a year, the problem of "serious overcrowding."[18]

Nearly all the interest groups found something objectionable in the new legislation. It had no provision for teachers' salaries and hence earned the disapproval of the National Education Association (NEA). At the same time, as Sorensen told the president, influential congressmen, such as Speaker Sam Rayburn (D-Tex.), were "strongly opposed" to using federal funds to pay teachers' salaries. Catholics found the measure "discriminatory," as Hugh Graham puts it, because it gave money to construct public but not parochial schools. Even so, as Sorensen noted, Senators Morse and Humphrey expressed bitter opposition to letting the "Catholic Church exercise a veto power over the Senate passed Administration bill." House Republicans thought that the administration wanted to railroad a law through Congress without sufficient consideration. The Democrats carped that the administration failed to give education the leadership it gave to foreign policy.[19]

Although the emergency legislation floundered for many reasons, Cohen put most of the blame on the civil rights issue. If the southerners could somehow be persuaded to endorse the measure, it or a similar bill would pass.

"The issue of slavery was one of the main reasons why we were unable to get any of the three education bills enacted by Congress this session," he told Harlan Hatcher, president of the University of Michigan; Cohen referred to the southern fear that the federal government would require that all schools receiving federal funds be integrated. It made for an uneasy political session, with the administration reluctant to back civil rights measures for fear of alienating southern support and with the southerners unwilling to vote in favor of measures that even hinted of approval of integration.[20]

Cohen understood above all the virtue of patience. He consoled Sterling McMurrin, Kennedy's appointment as commissioner of Education, by noting that passage of new legislation took time. Cohen recalled his seventeen-year struggle to pass disability insurance: "So it goes," he said, the veteran of many legislative battles to whom the less-seasoned political appointees turned for advice.[21] "Politics is not like an athletic event," he told his son Chris, who had complained about one of the key congressmen involved in education legislation. "There is always a tomorrow when you must try to get support from someone who has opposed you today."[22]

1961: MEDICARE

Similarly, Cohen tried to be conciliatory on Medicare. His earliest statements took the form of reassurances to the effect that he had no intention of putting doctors out of business and replacing the excellent American medical system with socialized medicine; indeed, he wanted to give doctors stipends for education, scholarships, and research fellowships. As for the administration's proposals, they in fact demonstrated the "conservative and responsible" Social Security approach. They did not allow the government to provide a single medical service, nor did they even cover physicians' services. The government would exercise no "supervision or control" over the hospitals.[23]

Reassuring everyone that he could on the subject of health insurance, Cohen worked with Robert Ball of the Social Security Administration and Nelson Cruikshank of the AFL-CIO to draft legislation. The three had known one another and collaborated on previous health insurance proposals ever since the 1940s, and each had his specialty. Cohen was the link between the administration and Congress. Ball, soon to become commissioner of Social Security, was the chief bureaucrat in charge and also a sophisticated advocate for the SSA in congressional relations; he had the job of convincing Congress that the SSA was up to the task of running the Medicare program. Cruikshank was the political muscle: it was his job to put the considerable strength of organized labor behind the movement for Medicare.

By February 1961 Cohen had a Medicare bill to show Secretary Ribicoff that built on the Kennedy bill of 1960. The specifications included coverage for people sixty-five years or older who were covered by Social Security, and the benefits included 90 days of care in a hospital and up to 180 days in a skilled nursing facility. The bill made no provision for doctors' services except for those such as radiology and anesthesiology that were provided in the hospital. To pay for the services, the administration proposed to raise the Social Security taxes.[24]

Just as in previous years, Cohen and his colleagues in his policy apparatus far from monopolized the conversation on health insurance for the elderly. Conservatives, such as Congressman Thomas Curtis, argued that aid should be limited to people in poverty and administered by the states, as in the Kerr-Mills legislation.[25] Liberal Republicans, such as Gov. Nelson Rockefeller and Sen. Jacob Javits of New York, held that people should have a choice, and Rockefeller proposed an option: a person should receive either a higher cash Social Security benefit or health insurance. To elect the cash benefit, a person would need to prove that he already had a health insurance policy that provided coverage at least as good as that offered by Medicare. Rockefeller's option added an element of voluntarism to the proposal, left more room for private health insurance, and encouraged more people to continue their health insurance plans after retirement. But as Robert Ball pointed out, it would also be hard to administer and might leave the Social Security system with the worst risks to insure, driving up costs.[26] Still, Cohen saw the option as an opportunity for compromise. Rather than dissuading Javits, as he had Curtis, he privately encouraged the senator to come up with a plan on which he and the administration might collaborate. Thus in November 1961 Cohen opened up a private channel of communication with Javits.[27]

Meanwhile, the Ways and Means Committee was conducting its business in public, its first order of business to raise Social Security benefit levels. The committee tackled the problem of early retirement and for the first time permitted men to receive retirement benefits at age sixty-two, but it stayed away from the question of health insurance. When it considered how high to raise Social Security taxes, Cohen worked hard to keep members from raising the rate too high to leave room for Medicare. The president, for his part, appeared to be more interested in using Social Security as a fiscal stimulus than in Medicare. He and his economic advisers wanted to make sure that the Ways and Means Committee bill would pump plenty of money into the economy by providing an excess of benefits over revenues. By adding over $1 billion to the economy over three years, the final bill, in Cohen's words, would "make a

On the edge of power: Assistant Secretary Cohen watches President Kennedy sign the Social Security amendments of 1961 into law. (Courtesy of Bruce Cohen)

significant contribution to the President's program to restore momentum to the economy."[28]

Consideration of health insurance was pushed back to summer after the passage of the Social Security amendments of 1961. Cohen saw the initial hearings on health insurance during the Kennedy administration as a dress rehearsal for the subsequent passage of Medicare. Around May he began to prepare during one of his more beleaguered periods on the job so that not until July did he focus on Senator Ribicoff's testimony. The hearings themselves began July 24, just six days after the disastrous vote on education in the House Rules Committee, and Ribicoff, with Cohen by his side, dutifully led them off. Nine days of hearings and over 1,800 pages of testimony followed, and as one historian of Medicare has noted, "They changed no one's mind."[29] By the end of summer, the administration did not even put Medicare on its list of top legislative priorities.[30]

EDUCATION IN 1962: THE SECOND ROUND

The 1961 debate had taught Cohen the necessity of moving toward the goal of federal aid to education by indirection. Just as in the health insurance area, less controversial legislation had to pave the way for the more controversial. With health care, Cohen believed that the 1946 Hill-Burton hospital construction program, which increased the supply of hospitals in rural areas, had helped to do this for national health insurance. He saw this legislation, in which money went to Catholic and non-Catholic hospitals alike, as a useful analogue for education: a noncontroversial, intermediate step. After some consideration, Cohen came to feel that aid to higher education might provide just such a step since private colleges and religious schools already received federal research funds.[31] He later told an interviewer that after the 1961 defeat he met with Sorensen, and together they decided "the key was to get a higher education bill passed along the lines of Hill Burton. . . . Nobody raised a constitutional question of giving federal money for a building in which you have crosses and religious things, altars and prayers."[32] Secretary Ribicoff also concluded that the administration should back off from a general aid to education proposal in favor of a higher education bill. "If brought up early and by itself, it should succeed," Ribicoff wrote to the president."[33]

Cohen, like Ribicoff, understood that powerful members of Congress could be pushed only so far. As he put it in an unusually reflective letter to his oldest son, "It is easy for a newspaper columnist or editor to talk about Presidential leadership, but Senators like Harry Byrd, Eastland, Stennis, and others don't need the President—the President needs them." Adam Clayton Powell for example was "almost unbeatable," and attacks upon him only made him more popular with his constituents. Indeed, Cohen knew just how fragile the president's power was, observing that he "must use his great Power wisely, appropriately, sparingly. . . . He is best advised to use his influence when the issue is close and he can tip the scales by his personal intervention and his personality and power. But to use it too often in adventures doomed to failure is neither wise for a President nor any human with feelings and a future."[34] Aid to elementary and secondary education was not close enough for the president to spend his political capital.

In January 1962 Kennedy made a token gesture toward aid to elementary and secondary education, noting that it had passed the Senate and that he saw "no reason to weaken or withdraw that bill." He reserved his persuasive powers, however, for a higher education bill that would provide federal loans for the construction of academic facilities and initiate federally financed scholarships.[35] By the spring of 1962 Congress had made substantial progress on the higher education bill yet still faced a deadlock. The House passed a bill by a substantial margin at the end of January, and the Senate approved one early in February. Unfortunately, the two differed: the Senate conferees wanted loans, rather than grants, for private colleges; the House conferees insisted on grants. And the former wanted scholarships for worthy college students; the latter opposed federal financing of scholarships.[36]

Cohen kept looking for the compromise that would spring the legislation from the conference committee, a familiar role for him, one he had played on Social Security legislation for more than twenty years. Once again, he faced a question related to the boundaries of public and private power, just as he had in 1952 with the question of the disability freeze. He discovered, however, the conferees on higher education did not feel the same pressure to pass legislation as the conferees on Social Security had. The legislators responsible for education leaned toward doing nothing rather than crossing an undesirable threshold. Edith Green (D-Oreg.), a congresswoman with much influence over the House delegation, characterized the conference on July 20, 1962, as "almost hopeless" and suggested that the two sides should stop meeting. According to Mike Manatos of the White House congressional liaison staff, Sen. Pat McNamara expressed the "same feeling of hopelessness" and said that the "conference should agree to disagree."[37]

Neither Cohen nor the president saw it that way. Cohen worked on a possible compromise that included loans, rather than grants, for the construction of academic facilities, and loans, rather than scholarships, for college students. In each case, he modified his suggestion so that the loans contained low interest rates and liberal forgiveness features; thus, the loans came to resemble construction grants in one case and student scholarships in the other.[38] Meanwhile, the president tried to interest Senator McNamara in the idea of categorical grants limited to science and library facilities.[39]

Adding to the disarray, Ribicoff left in the summer of 1962 and Anthony Celebrezze replaced him. Late in July Cohen tried to bring Celebrezze up to date on the issue, describing higher education legislation as "the most immediate, important, and controversial legislative issue awaiting your attention." The controversy concerned the "explosive" issue of aid to church schools and the "controversial" issue of federal support for scholarships. As Cohen noted, the president "personally has been discussing compromises with individual Senators."[40]

With the president involved and an election approaching, higher education legislation became a high-stakes political gamble. Cohen shuttled between the House and Senate conferees, searching for a compromise that could be described by the administration as a victory and working closely with Edith Green, Ted Sorensen, and the lawyers in HEW. By August, for example, Cohen's student loan proposals included such features as no interest on the loans, annual repayments limited to 5 percent of the borrower's taxable income, and forgiveness of 10 percent of the unpaid balance for each year of service in an area of "critical manpower need in the national interest."[41] Eventually, the conferees used this notion as a way around the scholarship issue, in effect, recommending loans that were so liberal in their terms that they were similar to outright scholarships. They also arrived at a compromise that provided construction grants for public and private colleges that were limited to science, engineering, and libraries. The conferees filed their report on September 17, 1962.

Despite the hard work done by Cohen and others, the conference report failed to attract the support of the National Education Association because it recommended aid to private colleges and of southern Democrats and conservative Republicans who remained wary of any sort of federal aid to education. The House voted to kill the legislation on September 20, 1962. Using a boxing metaphor, Irving Bernstein has written that in 1962 President Kennedy "went down for an eight count" on the education issue. If one were to employ Cohen's imagery, derived from Richard Neustadt's view of presidential power, then one could say that the president had used some of his precious political capital, failed to persuade Congress, and, in the process, lowered the future value of that capital.[42]

MEDICARE IN 1962

The administration appeared to be in considerable disarray on Medicare in 1962, just as it was on education. Cohen continued to work along lines that might be described as the inside track, his goal to persuade Wilbur Mills to accede to Medicare either by taking the lead himself or by allowing someone else within the committee to handle the matter. In early January Cohen and Ribicoff visited Mills, who told them that he saw little possibility of getting Medicare out of his committee, but he showed great interest in the welfare reform bill that Cohen was developing. He did not expect that welfare reform would be controversial and suggested that it be given priority over Medicare. Once the House passed welfare reform, Sen. Clinton Anderson's (D-N.Mex.) Medicare proposal could be inserted as an amendment in the Senate. In conference Mills hinted that "after protracted discussion and some compromises," he would accept "some health insurance provisions." He would tell his constituents that the health insurance provisions were the price of getting the welfare amendments that would bring tangible benefits to Arkansas. "This formula," Cohen reported to Myer Feldman, "would appear to take Mr. Mills off the hook in connection with his commitments to Arkansas." Ribicoff thought it "might break the deadlock."[43]

In the first half of 1962 Cohen continued the course of modifying the Medicare proposal so as to find the compromise that Mills would reluctantly accept. He and the administration also worked on other members of the Ways and Means Committee, such as Burr Harrison (D-Va.). Of the four major undecided Democratic votes on the committee, administration officials considered Harrison's to be the most promising.[44] Harrison's concerns about Medicare resembled Mills's: he wanted to guard the program against financial pressures, and he worried about the provisions that allowed those retirees on Social Security to receive health insurance even though they had made no contributions to pay for it. Harrison wanted to tie eligibility for Medicare to the payment of payroll taxes, maintaining that only those people who had paid into a special trust fund for five years should receive Medicare; even those already over sixty-five would need another year-and-a-half of payments to qualify. He also favored an arrangement that would allow hospitals to designate private, voluntary Blue Cross plans as their agents so that the money went from the federal government to Blue Cross rather than directly to the hospitals.[45]

In June 1962 Cohen began to broaden his scope of attention to influencing the Senate to amend the House welfare reform bill. He worked on a change in the administration's Medicare bill, along the lines that he had suggested to Congressman Harrison, that would allow hospitals to designate an organization to act as their intermediary, which in turn would handle billing arrangements and intercede between the government and the hospital. This arrangement closely resembled the billing system that many hospitals already practiced: they collected a person's Blue Cross number when he entered the hospital and then sent the bill to Blue Cross rather than to the patient. Cohen fully expected that most hospitals would continue to use that same organization, Blue Cross, as their intermediary under Medicare. His proposal further removed the administration's King-Anderson bill from the charge that it was a form of socialized medicine. Although the government would set the rules for program eligibility and reimbursement, hospitals could treat their Medicare patients just as they did their other insured patients.[46]

Organized labor appeared willing to go along with this change, yet even Cohen's close friends in his policy apparatus could not agree on how much further to go in order to get first the Senate and then the House in conference to accept Medicare. One idea, for example, was for the federal government to make payments directly to private insurance carriers for those people already covered by private insurance. Nelson Cruikshank argued that this idea was "completely unacceptable" because it cost private health insurance companies too much to administer coverage; as little as thirty-nine cents of every dollar they collected would go to doctors and hospitals.[47] Even at the risk of splitting his own coalition, Cohen pursued a compromise with Jacob Javits that included private health insurance companies. Sen. Clinton Anderson, on behalf of the administration, held a series of meetings with Javits in an effort to obtain a truly bipartisan measure. Cohen realized that such a measure would appeal to Mills, who prided himself on reaching a consensus before reporting out a bill or agreeing to a measure in conference. The key agreement, reached on June 28, 1962, included an option for reimbursement to private plans. If a person was covered by an approved private health insurance plan, one that contained the same or better benefits than specified in Medicare, then the person could continue the coverage at retirement. The federal government would pay part or all of the person's premiums by reimbursing the private health insurance company.[48]

The Javits amendment resembled the Kerr-Mills proposal of 1960 in its effect of dividing the proponents of Medicare. In both cases, Cohen advocated compromise, and Cruikshank and Ball had reservations. Indeed they felt more strongly about the Javits amendment than they had about the Kerr-Mills program. Kerr-Mills was harmless incrementalism; the Javits amendment defeated one of the main purposes of Medicare, which was to spread the costs of ill health among the elderly as widely as possible through the device of social insurance. As late as 5:00 P.M. on June 28, Cohen had still not heard the AFL-CIO's decision on the matter. Nor was Javits exactly sure what Anderson would propose.[49] By the next day, however, Anderson was ready to introduce the Anderson-Javits bill, complete with the compromise that allowed the federal government to reimburse the private insurance companies. Cohen told Sorensen that eighteen Democratic senators and five liberal Republicans, including Javits, had put their name on the legislation.[50]

By July the Senate debate had become an item of concern to Sorensen and Kennedy. Sorensen, who later wrote that Kennedy regarded the loss of Medicare as the most discouraging defeat he suffered during the administration, described the Senate debate that opened on July 2 as "desultory." Cohen continued to meet with the members of his apparatus and with key congressmen to draft further concessions that might permit them to pick up more Republican votes, concessions that made it easier for private plans to qualify for federal reimbursement under Medicare. At first, neither Javits nor Cruikshank found these revisions to be satisfactory.[51] Then, on July 11, Javits agreed to offer the revisions, and Cruikshank and Andy Biemiller, a former congressman and an AFL-CIO lobbyist, "reluctantly agreed to go along"; Anderson also concurred.[52] Meanwhile, Senator Kerr, according to Cohen, was "working hard" to obtain both Democratic and Republican votes against Medicare.[53]

On July 17 Medicare finally came to a vote in the Senate. All indications had pointed to a close contest, but the administration ultimately lost, 52 to 48. The key vote belonged to Jennings Randolph (D-W.Va.), a veteran senator with a strong attachment to Social Security proposals. If he had voted in favor of the bill, then Senator Hayden (D-Ariz.) would have also, and Vice-President Lyndon Johnson would have broken the tie.

Randolph voted against the Javits-Anderson amendment" to the public welfare bill for reasons that Cohen and Ribicoff understood but could do little to control. The complex situation concerned West Virginia's welfare program. The state had decided to take advantage of the Aid to Families with Dependent Children–Unemployed Parent program created in 1961, but state officials had broken the rules and required persons on welfare to perform work relief, although that requirement could not be validly imposed until October 1, 1962. That meant they owed the federal government $10 million. A special section of the Public Welfare amendments of 1962 forgave the debt, and Randolph worried that Kerr, the leading senator on the Finance Committee and certain to be on the conference committee after Senate passage of the Public Welfare amendments, would drop this section of the Public Welfare bill in conference. According to Cohen, "Senator Kerr probably never said this explicitly to Senator Randolph nor did he need to do so. Senator Randolph understood the situation very well." By getting Randolph's vote, Kerr succeeded in killing Medicare in 1962. Cohen later told Sorensen that even if the Senate had passed Medicare in 1962, it might still have proved impossible to get the measure through Wilbur Mills and a conference committee.[54]

EDUCATION IN 1963 AND CIVIL RIGHTS

The new Congress that would receive education legislation and Medicare in 1963 looked a lot like the old Congress. The Democrats had lost two seats in the House and gained four in the Senate, results described by one analyst as "random flux, with little evidence of party movement at all."[55] The elections, therefore, produced no new mandate for education legislation but indicated the need for continued political accommodation and compromise. It was commonplace among the president's advisers to believe that the administration should try a new approach to education legislation. Cohen thought that there should be a moratorium on proposals for general aid to education in favor of legislation for higher education and library services.[56] Officials in the Bureau of the Budget, in a similar spirit, noted that it was "essential that the Administration find a fresh approach to new Federal programs in education" since previous

President Kennedy confers with (*left to right*) Anthony Celebrezze, Francis Keppel, and Wilbur Cohen in Palm Beach on legislative strategy for the education bill at the beginning of 1963. At this point, the administration had almost nothing to show for its considerable efforts in this field. (Courtesy of Bruce Cohen)

efforts had only dredged up "in passionate form" issues of "public school versus private and segregation versus desegregation." Earlier efforts had also aroused supporters of "specialized groups and needs–without any gain in support for broader programs in education which are really needed."[57]

Officials in HEW and Congress, meanwhile, seemed to be spinning their wheels. Anthony Celebrezze, the new secretary, was unfamiliar with the ways of Washington, and a vacuum in leadership at the Office of Education augmented the indecision of policymakers. Two weeks after Ribicoff resigned as secretary, Sterling McMurrin left the job of commissioner of education, and it was not until December that Francis Keppel, the former dean of the Harvard School of Education, firmly settled into the position.[58]

Despite these difficulties, Keppel, Sorensen, and Cohen concurred in a new strategy for 1963, which they discussed with the president in Palm Beach over the 1962 Christmas holidays. Instead of presenting many separate bills, the administration would give Congress one large bill.[59] Cohen told Celebrezze that the omnibus bill, which included elementary, secondary, higher, and vocational education, would receive widespread support. "While the Catholic groups will press for providing Federal aid to parochial elementary and secondary schools and will oppose public school aid unless they are included," Cohen wrote, "we believe they will support practically all of our other elements and try to emphasize the affirmative elements."[60] The president endorsed the strategy, which was discussed at a cabinet meeting in the middle of January. Although the tax cut occupied the top position on the president's domestic agenda, education followed it. On January 18 Cohen and others in the department had completed a draft education bill and sent it to the Bureau of the Budget. Keppel and Cohen then worked on a message to send to Congress that would accompany the legislation. By the end of January Adam Clayton Powell, noting that previous approaches had been too fragmentary, stated that "some type of omnibus approach will be the only way"; he said that he would chair the hearings, slated to begin early in February, and "author" the bill.[61]

"I spent the most intensive 3 and half months of my life with Francis Keppel and all the other members of the staff working out the new proposal," Cohen confided to former HEW secretary Arthur Flemming in mid-February. By then the National Education Improvement Act of 1963 had been firmly launched, with Powell, Edith Green, James Roosevelt (D-Calif.), Wayne Morse, and Pat McNamara among its chief congressional sponsors.[62]

The strategy was simple, but the execution was difficult. The idea was to tie the needs of one interest group to the needs of another so that they would not sabotage one another's efforts. Fragmentation forced legislators to choose between Catholics and Protestants, whites and blacks. An omnibus bill softened the trade-offs and, so it was hoped, made it easier for an education bill to pass. As always, however, education proved to be a harrowing area of legislative endeavor with personal idiosyncrasies intruding on impersonal bureaucratic processes. Chairman Powell slipped in and out of town, sometimes presiding over his committee and sometimes allowing Edith Green to chair it.[63] Green, for her part, wanted to pass her own piece of legislation and objected to the administration's omnibus approach.

When Powell caucused with the Democrats on his Education and Labor Committee on February 19, he found, in the words of a member of Cohen's staff, that "everybody had a different view to express."[64] Soon the full committee broke up into subcommittees, each considering a piece of the bill and each threatening to develop separate legislation.[65] The subcommittee chairmen began to compete with one another over who could get legislation through the full committee first. Green, who had developed higher education proposals in the previous Congress, wasted little time in completing her work; by the end of

March, she had finished a proposal.⁶⁶ The other subcommittee chairmen were furious with her. Cohen and Keppel's legislative informants told them, for example, that Carl Perkins (D-Ky.) was "extremely annoyed" because she was trying to "beat him" in getting a bill to the full committee. Perkins, for his part, had begun hearings of his subcommittee on vocational education and adult basic education. He also expressed his displeasure with Congressman John Dent (D-Pa.), whose subcommittee was holding hearings on aid to elementary and secondary education, impacted-area legislation, and aid to public libraries. Perkins claimed that Dent had violated a promise to tie proposals for impacted-area legislation with general aid to elementary and secondary education, but Dent preferred to move first on impacted areas. If he refused to consider aid to elementary and secondary education, then Perkins threatened to have his subcommittee take up the matter. As for Chairman Powell, Perkins accused him of creating a "complete vacuum of leadership."⁶⁷

In the spring of 1963 no one quite knew if the omnibus bill strategy would remain intact.⁶⁸ Cohen worried that if a higher education bill were considered separately, the NEA would once again oppose it, and the situation would deteriorate as it had in the past. If the bill were broken up, then Cohen and Keppel favored taking up a "little" omnibus education bill first, which would contain as many of the noncontroversial features as possible, including an extension of the impacted-area legislation, vocational education, aid to libraries, NDEA amendments, and aid for the education of handicapped children. Cohen believed that such a bill could gain southern support and be enacted, giving the administration an education bill at long last. Before any action was taken, however, Keppel and Cohen wanted the subcommittees to report to Powell. Cohen described him as the "key to the situation. He will go along with the President if the President makes it absolutely clear what he wants."⁶⁹

In addition to this far-from-clear situation, the administration was contending with the issue of civil rights, which in the spring of 1963 emerged as a major concern that cut across nearly all its domestic proposals. The issue was not new, of course, but it became particularly pressing in this season of demonstrations in Birmingham. For Cohen, whose life was ordered in terms of passing education and Medicare legislation, civil rights figured to be an additional complication, a further wedge between northern and southern Democrats, whose support was crucial to the passage of any legislation.

Cohen himself was a northerner working among southerners and, like many northern liberals, he strongly opposed racial segregation in the South. "I always thought it was unfair to dislike people as a whole because of their religion or race or nationality," he once wrote in one of his self-conscious efforts to record his thoughts. "I just think that the Constitution under the 14th Amendment guarantees you your constitutional rights," he told an interviewer on another occasion.[70] Despite his straightforward personal beliefs, Cohen realized that he was a servant of Congress and of the administration, and neither entity appeared predisposed to advocate the passage of civil rights laws.[71] As much as he favored civil rights, he also strongly believed in the efficacy of the legislative process and saw his main job as passing education and health insurance legislation that would as a matter of course provide benefits to blacks. He did not want civil rights to envelop and derail those issues or to keep the Kennedy administration from creating and expanding social welfare programs. He therefore stuck to his traditional role of accommodating congressional leaders rather than challenging them on the issue of civil rights. He tried to be tactful to the southerners on the issue, never agreeing with their views but always being aware of the political realities. "One thing I've learned from experience," he said in commenting on civil rights issues, "you don't have to say everything that's true."[72]

If Cohen did not regard civil rights legislation as a moral imperative, he did worry about improving the economic conditions of African Americans. His remedies were the traditional ones: training and income maintenance. The expansion of welfare was to Cohen and to many of his fellow liberals an important vehicle of opportunity for blacks. Welfare, he noted, although not an adequate substitute for jobs, had helped blacks move from the rural South to the urban North and in this manner to respond to changes in agricultural life and technology; it also aided them in "meeting situations relating to desertions and illegitimacy." Indeed, African Americans consumed welfare benefits out of proportion to their share of the general population. In some regions, Cohen wrote, "the number receiving ADC is from 2–4 times their number in the population."[73] In 1963 such figures represented positive accomplishments for an administration eager to demonstrate its commitment to African Americans even though in the longer term, such figures would help to stigmatize both the welfare program and the African American beneficiaries. But in 1963 Cohen regarded his efforts to expand eligibility for welfare as a contribution to the civil rights movement.

Much as Cohen and Kennedy might have preferred to avoid the issue, civil rights kept coming up in the many hearings on the administration's omnibus education bill. During discussions on impacted-area legislation, for example, Green asked whether HEW was doing anything about the segregation of children who lived off base in military towns; congressmen also wondered what the department was doing to integrate libraries that received federal funds.[74] At the end of April a congressman asked Cohen during a hearing if the department objected to writing a nondiscrimination clause into the vocational education law. "I said I agreed with the principle," Cohen told the secretary, "that we would do everything along this line, and in general attempted to avoid answering the question." Pressed on the matter, Cohen said that a civil rights clause could cause the whole bill to be defeated. "The issue will surely arise again," he added.[75]

By the end of May, as the administration prepared to send a civil rights bill to Congress, the issue had become an explicit topic of consideration within the administration's domestic policy councils. Departments were expected to inventory their efforts in this field and discuss them with Robert Kennedy and Ted Sorensen. Cohen prepared a long civil rights memo for Secretary Celebrezze in which he considered the relationship between civil rights and the department's endeavors. Cohen advocated excluding segregated libraries from federal assistance even though it "might hurt us somewhat." In the field of vocational education, he urged more caution: the department should not move unilaterally on this matter but instead wait until the administration took "further action in the courts" and passed new laws "to aid in the desegregation of regular local school programs." Writing about the NDEA fellowships, Cohen foreshadowed some of the problems that would later arise in civil rights policy. The fellowships, he noted, presented an excellent chance "to give visibility to Negro opportunity." When HEW negotiated with graduate schools, it should be made clear that the grants were to be available to black students. "It would seem," Cohen continued, "that the Office could scrutinize and evaluate the graduate student body of the recipient university in terms of the kinds of enrollment record they have had, currently and in the past, with respect to minority groups."[76] In such thoughts lay the beginnings of executive action that would lead to the highly contentious affirmative action programs of the 1970s.

Cohen never debated the issue of civil rights at this philosophical level. In the spring of 1963 civil rights remained a sectional issue that, because of the hold of southerners on Congress, also affected the politics of federal aid to localities. At that point neither Cohen nor those in the Kennedy administration could have predicted the tremendous effect that urban riots would have on the nation's consciousness. Consequently, for Cohen, civil rights became just another of the many political considerations that went into legislative politics, and in the spring of 1963 education legislation stood at the top of the agenda. Cohen, Keppel, and Celebrezze tried to keep their eyes on the main chance: the passage of some sort of education bill. To some extent, Kennedy's endorsement of a comprehensive civil rights bill on June 11 helped them in this endeavor by shifting civil rights into a different legislative arena.[77]

Even without civil rights as a major consideration, education legislation continued to be a tactical nightmare although Celebrezze kept trying to hold as much of it together as possible. Congressman Dent came to believe in April that the White House would support a "small omnibus bill" with provisions for NDEA, handicapped children, adult basic education, impacted areas, and library construction. Powell announced in May that he thought there would probably be a higher education bill, a "little" omnibus bill with seven titles, and an elementary and secondary bill.[78] Congressman Philip Landrum (D-Ga.), who was devising some means to bring subcommittee chairmen Green, Perkins, and Dent together, thought in terms of considering vocational education in 1963 and higher education in 1964. When Cohen met with Landrum at the end of April to urge him to back a more general proposal, Cohen realized that he would need more guidance from the administration on which items to drop from the omnibus bill.[79]

Through this dizzying round of legislative jockeying, substantive policy issues still needed to be addressed, and Cohen personally intervened in the field of vocational education. Legislation in this area had begun in 1917, with matching grants to the states for programs in trade, agricultural, and home economics education. After World War II, Congress added such categories as programs in nursing education, fishery occupations, and "highly skilled technicians necessary to the national defense." Here was another barrel in which to put federal aid to education, and Congress tried to stuff it as full as it could. Cohen urged, as did a panel of consultants appointed by the president, that some of the rigidity and inflexibility be eliminated from the law. The panel recommended, in effect, that the existing system be scrapped and replaced with programs aimed at high school youths, high school dropouts, and others who needed "training or retraining to achieve employment stability." Cohen suggested, in testimony before Carl Perkins's subcommittee, that there be frequent review of the law so that it more effectively met the nation's most pressing manpower needs. In private, he told the secretary that the vocational education program needed "basic reorientation" and "new blood."[80]

In the spring and summer of 1963 Congress digested the various parts of the omnibus education bill. First to emerge from the process as a distinct entity was a higher education bill, which made it through Powell's committee in May. Cohen and Keppel were encouraged because twenty of twenty-five Republicans on the Education and Labor Committee supported the bill and Congressman Charles Halleck, the conservative Republican leader from Indiana, agreed to speak for the bill on the floor.[81] That began another struggle to get the higher education legislation past the Rules Committee and to the House floor. On

July 23 the House leaders, meeting with Adam Clayton Powell and the education subcommittee chairmen, agreed to seek a rule on the higher education bill. On July 25 Cohen went to see majority leader Carl Albert (D-Okla.), who said that if the participants agreed not to add provisions for community libraries to the bill, it might be possible to get a rule. At this point, the administration's "preliminary head count" indicated the "very real possibility of House passage of the bill."[82]

On August 6 the House voted on the relatively uncontroversial vocational education bill, and the large margin of victory provided a favorable omen for passage of the higher education legislation. On August 8 the House Rules Committee granted a three-hour "open rule" to the higher education legislation and thereby acquiesced in bringing it to the floor. Even though Cohen worried about opposition from such groups as the state superintendents of education, who were busy sending telegrams opposing the bill to their congressmen, he concluded that the higher education bill would pass.[83] When the House finally debated the bill on August 14, it endorsed the legislation by more than a 150-vote margin.[84]

Despite the tremendous effort that Cohen had already invested in passage of education legislation in the House, he needed to turn his complete attention to the Senate. Intensive meetings between Cohen and Keppel, representing the administration, and Senators Morse, Hill, Joseph Clark (D-Pa.), and Jennings Randolph began after Labor Day. Morse and Hill immediately said that they could not vote for the House higher education bill because it gave grants (not loans) to private colleges. They preferred to start with the House bill on vocational education and then turn to higher education.

Four days later Keppel and Cohen met with Morse's Subcommittee on Education of the Senate Committee on Labor and Public Welfare, which agreed to consider two bills. The first would be vocational education, with a number of other measures added to it, "making it," according to Cohen, "a little omnibus bill." The second would be a higher education bill, but once again Morse, Hill, and Randolph told Cohen that they would not vote for across-the-board grants to private colleges. Morse favored categorical grants in the fields of science, mathematics, and libraries but doubted that Hill would go along. The Senate subcommittee leaders preferred reporting out only loans and then "working out categorical grants in committee" or reporting out only categorical grants and "attempting to get the House to accept the Senate version."[85]

Having already held hearings on the original omnibus measure, the Senate subcommittee moved quickly to approve the education bills, and on

September 25 the full committee, meeting in executive session, voted to report out the "little omnibus bill." It included vocational education amendments, as worked out by the House, a three-year extension of the impacted-area legislation, and a three-year extension of various titles in the NDEA legislation.[86] On the same day the Senate Labor and Public Welfare Committee also gave approval to the higher education bill. Instead of accepting the House version, the Senate committee fell back on the text of the bill from the previous year, which included grants for the construction of facilities to be used for engineering, natural or physical sciences, or a library, and low-interest loans for the construction of other facilities.[87]

The final stages of the effort to pass higher education legislation coincided with the last two months of John F. Kennedy's life. On October 8 the Senate passed the vocational education/little omnibus bill, and on October 21 its version of the higher education bill. Although the bill itself cleared by a margin of 60 to 19, the Senate also included what Cohen regarded as a crippling amendment. Senator Sam Ervin's (D-N.C.) judicial review amendment would permit taxpayers' suits to test the constitutionality of loans or grants to religious schools. As Cohen noted, administration officials opposed the amendment, regarding it as unconstitutional, as a needless complication in administering the law, and as a source of delay in implementing the law. It was an issue of sufficient importance, Cohen believed, to warrant the intervention of the president.[88]

On October 24 the House Rules Committee agreed to send both the vocational education and higher education legislation to conference. Cohen believed there was a "reasonable chance of negotiating with the House to drop their across the board grants and the Senate to drop judicial review by arrangement before the Committee."[89] That proved to be the case, and the conference finished on November 4, after fashioning legislation with three primary titles. The first authorized $690 million over three years for the construction of academic facilities at colleges and community colleges. These grants followed the categorical framework favored by the Senate and could be used only for instruction or research in the natural or physical sciences, engineering, mathematics, and modern foreign languages and for libraries. Title two allotted $145 million in the form of matching construction grants for the establishment or improvement of graduate schools. Title three provided $360 million for loans to higher education institutions for constructing or improving academic facilities. Funds could not be used for athletic facilities or for "sectarian instruction or religious worship."[90] The House passed the final legislation two days later; passage of the measure in the Senate appeared to be certain.

NESTINGEN AND MEDICARE

The Kennedy administration may have won a partial victory on education in 1963, but it made little progress on Medicare. Cohen's strategy of concession and accommodation earned him considerable censure, even within the pragmatic Kennedy administration. HEW undersecretary Ivan Nestingen, in particular, viewed the handling of Medicare in 1962 as a complete disaster. Cohen had coddled Wilbur Mills, made all sorts of concessions to Javits and Harrison, and still the administration had absolutely nothing to show for its efforts except for an embarrassing public defeat on the floor of the Senate. Instead of accommodating Mills and the other policy insiders, Nestingen thought it might be better to confront them with the reality of Medicare's popularity; he wanted, in effect, to force them to pass it.[91] Nestingen believed that the administration should take its case to the public rather than relying on Cohen's private negotiating skills. He wanted, as he put it, to be "gung ho in taking the issues to the people" even though he knew that "Wilbur took a dim view of various grass roots efforts."[92]

Nestingen and Cohen had not gotten along from the very beginning of the Kennedy administration. Nestingen, like Cohen, came from Wisconsin, and he owed his appointment to the fact that as a Protestant he had supported Kennedy in a state that mattered; indeed, he had chaired the Kennedy for President Club there. From Cohen's point of view, it was a political appointment, pure and simple. Although a graduate of the University of Wisconsin and a trained lawyer, Nestingen had a strictly political résumé, one that included service on the Madison Common Council and in the Wisconsin Assembly in addition to being elected three times as mayor of Madison.[93] Cohen thought that Nestingen was "completely incompetent. He might have been a good post office man or something like that." Nestingen, for his part, conceded that Cohen was "very able; . . . very knowledgeable as far as the Federal Government is concerned. He and I have two different types of personalities, though, and I doubt that either has an overly fond regard for the other."[94]

Nestingen not only rankled Cohen, but he also threatened to undermine Cohen's relationship with his major clients in Congress. Medicare was too important to Cohen for him to tolerate meddling by his own department. It was difficult enough always to be obliging to Mills, and it was part of the job to work with Sorensen, who could be very prickly, but it was simply intolerable for Cohen to cajole Nestingen as he blundered into areas where in Cohen's opinion he did not belong. Cohen managed the politicians who found themselves temporarily stationed at HEW; he had no interest in being managed by them.

Cohen feared that Wilbur Mills would not work with Nestingen, and that refusal, quite simply, would mean the end of Medicare. Indeed, Cohen claimed that "Mr. Mills called me up and said, 'You better call those guys off over there. They're complicating my program, Wilbur.' " Whether Mills actually said that, the quotation reflected Cohen's view of him: Social Security was Mills's program. Cohen understood, in ways that Nestingen might not have, just how seriously Mills took his duties as chairman of the House Committee on Ways and Means and just how cautious he was about policy departures in Social Security. Cohen instinctively saw Mills as a permanent member of Congress, with essentially sound instincts. In Cohen's view, the administration had nothing to trade with Mills. As he put it, "You cannot say to Wilbur Mills during the Medicare fight, 'If you don't vote for us we'll defeat you in the next election.' Absolutely preposterous point of view."[95] Yet Nestingen and his unschooled "eager beavers" wanted to "chop Mills up, grind him, put the pressure on him, and the thing would fall in Kennedy's hands." Cohen thought they were "naive and simplistic" men of "limited experience." In contrast, he had a long-range plan by which he would "build slowly." Mills, a rational man, would come to see the logic of Medicare as a reasonable expansion of Social Security.[96]

Nestingen's partisans in Congress, such as Sen. Pat McNamara, and in the White House, such as political operative Kenny O'Donnell, accepted little or none of Cohen's analysis. Mills could stall until the millennium; he would not move until he was pushed. The Nestingen backers saw themselves as the ones with the political sense. William Reidy, a classmate of Cohen's at the Experimental College and a staffer on the Senate Committee on Labor and Public Welfare, thought it was Cohen rather than Nestingen who was naive. According to Reidy, Cohen believed that as a loyal servant of the Finance and Ways and Means committees, he had debts coming due and that he could approach those committees and "they'd say, 'Yes, we do owe you something Wilbur.' Wilbur is just politically naive – we think politically stupid."[97] The Nestingen proponents believed Cohen was ineffective, badly miscalculating the 1962 Senate vote, and overly conciliatory, hence dangerous, on the substantive points of policy. Reidy thought that without the Nestingen faction around to keep Cohen honest, "Wilbur would have given away 99% of the bill." According to a close associate, Nestingen considered the Javits compromise particularly "dangerous."[98] Nestingen himself told an interviewer that Cohen "carried the compromise discussion too far and very seriously amended the legislation to the point where the amendment would be harmful."[99]

Sen. Pat McNamara agreed with Nestingen on many of the substantive points of policy, opposing, for example, any sort of deductible in health insurance. Unlike Nestingen, whom Cohen regarded as a blunderer and an interloper, McNamara, an important member of Congress, required Cohen's direct attention. To appease McNamara, he suggested to Sorensen a complicated plan that provided a uniform benefit with no deductible but that also allowed individuals to elect, once a year, a longer duration of benefits with a deductible. Robert Ball thought this plan so administratively unworkable that he requested an appointment with Kennedy to dissuade him from endorsing it. It was, Ball later admitted, "probably a dumb thing to do." When Ball arrived in the Oval Office, he found Cohen already there, and in the words of Sen. Edward Kennedy, Ball "knew he had been had." The plan, Ball said, would lead to administrative chaos. "Well, then, let's have a little chaos," JFK replied.[100] Although the story became one of those anecdotes that admirers of Ball, Cohen, and Kennedy would later tell fondly, it indicated how deeply the effort to accommodate Senator McNamara split the Medicare coalition. Nor was McNamara ever satisfied; throughout the battle to pass Medicare, he continued to object to Cohen's efforts to appease a wide variety of people.[101]

After the 1962 defeat, with both Nestingen and McNamara "critical of my views and my strategy," Cohen entered a period of personal peril on Medicare. Ribicoff had left the department to run for the Senate, and Celebrezze, the new secretary, naturally hoped to rely on his undersecretary for advice on sensitive political matters like Medicare. Sorensen and Kennedy were annoyed at the defeat on the floor of the Senate, which, coupled with the defeats on education legislation, made the administration look particularly ineffective on domestic policy. It was a political year, and the administration faced the midterm elections without a single victory in a high-stakes contest on domestic policy. Nestingen claimed that after the defeat the administration turned the legislative aspects of Medicare over to him. He said that "President Kennedy blamed Wilbur Cohen for its defeat because of the compromise aspects of the bill and the legislative processing."[102]

Cohen reacted to Nestingen's ascension with concern. A stressful time for him, it was, he said, "impossible for me to conduct the negotiations without having to spend a lot of time always looking behind me to see if somebody was cutting my throat while I wasn't looking." Cohen continued his work with Sorensen and with Lawrence O'Brien but said that "quite frankly I considered all of these other people as being interlopers and interferers into the process for which I was being held responsible."[103]

Ultimately, Nestingen was a little too hot for the cool style of the Kennedy administration. On numerous occasions, he overplayed his hand, failing to heed instructions from first Ribicoff and then Celebrezze.[104] Nestingen eventually alienated enough people to lose his job in 1965: "Nestingen Resignation

Rumored Not to be Voluntary," read the headline in the Milwaukee paper. In 1963 and 1964, according to the account in the *Milwaukee Journal,* Nestingen "reportedly accused Cohen . . . of working behind his back with the committee." Cohen finally won his fight with Nestingen but not before he had engaged in a debilitating battle with him throughout 1963.[105]

Despite the considerable administrative infighting, the year passed without major developments on Medicare. In December 1962, Cohen told Sorensen that Celebrezze wanted to resubmit the Anderson-Javits bill without the "option" provision for the continuation of private insurance. The secretary believed that the administration should send up the basic bill and then "let the Congress make any substantive changes in the scope of the benefits" that would drive up its costs. Senator McNamara, for example, planned to introduce a bill that would eliminate all deductibles, cut back the number of hospital days to forty-five, and restore nursing home benefits. Senator Anderson, meanwhile, appeared willing to continue to sponsor whatever bill the administration, with the assistance of Nelson Cruikshank, agreed upon.[106]

In the spring of 1963 Cohen wrote Kennedy that a number of alternative proposals to the Anderson-Javits bill had appeared. Cohen took this as a hopeful sign, indicating "that we are probably getting closer to obtaining some Congressional action." Senators George Smathers and Russell Long were among those toying with alternatives. Long proposed what would become known as a "catastrophic" plan, one that paid only medical bills that exceeded 20 percent of a person's income. Cohen did not like this plan because he believed that it would provide an incentive to raise costs to the point where medical bills would be paid from the fund; nonetheless, he held discussions with Long and offered help in drafting a bill. As one congressional staffer described it, Cohen realized that Long and Smathers would probably be on a conference committee related to Medicare, and he needed their cooperation; hence, he did not want to "denounce or antagonize" either senator.[107] At the same time, Cohen, Ball, and Myers carefully tracked Senator Javits's latest activities as well as those of the undecided members of the Ways and Means Committee. In Cohen's judgment, "We probably can't get a final bill out of a conference committee (with the Senate conferees being Harry Byrd, Russell Long, and Smathers) without making modifications in our basic proposal."[108]

Cohen spent a great deal of time in 1963 following the deliberations of the National Committee on Health Care of the Aged, which Senator Javits had formed after the July 1962 Senate debate. When the Javits report appeared in November 1963, Cohen hailed it as a "strong endorsement of the President's proposals." Cohen, who described the differences between the Javits and the administration plans as "minor," found it encouraging that a group containing three members of Eisenhower's administration, representatives of hospitals, administrators of Blue Cross plans, and private insurance executives could recommend a plan so similar to the Anderson bill.[109]

None of these maneuvers mattered much without the consent of Wilbur Mills, who continued to raise various objections. In April, for example, he told Cohen that if any hospital insurance were to be passed, it should be funded through higher tax rates rather than through expanding the amount of a person's wages on which Social Security taxes were paid. Mills did promise to hold hearings on Medicare as soon as he disposed of the president's tax bill, perhaps around July.[110]

As the alternatives to Anderson's bill mounted, Anderson himself became restive, expressing particular concern because Smathers, whom he described as chairman of the Senate Special Committee on Aging and "close friend of the President," appeared to be speaking against the Medicare bill. "Has the administration dropped support for its own bill?" Anderson asked. Cohen tried to reassure him, disavowing Smathers and telling Anderson that the president wanted to do "absolutely everything which is humanly possible to achieve early passage of your bill." Cohen reminded Anderson that the strategy for 1963 was to get the legislation through the House Committee on Ways and Means first, even though, as Cohen fully realized, Mills kept stalling.[111] He did not announce hearings on health insurance until October 29 and set November 18 as the date for them to begin. He asked Celebrezze to be the first witness. The hearings ended abruptly after the president's trip to Dallas.[112]

At the conclusion of the Kennedy administration, the Medicare legislation, like aid to education, remained in a highly fluid state, with few assurances that it would ultimately pass. Cohen had followed the education legislation through three punishing rounds, with only the possibility of a victory on higher education and some minor education bills to show for his efforts. The Kennedy program, said Dean Coston of Cohen's staff, was "going nowhere . . . and he was not positioned to drive it very far."[113] Nonetheless, Cohen continued to ride the Kennedy program, looking for a way through the congressional maze. Between 1961 and 1963 he persevered through personal attacks and through almost endless congressional bickering and tactical maneuvering. Congress clearly tested Cohen's reserves of patience and his famous penchant for compromise. Yet during these same years, despite the bleak record of legislative success, Cohen, more than any other person in his department, refined a social agenda that, contrary to the weariness and pessimism of 1963, would soon meet with extraordinary congressional approval.

9
LBJ, POVERTY, AND EDUCATION

After John F. Kennedy's assassination, Wilbur Cohen's world collapsed. On November 23, 1963, he and Eloise went to the White House to view the president's bier, and he spent the next day watching television: "I just couldn't get out to go to the Capitol or elsewhere. It was too terrible, too unreal, too preposterous." On November 25, after seeing the funeral on television, Cohen got a call from a member of Lawrence O'Brien's staff asking him to bring a memo on Medicare to the White House for President Johnson to see. Cohen, along with Eloise, arrived at the White House at six in the evening and went to the second floor of the West Wing where O'Brien's office was located. There Cohen encountered a number of JFK's aides, many of whom were drinking. He returned to the first floor and stopped at Sorensen's office: "He was there alone," Cohen recalled, "a white numbed pallor on his face. . . . When we remarked what a great loss had occurred, he said that President Johnson needed all of us."[1]

Johnson, outside the loop during JFK's presidency, needed to be informed quickly on the major domestic policy initiatives of the Kennedy administration. The areas of education and Medicare, which contained so many pieces of uncompleted business, were particularly critical; in a short time, President Johnson mastered both. In the field of education, he succeeded not only in getting a general federal aid to education bill through Congress but also in initiating a major effort aimed at reducing the level of poverty in America.[2] Wilbur Cohen, in his usual role as legislative liaison, helped to ensure continuity between the 1961 proposals of President Kennedy and the 1965 triumphs of President Johnson. He participated enthusiastically in writing the final version of an aid to education bill. Although he approached the poverty bill with similar zeal, he eventually came to regard it as an ill-advised attempt to circumvent Congress and to place power in the hands of the president. Consequently, he voiced opposition to it within inner administration councils and gave it a low priority in his work with Congress. As always, he favored incremental over innovative policies.

LBJ AND EDUCATION

Wilbur Cohen, as stunned as anyone by the events in Dallas, never gave much thought to resigning. That November, in the middle of developing a legislative program for 1964, he had so many ongoing projects that he could not conveniently conclude them on short notice. Further, Cohen worked in an executive agency rather than in the White House; he was a program man, not one of the president's men. He did write out a short pro forma letter of resignation, which Johnson ignored as he did almost all the others that he received in November.[3] Johnson wanted to keep Kennedy's legislative team together and to use the tragedy of Kennedy's death to get the controversial items of the late 1950s and early 1960s through a recalcitrant Congress.[4]

As with nearly everyone else who worked for LBJ, Cohen found Johnson to be a challenge as a boss. The new president, unlike the somewhat remote Kennedy, had a mercurial personality that Cohen described as complex and contradictory. Johnson could be crude but "five minutes later you could stand on the hillside . . . watching the sunset and you'd find a man who was a poet in describing the sunset." Cohen also noted Johnson's penchant for making big decisions without comment but agonizing over small ones, such as who should belong to a particular advisory council.[5] Cohen, a prodigious worker, even had difficulty matching Johnson's energy and appetite for work. The president liked to call people at all hours of the day or night, and Cohen learned how to accommodate LBJ's often impetuous requests for information or action. If necessary, he took a nap in the late evening so he would be ready for the president's call after midnight. Working for Johnson required Cohen to put in twelve-hour days and still be ready "to take a call from the president at two o'clock in the morning."[6]

Cohen had his first real glimpse of Johnson's vitality on December 10, 1963, at a meeting of departmental legislative liaison officers in the White House. The president spoke of how important it was to continue Kennedy's program, shook hands with those around him, and then, to Cohen's surprise, shook the hands of the forty-odd people in the room. Approaching Cohen, he mentioned that "I had dinner with Wicky the other night."[7]

Elizabeth Wickenden, who had known LBJ since his days at the National Youth Administration, proved to be a crucial contact between him and Cohen. When Johnson was still the Senate majority leader, Wickenden wrote him a letter urging him to rely on Wilbur Cohen's advice in the field of Social Security. According to Wickenden, although Johnson had not known Cohen before that incident, he continued to associate him with Wickenden after it.[8] She in turn encouraged Johnson to equate Cohen with Social Security, the

New Deal, and aid to the elderly–all matters to which the president was favorably predisposed. Cohen later claimed that these associations exempted him from much of the harassment and humiliation to which Johnson often subjected subordinates.[9] Unlike Hubert Humphrey, for example, Cohen never had to hunt deer on the ranch, swim naked in the White House pool, or take reckless spins in a car with the president guzzling scotch.[10]

Lyndon Johnson took over the presidency just as a big batch of Kennedy education legislation cleared Congress. On December 10, the same day that Cohen met with Johnson, the Senate passed the aid to higher education bill and sent it to the president for his signature. Cohen's role in this legislation had centered on overcoming political obstacles and facilitating agreement among the key players. He had helped to develop the strategy of bundling pieces of education legislation and using established programs as a lure to create new programs. He, among others, had suggested making higher education the entering wedge for federal legislation. The Kennedy administration, in the interest of obtaining some sort of success, had tacitly laid aside general aid to elementary and secondary education. Even in higher education, the administration, despite substantial effort, had failed to secure government-financed scholarships or student loans.

Despite its limitations, as Cohen liked to point out, the higher education law amounted to a substantial legislative achievement: the first nondefense, general aid to education legislation since 1945.[11] A haggard Sorensen, still in shock over the assassination, pressed Cohen on December 11 to tell him if the higher education act constituted the most important education bill in the nation's history. Cohen, with his usual objectivity on these matters, could not quite agree; instead, he termed the act the most significant legislation in the field since 1862, when the Morrill Act initiated the land-grant program.[12]

If one counted bills passed just after Kennedy's death, such as aid to higher education and the vocational education law, the Kennedy administration succeeded in passing nearly half the twenty-four items in the 1963 omnibus education proposal. By passing four major education laws in 1963, Congress authorized the expenditure of $4.1 billion, compared to the $255 million that had been appropriated under the Morrill Act throughout its entire history.[13] In 1964, with America on the verge of the Great Society, such figures were an unambiguous source of pride and evidence of progress.

Nor was President Johnson through with education legislation; on the contrary, he picked up the theme without shuffling his feet. As one of his biographers later put it, "LBJ was the first national politician to place education as subordinate to nothing else."[14] Even in the chaotic period just after the assassination, Johnson fought to get more of the education program enacted.

Cohen and O'Brien told him on December 11 that the administration could still succeed with one piece of the omnibus law in the form of the public community library bill. Passage of this bill depended, according to Cohen, on President Johnson's willingness to intervene with the Speaker and Judge Howard Smith (D-Va.) of the Rules Committee.[15] Regardless of whether the president made the calls, the legislation, which allowed federal grants to the states for the construction of libraries and the improvement of library services, passed in January 1964.[16]

Early in 1964 Cohen, Keppel, and Celebrezze made plans to press for the rest of Kennedy's education legislation. It was the common wisdom of the group that the Eighty-eighth Congress had probably gone as far as it wished to go on aid to education and did not want to take on controversial legislation before a presidential election. Still, the HEW team continued to fine-tune its proposals for aid to elementary and secondary schools. One draft contained the measures carried over from 1963–money to increase teacher salaries, build schools, and improve educational quality through special projects–and also a new feature that reflected the administration's interest in reaching out to parochial schools. For the first time, the administration explored specific linkages between aiding education and ending poverty and toyed with the idea of initiating federal grants to urban or rural areas designated as "pockets of poverty." Cohen and his associates wished to encourage projects such as "educational improvement centers," guidance and counseling programs for "culturally and economically deprived children," after-school study centers, work-study, and summer programs. Although each of these programs would need to be under public supervision and control, students in both public and private schools would be eligible to participate. That was the key point. With the president no longer quite so concerned about restricting aid to parochial schools, a general aid to education bill might include something for Catholics.[17]

THE POVERTY PROGRAM

The new education proposal meshed with the administration's efforts to pass a legislative program geared to reducing poverty in America, an initiative that had begun in the Kennedy administration and that reached a climax in the Johnson administration. Although in later years the War on Poverty would come to symbolize the social policy of the 1960s, it was little more than an incidental concern for Wilbur Cohen and others who were trying to pass Kennedy's education and health legislation in 1963. Like civil rights, poverty legislation

Wilbur Cohen meeting with President Johnson and members of the Council of Economic Advisers. The council proved a formidable bureaucratic foe in the creation of the War on Poverty in 1963 and 1964. (Courtesy of Bruce Cohen)

cut across several areas of departmental initiative and complicated legislative campaigns that were already well advanced.

One difference between Cohen and most other individuals in the Kennedy administration was that he could lay claim to some expertise on the subject of poverty; before 1964 he had often spoken and written on the subject. In the 1962 book on income and welfare in the United States, produced with his University of Michigan colleagues, Cohen had written, "The United States has arrived at the point where poverty could be abolished easily and simply by a stroke of the pen." He estimated the cost at about $2 billion a year, less than 2 percent of the gross national product (GNP). Cohen noted, however, that there was a difference between "the short-run alleviation of poverty" and the long-run "elimination of dependency."[18] This conflict between income maintenance and rehabilitation would haunt the War on Poverty throughout its history. Early in 1963 Cohen had given a speech on the elimination of poverty that reflected the administration's prevailing view on the subject. America had the necessary abundance to end poverty, including "huge technical capacity" and great "wealth of potential human resources." Ending poverty was a matter of allowing more people to participate in the prosperity so as to improve central cities in which "blight" formed such a stark contrast to "high-rise luxury apartments" and of discovering ways to allow more people to take advantage of "significant advances in the health and medical fields." In the way of specific legislative remedies for poverty, Cohen mentioned the administration's plans for a tax cut and the passage of Medicare.[19] As Cohen's short list implied, the general goal of ending poverty had become subsumed under the more specific goals of cutting taxes, passing aid to education and Medicare, and implementing the 1962 public welfare amendments. It was revealing that neither Cohen's analysis of the problem nor his specific legislative remedies featured the problems of race or of what later generations would call the underclass. The relationship between civil rights and the rehabilitation of the poor would be another conflict that would undermine the War on Poverty.

When Cohen learned at the end of October 1963 of the administration's serious interest in antipoverty legislation, he probably conceived of the situation as similar to Kennedy's interest in mental retardation. Poverty, like mental retardation, was a problem whose policy dimensions stretched across many parts of HEW. A coherent response would require new priorities in several agencies but would be complementary to the department's on-going activities. In initial meetings with Sorensen, the focus appeared to be on the problems of eastern Kentucky, which President Kennedy planned to visit in late November. Sorensen and Cohen saw the department's mission, at least in the short term, as making the residents of thirty-three counties there aware of the social welfare benefits available to them. Federal teams could search out those eligible for, but not receiving, Social Security, veterans', and vocational rehabilitation benefits.[20]

Unlike the mental retardation program, the poverty program would be directed from the White House and not from the Department of Health, Education, and Welfare. Legislative planning became the responsibility of a task force headed by Walter Heller of the Council of Economic Advisers (CEA).[21] Cohen did not perceive the council as a rival organization, and he got along reasonably well with Heller. Both Heller and Cohen had studied economics at the University of Wisconsin, even though the two men had taken different courses and worked with different people; Heller had focused on the emerging field of macroeconomics, and Cohen had concentrated on institutional economics. Heller had become an early Keynesian and Cohen a disciple of Edwin Witte.[22] Despite these intellectual differences, Cohen told an interviewer, "Having been trained initially as an undergraduate as an economist myself, I felt that I could reasonably understand the economist's point of view."[23]

Further, Cohen, well versed in bureaucratic politics, quickly sized up Heller's importance to the president. "In many ways," he said, "the Budget Director and the Chairman of the CEA were many times more important than the Secretary. . . . They had the ear of the President many times more intimately, more frequently, and more sensitively than the Secretary did." Medicare, which fell into Cohen's bailiwick, was a departmental concern, but economic growth was a presidential one; Heller undoubtedly spoke to Kennedy and Johnson many more times about economic growth than Cohen did about Medicare or education.[24]

Cohen therefore paid attention to Heller's request when he asked Secretary Celebrezze to help him "pull together for the President's consideration a set of measures that might be woven into a basic attack on the problems of poverty and waste of human resources as part of the 1964 legislative program."[25] Cohen had little to fear from such a request and much to gain. He worked for the agency that everyone conceded to be the center of the federal government's antipoverty efforts; he had a definite legislative agenda, including Medicare and education, that could be wrapped inside a poverty package; and he knew how to phrase matters so as to appeal to economists.

To facilitate poverty legislation, Heller turned to his subordinates and Cohen to his staff. William Capron and Burton Weisbrod, two young economists, headed a special CEA task force on poverty, and Cohen mobilized his many contacts in the department to solicit ideas to feed to them. Phillip Des Marais, who worked on Cohen's small staff, recommended to Cohen that he push school-health programs and special school-enrichment projects as antipoverty measures since they fit the mold for the department's latest education initiatives. Other suggestions from Des Marais included incremental expansions of traditional HEW programs, such as making old-age assistance available at age sixty-two and making the definition of disability in Social Security more lenient. To Des Marais, as to Cohen, ending poverty meant expanding HEW's programs.[26] The poverty program would be a convenient umbrella for passing HEW's proposed legislation and augmenting existing programs.

Nothing in the Council of Economic Advisers' initial responses to the Department of Health, Education, and Welfare gave Cohen any reason to suspect that the War on Poverty would complicate his legislative plans for 1964. In November 1963 Heller and his associates were using such labels as "human conservation and development" and "wider participation in prosperity" to describe their program. The analysis of who was poor depended very much on Cohen's study of income and welfare in the United States; the data showed, not surprisingly, that race and region were strong predictors of poverty. People who were black and from the South were more likely to be poor than those who were white and from the North. Ending poverty, according to the economists, would be an investment in the nation's future that would pay dividends in the form of reduced crime, delinquency, and wider participation in the military.

This analysis did not differ appreciably from that of the Rockefeller report on which Cohen had worked in the mid-1950s. As for practical programs to reduce poverty, the Council of Economic Advisers turned to the ideas that it had received from the Department of Health, Education, and Welfare, such as "flexible and imaginative work with public assistance" and raising Social Security benefits. The poverty effort appeared to be moving in Cohen's direction.[27]

Heller encouraged administration officials to think small but to seek large results. He wanted to concentrate efforts on "such areas as Eastern Kentucky" and "major urban slums," which had become the shorthand descriptions of the places in which the poor lived. Heller also wanted officials to think in terms of "self-help." "Success of the total effort depends on minimizing passive acceptance of 'handouts' and maximizing the pride that individuals and community can take in their own efforts to eradicate poverty," he said. This effort, then, was not to be conducted in the depression mode of the New Deal with its emphasis on relief but in the optimistic style of the postwar era. People would not receive temporary palliatives so much as permanent cures; poverty would be eradicated, not just controlled. Still, Heller implied that there could be no universal response to poverty, and each place would need to define its own program. Although Heller mentioned increased Social Security benefits as an antipoverty device, he appeared to be thinking more in terms of rehabilitation than of income maintenance, and he seemed to favor flexible over universal programs.[28]

Undeterred by Heller's calls for flexible programs, each of the constituent agencies within HEW continued to feed Heller ideas that meshed with their missions. Ellen Winston, in charge of the Welfare Administration, said that states needed higher benefits and more services. There should be federally defined minimum payments and the elimination of arbitrary reductions.[29] Winston was apparently making the logical point that what the poor needed most was money, despite Heller's admonitions against temporary palliatives. She, like many of her HEW counterparts, wanted to expand the established program.

On November 19 Cohen sent Heller in effect the department's official response to his request for suggestions for antipoverty programs. Cohen led with the statement that HEW's programs were directed "toward the conservation and development of human resources"; in other words, any program that HEW administered counted as an antipoverty effort. With his eye for historical analogy, Cohen compared the situation to the Employment Act of 1946, which had declared the nation's commitment to attain full employment. The poverty legislation should announce the new intention of moving beyond full employment so as to include those individuals who had dropped out of the labor force. When it came time for specific suggestions, Cohen stayed with the items already on the department's agenda, Medicare and raising the level of Social Security benefits. Next came the department's education legislation and then its vocational rehabilitation program. In other words, Cohen responded to Heller's request for innovative antipoverty measures by reciting the department's legislative proposals that were already under way. If Cohen had his way, the antipoverty program would be little more than putting a new label on the old program.[30]

As the antipoverty program took shape late in 1963 and early in 1964, the economists in charge moved away from recommending a simple extension of HEW's programs.[31] William Capron later commented that what he received from HEW and the other departments was "garbage."[32] The economists disliked the way in which the HEW programs had developed funding patterns and priorities that did not necessarily put the needs of the poor above others.

By the end of November it had become apparent that specific decisions needed to be made about the contents of the administration's antipoverty proposals. The rhetoric of the effort had begun to escalate, just as administration officials, in the period after Dallas, found themselves in considerable disarray. "A national problem—a blight on our conception of social justice—demands a national program: a declaration of war on poverty," wrote Capron and Weisbrod early in December.[33] What had begun as a demonstration had become a war. And, just as the war was about to be declared, the key decision makers, such as Ted Sorensen, were operating at less than full capacity for a new and untrusted boss.

At this point, Cohen began to develop serious doubts about the program. The Council of Economic Advisers was moving toward recommending that the federal government provide funds to communities for local development corporations that became known as Community Action Programs (CAPs). Cohen thought this idea to be seriously misguided, pointing out to Capron and Weisbrod that some people needed transfers of money rather than rehabilitative or civil rights measures if they were ever to rise above poverty. Cohen even quoted one of the CEA's own staff members who had said that the only way to improve the situation of one-third of those in poverty was to transfer money to them. There were other problems as well. The administration appeared to be committing itself to a poverty standard that Cohen regarded as unrealistically high, and he felt that the poverty planners were neglecting the 1962 Public Welfare amendments already established.[34]

The line agencies in HEW reacted to the idea of community action with similar disdain. Ellen Winston, speaking with revealing candor, noted that the CEA proposal "does not do anything to help our programs in any substantial way. . . . We must not be deluded into too much enthusiasm about organized local action." She believed that ghetto communities lacked the leadership to develop antipoverty programs and that expertise would need to be imported. She also expressed skepticism about the results of more research on poverty: "We already know more about the sources of poverty and ignorance than we are prepared to do anything about constructively."[35] Robert Ball, head of the Social Security Administration, echoed Cohen's thinking that "what is mainly needed is expansion and additions" to HEW's existing programs; he did not believe that the Johnson administration should emphasize the "development corporation approach."[36]

Heller disagreed with the HEW bureaucrats, and his approach carried the day. On December 20, 1963, he formally recommended to Sorensen that the president include a major " 'Attack on Poverty' as a central feature of his 1964 legislative program." To carry it out, Heller proposed a "coordinated community action program which is aimed at specific local areas of poverty, relies on well-organized local initiative, action and self-help under Federally-approved plans and with Federal support." He continued to hope that these Community Action Programs would function as demonstration projects, with about ten of them spread across the country. Each would receive about $10 million a year for no more than five years, and each would be evaluated to determine what worked and what did not work in ending poverty. Heller believed that his proposal would bring "focus, consistency, and continuity" to the nation's response to poverty.[37]

Despite Heller's desires, Cohen still hoped to use the interest in poverty as a way of passing HEW's education legislation. Where Heller pushed CAPs as the centerpiece of poverty legislation, Cohen advocated aid to education. The Council of Economic Advisers wanted to make community action the first title in a poverty bill, but Cohen hoped to make federal aid to schools located in pockets of poverty the first: "Elementary and secondary education should have the highest priority as part of an anti-poverty and illiteracy campaign," he said.[38] Education programs would raise people's competence and erase illiteracy and were therefore better vehicles to drive the poverty programs than were Community Action Programs. "In other words, I would make the community action program the second string to the bow rather than the first string," said Cohen.[39]

Asked to make a general evaluation of the poverty bill as it stood at the end of 1963, Cohen characterized it as "weak." In his opinion, it did not do enough "for children, broken families where the women have to work to support the family, minority groups and special problem areas like alcoholics, delinquents, and the mentally ill." Heller did not want to classify the poverty program in these specific ways, preferring a more flexible, general, and global approach over Cohen's categorical view.[40]

LEGISLATING THE WAR ON POVERTY

As it became clear that President Johnson would recommend a poverty program as part of his 1964 legislation, bureaucratic infighting began in earnest over which department would take charge of the program and how it would be presented to Congress. Two issues consumed much of Cohen's time: the first concerned whether HEW would be the lead agency in the War on Poverty; the second involved the specific relationship between legislation on poverty and on education.

Cohen argued that his department should coordinate the War on Poverty. As Cohen saw it, the secretary of HEW should chair an Interdepartmental Committee on Poverty, which, among other things, would approve and regulate Community Action Programs. To staff this committee, Congress should permit HEW an extra assistant secretary who would serve as executive vice-chairman and as the program director for the War on Poverty.[41] William Capron of the CEA disagreed with Cohen and instead urged "an independent Presidential appointee of stature outside the existing bureaucracy." This appointee would operate with a lean staff but with real power over approving and coordinating local CAPs. Capron hoped in this manner to involve all the federal agencies concerned with poverty and to avoid being bogged down in the "bureaucratic, pressure group morass of the existing agencies." He specifically mentioned the National Education Association as a pressure group that put its own needs above those of the nation. Capron, who worked in the White House, hoped to identify the new initiative as the "Johnson attack on poverty," rather than "just a somewhat beefed-up HEW operation."[42]

Cohen's disagreement with Capron stemmed partly from defensive bureaucratic behavior and partly from his belief that programs should be based in established departments rather than in the White House. He believed in working through channels, and other members of Cohen's apparatus readily agreed with him.[43] When Johnson became president, Elizabeth Wickenden had urged him to sponsor a major conference, "Freedom from Want," that would expand upon President Roosevelt's four-freedoms speech of 1941. She wanted to highlight future goals rather than specific legislative proposals. As the poverty planners moved toward the community action idea, Wickenden urged them to reconsider. She told Walter Jenkins, a key aide to LBJ, that the poverty bill would become the "most vulnerable part of the Johnson program"; because it bypassed the governors and the normal federal-state-local channels, it would be "labelled as a Presidential power grab or slush fund."[44]

Cohen and Wickenden lost the bureaucratic battle over running the War on Poverty. Instead of having HEW administer the program, Charles Schultze of the Bureau of the Budget and other administration officials decided that there would be a director of Community Action Programs who would work from the White House.[45] Eventually, the director became the head of the Office of Economic Opportunity (OEO). Johnson named the charismatic Sargent Shriver, Kennedy's brother-in-law, to the post.

Perhaps because of Cohen's premonitions about the War on Poverty, he fought hard with the Bureau of the Budget in January 1964 to remove the administration's education proposals from the poverty bill. The Council of Economic Advisers staff, such as Capron, wanted the new antipoverty special projects that Cohen and Keppel had developed to be in the bill, however. Capron reasoned that, as part of an aid to education bill, the special projects stood little chance of passage, but Cohen thought, even if general aid to education failed to pass Congress, the special projects would pass and give Johnson his first successful education legislation.

Like all intramural governmental debates, this one involved more than the protection of turf; it also contained a more ideological dimension. The economists encouraged a deliberate vagueness in the poverty legislation so as to remove as much of the War on Poverty as possible from the direct control of Congress. They hoped that experts in the executive branch, not the congressional chieftains, would make the key decisions about resource allocation. Capron said and Cohen admitted that if special projects were in an education bill, they would be encumbered by formal administrative requirements. Capron hoped to exempt the projects, and the entire antipoverty effort, from these sorts of political specifications that were the means by which Congress imposed its will on the allocation of federal funds. At the same time, Capron realized that the passage of poverty legislation was a political exercise, and he thought that the funds for education projects would add to the political attractiveness of the poverty legislation. They would increase the authorization by $200 million and add a specific note to "what otherwise is going to look (necessarily and desirably) pretty open-ended and non-specific to the Congress."[46] Cohen, whose view of the world was heavily influenced by a need to accommodate Congress, saw Capron's belief that experts could somehow circumscribe congressional leaders as naive. Successful programs required strong congressional defenders.

Cohen urged Kermit Gordon in the Bureau of the Budget and Theodore Sorensen in the White House to include the special projects in education, rather than in poverty, legislation, arguing that this strategy offered "the best chance to pass the [education] bill in 1964."[47] Unfortunately, Sorensen, still staggered by the assassination, was not attentive to the details of the dispute and at one point suggested that education grants for antipoverty projects be put into separate legislation rather than in the poverty bill or a general federal aid to education bill. Celebrezze, Keppel, and Cohen quickly agreed. When Celebrezze tried to call Sorensen to tell him of HEW's approval, the secretary found that he had already left the office. In the end it was Bill Moyers, LBJ's man, rather than Ted Sorensen, JFK's man, who made the decision. The special education projects would go into the poverty bill because, as Moyers reported, Johnson felt that he needed the "additional support of the educational proposal to beef up the poverty bill."[48]

After this key decision was made, Cohen turned his attention to Medicare and let others handle the War on Poverty. In effect, Cohen understood that Johnson had made a tacit decision not to push for a general aid to elementary and secondary education bill in 1964 and to highlight the poverty bill instead. Cohen assigned Dean Coston, a member of his staff whom he had recruited from Ann Arbor, to monitor the poverty legislation, which quickly receded into the background as a departmental priority.[49]

In the early months of 1964, without Cohen's input, the poverty bill acquired shape and weight. In addition to community action, the legislation gained a measure that William Capron described as a "program to educate and train 17 year-olds largely in reactivated army camps, but with civilian orientation and staff." This idea emerged in the final legislation as the Job Corps and became the first title in the bill.[50] The bill that Congress considered contained community action, the Job Corps, and four other titles, including work-training programs, work-study programs, special programs for rural areas and small businesses, and a workfare program based on the 1962 Public Welfare amendments. In March the president issued the bill with a special message on poverty, and hearings began in the House Committee on Labor and Public Welfare.[51]

By the standards of the era, the bill moved through Congress with reckless speed and none of the contentiousness that marked either education or Medicare legislation. Congress made what were at most marginal adjustments, such as deciding that women should be allowed to participate in the Job Corps. Yet this was the same group of people who had so delayed the education legislation. After the Kennedy assassination, with a new president who was simultaneously at the beginning and the end of his first term, these congressmen accepted direction from the White House with only a minimal display of proprietary behavior and ego. The Rules Committee granted a rule for the bill even though conservatives raised significant questions about its efficacy. After this easy trip through the House, the Senate decided in June 1964 not to hold hearings on the legislation. In the end, Congress passed a law that, according to political analyst Michael Barone, would not have been passed in "normal times."[52]

In its haste, Congress affirmed the measure without looking deeply into its contents. In the Rules Committee, for example, a congressman asked Phil Landrum, who skillfully piloted the poverty bill, exactly what jobs sixteen-year-old girls would be trained for in the Job Corps; Landrum replied that vocational experts, not he, would design the program. Unlike its ponderous and careful handling of education, in which years of hearings and thousands of pages of testimony preceded legislation, Congress took the efficacy of poverty legislation on faith. It was a presidential initiative, not a congressional or executive agency effort.[53]

For Cohen, who observed the passage of the Economic Opportunity Act at some remove, the poverty program became a source of great personal frustration. "The anti-poverty bill has been all messed up," Cohen told Sorensen, who was at Harvard writing a history of the Kennedy administration, in May 1964.[54] Part of the problem was that Sargent Shriver, head of the Office of Economic Opportunity, had convinced the president to sell the idea not as an experimental or pilot program but as a "full-scale effort to give millions of Americans an immediate opportunity to lift themselves from the ranks of the poor."[55] Cohen, who liked Shriver personally, doubted his ability to bring off such a large project. Like Bobby Kennedy, Shriver had "lots of charisma, people flocked to him like the Pied Piper attracted children." Yet despite his charm, Shriver did not know how to manage people well, according to Cohen, who worried that he lacked a conceptual framework from which to pursue the War on Poverty.[56]

Another part of the problem was that Shriver and the OEO acted at cross-purposes to Cohen and HEW. Shriver maintained that the War on Poverty could not be won by expanding existing programs, yet Cohen's experience with Social Security showed just how effective such expansion could be. Shriver believed that poor people should have a "democratic voice" in determining social services, a stark contrast from the way in which Cohen and Wilbur Mills operated. Shriver further argued that poor people had a right to benefit from available social programs and that these services should be packaged so as to facilitate "one-stop shopping." Cohen, like Arthur Altmeyer before him, also emphasized the right of poor people to receive benefits, but he knew from personal experience how each of the bureaucratic agencies wished to preserve its distinctive identity and resisted being merged with other agencies. Still another part of the problem was that Shriver spoke in language that Cohen regarded as blatantly antipolitical and that could only lead to antagonism between the poverty warriors and the politicians at all levels of government. One example of Shriver's ill-considered language, as Cohen perceived it, was his notion of special help for the disadvantaged. Shriver said that his poverty program would adopt "a discriminatory approach, seeking consciously not to spread benefits evenly, but to provide progressively greater advantages in inverse correlation to income." Such an attempt was the very antithesis of the social insurance method that Cohen perceived as the most effective way to redistribute income in America.[57]

James Sundquist, the Brookings political scientist who had helped to create the program, later argued that the quick way in which it was passed left the poverty program with an "uncertain underpinning." It was the president's program, with few congressional proprietors. When it came under attack, as it did from many directions in a short time, there was no Lister Hill or John Fogarty or Wilbur Mills around to defend it. Those defenders it did have tended to concentrate on an individual component of the omnibus program and to favor appropriating money for that component alone. In effect, they wanted to protect parts of the program in the traditional manner, which in turn undercut the flexible approach that the economists hoped to bring to the problem. Although Cohen could do little to stop the legislative juggernaut in 1964, he spotted these and other problems in the program long before they came into public view. Cohen was an architect of the Great Society but not a defender of the War on Poverty.[58]

EDUCATION LEGISLATION

If nothing else, the enthusiasm for antipoverty legislation in 1964 helped to supply the rationale for the major breakthrough in education legislation that occurred in 1965. The same set of legislators had charge of both, and inevitably, the experience of passing one piece of legislation influenced their perceptions of the other. Congressman John Dent, who had helped to design an allocation formula for the community action title of the poverty bill, thought that this formula might also be useful in the stalled education legislation. He concurred in Sen. Wayne Morse's idea of adding a new category of payments based on the number of low-income families in a school district to the impacted-area law. Children in families in which the parents received welfare or unemployment compensation might qualify.

Both Dent and Morse saw political advantages to this approach. First, it was the sort of incremental expansion of an existing program that might not attract too much opposition. Second, the legislators reasoned that if payments were based on the number of poor children regardless of whether they attended public school, both public and parochial school interests might come to accept the approach. Moreover, Dent and other observers realized that the imminent passage of the Civil Rights Act (in July 1964) would ease southern fears about aid to education. Since Title VI "required nondiscrimination in any federally aided program," Cohen believed he could neutralize southern legislators by saying, "Well, the Civil Rights Act of 1964 is passed anyway. If you now vote to deny Federal aid to education, you are not helping yourself, you are just making it worse, because you might comply in some places and you might as well pick up that money."[59] Responding cautiously, the bureaucrats in the Department of Education agreed to provide technical assistance to Morse and Dent, yet they felt that if the approach had merit the administration should develop its own legislation and introduce it in the next Congress.[60]

The 1964 election results made Cohen feel more confident of victory on federal aid to education. President Johnson gave education legislation a high priority: "I want and I intend," he told his cabinet, "education to be the cornerstone on which we build this administration's program and record." According to John Gardner, who became Secretary of Health, Education, and Welfare in 1965, the president said early in the new administration, "Education is the number one priority in the country." "Well no other president had ever said that before," Gardner noted, "and it was an electrifying thing for a President to say."[61] Johnson pressured his staff and his cabinet to produce substantive legislative results. At one cabinet meeting in February 1965, he spoke of the importance of having a good legislative liaison in each department: "If we are to get our legislative program through," he said, "you must have heavyweights in these jobs—people with political sensitivity and substantive knowledge of your programs."[62]

Cohen qualified as a heavyweight. By the time Johnson spoke to his cabinet, Cohen had talked with key people in the department, the White House, the Bureau of the Budget, and the Congress about how to make the final push on federal aid to education. Dent's proposal, cosponsored with Morse and introduced in 1964, supplied the agreed-upon approach for the 1965 legislation.[63] No longer would the administration try to pass a general federal aid to education measure; instead, it would push the new idea that aid should go to children who lived in conditions of poverty. Francis Keppel, in the Office of Education, concurred in the decision that the Morse-Dent approach should take precedence over the old strategy of federal grants for classroom construction and teachers' salaries.[64] Within the Office of Education, experts on school finance began to draw up specific formulae that would link low family income in a school district with federal aid for education to that district.[65] As one historian of the measure put it, "So finally HEW dropped general aid to education for a poverty-oriented school bill."[66]

Cohen, Keppel, and the president received additional advice from an Education Task Force, headed by John Gardner, which reported soon after the election and included several ideas that would later find their way into federal legislation. In particular, Gardner proposed the creation of supplemental education centers, funded by federal grants to local school systems, that would help school districts deal with special problems by providing counseling and guidance centers or, perhaps, library services and a diagnostic reading center. The idea resembled the special education projects that had been discussed since at least 1963. Other Gardner proposals included urban university extension services that would focus on urban problems. In short, Gardner, like Cohen and Keppel, wanted to help the "disadvantaged segments of our population" by bringing them the benefits of education.[67] Indeed, Gardner later commented that the task force owed its success to the way in which HEW bureaucrats quickly picked up on its ideas. "Wilbur Cohen was in very close touch," Gardner said.[68]

John Gardner became a central figure in Cohen's life. During World War II, Gardner, who held a doctorate in psychology from Stanford, had joined the marines and worked in the OSS. After the war he took a job with the Carnegie Corporation, specializing in education policy. In the 1950s he emerged as a leading figure in the field, a natural choice to serve on blue-ribbon panels such as the one put together by the Rockefeller brothers and later the one that advised Kennedy during the 1960 transition. Cohen liked to compare John Gardner to John Winant, the first head of the Social Security Board. Both of these men, according to Cohen, had "the ability to infuse into an organization a sense of great leadership" that derived from the "mystique" that each of them had. Gardner was an intense man, given to aphorisms and to occasional outbursts of indignation and temper.[69]

Gardner's task force later was much celebrated by historians and other academics who applauded the application of expertise to the solution of social problems.[70] Cohen himself had trouble remembering the various task forces with which he had been associated: "They kind of telescope in my mind," he said.[71] The task forces in fact were not that important; for Cohen they were just one more incidental detail. Like the blue-ribbon commissions on which Gardner and Cohen had served during the 1950s, the Education Task Force owed its success to its restatement of the common wisdom and its contribution to an emerging consensus, not to its innovative proposals. Nor was the report the major source for the 1965 legislation, as Gardner readily admitted: "The formula—the final thing that broke the log jam—really came more out of Frank Keppel and perhaps Wayne Morse than it did out of the task force."[72]

Far more important to Cohen than Gardner's ideas were the predilections of President Johnson. After the election, Cohen found out what he could about Johnson's preferences during a State Department party. As Eloise chatted with Sen. Eugene McCarthy (D-Minn.), the president beckoned to Cohen. After the two discussed Medicare, LBJ asked Cohen if he had come up with a good education program; Cohen said that he had. Johnson wanted to know how much the program would cost, and the two men briefly batted around various proposals worth billions of dollars. Then the president told Cohen to be sure to keep him out of the parochial school issue.[73] According to Cohen's embellished account after the fact, the president said, "By the way, Wilbur, be sure that whatever you do you don't come out with something that's going to get me right in the middle of this religious controversy. I don't want to have the Baptists attacking me from one hand the Catholics from another." "Mr. President, I think we're working on something that will keep you out," Cohen replied. "That's the only thing I want you to keep in mind. That's the primary thing I want you to keep in mind," the president said.[74]

In later years, Cohen claimed credit for the idea of basing federal aid to education on the number of poor children in a school district. Like many ideas, however, it came from a number of different sources. Francis Keppel noted that the National Education Association, the Catholic groups, and he himself believed that they had started it. "I don't know," said Keppel; "it just got put together." Keppel's recollection indicated the strong forces that supported the idea; by buying into it, they gave it legitimacy and in effect created it. Cohen, however, continued to see the idea as distinctively his. In his account, he heard about Dent and Morse's bill, which based aid on the number of children receiving welfare or unemployment compensation, and then said that it would be better to substitute a simple income measure of poverty. In other words, aid should be based on the number of poor and hence educationally disadvantaged children in a particular district, regardless of whether they went to public or private school. Cohen claimed that he owed this idea to his studies of poverty at the University of Michigan.[75] It seems more likely that the idea reflected Cohen's careful reading of congressional sentiment and his desire to come up with a measure that would please all parties to the dispute.

According to Hugh Graham, President Johnson decided to move on education legislation in November 1964. After Thanksgiving, he talked with Celebrezze, Labor Secretary Willard Wirtz, Cohen, Keppel, Bill Moyers, and Bill Cannon from the Bureau of the Budget and gave his assent to "press ahead on the legislative strategy and program for education."[76] He wanted to introduce education legislation in January.

Cohen rushed to brief Congress on the details of the bill. Early in January Morse specifically asked that Cohen and Keppel meet with the Democrats on the Senate's education subcommittee so that they could obtain a "clear picture of the legislative components of the education program."[77] Within a matter of days, the House began consideration of the Elementary and Secondary Act. Doug Cater of the White House staff told LBJ at the end of January that the hearings were "going well."[78]

LBJ exhorted his staff to push Congress to move as quickly as possible. He wanted to slip as much legislation as he could through what he perceived to be a brief window of opportunity. During the period between February and June 1965, Cohen worked as hard as he ever had in his life. The legislative bonanza that would leave a distinctive mark on the American state was at hand. Cohen, normally extremely patient with the meanderings of Congress, wanted to close the books on stories that had taken a generation to write.

"Now look," Cohen remembered LBJ as saying at the beginning of 1965; "I've just been reelected by the overwhelming majority. And I just want to tell you that every day while I'm in office, I'm going to lose votes. I'm going to alienate somebody. . . . The President begins to lose power fast once he has been reelected, and I'm going to do that too. It's going to be something. . . . We've got to get this legislation fast. You've got to get it during my honeymoon."[79] Johnson had been elected to Congress at the height of the battle over Roosevelt's Court-packing plan and knew how fast legislative opportunities could fade. Cohen also understood. As one of his associates put it, "Wilbur Cohen recognized this singular moment in history. Several times during 1965 he told me to push the people I was working with as hard as I could, whether they protested or not; that we were to work any day, any hour, to do whatever was necessary to pass the legislation."[80]

Unlike his young associate, Cohen had witnessed another legislative blitz in 1935, and no doubt one situation reminded him of the other; there were, however, important differences. In 1935 Congress dealt with legislation that the president and his agents either wrote themselves or with legislation that concerned subjects of relatively recent origin. In 1965 Congress handled legislation that had been developed over a longer period of time and bore more of Congress' imprint. The 1935 Social Security Act contained a number of proposals, such as old-age insurance, that were almost completely new. The Elementary and Secondary Education Act of 1965 and Medicare reflected legislative transformations of proposals long under consideration. Both sets of legislation bore the distinctive imprints of their era. The legislation of 1935 reflected the concern for jobs and income security; the legislation that followed thirty years later built on this drive for security but added the new goal of opportunity. The New Deal concerned security for those people in the labor force, and the Great Society centered on bringing opportunity to those outside the labor force.

In 1965 Cohen, with little time to reflect on broad intellectual trends, instead put himself through a succession of impossibly long days. His staff members told of having to arrive at 8:15 in the morning in order to see him for a few minutes before he began making phone calls to the Hill, the White House, or other places in his policy network. Cohen's phone logs from this period showed the extent of this network. On a typical day in March 1965 he received calls from three different congressmen, from lawyer Lloyd Cutler, from staff members in Sen. Fred Harris's (D-Okla.) and Congressman Adam Clayton Powell's offices, from HEW officials Robert Ball and Francis Keppel, from Bill Moyers in the White House, and from Loula Dunn of the American Public Welfare Association. Cohen returned the call to Adam Clayton Powell's office at 7:30 in the evening. By then, if the day were like most days, he had probably come back from a meeting or from the Hill at 6:30 and then begun to make other calls and talk with members of his staff.[81]

In step with the frenzied legislative atmosphere in 1965, the education legislation sped through Congress. As expected, Carl Perkins took control of the elementary and secondary education bill and did what he could to expedite the proceedings. Douglas Cater, watching from the White House, learned that Perkins would do "nothing to harm the package" and that Adam Clayton Powell was "obliging." Cohen hoped that the House would pass the bill quickly and then the Senate, without need for a conference. He met with key senators, such as Robert Kennedy, in February in an effort to smooth out problems before they arose. Cohen, in common with others who had watched education legislation over the years, wanted to avoid a situation "so complicated that the whole bill gets lost."[82]

The situation did get complicated, in part because the issues were complex. The trick was to obtain agreement before the euphoric postelection bubble burst, and the entire gestalt changed. The participants were haunted by the possibility of a sudden shift in scene in which consensus turned to conflict. Cohen and Keppel worked with Henry Wilson of the White House congressional liaison staff, with Cater of the White House staff, and with Des Marais of Cohen's office to keep matters under control. Any change needed to be evaluated in light of its potential to upset the fragile consensus on the bill.

It was basically a matter of money. Nonsoutherners, such as Sen. Robert Kennedy and Congressmen Phillip Burton (D-Calif.), Powell, Dent, and

Pucinski, objected to the formula in Title I, which based aid to local school districts, intended to meet the special needs of educationally deprived children, on the number of children in families with incomes under $2,000. Each school district would be eligible for payments equal to one-half the average per pupil expenditure in that state multiplied by the number of children in families with annual incomes under $2,000. That idea had been the Cohen masterstroke, the great simplification of a politically contentious matter. Northern congressmen thought it a bit too simple and wondered about their constituents in New York, or Los Angeles, or Chicago who were on welfare and whose income thus might rise above $2,000 and reduce the subsidy to the city schools. If the formula were changed, however, then southerners, with fewer people on welfare and lower welfare benefits in their districts, might object. Lawrence O'Brien admitted that the formula as written was slanted toward the southern states; indeed, Texas got almost as much as New York. As Cohen put it, the objections of these legislators had merit but had to be handled "so as not to run into opposition from the southerners."[83]

The bill also contained the potential for religious controversy. The second title of the bill concerned school library resources, textbooks, and other instructional materials. Representatives from Protestant districts wondered if the title permitted federal funds to be used to purchase books that would serve religious purposes in Catholic schools. A New York congressman from a heavily Jewish district worried that Jewish children would have to read about Christmas celebrations in their primers.[84]

Everyone who tracked the bill was concerned that it would fall apart, just as it always had. Beyond the real issues of religion and resource allocation, there were the eccentricities of Adam Clayton Powell and the impetuous demands of Congressman Green to consider. Powell came through, pushing his committee hard to mark up the bill early in February, and then, just when he was about to get it through the committee, he canceled a meeting and did not answer phone calls from Speaker John McCormack or from Lawrence O'Brien. O'Brien, for his part, began to think of ways to take the committee away from Powell, keeping it in session without his presence. As O'Brien tried to track him down he held his breath. The situation looked good, O'Brien told the president, but the "religious matter continues to be troublesome. . . . And it's hard to believe we'll get through this without racial troubles." Congressman Landrum shared O'Brien's concerns and worried about a last-minute flare-up of the religious issue.[85]

Reflecting the heavy influence of urban interests on Powell's committee, the House made some substantive changes in the administration's bill. The northerners on the committee managed to modify Title I—grants for education of children of lower-income families–to take families of welfare recipients into account. The congressmen also sought to ensure that all textbooks purchased by federal money became the property of a public school district and then be lent to private schools. Other titles included supplementary educational centers and services, as proposed by John Gardner, grants for educational research and training, and grants to state departments of education. The big title, however, was the first one, to which Congress authorized more than $1 billion. It received the most intense scrutiny from Judge Smith and William Colmer (D-Miss.) of the Rules Committee when they considered the legislation in March.[86]

Congress adjusted the legislation but did not derail it. It was early in the legislative session; the battle over the Civil Rights Act was over; Congress owed the president a quick response to one of his most urgent requests. The Senate, as promised, passed the House bill and inserted the views of individual senators in the committee reports and in the floor debate but not in the bill itself. That cleared the way for President Johnson to sign the bill, in a typically dramatic manner, in April. Speaking before one of his elementary school teachers and some of his old classmates, Johnson said that no law he would ever sign would "mean more to the future of America."[87]

Cohen, still trying to get Congress to pass Medicare and many other bills, did not linger over the education bill. The window of legislative opportunity remained open, and more measures needed to be shoved through it. Even after the passage of the Elementary and Secondary Education Act (ESEA), the education committees in Congress, along with Cohen, continued to work through the summer on what became the Higher Education Act (HEA) of 1965. It included urban land-grant extension, taken from the Gardner task force; aid for university research libraries; aid to black colleges; and programs, such as guaranteed student loans, that provided financial assistance to students attending college.[88]

In time the money began to pour into the local school districts and the nation's universities. In the fall of 1966 the Johnson administration heralded the actions of the "great Congress," the one of "great achievement," that passed over 90 percent of the 200 major recommendations that the president had sent to it. Education headed the list. The Eighty-ninth Congress "broke through the roadblock that had stymied federal aid to elementary and secondary schools," and it provided federal scholarships to college students. If one believed the figures provided by White House staffers Joseph Califano and Lawrence O'Brien in 1966, then the Elementary and Secondary Education Act benefited 7 million disadvantaged youngsters and nearly 49 million children through the grants for libraries and textbooks. In just one year, the Higher

Education Act provided 134,000 scholarships to college students and helped 190,000 students with work-study assistance.[89]

For Lyndon Johnson it has been said that these numbers were sources of satisfaction in and of themselves. As subsequent observers have pointed out, however, there is no assurance that the 7 million students who received funds from the ESEA actually gained tangible benefits from the experience. The education legislation, like the poverty bill, would soon become embroiled in a major controversy over whether it authorized enough money for its purposes or whether that money was well spent.[90] Cohen, for his part, inhabited a world in which the passage of the legislation was the ultimate reward. He regarded the ESEA as a triumph if for no other reason than the fact that the administration had managed to get it through Congress. He realized that basing aid on the number of poor children in a school district served as an indirect way of beginning federal aid to education, yet it also provided a way around the objections of Catholics and, to a more limited extent, of southerners.[91] Of course, the passage of the law, itself an incremental product of discussions between 1961 and 1965, permanently altered the dynamics of federal aid to education. After 1965 Congress no longer debated the issue in terms of classroom and teacher shortages and the level of teachers' salaries; instead, these real concerns became subsumed under a concern for the disadvantaged child.[92] For Cohen, who trusted in the benevolence of the legislative process, the changes constituted a reasonable price to pay for breaking down the barriers against federal aid to education.

Although Cohen trusted in the legislative process to produce useful results, he fought a rearguard action from within the administration against the War on Poverty. He feared it was too weak a foundation for future legislation. With his usual resilience, he was nonetheless able to synthesize the lessons he had learned from the formulation of the War on Poverty and to apply them to the field of education. Unlike Lawrence O'Brien and others who worked on congressional liaison, Cohen functioned as more than a lobbyist, coaxing the members to pass the administration's program. Versed in the details of social welfare programs, he possessed a panoramic view of social policy. Because he worked in so many areas, he could spot emerging trends more quickly than a program specialist who was limited to one field. Hence, he could move easily from the War on Poverty to the Elementary and Secondary Education Act.

The exact level of Cohen's influence on this act is impossible to measure. The very fact that so many people claim credit for Title I of the measure indicates the strong consensus that underlay the effort. It is abundantly clear, however, that Cohen, alone among the department's top leaders, was there from Kennedy's original proposals to Johnson's final triumphs. The secretary's job turned over;

so did the job of commissioner of education. The president's advisers changed from Sorensen and Myer Feldman to Doug Cater and Bill Moyers. Through all the changes, Cohen provided a source of continuity and kept the conversation going, even if he neither dominated nor monopolized it.

And through it all Cohen never lost his sense of wonder, his amazement that he should be moving in such circles. A high point in the battle for education legislation came in the campaign summer of 1964. One August afternoon Cohen attended a briefing for Democratic governors and sat between Walter Heller and Kermit Gordon, director of the Bureau of the Budget. When the governors started a political discussion, Jack Valenti asked Cohen to leave. With Frank Keppel, Cohen started to wander about the White House, playing with the lights, dimming them, sitting in the Red Room, like children exploring Disneyland. Later that night, Cohen returned to attend a formal White House dinner for the governors. Afterward, he walked into the reception hall, where Averill Harriman came up to him and said hello. Cohen then spotted Governor Reynolds of Wisconsin and had coffee with him in the Red Room. Reynolds remarked that he had seen Aaron Cohen in Milwaukee, who told him how proud he was of Wilbur. It was the perfect compliment delivered in a perfect manner in a perfect setting. No doubt Cohen felt a sense of satisfaction as he led Mrs. Fortas around the dance floor while Abe Fortas danced with Mrs. Johnson.[93]

It was a rare moment of glamour in a life of twelve-hour days spent largely in the service of others. Cohen seldom inflated his importance; he was a servant of the administration. Still, one could not remain unchanged by the proximity to the White House or by the experience of fighting such a prolonged battle to secure a piece of legislation. Wilbur Cohen, the son of a Milwaukee grocer, had gone to dinner at the White House, where the son of a fabulously rich railroad magnate, who was himself a big-time figure on Wall Street and the former governor of New York, had personally greeted him.

Even in the narrow professional sense by which Cohen defined himself, passage of education legislation had a transforming effect on him, altering his professional identity. He began the Kennedy-Johnson years as an expert on aging, Medicare, and Social Security. By 1969 he had become an expert in education policy, and he felt comfortable enough to take a job as the University of Michigan's Dean of Education. In the interim, he helped to pass a series of laws, including the Elementary and Secondary Education Act of 1965, that greatly expanded and redefined the federal role in education.

MEDICARE– LEGISLATIVE TRIUMPH

Congress took slightly longer to pass Medicare than to approve the Elementary and Secondary Education Act. It had hesitated to tamper with the administration's education bill for fear of undoing a delicate political deal, but Wilbur Mills continued to exercise considerable personal discretion over Medicare, right up to the final minute of passage. Despite Cohen's best efforts, Mills succeeded in blocking Medicare, and only in 1965, after the 1964 presidential landslide, did he change his mind. Having made the switch, Mills became not only a supporter of Medicare but its leading advocate in the House of Representatives.[1]

Once Mills decided to endorse Medicare, he knew he could rely on Cohen to help him fashion a law to his specifications. Mills personally directed the writing of the Medicare bill, although Cohen was in the room, quite involved, the point of contact between Mills and the lawyers who drafted it. But it was Mills, not Cohen, who put the final legislative transformation into the bill. Cohen, who maintained he was the true author of the 1965 education legislation, never once claimed to be anything other than Mills's lieutenant in the 1965 Medicare legislation. For him, the story behind passage of Medicare involved the wooing of Wilbur Mills after so many years of unsuccessful courtship.

SENATE PASSAGE, HOUSE DEFEAT

At the beginning of 1964 the new administration, like the old one, did not know if it could get a Medicare bill through the Ways and Means Committee. One possibility was that Mills would report a Social Security bill that did not contain Medicare. If so, the situation would be similar to 1962, with the administration trying to pass the measure in the Senate and then attempting to get some form of it through Mills in the conference committee. The legislative situation indeed was more complicated in 1964 than in 1962 because of the possibility that the administration might succeed in passing a tax cut. If that happened, President Johnson would not want the increased payroll taxes for Medicare to undercut the effect of the tax cut on the economy.[2]

At the heart of it all was Mills, who had become like some sort of Chinese puzzle that the administration needed to solve. In 1964, as Mills prepared to resume hearings on health insurance, he appeared to have more interest than before in fashioning a health insurance bill, one that would be acceptable to his committee and to the administration. Still, he worried that hospital costs would keep rising faster than wages. Taxes on working Americans would have to keep going up to pay for the hospital stays of retired Americans. As costs went up, it would be harder and harder to keep the Social Security system, including the cash benefits, solvent. Adopting the prevailing puzzle metaphor, Lawrence O'Brien told President Johnson, "This actuarial soundness thing is likely crucial to solving Mills."[3]

Johnson was in the first flush of full activity, reaching out to the various constituencies that would define his presidency. Among those with whom he met early in 1964 were leaders of senior citizens' organizations. Ivan Nestingen and Ray Henry, one of Nestingen's supporters in the White House, arranged the details of the meeting with the guest list including Celebrezze, Nelson Cruikshank, and Robert Ball. Not on the guest list, Cohen went anyway; Celebrezze simply took him. At the gathering, Johnson endorsed Medicare and worked the crowd, kissing Elizabeth Wickenden on the cheek. The meeting was an indication both of Johnson's strong interest in Medicare and of Cohen's refusal to be shut out of the policy action.[4]

As the 1964 legislative session began, Cohen, although fully occupied by both the poverty and education legislation, kept his eye on Medicare. He became bolder in his dealings with his rival, Nestingen, at one point writing him a note reprimanding him for issuing a memorandum without Celebrezze's approval. In a pointed rebuke to a nominal superior, Cohen told Nestingen that he was writing at Celebrezze's specific request.[5] Even as he attended to Nestingen, he also kept track of the legislative situation, noticing that Jacob Javits had introduced the latest version of his health insurance bill. Closely modeled on the recommendations of Javits's commission, the bill differed only slightly from the administration's King-Anderson bill. Nelson Cruikshank said that Javits had made a "real contribution" to the debate.[6] Another Republican proposal that surfaced in January 1964 contained the old idea, associated with potential Republican presidential candidate Nelson Rockefeller, of a choice or option between Medicare on the one hand and increased cash benefits to purchase private health insurance on the other.

The two 1964 liberal Republican measures differed from one another in subtle ways. The Javits bill gave Social Security beneficiaries no choice about accepting Medicare. Rockefeller's bill, introduced by Congressmen John Lindsay (later to be mayor of New York), offered a choice between public or private hospital insurance. The Javits bill, unlike the Rockefeller bill, had a mechanism to encourage the purchase of supplementary private insurance to cover doctors' bills and other expenses not handled by Medicare. Javits wanted this insurance to be private but nonprofit, and he hoped it would be available at low cost. Javits, like Rockefeller, believed that he could appease both senior citizens and private insurance companies, arguing that his complementary "national private insurance program" provided a "built-in limit" to the expansion of Medicare. The government would be limited to hospital insurance and prevented from paying for doctors' bills.[7]

Although Cohen did not see either the Javits or the Rockefeller bills as the solution to the Medicare puzzle, he began to grow more optimistic that it could be solved. He did not know how the private insurance companies would react to the Javits proposal and noted, too, that neither of the Republican bills had caught the interest of Mills or any of the Republicans on the Ways and Means Committee. At the same time, Cohen started to sense that the legislative process was gaining momentum.

At the end of January 1964 Cohen reported to the White House that the public hearings on Medicare had ended and that Mills was preparing to take his committee into executive sessions to discuss the issue. Privately, Mills told Cohen that he might report a bill by late March or April. The pattern fit the usual pace of Social Security legislation. Mills wanted some sort of bill for the Democrats to take into the 1964 elections.[8]

On February 5 Cohen met with the president to discuss LBJ's health message with Celebrezze, Elmer Staats of the Bureau of the Budget, Myer Feldman, and Henry Hall Wilson of the Legislative Liaison Office. Inside the Oval Office, Feldman handed Johnson a draft of the health message. Unlike Kennedy, who would have read it, Johnson sat passively and glanced at the text in front of him. Then he started to talk politics and wanted to know how Celebrezze and Cohen were progressing with Mills. Cohen told the president that he had had three different meetings with Mills and believed that there was an excellent chance that he would report out a bill with hospital insurance in it.[9]

Five days after the meeting, Cohen had the responsibility of giving a background press briefing on the President's Message on Health at the White

House. "The fundamental principles have been agreed upon . . . that [Medicare] should only cover hospitalization, leaving private enterprise the supplementation of physicians' services," he said. The issues had "worked themselves out," according to Cohen, who noted that for the first time in thirteen years, he felt confident of Medicare's passage. A reporter wanted to know if the administration could pass Medicare without Mills's support. "Any discussions that did not include Wilbur Mills would not be very important discussions," Cohen replied.[10]

In February the president put Cohen, not Nestingen or Celebrezze, in full charge of the administration's effort to pass Medicare. Johnson called Cohen and told him to meet with Mills and work out a bill that Mills and organized labor could support. The next month Larry O'Brien telephoned Cohen and repeated the instructions: the president wanted Cohen to get together with Mills and negotiate a hospital insurance bill.[11] Early in April Cohen prepared for daily executive sessions of the Ways and Means Committee to consider Medicare, benefit increases in Social Security, and the Kerr-Mills program, expecting about six weeks of intensive work. It was almost as if he were back in his old job working for Arthur Altmeyer and trying to pass the 1950 Social Security amendments. The difference was that he was reporting to the president, not the commissioner of Social Security, and that in 1965, unlike in 1950, he had to stay abreast of developments in education, the War on Poverty, and scores of other legislative items. "I am still optimistic that we can work something constructive out with Wilbur Mills—but only time will tell," Cohen told his former colleague Falk.[12]

A period of crushing staff work followed. Once again Mills put Cohen and the staff of the Social Security Administration through its paces, demanding background memos on all sorts of policy alternatives and cost estimates for many varieties of changes in the Social Security program. Among many other details, the staff worked up a plan for Mills that became the first draft of a new program to provide health insurance for welfare recipients. It would become known as Medicaid, and its origins would become so obscure that even Wilbur Cohen would lose track of them.[13]

Mills apparently had not yet made up his mind about Medicare, and in his ambivalence he kept probing various options and proposals. "Mills has been reasonably cooperative," Cohen told Sorensen in May; "I've worked out a number of solutions. I hope he will take one but I wouldn't be sure until the last minute."[14] On May 5, for example, Cohen worked with Mills on a plan that included an option to elect higher cash benefits or hospital benefits and that used Blue Cross as an intermediary.[15] On May 15 Mills called Cohen at 6:30 P.M. to ask him whether he had spoken with Walter McNerney of Blue Cross about the company's serving in that capacity. "No," Cohen replied, reminding Mills that he had asked him to wait. Mills then said that he wanted to sell McNerney on the idea of Blue Cross' administering the hospital insurance plan, provided that the hospitals were not to receive more than 99 percent of their costs. He argued that if the law were written that way, then no private insurance company could be the administering agent; instead, the nonprofit Blue Cross plans across the nation would assume that role. After listening to Mills, Cohen called Robert Ball, who agreed that Mills's suggestion was a brilliant way of meeting Celebrezze's and Cruikshank's concerns over the involvement of private insurance companies in Medicare and also of obtaining the support of Blue Cross for the program.[16]

In the middle of these discussions with Mills, Cohen took the time to reply to a routine letter in which the writer complained that Cohen was a proponent of socialized medicine. It was an old charge, and he had long since developed a rote response stressing the conservative nature of Social Security. It was particularly ironic that Cohen, who was making every conceivable effort to placate Mills, should be accused of being a radical; hence, he found it appropriate to add a few lines to his routine reply. "May I say in passing," he wrote, "that I do not really think I am a frustrated professor nor do I think that I am one of those whose single-minded purpose is to socialize medicine. Nor do I think I have been inflexible."[17]

On May 22 Cohen traveled on the president's plane to Ann Arbor where Johnson was scheduled to give the commencement address. It was to be an important occasion in which, as Theodore White later wrote, the phrase "Great Society was elevated to capital letters in the text and hoisted by Lyndon Johnson as the banner over his purpose."[18] During the plane ride, LBJ–aide Jack Valenti invited Cohen into the president's cabin, where Cohen found Johnson seated at a desk across from Sen. Pat McNamara. The president asked Cohen how negotiations were going with Mills, and Cohen said he was hopeful. McNamara then flew into a rage, claiming that the compromise bill, with its various options and its expansion of the Kerr-Mills program, had a means test in it. Each time Cohen explained that there was no means test, McNamara interrupted him, exclaiming that he would never vote for the bill. Johnson listened patiently and quietly. When Cohen asked the president whether he would like to read a summary of the bill, Johnson replied that he would. Cohen, in characteristic manner, had one in his pocket and handed it to the president. He told Johnson that he believed fewer than fifteen congressmen would vote against Mills's bill, which he expected would be completed in two or three weeks.[19]

As Cohen waited for Mills to complete his bill, he met with the economists, seeking to convince them that health insurance, an expansion of Kerr-Mills, and a Social Security benefit increase would not burden the economy or negate the effects of the 1964 tax cut. He realized that it made little sense to raise a worker's takehome pay through the general tax cut and simultaneously to lower it through increased deductions for Social Security. In general, Cohen favored raising the wage base on which workers paid Social Security taxes rather than raising the level of the taxes themselves. In this manner, lower-income workers would not be affected by the legislation, since their payroll deductions would remain the same, yet substantial revenues would be generated. Cohen told Celebrezze that raising the earnings base to $12,000 would fully finance Medicare and the other provisions that might come from Mills.[20]

At this point, Cohen still believed that Mills would come out in favor of Medicare. "Despite what you read in the newspapers," Cohen told Altmeyer at the end of May, "I think still we have a better than 50–50 chance to get Wilbur Mills to go along with the principle of insuring some hospital costs under social security." Cohen confided that the work had been trying, not so much because of Mills but because of "our liberal friends continually giving me the advice – don't sell out on any bad compromise." Should the effort fail, Cohen noted, the liberals would then say that he should have compromised more. "The whole experience," he noted, "has certainly led me to get annoyed at the professional liberal who has such easy slogans for both victory and defeat." Despite Cohen's annoyance and his volatility as Congress stood on the verge of a major decision, he remained, in his words, "a perennial optimist" who looked forward to the appearance of a "reasonably good package" from Mills.[21]

The situation remained fluid in early June. Mills kept juggling various proposals, constantly changing the size of the deductible, the age at which a person would become eligible for Medicare, and the amount of the increase in cash benefits for Social Security beneficiaries. Cohen continued in his role as the administration's seer. He would present Mills with twelve to fifteen variations on the Medicare plan and then predict which of these combinations would most appeal to him. Meanwhile, Cohen tried to pressure as many other members of the Ways and Means Committee as he could, without at the same time offending Mills.[22]

By June 9 the negotiations with Mills had become intense, and Cohen met with Speaker John McCormack and other congressional leaders in an effort to decide on policy. At one point, Congressman Eugene Keogh (D-N.Y.) asked Mills what he intended to vote on the next day. "I am only the Chairman of the Committee," Mills snapped. "It is up to somebody else to make the motion." Mills, as usual, was evasive, and he quickly absented himself from the meeting. Hale Boggs, the majority whip, suggested that the president invite the Democrats on the Ways and Means Committee to the White House that evening, so

McCormack decided to call Johnson. When McCormack reached him, the Speaker learned that the president had already spoken with Mills that morning, who told him that the committee was making progress. Still, Mills would make no specific commitments. After the meeting, Nelson Cruikshank and Andy Biemiller of the AFL-CIO went to see Mills, who told them that he wanted to talk with John Watts (D-Ky.) and A. Sidney Herlong (D-Fla.) before he brought Medicare to a vote. At about the same time, Cohen learned that Watts, normally a reliable Mills ally, might not vote in favor of Medicare because of pressure from the AMA and the tobacco industry.[23]

Then the delicate situation fell apart. Perhaps because Congressman Watts announced that he could not support the measure, Medicare never came up for a vote in the Ways and Means Committee in 1964. As journalists Rowland Evans and Robert Novak put it, "Medical care proponents avoided a roll call vote rather than suffer sure defeat." In the end, for whatever reason, Mills could not bring himself to vote for Medicare, and his opposition effectively killed the measure in the House. Evans and Novak reported that Cohen was "deeply shocked" by what had happened; his long courtship of Wilbur Mills had ended in rejection.[24]

Instead of Medicare, Mills's committee reported a traditional Social Security bill, with a benefit increase but without any changes in the Kerr-Mills program. The only victory for the administration came in defeating a measure to raise Social Security benefits by 6 percent (the final bill contained a 5 percent increase), which would have made it hard for the Senate to add Medicare to the final bill.[25] Cohen tried not to brood in public. Pausing only momentarily, he proceeded to outline two possible strategies, first for the Senate Finance Committee and later for the entire Senate to follow. One was simply to add the administration Medicare bill to the House bill in the hope that Mills might agree to a compromise plan in conference. The other strategy was for the Senate, either in the Finance Committee or in an amendment to the bill on the floor, to pass a modified Medicare measure offering individuals a choice between accepting the Social Security benefit increase or health insurance. Cohen believed that Mills might accept the second strategy without even going to conference.[26]

Both strategies had their share of complications. If Medicare were simply added to the House bill, with its increase in cash benefits, then the cost of the bill became considerable. Social Security tradition required that future tax rates be written into current legislation. That meant, according to the actuarial rules developed by Robert J. Myers and cleared with Wilbur Mills, that the 1964 law would have to specify, for example, a 1971 combined tax on employers and employees of 11 percent of the first $6,600 of an employee's wages. Nor was it at all certain that Mills would agree to such a plan. The second strategy would be complicated to administer and might also be very expensive.[27]

Cohen realized that he needed advice from the president on how to handle the situation. He asked Larry O'Brien to arrange a meeting with Celebrezze and the president, which took place on July 16. LBJ came into the Oval Office, sat down in a rocking chair, and asked Celebrezze what he thought of the Republican convention, which would nominate Barry Goldwater. Then LBJ asked, "What are we going to do about Medicare?" Celebrezze began to summarize the long negotiations with Wilbur Mills. Before he could get too far, a woman came in and brought the president a pile of items from the press ticker, which LBJ immediately began to read. He offered his guests refreshments, ordered a large orange drink for himself, and then asked again about Medicare. Larry O'Brien gave the president two memos that Cohen had prepared on the two strategies, saying that they were complicated. As he started to explain them, LBJ asked, "What do you want me to do?" Cohen took over. He told the president that the important point was to get a commitment from Mills either to accept a compromise version in conference or to accept a substitute version of Medicare without going to conference. Johnson continued to show little interest in the substantive issues, which were, in fact, inordinately complex. He had started to look at Cohen's memos but soon forgot about them and rolled them up in his large hands. Cohen said that only the president could get a commitment from Mills, and LBJ replied that he had not been very successful in getting Mills committed to anything. The president then ended the meeting, walking into the next office, joking with the secretaries.[28]

The meeting made it clear that neither the president nor Lawrence O'Brien could offer Cohen much guidance. Just as it appeared that he would have to act completely alone, Abraham Ribicoff, who had been elected to the Senate in 1962 and who was familiar with the issue from his HEW days, stepped in as a major player. He told the president that the Mills increase in Social Security benefits would be difficult for the senators to vote against; increasing the payroll taxes to pay for the benefit increase would, however, put a "real squeeze on Medicare." Ribicoff therefore proposed the option plan that Cohen and Ball had developed. As he explained, "This achieves health insurance under social security, keeps the cash benefit increase of the Mills bill for those who prefer it, and makes medicare available to all but not forced on anyone." Ribicoff, still a freshman senator, knew enough to defer to Clinton Anderson on the issue. As he told Anderson, he remained hopeful that the New Mexico senator's bill could be passed, yet if that were not possible, it would be a "mistake to see the Mills Bill passed without any other effort being made to include hospital insurance."[29]

Above all, as Ribicoff noted, the administration supporters needed to be in complete agreement or the Medicare measure would come undone, as it had in 1962. It was Cohen who had to maintain the agreement. He talked with Senator Anderson's staffer and assured him that Ribicoff's proposal was receiving serious attention but that no final draft amendment had been prepared. Cohen also remained in touch with Senators Smathers and Long and from his conversations with them concluded that it would be better to fight for Medicare on the floor of the Senate rather than in the Finance Committee.[30]

For the third straight time, it appeared that a dramatic battle over the expansion of Social Security would occur on the floor of the Senate in a presidential election year. As the Senate carefully worked its way around election-year recesses for the political conventions and as the Senate Finance Committee held hearings that did not begin until August 6, Cohen focused his attention on the conference committee, trying to determine whether Mills would accept Medicare in conference. By August 13 he had decided that Mills would not and wrote O'Brien that he had received three separate reports that "under no circumstances" would Mills accede to Medicare in a conference committee. To Cohen that meant it was desirable to have the bill pass the Senate in a form that would "give the least grounds for objection to Mills." That, in turn, implied that the Senate should pass some variation on what was now called the Ribicoff amendment—which offered the choice between a benefit increase and Medicare—rather than some variation on what was now called the Gore amendment—which was most similar to the administration's original King-Anderson bill.[31]

The administration gathered that the Senate leaders on Medicare, such as Mike Mansfield, Hubert Humphrey, Clinton Anderson, and Ribicoff, favored the Ribicoff approach. As Anderson told Mike Manatos of the White House legislative liaison staff, King-Anderson was a hard vote for many Democratic senators in an election year. The Ribicoff amendment, in contrast, made an attractive campaign issue because it was voluntary and elective. The senators also cautioned that rather than pass a benefit increase without Medicare, the increase should simply die; if it became operative, claimed the senators, then medical care would be lost for all time.[32]

A week later, the Senate Finance Committee had reported out a largely unchanged version of the Mills bill, the Democrats had held their convention, and the full Senate was preparing to take up Medicare. Even at this late date, Cohen did not know whether the Gore or the Ribicoff amendment would be offered. He leaned against the Gore amendment because its Senate passage might "give Mr. Mills the basis to argue that a Ribicoff-type compromise is not in conference." Cohen also noted that Senator Long might offer a third amendment that would increase Social Security benefits above the 5 percent in the House bill and in so doing, "certainly hurt the chances of obtaining Medicare."[33]

As matters turned out, Long did offer his amendment, which put the pro-Medicare forces into considerable disarray. Humphrey (the Democrat's vice-presidential candidate by virtue of the previous week's convention), Gore (D-Tenn.), Anderson, and Cohen then whipped up another version of Medicare. In his memoirs, Senator Anderson described Cohen, who sat in on the strategy meetings in a position of full equality with the senators, as "the government's chief expert on Social Security arithmetic in general and on Medicare in particular." The senators needed expert help quickly, and Cohen, with his connections both to the White House and to Ball and the SSA, was able to supply it. He put together an amendment that included a flat $7 increase in Social Security benefits with Medicare built in on top of that, with an accompanying wage base of $5,600 and an ultimate combined contribution rate of 10.4 percent. Senator Gore (father of the future vice-president) offered this version on August 31 as a substitute to the Long amendment.[34]

The Senate passed Gore's amendment, complete with the provisions for Medicare, on September 2. Cohen experienced a feeling of elation after the Senate vote, recognizing that an important milestone had been reached. The politics worked well for the Democrats, since Barry Goldwater, the Republican presidential candidate, cast one of the votes against the amendment. The Democrats had succeeded in making Medicare a campaign issue, but there were still considerable problems to be worked out with Wilbur Mills. If Medicare were to become law, Mills would have to accept some sort of compromise in conference even though he had already signaled his reluctance to do so.[35] On September 10 Cohen went to see Mills and talked with him for two hours about the Senate-passed bill.[36]

The House and the Senate assembled their conferees. On the Senate side, Russell Long assured his colleagues that although he had not voted for the Gore-Anderson amendment, he would nonetheless uphold the Senate's position in favor of Medicare. Long told administration officials that he was leaning toward some sort of compromise position in the manner of the Ribicoff amendment on which the Senate had never voted. Senator Gore contemplated killing the whole bill rather than agreeing to a benefit increase without Medicare.[37]

Cohen, Ball, and Sidney Saperstein, a departmental lawyer, drafted another compromise to which they hoped to get Mills's assent. This plan involved two elements: the first was the creation of a Medicare trust fund, separate from the rest of Social Security, into which the working population would pay and from which this population would eventually receive Medicare; the second involved the retired population, which would have the option of deducting payments for Medicare from its Social Security benefits.[38]

The immediate issue hinged on whether Mills could be convinced that such a compromise plan was "in conference." The parliamentarian advised Mills that the plan would be subject to a "point of order" in the House. Despite the admonitions of Gore, Anderson, Hale Boggs, and Cecil King (D-Calif.), Mills said that he was unwilling to ask the Rules Committee for a rule waiving "points of order in the House debate." On September 24 Cohen, along with Saperstein, met with the House parliamentarian, Speaker McCormack, and majority leader Carl Albert to see if anything could be done to overcome Mills's objections. They fiddled with a number of complicated, legalistic suggestions, and as Saperstein recalled, "I don't remember what the ruling was, but Wilbur Mills wouldn't go along with it." That ended the matter.[39]

The conference committee adjourned, and no Social Security bill was passed in 1964. The Democrats decided to go into the election without an increase in the program's benefits to offer the voter, perhaps figuring they did not need this bit of largesse to win. Barry Goldwater, after all, had entertained the idea of making Social Security private, and he had voted against Medicare on the Senate floor in September. As Theodore White noted, "Out of the vast mass of his many statements, [the Democrats] chose to hook and hang [Goldwater] on one issue: Social Security."[40]

FINAL PREPARATIONS

When Johnson won the election, he might have used his 150-vote margin to work around Wilbur Mills and pass Medicare. Apparently, that strategy never occurred to the president, who saw no point in antagonizing Mills.[41] Late in 1964 Cohen began one last inclusive sweep of his policy apparatus to write the plan that everyone hoped would be the definitive version of Medicare. The starting point was the plan that Cohen and Ball had prepared for Mills to use in the conference committee that had failed to reach an agreement. Even as this plan became modified, certain of its features remained in the law that Congress eventually passed. In particular, Cohen and his colleagues decided to retain the idea of a separate hospital insurance trust fund, as "suggested by Mr. Mills." "We could then say that hospital insurance was financed under *social insurance* rather than under Social Security," explained Cohen to the secretary.[42]

Although Cohen did not try to push Mills, he did insist that Medicare go the head of the legislative agenda. When Cohen saw the president after the election,

Johnson told him that Medicare would be our "number one priority" and expressed his hope that Mills would make Medicare the first item of business in the Ways and Means Committee. Two days later, the president talked with Cohen again and urged him to "touch base with everyone concerned" and to inform everyone in the cabinet about Medicare. He clearly wanted to move on Medicare and make it part of the legislative blitz for 1965.[43] Senator Anderson also urged Cohen to "put all possible speed and effort into the preparation of a new King-Anderson version." Anderson informed Cohen that he intended to introduce Medicare as Senate bill 1 and thought that Congressman Cecil King would get a low number for his Medicare bill as well. Anderson asked Cohen to send him copies of completed bills so that "I can check them." In this manner, Anderson deferred to Cohen and his policy apparatus on the style and on much of the content of the bill.[44] At the same time, Cohen was in touch with the leadership in the House, urging Speaker John McCormack formally to designate the Medicare bill as HR1. That, along with a change of membership in the Ways and Means Committee, would "assure very early passage of the bill," Cohen hoped. He also informed the Speaker that although the members of Cohen's policy apparatus wished to defer to Wilbur Mills, they felt no need to accede to all his wishes. If Mills wanted a separate tax for hospital insurance, for example, he would have to obtain it on his own.[45]

Setting to work on the new bill, Cohen met first with Robert Ball and then with Nelson Cruikshank. Together they fashioned the specifications for the latest in a seemingly infinite series of drafts of Medicare legislation. Actuaries, led by Robert Myers, and lawyers, led by Sidney Saperstein, fleshed out the details.[46] On November 24 Cohen had a summary of the bill ready for the president, the Speaker, Senator Anderson, and Congressman King. The bill included three of the prominent features that had been added in the period between 1961 and 1964. First, the draft allowed beneficiaries to select one of three options: they could have 45 days of hospitalization per year with no deductible, 90 days with a deductible of $10 a day up to a maximum deductible of $90, or 180 days with a flat deductible of $100. Second, it included provisions for intermediaries such as Blue Cross to administer the program. Finally, the draft contained the Javits provision that permitted associations of private health insurance companies to sell on a nonprofit basis policies covering costs, such as doctors' visits outside the hospital, not covered by Medicare. In addition to these three features related to Medicare, the draft also contained a benefit increase of 7 percent, which would be paid retroactively to January 1, 1965.[47]

A letter with the draft of the legislation went from Celebrezze to President Johnson, but the secretary made it abundantly clear that Assistant Secretary

Cohen was in charge. In the president's mind, Cohen was the principal administration strategist on the content of the Medicare legislation, and the others involved took their cues from him.[48] Senator Anderson, for example, continually questioned the notion of combining Social Security benefit increases and health insurance in one bill but told Cohen, "Since you and Nelson Cruikshank and apparently others think this is the way to go, I am not going to cause any difficulty."[49]

Although Cohen orchestrated the details, he lived in a collaborative universe in which consensus was the desired goal.[50] When he went to see Hubert Humphrey to gain his approval, Cohen brought Andy Biemiller of the AFL-CIO along with him.[51] Before advising the president on his negotiations with Jacob Javits, Cohen checked to see how Anderson, Humphrey, McCormack, Albert, Cruikshank, and Biemiller felt about the issues involved. As he handled these matters, Cohen reported to Secretary Celebrezze and President Johnson on almost a daily basis.[52]

On most issues, the politicians recommended that Cohen stick with what had already worked, meaning that the administration bill should be closely modeled on the bill that had passed the Senate. Since it had included a Javits provision, allowing private insurance companies to market policies to fill in the gaps left by Medicare, Cohen and his cohort of politicians thought the new bill should also include such a provision.[53] Cohen, however, told Myer Feldman that Anderson and Cruikshank had both advised him that the administration should not negotiate with the private insurance companies and that he did not expect Javits's proposal to survive in the final legislation. Regardless of Cohen's personal views, the Javits provision remained in the bill, which represented a collaborative patchwork, not an expression of Cohen's best wisdom on how to write a health insurance policy for the elderly.[54]

As the year drew to a close, Cohen appeared to sense that he was on the verge of a historic development. Always a meticulous compiler of notes and memorandums, he began to make special notes for the record as though he were aware that historians would someday be staring over his shoulder. When Cecil King called to give his assent to the specifications for the new Medicare bill, Cohen noted it and put it in the files. He was compiling his own personal record of what shaped up to be a legislative session of record. Neither Cohen nor his allies stumbled unaware into the big bang of legislation that occurred in 1965; they heard it coming. It would be a replay of 1961 but with an acquiescent rather than a rebellious Congress; this time the measures of the president's domestic agenda would be passed into law rather than passed over. Indeed, much of the hard work had already been done, such as the Senate's passage of Medicare and the passage of the 1964 Civil Rights Act.[55]

In December most of the congressional barons rested at home as they awaited the start of the new Congress and the inaugural festivities; Senator Anderson was in Albuquerque, Wilbur Mills in Arkansas. White House functionaries and labor union lobbyists remained behind in Washington, writing the documents that would become the laws passed by the Eighty-ninth Congress.

Cohen remained alert for news that might affect the shape of the Medicare bill and for confirmation that Wilbur Mills understood its inevitability. On December 2 the congressman gave a speech to the downtown Little Rock Lions Club, "Financing Health Care of the Aged." Cohen read the transcript the way that sinologists studied statements from Mao. Underlining with a sharp red pencil passages he thought were key, he noted Mills's pronouncement that "I can support a payroll tax for financing health benefits just as I have supported a payroll tax for cash benefits." He observed, too, how Mills continued to hedge his bets, preferring a separate Medicare tax rather than one combining Social Security and Medicare and raising the possibility of beginning benefits at age sixty-eight rather than at sixty-five. Mills also mentioned the possibility of providing preventive services, such as x-rays, on a universal basis and relating other benefits to a person's ability to pay. He dropped hints that Cohen perceived as directed toward him, for example, that the legislation should define "qualified hospitals and hospital practitioners." Cohen underlined that passage of Mills's speech in red.[56]

One important item that floated about in the planning documents for 1965 was called the Child Health Act, which included an extension of medical assistance for needy children similar to the coverage already provided for the elderly in the Kerr-Mills program. Formulating this legislation, Cohen relied upon a group within the bureaucracy different from the one in charge of Medicare. The impetus for the extension of Kerr-Mills to cover the needy disabled, blind, and children came from Ellen Winston in the Welfare Administration and others associated with the Public Health Service. Because of its pedigree, it lay beyond the immediate purview of Social Security Commissioner Robert Ball and AFL-CIO official Nelson Cruikshank. As Cohen told Myer Feldman, Mills supported this legislation even if the legislative tacticians at the White House were "not very enthusiastic about it."[57]

In addition to preserving the services that later became Medicaid as part of the administration's program, Cohen also kept his eye on what might be described as traditional medical legislation and urged that it, too, be put on Congress' plate in 1965. These programs included money for research and services related to heart disease, cancer, and stroke, institutional support for medical schools, and grants to construct medical libraries. Cohen was determined not to waste the moment of legislative opportunity, and he saw a need to accompany Medicare with companion measures that would build up the medical infrastructure by expanding the supply of doctors and the number of hospitals with advanced treatment facilities.[58]

Before Congress returned, Cohen met with influential individuals or groups in Washington to reassure them about the legislation and to solicit their views and support.[59] He attended a meeting of liberal doctors, associated with such causes as prepaid group health and preventive medicine, and listened to their critique of the Medicare bill. They urged that the various political concessions be removed, and they wanted no deductibles and a single hospital benefit rather than the three options in the administration bill. They also favored alternative forms of care, such as home health services, over institutionally based care. Cohen, Ball, and Cruikshank, the central proprietors of the Medicare enterprise who knew many of the doctors in attendance personally, thanked them for their input but took none of their suggestions seriously. They were simply touching base, as they did with Dr. Montague Cobb, head of the organization that represented the interests of black doctors, and with Sen. Richard Russell (D-Ga.).[60] By the end of 1964 Medicare was primarily a political undertaking in which items gained value according to their political appeal, not from their worth in pushing the American health care system toward such goals as preventive medicine.

On New Year's Eve Cohen distributed the latest version of the "Hospital Insurance, Social Security, and Public Assistance Amendments of 1965," which provided one set of basic benefits rather than the option of three choices included in the previous draft. The bill provided for inpatient hospital services for up to sixty days, with a deductible equal to the average cost of half a day of hospital care. Other aspects covered included physician services associated with hospital care, such as pathology and radiology, outpatient hospital diagnostic services, up to sixty days of posthospital extended care in a nursing home or similar recuperative facility, and up to 240 home health visits a year. The notions of a private intermediary to receive bills for services from hospitals, of a separate hospital insurance trust fund, and of complementary private insurance remained in the bill from the previous drafts. It also included a 7 percent across-the-board Social Security benefit increase. All in all, it amounted to a large, complicated, and expensive package, as big a Social Security bill as Congress had considered in at least twenty years.[61]

The year began with two endorsements of Medicare, one expected and the other anticipated but by no means taken for granted. On January 3 the Advisory Council on Social Security released a report that recommended Medicare be enacted. At almost the same time, a story came in over the AP wire that featured an interview with Wilbur Mills. "I assume the committee would be able to work something out," Mills had told the AP reporter. If that were the case, the reporter noted in his dispatch, then the "decade-long controversy in Congress over health care for the aged could be settled by mid-1965." The story received wide notice. In fact, Mills went little beyond his remarks to the Little Rock Lions Club and continued to insist, for example, that he wanted the Medicare program to be separately financed from the rest of Social Security.[62]

THE MILLS MODIFICATION

In contrast to previous years, this time Wilbur Mills got off to a prompt start on Medicare: no sooner had legislation been introduced in January than he convened his committee. Other than Mills, few of its members could follow all the details, yet he pushed them, day after day, section after section, to accompany him in writing what became the most comprehensive Social Security bill to pass the Ways and Means Committee since 1935.

For Wilbur Cohen, the experience resembled that of a lawyer in the middle of a trial. Each day he would go to the hearings or to the executive sessions, and sometimes Mills held two of these a day. During the recesses, Cohen met with the committee members and with Mills; then, returning to his office, he often had to arrange for the preparation of materials that Mills would need for the next day. Always, Cohen had to write a memo that summarized the day's events for the secretary and for the White House. And, like a lawyer consumed with a trial, Cohen had in the interstitial moments to cope with the rest of his life: to return the phone calls relating to the education bills, to talk with the members of his staff about other pieces of legislation, to answer his mail. The work was relentless. Mills demanded that Cohen pay total attention to the Social Security bill, and Cohen realized that Mills's hearings would be followed by preparations for the floor debate, for the Senate Finance Committee hearings, for the Senate debate, and then for the conference committee. The entire process took almost exactly seven months.

The process unfolded in an atmosphere in which the participants knew that they were writing a law rather than positioning themselves in a political debate and laying the groundwork for future legislation. The major players understood that Medicare would pass, barring political catastrophe. Even so, many details remained to be debated, not just on Medicare but on many other matters related to Social Security and welfare, as, for example, whether to make the definition of disability more liberal.

Cohen waited to see how the Republicans would respond to the administrative bill, knowing it was unlikely that they would simply acquiesce in its passage without first offering some sort of alternative. Senator Javits's ideas, already contained in the legislation, failed to spark the imagination of key Republicans on the Ways and Means Committee. A staff member for ranking minority member John Byrnes (R-Wis.) asked Cohen why the administration did not support what Cohen later described as a "commercial-insurance-type proposal." Soon after the committee went into executive session on January 27, Byrnes revealed such a proposal, which became the Republican counter to Medicare.[63]

The Byrnes proposal was based on a plan available to employees of the federal government through the Aetna Insurance Company. Passed in 1959, the federal program offered employees a variety of choices for health insurance, including the Aetna plan. It was a classic indemnity plan in which employees paid monthly premiums, deducted from their paychecks, and the federal government contributed a percentage of the premium as well. When an employee got sick, the plan paid the doctor and hospital bills, minus a portion that the employee was expected to pay himself. Byrnes proposed to offer this sort of protection to the elderly. It would be voluntary, subsidized in part by the federal government through general revenues, and comprehensive in that it covered both doctor and hospital bills. It would also involve out-of-pocket payments by the elderly both for the premiums (analogous to the payroll deductions) and for the costs of medical care that they were expected to share with the insurance plan. Cohen objected to the voluntary nature of the plan, the costs to the general revenues, and the way that it would pay doctor and hospital bills based on "charges" rather than on "costs" (it was an item of faith at the time that the elderly cost less to serve than did younger people). Above all, Cohen and the members of his policy apparatus thought it inadvisable to make a person pay for health insurance during his retirement "when his income is lowest." The administration plan, in contrast, required a person to pay for health insurance during his working lifetime and enabled him to earn a paid-up policy upon retirement.[64]

Even though Cohen railed against the Byrnes plan, he could see that it made good politics. In particular, it was, in the manner of previous Republican alternatives to Social Security, straightforward in its approach to financing. Since it relied largely on general revenues and current taxes, it had none of the problems of maintaining large reserves that so complicated Social Security financing. The budget could be observed from year to year without the complication of thinking about future obligations. Even more important, the Republicans outcompeted the Democrats on the range of benefits. The Byrnes plan contained crucially important surgical benefits that the administration plan did not. Although the administration offered to pay hospital expenses, these did not include a surgeon's bill for his services. The Republicans could therefore claim to be both fiscally and socially responsible. The Democratic response, to encourage private companies to offer nonprofit plans to pay doctors' bills, through the Javits provision, was a weak one. No wonder, then, that the Republicans on the Ways and Means Committee adopted the Byrnes proposal; five members of the committee immediately announced their support for it.[65]

Mills appeared unflappable, taking his committee into executive session at the end of January and keeping it there for the entire month of February and much of March. He patiently worked on problems, such as expanding Social Security benefits to cover students between the ages of eighteen to twenty-two in families where the worker had died before retirement age. His major interest appeared to be in the tax rates that the committee would propose. He wanted the accounts to show that the rates would be 9.5 percent of covered payroll for old-age, survivors', and disability insurance (OASDI) and 1 percent for hospital insurance. It was important to him that the OASDI rate be below 10 percent since he and others in the policy apparatus believed that that number represented a psychological barrier that could never be broken.[66]

Even in executive session, Mills continued to call upon witnesses to advise him on different parts of the legislation. On February 4, 1965, for example, J. Henry Smith, a vice-president of Equitable Insurance and major spokesman for the industry, told Mills that insurance companies opposed the Javits amendment for supplemental private policies and recommended that it be dropped from the bill. It was the sort of thing that was easier for Smith to say in private than in public. He also attempted to preserve a large zone that the private market could exploit: he wanted patients to pay 10 percent of hospital costs, for example, in part because private companies could then offer plans, which came to be known as medigap policies, to cover this amount.

Cohen watched the testimony of insurance spokesmen such as Smith as more than a spectator. It was his job not only to predict what effect such testimony would have on Mills but also to formulate the administration's response. Cohen knew that at any time Mills might turn to him and ask if he could accept a particular provision, acting on behalf of the administration. In the case of the insurance spokesmen, Cohen could dismiss many of their suggestions, such as the ones asking patients to pay more of their bills out of pocket, without need for extensive consultation. "We cannot accept any of these proposals," he flatly told the secretary.[67]

Mills kept his own schedule and offered nearly all the interested parties a chance to testify in executive session. Soon after the private insurance industry spokesmen had appeared, representatives from the Blue Cross Association, the American Hospital Association, and the American Medical Association testified. Like the Republicans, the AMA had its own bill, written by the association and introduced by two sympathetic congressmen, Democrat Sidney Herlong and Republican Thomas Curtis. The AMA approach, known as Eldercare, allowed states to expand their Kerr-Mills programs in order to pay the doctor and hospital bills of the needy elderly. Although it called for state administration and contained a means test, the AMA bill, like the Byrnes bill, covered the cost of both doctor and hospital bills.[68] Aware that Eldercare did not stand too much of a chance of passage, Dr. Donovan Ward, AMA president, spoke against the inclusion of radiologists, pathologists, anesthesiologists, and psychiatrists in the hospital services that were covered in the administration bill. In this way, the AMA made both a broad ideological statement and tried to condition the administration bill.[69]

Cohen kept his eye on the clock. The longer that Mills stretched out the executive sessions, the less his committee and hence Congress could do in what was obviously a crucial session for the administration. Mills, extremely careful in writing legislation, acted as though he were the captain of a hockey team that was one player short and killing time on a penalty. Congress observed its usual calendar, which meant committee recesses so that, for example, the Republicans could make Lincoln-day speeches. The longer the deliberations, the more opposition to Medicare could arise. "We should try and keep the bill as it is," Cohen advised the secretary, "and we should continue to press Mills to expedite the bill."[70]

Cohen's sense of urgency meant that many larger, more philosophical considerations related to health care received little attention. One issue that was swept aside involved the promotion of alternative forms of health care provision, such as health maintenance organizations (HMOs). Representatives of both the Group Health Association and the Kaiser-Permanente health plans testified in executive session, and Kaiser proposed a capitation, a payment for each of its members enrolled in Medicare, equal to the average cost per Medicare recipient in a given area. In return for this payment, Kaiser agreed to supply all the benefits specified in the legislation. As Cohen noted, "They think they can turn a profit." Although he knew that the Kaiser plan had powerful allies, such as Walter Reuther in the labor movement, he still felt he had to oppose the Kaiser recommendation because it represented a subsidy from the general public to Kaiser. Cohen did not reveal that he was himself a member of the Group Health Association of Washington D.C. or that others in his apparatus, such as Nelson Cruikshank of the AFL-CIO, also belonged to Group Health. Neither Cohen nor Cruikshank allowed his personal preferences to influence his political decisions on Medicare.[71] Even though Cohen believed in prepaid group health and approved of Kaiser, he also felt that there would be "no way to keep other plans from profiting by insuring only the best risks, or by covering care only in the cheaper hospitals." And Cohen did not want to encourage cheap care; the whole thrust of Medicare was toward quality care for the elderly. Cost reduction, which would become so important to the health care debate in future years, figured only at the edges of the 1965 debate.[72]

Mills, meanwhile, looked carefully at each of the major health insurance bills, completing his review on March 2.[73] At that afternoon's meeting in Room H 208, Cohen sat in the center of a group of departmental experts at a long table placed before the congressmen, who were arrayed behind a raised horseshoe table.

Something happened that afternoon. "Without any advance notice," according to Cohen, "Mills asked me why we could not put together a plan that included the administration's Medicare hospital plan with a broader voluntary plan covering physician or other services."[74] Cohen and many of the others in the room were stunned by this suggestion to combine the Byrnes plan and the administration plan..Robert Ball and Arthur Hess of the Social Security Administration called the development "unexpected." Fred Arner of the Congressional Research Service turned toward the chief legislative draftsman and said, "He's kidding, isn't he?"[75] No, he was not. Mills wanted a health insurance bill that contained three principal elements—Medicare for hospital services, the Byrnes bill for doctors' services, and an expanded Kerr-Mills program for those on welfare.

Cohen did not quite know how to react. He stalled for time because he could not immediately unscramble the politics of the situation, and he had no clear instructions on how to proceed. It was a moment of existential freedom of the sort that he liked to emphasize in his accounts of legislation. Cohen was, at least temporarily, free of authority, just as he had been in the conference committee in 1952 when it had considered disability insurance. He decided to seize the moment and agreed to provide specifications for the bill the next morning.[76] Mills adjourned the committee for the day, and Cohen raced out of the room. He met with Robert Ball and with the lawyers and technical experts, who would forge the specifications for Mills. Sidney Saperstein worked until two in the morning to have material ready for Mills.[77]

As the technical specialists spent the night writing up specifications, Cohen wrote a memorandum for the president. He explained that Mills had become concerned that the Republicans would attack Mills's bill as inadequate and point out that their bill was "more liberal . . . and a better total package than the Administration's program." Mills's augmented bill would be, as Cohen put it, "unassailable politically from any serious Republican attack. . . . The effect of this ingenious plan," Cohen concluded, "is . . . to make it almost certain that nobody will vote against the bill when it comes to the floor of the House."[78]

Mills's motivation would later become the object of considerable speculation. In fact, his actions were foreshadowed in part by his earlier desire to expand Kerr-Mills and in part by his interest in protecting Social Security's financing. As the new plan was structured, doctors' bills were financed completely separately from hospital bills through voluntary contributions and general revenues. Mills had been interested in a separate taxing system for health benefits throughout the legislative session. He perhaps understood that he would have to accept Medicare, and he did what he could to protect the fiscal integrity of that program by surrounding it with other programs to handle doctors' bills and the care of the poor.

Ever the exacting legislative craftsman, Mills began another review of the bill in March, taking the committee through each page of the legislation. On a typical day they made it through thirty-three pages, with Mills asking for numerous revisions.[79] Even then, the measure did not move through Ways and Means without controversy.

One major point of contention concerned Mills's desire to have all doctors' payments, including the services of radiologists and pathologists, handled through the voluntary health insurance part of the bill rather than through the compulsory hospital insurance part. When the president read an item in the *Herald Tribune* that suggested that Mills's handling of the matter would raise the costs of health care, he mentioned his concern to Bill Moyers, who passed it along to Cohen.[80] Cohen talked to Mills about the matter and found him to be adamant. During a meeting in the Speaker's office, Mills did agree to require that all physicians' charges under voluntary health insurance be "reasonable" and similar to those made to other patients and payers. But when the Speaker called the president and asked Cohen to explain the situation to LBJ, Mills abruptly left the room. When he returned, he was, according to Cohen, "boiling mad" because of the president's criticism of him. Mills remained firm on the matter; he did not want any physicians' services to be covered under Social Security. Lawrence O'Brien told Johnson that the matter could not be resolved without a direct discussion between the president and Mills, and "frankly at this point Cohen's view is Mills is completely opposed." Once again, Cohen served as the administration's resident expert on Mills.[81]

A second point of contention concerned the effect of the Medicare legislation on the economy. The administration economists, including Kermit Gordon and Gardner Ackley, worried that the bill would take more money from the economy than it put in and create a "fiscal drag" on its continued growth. Cohen had already told the president that Mills's actions added to the cost of the program by as much as $.5 billion, and the president had reacted impassively.[82] Celebrezze, concerned that the criticism of the bill by the economists was a sophisticated way of derailing the passage of Medicare, once again appealed to LBJ for help. Johnson typically saw the matter in political rather than in economic terms. "Please ask Ackley and Fowler [secretary of the treasury] to ask their friends to pipe down," the president commanded. Meanwhile, Gordon, Ackley, and Fowler met with Cohen and White House officials to negotiate a means of reducing the predicted $2.4 billion drag on the economy in 1966. One way to accomplish this result was to raise the taxable wage base and reduce the tax rates written into the bill.[83]

A third complication arose over the more fundamental matter of civil rights. Senator Byrd wanted to know whether Title VI of the Civil Rights Act of 1964 would apply to the Medicare program; as a recipient of federal grants in the form of Medicare payments, would a hospital have to be integrated? The question did not even come up until after the bill had made it through the House of Representatives. The administration did not want to include a specific civil rights amendment in the Medicare legislation because, as White House staffer Lee White put it, they did not want to "jeopardize" the bill. Ultimately, the matter was settled through an exchange on the Senate floor rather than through formal legislation.[84]

As these issues lingered in the background, Mills marched the committee through the draft bill, and early in April the House voted on the measure. Cohen, who recognized the historical significance of the House's approval of Medicare, wrote a sentimental note to Harry Truman, letting the former president know that twenty years after Cohen had helped draft Truman's health care message of November 1945, "we are finally coming close to victory." Cohen also dropped Congressman John Dingell a line, pointing out that it was appropriate for him to preside over the Medicare debate in the House since his father had done so much to start the movement.[85]

Such sentiment aside, Cohen needed to court the barons of the Senate and gain their approval of the legislation. Russell Long, for instance, hoped to make major changes in it. Among other ideas, Long entertained the notions of broadening the legislation to include payments for prescription drugs and of eliminating the copays that had been put into the bill. "I begged, cajoled, argued to get the Senator not to touch the basic King-Anderson portion of the bill," Cohen told Larry O'Brien, and he arranged for Cruikshank to see Long as well.[86] Clinton Anderson also needed attention, and Cohen paid him a special visit early in May and listened to his various concerns. Unlike his approach to Senator Long, whose motives neither Cohen nor the others in his policy apparatus trusted, Cohen tried hard to accommodate Anderson and relied on him to offer amendments of interest to the administration, such as the proposal worked out with the economists raising the taxable wage base.[87]

Long provided the most trouble in the Finance Committee. On June 17 the committee voted to adopt Long's amendment, which transformed the Mills proposal into a catastrophic health care plan. In return for a variable deductible related to a person's income and a cost-sharing provision, the Long plan allowed a person to receive unlimited hospital care, posthospital extended care, and home health services. Cohen and his apparatus lobbied hard against the Long plan, and he told the president that he was working with Cruikshank, Elizabeth Wickenden, and the American Hospital Association to obtain a reversal. The effort paid off on June 23 when the committee voted to defeat Long's amendment, although not without agreeing to add another sixty days of hospital coverage to Mills's bill (with a ten-dollar-a-day copay during those additional days).[88]

Both Anderson and Cohen grew restive as the bill approached the Senate. Anderson was worried because Long would serve as the floor manager and might accept crippling amendments from Sen. Vance Hartke (D-Ind.) and others. "Because of the unpredictable situation," a nervous Cohen wrote to Lawrence O'Brien on July 6, "I probably will plan to go to Senator Mansfield's office to be available during the debate for any unexpected developments."[89] None occurred.

On July 9 the Senate passed Medicare, and the two Houses moved quickly to a conference to resolve their differences, reporting out a compromise bill July 21. As usual, Cohen was heavily involved in the negotiations, which concerned a broad range of Social Security matters. Cohen advised the president against accepting Robert Byrd's notion of allowing early retirement at age sixty and concurred with Mills in opposing Senator Hartke's idea that blind people should receive disability insurance on a more liberal basis than other applicants. Of more immediate importance were the boundary decisions to be made about Medicare. In particular, the conference needed to decide whether a specialist's services should be handled under hospital insurance or Supplementary Medical Insurance. A person who went to the hospital for an operation typically received a bill from a surgeon, another from an anesthesiologist, another from a radiologist, and still another from the hospital itself. The conferees agreed that the hospital bill should be paid through hospital insurance and the surgeon's bill through Supplementary Medical Insurance. At issue were the other doctors who routinely saw a patient in the hospital, such as the pathologist who interpreted the results of a biopsy or the anesthesiologist.

Cohen thought instinctively of the compromise that would spring the legislation: it was his notion to split the difference. Radiologists and pathologists would come under hospital insurance, anesthesiologists and physicalmedicine doctors under Supplementary Medical Insurance. Although Cohen thought Mills would go along, somehow the agreement came undone. Mills and Hale Boggs, with the help of Senators Long and Smathers, were able to obtain the conference's approval of the House version. "The conferees action, of course, will make the AMA happy and the result will be viewed as a defeat for the Administration," Cohen noted.[90]

On the whole, an exhausted Wilbur Cohen would probably have agreed with Senator Anderson's assessment that the "bill came through conference in generally good shape."[91] The scope of the legislation was amazing. In addition to starting Medicare (hospital insurance), Medicaid (the expansion of the Kerr-Mills program), and Supplementary Medical Insurance (for doctors' bills), it also raised the earnings base on which Social Security taxes were paid, contained a substantial 7 percent increase in Social Security benefits, made it easier for beneficiaries to work without losing their benefits, liberalized the definition of disability, began a program of rehabilitation services for people on disability insurance, extended the scope of childhood disability benefits, and lowered the age at which widows could receive benefits. The bill increased federal payments for welfare and expanded the maternal and child health and children's services programs. On July 28, 1965, the measure, the most far-reaching amendment to the Social Security Act since its passage in 1935, received final approval from Congress and reached the president's desk.[92]

As Cohen realized, the 1965 amendments marked the high tide of Social Security expansion. Although the entire debate centered on Medicare, the incremental engine that expanded Social Security continued to operate throughout the process. As in all Social Security legislative exercises, prosperity played a major role, and in this regard the bill resembled the Elementary and Secondary Education Act. In both cases, prosperity enabled the federal government to make generous investments in the nation's future and to fulfill the items that had been on Cohen's agenda at least since the 1950s. In the case of Medicare, it was the expanding economy that permitted program administrators such as Robert Ball to recommend and Congress to accept a raise in benefit levels, combined with reduced tax rates. As the law was written before July 1965, the combined employer–employee Social Security tax rate was to have been 8.25 percent in 1966; in the new law, Congress reduced the rate to 7.7 percent, and even after adding in the new hospital insurance program, the total 1966 rate was only 8.4 percent. As projected in 1965, the 1968 rates for hospital insurance and Social Security would actually be lower than the rates that had earlier been projected for Social Security alone. Prosperity enabled the program's benefits to rise by $1.4 billion, the elderly to have most of their hospital bills paid, and hospitals and doctors to receive generous subsidies without raising long-term tax rates on workers.[93]

Cohen had little chance to dwell on his legislative prowess as efforts to implement Medicare began even before its passage. Before the conference committee finished its work, Cohen decided that it was an appropriate time for the president to meet with the representatives of the American Medical Association since he realized that the successful implementation of Medicare would require the "full cooperation of the physicians."[94] As he knew from his previous experience with the disability insurance amendments, the politics of Medicare would soon shift. The AMA, which had done so much to oppose the legislation, would work to make sure that the law functioned in the interest of its member physicians. The government had every reason to enlist the goodwill of the doctors because of the strong desire within the federal bureaucracy to make Medicare a success. The two groups might continue to fight about health insurance for the working population, but they made common cause over Medicare.

Perhaps that insight caused Cohen to oppose the harmless bit of symbolism in Jack Valenti's suggestion that President Johnson sign the Medicare legislation in the presence of Harry Truman. Valenti played to Johnson's love of the dramatic gesture, but Cohen worried that people would associate Medicare with Truman's bill and conclude that Johnson wanted to extend it to cover the entire population. That, Cohen believed, was exactly the wrong signal to send the AMA; instead, the president should emphasize that the new legislation permitted no interference in medical practice and allowed the patients to pick their own physician. Further, it permitted the doctors to work through Blue Shield and other designated "carriers" for the collection of payments. The law also guaranteed that doctors would be paid their "reasonable and customary charges" at the prevailing rates for their area. Cohen wanted the president to make love, not war.[95] In the end, LBJ, who just could not resist the opportunity, decided to sign the law in Independence, and Cohen made the trip with the other Washington dignitaries, waited in line, and received one of the signing pens.[96]

Looking back on the experience of passing Medicare and aid to education, Cohen saw a link between the two areas of legislation. He said that Medicare owed its existence to "middle class anxiety," which, as Cohen described it, drew

Cohen receives his pen at the signing ceremony for Medicare in Independence, Missouri, on July 30, 1965. He later hung this photo in his office, underscoring the fact that Medicare was the legislative accomplishment of his life. (Courtesy of Bruce Cohen)

heavily on his personal concerns. Children of aged parents were caught in the middle between paying their parents' medical bills and setting money aside for their children's college education. The Great Society eased both of these concerns, helping to bring down the out-of-pocket costs and to raise the quality of both education and medical care.[97] Cohen's analysis said a great deal about his view of the world, one composed of middle-class families with generations tied together by mutual obligation. Distinctions between rich and poor and white and black were subsumed under the category of family. Successful federal laws were really ways of helping families by coming to the aid of the average tax payer.

Indeed, as Cohen implied, the new laws of 1965 were in fact quite traditional in the sense that they reflected a profound faith in the status quo. The planners believed that prosperity was destined to continue; the nation's problems were assumed to be those of harnessing prosperity rather than coping with recession. Hospitals and schools were not challenged to do better so much as they were encouraged with generous financial incentives to do more. The means to solve the nation's problem were at hand: it was just a matter of ensuring access of the elderly to hospitals or of inner-city children to high schools and colleges.

For Cohen the questions that led to the 1965 legislation were never ideological so much as they were tactical. The key to progress lay in overcoming practical political barriers, not in determining the best form of federal aid. Above all else, Medicare reflected a desire to accommodate Wilbur Mills and still retain health insurance for the elderly funded through Social Security. Aid to Elementary and Secondary Education owed its ultimate design to the wishes of its sponsors to overcome longstanding congressional objections related to local autonomy and religious preference. The triple play of Kennedy's death, Johnson's electoral triumph, and passage of the 1964 Civil Rights Act created a window of opportunity to pass these and other items on the liberal growth agenda. Prosperity created the additional advantage of being able to use the federal government as a financier of social projects.

Wilbur Cohen was as responsible for the core legislation of 1965 as anyone. If he erred as a social prophet, it was in placing too much faith on the incremental political process to correct the problems in the legislation. For him, it was important to cross thresholds, and he trusted in the popularity of the programs he created to ensure their continued maintenance and improvement. He was right about the historical importance of crossing thresholds: 1965 was a landmark year in the creation of an American state, with the federal government in a central administering and financing role. He was perhaps less right about the benevolence of the political system in maintaining these landmarks and in the persistence of postwar economic conditions. In the years ahead, Cohen's programs would be severely tested.

In the Johnson years, however, Cohen was not above enjoying some of his accomplishments. One person wrote to him that "as a woman of 87, alone in the world and utterly unable to meet doctor bills, I wonder what I would have done had it not been for the angel of mercy and compassion known as Medicare."[98] Whether or not Medicare was an angel of mercy, Cohen helped bring it to earth.

11
IMPLEMENTING
THE GREAT SOCIETY
IN A TIME OF TROUBLES

It was almost as if Cohen had lived in a cave for much of 1965 since he had spent so much of his time dealing with Congress on the passage of legislation. Nor did Medicare and the Elementary and Secondary Education Act exhaust the list of accomplishments. Since Cohen and his colleagues wanted to get as much legislation on the books before congressional tolerance for presidential initiatives abated, they continued to bargain with congressional leaders until the end of the session and to win impressive victories. As if to underscore Cohen's triumph, President Johnson appointed him undersecretary of HEW in the spring of 1965.

In this capacity Cohen faced the hard task of implementing Great Society legislation. As early as 1966 he discovered that Congress was much less compliant toward the administration than it had been only a year before. Part of the reason for the dissatisfaction was the war in Vietnam, which cut down the available funds for existing programs and had the effect of diminishing President Johnson's popularity. Another reason for congressional recalcitrance was the shift in the focus of the civil rights movement from the South to North and a growing fear of civil disorder in the nation's cities. As conditions changed, liberal and conservative critics charged that the programs themselves might not be capable of meeting their objectives. By the end of 1967 the euphoria of 1965 had been replaced by a feeling close to despair. Even the administration's Social Security proposals, closely superintended by Cohen, ran into obstacles related to civil rights, the growth of the welfare rolls, urban riots, and the politics of the Vietnam War. Cohen's own transition from elation to depression followed the path of the Great Society's political fortunes.

COHEN AS UNDERSECRETARY

In 1965 it seemed as though Cohen worked on every policy. A good example concerned water pollution legislation, a topic about which he knew nearly nothing. In this field, Sen. Edmund Muskie (D-Maine) and Congressmen John Blatnik (D-Minn.) and John Dingell were the congressional leaders, underscoring the impression that in effect a different Congress legislated on water pollution than on education or Social Security. The issues concerned such matters as whether the federal government should set water quality standards for the states and localities. Blatnik, according to Cohen, thought it more important to establish a new entity called the Water Pollution Federal Control Administration than to argue about water quality standards, but characteristically Cohen saw the need to enact the standards. The time for action, whether on water pollution or federal aid to education, was 1965. Since the House committee had not put pollution standards in the bill, Cohen favored amending it on the House floor to include them.[1] In the end, he used his negotiating skills to broker a deal between Muskie and Blatnik on federal standards for water pollution. Thus was born the Water Quality Control Act of 1965, which authorized the federal government to set clean water standards for states that did not set their own. Cohen ranked it as among the five most important acts passed that year.[2]

Not content to stop there, Cohen turned almost immediately to negotiations with Senator Muskie over what became the Clean Air Act amendments and the Solid Waste Disposal Act of 1965.[3] It was a wonder that he could even keep the various pieces of legislation straight; even he admitted that his stock of ideas on which to base policies had diminished. He told British social policy expert Brian Abel-Smith that he just did not have time to exchange ideas because legislative politics occupied all his time, "25 hours a day and 8 days a week." Even in Social Security Cohen felt that he was coasting on his reputation. Most people, he noted, "have the mistaken idea that I still am an expert on social security." Like the other workaholics in Washington, Cohen was dependent on short memos and short conversations to stay abreast of current events.[4] He conceded that he was fatigued and needed his "batteries recharged," yet he relished his accomplishments. "During the past year," he told Brian Abel-Smith in a matter-of-fact manner, "I was responsible for getting 21 new laws through Congress."[5]

In a subtle way, Cohen's core project had already begun to shift from the passage of legislation to its implementation and continued management. As undersecretary of HEW, he became concerned with matters related to departmental personnel, reorganization, and budgeting. To a great extent, his responsibilities followed the cycle of legislative innovation that marked the Johnson years. In 1965 the main legislation of the Great Society became law, and in subsequent years the laws were put into effect. The situation required the presence of someone who, in the words of Dean Coston, Cohen's deputy, was delegated to stay in Washington and "run the place."[6] That, more than anything else, was Cohen's job after the summer of 1965.

Cohen owed his appointment as undersecretary in part to Abraham Ribicoff. In a letter to John Macy, the administration's director of personnel, Ribicoff called attention to the fact that the 1965 wave of legislation would leave HEW with over 150 different programs to administer and over $30 billion to disburse in 1967. As a result, the secretary would find himself overwhelmed with problems of all sorts and in need of a competent undersecretary who had the confidence of the civil servants and political savvy. Ribicoff, who described Cohen as "my right arm when I was Secretary," knew that Cohen would want to return to Michigan after the passage of Medicare. "I believe you could keep him if you offered him the position of Undersecretary," concluded Ribicoff.[7]

In this manner, a campaign began to replace Ivan Nestingen with Wilbur Cohen. On April 27, 1965, John Macy formally recommended to Johnson that Cohen be promoted to the post of undersecretary.[8] By the end of May Cohen's nomination had been approved by the Senate, handled as a pro forma matter. "Not a single person said anything on my nomination," Cohen reported to Sorensen. "Bob Weaver [soon to be the first black member of the cabinet] called me up and said it must be because I am getting too conservative."[9] On the first day of June Cohen officially assumed his duties as undersecretary of HEW. John McCormack, the veteran congressman from South Boston and Speaker of the House, administered the oath of office, marking the first time, according to Cohen, that McCormack had performed such a function for anyone other than a congressman.[10]

Only a few weeks after Cohen took over as undersecretary, John Gardner became the new secretary of HEW. Cohen found that his own practical, detail-oriented style meshed well with Gardner's loose management directives. The new secretary wrote beautiful speeches and made memorable remarks, but it was Cohen who transformed Gardner's epigrams and metaphors into practical policies.[11] As always, Cohen embraced a change of activity with enthusiasm; he would handle major employee-dispute cases, perform budget reviews, and make organizational changes—the minutiae of bureaucracy for which people like John Gardner had only limited tolerance. "I never thought I would do it or like it," wrote Cohen. "But I do!"[12]

Undersecretary Cohen could not spare many moments from his desk. He was named to the post in summer 1965 when the Great Society was at high tide. (Courtesy of Bruce Cohen)

IMPLEMENTING MEDICARE

As undersecretary, Cohen faced the consequences of the programs he had done so much to pass. First on his mind was Medicare. Along with nearly all the other participants, he took great pride in the way the administration put the program into effect. The tasks were as daunting as any that the government had ever attempted in a time of peace. People needed to be contacted about the voluntary, Supplementary Medical Insurance program and offered every chance to participate. Fiscal intermediaries and carriers who would help to administer the program had to be selected. Hospitals would have to be in-spected to see if they met the criteria for participation. And these efforts would be carried out simultaneously with preparations for effecting many changes in the basic rules of Social Security. Robert Ball later noted that his agency opened 100 district offices, hired thousands of people, and issued 19 million Medicare cards. "As I look back on it . . . I don't know how in the hell we did it, to tell you the truth," Ball said. Cohen compared beginning Medicare on July 1, 1966, to planning the invasion of Normandy: "We did a better job of preparation than we did for almost any other program."[13]

With Robert Ball handling much of the implementation effort, Cohen served as the link between the bureaucracy and the White House and between the Social Security Administration and Congress. He had the job of explaining the rules for the reimbursement of hospitals to Wilbur Mills in Congress and to Doug Cater in the White House. In a typical bit of service, Cohen met with the Oklahoma congressional delegation about the problems of certifying Okla-homa hospitals that did not have around-the-clock nursing care supervised by a professional nurse. More important, he reassured the president that Medicare would work.[14] As Johnson read a spate of stories about the possible lack of enough beds for the Medicare patients who would suddenly materialize on July 1, he became progressively more concerned. Bowing to pressure from the White House, the Social Security Administration was forced to identify hospi-tals with high occupancy rates by means of pins on a map of the United States. In those areas, Ball and his associates alerted the army and veterans' hospitals and even readied helicopters to move people from one place to another.[15] There was, as it turned out, little reason for concern. "We put Medicare into opera-tion at 12:01 this morning. It is a great day," wrote Cohen in an exuberant note to Vice-President Hubert Humphrey on July 1.[16]

Medicare occasioned a silent social revolution that went largely unheralded. Hospitals, like other public facilities, were among the most segregated of institutions in the South; if they expected to receive Medicare funds, they would have to admit blacks. The process of certifying hospitals for Medicare became politically charged, and Cohen often found himself designated as the intermediary between the federal government and southern congressmen. In March of 1966, for example, he received a phone call from Joseph Califano, who had emerged as the president's chief assistant for domestic affairs, instructing him to meet with Congressman Mendel Rivers (D-S.C.) on a matter related to civil rights. Rivers, a friend of the administration, took particular exception to an investigation of the hospitals in his district, yet the fact remained that those hospitals were admitting black patients only to rooms with other black patients. Cohen had somehow to mollify Rivers and to ensure the integration of the hospitals in his district.[17] It was a scene that would be repeated throughout the implementation process. Speaking metaphorically, Cohen later said that on the day Medicare went into effect the signs reading "white" and "colored" came down from the hospitals in the South. "In one day," he claimed, "Medicare and Medicaid broke the back of segregated health services."[18]

The night before the start of Medicare, Cohen met with Ted Sorensen, veteran of the Medicare battle from the Kennedy administration. His book on Kennedy finished, he had turned to the worldly matter of making money. Speaking with Cohen as the counsel to the proprietary (for-profit) hospital group, Sorensen asked Cohen about ways to guarantee the hospitals more of a profit. As the conversation indicated, the issues were shifting from those of implementation to the less dramatic and in some ways more difficult matter of containing costs. The euphoria of accomplishing a difficult task was giving way to the reality of maintaining a costly and complicated law, and in a time-honored Washington manner, former allies such as Sorensen had become the representatives of interests that needed to be accommodated.[19]

Indeed, Medicare, like most of the Great Society programs, would soon attract considerable criticism. Historian Allen Matusow described the program as "a ruinous accommodation between reformers and vested interests" that produced run-away inflation in health care costs. To be sure, the Medicare program grew expensive quickly. The hospital insurance part of the program cost $1 billion in (calendar year) 1966, $3.4 billion in 1967, and $4.3 billion in 1968, and in those same years, expenditures on Supplementary Medical Insurance increased from $200 million to $1.7 billion.[20] And of course these rising costs attracted the attention of Wilbur Mills and Lyndon Johnson. In March 1967, for example, the president approached Cohen at a departmental ceremony, complaining that Wilbur Mills was "all over the ticker" on the increased costs of hospital care. Cohen could only reply that he hoped the increases would not continue and that he did not think it would be necessary to increase the payroll taxes for Medicare. Mills, for his part, was genuinely worried that his fear had been realized: rising hospital costs would cut into the money that might otherwise have gone to raise basic Social Security benefits.[21]

Other problems surfaced as well. The carriers who were to implement the Supplementary Medical Insurance (SMI) program often proved inadequate to the task, not handling the claims swiftly or accurately enough. Adverse publicity attracted the president's attention and created problems for Cohen.[22] Nursing homes proved to be difficult institutions to regulate.[23] Medicaid, a program that differed significantly from state to state, proved even more difficult for the federal government to manage. Some states, such as New York, started ambitious but costly programs that for example guaranteed medical care to any needy citizen regardless of whether the person was on welfare, which soon became prohibitively expensive.[24] In general, charges to patients increased in all the health insurance programs, the first increases in copayments and deductibles becoming effective in 1968.[25]

Cohen, who watched the problems develop, nonetheless continued to defend Medicare. Twenty years later, he still gave it "a very good overall rating," in part because it laid the "basic foundation to secure incremental improvement even in relatively conservative administrations."[26] Unlike later critics, Cohen understood the historical context in which Medicare was created. At the time, the object was to ensure access to health care for the elderly population, not to control health care cost inflation or to reform health care delivery. If the government had attempted to change the health care financing or delivery systems, Congress would certainly have objected and probably have defeated the measure, as it had done in 1957, 1960, 1962, and 1964. Medicare resembled the Blue Cross plans enjoyed by working Americans, and few people in 1965 regarded such plans as breeding inflation. Indeed, the preoccupation with inflation was largely a post-1965 phenomenon; only in retrospect would Medicare appear to be flawed. Cohen regarded it as the best that could be done at the time and as a base from which to push for national health insurance.

In contrast, he seldom came to the defense of the Economic Opportunity Act. Just as he had foreseen, antagonism between the poverty warriors and the politicians, abetted by the urban violence of the 1960s, soon developed. Almost from its inception, President Johnson heard distressing reports about the Office of Economic Opportunity, such as the rumor that some of the race rioters in northern cities were being financed by OEO funds.[27] As early as 1966 the president complained to his cabinet that the program was not being run to his satisfaction and that it was difficult to explain to an apple farmer in Washington State just why the poverty program should hire someone to administer it for $26,000 a year.[28] In 1968 Johnson told Cohen that he could not appoint a person whom Cohen regarded as perfectly competent to a federal post because of that person's association with the OEO. "These fellows are all disloyal," the president said.[29]

Congress, which had never shown much sympathy for the poverty program, soon developed an antagonistic relationship with the Office of Economic Opportunity. Bureaucratic warfare among OEO, the Department of Labor, and HEW, which had begun even before the act was passed, spilled over to Congress. The Department of Labor claimed jurisdiction over manpower programs; HEW sought to control all programs that involved health, education, or welfare; OEO believed it should run all programs involving poor people. "These claims obviously overlap," noted an exasperated Bureau of the Budget official in 1966.[30] The very structure of the legislation, with its many different education and manpower programs, invited bureaucratic competition that produced conflict in Congress and confusion at the local level.[31] Not surprisingly, in 1967, as Congress considered major amendments to the poverty program, the Republicans appeared interested in removing programs from the control of OEO and placing them in HEW and other established departments. The American Vocational Association meanwhile wanted to dismantle the Job Corps, and HEW and the Department of Labor were engaged in protracted negotiations over how to coordinate Title V of the Economic Opportunity Act and the provisions in the Manpower Development and Training Act.[32] By 1967, therefore, much of the confusion that Cohen had predicted had materialized, and the program had developed into the bureaucratic nightmare – the fiasco – that he had anticipated and dreaded.

The experience with the War on Poverty served to confirm his opinions. Successful programs, in his conception, had firm bases of congressional support and appealed to middle-class values. Subsequent commentators on the War on Poverty would evaluate the entire run of social policy legislation between 1965 and 1980 and ask if the programs helped to alleviate poverty or to improve the conditions of minority groups.[33] Cohen's focus was on building a permanent relationship between the government and the majority of its citizens, as in the Social Security program, rather than on the specific goals of ending poverty in inner cities or aiding minorities. It seemed axiomatic to him that programs in aid of minorities would never develop the mass appeal that could sustain them over time.

Cohen may have evinced little enthusiasm for the poverty program, but he was prepared to work hard on the successful implementation of the Elementary and Secondary Education Act. Just as he believed that programs for poor people made poor programs, so he assumed, with equal fervor, that education was the fundamental solution to income inequality and other social problems. Cohen, himself the product of inner-city schools, could not help but be optimistic that federal aid to the nation's schools would produce improvements in the system and ultimately in the students themselves. In 1966, however, a report by sociologist James S. Coleman, commissioned by the federal government, argued that a student's home environment and the quality of his fellow students mattered far more to educational achievement than did such concerns as school facilities and curricula. In short, one could not simply buy better schools and produce better students. The process was a complicated one that involved politically contentious matters such as changes in the black family (as Daniel Moynihan would soon discover, to his chagrin). Put more bluntly, the solution to income inequality might be beyond the reach of legislation except through overt income redistribution measures, but as Cohen noted, "During the sixties there was no policy window open for basic redistribution of income in any striking way." And, even if one did not accept the findings of Coleman and others, few people even in the 1960s believed that urban school systems were improving. As historian Michael Katz later reported, "Massive flow of funds to schools that served poor children made no dramatic impact on the quality of urban education, which, as report after report has documented and despite a few shining exceptions, remains a scandal."[34]

Here was a true dilemma for the architects of the Great Society, yet Cohen simply ignored it. He could not bring himself to question the beneficial effects of education and instead continued to work on the specific political problems of implementing education legislation. Since Cohen placed great validity on the very existence of legislation that had survived so many tough political fights, he fought hard for the preservation of the ESEA in 1966 and 1967. Like many people in the administration, he worried that the political compromise between public and private schools that had been reached in 1965 would somehow come undone.

As in any fragile consensus, both liberals and conservatives had plenty of grounds for complaint. Liberals objected to the way in which the Vietnam War made it impossible to fund ESEA at the levels originally intended. The Johnson administration had hoped to spend $5 billion by 1969, but when the time came, expenditures amounted to less than $2 billion. As early as 1966 Charles Schultze, Johnson's budget director, had counseled the president on the need to keep Congress from adding to budget expenditures for education. Cohen, who had worked so hard to get the program passed in one year, had to work on restraining the appropriations for the program in the next year. It was his job to ask Secretary John Gardner to see a coterie of liberal senators, including Jennings Randolph, Joseph Clark, Robert Kennedy, Jacob Javits, and Winston Prouty (R-Vt.), "to try to press down the increases."[35] In both 1966 and 1967 these senators fought with the administration in an effort to raise education appropriations beyond the amount requested. As Senator Morse put it in 1966, the country should not pay for Vietnam at the expense of school children.[36]

In dealing with the liberal senators, Cohen couched his arguments not as a defense of the need for guns and butter but in terms of administrative capacity, telling Morse in 1966, for instance, that it was not clear that the local school districts could even spend the additional billion that the senator wanted to give them. Apparently the school districts were investing in equipment rather than providing more services to students, and in general, the projects funded under Title I "were necessarily developed hastily to get this program moving in the past school year." Morse's committee also wanted to spend $150 million on a new program for the education of the handicapped. Cohen, coached by departmental and Bureau of the Budget officials, said that the administration needed more time to study the matter. As an administration official put it, "Merely turning over $150 million to the states in formula grants doesn't insure good services for the handicapped."[37]

Conservatives were sympathetic to the argument that one could not simply throw money at problems. In 1967 Congressman Albert Quie (R-Minn.) proposed to do away with the various titles in the ESEA legislation and substitute a block grant to the states for educational purposes. At least in theory that would give the states and localities more discretion over how to spend the money and make them less subject to the latest social engineering and civil rights mandates from Washington. After mobilizing the support of organized labor, civil rights groups, and private school groups, the administration defeated Quie's proposal.[38] The basic framework of the ESEA held.

Lingering in the background of the disputes over education was the explosive matter of school desegregation, as few issues attracted as much attention in 1965 and 1966. Almost as soon as the ESEA was passed, the disputes began, including a dramatic confrontation between the federal government and the city of Chicago in the fall of 1965 over cutting off the city's $32 million worth of Title I funds. Education commissioner Francis Keppel announced this decision on October 1, and an angry Richard Daley confronted the president two days later. The president assured the mayor, to whom he owed considerable political debts, that he would look into it. That evening Johnson summoned Gardner, Keppel, Cohen, Cater, and Attorney General Nicholas Katzenbach to the White House to discuss the situation. Johnson promptly assailed Keppel for his failure to notify Daley of his intentions to remove the federal funds from Chicago and told White House aide Joseph Califano to let Daley know that the funds would not be cut off. Then, ignoring Keppel, he turned to Cohen: "Wilbur, you know anything about Chicago?" "No, Mr. President," replied Cohen. "I know a little about it, but if you want me to know anything about it,

I'll know everything I can about it as quickly as possible." "Well," said Johnson, "you're going out to Chicago to resolve this situation." In this manner, Cohen once again found himself in demand as a negotiator. He flew to Chicago and managed to win what one historian describes as a "few desegregation concessions" while also giving Daley most of what he wanted. In his account, Cohen explained that he was given complete authority to resolve the matter and did so in a way that won praise from Lyndon Johnson.[39]

Cohen's narrative of events reveals both the intensity of feeling that underlay the decisions to withhold federal funds from local school systems and the value that Cohen placed on freedom. As someone who worked for much of his life in a large bureaucracy in which consensus ruled and caution governed most actions, he relished the moments when he was free of supervision and control. Like Francis Macomber in the Hemingway short story, he defined his life by those times in which he broke free of restraints and the outcome depended on his instincts. He relished the role of negotiator who followed his gut rather than an elaborate set of instructions. In Cohen's short and happy life, such moments were rare and consequently cherished all the more.

SOCIAL SECURITY AND THE LEGISLATION OF 1967

Along with his new responsibilities as undersecretary, Cohen continued to take the lead on Social Security legislation. More than any other project, the passage of the 1967 Social Security amendments, which contained major changes in Social Security and welfare, framed his life in 1966 and 1967. Working on these, Cohen encountered nearly all the cross-currents of the politics of the era, yet despite the considerable frustrations, he never once considered relinquishing this aspect of his work to someone else. "I not only like this part of the work," he noted, "but the . . . President expects me to do it because he associates me so closely with social security, medicare, and public welfare programs."[40] Preparations for the legislation began as early as March 1966 when he urged the president to consider the expansion of Social Security. Cohen's wish list included the usual incremental items, such as increases in the wage base and in the basic level of benefits. Even though Medicare was new, not even put into effect, he did not hesitate to suggest ways it should be expanded, for instance by covering disabled workers.[41]

Cohen was astute about the politics of economics. When he sent Johnson his proposals for Social Security expansion, he also tried to convince the president that the program was anti-inflationary and revenue enhancing, key virtues during the early phases of the Vietnam buildup. The Social Security tax, he explained, generated a great deal of revenue; a 1 percent increase in the payroll tax could yield as much as $3.5 billion a year.[42] Pursuing his campaign, Cohen told Charles L. Schultze and Gardner Ackley, the administration's chief economists, that an increase in the maximum earnings base for Social Security taxes from $6,600 to $15,000 would produce $4.5 billion in additional tax revenues in 1966. Not only would it dampen the inflationary effect of wage increases beyond $6,600, but it also would be acceptable to many people who believed that unlike with other taxes they received something in return from these.[43] Cutting the cloth to suit the customer, he told LBJ that he did not know how Schultze and Ackley would react to his economics, but he was sure that his recommendation to raise the taxable wage base made for good politics. First, the AFL-CIO backed raising the earnings base. Second, the administration needed something to counter the effect of the deductions from Social Security paychecks that would begin in July 1966 to fund Supplementary Medical Insurance (the voluntary contributions would come from Social Security paychecks) because people would perceive these deductions as a benefit cut. By raising the earnings base, LBJ could finance a Social Security benefit increase in a noninflationary way.[44]

Cohen did not relent in his effort to interest the president in Social Security legislation. When a minor tax bill came to Johnson's desk in April, the undersecretary recommended a signing ceremony in a Texas Social Security office as a way of signaling the president's intention to recommend major improvements in the program in 1967. Cohen urged Johnson to "serve notice to Vietnam critics that you intend to pursue your Great Society program." Robert Kennedy was already planning to introduce a big Social Security bill, and LBJ needed to "keep the initiative."[45]

As Cohen pressed the campaign to increase Social Security benefits, he also addressed welfare policy, realizing that Congress would conduct a major investigation of those programs in 1967 since many of the items in the 1962 Public Welfare amendments would need to be reauthorized in 1967. In an effort to condition the debate, Cohen criticized state practices, such as midnight raids on welfare recipients to see if a man was living in the house, which, he believed, diminished the "self-esteem" of welfare recipients and made it harder for them to go off the rolls.[46] For Cohen, welfare involved a delicate balancing act between alleviating financial need and creating incentives to work; work incentives in turn had to be reconciled with the right of mothers to stay home and care for their young children. Welfare programs therefore needed to encourage independence without undermining family security, a difficult, perhaps impossible task, yet Cohen optimistically believed that "we should come up with a constructive legislative proposal."[47]

In the second half of 1966, Cohen monitored and directed developments in both welfare and Social Security in preparation for the presentation of a comprehensive legislative package in 1967. Among the ideas he bandied about were federally mandated minimum benefits in the Aid to Families with Dependent Children program, mandatory state participation in the Unemployed Parents segment of that program, the elimination of the man-in-the-house rule, a work-training program in each state, and higher public assistance benefits for the elderly. For Social Security, which he called the "original anti-poverty program," he recommended a large increase, as much as 19 percent on average, in the basic benefit.[48]

Although the Democrats fared badly in the midterm elections, 1967 began as Cohen had expected. The Republicans gained forty-seven seats in the House, ten above the average increase for the party out of power over the course of sixty previous years. The number of northern Democrats, crucial to the chances of Great Society legislation, fell from 191 to 156.[49] Undeterred, the president asked Congress for an increase of at least 15 percent in Social Security benefits to begin on July 1, 1967, proposing to fund it through a rise in the Social Security tax rate in 1968 and a gradual augmentation of the taxable wage base. He also asked Congress for many other liberalizations in the program, including the extension of Medicare to disabled workers.[50] Cohen contributed to the effort by mobilizing his network in support of the president: he received a promise from Mills for an early hearing date and assurances from AFL-CIO representatives that labor would support Johnson. Elizabeth Wickenden sought support from voluntary welfare agencies, and Cohen addressed a National Council of Senior Citizens rally, getting them to back the president as well.[51]

In other years, the president's suggestions might have sped through Congress and become law in short order, but in 1967 problems developed that delayed and nearly derailed the law, just as with nearly all of Johnson's domestic legislation. Title I of the Elementary and Secondary Education Act almost came undone in the battle over the Quie amendment, and the Economic Opportunity Act also received considerable congressional criticism. In each case, Congress showed an unwillingness to follow the lead of the administration, even in areas such as Social Security and welfare that had previously generated little conflict. In this regard, 1967 marked a year of transition, away from the consensus that underlay the Great Society and toward the polarized politics that Americans would later come to associate with the 1960s. In welfare reform, to cite a primary example, wide gaps were developing between liberals and conservatives. On the left, the new concept of welfare rights began to gain sway; on the right, the old concept of the welfare loafer came back into fashion.

A product of both the civil rights movement and the War on Poverty, welfare rights began with the notion that people, and in particular black people living in northern ghettos, should be encouraged to seek welfare not as some sort of temporary expedient for acute economic distress but as a permanent right of citizenship. As two of the founders of the movement expressed the idea, "Activists of all kinds should join in a massive drive to mobilize the unaided poor to disrupt the relief system all the more by demanding relief." Toward this end, George A. Wiley, formerly of the Congress of Racial Equality (CORE), founded what officially became the National Welfare Rights Organization (NWRO) in August 1967.

For Cohen the idea of organizing a movement that tied a person's political identity to the receipt of welfare made little or no sense. It mocked liberal hopes of endowing citizens with civil rights that would allow them to participate in the larger society around them; it rejected totally the ideal of rehabilitating welfare recipients so as to make them economically independent. To Wiley and others in the movement, liberalizing welfare laws was less important than expanding welfare rolls. Wiley saw the welfare rights organization as the economic arm of the civil rights movement. In effect, he regarded welfare as the black form of Social Security and therefore believed that the expansion of welfare had as much if not more legitimacy than the expansion of Social Security. To achieve his ends, Wiley did not hesitate to engage in the confrontational rhetoric that had become characteristic of the civil rights movement and in this vein portrayed most of the Cohen/Johnson suggestions as "too timid, token, tardy and toothless."[52]

As if in direct response to Wiley, Ronald Reagan, the recently elected conservative governor of California, declared in a major speech that the public welfare system "must be judged a failure." Welfare, he said, should no longer be considered an "inalienable right" of the poor but as "something of a gift" from people who earned their own way to those who could not earn theirs.[53] Between Wiley's idea of welfare as a right and Reagan's conception of it as a gift, the battle lines were drawn. The polarization made the passage of liberal welfare reform even harder.

Although Cohen knew it would be a difficult year, he failed to predict just how difficult. In February 1967 he wrote to an academic friend that he was involved in "another big legislative program." He spoke with pride of how important congressmen continued to call upon him for advice and of how the White House "deals with me on major policy and political matters." Overall, the congressional session was shaping up as another one that would illustrate the ultimate benevolence of the American political system.[54]

Cohen knew that as always the Social Security law would come down to a negotiation between the Johnson administration and Wilbur Mills. The press noted that Mills and his committee were "somewhat skeptical" about passing the largest benefit increase in the program's history. Most people thought that some sort of compromise would probably emerge, with benefits raised somewhere between 8 percent, as the Republicans wanted, and 15 percent, as the administration desired. Cohen said that a benefit increase in the "neighborhood of only 10 or 11 percent" would generate "tremendous criticism" from organized labor and help the Republicans. He hoped to get a promise from Mills to stick with a "firm 12.5 benefit increase" but did not know if the congressman would agree.[55]

As Cohen and Mills negotiated over Social Security, the undersecretary also began to concentrate on a major departmental reorganization. With Congress unwilling to pass major new laws, bureaucratic reorganization represented one of the available means for Cohen to influence policy. The departure of Ellen Winston as commissioner of welfare prompted him to rethink the ways in which the department administered that program. As early as the end of February, departmental planners had begun to circulate a memo that called for the establishment of the "Social and Rehabilitation Service."[56] Although the details were sketchy, the plan was to bring vocational rehabilitation, aging, and welfare programs together. Mary Switzer, since 1950 the head of the vocational rehabilitation program and an accomplished administrator who had earned John Gardner's confidence, stood at the top of the list of potential directors for the new Social and Rehabilitation Service (SRS).[57] The idea, as in 1962, was to emphasize the need for social services rather than simply for money in responding to the problems of people on the welfare rolls. With Mary Switzer in charge, the new agency would highlight the value of work rather than continuing to stress the connection between welfare and income maintenance. Switzer, as head of the vocational rehabilitation program, had won a reputation as a hardheaded devotee of training people with disabilities for employment; it would be her job to extend similar considerations to mothers on welfare.

In the spring of 1967 Cohen, who had spent those busy months on Social Security, an education bill, and departmental reorganization, felt the usual fatigue at the end of one of his activity spasms. As he told Gardner, he was getting stale "and needed a brief vacation."[58] So far, nothing out of the ordinary had happened to change Cohen's mind that the congressional session would be reasonably productive. Toward the end of June, the Ways and Means Committee completed its initial consideration of Social Security and made plans to turn its attention to welfare; everything was on track for a bill to emerge by the end of July.[59]

In June Cohen busied himself with preparing welfare proposals and completing plans for the department's reorganization. Nearly all of his proposals built upon the 1962 welfare amendments. He wanted, for example, to ensure that there was a comprehensive plan for each family on welfare, and he wished to promote work incentives by allowing recipients to keep some of the money that they had earned without penalty.[60] In these suggestions Cohen showed both faces of his approach to welfare reform: he hoped to raise the basic level of welfare benefits and to promote the idea that expenditures "for social welfare are a good investment."[61]

Even as he issued his welfare wish list, Cohen also produced countless iterations of a timetable for a reorganization of the Welfare Administration. The process would begin with a memo from the Secretary of HEW to the White House, followed by a round of consultations with leaders on the Hill, state administrators, and affected federal employees. Then there would be a White House press conference to announce the new Social and Rehabilitation Service and to introduce Mary Switzer to the press. The process would begin in mid-July and culminate in mid-August.[62] Once created, the SRS would implement the welfare amendments Congress would produce as part of an omnibus Social Security bill. Simultaneously, HEW would launch a major publicity blitz explaining its modern, realistic, yet humane approach to welfare.

In July Cohen told the president that since Wilbur Mills was "most cooperative," the administration was doing "very well" on the Social Security bill. According to Cohen, it would contain the biggest single annual dollar increase in Social Security cash benefits ever enacted. Mills would agree to raise benefits by 13 percent, and Russell Long might gain approval for an even bigger raise in the Senate. Mills, advised Cohen, "takes this into account in making certain changes in the administration proposals." Although the committee backed away from some of the department's recommendations, such as paying Medicare to disabled Social Security beneficiaries, and scaled down the administration's recommended benefit increase, Mills did indeed deliver what he had promised Cohen: a 13 percent increase.[63] In the area of welfare, Cohen told the president that the bill would strengthen the programs and emphasize "rehabilitation and work incentives." Cohen confided to Elizabeth Wickenden on July 15, that the Ways and Means Committee, beginning its final round of deliberations on the bill, was prepared to make important changes in the welfare program, and he believed that she would approve of them.[64]

In the White House, administrative observers shared the sense of optimism about the emerging legislation. Unlike Cohen, who put substantive changes in Social Security and welfare at the head of his wish list, the White House staff members tended to judge the legislation in terms of its potential impact on the economy. Above all else, the president and his advisers were concerned that the bill generate a surplus of revenues over expenditures and ease some of the pressure on the federal deficit.[65]

In the middle of technical discussions about the details of the legislation, the situation underwent a dramatic shift. On the evening of July 12, the arrest of a black cab driver in Newark for a traffic violation touched off riots that lasted for a week. Then on Sunday, July 23, race riots erupted in Detroit and for a week galvanized the nation's attention. Almost overnight, the spirit of close cooperation that had characterized Social Security legislation faded. By Thursday, July 27, on the same day that the president announced the formation of the Kerner Commission to study the causes of urban riots in Detroit, Newark, and elsewhere, the *Wall Street Journal* reported that the Ways and Means Committee wanted "to kill a major proposal to liberalize welfare." The tone of the debate appeared to have been altered. Mills wanted mandatory referrals of welfare mothers to training programs and, according to the *Journal*, to throw recalcitrant adults off the rolls entirely. An anonymous source said that the committee would crack down on people "who are able to work but who make welfare a way of life." The committee, which had been lavish with Social Security benefits the week before, billed its approach to welfare as "tough." Although the connection with the riots was not emphasized by either the politicians or the press, the fact that the committee considered welfare just after the riots ended in Newark and just as they started in Detroit (43 dead, 7,000 people arrested) clearly changed the entire tone of the legislative process. To many observers in Congress, the riots indicated a failure of social policy and called for a tough response, such as cracking down on "permissive" welfare policies. Mills, already under pressure to cut domestic spending to pay for the Vietnam War, obliged.[66]

Still deeply involved in the Social Security legislation, Cohen turned his attention to a crash program to push federal aid in the urban ghettos. Among the ideas he raised was one to expand emergency financial assistance for welfare from 30 to 120 days and to raise the federal share for such aid from 50 to 75 percent. He also talked about establishing round-the-clock programs in local schools for summers and weekends. An atmosphere approaching panic was coming to engulf the government as the administration hoped to make it through the summer without more violent clashes between whites and blacks.[67]

In this atmosphere the House voted on the Mills omnibus Social Security measure. It included the mandatory referral of some welfare mothers to work-training programs and a little-noticed provision that in effect "froze" the number of dependent children that could be aided by federal funds. Despite an impassioned plea from John Gardner that it reconsider, the House, acting with strong support from the Republicans, passed the bill on August 17 under the usual closed rule provision for Social Security. In an uncharacteristic manner, welfare, rather than Social Security, dominated the debate.[68]

Cohen shifted his attention to the Senate and to the normal business of Social Security, courting Russell Long, who over the course of the decade had emerged as a successor to Robert Kerr as the most powerful senator on the Finance Committee. Cohen saw his job as convincing Long to recommend a 17.5 percent rise in the average Social Security benefit and a ninety dollar minimum benefit, so as to emerge from conference with a 15 percent across-the-board increase and the seventy dollar minimum that the president wanted. Long, like Mills, was obliging, willing to do his part to raise benefits.[69]

The calm decorum and inside politics of Social Security received another blow at the end of August, however, when the National Welfare Rights Organization, holding a founding convention in Washington, decided to confront the senators on the welfare amendments. Its members made the explicit charge that if welfare benefits were not raised, then more riots might occur in the cities. The welfare freeze and mandatory training requirements triggered the rallies held at the Department of Health, Education, and Welfare and at the Capitol. "It's another form of slavery, baby. But I'm black, and I'm beautiful. They're not gonna take me back," said Mrs. Margaret McCarty of Baltimore. Neither Gardner nor Long would meet with the welfare demonstrators although Gardner offered to send Cohen in his place and Wiley declined. Long refused to back down; arguing that "people who can work ought to work," he opted to take a long Labor Day holiday.[70]

The confrontation over welfare rights tended to put a damper on Cohen's plans for departmental reorganization and the public unveiling of the Social and Rehabilitation Service. In a background interview with the *New York Times*, Cohen spoke of how much rehabilitation could accomplish: "Psychologically," he said, "testing and adjusting are advancing people who 10 or 20 years ago were believed to be beyond rehabilitation." Cohen's rhetoric, which smacked of the lessons taught in social work school, was much too cool to match the warm temper of the times. The actions of the Ways and Means Committee, the urban riots, and the welfare rights demonstrations appeared to make SRS obsolete even before it opened.[71]

The situation continued to deteriorate. On August 29 Robert Kennedy told the Senate Finance Committee that the House-passed bill should simply be scrapped, and he proposed larger rises in Social Security benefits than were advocated by either the administration or Russell Long. The next day Cohen attended a cabinet lunch at which the topic was a demonstration planned for October to protest the Vietnam War. Attorney General Ramsey Clark reported that he expected at least 100,000 people to show up; the organizers of the march hoped to attract 250,000 people to Washington. Robert McNamara, the beleaguered secretary of defense, expressed his concern about how the administration should handle so many people, some of whom would engage in "nonviolent disobedience" by blocking streets. Larry O'Brien said that the Democratic party had lost the ability to communicate with the middle class. O'Brien, like the other cabinet members, had no solutions; he only knew there were problems.[72] Deciding to escape from such turmoil and his legislative problems, Cohen took a trip to South America.[73] Normally, he found foreign travel a tonic and came home buoyed by the comparison between affluent America and the rest of the world; this time, when he returned on September 14, he discovered chaos.

The hearings in the Senate Finance Committee had resumed at a shrill pitch. Mayor John Lindsay of New York said that if the Senate adopted the House's version of the bill, the result could be a "flaming crisis."[74] On September 19 the National Welfare Rights Organization received permission to present thirty minutes of testimony. At first, George Wiley was scheduled to testify, but he decided to bring six other witnesses who were welfare mothers with him; Russell Long and Fred Harris listened to the testimony. One of the welfare mothers called the House-passed bill a form of "dictatorship" that imposed "changes on our lives, our children, our husbands, and yet we haven't been asked about them." The women objected to the fact that the Senate hearing was so sparsely attended and also took exception to the interruptions for quorum calls that were interspersed through the proceedings. After one such interruption, Senator Long failed to return and left Harris in charge. At one o'clock, with the hearings in temporary recess and the NWRO testimony apparently over, the women decided not to surrender the witness table and staged a sit-in that lasted until 3:45 P.M.. The Capitol police, according to Wiley, threatened to arrest the group with "unlawful entry" if they did not leave. It made for a confusing and unsettling scene. It was remarkable that such a confrontation could take place in one of the inner sanctums of power on a hearing devoted to a subject that was usually discussed calmly in a technical patois spoken by only a few.[75]

Senator Long professed to be unintimidated by the welfare group: "If they can find time to march in the streets, picket and sit all day in committee hearing rooms, they can find time to do some useful work." He suggested that they pick up the litter in front of their houses instead of obstructing the work of Congress.[76] No stranger to the use of invective and political innuendo, Russell Long showed that he knew how to use the confrontational spirit of the time to his advantage.

The very evening of the sit-in, Wilbur Cohen put on evening clothes, drove to a hotel in a leafy, affluent area of northwest Washington, and served as toastmaster for a testimonial dinner in honor of Mary Switzer.[77] It was her coming-out party as the head of the Social and Rehabilitation Service, the agency that was expected to deal with the situation that could now be called a welfare crisis. It was her unfortunate assignment to be asked to administer the welfare program to the satisfaction of Robert Kennedy, Russell Long, Wilbur Mills, George Wiley, and the millions of people who depended on welfare for their very existence. Switzer, described by the *Des Moines Register* as a sixty-seven-year-old administrator with graying hair and candid blue eyes, began her new job by barnstorming the nation. Wherever she went, she talked about the creative blend of rehabilitation and income maintenance that would solve the welfare problem, trying hard not to alienate either Senator Long or her new constituency of welfare recipients. She opposed the "welfare freeze," but she favored a "work-oriented program."[78] "Mary's appointment was a very smart move," Elizabeth Wickenden confided to Cohen. Charles I. Schottland, the former Social Security commissioner, added that "Mary really knows how to get things done and whatever she sets out to do will certainly be pro bono publico."[79] It was unclear, however, that even competent bureaucrats such as Wilbur Cohen and Mary Switzer could handle the polarized politics of 1967. People with the ability to romance Congress and to move programs through orderly channels could do less in an era when the congressional institutions were themselves under attack than in an earlier era when the passage of legislation was equated with progress.

Although Cohen persevered in his negotiations with Senator Long and others, he yielded at times to an uncharacteristic sense of despair. In a letter to Wickenden, Cohen finally let go and vented his feelings: "I have never experienced frustration as I am now," he complained. The situation was worse than in the Eisenhower administration. Then, Cohen's frustration stemmed from "neglect and apathy"; in 1967, the problems were more fundamental and came from the fact that the country was "torn apart" on a whole host of issues. It made for the most "difficult legislative happening" in his thirty-three years of experience, and he felt like an unappreciated "intermediary" among contending parties.[80]

With Wickenden, Cohen could indulge in self-pity, but with his congressional clients, he continued to show up for work with a shoeshine and a smile. Regardless of the fate of the welfare amendments, Cohen knew he must continue to push for the Social Security benefit increase. The strategy consisted of urging the Senate Finance Committee to back a high increase that would give Russell Long room to maneuver with Wilbur Mills in Congress. Cohen told the president that he thought Long would go along because he too wanted the increase. He would also raise Social Security taxes because he wanted to show that he was fiscally responsible. Similarly, the conservative John Williams (R-Del.) would want to increase benefits and taxes to emphasize the connection between revenue and spending.[81]

Despite the disputes over welfare, the administration needed the Social Security legislation badly for its tax revenues. It was increasingly clear that since the president would be unable to obtain a general tax increase, the Social Security tax would have to serve as a substitute. Thus it was even more important for any bill to provide a Social Security benefit increase and to yield an excess of revenues over expenditures. One idea was to raise taxes but to defer increased benefits until April 1968, an action that would give "the maximum anti-inflationary effect" in the first quarter, as Cohen described it. It was, however, a difficult political maneuver to pull off. Senator Long needed room to bargain with Mills, and he also had to contain the antiwar sentiments of liberal senators such as Vance Hartke (D-Ind.) and Eugene McCarthy (D-Minn.). Hartke's proposal was the opposite of the administration's; he wanted to raise benefits immediately but postpone tax increases until 1969, maintaining that the administration's scheme was a "cruel hoax" on low-income persons designed to finance the war. The increase in Social Security taxes, he said, was a substitute for a new tax bill and marked the first time that the program had been used for fiscal policy purposes.[82]

Cohen knew that Hartke and his fellow liberals could make political trouble for the administration. Tax raises were never popular, and senators who had to run in 1968 would have particular reason to oppose an increase in Social Security taxes. Further, the administration had not taken a consistent position on the question of the level and timing of tax raises. Cohen reminded the president that "we . . . are now changing our recommendation in view of the failure of passage of the tax bill."[83]

Cohen's allies soon confirmed his sense that it was unwise to raise the taxable wage base and to increase the basic tax rate from 8.8 to 10.0 percent as the Senate Finance Committee had tentatively decided. George Meany of the AFL sent word that he was concerned about the financial impact of higher Social Security taxes on his members. Cohen believed that it might be better to skip the tax rise and to recommend instead only a rise in the taxable wage base.[84] As usual, the details were too technical for most people to follow. At the same time, Hartke's argument that the administration was using Social Security to pay for the war and in effect was financing the war on the backs of the working class had a great deal of resonance. The contrast between workers, paying higher Social Security taxes, and welfare recipients, complaining that their benefits were too low, was particularly striking. The Senate Finance Committee met with Cohen and decided to reverse its earlier decision to have both a rise in the taxable wage base and a Social Security tax increase.[85] In working out the complicated changes, Cohen lost some of the customary goodwill that he brought to the legislative process, particularly from the leaders of the Ways and Means Committee who were angry with him and Gardner for changing their minds on the advisability of a tax increase.[86]

The conflict over the Social Security amendments continued through Senate passage, the work of the conference committee, and into the next year. The Senate passed a liberal version of the House bill that discarded many of its harsher elements. Under the terms of the Senate bill, welfare mothers would not be required to work, and there would be no welfare freeze. "If the Social Security bill emerges from the conference in substantially the form in which it has just passed the Senate," editorialized the *New York Times*, "it will rank as the year's outstanding legislative achievement." The *Times* praised the spirit of cooperation "of a kind rarely seen in the Ninetieth Congress between legislators and the administration" and applauded the efforts of Gardner and Cohen.[87]

It was now time for Long and Mills to meet in conference to decide the final shape of the bill. Cohen attended as usual and reported on the results to the White House. By December 8, 1967, the conference had reached some major decisions. On Social Security, the conferees agreed on a 13 percent across-the-board increase with a $55 minimum. Cohen characterized this result as 75 percent of what the president had requested and "a very substantial achievement." It would be financed by raising the taxable wage base from $6,600 to $7,800, effective on January 1, 1968, and by raising the tax rate in 1969. The increase in benefits would not be paid until March, which gave the administration something of what it had asked for in the way of an anti-inflationary measure and the liberals something of what they had requested through no immediate rise in the tax rate. Welfare proved a more contentious matter. The conferees tempered the provisions in the House bill, but only somewhat: the AFDC freeze would not begin until July 1, 1968; referral to training programs would not be mandatory but would apply only to cases that state welfare directors regarded as "appropriate."

Even though Cohen saw trouble ahead, he tended to believe that the administration should support the conference report. He knew that liberal senators, such as Kennedy, Javits, Ralph Metcalf (D-Mont.), and Millard Tydings (D-Md.), would attack it. As a partial response, he advised the White House that the president should announce the establishment of a commission on income plans at the same time that he signed the law; such an action might "take some of the sting out of the criticisms of the liberals, the social workers, and even the Governors of the 'tough' provisions in the bill on welfare."[88] On December 9 he told state welfare officials that the administration believed it best to live with the law, at least for a short period. "New Congresses may always reconsider what past Congresses have done," he said.[89] Mary Switzer also lent her support to the conference report.[90]

By December 11 Cohen, perhaps taking his cues from George Meany–who denounced the bill and resolved to fight it–had changed his mind and recommended instead that the administration try to alter the bill. He wrote Wilbur Mills that approving it would cast the administration as anti-Negro in an election year and reminded him that nineteen governors had come out against the welfare freeze. Mayors worried that the harsh welfare provisions might occasion the next round of urban riots. Liberals and civil rights groups would use the bill to demonstrate that Lyndon Johnson, despite his accomplishments, was really anti-Negro. Fred Harris told Cohen that he "would filibuster to death if necessary against the bill" and expected Senators Metcalf, Kennedy, Morse, and Hartke to help him.[91]

A formal campaign against the conference report began. On December 11 Mayor John Lindsay talked with his colleagues in Chicago, Pittsburgh, and elsewhere, and they agreed that the report should be opposed. John Gardner decided it was time to appeal directly to the president, saying that he had tried to keep his appeals to a minimum but that the freeze and the compulsory features of the work and training programs needed to be opposed. "These are going to become celebrated issues in the liberal community. They will be perceived as anti-Negro measures by the Negro community," Gardner noted. The possibilities for "political exploitation of the issues" were "considerable, since the chief ones to suffer will be children and the effect of the compulsory features will be to place the State between mothers and their children, even infant children."[92]

Here was the politics of the late 1960s in microcosm. The 1967 legislation featured a big rise in Social Security benefits in a bill that organized labor, the administration's biggest supporter and collaborator on such legislation, felt compelled to oppose. Liberals, who strongly favored some features of the bill such as increased Social Security benefits and the notion of allowing welfare beneficiaries to keep some of their earnings, nonetheless perceived the measure as anticity and antiblack. Organized labor leaders and liberals joined in the cause of opposing higher Social Security taxes although for different reasons. Labor leaders worried about maintaining the income of the working man; liberals regarded higher Social Security taxes as a disguised way of financing the Vietnam War, and thus the unlikely vehicle of a Social Security bill became a means for them to express their opposition to that war. Conservatives, who very much wanted to contain welfare benefits, could not overlook the liberal features of the law. Hence, the bill, the very sort of bill that would have been inordinately popular a few years before, stirred up controversy.

The situation indicated how the Vietnam War complicated the politics of the 1960s by separating liberals from measures they ordinarily would have supported. It also demonstrated the racial polarization of the period after the riots of 1967. Stripped to the ugly essentials, the situation featured blacks threatening riots in the cities and whites threatening to retaliate by cutting welfare benefits. Meanwhile, the administration, which was making a sincere effort to raise Social Security benefits, to finance the war, and to create a blend of rehabilitation and income maintenance in the welfare program, earned the enmity of nearly all sides. The administration was distrusted by everyone, even by its traditional allies.

Although the president sympathized with Cohen and Gardner, he wanted the legislation to pass. He distrusted Robert Kennedy and his motives, needed the revenue that the bill offered, and genuinely wanted to raise Social Security benefits. As one of his political advisers told him, a Senate filibuster would give the administration the worst of both worlds. In the opinion of Edmund Muskie, it would inflame black militants and irritate Social Security recipients. Fred Harris, LBJ's aide told him, was simply acting as "Bobby Kennedy's agent."[93]

Carping over the bad choices available, the Senate passed the bill. Approval of the conference committee measure in the House was never in doubt. Johnson delayed for two weeks after final passage of the bill before he signed it on January 2, 1968. The president issued a tempered statement in which he said that he was "directing Secretary Gardner to work with state governments so that compassionate safeguards are established to protect deserving mothers and needy children." If the president had waited two more hours to sign the bill, it would have died by pocket veto.[94]

Undoubtedly the confrontational politics of 1967 tempered some of Cohen's enthusiasm for legislative politics. He realized that the bonanza of 1965 was over, and in its place was bitterly divisive form of politics that made his job much more difficult. Not only did it make it harder to pass new laws, it also made it more arduous to administer existing laws. Ironically, this confrontational politics arrived just as Cohen was to achieve a position of true national influence. A generation of New Deal bureaucrats was about to come to full power at a time when the ideas that had served them so well for over a generation were beginning to lose their sway over social policy.

12
SECRETARY COHEN

Cohen accepted the position of Secretary of the Department of Health, Education, and Welfare in the spring of 1968. It was a prize tarnished by the brutal events of that year and by the president's announcement of his decision not to seek reelection. Cohen understood that under different circumstances Johnson would not have chosen him, but the president wanted to reward him for his service and shore up the programs under the direction of HEW. His appointment was symbolic recognition of the work accomplished by the group of people who had entered public service in the 1930s and who came to positions of influence in the 1960s. As Secretary of HEW, Cohen rode out the events of 1968, not so much influencing the nation's social welfare policy as responding to events that were well beyond his control. By the end of his brief term as secretary, he had no signature pieces of legislation to show for the experience, but he did have the considerable satisfaction of reaching the top of a department he had entered in 1934 as little more than an office boy.

When he was undersecretary, Cohen attracted little national attention. He made his share of important appearances before hospital planners, welfare administrators, and the like, and his remarks were often taken quite seriously by these professionals as indicators of trends in federal health, welfare, or Social Security policy.[1] Journalists who wanted the inside story on legislation turned to him for advice.[2] Cohen even picked up his share of awards, such as a Rockefeller public service award in 1967 that netted him and four other anonymous public servants $10,000 and a brief flurry of attention.[3] Yet the perception of Cohen remained as that of a technical expert, a competent assistant to John Gardner, rather than an important personality in his own right.

In this regard, Wilbur J. Cohen tended to follow the examples of his mentors. Arthur Altmeyer had been a faithful public servant who strived for anonymity and, despite considerable accomplishments in building Social Security, achieved it. Edwin Witte was downright unassuming and did not like calling attention to himself.[4] Cohen, too, consciously tried not to be arrogant, in part because of his long training as a legislative liaison who had constantly to deal with people of large and expansive egos. He developed a determined drabness, in striking contrast to intellectual celebrities such as Daniel Patrick Moynihan or activists such as Jesse Jackson, both of whom crossed Cohen's path in 1968.

Sid Johnson, who went to work for Cohen in 1967 and remained with him through the beginning of 1969, liked to tell a story about Cohen's manner when he appeared in front of congressional committees. When an academic testified on welfare and received a great deal of favorable publicity, Johnson asked Cohen why he did not use his testimony to dazzle the senators in a similar manner. He deliberately did not do that, Cohen replied; he liked to talk around and around a subject, to speak at length and be plodding. Then, finally, a congressman would interrupt and say, "Cohen, why don't you do thus and so?" "Let me work on it," Cohen would answer. As Cohen explained to Sid Johnson, that way the idea came from the congressman.[5] If the story revealed some of Cohen's charm, it also indicated that he had his own kind of arrogance. Although he did not call attention to himself, he took pride in his ability to control a situation and bend the policy process to his ultimate purposes. Nearly always, Cohen thought himself the intellectual equal of his partner or adversary, believing there was an inner light within him that separated him from the great majority of individuals. Little had happened to him since he had left Milwaukee to weaken his sense of confidence.

At the same time, Cohen had few financial, social, or political ambitions. It was enough that he could guide legislation and make policy; he did not require his name in the press. Paradoxically, because he was so relaxed about his social ambitions, he could take genuine delight in his proximity to power and glamour. He did not expect to travel first class or to receive an invitation to a White House dinner, but when those things happened, he savored them. He worried little about acting inappropriately or revealing himself as unrefined or middle class. As a result, he could let go when others were often uptight, a quality that served him well in 1968.

GARDNER'S DEPARTURE AND COHEN'S ARRIVAL

John Gardner gave few signs of disengagement in the early days of 1968. On January 11 the secretary appeared to be deeply involved in an effort to reorganize his department, seeking to strengthen what a journalist called the department's "superstructure" so as to limit the power of outside interest groups and to coordinate the department's approach to health and welfare. Gardner had the idea that there should be an undersecretary in charge of health, another in charge of education, and still another in charge of welfare. With the possible title of deputy secretary, Cohen would be the person to whom these under-secretaries reported.[6]

The beginning of the year found Cohen engaged in his traditional activities. He assisted Gardner in reorganizing the department's health functions in three principal agencies headed by an undersecretary. He talked with Wilbur Mills about ways to temper the welfare freeze that was scheduled to go into effect in July. As was his custom, he also worked on the incremental and expansion of existing programs, in this case Medicare. His pet project, dubbed kiddycare, was to extend Medicare and Medicaid so that the government paid for prenatal and postnatal care of all mothers as well as for the costs of delivering the baby and the baby's care during its first year of life. Although Cohen knew the measure would be controversial, he also knew the political appeal of providing benefits to mothers and children so that every child could "be born with the best medical care and have a good start in life."[7] Using the reasoning that he had learned over a lifetime, Cohen advised that kiddycare should not be limited to the poor and that the plan's benefits should be funded through payroll taxes to create a "contributory, earned right." It was important, he said, to give people the "psychological feeling that they have helped to pay for *their* protection. It is the reason why social security has been so popular and well accepted."[8]

Then on January 25 John Gardner resigned as Secretary of HEW. He left on the last day of February, and stepping into the corridor of the fifth floor of the HEW North Building at 5:50 P.M., he found a crowd of 300 employees lining the halls who broke into applause. Gardner waved, shook people's hands, and without a word, got into the elevator and went home. He soon started to work for the Urban Coalition, created to cope with what he perceived to be a domestic crisis.[9]

Cohen, who prided himself on his sensitivity to people's needs, was as surprised as anyone by Gardner's departure. "I guess I was just about the last person to know," he said. He thought that some dynamic in the relationship between Gardner and Doug Cater, the White House staffer, precipitated Gardner's decision.[10] Other observers thought Gardner acted from a general feeling of weariness and despair over the Vietnam War. The news came at a particularly bad time for the president, who had also to contend with the resignation of Secretary of Defense Robert McNamara and, at the very end of January, the beginning of the Tet offensive in Vietnam. The simultaneity of

Acting Secretary Cohen attends a cabinet meeting on March 10, 1968. (Courtesy of Bruce Cohen)

events made it appear as though the nation was losing both the war in Vietnam and the War on Poverty.[11]

Distracted by news of epochal importance, Washington insiders still found time to speculate on Gardner's replacement. Cohen's name invariably appeared on lists of possible HEW secretaries, along with such other names as Ben Heineman, chairman of the Chicago and North Western Railway, Housing and Urban Development (HUD) secretary Robert Weaver, Radcliffe president Mary Bunting, and Congresswoman Edith Green. One line of thought held that Cohen would be given the job on an interim basis, until Johnson started his second term in 1969. Gardner himself permitted Cohen to assume his duties just as soon as he announced his resignation. "You take charge," he told Cohen in January, "act like you are running the department." Even before Gardner's formal departure, Cohen had become the real head of the department.[12]

When Gardner left, Cohen officially became the acting Secretary of HEW and on March 4, 1968, appeared before the House appropriations subcommittee to explain the department's budget requests. It was a command performance in front of Congressman Dan Flood (D-Pa.), who, with his distinctive handlebar mustache, looked a little like a villain in a melodrama. With elaborate congressional courtesy, Flood welcomed Cohen and noted, "As far as I am concerned, I would like to see him Secretary of Health, Education, and Welfare."[13] Cohen, who had attended many such sessions, led the congressmen through an overview of the nation's health, education, and welfare activities. He liked being at the center of the table, in marked contrast to his appearance in April 1961 with Abraham Ribicoff. On that day, Ribicoff had made the sweeping philosophical statements, and Assistant Secretary Cohen had answered technical questions.[14] In 1968 he was auditioning for the role of secretary. Sensitive to congressional concerns, Cohen began with the growth in the welfare rolls and also talked about medical research, child health, and the problems of the nation's cities. Always, he tried to show the congressmen what they were buying with their appropriations. In 1967 Social Security benefits helped keep 5.7 million people out of poverty, and the new amendments would lift .5 million more out. Medicare, in its first eighteen months, had paid more than 28 million medical bills, amounting to over $1.3 billion. Ninety-three percent of the elderly had signed up for the voluntary Part B of Medicare. Nine million disadvantaged children were aided by the special projects of Title I of the Elementary and Secondary Education Act in 1967.[15]

In the days when John Fogarty had run the appropriations subcommittee, the numbers would have served as the talisman to earn increased appropriations, which would have led to higher numbers in a continuous parade of progress, but in 1968 there were more ambiguities in the situation. The numbers told of progress, yet the cities, as Cohen admitted, were in deep crisis. There were rising welfare loads, high unemployment among the young and untrained, high rates of crime and delinquency, unrest, and alienation. In the past these matters might have been agreeable challenges that required legislative initiatives and increased appropriations; in 1968 these problems seemed less amenable to new laws, bigger numbers, higher appropriations. As an example of a new difficulty with no apparent remedy, Flood mentioned that parents were placing advertisements in magazines read by what the congressman referred to as "the so-called 'hippy' set" in a desperate effort to reclaim their children. He worried about the young people who became flower children "in apparently astonishing numbers."[16]

Cohen confessed that he was still "groping for solutions" to the nation's problems, yet like the congressmen, he fell back on the verities of his own life and recommended more of the same. He supported vocational education, for example, because he had always supported it. He told the committee that he had gone to primary school right across the street from the Milwaukee Vocational School, had visited the building many times, and had many friends who had gone there. "I would say it would be great if we could have something like the Milwaukee Vocational School in every area of the country," he said. In telling this story, Cohen was engaging in the sort of selective memory that often marked the effort to go from personal experience to national policy. He had perhaps forgotten his strong advice to his brother not to attend such a school in the 1930s because nothing could be gained "from a cultural point of view."[17] Similarly, Cohen repeatedly relied on his personal experience as a guide to future action, despite the deep differences between his depression generation and the generation that grew up in postwar affluence. When he was a boy, he had had the "privilege" of working in his father's store. He lamented that his children had less opportunity to be of help, but then again, as Cohen realized, their father did not work on a "farm, ranch, or . . . store."[18] Despite these differences, he thought in terms of policies that would somehow replicate his depression experience.

Cohen spent the month of March prodding the president on personnel matters, putting the first stages of the health reorganization into effect, and cajoling Wilbur Mills to postpone the welfare freeze.[19] As these activities occurred more or less in public, the president's advisers debated, more or less in private, the merits of appointing Cohen as secretary. Doctors, as usual, objected. Within a week, the president received 163 letters claiming Cohen was a Socialist; these appeared to be connected with the Association of American Physicians and Surgeons (AAPS), which had published a bulletin headed "Stop the Appointment of Wilbur J. Cohen as Secretary of HEW." Relying on the analysis of Marjorie Shearon, the bulletin implied that Cohen wanted to put all doctors on salary. It followed the theme of Shearon's privately published *Wilbur J. Cohen and the Pursuit of Power,* which she described as "the story of a man without professional training in *any* field, who set out to be Czar of Medicine." John Macy, White House director of personnel, told the president that the members of AAPS, who opposed the administration anyway, should not influence the nomination. Cohen wrote those doctors who corresponded directly with him that he was not a Socialist. Shearon's book, in his opinion, was "biased, slanted, and prejudiced."[20] He did receive support from members of the medical community such as Dr. Morris Fishbein and the dean of the Medical School at George Washington University. In addition, a Democratic national committeeman for Oregon, one of Cohen's friends, advised Johnson that Cohen was known as a liberal. As matters stood, liberals had developed such "religious fanaticism about Vietnam that they're forgetting the rest of the ball game," and Cohen's appointment would help them remember, bring them back for the election, and boost the morale of the civil service. The president received a telegram in a similar vein from Darwin Huxley of Milwaukee; the writer apparently did not feel it necessary to mention that he had changed his name after military service and that he was, in fact, Wilbur Cohen's brother.[21]

On March 22, 1968, Lyndon Johnson nominated Wilbur Cohen to become the seventh person ever to serve as Secretary of the Department of Health,

Education, and Welfare. As Cohen recalled, Johnson called him into the Oval Office and said, "Wilbur, I've made up my mind what to do. . . . I have a great deal of confidence in you. . . . Therefore, I'm going to appoint you Secretary. We're going to announce it at 5:30." And thus LBJ pulled one of his much-loved surprises on the press. Cohen came to believe that the president had already made up his mind not to seek another term and therefore felt he could get by with the appointment even though Cohen had no political standing.[22]

The press treated Cohen with respect. The *New York Times* set the tone by calling him "one of the country's foremost technicians in public welfare." The *Chicago Daily News* referred to him as a "practical visionary." *Chicago's American* sounded one of the few dissonant notes, pointing out that Cohen had "impeccable credentials" but that he was "obviously a second choice which the President forced upon himself by his failure to attract badly needed new blood." In the sudden glare of publicity, the press sought to reinvent Cohen and make him into an interesting Washington character whose continuing adventures, along with those of his wife Eloise, would be of interest to readers. Many writers highlighted the contrast between the tall and aristocratic Gardner and the short and ordinary Cohen. He was, as the *Chicago Daily News* put it, a "small round man with a fringe of curly hair on his baldish head." Those were the adjectives of choice: Cohen was "short, balding, and plain," or he was "short, plump, and balding." He was a Jewish man of the people of whom it was said, in an inspired moment of public relations creativity, that he liked to go across the mall and grab a lunch of matzo ball soup and corned beef on rye. He was "easily approachable," and most people called him by his first name. He led a "casually informal existence," chopping wood on weekends on his three-acre Silver Spring property, living in the same house he had owned since 1948, the very house he had bought from Esther Peterson, who became the head of the Women's Bureau.

Eloise Cohen was portrayed as a cross between Lady Bird Johnson and Eleanor Roosevelt. She was a "red-haired" or "titian-haired" Texan who thought she could ease her husband's burdens by "having his headaches for him." Mrs. Cohen, it was reported, did all the family cooking but was one of those women who, according to the *Charleston West Virginia Gazette,* was "constitutionally unable to sit still and watch the world go by." Like Mrs. Roosevelt, she was involved in the improvement of Appalachia and was actively political, vowing to make campaign speeches on LBJ's behalf. Just as with the Roosevelts, in the words of the *Washington Post* headline, the nation "got two for one with the Wilbur Cohens."[23]

Time Magazine, which had time to peruse the various press accounts, ran a short item that provided Cohen with one of the tag lines that eventually came to define him: *Time* called him "the salami slicer." He was willing and able "to sacrifice cherished legislative objectives so long as he gets at least a small piece of what he wants." He had the gift of taking a morsel and fattening it year by year until he ended up with what he wanted in the first place. The magazine quoted an aide who called Cohen's technique " 'salami slicing.' . . . One slice does not amount to much but eventually there is enough for a sandwich." The article provided an enduring portrait to which Cohen himself liked to refer in speeches and interviews, saying that the salami metaphor reflected his idea of the "evolution of social legislation; to take a bit at a time and digest it."[24]

As secretary-designate, Cohen discovered that the press was interested in his views on a broad range of issues, not just on the narrow questions of social policy. He no longer commented exclusively on such matters as whether Congressman Mills or Senator Long would support a particular modification of Social Security. As a frontline member of the administration, he was expected to speak on broader, more consequential issues. At the time of Cohen's nomination, the story of interest was the administration's reaction to the situation that people were starting to call the urban crisis. In particular, the media wanted to know how the administration would respond to the recommendations of the Kerner Commission that had been released at the beginning of March. Hubert Humphrey had already indicated his view that this report on civil disorders, with its tag line that the nation "was heading toward two societies, one black, one white – separate and unequal," overemphasized white racism. Cohen followed up on Humphrey's comment on March 25 at his first postnomination press conference: "I've thought a good deal about the term 'white racism,' " he said. "It bothers me a good deal because I think you could also say there is black racism and brown racism and red racism." Cohen continued, "I believe the problem is more complicated than white racism." It was "no great help" to use "slogans" to cope with complex problems; the report "oversimplified" the cause of urban problems, and people in the ghettos should direct their energies "away from rioting and toward obtaining jobs and schooling."[25]

Other than a desire to defend the administration, it was difficult to say what motivated this outburst. Cohen did believe in social programs and felt that glib slogans too often became excuses for inactivity, but whatever his motivation, he exhibited extremely unorthodox behavior for a cabinet nominee who as a general rule was not supposed to comment on matters so close to the surface of the nation's sensitivity. He soon found his words splashed across the pages of the country's newspapers. Carl Rowan, the columnist, noted that minorities placed more trust in presidential candidate Robert Kennedy (who had entered the race on March 16) than in presidential candidate Lyndon Johnson, in part because of the performance of people such as Wilbur Cohen. Rowan charged that Cohen got off "to a disturbingly inauspicious start by delivering a gratu-itous attack" on the Kerner Commission report. Rowan objected particularly to Cohen's comment that the commission put too little emphasis on how the poor could "lift themselves up by their own bootstraps." It sounded to Rowan and to many other observers as though Cohen was, in a phrase that would soon be bandied about in discussions of the nation's social policies, blaming the victim. "In this revolutionary era," wrote Rowan, "men who hunger for either food or dignity cannot be satisfied with bureaucratic legalisms or Horatio Alger cliches."[26] Aware that he had made a mistake, Cohen found it necessary to backtrack, telling an American University audience on April 2 that the report was a "valuable contribution to our thinking" and did the nation a service by calling attention to the formation of two societies, one black, one white.[27]

By this date Cohen's remarks almost did not matter. On Sunday, March 31, President Lyndon Johnson addressed the nation: "I want to speak to you of peace in Vietnam," he began. "Accordingly I shall not seek, and I will not accept the nomination of my party for another term as your president," he concluded. *Newsweek* reported that those were the "20 words that shook the world."[28] Cohen had apparently been called by the White House right after the president's speech. After a long pause, he mumbled, "thanks for calling"; then he and Eloise drove to the White House. As Eloise recalled, the gates were open, and they were able to drive right into the White House grounds. Once inside, they found other members of the administration, such as Walt and Elspeth Rostow, looking a little stunned. When Cohen saw the president he did not know quite what to say, but Johnson put him at ease. "Wilbur," he said, "I absolutely and completely forgot when I appointed you . . . that your wife was from Texas." "Mr. President, I thought that was the only reason I got the job." LBJ continued: "I'm working on that housing in Johnson City, you and your wife and me are going to live in them and need them." "You're a great President, we wish you could be our President for four more years," said Cohen. Characteristically, he could not quite believe he was so close to the very stuff of history. He unabashedly collected the moment and polished it into a practiced anecdote. Without any trace of self-consciousness, he later wrote up the incident and sent it to *Reader's Digest* in the hope they would run it in their "Humor in Uniform" feature.[29]

Even before he was confirmed by the Senate and sworn into office, the value of Cohen's nomination was reduced. Although the administration received something of a boost from the president's announcement that he would not run, the assassination of Martin Luther King in Memphis on April 4 once again plunged the nation into crisis. In short order, Cohen found himself dealing with one of King's legacies. In December 1967 the civil rights leader had announced that he planned to launch the Poor People's Campaign in the spring. Part of King's broadening critique of American society that included his condemnation in the spring of 1967 of the Vietnam War and his encouragement of passive resistance of the draft, the campaign would appeal to America's conscience and force the government to provide jobs and other supports to all who needed them. Although he would pursue his goals nonviolently, King hoped to "develop massive dislocation" that would lead to government action.[30] After King's death, the Reverend Ralph Abernathy decided to proceed with the Poor People's Campaign, initiating the project with the Poor People's March on Washington that included visits to cabinet officers. Since a guaranteed annual income was one of the campaign's central demands, Abernathy targeted the Department of Health, Education, and Welfare. Accordingly, Cohen, Switzer, and other high-ranking departmental officials met with representatives of the Poor People's March on April 30.

Cohen presided, trying to bring a sense of dignity to the proceedings, treating the representatives of the Poor People's Campaign as though they were congressmen or diplomats. The people from the campaign were deferential, yet they spoke in the confrontational idioms of the 1960s. They were not there to discuss social policy; instead, they presented a series of demands. Jesse Jackson, who identified himself as a member of the Southern Christian Leadership Conference (SCLC), began by treating the departmental officials to the rhetoric that would later make him famous.[31] He launched into a list of nine demands, including expanding Medicare to cover all the medically indigent, applying civil rights guarantees to hospital admissions, involving the poor in planning bodies for social programs, and training poor people for jobs.[32] A few minutes later, George Wiley, the executive director of the National Welfare Rights Organization, took the floor and highlighted the case for welfare rights, urging Cohen to favor "a guarantee [of] minimum income for every citizen without any exception, whether they work or not, whether they're able to work or not."[33]

In making this basic plea, Wiley put the Poor People's March squarely in the tradition of the bonus marchers and others who had petitioned the government for help in a time of trouble. This time, however, the marchers came in an era of abundance rather than of scarcity; their primary means of identification was race rather than national service; they urged that the demands of the Vietnam War be forgotten rather than reminding the nation of their service in a time of war. As Mrs. Pulah Glover of Toledo put it, "I feel that we, as Americans, . . . in a land of plenty, should take care of our own and forget about Vietnam. Do your work here first."[34]

Cohen, unflappable, thanked the participants for an "unusual two and a half hours" and then charmed the crowd by making a short remark in Spanish. He promised that the department would study the suggestions and that "we'll be back with you and see how we can make some constructive progress."[35]

Despite the flurry of attention occasioned by his meeting with the representatives of the campaign, Cohen found that the press, with so many tumultuous events to cover, showed little interest in him. Political reporting focused instead on the candidates who remained in the presidential race and on newly aggravated racial tensions. On April 24 Cohen gave a speech at the National Press Club in which he engaged in self-deprecating humor, saying that he was the "only cabinet member you've ever seen who is a lame duck before he's even been confirmed." He then said he would "do everything I can to help Hubert Humphrey become the next President of the United States." That part of the talk made news in stories that centered on the presidential race, not on social welfare policy.[36]

Although the president wanted his cabinet officers to maintain a position of neutrality, it was logical for Cohen to favor Humphrey for the presidential nomination. He had worked with him and his staff on Social Security in the 1950s and on a broad array of social legislation in the 1960s. Humphrey deserved Cohen's support if only because he was the administration's representative. Beyond a sense of duty, Cohen's endorsement of Humphrey reflected his opinion that he was the best candidate in the race. Robert Kennedy, the brother of the man whom Cohen held in the highest respect, had never impressed him as a practical leader but as a person of great charisma, good intentions, and bad execution.[37] Sen. Eugene McCarthy had never been one of Cohen's special clients, and that left Humphrey. Unlike in 1960, when Cohen might have supported Kennedy, Humphrey, or Johnson, he felt no ambivalence in 1968.

COHEN AS SECRETARY

When Cohen spoke to the representatives of the Poor People's Campaign at the end of April, the Senate had still not acted on his nomination, but the Finance Committee soon took up the matter and decided not to hold public hearings; within a week, the full Senate confirmed him by voice vote. Strom Thurmond (R-S.C.) and Carl Curtis spoke against him, but Curtis said that he did not oppose the nomination. Only Thurmond, disturbed about the integration of public schools, asked to be recorded as opposed.[38]

Even before formal confirmation, Cohen wrote to LBJ and asked if Hubert

Wilbur Cohen is sworn in as Secretary of Health, Education, and Welfare by Vice-President Humphrey on May 16, 1968, in the East Room of the White House. *Left to right:* Stuart, Eloise, Bruce, and Chris Cohen look on. (Courtesy of Bruce Cohen)

Humphrey could swear him in as secretary; LBJ readily agreed. On May 16, 1968, at 1:06 P.M., Cohen took the oath of office from Humphrey in the East Room of the White House. The president joked about Cohen's choice of Humphrey: "Usually I can figure out what he is up to. But for the life of me, I just couldn't understand why he chose the man he did to administer the oath." Johnson referred to Cohen as a "planner, an architect, a builder and a repairman on every major piece of social legislation in the last 35 years." Cohen, in turn, praised the president: "You have done more for health, education, and Social Security than any President in the history of the United States."[39]

Cohen turned the ceremony into a family celebration. His father, stepmother, and brother came from Milwaukee, and his three children attended. Thirteen members of the Cohen family posed for a photograph in front of the White House. Aaron stood on the bottom row, dapper in his dress suit with a pressed handkerchief in the front pocket. Cohen was one step above him, his tie fashionably striped, his hair slightly less gray, not as bald as his father. Eloise did not look at the photographer; instead, she turned to her left and watched Wilbur. In three quarters of a century, the Cohen family had gone from steerage to a seat in the cabinet.[40]

The ceremony provided a diversion from Cohen's usual routine of constant work, but one project that demanded his attention was the response to

President Johnson gives the new secretary his marching orders. *Left to right:* Humphrey, Aaron Cohen, Ann Cohen (Wilbur's stepmother), Stuart, Wilbur, Eloise, and Chris look up at Johnson; Wilbur's brother Darwin stands just behind Aaron Cohen. (Courtesy of Bruce Cohen

the demands of the Poor People's Campaign. Operating in his typical fashion, he wrote a memo to the president in which he summarized the marchers' demands but highlighted the items on his own reform agenda. Although no one had mentioned it, for example, he stressed the need to extend Medicare to the disabled. Another related project concerned reforming the welfare system. Cohen told the president that the Supreme Court would soon invalidate the "man in the house" rule so that in the future a male's presence in a house would not be a reason for removal from the welfare rolls. The Court would also circumscribe the residence requirements that restricted welfare payments. Since these legal developments would reopen the question of welfare financing, Cohen asked permission to talk with Wilbur Mills about recommending "*a completely Federal system of welfare* with 100% Federal financing and administration," thinking that the congressman might be ready for the change because of his disappointment with the failure to contain welfare costs.[41]

The federalization of the welfare system became the first of the trial balloons that Cohen floated as secretary, selling the idea as an approach combining fiscal prudence with equity for welfare recipients. The federal government could keep a tighter control over welfare costs than the states, and recipients would benefit from protection against the low level of benefits that characterized the Deep South. If welfare benefits were more uniform, then the migration of poor families to the North might be halted. The states would be free to concentrate on job training and other positive measures for potential welfare beneficiaries. In time, Cohen hoped, the words welfare and relief "will be eliminated from our vocabularies."[42] Despite the sales pitch, Cohen's suggestions met a hostile reaction from many of the key actors. As a member of the National Welfare Rights Organization put it, welfare recipients thought there was "a lack of bona fide" in HEW's efforts.[43] Nor did the welfare mothers believe that Wilbur Mills or Russell Long would ever pass laws that operated in their favor.

Enactment of major new laws was in fact difficult, as the fate of Cohen's welfare reform proposals revealed. In June Congresswoman Martha Griffiths (D-Mich.) echoed Cohen's call for a federal takeover of welfare financing, the *Washington Post* noting that her actions showed that his proposal was receiving "serious legislative attention." It proved hard for Congress to maneuver, however, in an era when the cost of the Vietnam War constrained expenditures and in which George Wiley was urging Congress to create a guaranteed income of $4,400 for a family of four at a cost of at least $20 billion a year. Congressman Richard Bolling (D-Mo.) told Wiley that his presentation was "sensible" but politically impossible to enact. The conservatives who dominated the key congressional committees, said Bolling, thought that "anyone who is not earning his own living is bad." As Cohen had long understood, it was necessary to accompany benefit increases with promises to rehabilitate welfare beneficiaries, but such measures were stunted in an environment where, as Mrs. Beulah Sanders of the NWRO put it, she would not mind working in a job for which she was qualified but she was not "going to be pushed into housework."[44]

Apart from Congress, even within Cohen's own department, some people doubted the ability of HEW to affect genuine reform. As Jonathan Spivak, the journalist who was closest to the mood of the department, reported, the "young turks" were convinced that Cohen was "out of date and out of touch . . . isolated by years of Washington service and sullied by the compromises that politics requires." One young staff member said that Cohen was "a politician, not an idealist." The old-timers in the department believed that he was "the hometown boy who made good." The dissidents, described as men and women in their twenties who did not hold policymaking positions, thought that he symbolized the "survival of the old system in which important issues are evaded and powerful political interests are reconciled."[45]

Basically, the dissidents blamed Cohen for not being John Gardner, and they were right. The two men did not disagree on matters of policy; if anything, Gardner, a Republican, was more conservative than Cohen, a liberal Democrat, on questions related to welfare rights and the expansion of income

The official countenance of Secretary Cohen shines down upon the Department of Health, Education, and Welfare. (Courtesy of Bruce Cohen)

maintenance programs. The gap between the two was a matter of rhetoric and style. Where Gardner concentrated on the grand vision, Cohen looked for the incremental step that would lead to change. Gardner's rhetoric soared; Cohen spoke like a reporter, and his words seldom approached poetry. It was the same sort of difference that divided the mystical Robert Kennedy from the politically pragmatic Lyndon Johnson. It did not matter that Cohen and Johnson were much closer to the experience of disaffected Americans than were Kennedy or Gardner. Since both Cohen and Johnson were so tightly bound up in the status quo, it was difficult for them to disparage the system that had done so much for them. Kennedy and Gardner implied the possibility of escape from a world that had once been right and had now gone wrong.

Cohen might not have inspired people, but he did a good job in containing conflict in his immediate bailiwick. His response to the Poor People's March was a case in point. After the representatives of their campaign met with Cohen, their march on Washington began to fall apart in the midst of what one reporter described as "organizational chaos." At the end of May the remaining residents of Resurrection City, living in plywood shacks that had been erected in Potomac Park and plagued by squalid conditions, decided to stage a sit-in at HEW. Sidney Johnson had kept Cohen posted on the activities of the Poor People's Campaign. Discussing matters with the White House, Sidney Johnson had received strict instructions to keep the marchers away from government buildings and to meet with them only in small groups, but none of these control devices appealed to Cohen. When the group of about 470 protesters reached the HEW Auditorium at 4:30 P.M., they announced that they were tired of talking to assistants and wanted to see the man in charge, chanting "we want Cohen, we want Cohen." Johnson went upstairs and told the secretary that he should come down, and Cohen agreed. When he reached the auditorium, he was stopped by one of the guards, ironically called a "peace brother," from the Poor People's Campaign. "I'm Cohen," he said, and he walked into the auditorium on the arm of the young black guard just after six o'clock.[46] According to press accounts, Cohen apologized for the delay and "won loud applause when he presented his 35-page reply to the Campaign's demands." He talked about his idea for federal control of welfare payments. His appearance, according to the *Washington Daily News,* turned a "potential confrontation with police into a cordial talk session."[47]

Impressive as Cohen's performance was, it amounted to little more than damage control. With Congress unwilling to pass kiddycare or to federalize the welfare programs, Cohen faced limited options: he could condition the policy environment, manage existing programs, and reorganize the agencies in his department. Although his powers were circumscribed, he nonetheless delighted in his official duties. On June 14 he flew to the LBJ ranch and talked with the president for an hour about how to organize HEW's health programs. The next day Johnson announced "a shakeup of the Public Health Service." According to the front-page headline in the *Washington Star,* the shake-up gave Cohen "vast power." In particular, the president named him as his "first chief adviser on health policy." Cohen would chair a council, composed of the heads of federal agencies with responsibilities for health policy, such as the Veterans Administration and the Department of Defense.[48] Then on August 14 Cohen presided over a celebration of Social Security's first third of a century and presented Arthur Altmeyer, seventy-seven years old, with an award from the department. He also established the Arthur J. Altmeyer award for outstanding contributions to economic security and named Robert Ball as the first winner.[49]

As much as he enjoyed the ceremonial duties, Cohen also thought it important to condition the policy environment. His efforts were described in a piece that appeared in the *New York Times Magazine* on June 23 featuring Cohen's picture, with the caption "Mr. HEW," and containing cartoons that depicted his desires to simplify welfare administration, establish a federal welfare system with nationwide standards, and raise the minimum benefit levels in Social Security. The article described him as someone who knew "everyone in the field" and exuded "boundless energy, infectious enthusiasm, and a drive for action."[50] The article afforded Cohen, the background man and technical expert, unusual visibility.

Despite his satisfaction in the job, Cohen realized that the world he and Altmeyer had made was beginning to fade. In the summer of 1968 James Shannon, director of the National Institutes of Health (NIH), retired. He had enjoyed a remarkable thirteen-year tenure, presiding over NIH in an era in which the nation believed strongly in the efficacy of medical research. The NIH budget grew at an annual rate of 30 percent, from $98 million to $1.2 billion. John Fogarty and Lister Hill had "force-fed" the agency through the congressional appropriations process, and everyone conceded that Robert Marston, Shannon's successor, faced a much harder job. Pay at NIH was low compared to academia. In the absence of Fogarty and the presence of the Vietnam War, NIH appropriations were being cut. The emphasis in health policy was shifting away from research and toward the economics of health care delivery.[51]

The National Institutes of Health had poured millions of dollars into America's medical schools, and HEW programs had provided untold grants and contracts to academics of all types. Yet the recipients of this largesse, like the welfare recipients, were angry at the administration. The chief issue was the war. Even Cohen, who administered domestic policy, found himself attacked for his association with the Johnson administration. When, for example, Cohen gave an address at the 1968 meeting of the American Sociological Association, he was picketed by a group of young sociologists. When he argued that changes could be made through the electoral system, many in the audience laughed at him and walked out. Wearing paper arm bands, sixty members of the Sociology Liberation Movement stood outside the Boston hotel in silent protest as Cohen spoke.[52] It looked as though the era of confidence in the government was ending at the exact moment that Cohen was coming to power.

Despite the polarized politics of the era, Cohen thought it important to continue to produce suggestions for reform. In a revealing letter to one of his detractors, he wrote, "Some would argue that the constrained budgetary climate or other circumstances make social progress impossible or at least improbable at this time. . . . But in my judgement, future social programs can be influenced just as much by decisions that are made this year [as] . . . by the decisions made in 1965 about what legislative proposals should be presented to the Congress."[53] The strained syntax of this passage showed the spontaneity of its composition and indicated that Cohen was writing close to the surface of his emotions. Simply put, he felt that the presence of the war was no reason to abandon social progress. He rejected the analysis of radical critics who argued that American imperialism linked the exploitation of blacks in the ghettos and the pursuit of an immoral war in Asia.[54] Even in 1968 he believed in the benevolence of the American government. Although he hoped for an early end to the war, he continued to dedicate himself to his work at HEW.

Although the circumstances were often trying, Cohen kept the president supplied with ideas to recommend to Congress. During the summer of 1968 he witnessed, at a distance, the Democratic convention in Chicago. After the assassination of Robert Kennedy on June 5, Hubert Humphrey had emerged as the undisputed front-runner. The convention that nominated him late in August became another celebrated event of the era and another public relations disaster for the Democratic party. Cohen confided to his friend Bill Haber on August 29 that he was a "little apprehensive about things and I am even more apprehensive after watching the Democratic Convention last night."[55] As Humphrey's campaign got off to a bad start, Cohen remained in Washington, continuing his efforts to condition the policy environment and to achieve incremental expansion of the welfare system.

In September Cohen sent the president a detailed memo on programs aimed at children, leading off with the notion of extending comprehensive prenatal care to all women in low-income families. Next came the idea of providing medical care for all children of low-income families for the first year of life. He also hoped to expand family planning services, provide preschool experience for all children by 1976, and increase Social Security benefits so that no survivor of a covered worker would be in poverty. As always, he expressed his suggestions not as immediate, nonnegotiable demands but as proposals that could be phased in over time.[56]

As Cohen understood, it was a time to influence the future rather than to dwell on the present. His memo to Johnson resembled the wish lists he had compiled for JFK and his other clients during the 1950s; this memo outlined a scenario for the next period of legislative activity, the next big bang. Cohen explained that the past year had been "particularly rough . . . especially with regard to appropriations." In the face of difficulties, he tried, as he put it, "to be concerned about the long-run impact on programs. . . . I am never really unhappy," he added, "if I have to standstill for a short time or take a step backwards if I can see my way to taking two steps forward in the near future."[57]

SUMMING UP THE JOHNSON YEARS

Soon after Cohen delivered his comprehensive memo to the president, he had the opportunity to conduct an "off the record review" of HEW's programs. The audience at the White House consisted of the president, who took an active role in the discussion, and a select group of staffers. Cohen gave an overview of the department's activities in the same tone that he adopted in congressional appropriations sessions, with added flattery for the president. He noted that the Johnson administration included 49 landmark enactments and 100 legislative actions in the HEW field. The Johnson years had witnessed an increase in HEW expenditures from 18 to 25 percent of the federal budget and from 3.5 to about 5 percent of the GNP. During those years, the nation had opened twelve medical schools, and infant mortality had declined by 12 percent. The nation had also started twelve public television stations and doubled the annual number of rehabilitated handicapped people. The Medicare program had been passed, implemented, and put into full operation, and the Social Security Administration had paid 10 million hospital bills and 45 million physicians' bills.[58]

Clearly enjoying himself, Johnson listened attentively and often interrupted Cohen to ask a question. The president saw the briefing as a way of identifying the achievements of the Johnson administration and of beginning a program of public education to spread the story of the administration's success. Cohen characteristically regarded the discussion as a chance to advance his reform agenda, and it allowed him an unusual opportunity to repeat his proposals, such as the plan to federalize welfare, directly to the president. He concluded with a plea for the expansion of social welfare expenditures, suggesting that the nation should spend 25 percent of its GNP on social welfare by 1976. He believed that continued economic growth would make it possible both for family income to expand and for the government to increase its social welfare expenditures.

Toward the end of the briefing, the president asked him when he had come to Washington, and Cohen said that he had arrived in 1934. LBJ then asked him to name the five most "comprehensive and constructive and beneficial public acts" since 1934, and the two men quickly agreed on the Social Security Act, Medicare, and the Elementary and Secondary Education Act of 1965. Strikingly, Cohen had worked on the passage of all three. There was some disagreement about the other pieces of legislation to put on the list. Johnson mentioned the Economic Opportunity Act, but Cohen called it a "minor aspect of the total poverty program." Only after some minutes did Harry McPherson put the Civil Rights Act of 1964 on the list. The president added the Fair Labor Standards Act.

As Johnson indulged himself in his accomplishments and contemplated his retirement, Cohen became involved in the coming election and later told an interviewer that he had campaigned "very vigorously" for Humphrey. He helped Bob Nathan, a Washington consultant and an old New Deal hand, in writing campaign task force reports and served as vice-chairman of the Older Americans for Humphrey-Muskie. He also attended the morning meetings that Orville Freeman held in the basement of the Agriculture Department to plan strategy and to supply ideas for the campaign. When he could, he delivered partisan shots at Nixon, reminding voters that "Mr. Nixon stood four-square against the passage of Medicare." Eloise also campaigned actively for Humphrey.[59]

Nixon won the election for reasons that political scientists must fully unravel. One factor, surely, was public dissatisfaction over the course of the Vietnam War; another, just as surely, was a backlash against the social welfare legislation that the Johnson administration had helped to pass. As the election approached, the public learned of increasing welfare expenditures in cities such as New York: in October the *Times* reported that the city relief rolls had passed the 900,000 mark and would soon reach 1 million. In an ironic commentary on the outcome of the Great Society, the paper reported on November 1 that welfare had replaced education as the city's biggest expense item.[60]

Cohen took Humphrey's defeat with equanimity. He began almost immediately to pack his mementos and to make a last effort to tighten HEW regulations to limit the new administration's flexibility to undo the Great Society programs. In a typical action, he wrote President Truman and asked him to autograph a picture of the Medicare signing ceremony; in return, he offered the former president a copy of the memo on health policy that I. S. Falk had prepared for him in 1945.[61] In a news conference, Cohen said that the Johnson administration had "built the momentum. We must go forward" and indicated that he would return to the University of Michigan in January.[62] "I've had a wonderful, wonderful time," Cohen told a reporter from the *New York Times*.[63] He could use two more years to "clean up some things I've started," he told the *Washington Post*. Still, he appeared content to return to the University of Michigan, where it was reported he had his choice of four major assignments. The *Post* described Cohen as "bouncy, ebullient, and energetic," in stark contrast to the other spent members of the administration.[64]

In the middle of making his own plans, Cohen had also to consider what sort of program the Johnson administration should recommend to the new Congress. He worked on a comprehensive Social Security proposal that included a 7 percent across-the-board increase in benefits and an increase in the minimum payment paid by the program. He also attended to the completion of the health reorganization plan that had gone into effect in July. Finally, he made suggestions on Johnson's State of the Union message, advising that it not deal with specific legislative items but with "broad longer-run goals and objectives."[65]

Secretary Cohen's last days were taken up with more than sentimental gestures and symbolic statements about the future; he also faced a number of hard policy choices. Perhaps the most difficult concerned whether to raise the monthly premium for Part B of Medicare from $4.00 to $4.40 a month. Both Myers and Ball recommended the raise, but Cohen resisted it because, as he put it, "publicly predicting that physicians' fees will increase . . . is making it almost certain that they will." He preferred to take the position that physicians had already received significant increases in the past two years and should "voluntarily forego any further increase." Cohen favored an increase in the coinsurance rate, the amount the patient paid out of pocket, over an increase in the premium rate since Congress legislated the coinsurance rate and he promulgated the premium rate.[66] On December 31 Cohen announced his decision to keep the premium rate at $4.00: "I took this step," he explained, "in the face of actuarial advice that physicians' fees are likely to increase substantially next year and in 1970 over current levels." He said that if doctors did not show more restraint in increasing their fees and incomes, "I can only believe that Congress will do something more and it may be something they do not like."[67]

As Cohen made last-minute changes in the public assistance regulations and attended to other substantive matters, he also began a long series of thank-you notes. Having received so many such letters from a succession of HEW secretaries, he understood the drill. He told the president that "boys and girls yet unborn will benefit from your vision, your leadership, and your emphasis on social justice" and sent Johnson a complete list of the 102 HEW laws passed during his administration. He thanked the *Wall Street Journal* for putting Jonathan Spivak on the HEW beat and for writing such conservative editorials, thus inspiring him to produce liberal counterproposals. He wrote to his mentor Arthur Altmeyer and to the three HEW secretaries who had preceded him in the Kennedy and Johnson administrations. He recognized the "wonderful help" that Elizabeth Wickenden had given him.[68] Taking advantage of the position and the stationery, Cohen sent letters, suitable for framing, to the members of his family, including his wife, an indication that he still delighted in the trappings of office and did not expect to be back in a position of such prestige anytime soon. He gave little thought to being gauche. "For us in our family," he wrote, "it has meant a shared experience." To his son Stuart, Cohen said simply that "I did my best for you, my family, my friends, and my country."[69]

In January Cohen met with Robert Finch, Nixon's choice as Secretary of HEW. He told LBJ that the meetings had gone well and that Finch was not opposed to the administration's major programs. He thought it very likely that Finch would ask the department's comptroller to remain in the government and that he would keep Robert Ball as commissioner of Social Security. "I don't want to disturb social security," Finch told Cohen in an unconscious tribute to the administrative standards that Altmeyer and Cohen had helped to establish.[70]

Sometime in January Cohen made a final decision about his next job. As he told the president of Brandeis, who had apparently asked him to take a position at the social welfare school there, he had decided to return to Michigan as dean of the School of Education. Bill Haber had helped convince Cohen to accept the job, one that University of Michigan president Robben Fleming had urged upon him.[71]

As Cohen signed memos from a large stack on his desk in a desperate effort to beat the January 20 deadline, he could not resist the sentimental gesture. "My father came here from Great Britain as a small boy," he wrote the president. "Both my paternal and maternal grandparents found a haven of freedom and opportunity in this country. I spent my boyhood in Milwaukee and my University days in Madison, Wisconsin, where I learned from great teachers that public service is the greatest privilege and the highest duty. I have tried to remain true to those teachings." With those words, Cohen left public service.[72]

During his short stint as secretary, not much happened at HEW compared to the extraordinary series of events that took place outside the department. Cohen, like millions of others, watched the events tumble one after another. It was not his sort of year in that it did not feature a major legislative campaign. Instead, it was a time for him to consolidate and to strengthen the legislative programs of the Great Society. He acted through reorganization and regulation, not legislation. Nonetheless, his tenure as secretary gave him a brief moment in the public spotlight and allowed him an opportunity to condition the social policies of the Nixon era and beyond. Cohen was only fifty-five, and another career lay ahead of him.

13
AFTERMATH

Wilbur Cohen lived for another nineteen years but he never held another permanent government post. Instead, he watched the slow disintegration of the powerful apparatus that had supported the growth of the Social Security and Great Society programs. As early as 1965 Nelson Cruikshank had retired from his job at the AFL-CIO, and in 1973 Robert Ball left his post as head of the Social Security Administration. Finally, Wilbur Mills lost his power and eventually his seat in Congress. Meanwhile, the Democrats lost their hold over the presidency, and even Jimmy Carter, the only Democratic president in this period, showed considerably less sympathy toward Social Security than had his predecessors. Indeed, Cohen began the Carter years in close touch with the administration but ended them as a bitter opponent of the president. The remnants of Cohen's apparatus fought a pitched battle with Carter at the end of 1978 that led to the establishment of an organization designed to lobby against the administration. Hence, during this period, Cohen's status changed from that of the consummate insider to that of an outsider. At the end of his life, as a professor at the University of Texas, he spent much of his time defending the Social Security program from hostile attacks.

DEAN OF EDUCATION AND POLICY EXPERT

Cohen's life after he left Washington was concerned with the major social welfare issues of the era, such as national health insurance, welfare reform, and Social Security financing, yet he spent the years between 1969 and 1978 as dean of the School of Education at the University of Michigan. In May 1969 Cohen gave what amounted to an inaugural address as dean to the Board of Regents at the university, devoting it to an explanation of why he had taken the job. "I come from stock which has long respected learning and scholarship," he said. As Secretary of HEW, he continued, "I have had the advantage of a rather high

Wilbur and Eloise, finishing some business during the 1970s. (Courtesy of Bruce Cohen)

level course of instruction in the needs of the American educational system." This experience convinced him that Americans were not allowing education "to make its full contribution." Part of the problem was a lack of leadership; as dean of the School of Education, Cohen hoped to supply some of that leadership.[1]

Cohen began his tenure at the height of the period of campus protest, and he quickly came into contact with a group of students whom he described as "very militant, very noisy, and very articulate." They wanted their demands met immediately and, according to Cohen, could never be satisfied. He said that it was nonetheless "essential to work with them" because they could "very easily precipitate a major calamity in the University community." This group attracted the most notice, but the majority of the students, according to the new dean, were "apathetic." As with the students, so it was with the faculty. A small group of bright faculty members was "discontented with everything and everybody"; another was close to retirement and reluctant to make many changes. Some faculty members worked hard, but others did nearly nothing. "The distribution of effort," Cohen said, "was largely determined by the individual's own decision."[2] Responding to the various student and faculty groups, he used the methods that had worked for him in the past: he kept his door open and agreed to meet with nearly anyone who wanted to see him. This policy, he admitted, was "time-consuming," but time had always been his long suit.[3]

So far as Cohen had a personal agenda, it consisted of focusing more of the school's attention on urban education. He hired two black staff members to assist in the effort, and he tried to have more teacher training take place in inner-city schools. He also decided to close the University Laboratory School as a way of redirecting his priorities "from the upper-middle class white student in a University laboratory setting to teacher preparation on the firing line in the inner-city."[4] In accomplishing these goals, Cohen hoped to rely on his many contacts in the education and philanthropic communities and spent a considerable amount of time in the early days of his job writing to potential funders in the government and in the foundation community. He explained to Alan Pifer of the Carnegie Corporation that he wanted to "jazz things up. . . . I don't have anything to lose, and I'm willing to try and experiment."[5]

Even with his high-level contacts, Cohen soon became involved in the minutia of university administration. His life consisted of making decisions about space allocation, such as moving the dean's offices from a downtown bank building to the School of Education building. He awarded travel funds to faculty members and worked on promotions and tenure, an area he found particularly "difficult and time-consuming." He oversaw revisions in the faculty by-laws. When it came time to report on these developments, he chose to quote from John Gardner's new book, *The Recovery of Confidence*. "No people," Gardner wrote, "has seriously attempted to take into account the aging of institutions and to provide for their continuous renewal." Renewal became one of Cohen's buzz words in 1969: he hoped to renew the School of Education.[6]

Cohen's situation in the 1970s resembled that of the early 1950s. Then he had served as director of research and statistics for the Social Security Administration, yet his real responsibilities had extended far beyond his assigned areas. In the 1970s he served as dean, yet his work involved far more than education as he remained vitally involved in all areas of social welfare. In the 1950s he had helped with the transition from Truman to Eisenhower; in the late 1960s and early 1970s, he assisted in the transition from Johnson to Nixon. During both eras, he moved to Ann Arbor but kept his house in Washington and made frequent trips to consult with congressional and other leaders.

It was typical of Cohen that he began his duties as dean on July 1 but still planned to return to his house in Silver Spring for the Fourth of July holiday. He maintained an active correspondence with HEW Secretary Robert Finch about department personnel matters and about appointments to advisory boards.[7] The tone of Cohen's interchanges with Finch was always amiable; he strived for the same sort of helpful note that he had achieved in his dealings with Nelson Rockefeller in the early 1950s. Characteristically, however, he also advised his congressional clients, such as Abraham Ribicoff and Wilbur Mills, on just how they should respond to the Nixon policy proposals.[8] Reporting to President Johnson on his first few months out of government, Cohen made it seem as if little about his life had changed. He told the president that the problems of a large university resembled those of running HEW, adding that he had been to see Wilbur Mills three times concerning child health and Social Security bills that had been initiated in the Johnson administration.[9]

Much as the reports must have cheered up Lyndon Johnson, the fact remained that the action in social policy had shifted from him to Nixon. The summer of 1969 marked the unveiling of President Nixon's bold new welfare initiative. Called the Family Assistance Program (FAP), it would have replaced the old AFDC program with a guaranteed annual income for families with children (including working families). Cohen had a direct line to the internal White House discussions of FAP through Nixon adviser Daniel Patrick Moynihan. When Cohen had been an assistant secretary at HEW, Moynihan had been an assistant secretary at the Department of Labor; hence, Cohen received advance word of FAP from Moynihan, who sent him a telegram offering to brief him on the new program. Cohen became an early advocate of FAP.[10]

Typically, this role did not prevent him from suggesting that the Democrats ask for more. In this regard, his behavior resembled his standard mode of operation in the 1950s, when he would prepare one proposal for Republican Robert Kean and a more liberal proposal for Democrats such as Herbert Lehman. By October 1969 Cohen had written a complete analysis of FAP for Wilbur Mills and his staff in which he pointed to problems in the legislation that Mills might want to highlight and ultimately to correct.[11]

Cohen stayed with the fight for FAP until the end. "I do hope Family Assistance makes it," Moynihan told Cohen in June 1970. "We are so close. But we desperately need help from some of the liberal Senators." After receiving Moynihan's note, Cohen visited Russell Long, head of the Senate Finance Committee, and Elliott Richardson, the new Secretary of HEW, hoping to assist in some compromise measure that would clear Congress. Cohen told Moynihan that the bill needed a "substantial number of specific changes" if it were to pass.[12] As it became clear that FAP would not make it through the Senate, Cohen continued to work with Senator Ribicoff on welfare reform. Unlike in 1962, when Ribicoff and Cohen had teamed up to pass significant new welfare amendments, they could do little in 1970. Welfare reform, as conceived by Richard Nixon, died. It was the first of many legislative casualties of the 1970s.[13]

Cohen, with customary persistence, continued throughout 1971 to collaborate with Wilbur Mills and Ribicoff, among others, on a welfare reform bill. As always, he tried to sense what Mills wanted and then to present him with an agenda that meshed with ideas the congressman was already thinking about. In this manner, a February 1971 meeting with Mills led to an outline for a new welfare reform program. The general idea, Cohen wrote Mills in a letter marked "personal and confidential," was to separate welfare recipients into three groups. The first group, which included the aged, blind, disabled, and widows, would receive welfare more or less automatically. The second group consisted of the working poor and those looking for work, and payment of welfare for them would be linked with the state unemployment agency and paid in weekly installments. The third group contained families in which the parents had dropped out of the labor force or never entered it, and eligibility requirements would be developed that related to the care and education of the children. As in Cohen's previous welfare reform proposals, the payments would come from the federal government.[14]

In addition to welfare reform, the other pressing social policy topic in the first Nixon administration was national health insurance. In the late 1960s and early 1970s, its passage in some form carried an aura of inevitability. A nation that had already passed health insurance for the poor and for the elderly stood poised to expand the system to cover everyone. Cohen assumed his usual role as a contributor to a national health bill that came from the offices of the AFL-CIO. Nelson Cruikshank at the age of sixty-two had become president of the National Council of Senior Citizens, and Bert Seidman, another of the many labor economists trained in Madison, had replaced Cruikshank as head of the Social Security department at the AFL-CIO. In the summer of 1969 Cohen sent Seidman a detailed critique of the specifications that Seidman had prepared for a national health insurance program.[15]

The drive for national health insurance, like the effort at welfare reform, became bogged down in the poor economic conditions and uncertain congressional politics of the 1970s. Cohen offered many sorts of compromises, but none worked. In 1971, for example, Cohen suggested to Wilbur Mills that he might take an existing catastrophic care bill and add features relating to medical care for children.[16] Cohen was also enthusiastic about a catastrophic health care plan that he was developing for Senators Ribicoff and Long. In working on this plan, he positioned himself to the right of the others in his network on health insurance, just as he had on Kerr-Mills and on the early versions of Medicare. Cruikshank said that the catastrophic health proposal, which reimbursed people for expenses above a certain threshold rather than providing "first dollar" coverage, might be a step forward. "But I must confess," he added, "to some hesitancy about any program that apparently does little if anything to change the system of medical services and appears simply to pour more money into the existing system."[17] Cohen did not see it that way. Although Cohen backed the liberal Kennedy-Griffiths bill, he also regarded it as "desirable and practical to improve our health system on an incremental basis." It was best to extend Medicare and to begin a program of catastrophic coverage. Although it would not resolve all the problems or, to use one of Cohen's favorite expressions, bring about the medical millennium, it would "result in vast improvements for millions of persons."[18]

If Cohen had a core project in the 1970s, it consisted of expanding the basic Social Security program. Although the incremental engine of the program's expansion continued working in the first years of the Nixon administration, problems nonetheless developed, one involving a serious internal dispute among the program's supporters. At issue was whether Robert Ball should continue as Social Security commissioner in the Nixon administration. Robert J. Myers, the chief actuary of SSA and a Republican, made no secret of the fact that he wanted to become commissioner. Cohen believed that Myers's public challenge to Ball was unseemly and that it undermined public confidence in the program at a critical period of transition.

Myers, according to what Cohen could piece together, had decided he wanted the job and had gone to John Byrnes and Wilbur Mills of the Ways and Means Committee to ask about it. Mills believed that Myers had obtained the support of the Republican Byrnes. Reacting to this news, Cohen warned Mills against Myers, who, said Cohen, was not an administrator and would be a disaster as commissioner. Cohen also wrote Myers directly and told him that his attacks on Ball "were likely to have the effect of undermining public support for the Social Security Program and those who administer it." Mills told Cohen that he "wholeheartedly supported Robert Ball." Arthur Altmeyer, still living in retirement in Madison, noted that he was "distressed" by Myers's actions. The incident ended with Ball remaining as commissioner; Myers resigned in the spring of 1970.[19] The fact that Nixon kept Ball as commissioner throughout his first term indicated the strong bipartisan support that had developed for Social Security.

Cohen, as was his custom, mixed issue politics with presidential politics. He told Edmund Muskie, who had distinguished himself as a vice-presidential candidate in 1968, that he was willing to work on his 1972 campaign. Yet at the same time, Cohen also encouraged John Gardner to run. "I believe," he wrote in an unusually forthright letter to Gardner, that "you should be a candidate for

President. . . . I would hope that you would declare yourself a Democrat at an appropriate time. . . . John, this is no time to be shy or cautious. I need not tell you what a difficult situation we are in in this country. You have said this so much better than anyone else. You must do something *more* about it." Gardner, despite this encouragement, hesitated on the edge of becoming actively involved in politics.[20]

THE BIG CHANGE

Even by 1972 it was becoming apparent that a shift was occurring from the policies of the era of consensus to new, as yet undefined, social policies. Conflict had been apparent at least since 1967, when the Social Security bill had run into unexpected trouble at the time of the urban riots, but it had centered on welfare rather than on Social Security itself. In the 1970s, however, as members of the old apparatus began to drift into retirement, even Social Security and other forms of social insurance came under attack. Cohen's world began slowly to disintegrate. In 1972 Wilbur Mills decided to run for president, which made it much more difficult for Cohen to work with him. Early in March, for example, Mills wrote to Cohen requesting a Social Security report that he had done for Muskie. Cohen hastened to reassure Mills that his Social Security recommendations for Muskie were consistent with Mills's own proposals.[21]

As it turned out, 1972 marked the first year since Cohen had begun to vote that his favored candidate did not receive the Democratic nomination for president. Gardner decided not to run, and Muskie failed to advance far in the primaries.[22] In July Cohen told Ribicoff that although he was willing to do anything for the McGovern-Shriver ticket, he had many doubts about the candidate. McGovern needed "more specific and wider technical help in connection with the welfare proposal," and he also required considerable help to bolster his support among Jews. Cohen, who had made a recent visit to Israel in connection with his service on the Board of Governors of Haifa University, noted that "practically all the Israelis we met were very concerned about McGovern. Quite a number of the Americans who were in Israel shared the same doubts." McGovern, it was clear, faced a difficult election.[23]

Unlike Kennedy, Johnson, and Humphrey, McGovern did not appear predisposed to accept Cohen's advice on Social Security. Cohen received an invitation, at the behest of Ribicoff, to attend a meeting at Robert Kennedy's old house in Virginia on August 13. When he arrived at Hickory Hill, he found

McGovern in a bathing suit surrounded by a group that, according to Cohen, contained "lots of economists" discussing whether McGovern should repeat his proposal of a national income payment or "demogrant" of $1,000 per person.[24] At the end of the month, McGovern made a major speech on income maintenance. Reporting to Douglas Brown, Cohen said that McGovern's speech represented a "tremendous improvement over the earlier drafts which had many more specific items in it to which I objected." Yet Cohen was still troubled by the influence that economists such as James Tobin of Yale and Joseph Pechman of Brookings had over McGovern. "They are not only anti-welfare (which is understandable) but, in my opinion, they are also anti-social security," he complained.[25]

Even the traditional liberal supporters of Social Security were beginning to have their doubts about it. Where Cohen could be described as an incrementalist, the new generation of economists might be described as perfectionists; where Cohen put great stock in the symbolism of social policy, as in the notion of social insurance, the new generation regarded themselves as rational policy analysts. Therefore, according to Cohen, the Social Security system was "under attack from Harvard-Yale-MIT-Brookings economists who are relatively uninterested in differential benefits and attack the financing of payroll taxes for the program." The program they really wanted was a uniform national benefit, something like the demogrant that McGovern had proposed.

Cohen believed that the economists simply did not understand Social Security because they had come into the policy discussion too late. They analyzed it as though it were an ordinary tax, and as a tax it constituted a dubious form of social policy. It was, for example, highly regressive, placing a far heavier burden on low- and mid-income wage earners than on upper-income wage earners. The economists referred to Social Security as a "transfer" because it transferred the command over resources from the working to the retired population, and they tended to think there were more efficient ways to accomplish the transfer. Cohen, in contrast, regarded Social Security "as much more than a tax system and this is a point that is very difficult to get the tax economists to really understand."[26] He believed it to be a carefully constructed institution that redistributed income in a manner that accorded with American behavioral norms, both political and otherwise. Cohen, as always, put stock in policies that he believed Congress was predisposed to accept; the economists welcomed what Douglas Brown described as "clever inventions."[27] Social Security was an established institution that had Congress' blessing; the negative income tax, a conception of the economists, was a clever invention. The new economists stressed ideas such as marginal tax rates but excluded psychological, social, and ethical considerations. Contrary to the notions of the economists, Cohen believed that one could not solve social problems by "either macro-economic or microeconomic theories."[28]

He knew from personal experience how hard it was to establish new programs, having had first-hand knowledge of the difficulties of getting Congress to agree on federal funding for education or medical care. In his view, one did not have the luxury of choosing the best policy option; instead, one went with what worked. Economists, in contrast, elevated the concept of efficiency above political expediency. "We are now in the midst of a second generation of scholarly experts, students, and advisers who are reopening basic questions," Cohen explained to a perplexed William Haber. The experience applied in Social Security, welfare, and health insurance and meant that "nothing can be taken for granted with the new breed of scholars who find a great sense of satisfaction in challenging the fundamental postulates of their parents and peers."[29]

Cohen had already issued his challenge to the economists. He agreed to a debate with Milton Friedman, the conservative University of Chicago economist, in May 1971 as part of the American Enterprise Institute's rational debate seminars. The format was for each speaker to present a lecture and then to respond to questions from the audience. Friedman prepared for the event as he might for an academic symposium, writing an elegant, scholarly paper, complete with tables and appendixes. He argued that neither the taxes in Social Security nor the benefits would be popular in themselves, "yet the two combined have become a sacred cow. What a triumph of imaginative packaging and Madison Avenue advertising."[30] Cohen prepared for the event as though he were about to testify before Congress and wrote to Robert Ball asking for data and for help. In his presentation, he argued that "major institutions cannot be changed every day or even every decade—although perhaps, as Thomas Jefferson said, they might well be changed every 50 years or so."[31]

The event came alive during the rebuttal and discussion periods, when the liberal and the conservative used wit to appeal to the audience. They were an interesting pair: both were short, balding Jewish men almost exactly the same age who considered themselves economists. The difference was that Cohen followed the precepts of the long out-of-favor institutionalist school, and Friedman was perhaps the leading member of the monetary and market-oriented Chicago school. Friedman was far closer than Cohen to developments in the economics profession, but Cohen was far closer than Friedman to political developments. Not surprisingly, then, Cohen stressed the primacy of politics over economics: "Economists, do not determine all the choices and attitudes prevailing in the nation. . . . True, if you are an economist, you may exclude all matter of politics from your thinking. But to do so is not reality,

Milton." At another point, Cohen dismissed Friedman's arguments in a sweeping statement: "The point is simply that the social security system meets the test of insurance, it meets the test of equity, and it meets the test of social adequacy. And as to the fact that [Friedman] doesn't agree with it—well, he's not Congress, he's not the American people. He's only an economist." "Thank God for small favors," shot back Friedman.[32]

"You handled your side of the argument beautifully," Ball told Cohen and added that "I agree with you that we are really going to have to work on the whole area of economic criticism."[33] As it happened, Ball's job was soon to change and another part of Cohen's world to disintegrate. In late 1972 it became clear that the Nixon administration would replace him as commissioner of Social Security. As one of Ball's last actions, he arranged for Wilbur Cohen to receive the Arthur J. Altmeyer Award at the dedication of the new Arthur Altmeyer Building in Baltimore. Thanking Ball for the award, Cohen predicted that there would not be such a gathering of "distinguished old-timers again." Cohen, the boy wonder of 1934, was approaching his sixtieth birthday; he was a self-confessed old-timer.[34]

Robert Ball retired at the end of January 1973. Like the others in Cohen's apparatus, however, he had every intention of remaining active. He soon set up shop in downtown Washington as a scholar-in-residence at the Institute of Medicine where he continued his distinguished career as an expert on Social Security and Medicare. He kept in close touch with congressional leaders and with the members of the Social Security network, including Cohen.[35]

Cohen and Ball continued to recommend incremental improvements in Social Security, but the White House and the Congress were both changing, further undermining Cohen's working environment and making it difficult for him to find an audience for his policy proposals. A beleaguered Nixon devoted little attention to domestic policy.[36] Congress began to enter the "sunshine" era, in which, for example, more of its sessions were conducted in public. These changes complicated the enactment of such measures as a health insurance bill. The closed sessions of the sort during which Wilbur Mills had developed Medicare in 1965 were going out of style.[37]

So, rapidly, was Wilbur Mills himself. He began to encounter severe back pain and spent increasing periods of time away from Washington. "When I return to Washington, and right now I don't know when that will be," he wrote Cohen in October 1973, "I will be glad to talk with you" about catastrophic health insurance. But his doctor wanted him to remain in treatment for another thirty days and "frankly, I don't feel like going back yet." The era of Mills's inordinate power over Social Security legislation was over.[38] In October 1974 he suffered public humiliation when the police discovered him in the tidal basin with stripper Fannie Fox. He revealed that he was an alcoholic, and although he won reelection in 1974, he soon lost his committee chairmanship. Cohen kept supplying Mills with ideas for legislative proposals, but it was clear that he was no longer a factor in congressional politics.[39]

In March 1976 Cohen received the shocking news that Wilbur Mills would not seek reelection. "You deserve to retire and enjoy yourself," Cohen told him. As always, he deferred to Mills: "While there were times when we disagreed and I was overruled, I knew I had never run for elective office and I recognized the practicality of accepting the legislative wisdom." Cohen even offered to staff Mills's retirement, advising him on such matters as how to prepare his papers for archival use and urging him to do an oral history for scholars to use. Mills had known Cohen, the legislative technician. When the congressman retired, Cohen revealed another side of his character to Mills, the avid collector of Social Security antiquaria.[40]

Even before Mills's formal departure from office, Cohen's influence over social policy had begun to decline. To cite one example, his edited book on Social Security, produced in collaboration with William Haber, was out of print. Nor did the publisher express much interest in doing another edition, noting at the beginning of 1973 that the expected changes in the field, such as the enactment of the family assistance plan or national health insurance, had not taken place. Costs were rising fast enough to make "this kind of specialized volume marginal for commercial publishers to undertake."[41]

In 1974 Cohen retreated from the situation: he requested and received a leave for the spring semester. His stated project was to remain in Ann Arbor and write a short book on social policy. As always, however, other commitments intruded on his time, and he never wrote the book, which was to have been a defense of his view of social policy formation. He wanted to show that one could reach accommodation with the "vested interests" and still keep the "public interest" in mind. As it turned out, he could not bring himself to write on this abstract level. He could never resist the urge to return to the realities of current proposals in Social Security and health insurance.[42]

Instead of writing a monograph, Cohen entertained the notion of starting an outside group to lobby Congress on Social Security policy to be called the American Committee for Social Security. The title was a faint echo of an earlier organization, headed by Abraham Epstein, known as the American Association for Old Age Security. Cohen would be chairman of the board, and Robert Ball would be president. Nelson Cruikshank would be on the executive committee and Elizabeth Wickenden on the advisory council. Ball pointed out that the list of participants consisted entirely of "old-timers" and did not contain a single businessman. Like Cohen's monograph on social policy, the American Committee on Social Security never materialized.[43]

Wilbur and Eloise went on an extended trip to Paris and Israel in the spring of 1974. Travel was a favored mode for Cohen to take stock of his life and to relax, and the trip provided an opportunity for him to recreate his honeymoon and the world of his youth.[44] He could not help but reflect on the ways in which his world was coming apart. He complained to Douglas Brown, who, like Cohen, had been present at the creation of Social Security, that Richard Nixon and Caspar Weinberger, Secretary of HEW, were destroying the morale of the Social Security Administration.

And many of Cohen's heroes were beginning to fail him. Even John Gardner, whom he admired extravagantly, could not make much headway solving social problems. Gardner's new organization, Common Cause, was supposed to reform the political system; instead, its advisers could not even agree among themselves about policies to recommend. Cohen wrote Gardner that he was "very discouraged about the tone, attitudes and level of discussion" of the Common Cause Board. In a statement completely out of character, he said that he lacked the "emotional stamina" to attend the meetings.[45]

Cohen hoped that things would change with a Democratic victory in the 1974 elections.[46] Despite the resurgence of the party, the passage of welfare reform and health insurance proved illusive, and he remained in full retreat.[47] He began to give serious consideration to resigning as dean and beginning something new, but William Haber, his oldest friend on the Michigan faculty, advised him against it and he decided to continue as dean, at least for the moment.[48]

With the economy deteriorating badly and faith in the political system weakened by Watergate, Cohen did what he could to restore confidence in social programs. When, for example, Caspar Weinberger blasted the welfare state in a farewell address as Secretary of Health, Education, and Welfare, Cohen prepared a lengthy reply, taking particular exception to Weinberger's pessimistic forecasts about the future. He continued to accentuate the positive, in part because he had found it so useful to formulate policies based on the expectations of prosperity. "There is no evidence that I know of that energy, daring, or ingenuity has declined or reached a plateau in the United States," Cohen asserted. He concluded his argument by means of historical analogy: in the past people had cried doom and proved to be mistaken; similarly, Weinberger would prove to be a false prophet.[49]

THE CARTER ERA AND
THE LAST STAND OF THE APPARATUS

In 1976, a presidential-election year, the bicentennial year, and a year of considerable national celebration, Cohen once again played a role in the campaign. In January he prepared a lengthy draft of a document he described as a "democratic approach to improving the health, education, and welfare of all the American people," and he worked as the chairman of a study group that reported to the Democratic Advisory Council of Elected Officials.[50] The document mentioned the Ford recession, but it could as easily have appeared in 1965 although it was a bit more tempered than a report from the Johnson administration would have been. "We cannot and should not recommend the millennium," the document stated in a line that used one of Cohen's expressions. Still, the statement went on to present "some immediate imperatives." First and foremost was the need to put Social Security on a sound financial basis. This issue was relatively new, a product of the big benefit increases of the Nixon era combined with the poor performance of the economy in the 1970s. The other issues had been on Cohen's agenda for most of his life and included a "nonpartisan effort to reform the welfare system" and a "comprehensive health insurance system covering every person in the nation."[51]

Once again Cohen's candidate, Congressman Morris Udall, lost. Almost by default, Cohen turned his attention to Jimmy Carter, the unlikely front-runner, in the summer of 1976.[52] He served on a Carter campaign task force, staffed by two of his former employees at HEW, that was supposed to produce ideas on education policy. Despite this assignment, Cohen had few illusions about his influence on Carter. "I am drafting up innumerable proposals for Carter as are many others," he wrote William Gorham of the Urban Institute.[53] In addition to the work on education, he became involved in a Carter campaign initiative to "strengthen family life" and saw himself as able to advise the candidate on the best way to reorganize HEW to "carry out a constructive family policy." He also began to suggest names of people, such as Sid Johnson, whom the Carter administration might use to staff HEW.[54]

After Carter won the election, he deliberately distanced himself from the old guard Democrats. Robert Ball noted, for example, that Carter's transition team working on disability insurance was chosen precisely because its members had never had anything to do with the program. In this area, as in many others, Carter hoped to take a "fresh" look at the social programs of the Kennedy and Johnson era. Ball categorized the transition team's approach to Social Security as "perverse or naive" and "pretty weird."[55]

Although Cohen showed little interest in a Washington job, he spent a considerable amount of time offering advice to Joseph Califano, Carter's Secretary of HEW. From the beginning, he encouraged Califano not to regard HEW as "unmanageable" or as a "snakepit."[56] When Califano won confirmation in the Senate, Cohen sent him a congratulatory wire.[57]

On January 29, 1977, Cohen's father died of a heart attack at the age of eighty-nine. He went to Milwaukee to bury his father and to deliver a moving eulogy; Aaron, he noted, was the last of his generation.[58] Soon after, he announced that he would retire as dean at the end of the 1978 spring semester but that he would remain at the University of Michigan as a teacher and research professor until he reached seventy in 1983. In the meantime, he had plenty to do both at the university and in Washington. He saw one of his primary obligations as working with the new officials in HEW who, he noted, had "little background in connection with the past developments."[59]

Cohen did not hesitate to offer his advice to Califano, Undersecretary Hale Champion, new senator and Finance Committee member Daniel Moynihan, and anyone else who would listen. He suggested to Champion, a former California government official, that he should require all HEW officials to put their phone numbers on their letterhead; like nearly everyone who communicated with HEW, Cohen wasted a lot of time trying to get people on the phone. "No charge for the suggestion!" he added. He told Joseph Califano to be wary of proposals to start a new Department of Education. He had his students in a social welfare policy seminar write papers on ideas that should be brought to Califano's attention and dutifully passed them along. He wrote position papers on health insurance and welfare reform and distributed them widely.[60]

Cohen spent most of his time on legislation related to Social Security financing. Califano had set up competing teams to work on the problem of keeping the system solvent, one team consisting of Commissioner Bruce Cardwell and SSA employees, the other made up of economists led by Henry Aaron of the department's office for planning and evaluation. Cohen tried to stay informed. He told Douglas Brown that he had spoken with Treasury Secretary Michael Blumenthal and with Califano about the matter: "I am trying to develop a politically acceptable compromise which will satisfy the macroeconomists and ourselves," he said. "I don't want to see the Carter Administration botch up the program like the Nixon-Ford administration did," he told Califano. "I strongly urge you," he continued, "not to try to make social security subservient to economic policy which might undermine public confidence in the contributory, wage-related program."[61]

The lines of communication with Califano remained open. In April Cohen, along with Ball and Bert Seidman, met with Califano and Hale Champion to discuss the proposal. Cohen also kept in touch with Stuart Eizenstat in the White House and with Bruce Cardwell in the Social Security Administration.[62] The Carter administration, like Cohen, believed that some general revenue contributions should be made to the system. "I strongly support the general thrust of the President's proposals," Cohen told the Senate Committee on Finance in June. He disagreed with the president on details, but he saw the need for quick legislation to keep the system solvent and to maintain people's confidence in Social Security. Above all, he wanted to allay people fear's about the program's financial solvency. "Needless to say, we appreciate your support," Califano told Cohen after his testimony.[63]

The year ended amiably. In October the faculty of the School of Education celebrated Cohen's career as dean.[64] In the same month Califano selected Chris Cohen as HEW's regional director in Chicago. Chris had been elected twice as a Chicago alderman but had grown weary of machine politics. In 1976 Chris, along with his dad, had supported Udall and then had become involved in the Carter campaign; his reward was the regional directorship. Cohen was inordinately proud of his son, who had somehow managed to cross over the line from bureaucrat to elected office. "I want to take this opportunity to thank you for the appointment of my son, Christopher," he wrote Califano. "His mother brought him up right and consequently I think he will do a good job for you and the Department."[65]

The appointment of his son encouraged Cohen to become more engaged in the affairs of the Carter administration. Ray Marshall, secretary of labor, asked him to serve as chairman of the National Commission on Unemployment Compensation, and Cohen agreed. And Califano asked him to serve as chairman of the White House Conference on Families.[66]

Neither of these assignments went well. The National Commission on Unemployment already existed when Carter came into office. At the beginning of his administration, however, some of the members resigned and gave Carter a chance to appoint the chairman. Cohen took the job only to find that the various interest groups had "hard positions," and he thought many times of resigning but hesitated because something constructive might come of the commission's report. "I was completely wrong in my optimism," he later concluded. Unemployment compensation, according to Cohen, was an antiquated program kept alive by the interest groups. Its development, from Cohen's undergraduate days in Madison through his service on the Committee on Economic Security to the 1980s, was one of his "great disappointments."[67]

The White House Conference on Families also became a celebrated failure of public policy. Cohen had always believed that legislation, such as Social Security, should be directed toward the family. When he thought of a family, he tended to imagine a working father, a mother, and a number of children, in other words, an image of his own family. That nostalgic image no longer meshed with either social realities or the political aspirations of minority groups: black leaders, for example, resisted efforts to describe families headed by women as unnatural or pathological. The conference soon fell victim to the complicated politics that surrounded the definition of family in the 1970s. As soon as Cohen was appointed, representatives from the black and Hispanic communities pressured him to represent their groups on the advisory staffs. More controversy arose when Califano promised a young black woman that she could be executive director of the conference; she was divorced, however, and her appointment sparked considerable protest from Catholic groups. As the politics surrounding the conference intensified, Cohen began to have increasing doubts about remaining as chairman. He was not feeling well. Medication that he was taking for a thyroid condition left him dizzy, tired, and irritable, and during one convalescent period, Cohen received a letter from a black representative "impugning my impartiality and criticizing me for failure to meet his demands." Cohen considered the matter over the 1978 Memorial Day weekend; then he called Califano and announced his resignation.[68]

It was neither unemployment compensation nor family policy that led to Cohen's break with Califano and the Carter administration. The dispute that led him to denounce Califano as the worst secretary in the history of HEW concerned Social Security. The 1977 amendments had left the system with sharply higher taxes than previously planned. Instead of following the advice of Cohen or the Carter administration, Congress rejected the idea of introducing general revenues into Social Security and raised future tax rates so that, for example, employers and employees would each contribute 7.15 percent of their covered payrolls rather than 6.45 percent in 1986. When Congress reconvened in 1978, a movement developed to roll back the tax increases. For Ball and Cohen, continued discussion of Social Security finances only served further to undermine people's faith in the program.[69]

In August 1978 word began to reach Cohen that the administration was considering major Social Security proposals for submission to Congress in 1979. There had been staff discussions of changes in the disability insurance program, elimination of student benefits, and even elimination of the early retirement provisions.[70] Cohen remained in touch with his apparatus: Ball, Cruikshank, Wickenden, and others. In November, Cruikshank, who worked in the White House as an adviser on aging, tried to get an appointment with the president for himself, Ball, and Cohen.

On December 16, 1978, Cruikshank called Cohen and told him that the Office of Management and Budget (OMB) and HEW had submitted their

Social Security proposals and had discussed them with the president. Cruikshank had managed to secure an appointment with Carter for December 20, and Cohen flew in from Ann Arbor the evening before and talked with his old friend that night.[71] On December 20 he went to Cruikshank's office and signed a memo to the president that Ball had prepared and Cruikshank had revised, which went to Carter with their three signatures. For the last time, the apparatus that had been assembled in the 1940s prepared to fight a political battle over the expansion of Social Security.

The memo said that the administration could not gratuitously cut the program's benefits without discussing the matter with outside advisory groups. Social Security could not be handled like other items in the budget, nor could it be used to balance the budget. The memo also criticized each of the proposals from HEW and OMB, which included putting a cap on disability benefits, beginning a person's benefits with the first full month of entitlement, and phasing out postsecondary student benefits. Cohen and his allies countered that student benefits were not education grants to needy students "but benefits to make up for the loss of support of a Parent" who had died. As for the notion of phasing out early retirement benefits, the triumvirate called it "very damaging." It would not save money in the long run because these benefits were reduced below the level of regular retirement benefits. "The effect is almost entirely short-term and transparently designed for budget purposes," the memo stated. The fundamental issue went far beyond the details of policy and involved "no less than the confidence of people in the promises of government." The administration proposals, if enacted, "would undermine public confidence in the willingness of government to make good on the benefit promises."[72]

Armed with this rhetorical ammunition, Ball, Cohen, and Cruikshank met with Carter at 3:45 P.M. Ball led off the discussion, saying that Social Security deductions, unlike other budget cuts, would be permanent and affect public confidence. Ball called the HEW proposals "horrendous." The group urged Carter to wait before he endorsed the proposals. When the short meeting concluded, Carter, according to Cohen, "bent over in his chair and said in a questioning but affirmative quiet manner: 'But social security is not sacrosanct.' " The statement shocked Cohen and left him "emotionally exhausted." The three men parted company with the last Democratic president of Cohen's life.

Cohen and his allies took the battle to Joseph Califano, who, like them, had served in the Johnson administration. But Califano accepted Carter's point of view, believing that Social Security was not sacrosanct. He later wrote that as HEW secretary, he realized that "the days of expansion were over"; instead, the system required "sensitive disciplining."[73]

On December 22, 1978, a fabled confrontation took place between the old and new guard. Ball, Cruikshank, and Cohen, the key supporters of Social Security since the 1940s, met with Califano, Champion, and Stan Ross in Califano's office. A staff member was present who took notes that formed the basis of a long description of the meeting in Califano's memoirs of the Carter years. According to Cohen, Califano tried to restrict the discussion to the administration's proposals for disability insurance. Still, the talk strayed into the other administration suggestions, such as the elimination of the lump-sum death benefits. Ball, true to character, remained calm and focused on individual issues; Cohen, according to his own recollection, "tended toward the emotional and explosive comment." He said that he was ashamed of Califano and his colleagues for recommending proposals that undermined the public's confidence. According to Califano, Cohen said that if Califano persisted, "we're going to fight." "You'll destroy the Social Security program by what you're doing," Cohen said, "you're trying to dismantle it." At this point in the meeting, according to Califano, Cohen was "moving sideways and back and forth on the balls of his feet like a fighter ready to uncork a barrage of jabs."

Cohen did, in fact, decide to fight. Soon after the meeting, he attended another meeting of Social Security allies held in the Hilton Hotel in downtown Washington, sitting in the back of the room and listening as someone suggested that the group form a permanent organization. Cohen became the chairman. He wanted to use the name he had previously suggested, the American Association for Old Age Security, but Elizabeth Wickenden preferred Save Our Security (SOS). In 1979 the group was launched as the Save Our Security Coalition to Protect Social Security, with offices on K Street in Washington. Its membership consisted of senior citizen's groups and labor unions.

The coalition held, and the Carter Social Security financing proposals failed to gain congressional support. Still, a second battle developed in the Carter years over the administration proposals to reduce the cost of the disability insurance program. This dispute culminated in the passage of disability insurance legislation in 1980, over the objections of Wilbur Cohen and the Save Our Security coalition.[74] There were times during this fight that Cohen could not quite believe that he headed a conventional advocacy organization. At one point, for example, he became annoyed with Jake Pickle, the Texas congressman who chaired the Social Security subcommittee, for not consulting more closely with him. "Your staff members and you have known me for a long time; they know—and I trust you know—that I have been a party to resolving difficult legislative differences in the past. I still am."[75] But Cohen was no longer working Social Security legislation from the inside. He was not appearing as an academic or as a former Secretary of HEW or as a Social Security technician with

At the end of his life, Cohen found himself on the outside looking in. Here he rallies a group of citizens in front of the Humphrey Building, headquarters of the Department of Health and Human Services, in Washington, July 1981. (Courtesy of Bruce Cohen)

years of experience. He now headed an overtly political coalition that was asking not for a major expansion of the program, in the manner of Nelson Cruikshank's work for the AFL, but for the program to be spared from budget cuts.

There already had been cuts. The 1977 legislation reduced future benefits below the rates legislated in 1972. The later legislation, however, corrected what Social Security insiders referred to as a technical flaw, known as double indexing, that in times of inflation led to irrationally high benefit increases. The Carter administration wanted to go further and eliminate whole classes of benefits that had been won in hard political fights and that Cohen and his colleagues regarded as firm promises to future generations, promises that stood at the very heart of the welfare state. The alternative was for Social Security to struggle with the other programs each year for appropriations, which, Cohen believed, could only undermine confidence in the system.[76]

Many of those individuals who had built Social Security stood with Cohen. Ball was reluctant to surrender his reputation as an expert, yet he agreed to chair the advisory committee of SOS; Elizabeth Wickenden also served on it. Key labor leaders, such as Lane Kirkland of the AFL-CIO and Douglas Fraser of the UAW, agreed to put their names on the SOS letterhead. So did Wilbur

Mills, former Speaker John McCormack, and former HEW Secretary Arthur Flemming.

The insiders had become the outsiders. Wilbur Cohen, like Wilbur Mills, had left office as an important policy proprietor. In 1980 he was a figure from a time that no longer existed. The policy projects of the early 1970s such as welfare reform and national insurance had been abandoned, and retrenchment was the order of the day. Cohen had viewed programs such as Social Security as aids in the creation of economic growth and opportunity. But those people advising the new president, Ronald Reagan, believed that the social policies of the postwar era, such as federal aid to education, once regarded as the solutions, had become the problems.[77]

DECLINE AND DEATH

Cohen meanwhile had received an offer to teach at the LBJ School of Public Affairs at the University of Texas, and he agreed to start on January 1, 1980. When he took the new job, he was a little uncertain of the university's reputation. Still, he had major disagreements with the new dean of education at Michigan, who, Cohen believed, was undermining his accomplishments. The people at the University of Texas, such as Dean Elspeth Rostow (wife of Johnson's security adviser Walt Rostow), seemed genuinely to want him. As things turned out, he never regretted the move and remained at the LBJ School for the rest of his career.[78] Although he found it hard to reach Washington from Austin, he seemed to enjoy life in Texas. Characteristically, the Cohens did not sell their Ann Arbor house, returning there for the summers. Nor did they sell their house in Silver Spring since Cohen, as head of SOS, often went to Washington on business.

Only deteriorating health slowed Cohen down. In the summer of 1980 he spent a few weeks in the University of Michigan hospital undergoing tests for a heart condition. Doctors considered whether to recommend coronary bypass surgery, but Cohen resisted the suggestion.[79] As the decade continued, his heart problems grew slowly worse. He put on weight. His hair, which grew only on the sides rather than on the top of his head, turned white. He began to look old, and he began to wear the sort of clothes associated with grandparents in Miami Beach: white shoes, a white belt.

Cohen, however, remained active, fully engaged by his work. He taught courses on social welfare policy at the LBJ School, consulted on health care and other aspects of policy, gave talks across the country on aspects of Social Security, and served on corporate boards. His family urged him to consider a

Cohen spent some contemplative moments in the reading room of the Lyndon Baines Johnson Library. Toward the end of his life he began to write his autobiography but had not completed it by the time he died in 1987. (Courtesy of Bruce Cohen)

bypass operation, his brother Darwin begging him to consult his son Elliott, a cardiologist in Milwaukee, but Cohen resisted. When Eloise pleaded with him to cut down on his travel and his many speaking engagements, he told her that he was doing what he wanted to do; if it killed him, he would die reasonably content.

Cohen, who made so few concessions to his age, nonetheless receded further as a prominent Social Security figure during the 1980s. He was not on the cutting edge of political action. To be sure, he often appeared in Congress as the spokesman for SOS, balancing his testimony and public appearances with those of Arthur Flemming, who had become cochair of the organization. The two former Secretaries of HEW, divided by party, worked well together. Like Cohen, Flemming believed that Social Security was an intergenerational compact, the terms of which could not be violated, nor did he approve of the ways in which the Carter and Reagan administrations managed the Social Security Administration.

The major event in Social Security during the decade occurred in 1983. Legislation passed that year resulted from the work of a bipartisan commission

Wilbur and Eloise share a moment with Lady Bird Johnson. Cohen, who began his career in the shadow of Franklin Roosevelt and Harry Hopkins, ended it in the shadow of Lyndon Johnson at the Lyndon Baines Johnson School of Public Affairs. (Courtesy of Bruce Cohen)

established by Ronald Reagan after his social proposals, like those of Jimmy Carter before him, met with a hostile reaction in Congress. Within Social Security circles, the legislation was hailed as the salvation of the program. Its features, such as skipping one cost-of-living adjustment and raising tax levels (or moving up the dates for previously legislated tax raises), eased the short-term financial difficulties and restored many people's faith in the program. The legislation was acclaimed as artful work, a major compromise between Democrats and Republicans.[80]

Although it was a great compromise, it was not a Cohen compromise; instead, Robert Ball had taken the lead in developing the legislation and selling it to Congress. He, not Cohen, served on the commission, and he, not Cohen, explained the measure to the press. As always, Ball kept Cohen informed of what he was doing. Cohen did play a part in getting Congressman Claude Pepper (D-Fla.) and labor union leaders to back the measure, but he had relinquished his front-row seat in Social Security legislation. For the most part, he watched Ball perform.

To some extent, the events of 1983 followed the traditional division of labor between these two members of the Social Security apparatus. Ball's moments of greatest success had come during eras of Republican rule. He had put together the initial parts of the 1950 amendments in a Republican era, and he had demonstrated the logic of Social Security to Oveta Culp Hobby and others in the Eisenhower administration. He had performed a similar feat in the era of Ronald Reagan. Cohen, for his part, had achieved his greatest success working closely with the Democratic members of the Ways and Means Committee (on Medicare) or with other Democratic leaders (on disability insurance).

To a greater extent, the events of 1983 showed that Robert Ball, not Wilbur Cohen, was Washington's resident expert on Social Security. In much closer touch with political developments, he formulated strategy for the Social Security proponents. And, unlike Cohen, Ball retained his image as a skilled administrator rather than as a partisan figure.

In 1983, the year of the Social Security compromise, Wilbur Cohen reached the age of seventy. Despite his physical problems, he faced this milestone with a sense of joy. On his birthday, he even took the time to write down his thoughts, another bit of his personal history to add to his extensive collection. At this point of his life, Cohen viewed himself as a great collectible. He wanted to have the memos from the Committee on Economic Security, a complete set of the Columbia Oral History Interviews on Medicare, all the memos from the internal bureaucratic deliberations over Medicare. He was determined to write an autobiography, which he described as a book that would tell his grandchildren what their grandfather had done. Like many of his other book projects, this one too remained unfinished at the time of his death. What survived were autobiographical fragments that he had deposited in Austin, Ann Arbor, and Washington. The one on reaching age seventy revealed him in his attempts to celebrate the mundane: "I awaken very early," he wrote. "It is just becoming light. I am glad to be alive."[81]

The seventieth birthday was not Cohen's last hurrah. In 1985 he made an extensive circuit as a celebrant of the fiftieth anniversary of the Social Security Act. The *New York Times* ran a picture of him eating a large piece of cake at a ceremony that marked the twentieth anniversary of Medicaid and Medicare. He went to a special symposium on Social Security in New Mexico and spoke at a commemorative celebration sponsored by the American Federation of Government Employees in Baltimore.

On the day before the fiftieth anniversary, Cohen testified in Pittsburgh at a hearing before Sen. John Heinz (R-Pa.) before taking a plane to Baltimore. As he walked through the long airport corridors in Pittsburgh, leaving plenty of time to catch the plane, he experienced shortness of breath, a constant reminder of his heart condition. Once settled in a friend's house in Baltimore, he planted himself in front of the telephone and called his office in Austin to get his messages. Radio talk-show hosts and newspaper reporters had called, looking for material for stories to appear on August 14, the date of the anniversary.

In 1985 Cohen gave numerous speeches and made many appearances in honor of the fiftieth anniversary of the passage of the Social Security Act. (Courtesy of Bruce Cohen)

Cohen returned the calls and gave interviews to those who wanted them. Robert Ball called from Washington; the two discussed Robert Pear's story, which would appear the next day in the *Times* and featured a quote from Cohen. "The thing I'm most worried about today is the failure of young people to understand the value of social security," he said. That explained the need for the appearances: he wanted to make the young understand.[82]

The next morning Cohen drove to the Arthur J. Altmeyer Building in nearby Woodlawn; he had attended the dedication of this massive building. A Social Security official took him to a holding room, where important figures waited for the ceremony to begin. There was Douglas Brown, leaning over to talk with Murray Latimer, his colleague on the staff of the Committee on Economic Security in 1934; the two men, both seated in wheel chairs, shared memories and swapped stories about old age. Cohen also talked with Robert Ball and Bob Myers. Then he walked on the stage and, along with the current Reagan appointees, watched a formal ceremony in which a special postage stamp celebrating the anniversary was unveiled. From his position on the postal advisory committee, Cohen had fought to get the stamp approved. After the ceremony he went with his longtime colleague Ida Merriam, his successor as director of research and statistics at SSA, to Washington, where more work awaited him.

Nearly two years later, in May 1987, Cohen attended another anniversary celebration. This one, in the stately old Shoreham Hotel, was for the fiftieth anniversary of the Group Health Association (GHA), the pioneering HMO that Cohen had joined in 1937. He took his place on the rostrum for the formal luncheon and gave a short talk on GHA's importance in establishing the principle of prepaid group care. The featured speaker was Robert Ball. Maurine Mulliner, Cohen's close friend who had hosted parties in his honor after his three swearing-in ceremonies during the 1960s, introduced Ball, and the occasion gave Cohen a chance to chat with him about how they might approach Claude Pepper on a health insurance bill. The two oddly matched men–Ball, tall and somewhat aloof; Cohen, short, stout, and given to using his hands to reinforce his points–continued to hope that they could unlock the legislative door to national health insurance.

On the same visit to Washington, Cohen went to a meeting of Experimental College alumni, where he spoke about Alexander Meiklejohn and the concept of a liberal education. He also spent several hours working with Roberta Feinstein and the staff of SOS. The organization maintained offices on Sixteenth Street in the National Education Association Building, where Arthur Flemming also kept a finely appointed office. Down the street was the AFL-CIO headquarters and a bit further was the White House, where, in the West Wing, Cohen had met with Kennedy, Johnson, and, most recently, Jimmy Carter.[83]

Leaving Washington, Cohen traveled to Korea, where he was to speak at a symposium on aging and welfare for the aged. Asleep in Seoul's Plaza Hotel, he suffered a fatal heart attack.

For the last time Cohen reappeared in the news as a public figure as the press reported on his death. The *Times* tried to capture some of the ambiguities of his life: "Normally amiable and gregarious," wrote Wolfgang Saxon in the obituary, "he could take on an abrasive edge in his fervor, and there were many detractors who considered him a preacher of faded New Deal liberalism."[84] The next day the *Times* picked up the theme in an editorial devoted to Cohen. Pointing to his tenacity in defense of Social Security, the editorial writers noted, "An inexorable contradiction: the tenacity needed to pass social welfare laws may also blind one to changes in society–like the generational battle brewing over social security funding."[85] Most commentators chose to dwell on his sweet

A pensive Wilbur Cohen peers out of his office at the Lyndon Baines Johnson School of Public Affairs in the 1980s. (Courtesy of Bruce Cohen)

side rather than on the abrasive and on his social vision rather than on his blindness to change. Cohen had, as Congressman Pickle put it, "a clear vision of how we should care for each other as a nation. . . . He never lost his temperament or his composure or his poise."[86]

Bruce Cohen, the middle son, organized memorials in Texas, Michigan, and in the Ways and Means Committee Room in the Capitol, where Robert Ball presided. Ball had the ability to recognize by sight each of the many congressmen in attendance. Ted Kennedy, skilled at these sorts of occasions, told the story of Cohen's efforts to forge a compromise over disability in 1952 and of a meeting with President Kennedy to discuss Medicare. Former secretaries Arthur Flemming, John Gardner, Elliott Richardson, and Joseph Califano spoke about Cohen. Gardner mentioned his ability to tolerate a wide range of people; Califano spoke of how he and Wilbur had fought but of the bond of affection that underlay the friction. It was Califano's way of making peace with the family and with Cohen's memory.

The most moving speech was made not by a Washington official, but by one of Cohen's students at the LBJ School who told a simple story that rang true. Wilbur had noticed that she also had a middle name that began with the letter J. He had found it a big advantage to sign his name by linking the J to the C in Cohen and had told her that she, too, could sign her name in a distinctive way, offering to help her practice her technique. Nothing better expressed Cohen's lack of pretense than this unabashed attempt at self-improvement and his offer to help a student. As she told the story, she began to sob, and a wave of nostalgic sadness ran through the audience: Wilbur Cohen was dead.

An overflow crowd paid tribute to Cohen that day, and longtime SSA employees such as Ida Merriam mixed with Darwin Huxley and other family members. It was an eclectic gathering. In one row sat Herbert Stein, the economist and former chairman of the Council of Economic Advisers for Richard Nixon. Two rows in front of him was Judith Martin, the Miss Manners columnist for the *Washington Post,* whose maiden name was Perlman and who was the niece of Selig Perlman, Cohen's professor in Madison.

A final tribute came on April 28, 1988, when, under threatening skies, a building long known as HEW North was dedicated as the Wilbur J. Cohen Federal Building. Because of the inclement weather, the ceremony was moved indoors to the auditorium, which was located on the ground floor of the building where Cohen had worked for many years, first as a Social Security staffer and later as a department official. At the ceremony, the Social Security Administration Chorus sang, just as it had in 1961 when Cohen was sworn in as assistant secretary. A Unitarian minister gave the invocation, and a rabbi delivered the benediction. Congressman Pickle and Senator Moynihan spoke;

Wilbur Cohen's memorial in the Cohen family plot in Milwaukee, Wisconsin.
Wilbur's brother Darwin provided the inscription. (Courtesy of Bruce Cohen)

Moynihan told the audience that Cohen was a man "not without honor in his own time."

The downtown headquarters of the Department of Health and Human Services comprised three major buildings. One, the newest and the site of the secretary's office, was named for Hubert Humphrey. The second, formerly known as HEW South, was renamed in honor of Mary Switzer, Cohen's longtime colleague and the commissioner for SRS during Cohen's tenure as secretary. The two had often fought over the design of social policies. In 1988, after the dedication ceremony, the Switzer Building faced the Cohen Building; bureaucrats who had never heard of either Switzer or Cohen passed in and out.

Before Cohen died, he had given careful instructions that he wanted to be cremated and to have his ashes scattered over Eloise's family ranch in Ingram, but Darwin, his brother, thought something more was required and took it upon himself to have a stone carved for Wilbur in the family plot in Milwaukee. A little uncertain about inscribing the stone, Darwin solicited advice, but everyone assured him that his choice was fine: "In honor, Wilbur Joseph Cohen, born Milwaukee, Wis., June 10, 1913, for his contributions to improve the health and well being of the nation; the seventh secretary of Health

Education and Welfare; architect of social security and father of medicare; distinguished educator, administrator and counsellor to presidents; an eloquent voice for the progressive vision of America; a man of insight and compassion who gave much of himself because he cared deeply for others; remembered by his friends with affection, his associates with respect, his country with gratitude, and his family with love."[87]

POSTSCRIPT

Wilbur Cohen did not choose to follow the religion or the occupation of his parents, nor did he decide to remain in his hometown. His professional identity as an expert in social insurance superseded both his religious and regional identities. The most important difference between Cohen and his parents was that he went to college, and they did not. There he came into contact with a group of professors who provided the opportunity for him to go to Washington and obtain a job with the Social Security Board. If the times had been more prosperous, he might have been tempted to participate in his parents' businesses, but as matters stood, the depression put a premium on finding a secure job. Because of the long presidency of Franklin Roosevelt and the development of social welfare politics, the Social Security Board proved to be a secure and fulfilling place for Cohen to work. Once in Washington, furthermore, he no longer felt bound by the rules of his parents' world. That relative freedom enabled him to marry outside his religion and to arrange his social life around his collegiate and professional acquaintances.

But he never completely transcended his Jewish immigrant background or his family circumstances. Because he was instantly identified as Jewish, Cohen felt that his ethnicity limited his occupational options. Despite an interest in politics, for example, he never imagined that he would run for office or become a frontline political executive. As a member of a minority group, he realized that he would have to play a secondary role: he would be a technocrat who facilitated social change by serving others. Hence he began as a research assistant, continued as a legislative observer, and found steady employment as an assistant to the head of the Social Security Board.

Indeed, Cohen displayed a special talent for finding and holding mentors. He had the capacity to give himself over completely to them, to be swept up in their presence. Perhaps because he saw his own father as intimidating and remote, he was receptive to approaches from surrogate fathers who wanted to make him over in their image. As a first son somewhat unsure of his father's affection, he sought always to please his mentors and those individuals who had authority over him, such as Lyndon Johnson and Wilbur Mills. He became a disciple of Meiklejohn, Perlman, Witte, and Altmeyer. Cohen's own views seemed to be malleable. Looking to his mentors for ideas to guide social policy, he invested his ego in achieving practical results. It was particularly striking that, given his extraordinary loyalty to the institutions and individuals with whom he came into contact, he did not extend that same loyalty to his parents or to their occupational endeavors. He wanted to escape from a life in the retail trade, and he never looked back. Only toward the end of his life was he able to bathe his childhood in a warm, nostalgic light.

Once in Washington, Cohen joined a group of people who came to town during the New Deal mobilization of professional talent. Edwin Witte, who brought Cohen to Washington, was only a temporary resident who soon returned to Madison and resumed his academic career. Cohen, in contrast, maintained a Washington residence nearly continuously between 1934 and 1987. Even when he lived in Ann Arbor or Texas, he still thought it important to keep a house in Washington, D.C. In part, Cohen's attachment to Washington was a serendipitous result of history: he graduated from college at the moment when the enduring programs of the second New Deal were being formulated. Hence, he gained admittance to the Social Security Board just as it was getting started. He soon encountered other young people who had moved to Washington (or Baltimore) and invested their energies in the Social Security program.

Thus an apparatus in support of the program began to form in the late 1930s and early 1940s. Without exception the members were people who had been swept up in the politics of the organized labor movement and of Social Security. Both Nelson Cruikshank and Robert Ball spent time in grassroots activities before feeling the pull of the central offices of the bureaucracies in which they served, and Elizabeth Wickenden worked in the Washington offices of the first New Deal welfare programs. Along with Cohen, they formed the nucleus of a group that lobbied on behalf of Social Security from 1943 through the late 1970s. To some extent, the group matched the characteristics that political scientists ascribe to the iron triangles that perpetuate social programs. Ball and Cohen operated from inside the bureaucracy; Wickenden and Cruikshank represented important outside interest groups. Only strong congressional support was lacking. In fact, the group originally came together not to perpetuate the existence of a successful program but to drum up congressional interest. In the 1950s, when Wilbur Mills and his staff began to support the program, the triangle was complete. By then the incremental growth of the program that marked the period between 1950 and the mid-1970s was under way.

If Cohen was a creature of the bureaucracy, he was also a devoted follower of Congress who internalized many of its rules and operating assumptions. On the one hand, he valued the professional virtues of efficient public administration and reasoned policy analysis; on the other, he appreciated the constraints that politics placed on public administrators. For that reason he strived to blend political expediency and administrative efficiency with full realization of the trade-offs that were involved. Although he thought of himself as a technocrat and often argued that problems of social policy were technical rather than ideological by nature, he never shied away from the political side of his work. For Wilbur Cohen, Social Security and national health insurance remained political causes rather than rational solutions to social problems. Unlike many of the economists who offered the negative income tax in the late 1960s and the 1970s, he always factored congressional politics into his policy recommendations. For him, selling a proposal to Congress was agreeable work, not an unpleasant necessity.

Throughout his life Cohen maintained a rhythm in which he alternated between contemplative research and active political tasks. Often he would perform background research, help to pass a law, and then write an essay reflecting on the experience. If his first assignment was as a research assistant, his second one consisted of assisting Congress (in a very junior capacity) in the passage of the Social Security Act. After that he worked within the bureaucracy as Arthur Altmeyer's staff assistant, but by 1939 he had made congressional liaison his particular specialty. For the rest of his career, although he was never far away from the congressional deliberations over Social Security, he worked in the research and statistics division of the Social Security Administration and in academia.

Because of his long association with Congress, Cohen came to favor incremental over innovative policies. That meant, for example, that he preferred to expand an existing program, such as the impacted-areas program, rather than to create a new one, such as the Community Action Program. At the same time, he believed in the importance of crossing thresholds rather than in attempting to achieve a major legislative project all at once. It made perfect sense to him to approach the eventual goal of national health insurance by starting with such projects as federal aid to hospitals or federal assistance to pay the medical bills of the indigent elderly.

If Cohen had not developed the political side to his persona, he would have been content to stay in the bureaucracy and work as the head of the research and statistics division of the Social Security Administration. Throughout his career, however, he shaded the line between the policy technician and the policy advocate. In the Eisenhower administration, he conducted a campaign in which, as he put it, he tried to ride a donkey and an elephant at the same time. He worked within the bureaucracy on projects officially sanctioned by the Republicans, and he developed support within Congress for projects led by Democrats and not fully approved by the administration. Even by the time of the 1954 amendments, Eisenhower officials considered him too much of a partisan figure to participate in the congressional hearings. In a move that had fateful consequences, he decided that he was too much of a Democrat to remain in the Eisenhower administration. As a result, he accepted a job in academia that solidified his contacts with Sen. John F. Kennedy and enabled him to step over the line completely in 1961 to become a member of a Democratic administration. It was typical of Cohen's career that a stint in academia, which many people assumed to be the home of nonpartisan analysis, enabled him to become an unabashedly partisan figure.

Although Cohen operated in large bureaucracies and as the servant of congressmen and other politicians, he managed to leave a personal imprint on the legislative process because he never completely subverted his own ego. Even though he wanted to please people, he also sought to bend them and the political process to his will. By trying to achieve these two objectives simultaneously, he gained a reputation as someone who composed compromises between contending parties. As his memoirs reveal, he treasured the moments when he could shape the legislative process even if the basic context was largely framed by others. He enjoyed making the spot decisions that fell to him because he was the only Social Security or administration official on the scene. In 1965, for example, it was he who had to decide whether to encourage Wilbur Mills in developing a comprehensive Medicare package that blended Republican and Democratic, social insurance, and public assistance elements.

The Cohen compromise, his legislative signature, figured prominently in the Social Security amendments of 1952, in the Kerr-Mills legislation of 1960, and in many other pieces of legislation. Cohen could mediate disagreements because the leaders of the Social Security bureaucracy and of the administration knew that he understood the principles involved and shared their basic goals. At the same time, congressmen appreciated his sensitivity to political concerns and realized that he was not out for direct political gain. They knew, for example, that he had no plans to run for political office, and they knew also that he did not sit in judgment of them. On the contrary, he had seen them at their worst moments in closed sessions and had emerged from the process with his admiration for the institution of Congress intact. For Cohen to denigrate Congress was to attack the very system that gave him his identity and that rewarded him for his efforts. He even managed to approach subjects that others viewed as moral imperatives, such as civil rights legislation, as a practical political matter.

Although Cohen's contributions were functions of his ability, his innate personality, and the psychological forces that framed his life, they also were products of historical circumstance. The prosperity of the postwar era facilitated the growth of Social Security. Cohen's actions affected the shape of the program. Without Cohen there might not have been fiscal intermediaries in the Medicare program, or a disability freeze between 1952 and 1960, or a major new welfare law in 1962. Each of these actions generated policy feedbacks that influenced the subsequent course of social welfare. Someone needed to serve as the link between the Social Security bureaucracy and the Congress, and not everyone had the essential skills. Undersecretary Ivan Nestingen, to cite an example, conducted a feud with Wilbur Mills that made it difficult to pass Medicare, in part because Nestingen thought of himself primarily as a politician, not as a staff member. Still, the Social Security program grew not because of Cohen but because there was a basic consensus in Congress that the program should be expanded. When fundamental political and ideological roadblocks existed, as they did on Medicare between 1960 and 1964, Cohen, for all his conciliatory skills, could do little about them.

Furthermore, historical circumstances had a transforming effect on Cohen. His time at the University of Michigan was crucial, permitting him a chance to step out from under Altmeyer's shadow and to be regarded as an independent policy adviser. Quick to absorb the prevailing culture, he also acquired some of the intellectual trappings of the Michigan social work school at a time of great professional self-confidence in the therapeutic power of social services. Social work, as Cohen observed it in the 1950s, was not about protecting people against economic scarcity so much as about helping people to share in the blessings of prosperity. As a consequence, Cohen adjusted his views on welfare so that he advocated it as more than a pension to shield people from the stresses of the labor market. Like social work itself, it should be a source of social services that would facilitate participation in rather than disengagement from the world of work. Arthur Altmeyer, a man whom Cohen greatly admired, disagreed with this analysis. The differences between Altmeyer and Cohen were similar to the differences between politicians of President Roosevelt's generation and younger, liberal politicians, such as Kennedy. Unlike Altmeyer, Cohen accepted the prevailing reality of prosperity and learned how to adopt his policy proposals to suit this reality. In so doing, he made the transition between the New Deal and the New Frontier.

In making this change, Cohen expanded his core projects to include education as well as Social Security and Medicare. Between 1961 and 1969, he devoted almost as much time to securing federal aid to education as he did to passing Medicare and expanding Social Security. The change in Cohen's portfolio permitted him eventually to accept a job as dean of the School of Education at Michigan. At the same time, it was striking that the rise of the civil rights movement in 1961 did not affect him as decisively as did the intellectual events of the 1930s and the 1950s: his two academic contemplative periods. In government service, he was so occupied with his core projects that he simply did not have time to acquire much new intellectual capital. Organized labor and Social Security, not civil rights, remained his great causes.

Strikingly, too, he never really abandoned his faith in the American economy and in Congress that he had acquired in the 1950s. Cohen had, after all, observed the progression from the depression in the 1930s to postwar prosperity. He was therefore unwilling to believe that some sort of climacteric had been reached in the 1970s that would permanently alter America. When circumstances in Congress and the country changed, Cohen regarded the changes as temporary rather than as fundamental. Just as Social Security had entered a moribund period between 1935 and 1950, so, according to Cohen, did social policy continue to follow a cyclical course. Ultimately, Cohen remained true to his mentors and prepared for the next big bang of legislative activity that, he was confident, would match in intensity if not in exact contents those acts in 1935 and 1965 that had determined the course of his life.

NOTES

What follow are source notes rather than the usual academic commentaries on the text. I have tried not to add too many references to secondary sources, with the exception only of the notes that accompany the preface, which list some of the basic secondary sources in Social Security and social welfare history. In addition, I have included some selective material in the notes that expands on the material in the text.

Most of the material on which I have drawn comes from the Wilbur J. Cohen Papers in the Wisconsin State Historical Society, the central repository for materials related to Cohen. They are extremely well organized, and an excellent finding aid directs the researcher to the topics of most interest to him or her. When I began my research, the papers were just being put together so that I was not always able to get box numbers for the material I cite. Although I have made every effort to cite the right box number, that has not always been possible. Among the Cohen Papers, I have benefited in particular from the chronological files that Cohen kept of his correspondence, particularly for the period between 1961 and 1969 and from his correspondence with Arthur Altmeyer. In addition, the Wisconsin State Historical Society contains related manuscript collections that include the papers of Edwin Witte, Arthur Altmeyer, Nelson Cruikshank, Elizabeth Wickenden, and Merlyn Pitzele. Witte's and Altmeyer's papers are particularly useful for a biography of Cohen.

Wilbur Cohen left the papers that were in his Texas office at the time he died to the Lyndon Baines Johnson Library. These are less valuable than the materials in Wisconsin, but they include a complete set of the interviews that Cohen gave throughout his life under various auspices and a set of notes taken from the Columbia Oral History Project that the Social Security Administration commissioned to record the passage of Medicare. I found these notes, made by Cohen and his research assistants, particularly helpful in gaining a perspective on Cohen's feud with Ivan Nestingen. When I did my research, I should add, Cohen's papers at the LBJ Library had not been fully processed.

Cohen donated still another set of personal papers to the Bentley Historical Library at the University of Michigan. These contain materials related to his various stints at Michigan although much of the material is duplicated at the Wisconsin State Historical Society; I refer to these as the Michigan Papers. In addition, some primary materials related to Cohen remain in the possession of Mrs. Eloise Cohen and are still housed in Cohen's residences in Austin and Ann Arbor. Darwin Huxley, Cohen's brother, also retained some letters and other memorabilia related to Cohen, which are now in the possession of Mrs. Esther Huxley in Milwaukee, Wisconsin. I suspect that most of this material, on which I relied heavily to understand Cohen's activities in college and during the 1930s, will eventually find its way to the Wisconsin State Historical Society. I refer to these sets of documents as the Eloise Papers and the Darwin Papers. Finally, the University Archives at the Wisconsin Memorial Library contains the papers of the Experimental College, which include a nearly complete set of Cohen's undergraduate papers.

Elizabeth Wickenden maintained a lifelong correspondence with Wilbur Cohen that is invaluable for understanding how the Social Security apparatus operated. Although some of the key letters are in Madison, some remain in her personal possession.

Cohen enjoyed giving oral interviews. His various interviews in the Lyndon Baines Johnson and John F. Kennedy libraries are particularly useful for understanding his perspective on the policy process. The interview conducted by the Eisenhower Library contains illuminating material on Cohen's work for the universal training commission in the Truman administration. Cohen also gave many helpful interviews on the subjects of Medicare, disability policy, welfare reform, unemployment compensation, medical care, and civil rights to various oral historians, transcripts of which are available in the Cohen Papers, Lyndon B. Johnson Library.

My own interviews in preparation for writing this book include the following subjects and dates:

Robert Ball, May 20, 1992, Washington, D.C.
Bruce Cohen, October 19, 1990, Wilmette, Illinois
Christopher Cohen, October 20, 1990, Glencoe, Illinois
Eloise Cohen, December 8, 1990, Austin, Texas, and March 13, 1991, Ingram, Texas
Dean Coston, October 10, 1990, Washington, D.C.
Julius Edelstein, October 2, 1990, New York City

Myer Feldman, April 11, 1994, Washington, D.C.
Robert Frase, April 14, 1994, Washington, D.C.
Darwin Huxley, August 22, 1990, Milwaukee, Wisconsin
Sid Johnson, September 6, 1991, Washington, D.C.
Harold November, October 27, 1990, Baltimore, Maryland
Merlyn Pitzele, November 6, 1990, Beacon, New York
Elizabeth Wickenden, October 16, 1991, Haverford, Pennsylvania

Other archival collections consulted for this book proved helpful:

Dwight D. Eisenhower Library, Abilene, Kansas: White House Central Files, Oveta Culp Hobby Papers, President's Commission on National Goals Papers

Lyndon B. Johnson Library, Austin, Texas: White House Central Files, "Administrative History of HEW," Joseph Califano Papers, John Macy Files

John F. Kennedy Library, Boston, Massachusetts: White House Central Files, Theodore Sorensen Papers, Myer Feldman Papers, and Related Papers of Walter Heller

Rockefeller Archives, Pocantico, New York: Nelson A. Rockefeller Papers and Papers of the Rockefeller Brothers Fund

Library of Congress, Washington, D.C.: Clinton Anderson Papers

National Archives, Washington, D.C.: Record Group 235, Federal Security Agency; Record Group 47, Social Security Board; Record Group 174, Department of Labor

Washington National Records Center, Suitland, Maryland: Record Group 235, Department of Health, Education, and Welfare, and Record Group 47, Social Security Administration

---

PREFACE

1. See Theodore R. Marmor, Jerry L. Mashaw, and Philip L. Harvey, *America's Misunderstood Welfare State: Persistent Myths, Enduring Realities* (New York: Basic Books, 1990), and Merton C. Bernstein and Joan Brodshaug Bernstein, *Social Security: The System That Works* (New York: Basic Books, 1988).

2. Richard Hofstadter, *The Age of Reform: From Bryan to FDR* (New York: Alfred Knopf, 1955).

3. Louis Galambos, "By Way of Introduction," in Galambos, ed., *The New American State: Bureaucracies and Policies since World War II* (Baltimore: Johns Hopkins University Press, 1987). Other key works that discuss American state building are Stephen

Skowronek, *Building a New American State: The Expansion of National Administrative Capacities* (New York: Cambridge University Press, 1982); Galambos, "The Emerging Organizational Synthesis in Modern American History," *Business History Review* 44 (Autumn 1970): 279–290; Robert Wiebe, *The Search for Order, 1877–1920* (New York: Hill and Wang, 1967).

4. Important works on the history of Social Security that have influenced this one include Arthur Altmeyer, *The Formative Years of Social Security* (Madison: University of Wisconsin Press, 1968); W. Andrew Achenbaum, *Social Security: Visions and Revisions* (New York: Cambridge University Press, 1986); Martha Derthick, *Policymaking for Social Security* (Washington, D.C.: Brookings Institution, 1979); Edwin Witte, *The Development of the Social Security Act* (Madison: University of Wisconsin Press, 1963); Carolyn L. Weaver, *The Crisis in Social Security* (Durham, N.C.: Duke University Press, 1982); Jerry Cates, *Insuring Inequality* (Ann Arbor: University of Michigan Press, 1983); Robert J. Myers, *Social Security*, 3d ed. (Homewood, Ill.: Richard D. Irwin, 1985); Robert Ball, *Social Security: Today and Tomorrow* (New York: Columbia University Press, 1968); Theron Schlabach, *Edwin E. Witte: Cautious Reformer* (Madison: Wisconsin State Historical Society, 1969); Mark Leff, "Taxing the 'Forgotten Man': The Politics of Social Security Finance in the New Deal," *Journal of American History* 70 (September 1983): 359–381; Arthur M. Schlesinger, Jr., *The Coming of the New Deal* (Boston: Houghton Mifflin, 1959); Irving Bernstein, *A Caring Society* (Boston: Houghton Mifflin, 1985); William Graebner, *A History of Retirement* (New Haven, Conn.: Yale University Press, 1980).

5. Alicia Munnell, *The Future of Social Security* (Washington, D.C.: Brookings Institution, 1977), p. 6.

6. On iron triangles, see Louis Galambos, *America at Middle Age: A New History of the United States in the Twentieth Century* (New York: McGraw Hill, 1982).

7. In this regard, it is interesting that there is no entry for Social Security in the index for Mary Beth Norton et al., *A People and a Nation: A History of the United States*, 2d ed. (Boston: Houghton Mifflin, 1986), a leading history text; the index lists C. Wright Mills but not Wilbur Mills, the influential chairman of the House Ways and Means Committee.

8. The classic source on this point is Derthick, *Policymaking for Social Security*.

9. Theodore R. Marmor, with Philip Fellman, "Entrepreneurship in Public Management: Wilbur Cohen and Robert Ball," in Jameson Doig and Erwin Hargrove, eds., *Leadership and Innovation: A Biographical Perspective on Entrepreneurs in Government* (Baltimore: Johns Hopkins University Press, 1987), pp. 246–281.

10. Two excellent overviews are David Farber, *The Age of Great Dreams: America in the 1960s* (New York: Hill and Wang, 1964), and Allen J. Matusow, *The Unraveling of America: A History of Liberalism in the 1960s* (New York: Harper and Row, 1984).

11. Herman Somers, interview with Peter Corning, Columbia Oral History Collection, p. 70, annotated copy available in Box 394, Cohen Papers, Lyndon Baines Johnson (LBJ) Library, Austin, Texas.

12. Wilbur Cohen, "Social Security in 1995," in Edward Berkowitz, ed., *Social Security after Fifty: Successes and Failures* (Westport, Conn.: Greenwood Press, 1987), p. 144.

13. James L. Sundquist, *Politics and Policy: The Eisenhower, Kennedy, and Johnson Years* (Washington, D.C.: Brookings Institution, 1968), p. 393.

14. James T. Patterson, *America's Struggle against Poverty* (Cambridge: Harvard University Press, 1981), p. 130; Hugh Davis Graham, *The Uncertain Triumph: Federal Education Policy in the Kennedy and Johnson Years* (Chapel Hill: University of North Carolina Press, 1984), p. 34; Stephen K. Bailey and Edith K. Mosher, *ESEA: The Office of Education Administers a Law* (Syracuse, N.Y.: Syracuse University Press, 1968), p. 29;

Martha Derthick, *Uncontrollable Spending for Social Service Grants* (Washington, D.C.: Brookings Institution, 1975), p. 13.

15. As the notes for chapter 8 indicate, I have relied heavily on Graham, *Uncertain Triumph*.

16. Readers who want more of an interpretive framework or more details on individual programs might refer to my previous books on social welfare policy, including *Creating the Welfare State: The Political Economy of Twentieth-Century Reform* (Lawrence: University Press of Kansas, 1992), written with Kim McQuaid; *America's Welfare State: From Roosevelt to Reagan* (Baltimore: Johns Hopkins University Press, 1991); *Disabled Policy: America's Program for the Handicapped* (New York: Cambridge University Press, 1987); *Group Health Association: A Portrait of a Health Maintenance Organization* (Philadelphia: Temple University Press, 1988), written with Wendy Wolff; *Social Security and Medicare: A Policy Primer* (Westport, Conn.: Auburn House, 1993), written with Eric Kingson. I have also discussed ways of interpreting the welfare state in "How to Think about the Welfare State," *Labor History* 32 (Fall 1991): 489–502.

17. I am very aware of a renaissance in social-welfare history studies that owes much to the historians' interest in women's studies and the sociologists' interest in comparative studies of the welfare state. Although I do not choose to engage this literature here, I hope this book provides some data of use to both of these important enterprises. See, for example, Linda Gordon, ed., *Women, the State, and Welfare* (Madison: University of Wisconsin Press, 1990); Robyn Muncy, *Creating a Female Dominion in American Reform, 1890–1935* (New York: Oxford University Press, 1991); Anne Shola Orloff, *The Politics of Pensions: A Comparative Analysis of Britain, Canada, and the United States, 1880–1940* (Wisconsin: University of Wisconsin Press, 1993); Theda Skocpol, *Protecting Soldiers and Mothers* (Cambridge: Harvard University Press, 1993).

CHAPTER ONE. THE EDUCATION OF WILBUR COHEN

1. Cohen also went to great lengths to preserve pieces of his past. See Cohen to Robert G. Carroon, Milwaukee County Historical Society, July 8, 1977, Box 246, Cohen Papers, Wisconsin State Historical Society, Madison (hereafter cited as Cohen Papers). See also Wilbur J. Cohen, "Autobiographical Notes," n.d., Box 278, Cohen Papers; Cohen to Darwin Huxley, December 4, 1971, transmits copies of death certificates for his grandparents that Cohen managed to obtain (letter in personal possession of Mrs. Esther Huxley, Milwaukee, Wisconsin, widow of Wilbur's brother Darwin Mendel Huxley – hereafter these papers are cited as Darwin Papers). M. Davis Rubenstein, "The Jewish Sign Mogen David" (c. L. Boruszak and M. D. Rubenstein, copy obtained from Milwaukee Public Library), pamphlet written by Cohen's maternal grandfather. Cohen to Darwin and Esther Huxley, July 23, 1986, Darwin Papers; Cohen to Darwin Huxley, May 24, 1971, Darwin Papers, transmits an elaborate family genealogy; Cohen to executive director, Milwaukee County Historical Society, September 1, 1981, Darwin Papers, and Dr. Melvin E. Schwartz to Dr. Lowell E. Bellin, June 16, 1975, Darwin Papers, concern correspondence on the part of Cohen to locate his mother's birth certificate.

2. See, for example, Irving Howe, *World of Our Fathers: The Journey of the East European Jews to America and the Life They Found and Made* (New York: Harcourt Brace Jovanovich, 1976), pp. 5–7.

3. Here, as elsewhere, Cohen was his own best archivist. He requested information about the family from the commissioner of health for the City of New York, who dug up birth records for Rachel Rubenstein, Becy (*sic*) Rubenstein, and Harris Rubenstein, born to Davis Rubenstein in 1890, 1891, and 1893, at 183 Clinton Street. The commissioner also sent information from the New York City Business Directory of 1890 listing

Davis's occupation as a teacher and from a New York City police census, which listed Davis's age as thirty and Sara's (also known as Sarah and Sery) as twenty-six. See Schwartz to Bellin, June 16, 1975, Darwin Papers.

4. See Cohen to Darwin Cohen, May 14, 1971, Box 278, Cohen Papers, for Cohen's efforts to construct a family genealogy. The dates that he gives for the birthdays of his grandparents do not match those in the New York City census cited here.

5. The temple was Beth Israel. Darwin Mendel Huxley, interview with author, Milwaukee, August 22, 1990.

6. Rubenstein, "Jewish Sign Mogen David," p. 5.

7. In that year this territory belonged to Germany, and the surrounding towns had German rather than Polish names (from a family genealogy of the Cohen family, prepared in 1971 by Wilbur Cohen, Box 278, Cohen Papers). This material also contains the sketch of the house at 48 Grove Street, made in 1971.

8. This information comes from the genealogy of the Cohen family that Wilbur prepared (Box 278, Cohen Papers).

9. Wilbur collected his parents' certificate of marriage, which lists the wedding as having taken place on August 4, 1912, performed by a rabbi and witnessed by two residents of Ninth Street in Milwaukee. I take my sense of Aaron and Bessie's meeting from my interview with Darwin Huxley.

10. When Bessie Cohen died in 1941, Aaron had his brother Louis run the Wells Variety Store; after 1944 Aaron ran the store himself. In 1947 he opened a second branch on 4201 W. Capitol Drive, which lasted until 1968 (see the material in Box 278, Cohen Papers). See also "Fathers and Sons," a eulogy that Wilbur delivered for his father on February 3, 1977, at the Whitefish Bay Goodman-Bensman Funeral Home, Milwaukee, and the attached obituaries from the local Milwaukee newspapers. These include Greg Coenen, "After 86 Years Storekeeper's Still on the Job," *New Day, Milwaukee's Neighborhood Newspaper,* April 4–17, 1973, p. 8, and articles in *Milwaukee Sentinel,* February 3, 1977, and *Wisconsin Jewish Chronicle,* February 10, 1977, all in possession of Eloise Cohen, Austin, Texas (hereafter cited as Eloise Papers).

11. Julius Edelstein, interview with author, New York City, October 2, 1990.

12. I take this point in part from a conversation with Hugh Davis Graham, who interviewed Cohen for a book on public policy toward education. Graham marveled at Cohen's lack of ego, particularly compared to others he interviewed who had worked at the Johnson White House; without hesitation, Cohen attributed this trait to his mother. Cohen's own impressions come from his draft autobiography, July 1981, Box 278, Cohen Papers.

13. Cohen wrote an undated piece called "Aaron Cohen," from which I have taken the quotation (Box 278, Cohen Papers).

14. "Milwaukee Paper," p. 3 (1932), in Box 83, Experimental College Records, Memorial Library, University of Wisconsin.

15. Draft autobiography, July 1981, Box 278, Cohen Papers.

16. Ibid., and on Aaron's interest in boxing, see also Bruce Cohen, interview with author, Wilmette, Illinois, October 19, 1990.

17. Draft autobiography, July 1981, Box 278, Cohen Papers.

18. Bruce Cohen interview, and Chris Cohen, interview with author, Glencoe, Illinois, October 20, 1990.

19. Cohen, "Religion, Marriage, and Family," June 1976 and July 1981, Box 279, Cohen Papers.

20. Ibid.

21. Ibid.

22. Bruce Cohen, interview.

23. This view of Cohen's development is consistent with the work of Robert Wiebe, Louis Galambos, and other adherents of the organizational synthesis. In *The Search for*

Order (New York: Hill and Wang, 1967) and in *The Segmented Society* (New York: Oxford University Press, 1975), Wiebe writes about how occupation superseded location as a primary means of identity in the late nineteenth and early twentieth centuries.

24. Edelstein, interview.
25. Merlyn Pitzele, interview with author, Beacon, New York, November 9, 1990.
26. Wilbur Cohen, interview with author, Austin, Texas, November 12, 1984.
27. Bruce Cohen, interview.
28. Cohen, "Religion, Marriage, and Family."
29. Darwin Huxley, interview.
30. Pitzele, interview.
31. Edelstein, interview; draft autobiography, 1981, Box 278, Cohen Papers; "Milwaukee Paper," p. 6; undated autobiographical lists and annotations, Box 278, Cohen Papers.
32. "Milwaukee Paper," pp. 39, 70.
33. Desk calendar, November 12, 1965, Box 278, Cohen Papers.
34. Text of Cohen fiftieth reunion speech for Lincoln High School Class of 1930, Box 269, Cohen Papers.
35. Article by Hugo Autz in *Sporting Goods Dealer,* May 1968, Box 5, Cohen Papers.
36. Dedication, *Quill Yearbook,* 1930, Box 24, Cohen Papers.
37. "Milwaukee Paper," p. 29.
38. Ibid., p. 30.
39. Ibid.
40. Ibid.
41. Ibid., p. 34.
42. Draft autobiography, July 1981, Box 279, Cohen Papers.
43. Autz article, Box 5, Cohen Papers.
44. Ibid.; draft autobiography, July 1981, Box 279, Cohen Papers; "Wilbur J. Cohen," biographical statement prepared by Eloise Cohen, Box 5, Cohen Papers.
45. *Quill Yearbook* and other materials, Box 24, Cohen Papers; Cohen, "Growing Up in Milwaukee: 1913–1954," address to Milwaukee Historical Society, May 2, 1984, p. 9, Box 269, Cohen Papers.
46. *Quill Yearbook,* Box 24, Cohen Papers.
47. Undated notes from Cohen's Experimental College files, Box 83, Experimental College Records.
48. "Milwaukee Paper," p. 61.
49. Ibid., p. 57.
50. See Henry Adams, *The Education of Henry Adams* (Boston: Houghton, Mifflin and Company, 1919), intro. Henry Cabot Lodge; this appears to be the edition Cohen and his classmates read. Interestingly, the book begins with a whimsical reference to a fictitious high priest of Israel whom Adams calls Israel Cohen, noting that "he was born an eighteenth-century child" (p. 11).
51. "Milwaukee Paper," p. 57.
52. Cohen, "Growing Up in Milwaukee," p. 6. Cohen noted with pride that Stuart, his youngest son, did attend Harvard.
53. "Milwaukee Paper," p. 61; Autobiography, July 1981, Box 279, Cohen Papers. In some versions of the story, the newspaper was the *Milwaukee Journal.*
54. Undated notes in Cohen's Experimental College file, Box 83, Experimental College Records.
55. Undated, unpaginated autobiographical fragments in Box 269, Cohen Papers. Harold November, one of Cohen's classmates, said that the Experimental College contained a disproportionate number of easterners and Jews (interview with author, Baltimore, Maryland, October 27, 1990).

56. "Growing up in the central city I knew little about the South Side, Shorewood, Fox Point and other important places outside the third ward," Wilbur J. Cohen, "Growing Up in Milwaukee: 1913–1934; and Reflections on Its Longer Range Impact," typescript, May 2, 1984, in personal possession of the author.

57. Edelstein, interview.

58. Cohen himself wrote a history of the Experimental College that appeared in the *Wisconsin Daily Cardinal,* February 17, 1931, Box 268, Cohen Papers. See also Wilbur J. Cohen, "Unemployment Insurance and the University of Wisconsin: Reflections after 50 Years," presented at the Robert M. LaFollette Institute of Public Affairs, University of Wisconsin, September 15, 1984, typescript, pp. 2–3, copy in Box 269, Cohen Papers; *Summary Proceedings of the Experimental College Reunion with Alexander Meiklejohn,* May 10–12, 1957, Annapolis, Maryland, mimeographed copy in possession of Robert Frase.

59. Autobiographical fragments, Box 278, Cohen Papers; Charles McKinley and Robert W. Frase, *Launching Social Security: A Capture-and-Record Account, 1935–1937* (Madison: University of Wisconsin Press, 1970), p. xxii.

60. Cohen to Pitzele, May 31, 1940, Merlyn Pitzele Papers, Box 15, Wisconsin State Historical Society.

61. Cohen to Dr. Alexander Meiklejohn, May 3, 1962, Box 8, Cohen Papers.

62. November, interview, and Pitzele, interview. For Meiklejohn's attitudes, see the essays in *The Liberal College* (New York: Macmillan, 1920), quotes on pp. 33, 42.

63. Cohen to Alexander Meiklejohn, September 16, 1937, Box 70, Cohen Papers, and autobiographical fragments, Box 278, Cohen Papers. See also John Walker Powell and Alexander Meiklejohn, *The Experimental College,* Seven Locks ed. (Cabin John, Md.: Seven Locks Press, 1981).

64. Autobiographical fragments, Box 278, Cohen Papers.

65. Robert Cool, article on Experimental College, *Milwaukee Journal,* February 18, 1931, clipping in Cohen Papers.

66. November, interview.

67. "I still remember that historic occasion. Little did I realize then that a close relationship with Unemployment Compensation would continue for me for over fifty years" (Cohen, "Unemployment Insurance and the University of Wisconsin," p. 3). Raushenbush served as a tutor or as an adviser at the college and also taught in the economics department. Cohen, who encountered him in all his pedagogical roles, remembered that he had a "very commanding personality" ("Unemployment Insurance and the University of Wisconsin," p. 8). On Raushenbush, see also Paul A. Raushenbush and Elizabeth Brandeis Raushenbush, *Our "U.C." Story: 1930–1967* (Madison, Wis.: privately printed, 1979), pp. 3–4.

68. Adviser's report, February 21, 1931, by Donald Meiklejohn, Box 83, Experimental College Records.

69. June 15, 1931, final report, Box 83, Experimental College Records.

70. No name to Aaron Cohen, July 10, 1931, Box 83, Experimental College Records.

71. John Powell, November 12–February 8, 1931–1932, Experimental College, report of adviser, Box 83, Experimental College Records.

72. R. J. Havighurst, March 9, 1932, Box 83, Experimental College Records. Havighurst was echoing one of Meiklejohn's themes that activities must spring from studies and become the "fruits of the classroom" (Meiklejohn, *Liberal College,* p. 103).

73. No name to Aaron Cohen, June 28, 1932, Box 83, Experimental College Records.

74. "I am not in favor of concentrating the wealth of a nation in the hands of a few individuals, yet I believe I have a certain human impulse that urges me on to become a

millionaire," Cohen wrote, in "Conflicts about Wealth," November 10, 1930, (see Mr. Hart, adviser, Box 83, Experimental College Records).

75. Cohen, "Democracy," December 1, 1930, Box 83, Experimental College Records.

76. Cohen, paper due December 14, 1931, Box 83, Experimental College Records.

77. Cohen, undated paper, Box 83, Experimental College Records.

78. Edelstein, interview.

79. "We May Learn from the Russians," *Wisconsin Daily Cardinal* clipping, October 3, 1931, Box 268, Cohen Papers.

80. Edelstein, interview.

81. After his second year at the Experimental College, Pitzele transferred to the University of Chicago and became involved in a club that he described as "a group of crypto-communists, reading Marx." By graduation, Pitzele, in his own words, "bracketed as a communist" (Pitzele, interview).

82. For Cohen's support of the Groves bill, see his paper due December 14, 1931, Box 83, Experimental College Records.

83. Years later Cohen, in a characteristic manner, saw fit to comment on his association with the newspaper: "As I look back upon my undergraduate years, there is no extra-curricular experience I value more than my work as a reporter and member of the editorial board of the *Daily Cardinal* (1930–1934)" (Cohen to editor, *Daily Cardinal,* January 24, 1962, Box 12, Cohen Papers).

84. Pitzele, interview, and "Pitzele Requests Independent Help," clipping from *Daily Cardinal,* Box 268, Cohen Papers. "In high school he was a great 'activities' man, and he spent very little time in reading or in studying things that were not assigned to him. Here he has changed somewhat, although his recent election to the Student Council has given him an opportunity to get back to activities, which he enjoys greatly" (R. J. Havighurst, adviser's report, March 9, 1932, Box 83, Experimental College Records). The university archives also contain a copy of the 1932 *Badger,* the Wisconsin yearbook, that mentions his participation in the Student Council.

85. Pitzele, interview, and November, interview.

86. Herman Somers, interview with Peter Corning, Columbia Oral History Collection, p. 54, copy in Box 395, Cohen Papers, LBJ Library.

87. Pitzele, interview.

88. Cohen, "Milwaukee Paper," p. 87.

89. Ibid., p. 43.

90. I draw my account of Commons from John R. Commons, *Myself: The Autobiography of John R. Commons* (1934; rept., Madison: University of Wisconsin Press, 1963), and from Lafayette G. Harter, Jr., *John R. Commons: His Assault on Laissez-Faire* (Corvallis: Oregon State University Press, 1962).

91. Leon Fink, "A Memoir of Selig Perlman and His Life at the University of Wisconsin: Based on an Interview of Mark Perlman, Conducted and Edited by Leon Fink," *Labor History* 32 (Fall 1991): 520.

92. Commons, *Myself,* p. 3.

93. Edwin Witte quoted in Harter, *Commons,* p. 47. For a similar view of Commons, see the reminiscence of Raushenbush and Raushenbush, *Our "U.C." Story,* pp. 4–6.

94. Autobiographical fragments, Box 278, Cohen Papers.

95. Cohen, interview with Peter Corning, Columbia Oral History Collection, New York City, July 27, 1966, p. 37.

96. Commons, *Myself,* p. 3.

97. For example, Cohen said, "I had a difficult time following his efforts to integrate economics, law and ethics" ("Unemployment Insurance and the University of Wisconsin," p. 8, Box 269, Cohen Papers).

98. A partial list includes Harold Groves, Wayne Morse, William Haber, Elizabeth Brandeis, Theresa McMahon, Arthur Altmeyer, William Leiserson, Katherine Lenroot, Ewan Clague, Paul Rauschenbush, Alvin Hansen, Sumner Slichter, Florence Peterson, and Philip Taft (see Harter, *Commons,* p. 78).

99. Cohen, interview with Blanche Coll, Austin, Texas, October 19, 1985 (copy available from LBJ Library).

100. In my account of Perlman I draw heavily on the interview with his son Mark in *Labor History.*

101. Autobiographical fragments, Box 278, Cohen Papers.

102. Wilbur Cohen to folks, November 14, 1933, Eloise Papers.

103. Ibid., February 22, 1934.

104. A copy of the thesis is available in Box 268, Cohen Papers.

105. Cohen to folks, February 22, 1934, Eloise Papers, and Selig Perlman and Philip Taft, *History of Labor in the United States, 1896–1932,* vol. 4, *Labor Movements* (New York: Macmillan Company, 1935), p. 582.

106. Cohen to folks, November 14, 1933, Eloise Papers.

107. Cohen, interview with Coll; the dates of these various incidents remain obscure, but they clearly left an impression on Cohen since he told the story about his father's failed investment to his son Bruce (Bruce Cohen, interview).

108. Cohen to folks, November 9, 1933, Darwin Papers.

109. Cohen to folks, November 14, 1933, Eloise Papers.

110. Cohen to Darwin Cohen, November 2, 1933, Darwin Papers.

111. Cohen to folks, May 14, 1934, Eloise Papers.

112. The best source on Witte is Theron F. Schlabach, *Edwin E. Witte: Cautious Reformer* (Madison: State Historical Society of Wisconsin, 1969). For other biographical details on Edwin Witte, see the introduction by Robert J. Lampman to Edwin Witte, *Social Security Perspectives: Essays by Edwin E. Witte* (Madison: University of Wisconsin Press, 1962), and Cohen, "Edwin E. Witte," in Walter I. Trattner, ed., *Biographical Dictionary of Social Welfare in America* (Westport Conn.: Greenwood Press, 1986), pp. 785–787.

113. Cohen, "Unemployment Insurance and the University of Wisconsin," p. 8.

114. Cohen, interview with Coll.

115. This event wounded Perlman deeply; see Mark Perlman's reminiscence about his father in *Labor History,* p. 521.

116. Autobiographical fragments, Box 278, Cohen Papers, and Cohen, "Unemployment Insurance and the University of Wisconsin," p. 8.

117. Witte to Cohen, March 3, 1936, Box 25, Cohen Papers. Appended to this letter was a letter of recommendation that Witte wrote on Cohen's behalf.

118. Edwin E. Witte, *The Development of the Social Security Act* (Madison: University of Wisconsin Press), pp. 12–13.

119. W. Andrew Achenbaum, "Arthur Joseph Altmeyer," in Trattner, ed., *Biographical Dictionary of Social Welfare,* pp. 25–27, and Arthur J. Altmeyer, *The Formative Years of Social Security* (Madison: University of Wisconsin Press, 1966), p. ix.

120. Executive Order 6757, June 29, 1934, reprinted in *50th Anniversary Edition, the Report of the Committee on Economic Security of 1935 and Other Basic Documents Relating to the Development of the Social Security Act* (Washington, D.C.: National Conference on Social Welfare, 1985), p. 140, and Altmeyer, *Formative Years of Social Security,* p. 7.

121. Franklin D. Roosevelt, "Message to Congress Reviewing the Broad Objectives and Accomplishments of the Administration," June 8, 1934, reprinted in *50th Anniversary Edition,* p. 136.

122. Executive Order 6757.

123. Witte, *Development of the Social Security Act*, p. 12. Harry Hopkins was the federal relief administrator and confidant of Roosevelt; under Hopkins, the Federal Emergency Relief Agency provided $87,500 to finance the committee's work.

124. Autobiographical fragments, and "Venturing into the Unknown," autobiographical essay, Box 278, Cohen Papers.

125. Witte to Cohen, August 4, 1934, Box 25, Cohen Papers.

126. Somers, interview, p. 59.

127. In addition to the autobiographical fragments, see Wilbur J. Cohen, "FDR and the New Deal: A Personal Reminiscence," *Milwaukee History* 6 (Autumn 1983): 71–72.

128. Autobiographical fragment, Eloise Papers.

129. Cohen to folks, August 11, 1934, Darwin Papers.

130. Ibid.

131. Darwin Huxley, interview.

132. Cohen, "FDR and the New Deal," p. 71.

133. Altmeyer, *Formative Years of Social Security*, p. ix.

CHAPTER TWO. FORGING A CAREER IN NEW DEAL WASHINGTON

1. I examine the committee's work in detail in *America's Welfare State* (Baltimore: Johns Hopkins Press, 1991).

2. Wilbur J. Cohen, "The Social Security Act of 1935: Reflections Fifty Years Later," in *50th Anniversary Edition, the Report of the Committee on Economic Security of 1935* (Washington, D.C.: National Conference on Social Welfare, 1985), pp. 3–14, and Edwin Witte, *The Development of the Social Security Act* (Madison: University of Wisconsin, 1962).

3. Cohen to folks, August 14, 1934, Eloise Papers.

4. Ibid.

5. Cohen, "FDR and the New Deal: A Personal Reminiscence," *Milwaukee History* 6 (Autumn 1983): 73.

6. On the significance of the work of the Committee on Economic Security, see William Graebner, *A History of Retirement: The Meaning and Function of an American Institution* (New Haven, Conn.: Yale University Press, 1980); Abraham Epstein, *Insecurity: A Challenge to America* (New York: Random House, 1938); Paul H. Douglas, *Social Security in the United States* (New York: Da Capo Press, 1971); Daniel Nelson, *Unemployment Insurance: The American Experience, 1915–35* (Madison: University of Wisconsin Press, 1969).

7. Cohen, "FDR and the New Deal," p. 73.

8. Cohen to folks, August 14, 1934, Eloise Papers.

9. Cohen, "FDR and the New Deal," p. 74.

10. Cohen to folks, August 14, 1934, Eloise Papers.

11. Cohen to folks, August 20, 1934, Eloise Papers, and Witte, *Development of the Social Security Act,* pp. 9–10.

12. Cohen, interview with Blanche Coll, October 19, 1985, copy available from LBJ Library, and Cohen, interview with Peter Corning, Columbia Oral History Collection, p. 44.

13. Cohen to folks, August 20, 1934, Eloise Papers. The results of Cohen's work can be seen in *Social Security in America: The Factual Background of the Social Security Act as Summarized from Staff Reports to the Committee on Economic Security* (Washington, D.C.: Government Printing Office, 1937).

14. *Social Security in America,* pp. 521–523; appendix and supplement, *Report of the Committee on Economic Security,* pp. 265–267; Cohen, "Venturing into the Unknown," Box 278, Cohen Papers.

15. Witte was an advocate of the Wisconsin approach to unemployment and of the Wagner-Lewis bill, which featured a tax incentive. The incentive, originated in a suggestion by Justice Brandeis to his daughter, was to use a federal tax as leverage to obtain a state tax. In this case, the idea was to impose a federal tax on payrolls. This tax could be forgiven – not paid, in other words – if and only if a state agreed to levy another tax on those same payrolls and to use the money to pay benefits to the jobless. It was an indirect and apparently constitutional method of getting states to start unemployment compensation programs. See, for example, Arthur Altmeyer, *The Formative Years of Social Security* (Madison: University of Wisconsin Press, 1966), pp. 13–25, and Wilbur J. Cohen, "Unemployment Insurance and the University of Wisconsin: Reflections after 50 Years," speech presented at the Robert M. LaFollette Institute, University of Wisconsin, September 15, 1984.

16. Cohen to folks, August 25, 1934, Eloise Papers.

17. Cohen, "Venturing into the Unknown," and *Social Security in America,* p. 521.

18. Witte to Cohen, March 3, 1936, Box 25, Cohen Papers. The quote is from a letter that Witte wrote to Felix Frankfurter on March 3, 1936, which Witte enclosed in his letter to Cohen.

19. See Berkowitz, *America's Welfare State*.

20. Witte, *Development of the Social Security Act,* pp. 35–36.

21. Cohen to folks, October 25, 1934, Eloise Papers.

22. Ibid., August 25, 1934.

23. Cohen to Darwin Cohen, October 15, 1934, Darwin Papers.

24. Cohen to folks, August 25, 1934, Eloise Papers.

25. Cohen to parents, February 18, 1935, Eloise Papers; Ken Decker, "Three Bachelors," a reminiscence, February 24, 1986, Eloise Papers; Harold November, interview with author, Baltimore, Maryland, October 27, 1990.

26. Cohen to folks, August 25, 1934, Eloise Papers.

27. Ibid., August 14, 1934.

28. Ibid., August 25, 1934.

29. Cohen to Darwin Cohen, September 1, 1934, Darwin Papers.

30. Ibid., October 15, 1934.

31. Cohen to folks, November 22, 1934, Eloise Papers.

32. Cohen to Darwin, October 15, 1934, and April 4, 1937, Darwin Papers.

33. Cohen to parents, September 28, 1935, Eloise Papers.

34. Cohen to Darwin Cohen, August 4, 1937, Darwin Papers.

35. Cohen to folks, March 15, 1935, Darwin Papers.

36. Cohen to parents, November 22, 1934, Eloise Papers.

37. Cohen to folks, March 15, 1934, Darwin Papers.

38. Ibid., Memorial Day, 1935. On the Schecter decision, see Ellis Hawley, *The New Deal and the Problem of Monopoly* (Princeton, N.J.: Princeton University Press, 1966), p. 127.

39. Cohen to folks, March 15, 1935, Darwin Papers.

40. Cohen, interview with Coll.

41. Cohen, "Early Days of Social Security," autobiographical fragment, p. 5, Box 279, Cohen Papers.

42. Cohen to folks, Memorial Day, 1935, Darwin Papers.

43. Ibid.

44. Cohen to my dear Darwin, June 2, 1935, Darwin Papers.

45. Cohen to folks, June 17, 1935, Darwin Papers.

46. Witte, *Development of the Social Security Act,* p. 15; the Social Science Research Council also sponsored a participant account of the administrative steps taken to launch Social Security, written, among others, by Robert Frase, a friend of Cohen's from their

Experimental College days. This study was published in 1970, with a foreword by Cohen and with Cohen's encouragement. Cohen also helped to get Witte's account of the development of the Social Security Act published and wrote an introduction to it as well. Charles McKinley and Robert W. Frase, *Launching Social Security* (Madison: University of Wisconsin Press, 1970).

47. Cohen to folks, July 27, 1935, Darwin Papers, and Altmeyer, *Formative Years of Social Security*, pp. 41–45.

48. Cohen to parents, August 10, 1935, Eloise Papers.

49. Cohen, "Early Days of Social Security," p. 5; Elizabeth Wickenden, interview with author, Haverford, Pennsylvania, October 16, 1991; Witte, *Development of the Social Security Act*, p. 14. Witte refers to the Washington Auditorium, Cohen to the Municipal Auditorium, and Wickenden simply to the auditorium.

50. Although promised $3,200 a year by Altmeyer, the Civil Service granted him only $2,600. Youth, inexperience, and the lack of a graduate education combined to limit Cohen's salary to that of an associate economic analyst's (Cohen to folks, October 22 and 28, 1935, Darwin Papers.

51. Ibid., September 28, 1935.

52. The Social Security Act provided federal grants to states to start (or continue) welfare programs for needy elderly, dependent children, or blind citizens; it also included a tax incentive for states to initiate unemployment insurance programs. If the states wanted to receive money or other benefits from the federal government, the act required them to meet specified conditions. The Social Security Board, for example, needed to approve state plans for aid to dependent children and for old-age assistance. The state plans, in turn, had to contain such features as the right of rejected applicants to receive a fair hearing. On a more practical level, the states needed to draft new laws to take advantage of the Social Security Act, and they turned to the Social Security Board for help. See McKinley and Frase, *Launching Social Security*, and Altmeyer, *Formative Years*.

53. Cohen, "Early Days of Social Security," p. 9.

54. Cohen to folks, September 28, 1935, Darwin Papers.

55. Merlyn Pitzele, interview with author, Beacon, New York, November 6, 1990; the reference is to the central character in Max Shulman's novel, *What Makes Sammy Run*.

56. Herman Somers, interview with Peter Corning, Columbia Oral History Collection, p. 66.

57. Cohen to folks, October 28, 1935, Darwin Papers.

58. Ibid., December 2, 1935.

59. Ibid.

60. Ibid.

61. Cohen, "Early Days in Social Security," p. 11, and McKinley and Frase, *Launching Social Security*, p. 250.

62. Cohen, "Early Days of Social Security."

63. Cohen to folks, June 12, 1936, Darwin Papers.

64. See Altmeyer, *Formative Years of Social Security,* p. 68.

65. Winant, in his brief tenure with the board, made a lasting impression on the highly impressionable Cohen, who liked to compare him with Abraham Lincoln. Viewed through Cohen's eyes, Winant, the nominal Republican on the Social Security Board, was "idealistic, moody, and Lincolnesque in appearance and mannerism" ("Early Days in Social Security," p. 8). Not very eloquent, Winant nonetheless infused the Social Security Board with a high sense of mission. See Cohen, interview with David McComb, December 8, 1968, p. 6, LBJ Library.

66. Cohen, "Early Days of Social Security," p. 22, and McKinley and Frase, *Launching Social Security*, p. 359.

67. Operating bureaus administered individual programs, and service bureaus were responsible for such matters as legal advice, publicity, and research. See Altmeyer, *Formative Years,* p. 72, and McKinley and Frase, *Launching Social Security,* pp. 504–505.

68. Cohen to folks, June 12, 1936, Darwin Papers.

69. Cohen to Henry Ellenbogen, March 1937, Altmeyer to Hugo Black, May 10, 1937, Cohen to Altmeyer, January 14, 1938, Box 25, Cohen Papers.

70. Altmeyer, *Formative Years,* pp. vi–x, and W. Andrew Achenbaum, "Arthur Altmeyer," in W. Trattner, ed., *Biographical Dictionary of Social Welfare in America* (Westport, Conn.: Greenwood Press, 1986), pp. 25–27.

71. Linda Gordon, "The New Feminist Scholarship on the Welfare State," Institute for Research on Poverty Discussion Papers, Madison, Wis., 1989, p. 12. This essay, along with several other interesting pieces of new feminist scholarship on social welfare policy, is reprinted in Gordon, *Women, the State, and Welfare* (Madison: University of Wisconsin Press, 1990). See also Robyn Muncy, *Creating a Female Dominion in American Reform, 1890–1935* (New York: Oxford University Press, 1991). Standard biographies of Jane Addams include Allen Davis, *American Heroine: The Life and Legend of Jane Addams* (New York: Oxford University Press, 1973), and Daniel Levine, *Jane Addams and the Liberal Tradition* (Madison: State Historical Society of Wisconsin, 1971).

72. On these distinctions, which I think she uses too broadly, see Linda Gordon, "Social Insurance and Public Assistance: The Influence of Gender in Welfare Thought in the United States, 1890–1935," *American Historical Review* 97 (February 1992): 19–54.

73. Michael Katz, *In the Shadow of the Poorhouse: A Social History of America* (New York: Basic Books, 1986), discusses Jane Addams in the context of saving children and cities. He places Altmeyer's and Cohen's work in the context of reorganizing both the labor market and the nation.

74. On Altmeyer's affection for Cohen, see Altmeyer to Cohen, January 17, 1956, and May 2, 1966, Box 6, Cohen Papers.

75. Cohen to folks, November 29, 1936, Darwin Papers.

76. Somers, interview, p. 66.

77. Cohen to folks, March 15, 1935, Darwin Papers.

78. Ibid., Memorial Day, 1935, June 17, 1935, October 28, 1935, and December 2, 1935. Decker, "Three Bachelors"; and Cohen, "Religion, Marriage and Family," June 1976 and July 1981, Box 279, Cohen Papers.

79. Cohen, "Religion, Marriage, and Family."

80. I draw this account of Eloise Cohen's life from interviews with her in Austin, Texas, December 8, 1990, and March 13, 1991, and from Eloise Cohen, "A Letter I Would Like to Write My Mother," November 19, 1979, Eloise Papers.

81. Judith Sealander, "Sophonisba Breckinridge," in Trattner, ed., *Biographical Dictionary of Social Welfare,* p. 128.

82. The sight of Wilbur dressed up in riding clothes occasioned some laughter in the Social Security offices, but with characteristic enthusiasm, he described it as "great exercise and great fun" (Cohen to folks, April 4, 1937, Darwin Papers).

83. Eloise [Bittel] to mother and dad, October 17, 1937, Eloise Papers.

84. Ibid.

85. Cohen to mother and dad, February 16, 1938, Darwin Papers; Cohen to Darwin, March 16, 1938, Darwin Papers; Cohen to Bob Frase, May 3, 1938 (in personal possession of Robert Frase).

86. As Cohen later told the story, in the spring of 1938, Arthur Altmeyer and his wife prepared to travel to Europe. Part vacation, the trip also involved gathering data on foreign social insurance programs and meeting fellow social insurance administrators. Cohen did much of the staff work in preparation for the trip and then found out that he, too, might go to Europe. He went to New York and asked Eloise to join him. When she

agreed, they became engaged. See Cohen, "Religion, Marriage, and Family," and Frank Bane to Arthur Altmeyer, May 25, 1938, Box 25, Cohen Papers.

87. In fact, Eloise did not tell Wilbur about the conversation until years later, when he had already decided that his ashes should be scattered over the ranch in Ingram (Eloise Cohen, interviews).

88. Cohen to folks, April 17, 1938, and May 8, 1938, Darwin Papers, and Eloise and Wilbur to Dearest Bob [Frase], April 21, 1938, in personal possession of Robert Frase.

89. Cohen to Darwin, May 26, 1938, Darwin Papers; Eloise to mother and dad, June 21, 1938, Eloise Papers; Cohen to dearest dad, June 27, 1938, Darwin Papers.

90. Cohen to Darwin, May 26, 1938, Darwin Papers, and Eloise to mother and dad, June 21, 1938, Eloise Papers. Cohen used the data he gathered in Europe to write internal reports to the Social Security Board, such as "Old-Age and Survivors Insurance Program for Agricultural Labor, Domestic Service, and the Self-Employed," 1940, mimeograph.

91. Cohen to dearest dad, June 27, 1938, Darwin Papers.

92. It should be noted that work on the Advisory Council began well before Cohen left for Europe; the first meeting was November 5, 1937. On the significance of the council's process in the development of the Social Security program, see Martha Derthick, *Policymaking for Social Security* (Washington, D.C.: Brookings Institution, 1979), pp. 89–109. On the 1939 amendments, see Edward D. Berkowitz, "The First Advisory Council and the 1939 Amendments," in Berkowitz, ed., *Social Security after Fifty* (Westport, Conn.: Greenwood Press, 1987), pp. 55–78; Mark Leff, "Taxing the 'Forgotten Man': The Politics of Social Security Finance in the New Deal," *Journal of American History* 70 (September 1983): 359–381; Brian Balogh, "Securing Support: The Emergence of the Social Security Board as a Political Actor, 1935–1939," in Donald Critchlow and Ellis Hawley, eds., *Federal Social Policy: The Historical Dimension* (University Park: Pennsylvania State University Press, 1988).

93. See Wilbur Cohen to Arthur Altmeyer, October 13, 1938, File 025, Records of the Social Security Administration, Record Group (RG) 47, National Archives, Washington, D.C.

94. See Edward Berkowitz, *Disabled Policy* (New York: Cambridge University Press, 1987), pp. 56–60.

95. Cohen, interview with David McComb, LBJ Library, p. 15.

96. Cohen, "Early Days of Social Security," p. 22.

CHAPTER THREE. THE 1940S, SOCIAL SECURITY
APPARATUS, AND TRIUMPH OF 1950

1. Eloise Bittel Cohen, interview with author, Austin, Texas, December 8, 1990.

2. "The Cohen Family," n.d., Darwin Papers.

3. Eloise Cohen, "A Letter I Would Like to Write My Mother," Eloise Papers.

4. See Cohen to Pitzele, August 22, 1940, Box 15, Pitzele Papers.

5. Alvin Hansen to Arthur Altmeyer, November 8, 1937, and Altmeyer to Hansen, December 7, 1939, File 025, RG 47, Records of the Social Security Administration, National Archives, Washington, D.C.

6. "An Expanded Social Security Program," August 13, 1941, Box 26, Cohen Papers.

7. Ibid., and Cohen to Byron Mitchell, chief budget examiner, June 6, 1941, Box 26, Cohen Papers. One of the major factors that would lead to the surplus in Social Security was the elimination of experience rating under unemployment compensation, which would have created a large increase in the unemployment compensation taxes paid by employers.

8. "Comments on the Social Security Board's Legislative Proposals," September 30, 1941, Box 26, Cohen Papers.

9. See the citations in Edward Berkowitz and Kim McQuaid, *Creating the Welfare State,* paperback ed. (Lawrence: University Press of Kansas, 1992), pp. 153–154; Arthur Altmeyer, *The Formative Years of Social Security* (Madison: University of Wisconsin Press, 1966), pp. 141–145; Edward D. Berkowitz, "Domestic Politics and International Expertise in the History of American Disability Policy," *Milbank Memorial Quarterly* 67: suppl. 2, pt. 1 (1989): 207–214.

10. Altmeyer, *Formative Years,* p. 143. Among those who worked on the report was William Haber, a University of Michigan academic and Wisconsin economics graduate, who had written Michigan's unemployment compensation law and had served on the Advisory Council leading to the 1939 amendments; he became a close friend and collaborator of Cohen. Eveline Burns, who did much of the actual research, taught at Columbia; in 1934 she worked on the Committee on Economic Security staff. Mary Switzer, an assistant to the federal security administrator, also helped with the report. She had helped to staff the Interdepartmental Committee to Coordinate Health and Welfare Activities, on which Altmeyer had also served, that laid the groundwork for the federal government's first tentative proposals in the areas of health and disability insurance.

11. Altmeyer to the president, December 4, 1942, Box 26, Cohen Papers.

12. Fred Hoehler, director, American Public Welfare Association, to the president, December 4, 1942, Box 26, Cohen Papers.

13. Although the second title changed little about Cohen's job, it solidified an important link between the board's planning and legislative responsibilities. See Cohen to Howard L. Russell, director, American Public Welfare Association, February 19, 1947, Box 27, Cohen Papers.

14. Isidore S. Falk, a public health researcher and the Social Security Board's director of research, played a central role in drafting the SSB's health and disability proposals. For more on Falk, and on the health and disability proposals in general, see Daniel M. Fox, *Health Policies, Health Politics: The British and American Experience, 1911–1965* (Princeton, N.J.: Princeton University Press, 1988), pp. 48, 80; Daniel S. Hirshfield, *The Lost Reform: The Campaign for Compulsory Health Insurance in the United States from 1932 to 1943* (Cambridge: Harvard University Press, 1970), pp. 42–70; I. S. Falk, *Security against Sickness: A Study of Health Insurance* (Garden City, N.Y.: Doubleday, Doran and Company, 1936).

15. Wilbur Cohen, "From Medicare to National Health Insurance," in David C. Warner, ed., *Toward New Human Rights: The Social Policies of the Kennedy and Johnson Administrations* (Austin, Tex.: Lyndon B. Johnson School of Public Affairs, 1977), p. 144, and Monte Poen, *Harry S. Truman versus the Medical Lobby* (Columbia: University of Missouri Press, 1979), p. 32.

16. Cohen to Katherine Ellickson, July 7, 1943, Box 26, Cohen Papers.

17. Poen, *Truman and the Medical Lobby,* pp. 57–64.

18. Material from Cohen's response to FBI inquiry, December 10, 1947, Box 27, Cohen Papers.

19. Cohen to Sen. Robert Wagner, March 23, 1946, Box 27, Cohen Papers.

20. Memorandum on the Introduction of a Revised Health Bill, May 5, 1947, Box 27, Cohen Papers.

21. For an analysis of this legislative failure, see Paul Starr, *The Social Transformation of American Medicine* (New York: Basic Books, 1982), pp. 280–289, and Richard Harris, *A Sacred Trust* (New York: New American Library, 1966), pp. 31–33.

22. See Cohen to Wickenden, January 4, 1957, Box 81, Elizabeth Wickenden Papers, Wisconsin State Historical Society, Madison.

23. I draw this account almost entirely from an interview with Elizabeth Wickenden, Haverford, Pennsylvania, October 16, 1991.

24. Elizabeth Wickenden, untitled essay, in *SOS Bulletin* (June 1987): 4–5.

25. I discuss my concept of a grand design in social policy as a central theme in Berkowitz, *America's Welfare State* (Baltimore: Johns Hopkins Press, 1991).

26. Wickenden interview, and Public Welfare Association, "Objectives for Public Welfare Legislation, 1947," *Public Welfare,* April 1947, reprinted in William Haber and Wilbur Cohen, eds., *Readings in Social Security* (New York: Prentice-Hall, 1948), pp. 520–531; the quotation is on p. 531.

27. On Cruikshank, see Alice M. Hoffman and Howard S. Hoffman, *The Cruikshank Chronicles: Anecdotes, Stories, and Memoirs of a New Deal Liberal* (Hampden, Conn.: Archon Books, 1989); see also Edward Berkowitz, "How to Think about the Welfare State," *Labor History* 32 (Fall 1991): 489–502. Both of the quotations come from Martha Derthick, *Policymaking for Social Security* (Washington, D.C.: Brookings Institution, 1979), p. 126. For AFL support of Social Security and collaboration with Cohen, see Cohen to Altmeyer, January 11, 1949, Box 28, Cohen Papers.

28. Truman to Altmeyer, January 15, 1947, Box 55, Cohen Papers. Wilbur Cohen, interview with Maclyn C. Burg, March 31, 1976, Oral History Collection, Dwight D. Eisenhower Presidential Library, Abilene, Kansas. The people on the commission included the president of Princeton, the vice-president of Georgetown, and Judge Samuel Rosenman. It was probably Rosenman, who had prepared the president's health message, who recommended Cohen for the assignment.

29. Harry S. Truman, *Memoirs by Harry S. Truman,* vol. 2, *Years of Trial and Hope* (Garden City, N.Y.: Doubleday and Company, 1956), pp. 53–54.

30. Typically, Cohen sought advice from mentors such as Edwin Witte and J. Douglas Brown of Princeton. See Witte to Cohen, February 7, 1947, Brown to Cohen, February 10, 1947, Box 55, Cohen Papers.

31. "Early draft and tentative outline of report," February 18, 1947, Box 56, Cohen Papers.

32. Cohen, "Labor Market Aspects of Universal Training of Males," February 27, 1947, Box 56, Cohen Papers.

33. Cohen to Merrill G. Murray, March 10, 1947, and Cohen to Fiorello LaGuardia, March 13, 1947, Box 27, Cohen Papers.

34. Cohen to Judge Samuel Rosenman, June 2, 1947, and Cohen to Doug Brown, July 2, 1947, Box 27, Cohen Papers.

35. Cohen to Witte, September 25, 1947, Box 27, Cohen Papers.

36. Altmeyer, *Formative Years,* p. 163.

37. Cohen to Brown, June 21, 1948, Box 28, Cohen Papers.

38. William Wandel to Wilbur Cohen, June 2, 1947, Box 27, Cohen Papers.

39. Witte to Cohen, September 10, 1947, Box 27, Cohen Papers.

40. Cohen to Witte, September 25, 1947, and materials relating to FBI interview, December 10, 1947, Box 27, Cohen Papers. Cohen got as far as borrowing books on Japan and making preliminary preparations (see Cohen to Miss June Boeckman, January 5, 1948, Box 28, Cohen Papers).

41. Cohen to Roy T. Davis, Jr., embassy of the United States, December 3, 1947, and Cohen to Edward J. Howell, December 3, 1947, Box 27, Cohen Papers.

42. On Shearon, see Poen, *Truman versus the Medical Lobby,* p. 108.

43. Quoted in ibid., p. 110.

44. For the quotation and the general flavor of Shearon's politics, see Marjorie Shearon, prepared testimony, in *Social Security Act Amendments of 1949, Hearings before the Committee on Ways and Means, House of Representatives, Eighty-first Congress, First Session on HR 2893, Part Two* (Washington, D.C.: Government Printing Office, 1949); see also Shearon's lengthy testimony in *Nominations: Hearings before the Committee on Finance, United States Senate, Eighty-seventh Congress, First Session on Nominations of. . . . Wilbur J.*

Cohen, Assistant Secretary of Health, Education, and Welfare-Designate, March 22 and 23, 1961, pp. 139–143.

45. After leaving Salt Lake City, Mulliner danced in a company that specialized in modern ballet, and when she came to Washington, she went to work for Sen. Robert F. Wagner. She later worked at the Social Security Board and as an assistant to Gov. John Winant, first at the board and later in London, where he was the American ambassador, and at the San Francisco conference, attended by Alger Hiss, among others, that established the United Nations (based on conversations with Mulliner, Washington, D.C., April 1991).

46. Cohen to Witte, July 24, 1947, Box 27, Cohen Papers.

47. Cohen to Mrs. Mary Ross Gannett, October 14, 1947, Box 27, Cohen Papers, and Cohen to Jane Hoey and Katherine Lenroot, March 2, 1948, Box 28, Cohen Papers.

48. Theodore R. Marmor, with the assistance of Philip Fellman, "Entrepreneurship in Public Management: Wilbur Cohen and Robert Ball," in Jameson W. Doig and Erwin C. Hargrove, eds., *Leadership and Innovation* (Baltimore: Johns Hopkins University Press, 1987), pp. 246–281; Robert Ball, interview with David McComb, Washington, D.C., November 5, 1968, Oral History Collection, LBJ Library.

49. De Schweinitz, who had worked as Pennsylvania's secretary of public assistance and as head of the social work school at the University of Pennsylvania, had met Ball on a consulting assignment to advise the Social Security Board on its training procedures.

50. Much of the material on Robert Ball derives from my interview with him in Washington, D.C., May 20, 1992.

51. Cohen to J. Douglas Brown, October 1, 1947, Box 27, Cohen Papers.

52. For the report, see Haber and Cohen, eds., *Readings in Social Security,* p. 255.

53. Cohen to Witte, April 16, 1948, and Cohen to Sumner Slichter, October 25, 1948, Box 28, Cohen Papers.

54. Roger Shugg, editor, College Division, Alfred A. Knopf, to Cohen, February 21, 1946, Box 27, Cohen Papers.

55. Roger Shugg to Cohen, February 21, 1946, Cohen to Witte, September 25, 1947, and Cohen to William Haber, September 26, 1947, Box 27, Cohen Papers.

56. Cohen to Haber, September 26, 1947, Box 27, Cohen Papers.

57. Cohen to Miss Florence Peterson, March 9, 1948, Box 28, Cohen Papers, and Cohen to Falk, February 14, 1947, Box 27, Cohen Papers.

58. Cohen to Witte, April 16, 1948, Box 28, Cohen Papers.

59. Cohen to Haber, June 21, 1948, Box 28, Cohen Papers.

60. It is important to note a bureaucratic detail: a little more than a year after VJ Day, President Truman abolished the Social Security Board and replaced it with the Social Security Administration, headed by a commissioner. He chose Altmeyer as the first commissioner and, as he noted, "the immediate effect of the change was negligible." As for Cohen, he assisted a commissioner rather than the chairman of the Social Security Board (see Altmeyer, *Formative Years,* p. 159).

61. Haber and Cohen, eds., *Readings in Social Security,* and Cohen to Witte, October 25, 1948, Box 28, Cohen Papers.

62. Cohen, "Attitude of Organized Groups toward Social Insurance," in Haber and Cohen, eds., *Readings,* pp. 129–131.

63. Arthur Altmeyer, "Temporary Disability Insurance," in Haber and Cohen, eds., *Readings,* pp. 407–417, and Social Security Administration, *Annual Report,* in Haber and Cohen, eds., *Readings,* pp. 572–583.

64. Witte to Cohen, June 3, 1948, Box 28, Cohen Papers, and Merlyn Pitzele, interview with author, Beacon, New York, November 6, 1990.

65. Cohen to Prof. Charles McKinley, December 16, 1948, Box 28, Cohen Papers.

66. Witte to Cohen, January 27, 1949, and Red Somers to Cohen, February 12, 1949, Box 28, Cohen Papers.

67. Memorandum for Mr. Murphy, February 14, 1949, Box 28, Cohen Papers.

68. Wilbur J. Cohen and Robert J. Myers, "Social Security Amendments of 1950: A Summary and Legislative History," *Social Security Bulletin* 13 (October 1950): 7; this source also contains a complete list of committee reports and other documents associated with the amendments as well as a useful overview of the contents of the act and the legislative maneuvers involved in its passage.

69. Cohen to John S. Morgan, May 12, 1949, Box 29, Cohen Papers.

70. Cohen to Albert T. Sands, July 7, 1949, Box 29, Cohen Papers.

71. See Cohen to Robert L. Doughton, n.d. but undoubtedly 1949, Box 29, Cohen Papers.

72. Cohen to Mrs. Victor Hood, February 24, 1950, and Cohen to Witte, September 28, 1949, Box 29, Cohen Papers.

73. I have examined disability insurance in considerable detail in *Disabled Policy* (New York: Cambridge University Press, 1987) and choose not to dwell on it here. Cohen to Mrs. Abraham Epstein, March 7, 1950, Box 29, Cohen Papers.

74. Cohen to Louis Buckley, October 19, 1949, Box 29, Cohen Papers, and Cohen, "Social Security memoirs," p. 17, Box 279, Cohen Papers.

75. This was subject to many other complications, such as the number of the worker's dependents and the number of years he had been paying into Social Security.

76. There were many other technical parts of the legislation that did not meet SSA specifications. Altmeyer had hoped to retain the 1 percent increment in the size of a retired person's basic benefit for each year he had contributed to Social Security; the House permitted only .5 percent. Cohen had very much wanted to include benefits for the spouses and children of the permanently and totally disabled; the House eliminated dependents' benefits from its disability proposal. See Cohen to Witte, September 28, 1949, Box 29, Cohen Papers.

77. Cohen to Loula Dunn, July 14, 1949, and Cohen to Elizabeth Wickenden, August 29, 1949, Box 29, Cohen Papers.

78. Cohen to Doug Brown, September 30, 1949, Box 29, Cohen Papers.

79. Cohen to Witte, October 2, 1949, Box 29, Cohen Papers.

80. Cohen to C. B. Bragman, February 23, 1950, Box 29, Cohen Papers.

81. In particular, the Senate decided to eliminate disability benefits from the House bill and on this matter prevailed in conference. See Cohen to J. Douglas Brown, May 29, 1950, Box 29, Cohen Papers.

82. Altmeyer, *Formative Years,* p. 169.

83. Cohen to Walter Cooper, Industrial Relations Counselors, March 28, 1950, and Cohen to Robert Wray, September 21, 1949, Box 29, Cohen Papers.

84. See his statement on signing the bill, cited in Cohen and Myers, "Social Security Act Amendments of 1950," p. 1.

85. Cohen, "Income Maintenance for the Aged," *Annals of the American Academy of Political and Social Science* (January 1952): 154.

CHAPTER FOUR. THE NEW POLITICS OF SOCIAL SECURITY AND THE IKE AGE

1. This panel reported to the Wage Stabilization Board. Representatives of labor and management, drawn from the second echelon of company and union hierarchies, joined Cohen on the panel.

2. "Health, Welfare and Pension Programs under Wage Stabilization: Report to the Wage Stabilization Board by the Tripartite Panel on Health, Welfare and Pension Plans," October 22, 1951, Box 58, Cohen Papers, and Cohen to Richard Neustadt, March 21, 1952, Box 57, Cohen Papers.

3. Undated manuscript in Wage Stabilization Files, Box 58, Cohen Papers. See also Cohen, "Pensions and Welfare Funds under Wage Stabilization," an address before the Fourth Annual Conference on Labor, New York University, May 26, 1951, Box 249, Cohen Papers.

4. Cohen to Mrs. Phillip E. Lear (Dora Hershkovitz, whom Cohen had dated in 1935 and 1936), July 10, 1952, Box 31, Cohen Papers.

5. It should be mentioned that beginning in 1939 the Social Security Board (later the Social Security Administration) had become part of the Federal Security Agency. See Edward Berkowitz and Kim McQuaid, *Creating the Welfare State* (Lawrence: University Press of Kansas, 1992), pp. 138–141. On Ewing, see Monte M. Poen, *Harry S. Truman versus the Medical Lobby* (Columbia: University of Missouri Press, 1979), p. 114.

6. Cohen to Arthur Altmeyer, April 14, 1952, Box 6, Cohen Papers.

7. Between August 1950 and July 1951, prices increased somewhere between 6 and 7 percent. In 1950 Congress had decided not to raise welfare benefits for the elderly because the outbreak of the Korean War had made congressmen careful about increasing current government expenditures. In this case, war worked to the advantage of the Social Security Administration since Social Security coverage extensions brought more money into the federal treasury and public assistance benefit increases reduced the amount of money in the federal treasury. But this situation could not last indefinitely. Eventually, rising prices and the political appeal of helping the elderly would make a public assistance increase irresistible, just as it had been in 1946 and 1948. See Cohen, "Should Old-Age Assistance Again Outpace Old-Age Insurance?" *American Economic Security* (July-August 1951): a publication of the Chamber of Commerce, reprint in Cohen Papers.

8. See Cohen, "Should Old-Age Assistance Again Outpace Old-Age Insurance?" In this account of the 1952 amendments I have relied heavily on Wilbur J. Cohen, "The Legislative History of the Social Security Amendments of 1952," mimeograph, Social Security Administration, Division of Research and Statistics, June 1954, Box 249, Cohen Papers.

9. Cohen to Altmeyer, April 14, 1952, Box 6, Cohen Papers.

10. See Cohen to Miss Ann Geddes, April 14, 1952, Karl de Schweinitz to Cohen, May 9, 1952, Cohen to Helen Mysels, June 6, 1952, Box 31, Cohen Papers.

11. Cohen, "Legislative History of the Social Security Amendments of 1952," p. 11, and "Should Old-Age Assistance Again Outpace Old-Age Insurance?" Robert Ball, interview with author, Washington, D.C., May 20, 1992.

12. The House bill had included a freeze largely on the initiative of Congressman Kean, who had put the idea in a bill he had introduced, with the technical assistance of Wilbur Cohen, at the end of April. Doughton lifted the disability freeze idea from Kean and put it in his comprehensive bill (see my interview with Wilbur Cohen, Austin, Texas, November 12, 1984); Cohen, "Legislative History of the Social Security Act Amendments of 1952," pp. 17–22.

13. American Medical Association Bulletin no. 50, 82d Cong., May 23, 1952, quoted in Cohen, "Legislative History of the Social Security Amendments of 1952," p. 19, Box 249, Cohen Papers.

14. Cohen, interview with author; Cohen, "Legislative History of the Social Security Amendments of 1952"; Berkowitz, *Disabled Policy* (New York: Cambridge University Press, 1987); see also Deborah Stone, *The Disabled State* (Philadelphia: Temple University Press, 1984).

15. Bruce Cohen, interview with author, Wilmette, Illinois, October 19, 1990, and Cohen, interview with author.

16. Cohen to Elizabeth Wickenden, August 1952, Correspondence Files, Box 1, Wickenden Papers.

17. Cohen to Wicky, August 1952, and Witte to Cohen, September 6, 1952, Box 31, Cohen Papers.

18. "Basic Issues in Social Security," September 1, 1952, in Cohen to Wickenden, September 17, 1952, Box 1, Wickenden Papers.

19. Cohen to Wickenden, September 17, 1952, Box 1, Wickenden Papers. The Dewey brain trusters advising General Eisenhower felt the need to contact Fedele Fauri, the former Social Security expert at the Library of Congress reference service who was serving as dean of the social work school at the University of Michigan, for advice. He agreed to provide them with some background memos that were similar to those that Cohen prepared for the Stevenson campaign.

20. Cohen to Altmeyer, November 10, 1952, Box 6, Cohen Papers.

21. Cohen to Witte, November 12, 1952, Box 31, Cohen Papers.

22. See Cohen, "Around the World in 59 Days, November 17, 1952–January 15, 1953," Box 54, Cohen Papers.

23. Oscar Ewing statement, San Francisco, California, January 14, 1953, Box 54, Cohen Papers.

24. On the planning notion, see, for example, Margaret Weir, *Politics and Jobs* (Princeton, N.J.: Princeton University Press, 1992), and Otis L. Graham, Jr., *Toward a Planned Society* (New York: Oxford University Press, 1976). Examples of liberals who worked on domestic politics and international aid include Edward Hollander of the Americans for Democratic Action. In the 1950s and 1960s it was commonplace to send liberals, such as Chester Bowles and John Kenneth Galbraith, on missions to India, just as in the 1990s it would be commonplace to send conservatives on missions to Eastern Europe.

25. See the materials in Box 54, Cohen Papers, that describe the trip.

26. I draw this description from Cohen's own account in "Around the World in 59 Days," Box 54, Cohen Papers.

27. See Martha Derthick, *Policymaking for Social Security* (Washington, D.C.: Brookings Institution, 1979), pp. 144–157.

28. See M. Albert Linton to Robert L. Hogg, executive vice-president, American Life Convention, December 17, 1952, Box 26, Oveta Culp Hobby Papers, Dwight D. Eisenhower Library, Abilene, Kansas.

29. Elizabeth Wickenden, "Comments on Proposed Revised Policy Declaration by the United States Chamber of Commerce on Social Security for the Aged, December 9, 1952," Box 51, Cohen Papers; Arthur Altmeyer, *The Formative Years of Social Security* (Madison: University of Wisconsin Press, 1965), p. 206; *Improving Social Security: An Analysis of the Present Federal Security Program for the Aged and the Proposal of the Chamber of Commerce of the United States* (Washington, D.C.: Chamber of Commerce, 1953), p. 128.

30. Eisenhower statement quoted in Wilbur J. Cohen, Robert M. Ball, and Robert J. Myers, "Social Security Act Amendments of 1954: A Summary and Legislative History," *Social Security Bulletin* 17 (September 1954): 16.

31. Cohen to Wickenden, February 18, 1953, Box 31, Cohen Papers.

32. Derthick, *Policymaking*, p. 147; she also points out that the actual author of the chamber's proposal was Leonard Calhoun, a former lawyer at the Social Security Board, who had emerged as a leading conservative critic of the program.

33. See the résumé of clippings on Department of Health, Education, and Welfare, from March and April 1953, Box 57, Nelson A. Rockefeller Papers, Rockefeller Archives, Pocantico, New York.

34. Witte to Cohen, March 20, 1953, Box 31, Cohen Papers.
35. Cohen to Wicky, March 1, 1953, Box 33, Cohen Papers.
36. Ibid.
37. "Report to the New York Headquarters," Cohen to Wickenden, March 7, 1953, Elizabeth Wickenden Personal Papers (in her possession).
38. Cohen, interview with Macyln P. Burg, March 31, 1976, Oral History Collection, p. 17, Eisenhower Library.
39. Cohen to Wickenden, March 1, 1953, Cohen Papers.
40. Cohen diary, February 10 (including quotation), February 20, 1953, Box 1, Cohen Papers.
41. Ibid., February 25, 26, 27, March 2, 1953.
42. Cohen to Wickenden, March 12, 1953, and March 20, 1953, Wickenden Personal Papers.
43. Ibid., March 7, 1953.
44. Eveline M. Burns, "Comments on the Chamber of Commerce Social Security Proposals," n.d., Box 51, Cohen Papers; Cohen to Wickenden, August 1952, Wickenden Personal Papers; Arthur Altmeyer, "Social Security, the Republican Party and Eisenhower," draft manuscript for *Progressive Magazine,* n.d., Box 6, Cohen Papers.
45. He refrained from seeing Wilbur Mills because he doubted his credentials as a liberal (Cohen to Wicky, March 14, 1953, Wickenden Personal Papers).
46. Cohen diary, February 23, 1953, Box 31, Cohen Papers.
47. This line had been developed in a 1950 Brookings Institution monograph on Social Security. See Carl Curtis to Daniel Reed, December 22, 1953, Box 33, Cohen Papers, and Lewis Meriam, Carl Schlotterbeck, and Mildred Maroney, *The Cost and Financing of Social Security* (Washington, D.C.: Brookings Institution, 1950). Schlotterbeck was the subcommittee staff director.
48. Cohen to Wickenden, March 7, 1953, Wickenden Personal Papers.
49. Cohen to my dear Wicky, March 12, 1953, Wickenden Personal Papers.
50. Cohen to Wickenden, March 7, 1953, Wickenden Personal Papers.
51. Ibid., March 12, 1953.
52. Ibid., March 14, 1953.
53. Ibid., March 25, 1953.
54. Derthick, *Policymaking,* p. 149.
55. Cohen diary, April 10, 1953, Box 1, Cohen Papers; Cohen to Witte, April 10, 1953, Box 31, Cohen Papers; Altmeyer to fellow workers, April 10, 1953, Box 6, Cohen Papers. On Folsom and his role in Social Security, see Edward Berkowitz and Kim McQuaid, *Creating the Welfare State,* 2d ed. (New York: Praeger Press, 1988), pp. 106–141.
56. Central File 156-C, Social Security 1953, Box 848, Eisenhower Library, and Cohen, interview with Burg, p. 14.
57. Cohen to Wickenden, July 22, 1953, Wickenden Personal Papers, and Cohen to Wickenden, May 1, 1953, correspondence, Box 1, Wickenden Papers. According to a typescript in the Wickenden Papers, Cohen's change in status was reported by columnist Jerry Kluttz in the Federal Diary column, *Washington Post,* July 21, 1953.
58. Cohen diary, March 11, 1953, Box 1, Cohen Papers, and Cohen to Witte, April 10, 1953, Box 31, Cohen Papers.
59. Others in the Social Security Administration made far stronger efforts to remain in the government. Cohen's colleague Jane Hoey, head of the public assistance program, took her case to the public. In a letter that made its way into the *New York Times,* Hoey said that her real fear was not personal but that the nature of her job would be downgraded: it would be stripped of its professional and technical components so that it could be filled by just anyone rather than by a trained social worker. It was a battle that

Hoey lost. The Republicans, out of power for twenty years, needed all the presidential appointments they could get. See Rockefeller to Hoey, October 27, 1953, Hoey to Rockefeller, November 3, 1953, OF 236-B-2-Box 9092, Central Files, Eisenhower Library, and "Mrs. Hobby Ousts Key Aide," n.d., but probably November 3, 1953, in clipping file, Box 57, Nelson Rockefeller Papers.

60. Cohen, interview with Burg, and Cohen to Pitzele, April 7, 1954, Box 15, Pitzele Papers.

61. Cohen to Wicky, July 22, 1953, Wickenden Personal Papers.

62. Altmeyer, *Formative Years,* p. 215; Derthick, *Policymaking for Social Security,* p. 149; Consultants on Social Security, *A Report to the Secretary of Health, Education, and Welfare on Extension of Old-Age and Survivors Insurance to Additional Groups of Current Workers,* 1953; Robert Ball, interview with David McComb, Washington, D.C., November 5, 1968, Oral History Collection, p. 6, LBJ Library.

63. Nelson Rockefeller to Sherman Adams, October 29, 1953, Central Files, OF 236-b-2, Box 902, Eisenhower Library.

64. Cohen to Wickenden, February 2, 1953, and March 12, 1953, Wickenden Personal Papers.

65. Fedele Fauri to Wicky, February 11, 1953, Box 31, Cohen Papers.

66. Altmeyer to Cohen, November 18, 1953, Box 6, Cohen Papers.

67. Nelson Rockefeller to Sherman Adams, October 29, 1953, Eisenhower Library.

68. Cohen diary, June 20, 1953, Box 1, Cohen Papers.

69. Ibid., June 22, 1953; Altmeyer to Hon. John Dingell, June 23, 1953, and Altmeyer to Wilbur Mills, June 23, 1953, Box 6, Cohen Papers.

70. Altmeyer to Cohen, August 10, 1953, Box 6, Cohen Papers.

71. Altmeyer, *Formative Years,* p. 223.

72. Cohen to Altmeyer, November 3, 1953, Box 6, Cohen Papers.

73. Altmeyer to Leo Irwin (minority clerk, House Ways and Means Committee), November 22, 1953, Box 6, Cohen Papers.

74. Curtis quoted in Altmeyer, *Formative Years,* p. 234. Altmeyer's book also contains a lengthy description of his appearance before Curtis (pp. 225–234).

75. "Staff Memorandum: Some Major Findings," December 23, 1953, and Curtis to Reed, December 22, 1953, Box 33, Cohen Papers.

76. Roswell B. Perkins to the secretary, November 24, 1953, Box 32, Cohen Papers.

77. Eisenhower cabinet discussions, November 1953, quoted in Mark Leff, "Historical Perspectives on Old-Age Insurance," in Edward D. Berkowitz, ed., *Social Security after Fifty* (Westport, Conn.: Greenwood Press, 1987), p. 33, and Eisenhower to Edward F. Hutton, October 7, 1953, Central Files, file 156-C, Box 848, Eisenhower Library.

78. "Does Social Security Engage in Propaganda Activities," n.d., Box 33, Cohen Papers.

79. Cohen to Wickenden, February 23, 1954, Wickenden Personal Papers.

80. Description of this meeting drawn from Wilbur J. Cohen, "The First 25 Years of the Social Security Act," June 1959, Box 279, Cohen Papers.

81. Cohen diary, October 7, 1953, Box 1, Cohen Papers.

82. Cohen to Altmeyer, November 3, 1953, Box 6, Cohen Papers.

83. Altmeyer to Cohen, January 15, 1954, Box 6, Cohen Papers.

84. Cohen to Witte, April 5, 1954, Box 32, Cohen Papers.

85. Cohen's advocacy of higher welfare grants reversed his and Altmeyer's position of earlier years, when they had seen welfare as a threat to Social Security. He now argued that increased welfare payments did not "hinder" Social Security, "rather it has helped to get OASI increased." See Wilbur Cohen to Elizabeth Wickenden, March 8, 1954, Correspondence Files, Box 1, Wickenden Papers.

86. Altmeyer to Cohen, August 1, 1954, Box 6, Cohen Papers.

87. Ibid., August 25, 1954.

88. Ibid., August 1, 1954.

89. As an example of this close reporting, see Cohen, Ball, and Myers, "Social Security Act of 1954," pp. 3–18.

90. Cohen to Pitzele, April 7, 1954, Box 15, Pitzele Papers.

91. Altmeyer to Cohen, December 26, 1954, Box 6, Cohen Papers.

CHAPTER FIVE. A NEW LIFE

1. Altmeyer to Cohen, February 1956, Box 6, Cohen Papers.

2. John Kenneth Galbraith, *The Affluent Society*, 3d rev. ed. (New York: New American Library, 1976), p. 4.

3. Cohen to Altmeyer, October 22, 1954, Box 6, Cohen Papers.

4. Cohen, interview with Maclyn P. Burg, March 31, 1976, Oral History Collection, p. 43, Eisenhower Library (copy available in Box 23, Cohen Papers).

5. Cohen to Witte, April 5, 1954, Box 32, Cohen Papers.

6. On Folsom and the phenomenon of business support for Social Security, see Edward D. Berkowitz and Kim McQuaid, *Creating the Welfare State*, rev. paperback ed. (Lawrence: University Press of Kansas, 1992), and Sanford M. Jacoby, "Employers and the Welfare State: The Role of Marion B. Folsom," *Journal of American History* 80 (September 1993): 525–556.

7. See Edward D. Berkowitz, *Disabled Policy* (New York: Cambridge University Press, 1987), p. 67.

8. Altmeyer to Cohen, May 13, 1955, Box 6, Cohen Papers; Cohen, interview with author, Austin, Texas, November 12, 1984; "Memorandum for the Human Needs File: Telephone Conversation with Nelson Cruikshank," April 18, 1960, Records of the President's Commission on National Goals, Eisenhower Library.

9. Fauri had long been active in social welfare causes. A lawyer, he became the legal counsel for the Michigan Welfare Department in 1937. In 1943 he was promoted to state welfare director. He came to Washington in the mid-1940s to work with the Ways and Means Committee on a report about the Social Security program. On the staffs of the Ways and Means Committee and the Congressional Research Service, Fauri came to know and respect Wilbur Cohen. On Fauri, see his interview with Peter Corning, September 8, 1966, Columbia Oral History Project.

10. Shoring up the contact, Cohen also did his share of favors for Fauri, including writing numerous letters of recommendation. In one such letter, Cohen spoke of Fauri's "remarkable ability and intelligence, patience and the ability to suggest workable compromises" (Cohen to Robert Wray, September 21, 1949, Box 29, Cohen Papers).

11. Fauri, interview with Corning, p. 45.

12. Cohen, "The First 25 Years of Social Security," June 1959, p. 9, Box 279, Cohen Papers.

13. Cohen, diary, April 15, 1953, Box 1, Cohen Papers.

14. Cohen, "First 25 Years of Social Security," p. 9.

15. Altmeyer to Cohen, August 10, 1955, Box 6, Cohen Papers.

16. Cohen, "Memoirs–The University of Michigan, 1956–1960," Box 279, Cohen Papers.

17. Altmeyer to Cohen, June 18, 1957, and January 1958, Box 6, Cohen Papers, and Altmeyer to Proxmire, February 2, 1958, Box 6, Cohen Papers.

18. Cohen to Witte, September 25, 1947, Box 27, Cohen Papers, and Cohen, interview with Maclyn P. Burg, March 31, 1976, Oral History Collection, p. 22, Eisenhower Library.

19. "Professor Wilbur J. Cohen Beseeches Editor to Cease and Desist," letter from Cohen to Mrs. Shearon, March 22, 1960, published in *Challenge to Socialism*, March 31, 1960.

20. Merlyn Pitzele, interview with author, Beacon, New York, November 6, 1990.

21. "The Editors Reply to Wilbur J. Cohen," *Challenge to Socialism*, March 31, 1960.

22. Ibid.

23. "Interrogatory," December 9, 1948; Joseph F. McElvain, chairman, Board of Employee Loyalty of the Federal Security Agency, to Cohen, December 9, 1948; Cohen to McElvain, December 22, 1948; Cohen, sworn statement, December 10, 1947; Cohen, statement before Special Agent R. F. Ryan and stenographer Eileen Tyler, April 6, 1942 (I am grateful to Bruce Cohen for providing me with these materials, which were stored in the attic of Cohen's home in Ann Arbor).

24. Telegram quoted by Cohen, in edited transcript of an oral interview with C. T. Morrissey, November 11, 1964, for JFK Library Oral History Project, pp. 6–7, in Eloise Papers.

25. Cohen, "Memoirs–University of Michigan, 1956–1960," Box 279, Cohen Papers.

26. Altmeyer to Cohen, January 17, 1956, Box 6, Cohen Papers.

27. Cohen to Wickenden, January 16, 1956, Wickenden Personal Papers.

28. Nor was this the first time that Fauri had served as a special adviser to the Senate Finance Committee; he had also worked with the committee on the 1950 amendments. Cohen to Wickenden, January 16, 1954, Box 32, Cohen Papers, and Cohen to Robert Wray, September 21, 1949, Box 29, Cohen Papers.

29. On the development of the social work profession, see Stanley Wenocur and Michael Reish, *From Charity to Enterprise* (Urbana: University of Illinois Press, 1989), and Daniel J. Walkowitz, "The Making of a Feminine Profession: Social Workers in the 1920s," *American Historical Review* 95 (October 1990): 1051–1075.

30. Typically, he went on to say, "But I have kept myself pretty close to the long distance telephone, nevertheless" (Cohen to Max Kampelman, May 3, 1956, Box 63, Cohen Papers).

31. Altmeyer to Cohen, January 17, 1956, Box 6, Cohen Papers.

32. See the description of the passage of the 1956 amendments in chapter 6. Robert J. Myers was the chief actuary of the Social Security Administration.

33. Cohen and Fauri, "The Social Security Amendments of 1956," Box 250, Cohen Papers.

34. Wilbur J. Cohen, *Retirement Policies under Social Security: A Legislative History of Retirement Ages, the Retirement Test, and Disability Benefits* (University of California Press: Berkeley and Los Angeles, 1957).

35. Herman Somers, interview with Peter Corning, August 1968, Columbia Oral History Collection, p. 70.

36. Cohen, *Retirement Policies under Social Security*.

37. Cohen, "Memoirs–University of Michigan, 1956–1960," Box 279, Cohen Papers.

38. Cohen to Altmeyer, October 19, 1962, Box 6, Cohen Papers. The book, it should be noted, was far from a typical academic exercise; on the contrary, it provided empirical proof of the need for a War on Poverty (see chapter 11).

39. Fauri, interview with Peter Corning, p. 45.

40. Cohen to Altmeyer, September 28, 1956, Box 6, Cohen Papers.

41. Cohen to Mr. and Mrs. Arthur Goldschmidt, October 7, 1957, Wickenden Personal Papers.

42. Fauri, interview with Corning, p. 45.

43. Cohen, "Notes on Democratic National Convention, Chicago, Illinois, August 10–12, 1956," Box 70, Cohen Papers.

44. Cohen to Mr. Ken Hechler, July 12, 1956, Box 62, Cohen Papers.

45. Cohen to Altmeyer, September 28, 1956, Box 6, Cohen Papers.

46. James Sundquist, *Politics and Policy: The Eisenhower, Kennedy, and Johnson Years* (Washington, D.C.: Brookings Institution, 1968), p. 393.

47. Altmeyer to Cohen, November 22, 1956, Box 6, Cohen Papers.

48. Rockefeller to secretary, June 10, 1953, vol. 49, Rockefeller Papers, and Cohen to Kean, September 14, 1956, and July 12, 1956, Box 63, Cohen Papers.

49. This work for Senator Hill's Committee on Labor and Public Welfare took place between 1956 and 1957. Cohen accepted the assignment because it provided him with a regular means of coming to Washington and because it brought him "into contact," as he put it, with the current health proposals for the aged. His major political patron in the operation was John F. Kennedy, not Robert Kean. "He hadn't made up his mind about that whole business, about Kennedy and the sub-committee, and he called me in and asked me would I make a series of studies which would indicate whether that was a good idea" (Cohen, interview with Burg, p. 41). On the internal politics involved, see Sheri I. David, *With Dignity: The Search for Medicare and Medicaid* (Westport, Conn.: Greenwood Press, 1985), pp. 18–22.

50. Cohen to Kean, January 4, 1957, Box 63, Cohen Papers.

51. Altmeyer to Cohen, September 1956, Box 6, Cohen Papers.

52. Cohen to Altmeyer, September 26, 1956, Box 6, Cohen Papers.

53. Merlyn Pitzele, interview with author, Beacon, New York, November 6, 1990, and Tracy Copp to Mary Switzer, 1950, Mary Switzer Papers, Schlesinger Library, Cambridge, Massachusetts.

54. Altmeyer to Cohen, February 15, 1957, Box 6, Cohen Papers.

55. Altmeyer to Harry Page, March 20, 1957, Box 6, Cohen Papers.

56. Altmeyer to Cohen, March 5, 1957, Box 6, Cohen Papers.

57. Altmeyer to Harry Page, March 20, 1957, Box 6, Cohen Papers.

58. One reason that welfare requirements became tighter in the 1950s was that more blacks were entering the rolls, in part because of new legal requirements that they receive equal treatment under the law. In addition, their increased mobility from the South to the North brought more blacks into contact with the relatively liberal welfare systems of the North. Altmeyer to Cohen, April 20, 1957, Box 6, Cohen Papers.

59. Cohen to Altmeyer, October 25, 1957, Box 6, Cohen Papers, and Cohen to Jules Berman, chief, Division of Program Standards and Development, Bureau of Public Assistance, SSA, December 30, 1957, Correspondence Files, Box 1, Wickenden Papers.

60. Cohen to Altmeyer, n.d. but ca. April 1958, Box 6, Cohen Papers.

61. Ibid.

62. Wilbur J. Cohen and Sydney E. Bernard, "The Prevention and Reduction of Dependency," pamphlet published by the Washtenaw County Department of Social Welfare, September 1961, in Cohen Papers, Bentley Library, Ann Arbor, Michigan; the case study is on p. 28 (hereafter cited as Michigan Papers).

63. For more on Cohen's relationship with Senator Kerr, see chapter 6.

64. Cohen to Wickenden, October 18, 1958, Wickenden Personal Papers, and Cohen to Kerr, November 6, 1958, Box 63, Cohen Papers.

65. Nelson A. Rockefeller to Thomas A. McCabe, October 12, 1956, Rockefeller Brothers Fund Papers, Special Studies Project, Box 27, Rockefeller Archives.

66. McCabe to Rockefeller, May 13, 1958, Rockefeller Brothers Fund, Special Studies Project, Box 27, Rockefeller Archives.

67. Other names that Somers mentioned were Richard Lester, Clark Kerr, and Charles Myers—prominent labor and manpower economists of the era (Herman Somers

to Henry Kissinger, December 30, 1956, Rockefeller Brothers Fund, Special Studies Project, Box 28, Rockefeller Archives).

68. Memorandum for the Record, June 13, 1957, JIC, Joseph I. Coffey, Rockefeller Brothers Fund, Special Studies Project, Box 30, Rockefeller Archives.

69. Altmeyer to Cohen, January 17, 1957, Box 6, Cohen Papers.

70. As it turned out, Witte did not live much beyond the celebration of his retirement; he died in Madison, at the age of seventy-three, on May 20, 1960. It took little time for Cohen to compose a tribute in which he described Witte as a "patient and helpful teacher, a man of humility, and a man of absolute integrity." In the next few years, Cohen made sure that the University of Wisconsin Press posthumously published two of Witte's books. In a sense, Cohen helped to prepare Witte's legacy. Cohen, "Edwin E. Witte (1887–1960): Father of Social Security," *Industrial and Labor Relations Review* 14 (October 1960): 7 (offprint available in Box 252, Cohen Papers); Edwin E. Witte, *The Development of the Social Security Act* (Madison: University of Wisconsin Press, 1963); Witte, *Social Security Perspectives* (Madison: University of Wisconsin Press, 1972).

71. Wilbur J. Cohen, "The Future of Social Security," an address in honor of Prof. Edwin E. Witte, University of Wisconsin, Symposium on Labor and Government, Madison, March 28, 1957, Box 250, Cohen Papers.

72. Cohen, "Future of Social Security."

73. Cohen, "Social Policies and Social Services in an Expanding Economy," October 1957, Rockefeller Brothers Fund, Special Studies Project, Box 30, Rockefeller Archives.

74. *The Report to the President of the Committee on Economic Security* (Washington, D.C.: Government Printing Office, 1935), p. 35, and Cohen, "Social Policies and Services in an Expanding Economy." On the concern over juvenile delinquency, see James Gilbert, *A Cycle of Outrage* (New York: Oxford University Press, 1986).

75. "The Challenge to America: Its Economic and Social Aspects," Report 4, first published April 21, 1958, pp. 310, 316, 317, in *Prospect for America: The Rockefeller Panel Reports* (Garden City, N.Y.: Doubleday, 1961).

76. Wickenden to Cohen, January 4, 1958, Wickenden Personal Papers.

77. Aaron Cohen showed few signs of slowing down and gave no indication that he wished to retire from running his variety store; in 1960 he still had seventeen more years ahead of him. He had been married since 1944 to a non-Jewish woman, Anne Badura, whom he had met in Democratic political circles. Darwin Huxley, interview with author, Milwaukee, Wisconsin, August 22, 1990.

78. Bruce Cohen, interview with author, Wilmette, Illinois, October 19, 1990.

79. Maurine Mulliner, interview with Peter Corning, Columbia Oral History Collection, p. 100.

80. Cohen, interview with Burg, p. 38 (copy in Box 23, Cohen Papers).

CHAPTER SIX. COURTING JFK, EXPANDING SOCIAL SECURITY

1. Cohen, interview with Maclyn P. Burg, March 31, 1976, Oral History Collection, p. 38, Eisenhower Library (copies of these and other oral interviews are in Box 23, Cohen Papers).

2. Cohen, interview with Charles Morrissey, November 11, 1964, JFK Library (unedited transcript in possession of Eloise Cohen).

3. Ibid. (uned. transcript, p. 3).

4. Ibid., p. 4.

5. Cohen, interview with William Moss, May 24, 1971, p. 71, JFK Library.

6. Cohen to Wicky, February 1, 1954, Wickenden Personal Papers.

7. Cohen to Brown, February 27, 1956, Box 59, Cohen Papers.

8. Cohen, "The Situation in Social Security," February 15 (probably March 15), 1956, Box 70, Cohen Papers.

9. Cohen, "Situation in Social Security," and "The First 25 Years of the Social Security Act," June 1959, Box 279, Cohen Papers, and Cohen to Wickenden, March 4, 1956, Wickenden Personal Papers.

10. Brown to Cohen, April 2, 1956, Box 59, Cohen Papers.

11. Cohen to Brown, April 25, 1956, Box 59, Cohen Papers.

12. For Folsom's changing views, see "Arguments for Permanent Total Disability Insurance at Age 55," n.d., but probably 1950, Cohen Papers, which cites his testimony before the Senate Finance Committee on January 31, 1950; for a legislative history of the bill, see Wilbur Cohen and Fedele F. Fauri, "The Social Security Amendments of 1956," *Public Welfare,* October 1956 (reprint available in Box 250, Cohen Papers). It should be noted that Robert Ball contends that Folsom actually favored disability insurance but could not gain the administration's approval to testify in favor of it.

13. Cohen, "First Twenty-Five Years of Social Security," p. 12.

14. Cohen to Wickenden, March 4, 1956, Wickenden Personal Papers.

15. Cohen, interview with author, Austin, Texas, November 12, 1984, and "First 25 Years of Social Security."

16. Altmeyer to Cohen, May 17, 1956, Box 6, Cohen Papers.

17. Martha Derthick, *Policymaking for Social Security* (Washington, D.C.: Brookings Institution, 1979), p. 306, and Cohen and Fauri, "Social Security Amendments of 1956," pp. 2–3.

18. See American Medical Association, Special Report no. 84-21, May 10, 1956, Box 70, Cohen Papers.

19. Cohen, "First 25 Years of the Social Security Act"; I have told the story of the disability vote in *Disabled Policy* (New York: Cambridge University Press, 1987), in Berkowitz and Wendy Wolff, "Disability Insurance and the Limits of American History," *Public Historian* 8 (Spring 1986): 65–82, and in Berkowitz and Daniel Fox, "The Struggle for Compromise: Social Security Disability Insurance, 1935–1986," *Journal of Policy History* 1 (1989): 233–260.

20. Altmeyer to Cohen, August 9, 1956, Box 6, Cohen Papers.

21. Cohen to Sorensen, July 3, 1956, Box 67, Cohen Papers.

22. Cohen, interview with Morrissey, p. 7.

23. Sorensen to Cohen, June 28, 1957, Box 67, Cohen Papers.

24. Cohen to Theodore Sorenson (*sic*), January 10, 1958 (this has the quotation); Theodore C. Sorensen to Wilbur Cohen, June 5, 1958; Sorensen to Cohen, June 28, 1957; Cohen to Sorensen, July 3, 1956, Box 62, Cohen Papers.

25. Cohen to Sorensen, January 10, 1958, Box 62, Cohen Papers.

26. Cohen, interview with Morrissey, p. 8.

27. Ibid., p. 9; Paul A. Raushenbush and Elizabeth Brandeis Raushenbush, *Our "U.C." Story, 1930–1967* (Madison, Wis.: privately printed, 1979), p. 377.

28. Cohen, interview with Morrissey, p. 10.

29. As matters turned out, Kennedy's plan to extend ADC to children of the unemployed never made it to the Senate floor as a formal amendment to the Temporary Unemployment Compensation Act of 1958. The senator did manage to speak briefly about it in the course of the debate and tentatively decided to introduce the measure as a separate piece of legislation. Sorensen told Cohen that Kennedy "was most grateful to you for your suggestion and all your help and only regrets it could not have had a more successful conclusion" (see Sorensen to Cohen, June 5, 1958, Box 67, Cohen Papers).

30. Sorensen to Cohen, June 5, 1958, Box 67, Cohen Papers.

31. John F. Kennedy, "Ten Point Program for Older Citizens," *Congressional Record–Senate,* August 19, 1958, pp. 18422–18424, quote on 18424.

32. Kennedy, "Ten-Point Program," p. 18423.

33. John F. Kennedy, "The Missile Gap," speech delivered August 14, 1958, in Exhibition Materials, JFK Library.

34. Cohen, "Trends in Social Welfare Expenditures and Programs," *Commercial and Financial Chronicle,* Thursday, July 31, 1958, pp. 3–4 (reprint available, Box 251, Cohen Papers).

35. Cohen, "Urgent Needs in Retirement Financing," Twelfth Annual Conference on Aging, June 23, 1959, typescript, p. 2, Box 251, Cohen Papers.

36. Cohen to Theodore Sorenson (*sic*), September 2, 1958, Box 67, Cohen Papers; Cohen to Myer Feldman, September 2, 1958, and Myer Feldman to Wilbur Cohen, September 5, 1958, Box 61, Cohen Papers.

37. Cohen, interview with David G. McComb, December 8, 1968, tape 2, p. 5, Box 23, Cohen Papers.

38. Cohen to Arthur Altmeyer, December 27, 1957, Box 6, Cohen Papers.

39. Altmeyer to Cohen, May 17, 1956, Box 6, Cohen Papers.

40. For Cohen's views on Mills, see Cohen, interview with McComb, tape 2, p. 5, LBJ Library.

41. Cohen to Mills, January 8, 1958, and Mills to Cohen, January 17, 1958, Box 60, Cohen Papers.

42. Cohen, "Outline of Social Security Proposals for 1958," February 9, 1958, appendix D of Wilbur Cohen, "Materials for the Study of Factors Influencing the Social Security Amendments of 1958," Social Work 353, Social Welfare Policy, September 10, 1958 (hereafter cited as Course Materials), Box 69, Cohen Papers. This remarkable document, prepared for Cohen's students, gives an intimate view of the passage of the 1958 amendments, highlighting Cohen's role in the process.

43. This extended account of the 1958 amendments is based almost entirely on the Course Materials; a fuller and more comprehensive view is Wilbur J. Cohen, "The Social Security Amendments of 1958: Another Important Step Forward," October 17, 1958, Subcommittee on Income Maintenance and Social Security of the Coordinating Committee on Social Welfare Research, School of Social Work, University of Michigan, and Wilbur J. Cohen and Fedele F. Fauri, "The Social Security Amendments of 1958: Another Significant Step Forward," *Public Welfare,* Box 251, Cohen Papers.

44. The increase was permanent for those who received it.

45. Cohen, "Social Security Amendments of 1958: Another Important Step Forward," p. 17; on the behavior of Congress in avoiding Social Security tax increases, see Edward D. Berkowitz, *America's Welfare State* (Baltimore: Johns Hopkins Press, 1987).

46. Notes on the interview with William Reynolds, Columbia Oral History Collection, p. 15, in Box 394, Cohen Papers, LBJ Library.

47. Cohen, "Oklahoma," autobiographical fragment in Eloise Papers.

48. Born in 1905, Flemming had already worked as a journalist, civil service commissioner, university president, and director of Defense Mobilization. On Arthur Flemming, see Jarrold A. Kieffer, "Arthur Flemming's Leadership and Style," *Educational Gerontology* 14 (1988): 539–555.

49. Cohen and Fauri, "Social Security Amendments of 1958: Another Significant Step Forward," p. 1.

50. The Course Materials contain both the memo that Cohen wrote to Kerr and the president's statement on signing the bill.

51. Rudolph T. Danstedt to Cohen, October 10, 1958, Box 60, Cohen Papers.

52. Sidney Spector to Wilbur Cohen, December 31, 1959, Box 67, Cohen Papers.

53. Sherri I. David, *With Dignity* (Westport, Conn.: Greenwood Press, 1985), p. 21. Cohen, "Social Security Legislation, 1960: Issues and Proposals," March 12, 1960, mimeograph, p. 2, Box 270, Cohen Papers.

54. Cohen to Myer Feldman, January 13, 1960, Box 61, Cohen Papers, and David, *With Dignity,* p. 26.
55. Cohen to Mills, February 10, 1964, Box 64, Cohen Papers.
56. Wilbur J. Cohen, "Provisions Which Could Be Included in an Omnibus Social Security Bill in 1960," February 10, 1960, mimeograph, Box 274, folder 11, Cohen Papers.
57. Ibid.
58. Cohen to Mills, February 10, 1960, Box 64, Cohen Papers, and Cohen to Feldman, January 13, 1960, Box 61, Cohen Papers. The correspondence between Cohen and Mills and Cohen and Kennedy on health insurance is extensive. See Cohen to Myer Feldman, February 17, 1960, and February 22, 1960, Box 61; Feldman to Cohen, February 27, 1960, and Cohen to Feldman, March 10, 1960, Box 61; Cohen to Mills, March 14, 1960, Box 64; Feldman to Cohen, March 17, 1960, and Mills to Cohen, March 18, 1960, Box 61, Cohen Papers; Wilbur Cohen, Charles N. Poskanzer, and Harry Sharp, "Attitudes toward Governmental Participation in Medical Care," reprinted from *Health Needs of the Aged and Aging, Hearings before the Subcommittee on Problems of the Aged and Aging, Committee on Labor and Public Welfare, U.S. Senate, 86th Congress, 2nd Session,* April 1960, Box 65, Cohen Papers.
59. Richard Harris, *A Sacred Trust* (New York: New American Library, 1966), p. 109.
60. Altmeyer to Cohen, June 6, 1960, Box 6, Cohen Papers.
61. Cohen to Alfred Davidson, June 8, 1960, Box 60, Cohen Papers.
62. Feldman to Cohen, June 1, 1960, and Cohen to Feldman, June 6, 1960, Box 61, Cohen Papers.
63. Cohen thought that this proposal provided a means to get the principle of health insurance for the elderly, funded by Social Security, recognized while at the same time providing President Eisenhower the opportunity to sign the bill "on the grounds that it is a 'voluntary' plan which gives the individual a choice." Cohen's liberal allies, however, remained wary of the idea. As Douglas Brown noted, the proposal met a political need, but "no one can make such a decision wisely on reaching retirement for himself and his wife. It gives a 'class' climate to the whole business" (Cohen to Douglas Brown, May 26, 1960; Brown to Cohen, May 31, 1960, Box 59, Cohen Papers).
64. William Reynolds, interview with Peter Corning, Columbia Oral History Collection, p. 26, annotated notes available in Box 394, Cohen Papers, LBJ Library.
65. Harris, *Sacred Trust,* p. 111.
66. David, *With Dignity,* p. 37.
67. See Robert B. Stevens and Rosemary Stevens, *Welfare Medicine in America: A Case Study of Medicaid* (New York: Free Press, 1974).
68. David, *With Dignity,* pp. 36–37.
69. See Stevens and Stevens, *Welfare Medicine,* and Press Release, March 28, 1962, Box 133, Cohen Papers.
70. Harris, *Sacred Trust,* p. 110.
71. Clinton P. Anderson with Milton Viorst, *Outsider in the Senate: Senator Clinton Anderson's Memoirs* (Cleveland, Ohio: World Publishing Company, 1970), p. 267.
72. Cohen, "Memoirs–The University of Michigan, 1956–1960," Box 278, Cohen Papers; Cohen, "Some Policy Issues in Social Security Programs for the Aged," paper presented to the International Association of Gerontology, San Francisco, Tuesday, August 9, 1960; Cohen to William Reynolds, September 20, 1960, Box 66, Cohen Papers; Cohen, diary, August 7 and 8, 1960, Box 1, Cohen Papers.
73. Cohen, interview with McComb, p. 34.
74. These events are recounted both in David, *With Dignity,* and in Harris, *Sacred Trust.*

75. W. H. Lawrence, "Kennedy Pledges a Drive to Widen Social Security," *New York Times*, August 15, 1960, A-1.

76. On Cohen's ties to Humphrey and Johnson, see, for example, Cohen to Altmeyer, April 14, 1952, Box 6, Cohen Papers; Cohen to Max Kampelman, May 3, 1956, Box 63, Cohen Papers; Wickenden, interview with Michael L. Gillette, New York City, November 6, 1974, pp. 21–22, LBJ Oral History Collection, LBJ Library.

77. Cohen, interview with Morrissey, p. 8.

78. Ibid., p. 15, and Archibald Cox to Wilbur Cohen, July 26, 1960, Box 60, Cohen Papers.

79. Cohen diary, October 20, 1960, Box 2, Cohen Papers.

80. Theodore H. White, *The Making of the President, 1960* (1961; rept., New York: New American Library, 1967), p. 329.

81. Cohen, diary, October 21, 1960, Box 2, Cohen Papers.

82. Ibid., November 7, 1960. (This date might be recorded wrong by Cohen since the election took place on November 8 and Kennedy did not find out he was president until Wednesday, November 9.) Cohen to Kennedy, November 2, 1960, Box 63, Cohen Papers.

83. Ball to Cohen, November 9, 1960, Box 59, Cohen Papers.

84. Cohen, diary, October 21, 1960, Box 2, Cohen Papers.

85. Ball to Cohen, January 3, 1961, Box 59, Cohen Papers.

86. Cohen, diary, November 22, November 23, 1960, Box 2, Cohen Papers.

87. Cohen, interview with McComb, pp. 35–36, and Cohen, interview with Morrissey, p. 17.

88. Cohen to Sorensen, December 17, 1960, Box 67, Cohen Papers; "Progress Report of Task Force on Health and Social Security" (for a complete copy of the task force report, see "Health and Social Security for the American People," reprinted in *Nominations: Hearings before the Committee on Finance, United States Senate, Eighty-Seventh Congress, First Session on Nominations of . . . Wilbur J. Cohen, Assistant Secretary of Health, Education, and Welfare-Designate*, March 22 and 23, 1961).

89. Cohen, interview with Morrissey, p. 25.

90. Cohen to Ribicoff, January 4, 1961, Box 66, Cohen Papers.

91. Cohen, interview with Morrissey, p. 26.

92. See Cohen, interview with McComb, p. 38.

93. Cohen, interview with Morrissey, p. 20.

94. Cohen to Ribicoff, January 4, 1961, Box 66, Cohen Papers.

95. Cohen, interview with Morrissey, pp. 21–22.

96. Ibid., p. 22, and Cohen, "Memoirs–University of Michigan, 1956–1960."

97. Cohen, "Memoirs–University of Michigan, 1956–1960."

98. Ibid.

99. Cohen, interview with McComb, p. 39.

100. "Inauguration," January 20, 1961, in Cohen's Kennedy File, Box 278, Cohen Papers.

101. Cohen, third interview for JFK Library, with William Moss, Ann Arbor, July 20, 1972, p. 115.

CHAPTER SEVEN. THE NEW FRONTIER

1. Cohen, interview with William Moss, May 24, 1971, Oral History Collection, p. 69, JFK Library (this interview, like many of the others cited here, is also available in Box 23, Cohen Papers).

2. Ivan Nestingen, interviews with Peter Corning, 1966–1967, Washington, D.C., Columbia Oral History Collection, pp. 39–45. I used the annotated version of this interview from Box 392, Cohen Papers, LBJ Library.

3. Cohen, interview with Moss, p. 68.

4. *Labor-Health, Education, and Welfare Appropriations for 1962, Hearings before the Subcommittee of the Committee on Appropriations, United States Senate, Eighty-Seventh Congress, First Session on HR 7035, Making Appropriations for the Department of Labor and Health, Education, and Welfare and Related Agencies, for the Fiscal Year ending June 30, 1962, and for other Purposes* (Washington, D.C.: Government Printing Office, 1961), p. 195. Units housed within the Public Health Service and the Social Security Administration, such as the National Institutes of Health and the Children's Bureau, were themselves quite adept at protecting their particular interests. See Stephen P. Strickland, *Politics, Science and Dread Disease* (Cambridge: Harvard University Press, 1972); James T. Patterson, *The Dread Disease: Cancer and Modern American Culture* (Cambridge: Harvard University Press, 1987); Martha Derthick, *Policymaking for Social Security* (Washington, D.C.: Brookings Institution, 1977).

5. See "Administrative History of HEW," typescript, vol. 1, pt. 2, LBJ Library.

6. Blue Cartenson, interview with Peter Corning, February 23, 1966, Columbia Oral History Collection, p. 38, annotated copy in Box 392, Cohen Papers, LBJ Library.

7. Cohen to F. F. Fauri, January 24, 1961, Box 74, Cohen Papers.

8. Cohen to Richard Titmuss, Brian Abel-Smith, and Peter Townsend, February 28, 1961, Box 74, Cohen Papers.

9. Cohen to Marcia Kahn, June 27, 1961, Box 74, Cohen Papers.

10. Cohen to Dr. N. Hubbard, dean, Medical School, University of Michigan, February 22, 1961, and Cohen to Richard Titmuss, Brian Abel-Smith, Peter Townsend, February 28, 1961, Box 74, Cohen Papers.

11. Cohen to Raymond W. Houston, June 9, 1961, Box 74, Cohen Papers.

12. Cohen to Leona Gerard, May 22, 1961, Box 74, Cohen Papers.

13. Cohen to Fedele Fauri, May 2, 1961, Box 74, Cohen Papers.

14. Cohen to I. S. Falk, June 15, 1961, Box 74, Cohen Papers.

15. Cohen to Wallace Turner, July 14, 1961, and Cohen to Benjamin Linsky, February 22, 1961, Box 74, Cohen Papers.

16. Cohen, interview with Moss, p. 64 (for both quotations), and Cohen to the secretary, December 28, 1961, Box 75, Cohen Papers.

17. Cohen to Roger Lind, July 31, 1964, Box 81, Cohen Papers.

18. Wilbur Cohen to Leon A. Harris, Jr., December 7, 1970, and Bruce Cohen to Upton Sinclair, November 8, 1963, courtesy of Bruce Cohen. On Cohen's role in the food and drug legislation, see his interview with Moss, p. 77; Cohen to secretary, November 1, 1962–"Department of Health, Education, and Welfare, 87th Congress, 1961 and 1962, Report of Legislative Achievements and Activities," Box 165, Cohen Papers.

19. Cohen to Philip Hart, February 8, 1961, Box 74, Cohen Papers.

20. Dr. Robert Hardie, M.D., to President Kennedy, February 27, 1961, Macy Files (Cohen, File 2), LBJ Library.

21. Cohen, interview with Charles Morrissey, November 11, 1964, Oral History Collection, p. 27, JFK Library, and Sheri I. David, *With Dignity* (Westport, Conn.: Greenwood Press, 1985), p. 51.

22. Cohen, interview with Morrissey, p. 27; Cohen to Kennedy, March 6, 1961, President's Office Files, General Correspondence, Box 2, 1961, JFK Library.

23. Cohen to Melvin C. Pierce, March 21, 1961, Box 74, Cohen Papers.

24. *Nominations: Hearings before the Committee on Finance, United States Senate, Eighty-Seventh Congress, First Session on Nominations of . . . Wilbur J. Cohen, Assistant Secretary of*

Health, Education, and Welfare-Designate, March 22 and 23, 1961 (Washington, D.C.: Government Printing Office, 1961), p. 96.

25. Ibid., pp. 103–104, 111.

26. Ibid., p. 126.

27. Ibid., p. 143.

28. Cohen to Dean Coston, March 31, 1961, Box 74, Cohen Papers, and Cohen, interview with Morrissey, pp. 28–29.

29. Maurine Mulliner, interview with Peter Corning, Columbia Oral History Collection, p. 97 (copy obtained from Mulliner); Cohen to Elizabeth Springer, April 7, 1961, Cohen to Mr. and Mrs. Lloyd Ives, April 17, 1961, Cohen to Maurine Mulliner, April 20, 1961, Box 74, Cohen Papers.

30. Cohen, interview with Blanche Coll, October 19, 1985, Austin, Texas.

31. Cohen to David Levine (a professor at Florida State), February 7, 1961, Box 74, Cohen Papers.

32. Cohen, interview with Coll.

33. Elizabeth Wickenden, interview with author, Haverford, Pennsylvania, October 16, 1991.

34. For background on this matter, see Edward Berkowitz, *America's Welfare State* (Baltimore: Johns Hopkins Press, 1991).

35. Remarks of Thomas P. Curtis in 87th Congress, 1st sess., *House Report 28, Aid to Dependent Children of Unemployed Parents,* February 27, 1961 (Washington, D.C.: Government Printing Office), p. 13.

36. Cohen, interview with Moss, p. 107.

37. Ibid.

38. Cohen to Jane Hoey, May 22, 1961, Box 74, Cohen Papers.

39. See Berkowitz, *America's Welfare State,* and Gilbert Y. Steiner, *Social Insecurity: The Politics of Welfare* (Chicago: Rand McNally, 1966), p. 37.

40. Cohen to Mary Switzer, September 12, 1961, and Cohen to William Mitchell, September 12, 1961, Box 75, Cohen Papers; Martha Derthick, *Uncontrollable Spending for Social Services Grants* (Washington, D.C.: Brookings Institution, 1975), p. 79.

41. Cohen to the secretary, September 15, 1961, Box 75, Cohen Papers.

42. Abraham Ribicoff, memorandum for the president, November 1, 1961, Box 137, folder 2, Cohen Papers.

43. See Ribicoff, memorandum for the president, n.d., President's Office Files, Departments and Agencies, HEW 1961, JFK Library.

44. Derthick, *Uncontrollable Spending,* p. 75.

45. Cohen to Ted Sorensen, December 6, 1961, with attachments Secretary Ribicoff to William L. Mitchell, "Administrative Actions Necessary to Improve Our Welfare Programs," December 6, 1961, and "Bureau of the Budget Staff Analysis of HEW's Proposed Welfare Legislation for 1962," December 12, 1961, Box 34, Subject Files, 1961–1964, HEW, Theodore Sorensen Papers, JFK Library, and David Bell, director, Bureau of the Budget, to Wilbur J. Cohen, December 7, 1961, Box 137, folder 6, Cohen Papers.

46. Cohen to William Haber, December 19, 1961, Box 75, Cohen Papers.

47. Memorandum for Mrs. Eleanor Roosevelt, December 19, 1961, Box 136, folder 2, Cohen Papers.

48. Ibid.

49. Cohen, interview with Moss, p. 107, and Cohen to Ernest F. Witte, executive director, Council on Social Work Education, December 20, 1961, Box 75, Cohen Papers.

50. Memorandum for Hon. Wilbur Mills, January 17, 1962, and memorandum for Hon. Harry F. Byrd, January 5, 1962, Box 75, Cohen Papers.

51. Quoted in Berkowitz, *America's Welfare State*, p. 38. See also Steiner, *Social Insecurity,* p. 37.

52. Press release, Committee on Ways and Means, U.S. House of Representatives, February 1, 1962, and Ribicoff to the Speaker of the House, February 1, 1962 (with draft of public welfare bill), Box 143, Cohen Papers.

53. Statement by Abraham Ribicoff for Ways and Means, February 7, 1962, Box 144, Cohen Papers.

54. As it turned out, they had been corresponding about this matter. See Cohen to Anderson, March 9, 1962, Box 1101, Clinton Anderson Papers, Library of Congress.

55. Cohen to Sam Rabinovitz, executive secretary, Michigan Youth Commission, August 10, 1962, Chron. Files, Box 77, Cohen Papers.

56. Public Welfare amendments of 1962 (PL 87-543), described in Wilbur Cohen to the secretary, November 1, 1962, "Report of Legislative Achievements and Activities," Box 165, Cohen Papers. This document also contains the quotation from President Kennedy.

57. Cohen to Ellen Winston, January 13, 1962, Box 75, Cohen Papers.

58. Altmeyer to Cohen, February 18, 1962, Box 6, Cohen Papers.

59. As Ball later recalled, "Kennedy appointed me Commissioner of Social Security in 1962, not in 1961 when he took office. . . . The date is important. Bill Mitchell continued as Commissioner for well over a year, largely because Wilbur Cohen who was very influential on Social Security matters in 1961, believed strongly in not changing commissioners because of a change in political parties or a change in Presidents. He wanted to stress continuity and bi-partisanship" (Robert Ball to Robert J. Myers, August 21, 1993, in possession of author).

60. Cohen, interview with Coll.

61. Cohen to secretary, November 20, 1962, Cohen Papers.

62. Ball, meanwhile, took the occasion to transfer the staff and functions of the director's office of the Bureau of Old-Age and Survivors' Insurance to the commissioner of Social Security's Office. The bureau, which ran the basic Social Security program, had always been the major operating arm of the Social Security Administration. In a sense, Ball's actions helped to solidify the connection between the Social Security Administration and social insurance programs. See "HEW News Release," December 20, 1962, Box 137, Cohen Papers.

63. HEW press release, December 20, 1962, Box 137, Cohen Papers, and testimony by Dr. Ellen Winston, the American Public Welfare Association, February 13, 1962, Box 144, Cohen Papers.

64. Cohen to Altmeyer, May 6, 1963, Chron. Files, Box 79, Cohen Papers.

65. Cohen to Ellen Winston, March 16, 1967, Box 92, Cohen Papers; Cohen, interview with Coll; author's interview with Dean Coston, Washington, D.C., October 10, 1990.

66. Cohen to Myer Feldman, May 22, 1961, "A National Program for the Mentally Retarded for a Presidential Message," General Files, Mental Retardation, Myer Feldman Papers, JFK Library.

67. See Edward Berkowitz, "The Politics of Mental Retardation during the Kennedy Administration," *Social Science Quarterly* 61 (June, 1980): 128–143.

68. The new institute would be part of the National Institutes of Health (which was part of the Public Health Service). Cooke believed that pediatrics deserved its own National Institute of Health, a source of both prestige and, more important to someone who worked at a place like Johns Hopkins, a source of dedicated research funds. These were, of course, the glory years for NIH funding. See Strickland, *Politics, Science and Dread Disease.* On Cooke's desire to create the National Institute of Child Health and Human Development, see Berkowitz, "Politics of Mental Retardation during the Kennedy Administration," pp. 128–143.

69. Cohen to Luther Terry, February 20, 1961, Box 74, Cohen Papers.
70. Cohen to Feldman, May 22, 1961, General File, Mental Retardation, Feldman Papers.
71. Quoted in "Need for S. 2273 'To Authorize Grants, Contract, etc. for Research Relating to Maternal Child Health and Crippled Children's Services,' " August 3, 1961, Box 139, Cohen Papers.
72. Cohen to Myer Feldman, June 14, 1961, Box 28, Feldman Papers.
73. Cohen to Sen. Lister Hill, July 17, 1961, Box 74, Cohen Papers; PL 87-838 established the National Institute of Child Health and Human Development; PL 88-156 contained the research authorization for the Children's Bureau.
74. Although the bureau had enjoyed a fair amount of visibility in the Progressive Era and in the 1920s as an agency of the Department of Labor, President Truman decided in 1946 to transfer the bureau from the Department of Labor to the Federal Security Agency. The latter, the forerunner of the Department of Health, Education, and Welfare, had emerged between 1939 and 1946 as the executive agency most concerned with social welfare issues. After President Truman's reorganization, the Children's Bureau became an operating bureau of the Social Security Administration in the Federal Security Agency. The transfer buried the Children's Bureau one layer deeper in the federal bureaucracy and brought its leaders into direct communication with Altmeyer and Cohen, a situation that persisted throughout the 1950s. See Christopher Howard, "Sowing the Seeds of 'Welfare': The Transformation of Mothers' Pensions, 1900–1940," *Journal of Policy History* 4 (1992): 188–227; Richard Meckel, *Save the Babies* (Baltimore: Johns Hopkins University Press, 1990); James Gilbert, *A Cycle of Outrage* (New York: Oxford University Press, 1986), p. 7; *Social Security: A Brief Explanation of the Social Security Act* (Social Security Administration, 1947), reprinted in William Haber and Wilbur Cohen, eds., *Readings in Social Security* (New York: Prentice Hall, 1948), pp. 119–121.
75. Elizabeth Wickenden, interview with author.
76. *Departments of Labor, and Health, Education, and Welfare Appropriations for 1969, Hearings before a Subcommittee of the Committee on Appropriations, House of Representatives, Ninetieth Congress, Second Session, Part 2, Statement of the Secretary of Health, Education, and Welfare, Overview of 1969 Budget* (Washington, D.C.: Government Printing Office, 1968), p. 131.
77. See Cohen to Myer Feldman, June 20, 1962, Feldman Papers.
78. Cohen to Myer Feldman, January 11, 1963, "Mental Retardation Program for 1963," General File, Mental Retardation, January–May 1963, Feldman Papers.
79. Cohen to Mrs. Sargent Shriver, February 11, 1963, "Mental Retardation Progress Report No. 1," in General File, Mental Retardation, January–May 1963, Box 13, Feldman Papers.
80. Kennedy's message to Congress, February 5, 1963, quoted in Berkowitz, "Politics of Mental Retardation during the Kennedy Administration," pp. 138–139.
81. "Mental Retardation Progress Report No. 1," February 11, 1963.
82. Cohen, "New Frontiers for the Mentally Retarded," speech before the Eleventh Annual Convention of the Illinois Council for Mentally Retarded Children, Chicago, May 18, 1963, Box 13, Feldman Papers.
83. "Rehabilitation Programs in Arkansas," enclosure in Cohen to Feldman, n.d. (circa July 8, 1963), Box 13, Feldman Papers.
84. Senator Hill had consolidated education legislation related to special education, mental health legislation, and the mental retardation facility grants into one omnibus piece of legislation. See Cohen to Myer Feldman, May 6, 1963, Box 13, Feldman Papers.
85. Cohen to Mrs. Shriver, Mental Retardation Progress Report 11, May 1, 1963, Box 14, Feldman Papers.

86. The changes included a provision that the federal share of the planning grants be limited to 75 percent and another provision that a ceiling of $8 million a year be put on appropriations for research projects relating to maternal and child health and crippled children services.

87. The state share of 25 percent of the planning grants, Cohen concluded, could easily be made up through in-kind donations such as staff assistance, office space, and housekeeping services; the appropriations ceiling was as much as the administration would have asked for anyway. Cohen to Mrs. Shriver, July 12, 1963, Mental Retardation Progress Report 17, Box 14, Feldman Papers.

88. Berkowitz, "Politics of Mental Retardation during the Kennedy Administration," pp. 140–141, and Cohen to Myer Feldman, September 18, 1963, Box 13, Feldman Papers.

89. Cohen to Lawrence O'Brien, October 25, 1963, Box 14, Feldman Papers.

90. Cohen, interview with David G. McComb, March 2, 1969, tape 3, pp. 19–21, LBJ Library.

91. Cohen, "Recollections of My First Cabinet Meeting," Box 278, Cohen Papers.

92. Cohen, "Recollections of My Second Cabinet Meeting," Box 278, Cohen Papers. As usual, Cohen did much of the staff work for the secretary. He prepared a memo, "Legislative Situation," Cohen to secretary, June 11, 1962, Box 76, Cohen Papers.

93. See Irving Bernstein, *Promises Kept: John F. Kennedy's New Frontier* (New York: Oxford University Press, 1991).

CHAPTER EIGHT. EDUCATION AND MEDICARE IN THE KENNEDY ADMINISTRATION

1. Cohen to Congressman Fred Schwengel, July 24, 1962, Box 76, Cohen Papers.

2. James N. Morgan, Martin H. David, Wilbur J. Cohen, and Harvey J. Brazer, *Income and Welfare in the United States,* study by the Survey Research Center Institute for Social Research, University of Michigan (New York: McGraw-Hill Company, 1962), pp. 9–11.

3. Cohen sent his oldest son Chris to a large public high school in Ann Arbor, but Bruce and Stuart went to a much smaller, private school run by the University of Michigan. As for universities, Chris went to Michigan, one of the finest of the nation's public universities; Bruce went to Reed and Stuart to Harvard (Chris Cohen, interview with author, Glencoe, Illinois, October, 1992).

4. See Daniel S. Hirshfield, *The Lost Reform* (Cambridge: Harvard University Press, 1970), and Richard Harris, *A Sacred Trust* (New York: New American Library, 1966).

5. Eugene Eidenberg and Roy D. Morey, *An Act of Congress: The Legislative Process and the Making of Education Policy* (New York: W. W. Norton and Company, 1969), pp. 21–22.

6. Hugh Graham, *The Uncertain Triumph* (Chapel Hill: University of North Carolina Press, 1984), p. 119.

7. "Memorandum of Conversation by Jack Forsythe, Wilbur Cohen, and Mike Feldman," February 13, 1961, Box 61, Sorensen Papers, and JFK Speech Files, Education Message to Congress folder, February 11–20, 1961, JFK Library. It is worth pointing out that Kennedy thought that education was an important enough topic to warrant a separate transition task force. Among other measures, it proposed federal aid of thirty dollars per year for each pupil in average daily attendance, with bonuses for states with below-average personal incomes. Cohen, who chaired the task force on Social Security and Medicare, did not serve on the education committee,

chaired by Frederic Hovde, president of Purdue. Few of those on the education panel received appointments in the Kennedy administration. See Philip Meranto, *The Politics of Federal Aid to Education in 1965* (Syracuse, N.Y.: Syracuse University Press, 1967), p. 59.

8. Lee C. White to Larry O'Brien, February 23, 1961, President's Office Files, Legislative Files, Box 49, JFK Library.

9. Cohen to Myer Feldman, March 3, 1961, Cohen to Feldman, February 27, 1961, Box 11, Aid to Education folder, Feldman Papers; Cohen to Myer Feldman, General File, Higher Education, Box 28, Feldman Papers; Cohen to secretary, April 7, 1961, Box 74, Cohen Papers; Cohen to Theodore Sorensen, April 20, 1961, Education folder, Box 32, Sorensen Papers.

10. See Graham, *Uncertain Triumph*, p. 18, and Ribicoff to Kennedy, February 27, 1961, in Cohen to Feldman, March 3, 1961, Box 11, Feldman Papers.

11. "Summary of Proposed Amendments to Federal Impact Area Laws," n.d., in Ribicoff to the president, February 27, 1961, Box 11, Feldman Papers. In general, the administration failed to meet its goals with this program, with the president reluctantly agreeing to its extension at the end of 1961. See the material in Box 32, Subject Files 1961–1964, Education folder, August 9–November 2, 1961, Sorensen Papers.

12. Cohen to Feldman (with enclosures), March 6, 1961, Box 28, Feldman Papers.

13. Abraham Ribicoff to President Kennedy, April 20, 1961, Box 32, Education folder, Sorensen Papers, and Cohen to the secretary, April 7, 1961, Box 74, Cohen Papers.

14. The president received legal advice that, although grants to parochial schools were illegal, low-cost, low-interest loans were not. Moreover, the NDEA restricted loans to certain areas or categories and hence could not be construed as general aid to education (James Sundquist, *Politics and Policy* [Washington, D.C.: Brookings Institution, 1968], p. 193, and Julie Roy Jeffrey, *Education for Children of the Poor: A Study of the Origins and Implementation of the Elementary and Secondary Education Act of 1965* [Columbus: Ohio State University Press, 1978], p. 54).

15. See Graham, *Uncertain Triumph*, p. 22; Sundquist, *Politics and Policy*, pp. 192–193; Irving Bernstein, *Promises Kept* (New York: Oxford, 1991), pp. 232–233. It should be mentioned that, unlike the House, the Senate passed aid to education legislation.

16. Autobiographical fragment in Box 278, Cohen Papers; Hugh Davis Graham includes a similar anecdote in his definitive account of federal education legislation (see *Uncertain Triumph*, pp. 22–23).

17. Sorensen to the president, August 9, 1961, Box 32, Sorensen Papers.

18. Cohen to Sorensen, August 9, 1961, "Emergency Educational Act of 1961," Box 32, Education folder, Sorensen Papers.

19. Graham, *Uncertain Triumph*, p. 24, and Sorensen to the president, August 14, 1961, Box 32, Sorensen Papers.

20. Cohen to Harlan Hatcher, September 14, 1961, Box 75, Cohen Papers. Julie Jeffrey argues that "Republicans opposed to federal aid and southern Democrats fearful of upsetting race relations had joined forces to make general aid impossible" (*Education for Children of the Poor*, p. 63).

21. Cohen to Sterling M. McMurrin, September 14, 1961, Box 75, Cohen Papers. On McMurrin as weak and for an overview of education legislation in the Kennedy years, see Irving Bernstein, *Promises Kept*, p. 227; another useful overview of educational policy in the Kennedy and Johnson years is Graham, *Uncertain Triumph*.

22. Cohen to Chris Cohen, March 6, 1963, Box 78, Cohen Papers.

23. Cohen to Sen. Philip Hart, July 18, 1961, Box 74, Cohen to Dr. James K. Hall, August 19, 1961, Box 75, Cohen to Elliot Bell, publisher of *Business Week*, February 27,

1961, Box 74, and Cohen to editor, *Milwaukee Journal,* March 3, 1961, Box 74, Cohen Papers.

24. The administration wanted to raise taxes by ½ of 1 percent (that would get 0.5 percent of covered payroll) and to expand the amount of people's salaries on which taxes were paid from $4,800 to $5,000. In the technical parlance of Social Security, that would lower the level premium cost. The entire bill was estimated to cost 0.6 percent of covered payroll (see Cohen to the secretary, February 8, 1961, Box 74, Cohen Papers).

25. In effect, Curtis accused Cohen of sabotaging his own creation, a suggestion to which Cohen reacted with anger. Cohen said that he had worked hard to get the governor of Michigan to implement the provisions in Kerr-Mills, just as Governor Ribicoff had worked hard to start a Kerr-Mills program in Connecticut. "What did you do in Missouri?" Cohen asked Curtis (see Cohen to Congressman Thomas Curtis, November 9, 1961, and September 22, 1961, Box 75, Cohen Papers).

26. "Analysis of Proposals for Optional Feature in Health Insurance Plan for the Aged under Social Security," n.a., February 15, 1961, Box 140, Cohen Papers.

27. Cohen to Mr. Edward T. Chase, December 26, 1961, and Cohen to Javits, November 20, 1961, Box 75, Cohen Papers.

28. Cohen to Sorensen, March 29, 1961, and Cohen to Sorensen, "Social Security Revisions Being Drafted by House Ways and Means Committee," n.d. (but clearly March, 1961), Box 38, Subject Files, 1961–1964, Social Security File, Sorensen Papers.

29. Cohen to John Scott, May 8, 1961, Cohen to Raymond W. Houston, June 9, 1961, Cohen to Burr Harrison, June 9, 1961, and Cohen to Grover Wirick, June 20, 1961, Box 74, Cohen Papers; Sherri I. David, *With Dignity* (Westport, Conn.: Greenwood Press, 1985), p. 66.

30. Cohen to O'Donnell, July 20, 1961, and Wallace Turner, assistant to the secretary, to Kenneth O'Donnell, June 29, 1961, White House Central Files (WHCF), Box 336, JFK Library.

31. Autobiographical fragment in possession of Eloise Cohen, Austin, Texas.

32. Cohen, interview with William Moss, May 24, 1971, Oral History Collection, p. 70, JFK Library.

33. Abraham Ribicoff, "Memorandum for the President," October 6, 1961, President's Office Files, Departments and Agencies, HEW 1961, JFK Library.

34. Cohen to Chris Cohen, March 6, 1963, Box 78, Cohen Papers.

35. "Memorandum for Adam Clayton Powell," January 12, 1962, Box 75, Cohen Papers.

36. Cohen to the president, April 16, 1962, "Status of Higher Education Legislation," President's Office Files, Departments and Agencies, Box 79-A, JFK Library, and Bernstein, *Promises Kept,* p. 236.

37. Chuck Daly to Larry O'Brien, July 20, 1962, and Mike Manatos to Larry O'Brien, July 21, 1962, Subject Files, Education folder, February 9–July 30, 1962, Box 33, Sorensen Papers.

38. Cohen to Sorensen, July 20, 1962, "Higher Education Legislation–Conference Report," Box 33, Sorensen Papers.

39. "Arguments to Make on Higher Education Bill," drafted by Ted Sorensen, July 24, 1962, and used by the president in meeting with Senator McNamara, in Box 33, Sorensen Papers.

40. Cohen to the secretary, July 27, 1962, Box 76, Cohen Papers.

41. Cohen to Sorensen, August 3, 1962, Education folder, Box 33, Sorensen Papers.

42. Bernstein, *Promises Kept,* p. 237.

43. Cohen to Feldman, January 4, 1962, Box 75, Cohen Papers.

44. Theodore R. Marmor with Jan S. Marmor, *The Politics of Medicare* (Chicago: Aldine Publishing Company, 1973), p. 46, and "Current Status of the Health Insurance

Legislation before the Ways and Means Committee," n.a., n.d. (but 1962), Box 143, Cohen Papers.

45. Ribicoff to Kennedy, June 2, 1962, WHCF, Box 94, JFK Library. Similarly, officials turned their attention to John Watts (D-Ky.). Robert Ball, who could be extremely persuasive on the subject, had a long talk with Watts during which he told him about the merits of the Social Security approach. Although concerned about winning a primary election in May, Watts indicated "sympathy" for Ball's point of view and particularly liked his point that the passage of Medicare would make it easier for private insurance to cover working Americans. "Current Status of the Health Insurance Legislation before the Ways and Means Committee," Box 143, Cohen Papers.

46. Cohen, "Health Insurance Benefits–Use of Blue Cross and Other Private Organizations to Facilitate Payments to Hospitals and Other Providers," June 8, 1962, Subject Files 1961–1964, Medical Care for the Aged, June 6–13, 1962, Box 36, Sorensen Papers.

47. "Proposals to Modify Anderson-King," n.a. (but probably Nelson Cruikshank), June 12, 1963, Subject Files 1961–1964, Medical Care for the Aged, June 2, 1962–June 13, 1963, Box 36, Sorensen Papers.

48. Cohen to Sorensen, June 27, 1962, Box 36, Sorensen Papers; Cohen to Sorensen, June 28, 1962, Box 76, Cohen Papers; Clinton P. Anderson with Milton Viorst, *Outsider in the Senate* (Cleveland, Ohio: World Publishing Company, 1970), p. 276.

49. Cohen to Sorensen, June 28, 1962, Box 76, Cohen Papers.

50. Cohen to Sorensen, June 29, 1962, Box 36, Sorensen Papers.

51. Under the original Anderson-Javits proposal, a private plan had to offer the "exact" benefits of the Medicare program; the concessions allowed private plans to offer some variations on the Medicare program, such as forty-five days of hospital coverage with no deductible. Cohen to Sorensen, July 6, 1962, Box 76, Cohen Papers.

52. Cohen to Sorensen, July 11, 1962, Box 36, Sorensen Papers, and Cohen to Clinton Anderson, July 12, 1962, Box 1102, Anderson Papers.

53. Theodore C. Sorensen, *Kennedy* (New York: Harper and Row, 1965), pp. 342, 343, and Cohen to Sorensen, July 6, 1962, Box 36, Sorensen Papers.

54. Cohen to Sorensen, February 8, 1966, Box 87, Cohen Papers.

55. Michael Barone, *Our Country: The Shaping of America from Roosevelt to Reagan* (New York: Free Press, 1990), p. 348.

56. Cohen to the secretary, November 5, 1962, "Policy Issues in Education Legislative Program for 1963," Box 144, Cohen Papers.

57. "A New Federal Program in Education," November 7, 1962, Box 144, Cohen Papers.

58. On Keppel, see Bernstein, *Promises Kept,* pp. 238–240, and Cohen to Mr. Francis Keppel, December 12, 1962, Box 78, Cohen Papers.

59. Bernstein, *Promises Kept,* p. 239, and Cohen to the secretary, January 2, 1963, "Key Items in 1963 Education Proposal," Box 78, Cohen Papers.

60. Cohen to the secretary, January 9, 1963, Box 78, Cohen Papers.

61. Cohen to Claude J. Desautels, January 21, 1963, and January 28, 1963, in White House Staff Files (WHSF), Legislative Leaders Breakfast Material, Box 23, Lawrence O'Brien Papers, JFK Library; "Statement of Chairman Adam C. Powell," January 29, 1963, Box 144, Cohen Papers.

62. Cohen to Arthur S. Flemming, February 18, 1963, Box 78, Cohen Papers, and Cohen to Claude Desautels, February 4, 1963, WHSF, Legislative Leaders Breakfast Material, Box 23, O'Brien Papers.

63. Jim G. Akin to the secretary, February 18, 1963, House Hearings on Education Bill, Box 144, Cohen Papers.

64. Jim G. Akin to the secretary, February 19, 1963, Box 144, Cohen Papers.

65. Jim G. Akin to the secretary, February 28, 1963, Jurisdiction of the Subcommittee on the Big Education Bill, Box 144, Cohen Papers.

66. The bill included three titles: one provided both grants and loans for the construction of facilities in community colleges, junior colleges, colleges, and universities; another contained grants for the construction of graduate schools, medical schools, and dental schools; a third involved the provision of student loans. Cohen to Claude J. Desautels, April 8, 1963, WHSF, Legislative Leaders Breakfast Material, Box 24, O'Brien Papers.

67. Sam Halpern to Francis Keppel, March 25, 1963, Box 144, Cohen Papers.

68. See Cohen to Claude J. Desautels, April 8, 1963, WHSF, Legislative Leaders Breakfast Material, Box 24, O'Brien Papers, and Halpern to Keppel, March 25, 1963, Box 144, Cohen Papers.

69. Cohen to Sorensen, March 29, 1963, Box 33, Sorensen Papers.

70. Cohen, diary, Friday, November 12, 1965, Box 278, Cohen Papers, and Cohen, interview with Helen Hall, staff associate for the Civil Rights Documentation Project, Ann Arbor, September 4, 1969 (transcript available in Interview File, Cohen Papers, LBJ Library).

71. Allen J. Matusow, *The Unraveling of America* (New York: Harper and Row, 1984), chapter 3, contains a succinct overview of the Kennedy administration's cautious handling of the civil rights issue. The standard source is Carl Brauer, *John F. Kennedy and the Second Reconstruction* (New York: Columbia University Press, 1977).

72. Cohen, interview with Helen Hall.

73. Material for meeting with Hon. Theodore Sorensen and the attorney general, May 29, 1963, Box 79, Cohen Papers.

74. Cohen to Claude Desautels, April 15, 1963, WHSF, Legislative Leaders Breakfast Material, Box 24, O'Brien Papers.

75. Cohen to the secretary, April 30, 1963, Box 78, Cohen Papers.

76. Material for meeting with Hon. Theodore Sorensen and the attorney general, May 29, 1963, Box 79, Cohen Papers.

77. Among many accounts of this endorsement, see James Giglio, *The Presidency of John F. Kennedy* (Lawrence: University Press of Kansas, 1991), chap. 7.

78. Cohen to Claude Desautels, May 6, 1963, WHSF, Legislative Leaders Breakfast Materials, Box 25, O'Brien Papers.

79. Cohen to the secretary, April 29, 1963, Box 78, Cohen Papers.

80. Cohen to Myer Feldman, November 19, 1962, Subject Files, 1961–1964, Education folder, November 9, 1962–March 29, 1963, Box 33, Sorensen Papers; "1963: Year of Legislative Achievements in Education," *Health, Education, and Welfare Indicators,* October 1963–February 1964 (Washington, D.C.: Government Printing Office, 1964), pp. 41–42; Cohen to the secretary, June 28, 1963, Box 79, Cohen Papers.

81. Jim Akin to the secretary, May 27, 1963, in Cohen to Claude Desautels, May 27, 1963, WHSF, Legislative Leaders Breakfast Materials, Box 25, O'Brien Papers.

82. Cohen to Sorensen, July 25, 1963, Subject Files, Education folder, July 22–25, 1963, Box 33, Sorensen Papers, and Cohen to Desautels, July 29, 1963, WHSF, Legislative Leaders Breakfast Material, Box 27, O'Brien Papers.

83. Cohen to Desautels, August 12, 1963, WHSF, Legislative Leaders Breakfast Material, August 13, 1963, Box 28, O'Brien Papers.

84. Bernstein, *Promises Kept,* p. 292.

85. Cohen to the secretary, September 10, 1963, Box 144, Cohen Papers.

86. This legislation took the form of amendments to the Library Services Act, extending that act to urban areas and authorizing grants for the construction of public community library facilities.

87. Reginald Conley to Cohen, September 25, 1963, Box 44, Cohen Papers.

88. Cohen to Sorensen, October 25, 1963, Box 144, Cohen Papers.

89. Cohen to Claude J. Desautels, October 28, 1963, WHSF, Legislative Leaders Breakfast Material, Box 30, O'Brien Papers.

90. See "1963: Year of Legislative Achievements in Education," pp. 6–9, for a good description of the legislation.

91. Indeed, Nestingen had pursued this strategy in the spring of 1962. Working with Walter Reuther and other labor union officials, senior citizens' advocates, and Democratic party functionaries, he had helped to stage rallies from coast to coast. On May 20 the president himself spoke at Madison Square Garden, a performance that nearly everyone regarded as shrill and ineffective. Until that point, Senator Anderson had believed that the Medicare advocates "were launching a splendid public offensive" that surely would condition the debate; after that speech, George Meany and Nelson Cruikshank thought Kennedy had killed Medicare's chances for a year (Anderson with Viorst, *Outsider in the Senate,* p. 272, and David, *With Dignity,* pp. 71–72, 67–68).

92. Cohen and his allies cooperated with the publicity offensive even though they regarded it as irrelevant to the central business of persuading Mills. Cohen himself addressed a rally in San Diego, and Elizabeth Wickenden appeared at the Madison Square Garden rally. "They needed a woman," she explained. Instead of creating a ground swell of support, these and the thirty-odd other Medicare rallies did little to change legislators' minds. Elizabeth Wickenden to Myer Feldman, December 9, 1963, Box 125, Cohen Papers; Ivan Nestingen, interview with Peter Corning, 1966–1967, Washington, D.C., Columbia Oral History Collection, p. 21 (annotated copy in Box 392, Cohen Papers, LBJ Library).

93. Material on Ivan Nestingen from Nestingen File in the John Macy Papers, LBJ Library.

94. Nestingen, interview with Corning, pp. 39–45, and Cohen, interview with Moss, p. 74.

95. Cohen, interview with Moss, p. 73; Cohen, third interview with William Moss, Ann Arbor, July 20, 1972, pp. 112–113.

96. Cohen, third interview with Moss, p. 86.

97. William Reidy, interview with Peter Corning, Columbia Oral History Collection, p. 75 (annotated copy in Box 394, Cohen Papers, LBJ Library).

98. Ibid., p. 92. Blue Cartenson, interview with Peter Corning, Columbia Oral History Collection, p. 223 (annotated copy available in Box 393, Cohen Papers, LBJ Library).

99. Nestingen, interview with Corning, pp. 73–76.

100. Cohen, "Reflections on the Enactment of Medicare and Medicaid," *Health Care Financing Review,* 1985 Annual Supplement, p. 5; the quotation from Edward Kennedy comes from notes taken by the author of an informal eulogy he delivered for Cohen in the Ways and Means Committee Hearing Room in 1987. "Reflections on Implementing Medicare," a transcript of a discussion with Robert M. Ball and Arthur E. Hess, January 31, 1992, pp. 27–28, published in mimeograph by the National Academy of Social Insurance, Washington, D.C.

101. McNamara took particular exception to the strengthening of the Kerr-Mills program, a program that he had opposed from its very beginnings (Cohen, "Reflections," p. 9).

102. Nestingen, interview with Corning, p. 45.

103. Cohen, interview with David G. McComb, December 8, 1968, Oral History Collection, tape 2, p. 3, LBJ Library.

104. Dean Coston, interview with author, Washington, D.C., October 10, 1990, and Cohen, interview with McComb, tape 2, p. 3.

105. *Milwaukee Journal,* April 28, 1965; I am grateful to Darwin Huxley for providing me with this clipping. John Macy to the president, April 27, 1965, Macy Papers. The records also contain a letter of support for Cohen from Senators McNamara and Hart (McNamara and Hart to the president, April 26, 1965, Macy Papers).

106. Cohen to Sorensen, December 19, 1962, General File, Health Insurance folder December 1962–May 1963, Box 11, Feldman Papers, and Howard Bray to Clinton Anderson, December 20, 1962, Box 1097, Anderson Papers.

107. Howard Bray to Senator Anderson, May 7, 1963, Box 1098, Anderson Papers.

108. Cohen, "Memorandum for the President," n.d., Presidential Office Files, Departments and Agencies, Box 79-A, HEW 1963, JFK Library, and Cohen to the undersecretary, April 23, 1963, Subject Files, 1961–1964, Medical Care for the Aged, June 12–13, 1962, Box 36, Sorensen Papers.

109. The Javits group also proposed congressional action to facilitate the development of tax-free, low-cost special insurance plans to provide for the services not covered by Medicare, such as doctors' fees and catastrophic expenses. Cohen to Sorensen, November 13, 1963, Subject Files 1961–1964, HEW, March 29–November 22, 1963, Box 35, Sorensen Papers, and Cohen to the secretary, April 22, 1963, Cohen Papers.

110. Cohen to the secretary, April 23, 1963, Box 35, Sorensen Papers.

111. Anderson to Cohen, May 14, 1963, and Cohen to Sen. Clint Anderson, May 24, 1963, Box 1098, Anderson Papers.

112. Cohen to the secretary, October 29, 1963, Box 146, Cohen Papers. For a complete examination of the Medicare-related events in 1963, one that emphasizes the activities of Senator Anderson, see Sheri David, *With Dignity,* chap. 6.

113. Coston, interview with author, Washington, D.C., October 30, 1990.

CHAPTER NINE. LBJ, POVERTY, AND EDUCATION

1. Cohen, notes on November 23, 24, and 25, 1963, Box 278, Cohen Papers.

2. Historians in later years would note a tight association between President Johnson and federal education legislation. Paul Conkin, for example, has written that "broader educational opportunities for all youths" were an important goal of Johnson's Great Society. Vaughn Davis Bornet, another Johnson biographer, also underscores his faith in education, quoting LBJ: "If every person born could acquire all the education that their intelligence quotient would permit them to take—God only knows what our gross national product would be—and the strength we would add to our nation, militarily, diplomatically, economically is too large even to imagine." See Conkin, *Big Daddy from the Pedernales: Lyndon Baines Johnson* (Boston: Twayne Publishers, 1986), p. 209, and Bornet, *The Presidency of Lyndon B. Johnson* (Lawrence: University Press of Kansas, 1983), p. 125.

3. Cohen to the president, November 26, 1963, Chron. Files, Box 80, Cohen Papers.

4. Not surprisingly, Lawrence O'Brien, Kennedy's legislative liaison, remained in the White House, even as Sorensen, Press Secretary Pierre Salinger, and others close to JFK eventually left; Cohen, of course, stayed.

5. Cohen, interview with David G. McComb, March 2, 1969, Oral History Collection, p. 5, LBJ Library.

6. Cohen, third interview with William Moss, July 20, 1972, Oral History Collection, p. 116, JFK Library.

7. Meeting with President Johnson and the department liaison officers, Fish Room, the White House, December 10, 1963, informal autobiographical fragment, Box 278, Cohen Papers.

8. Elizabeth Wickenden, interview with Michael L. Gillette, New York City, November 6, 1974, Oral History Collection, p. 22, LBJ Library.

9. Cohen, interview with McComb, p. 2.

10. For a classic account of this side of Johnson's personality, see Doris Kearns Goodwin, *LBJ and the American Dream* (New York: Harper and Row, 1976), and Joseph A. Califano, Jr., *The Triumph and Tragedy of Lyndon Johnson: The White House Years* (New York: Simon and Schuster, 1991), pp. 20–23.

11. That is the opinion of Irving Bernstein; see *Promises Kept* (New York: Oxford University Press, 1991), p. 243.

12. See Cohen to Lawrence O'Brien, December 11, 1963, Box 80, Cohen Papers.

13. That was the amount at least between 1890 and 1964; the figure did not include the value of the land grants themselves. The four bills passed were the Higher Education Facilities Act, the vocational education legislation, the Health Professions Educational Assistance Act of 1963, and the part of the mental retardation legislation that included aid to teachers of handicapped children. See Cohen to Sorensen, December 11, 1963, Box 80, Cohen Papers.

14. Philip Reed Rulon, *The Compassionate Samaritan: The Life of Lyndon Baines Johnson* (Chicago: Nelson Hall, 1981), pp. xxii, ix–x.

15. Cohen to Lawrence O'Brien, December 11, 1963, Box 80, Cohen Papers.

16. Letter of transmittal from Cohen to Celebrezze, in *Legislative Achievements and Activities, 1964,* report to Secretary Anthony J. Celebrezze from Wilbur J. Cohen (Washington, D.C.: GPO, October 1964). This publication also has a good description of PL 88-269, the Library Services and Construction Act.

17. "Elementary and Secondary School Legislative Proposals," January 6, 1964, Box 80, Cohen Papers.

18. James N. Morgan, Martin H. David, Wilbur J. Cohen, and Harvey E. Brazer, *Income and Welfare in the United States,* a study by the Survey Research Center Institute for Social Research, University of Michigan (New York: McGraw-Hill Company, 1962), p. 3.

19. See Wilbur J. Cohen, "The Elimination of Poverty in the United States," an address before the Oregon State Conference on Social Welfare, March 25, 1963, copy in WHCF, Education, February 22–March 31, 1963, Box 94, JFK Library.

20. See "DHEW Actions Which Could Be Taken in an Emergency Program for Eastern Kentucky," Cohen to secretary, October 29, 1963, and Cohen to Mr. William J. Page, Jr., Box 149, Cohen Papers.

21. Julie Roy Jeffrey, *Education for Children of the Poor* (Columbus: Ohio State University Press, 1978), p. 28.

22. Wilbur Cohen, "Edwin E. Witte," in Walter I. Trattner, ed., *Biographical Dictionary of Social Welfare in America* (Westport, Conn.: Greenwood Press, 1986), pp. 785–787, and Irving Bernstein, *Promises Kept,* p. 123.

23. Cohen, third interview with Moss, p. 90.

24. Cohen, interview with David McComb, May 10, 1969, Oral History Collection, tape 5, p. 8, LBJ Library.

25. Walter W. Heller to Anthony J. Celebrezze, October 30, 1963, Box 149, Cohen Papers.

26. H. Phillip Des Marais to Burton Weisbrod, October 29, 1963, Box 125, Cohen Papers.

27. Draft memorandum to departments, "Wider Participation in Prosperity," November 2, 1963, and Heller to secretaries, November 5, 1963, "Widening Participation in Prosperity–An Attack on Poverty," Box 149, Cohen Papers.

28. Heller to secretaries, "Widening Participation in Prosperity."

29. Ellen Winston to Wilbur J. Cohen, November 19, 1963, Box 125, Cohen Papers.

30. Cohen to Heller, "1964 Legislative Program for 'Widening Participation in Prosperity—An Attack on Poverty,' " microfilm roll 37, Related Papers of Walter Heller, JFK Library. See also Legislative Background, Economic Opportunity Act of 1964, War on Poverty, Box 1, Papers of Lyndon Baines Johnson, President, LBJ Library.

31. Capron and Weisbrod to Heller, December 3, 1963, Box 149, Cohen Papers.

32. Quoted in Allen J. Matusow, *The Unraveling of America* (New York: Harper and Row, 1984), p. 120.

33. Capron and Weisbrod to Heller, December 3, 1963, Box 149, Cohen Papers.

34. Cohen to Capron and Weisbrod, December 5, 1963, Box 149, Cohen Papers. See also Ida Merriam to Cohen, December 4, 1963, Box 149, Cohen Papers.

35. Ellen Winston to Wilbur J. Cohen, December 17, 1963, Box 125, Cohen Papers.

36. Robert Ball to Wilbur J. Cohen, December 18, 1963, Box 125, Cohen Papers.

37. Heller to Sorensen, December 20, 1963, Box 149, Cohen Papers.

38. Cohen to the secretary, December 17, 1963, Box 80, Cohen Papers.

39. Cohen to Sorensen, December 26, 1963, Box 80, Cohen Papers.

40. Ibid.

41. Cohen to director of the Bureau of the Budget and chairman, Council of Economic Advisers, January 10, 1964, roll 37, Heller Papers, and draft of "Bureau of the Budget Proposal, Outline of a Proposed Poverty Program," January 2, 1964, Box 80, Cohen Papers.

42. William Capron to Walter Heller, January 4, 1964, roll 37, Heller Papers.

43. Cohen to director of the Bureau of the Budget and chairman, Council of Economic Advisers, January 10, 1964, roll 37, Heller Papers.

44. Wickenden to Myer Feldman, December 9, 1963, Box 80, Cohen to Myer Feldman, December 13, 1963, Box 149, and Elizabeth Wickenden to Walter Jenkins, February 18, 1964, copy in Box 149, Cohen Papers.

45. Cohen to the secretary, January 28, 1964, Box 80, Cohen Papers.

46. Capron to Heller, January 4, 1964, Heller Papers.

47. Cohen to Kermit Gordon, January 6, 1964, Box 80, and Labor and Welfare Division of the Bureau of the Budget to the director, January 8, 1964, Box 147, Cohen Papers.

48. Cohen to the secretary, January 29, 1964, Box 80, Cohen Papers.

49. Cohen to Edelstein, March 30, 1964, Cohen to Fedele Fauri, March 30, 1964, and Cohen to Bill Haber, April 2, 1964, Box 80, Cohen Papers.

50. William Capron to Walter Heller, February 12, 1964, roll 37, Heller Papers.

51. Burton A. Weisbrod to the Council of Economic Advisers, March 21, 1964, roll 37, Heller Papers.

52. Michael Barone, *Our Country* (New York: Free Press, 1990), p. 372.

53. Dean Coston to Wilbur Cohen, May 12, 1964, May 1, 1964, May 20, 1964, June 10, 1964, Box 149, Cohen Papers. Office of Program and Legislative Planning, Legislative Services Branch, "Report on Hearings of the Committee on Rules . . . on HR 11277," June 17, 1964, Box 149, Cohen Papers; 88th Cong., 2d sess., HR *Report 1458, Economic Opportunity Act of 1964* (from the Committee on Education and Labor), June 3, 1964 (Washington, D.C.: Government Printing Office, 1964); secondary sources on passage of the Economic Opportunity Act include Bornet, *Presidency of Lyndon B. Johnson;* Conkin, *Big Daddy from the Pedernales;* and James L. Sundquist, *Politics and Policy* (Washington, D.C.: Brookings Institution, 1968).

54. Cohen to Sorensen, May 5, 1964, Box 81, Cohen Papers.

55. "Statement by Sargent Shriver, Special Assistant to the President, Indian Treaty Room, Executive Office Building, Washington, D.C., March 14, 1964," Box 149, Cohen Papers.

56. Cohen, third interview with Moss, p. 105.

57. "The War on Poverty: Proposals Submitted by Sargent Shriver, 11/21/64," enclosed in Cohen to the secretary, November 23, 1964, Box 82, Cohen Papers. It should be pointed out that Social Security in fact rewarded lower-income workers more than higher-income workers, but as a general rule, the greater one's contributions, the greater one's returns.

58. Sundquist, *Politics and Policy*, p. 493. For another perceptive account of OEO and its problems, see David Zarefsky, *President Johnson's War on Poverty: Rhetoric and History* (Tuscaloosa: University of Alabama Press, 1986).

59. Matusow, *Unraveling of America* p. 189, and Cohen, interview with Helen Hall, Ann Arbor, September 4, 1969, Cohen Papers, LBJ Library.

60. Reginald C. Conley, assistant general counsel to Wilbur J. Cohen, June 6, 1964, Box 81, Cohen Papers, and Jeffrey, *Education for Children of the Poor*, p. 68.

61. Johnson, cabinet meeting of January 11, 1965, *Minutes and Documents of Cabinet Meetings of President Johnson*, Microfilm in Manuscript Collection, reel 1, p. 5, Library of Congress, and John Gardner, interview with David McComb, December 20, 1971, Oral History Collection, p. 17, LBJ Library.

62. Johnson, cabinet meeting of February 11, 1965, *Minutes and Documents*, Manuscript Collections, reel 1, p. 3.

63. "Existing Law and Pending Legislation for Federal Aid to Elementary and Secondary Education," July 30, 1964, Box 147, Cohen Papers.

64. Francis Keppel to the secretary, November 10, 1964, Box 152, Cohen Papers.

65. Albert L. Alford, School Finance Section, to Cohen, November 13, 1964, Box 152, Cohen Papers.

66. Jeffrey, *Education for the Children of the Poor*, p. 73.

67. "Education Task Force," November 15, 1964, in Box 165, Cohen Papers, and Hugh Graham, *Uncertain Triumph* (Chapel Hill: University of North Carolina Press, 1984), pp. 66–67.

68. Gardner, interview with McComb, p. 6.

69. Cohen, interview with David G. McComb, December 8, 1968, Oral History Collection, p. 7, LBJ Library. In the 1990s Gardner wrote a descriptive epithet about Wilbur Cohen: he was an "unarmed hero. A simple prescription for making government work: more Wilbur Cohens" (Gardner to author, July 24, 1991, personal correspondence). It should be underscored that Cohen genuinely admired Gardner and at one point in 1972 even urged that he run for president as a Democrat (Gardner was nominally a Republican, just as Winant was). The two had complementary skills. Gardner, for example, did not suffer fools gladly; Cohen had much more tolerance for long meetings and complex negotiations with people whom Gardner perceived as either greedy or not very intelligent.

70. "More than ever before in American history," wrote historian Paul Conkin, "an administration moved beyond crisis-induced legislative action, to a studied, carefully calculated effort to identify problems and to create the needed constituencies to help solve them" (*Big Daddy on the Pedernales,* pp. 209–210).

71. Cohen, interview with McComb, tape 4, p. 24.

72. Gardner, interview with McComb, p. 9; David Reisman, one of the task force members, called it a "legitimizing device" for legislation already in development (Jeffrey, *Education for Children of the Poor*, p. 75).

73. Discussion with President Johnson, November 17, 1964, about 9 P.M. at the State Department party for Ralph Dungan, Johnson memorabilia, Box 278, Cohen Papers.

74. Cohen, interview with McComb, tape 4, p. 15.

75. Graham, *Uncertain Triumph,* p. 77, and Cohen, interview with McComb, tape 4, pp. 14–16.

76. Graham, *Uncertain Triumph,* p. 71, and Stephen K. Bailey and Edith K. Mosher, *ESEA: The Office of Education Administers a Law* (Syracuse, N.Y.: Syracuse University Press, 1968), p. 41.

77. Morse to Cohen, January 4, 1965, Box 152, Cohen Papers.

78. Douglas Cater to the president, January 26, 1965, Box 13, Cater Files, LBJ Library.

79. Cohen, interview with McComb, tape 3, p. 16.

80. Michael L. Parker, "Operating Methods under Wilbur J. Cohen–A Personal Review," in *Administrative History of HEW,* vol. 1, pt. 2, p. 14, LBJ Library.

81. Parker, "Operating Methods under Cohen," and telephone log, March 4, 1965, Box 176, Cohen Papers.

82. Douglas Cater to the president, February 3, 1965, Box 13, Cater files; Phillip H. Des Marais to Cohen, February 10, 1965, Box 152, Cohen Papers; Cohen to Robert Kennedy, February 15, 1965, Box 82, Cohen Papers.

83. "Legislative Relations, Federal Aid to Education Proposals under the Kennedy-Johnson Administration," in *Administrative History of HEW,* vol. 1, pt. 3; Lawrence O'Brien to the president, March 8, 1965, WHCF EX LE/FA 2, Box 38, LBJ Library; Cohen to the president, February 23, 1965, Box 83, Cohen Papers.

84. O'Brien to the president, March 8, 1965, WHCF EX LE/FA 2, Box 38, LBJ Library.

85. Ibid., and March 6, 1965.

86. See Phillip H. Des Marais to Wilbur Cohen, March 17, 1965, Box 152, Cohen Papers.

87. Bornet, *Presidency of Lyndon B. Johnson,* p. 227.

88. Graham, *Uncertain Triumph,* p. 80.

89. "The Great Congress," White House press release, October 15, 1966, in Cohen Papers, and Lawrence O'Brien and Joseph A. Califano, Jr., "Final Report to President Lyndon B. Johnson on the 89th Congress," White House press release, October 24, 1966, Cohen Papers.

90. See, for example, Matusow, *Unraveling of America,* pp. 217–271, and Jeffrey, *Education for Children of the Poor,* pp. 97–198.

91. For a good overview of the politics of enactment, see Eugene Eidenberg and Roy D. Morey, *An Act of Congress* (New York: Norton and Company, 1969), and Philip Meranto, *The Politics of Federal Aid to Education in 1965* (Syracuse, N.Y.: Syracuse University Press, 1967).

92. Sam Halperin, "The Great Education Act: 10 Years Later," offprint in Box 15, Cohen Papers.

93. Cohen, "Meeting at the White House, Saturday, August 21, 1964, with Democratic Governors," in Box 278, Cohen Papers.

CHAPTER TEN. MEDICARE–LEGISLATIVE TRIUMPH

1. Robert Ball, interview with David McComb, November 5, 1968, Washington, D.C., Oral History Collection, p. 45, LBJ Library.

2. "Aging, hospital insurance, and social security," n.a., n.d. (ca. December 1963–this might be the memo that Cohen prepared for LBJ), Box 80, Cohen Papers.

3. O'Brien to the president, January 27, 1964, WHCF File LE/IS 1, Box 75, LBJ Library.

4. Press release, January 11, 1964, WHCF, File LE/IS 1, Box 75, LBJ Library, and Cohen, "Meeting in the White House, January 15, 1964," Box 278, Cohen Papers.

5. Cohen to Ivan Nestingen, January 17, 1964, Box 80, Cohen Papers.

6. Cohen to the secretary, January 14, 1964, and Cohen to I. S. Falk, January 17, 1964, Box 80, Cohen Papers. Cohen to Myer Feldman, January 29, 1964, RG 235, Records of the Department of Health, Education, and Welfare, Accession 69A-1793, File LL, Box 15, Washington National Records Center, Suitland, Maryland.

7. Cohen to Myer Feldman, January 29, 1964, RG 235, Accession 69A-1793, File LL, Box 15, Washington National Records Center.

8. Cohen to Claude Desautels, January 29, 1964, Box 80, Cohen Papers.

9. Cohen, "Meeting with President Johnson in the President's Office," February 5, 1964, Box 278, Cohen Papers.

10. Cohen, "Background Briefing on President's Message on Health" in the Fish Room at the White House, February 10, 1964, Box 278, Cohen Papers.

11. Cohen, notes on a call from President Johnson, February 24, 1965, notes on a call from Larry O'Brien, March 25, 1964, in Johnson memorabilia, Box 278, Cohen Papers; Cohen to Julius Edelstein, March 30, 1964, Box 80, Cohen Papers.

12. Cohen to Falk, April 8, 1964, Box 80, Cohen Papers.

13. Material in RG 235, Accession 69A-1793, Box 41, File AW, 1964, Washington National Records Center.

14. Cohen to Ted Sorensen, May 5, 1964, Box 81, Cohen Papers.

15. Cohen to the secretary, May 5, 1964, Box 81, Cohen Papers.

16. Ibid., May 15, 1964.

17. Cohen to Martin Thomas, May 19, 1964, Box 81, Cohen Papers.

18. Theodore H. White, *The Making of the President 1964* (New York: Signet Books, 1966), p. 463.

19. Cohen, "Plane Ride with President Johnson to Ann Arbor, May 22, 1964," Box 278, and Cohen to the secretary, May 25, 1964, Box 81, Cohen Papers.

20. Cohen to the secretary, May 25, 1964, Cohen to the president, May 26, 1964, and Cohen to the secretary, May 27, 1964, Box 81, Cohen Papers.

21. Cohen to Altmeyer, May 26, 1964, Box 81, Cohen Papers.

22. Henry Wilson to Lawrence O'Brien, June 8, 1964, WHCF, LBJ Library.

23. Cohen to the secretary, June 9, 1964, with enclosure "Meeting with Speaker McCormack," Tuesday, June 9, 1964, Box 81, Cohen Papers, and Sherri I. David, *With Dignity* (Westport, Conn.: Greenwood Press, 1985), p. 111.

24. Rowland Evans and Robert Novak, "Wilbur Woos Wilbur to Rescue Medicare," n.d., Box 278, Cohen Papers.

25. Cohen to Social Security experts, July 2, 1964, "Social Security Amendments of 1964," Box 81, Cohen Papers.

26. Cohen to the secretary, July 8, 10, 1964, Box 81, Cohen Papers.

27. Ibid., July 10, 1964; "A Substitute for the OASDI Benefit Increase in House Bill Which Would Give the Individual a Choice between Hospital Insurance and the Cash Benefit Increase," in Cohen to secretary, July 13, 1964, Box 81, Cohen Papers; Robert Ball to the secretary, July 23, 1964, RG 235, Accession A-1793, Box 43, Washington National Records Center.

28. Cohen, "Meeting with President Lyndon B. Johnson, the President's Office, the White House, July 16, 1964," Box 278, Cohen Papers.

29. Ribicoff to Johnson, July 20, 1964, WHCF, File LE/IS 1, Box 75, LBJ Library, and Ribicoff to Anderson, August 11, 1964, WHCF, File LE/IS 1, Box 75, LBJ Library.

30. Howard Bray to Senator Anderson, July 27, 1964, Box 600, Anderson Papers.

31. Cohen to Lawrence O'Brien, August 13, 1964, Box 81, Cohen Papers, and David, *With Dignity,* pp. 114–116.

32. Mike Manatos to Larry O'Brien, August 14, 1965, WHCF, File LE/IS, Box 1, LBJ Library.

33. Cohen to the secretary, August 28, 1964, Box 81, Cohen Papers.

34. Clinton P. Anderson with Milton Viorst, *Outsider in the Senate* (Cleveland, Ohio: World Publishing Company, 1970), p. 283, and Cohen to Lawrence O'Brien, August 31, 1964, Box 81, Cohen Papers.

35. Bill Moyers to LBJ, September 2, 1964, and Lawrence O'Brien to the president, September 2, 1964, both in WHCF, File LE/IS, Box 75, LBJ Library.

36. Cohen to Chris Cohen, September 11, 1964, Box 81, Cohen Papers.

37. O'Brien to the president, September 18 and 23, 1964, WHCF, File LE/IS, Box 75, LBJ Library.

38. Ibid., September 23, 1964; Cohen to O'Brien, September 24, 1964, WHCF, File LE/IS, Box 75, LBJ Library; Cohen to Clinton Anderson (and enclosures), November 3, 1964, RG 235, Accession 71A-3499, Box 1, Washington National Records Center.

39. Sidney Saperstein, interview with Janet Kerrtener, May 26, 1986, Silver Spring, Maryland, Oral History Collection, p. 34, LBJ Library, and Cohen to Lawrence O'Brien, September 28, 1964, Box 81, Cohen Papers.

40. Theodore H. White, *Making of the President, 1964,* p. 360.

41. Wilbur J. Cohen, "Reflections on the Enactment of Medicare and Medicaid," *Health Care Financing Review,* 1985 Annual Supplement, p. 5.

42. "Report on a Hospital Insurance Plan Discussed with the Conference Committee on H.R. 11865," in Cohen to Anderson, November 3, 1964, Box 82, Cohen Papers.

43. Cohen to the secretary, November 5, 1964, RG 235, Accession 69A-1793, File LL, Box 15, Washington National Records Center; Cohen, "November 15, 1964 – Party for Walter Heller," and Cohen, "Discussion with President Johnson, November 17, 1964," Box 278, Cohen Papers.

44. Anderson to Cohen, November 9, 1964, RG 235, Accession 69A-1793, Box 15, Washington National Records Center.

45. Cohen to Hon. John McCormack, November 19, 1964, Box 82, Cohen Papers.

46. Cohen to Clinton Anderson, November 18, 1964, Box 82, Cohen Papers.

47. "Summary of Major Provisions of 'Hospital Insurance and Social Security Amendments of 1965,' " in secretary to the president, November 24, 1964, Box 82, Cohen Papers.

48. Howard Bray to Senator Anderson, December 1, 1964, Box 1106, Anderson Papers.

49. Anderson to Cohen, December 1, 1964, Box 1106, Anderson Papers.

50. Cohen to Clint Anderson, December 1, 1964, Box 1106, Anderson Papers.

51. Cohen to Files, December 7, 1964, Box 82, Cohen Papers.

52. Secretary to the president, November 25, 1964, Cohen to Clint Anderson, December 1, 1964, Cohen to John McCormack, December 7, 1964, Cohen to Files, December 7, 1964, and Cohen to the president, December 8, 1964, Box 82, Cohen Papers.

53. Cohen to the president, December 8, 1964, Box 82, Cohen Papers.

54. Cohen to Feldman, December 8, 1964, Box 82, Cohen Papers.

55. Cohen to Files, December 9, 1964, Box 82, Cohen Papers.

56. "Remarks of Congressman Wilbur D. Mills before the Downtown Little Rock Lions Club," December 2, 1964, Box 151, Cohen Papers.

57. Cohen to the secretary, December 10 and 17, 1964, Box 82, Cohen Papers.

58. Cohen to Myer Feldman, December 15, 1964, Box 82, Cohen Papers.

59. Cohen to Clint Anderson, December 11, 1964, Box 82, Cohen Papers.

60. Cohen to the secretary, December 16, 1964 (describing a meeting with Drs. Furstenberg, Axelrod, Dearing, Clark, Esselstyn, Bailey, Mott, Sid Lee, Leslie Falk, and

Sheps held on December 13, 1964), and Cohen to Dr. Montague Cobb, December 16, 1964, Box 82, Cohen Papers.

61. "Brief Summary of 'Hospital Insurance, Social Security, and Public Assistance Amendments of 1965,'" December 31, 1964, RG 235, General Counsel Records, Accession 71A-3497, File Aw, Box 1, Washington National Records Center.

62. "Summary Highlights of the Report of the Advisory Council on Social Security," January 3, 1965, Box 194, Cohen Papers, and AP wire copy headed "Health," January 2, 1965, RG 235, Accession 1793, Box 43, Washington National Records Center.

63. Cohen, "Reflections on the Enactment of Medicare and Medicaid," p. 6.

64. Memorandum from Wilbur J. Cohen to the president, January 29, 1965, RG 235, Accession 69A-1793, File LL, Box 16, Washington National Records Center, and Edward Berkowitz and Wendy Wolff, *Group Health Association* (Philadelphia: Temple University Press, 1988), p. 89.

65. Cohen to secretary, February 4, 1965 (5:00 P.M.), Box 83, Cohen Papers.

66. Cohen to the secretary, February 3, 1965, Box 83, Cohen Papers.

67. Ibid., February 4, 1965.

68. Cohen to the president, February 25, 1965, RG 235, Accession 69A-1793, File AW-5, Box 41, Washington National Records Center.

69. Cohen to secretary, February 8, 1965, RG 235, Accession 69A-1793, File LL, Box 16, Washington National Records Center.

70. Ibid., February 3, 1965.

71. Cohen to author, October 28, 1986, personal correspondence, and Berkowitz and Wolff, *Group Health Association*.

72. Cohen to Douglas Cater, February 5, 1965, and Cohen to the secretary, February 15, 1965, Box 83, Cohen Papers.

73. Cohen to the secretary, February 9, 1965, Box 83, Cohen Papers.

74. Cohen, "Reflections on the Enactment," p. 6 (the recollections of Robert Myers come from an annotated copy of the essay that Myers sent Cohen in author's possession).

75. Richard Harris, *A Sacred Trust* (New York: New American Library, 1966), p. 187; Theodore Marmor, with Jan Marmor, *The Politics of Medicare* (Chicago: Aldine Publishers, 1973), pp. 64–65; Robert Ball and Arthur Hess, "Reflections on Implementing Medicare," National Academy of Social Insurance, mimeograph, 1993, p. 2; Fred Arner, "Wilbur Mills' Three-Layered Cake – It's [*sic*] 25th Birthday," unpublished manuscript.

76. Harris, *Sacred Trust*, p. 187.

77. Cohen, "Reflections on the Enactment," p. 6; Saperstein, interview with Janet Kerrtener, pp. 35–36. People who worked on the specifications included Larry Filson, Irwin Wolkstein, and Alvin David of the Social Security Administration and Ed Craft and Sidney Saperstein of the HEW general counsel's office.

78. Cohen to the president, March 2, 1965, Box 83, Cohen Papers.

79. Cohen to Larry O'Brien, March 11, 1965, Box 83, Cohen Papers.

80. Ibid., March 16, 1965.

81. Cohen to Lawrence O'Brien, March 17, 1965, RG 235, Accession 69A-1793, Box 16, Washington National Records Center, and Lawrence O'Brien to the president, March 17, 1965, WHCF, File LE/IS, Box 75, LBJ Library.

82. Harris, *Sacred Trust*, pp. 188–189.

83. Cohen to Lawrence O'Brien, March 17, 1965, RG 235, Accession 69A-1793, Washington National Records Center; Jack Valenti to the president, April 22, 1965, and Bill Moyers to the president, April 26, 1965, WHCF, LE/IS, Box 75, LBJ Library.

84. Lee White to the president, April 26, 1965, WHCF, LE/IS 1, Box 75, LBJ Library, and Ball and Hess, "Reflections on Implementing Medicare," p. 7.

85. Cohen to Harry Truman, April 11, 1965, Box 83, Cohen Papers, and Cohen to John D. Dingell, April 16, 1965, RG 235, Accession 69A-1793, File LL, Box 16, Washington National Records Center.

86. Cohen to Larry O'Brien, May 6, 1965, Box 83, Cohen Papers.

87. Ibid., May 17, 1965.

88. Cohen to the president, June 17, 1965, Box 83, Cohen Papers; Cohen to Lawrence F. O'Brien, "Amendment no. 188 to HR 6675 introduced by Senator Russell B. Long," n.d., Box 1104, Anderson Papers; David, *With Dignity,* pp. 137–138.

89. Clinton Anderson to the president, July 1, 1965, Box 1103, Anderson Papers, and Cohen to O'Brien, July 6, 1965, Box 83, Cohen Papers.

90. Cohen to Lawrence F. O'Brien, July 19 and 20, 1965, RG 235, Accession 69A-1793, File LL, Box 16, Washington National Records Center.

91. Anderson to the president, July 21, 1965, Box 1103, Anderson Papers.

92. For a sense of the tremendous scope of the 1965 legislation, see, for example, Robert Ball to the secretary, June 25, 1965, and Wilbur Cohen to Lawrence O'Brien, July 21, 1965, RG 235, Accession 69A-1793, Box 16, Washington National Records Center.

93. On the tax rates, see Cohen to Lawrence O'Brien, July 21, 1965, Box 83, Cohen Papers.

94. Cohen to Douglas Cater, July 16, 1965, Box 83, Cohen Papers.

95. Jack Valenti to the president, July 16, 1965, and Horace Busby to Valenti, Cater, Moyers, and Watson, July 22, 1965, WHCF, File LE/IS, Box 75, LBJ Library; Cohen to Doug Cater, July 26, 1965, Box 83, Cohen Papers.

96. Elizabeth Wickenden to LBJ, August 5, 1965, WHCF, File LE/IS, Box 75, LBJ Library, and Cohen to Cater, September 30, 1965, Box 84, Cohen Papers.

97. Cohen to Peter Corning, September 25, 1967, Box 93, Cohen Papers.

98. Cohen to Califano, February 15, 1968, Box 95, Cohen Papers.

CHAPTER ELEVEN. IMPLEMENTING THE GREAT SOCIETY IN A TIME OF TROUBLES

1. Cohen to Lawrence O'Brien, March 15 and 29, 1965, Box 83, Cohen Papers.

2. Cohen to the Speaker of the House of Representatives, September 9, 1965, Box 85, and Cohen to Larry O'Brien, November 5, 1965, Box 86, Cohen Papers.

3. In this field, Cohen needed to concern himself with the politically delicate matter of setting standards for emissions from automobile exhausts. Cohen to Senator Muskie, September 29, 1965, Box 85, Cohen Papers.

4. Cohen to Brian Abel-Smith, January 15, 1965, and Cohen to Miss Dorothy Allen, February 15, 1966, Box 82, Cohen Papers.

5. Cohen to Brian Abel-Smith, December 13, 1965, Box 86, Cohen Papers.

6. Dean Coston, interview with author, Washington, D.C., October 10, 1990.

7. Ribicoff to John Macy, February 18, 1965, Wilbur Cohen Files, John Macy Papers, LBJ Library.

8. Macy did note that there was some opposition to Cohen from some "interests," presumably representatives of doctors, and that Senator McNamara was less than totally enthusiastic about the appointment. Macy described Cohen as the "most thorough professional in HEW's social programs in the entire country." See McNamara and Hart to Lyndon Johnson, April 26, 1965, and Macy to the president, April 27, 1965, both in Cohen Files, Macy Papers.

9. Cohen to Sorensen, May 28, 1965, Box 83, Cohen Papers.

10. Cohen to Julius Edelstein, June 11, 1965, and Cohen to Maurine Mulliner, June 21, 1965, Box 83, Cohen Papers.

11. It should be noted that Cohen came greatly to admire Gardner as a leader, and Gardner returned the compliment: "Wilbur Cohen," he said, "was one of the most impressive leaders (and one of the most lovable human beings) I ever worked with" (Gardner to author, July 24, 1991).

12. Cohen to William Haber, March 1 and September 16, 1966, Box 87, Cohen Papers.

13. Robert Ball and Arthur Hess, "Reflections on Implementing Medicare," National Academy of Social Insurance, mimeograph, 1993, p. 4, and Cohen, interview with David G. McComb, December 8, 1968, Oral History Collection, tape 2, p. 11, LBJ Library.

14. Cohen to Cater, May 2 and 25, 1966, Cohen to the secretary, June 8, 1966, Cohen to Cater, June 8, 1966, Cohen to the secretary, June 10, 1966, Cohen to Lawrence O'Brien, June 15, 1966, and Cohen to the secretary, June 17, 1966, Box 88, Cohen Papers; DHEW press release, August 17, 1965, Box 127, Cohen Papers.

15. Robert Ball and Arthur Hess, "Reflections on Implementing Medicare," p. 14.

16. Cohen to Humphrey, July 1, 1966, Box 89, Cohen Papers.

17. Cohen to the secretary, March 21 and 25, 1966, Box 87, Cohen Papers.

18. Wilbur J. Cohen, "Random Reflections on the Great Society's Politics and Health Care Politics after Twenty Years," in Marshall Kaplan and Peggy Cuciti, eds., *The Great Society and Its Legacy: Twenty Years of U.S. Social Policy* (Durham, N.C.: Duke University Press, 1986), p. 116.

19. Cohen to Cater, June 29, 1966, Box 88, Cohen Papers.

20. Allen Matusow, *The Unraveling of America* (New York: Harper and Row, 1984), p. 228, and Social Security Administration, *Annual Statistical Supplement, 1992* (Washington, D.C.: Government Printing Office, 1933), pp. 291–292.

21. Cohen to the secretary, March 8, 1967, and Cohen to the president, March 8, 1967, Box 91, Cohen Papers.

22. Cohen to the president, June 1, 1967, Box 92, Cohen Papers.

23. Cohen to Mr. Pickens (a lawyer for the American Nursing Home Association), April 5, 1967, Box 92, Cohen Papers.

24. See Cohen to Douglas Cater, August 19, 1966, "New York Medical Assistance Plan," Box 89, Cohen Papers.

25. Cohen to the secretary, September 19, 1967, Box 93, Cohen Papers.

26. Cohen, "Random Reflections," pp. 116–118.

27. Bill Moyers to Marvin Watson, Bufford Ellingston, June 9, 1965, FG 11-15, Office of Economic Opportunity, Confidential File, Box 21, LBJ Library (see also Shriver to the president, September 15, 1967, and other correspondence in this file).

28. Cohen to the secretary, September 22, 1966, Box 89, Cohen Papers.

29. Cohen, third interview with David McComb, Silver Spring, Maryland, May 10, 1969, Oral History Collection, tape 4, p. 4, LBJ Library.

30. "Report on Meeting in BOB on Interrelationships of Education and Training Programs," November 28, 1964, Box 152, Cohen Papers.

31. Typical were reports that the Department of Labor offered Los Angeles more money for the Neighborhood Youth Corps if the city agreed not to run the program through the local Community Action Program. The Department of Labor ran the Neighborhood Youth Corps, the Office of Economic Opportunity administered CAPs, and the needs of Los Angeles became subsumed in the rivalry of the two organizations. Philip Hughes, deputy director of the Bureau of the Budget, to Califano, August 6, 1966, WHCF, EX LE/We 7, Box 165, LBJ Library.

32. See, for example, Stanley Ruttenberg to Wilbur Cohen, April 5, 1967, and related correspondence in Box 159, Cohen Papers. On other legislative problems with the Office of Economic Opportunity, see Samuel Halperin to Wilbur J. Cohen, July 31, 1967, Box 159, Cohen Papers; Shriver to the president, August 11, 1967, WHCF, EX LE/WE 7, Box 165, LBJ Library; Shriver to the president, September 15, 1967, FG 11-15, Office of Economic Opportunity, Confidential File, Box 21, LBJ Library.

33. Among many books, see Charles Murray, *Losing Ground: American Social Policy, 1950–1980* (New York: Basic Books, 1984); George Gilder, *Wealth and Poverty* (New York: Basic Books, 1981); Michael Katz, *The Undeserving Poor: From the War on Poverty to the War on Welfare* (New York: Pantheon Books, 1989); Christopher Jencks, *Rethinking Social Policy: Race, Poverty, and the Underclass* (Cambridge: Harvard University Press, 1992); John E. Schwarz, *America's Hidden Success: A Reassessment of Twenty Years of Social Policy* (New York: Norton, 1983).

34. Julie Roy Jeffrey, *Education for Children of the Poor* (Columbus: Ohio State University Press, 1978), pp. 144–148; Cohen, "Random Reflections," p. 115; Michael B. Katz, *In the Shadow of the Poorhouse* (New York: Basic Books, 1986), p. 258.

35. Schultze to the president, July 13, 1966, Box 157, Cohen Papers, and Sam Halperin, "The Great Education Act: ESEA 10 Years Later," offprint in Box 15, Cohen Papers.

36. Eugene Eidenberg and Roy D. Morey, *An Act of Congress* (New York: W. W. Norton and Company, 1969), p. 199.

37. Cohen to Senator Morse, July 15, 1966, Box 89, Cohen Papers; worksheet on elementary and secondary education amendments of 1966, July 13, 1966, Box 157, Cohen Papers.

38. See Harold Howe II, commissioner of education, to the secretary, May 3, 1967, and "Some Observations on the Elementary and Secondary Education Act Fight," n.a. (Howe?), May 25, 1967, Box 160, Cohen Papers.

39. "U.S. Gently Tells Chicago Its Schools Discriminate," *Baltimore Sun,* January 10, 1967, p. 6; Joseph Califano, *Governing America: An Insider's Report from the White House and the Cabinet* (New York: Simon and Schuster, 1981), pp. 221–222; Joseph Califano, *The Triumph and Tragedy of Lyndon Johnson* (New York: Simon and Schuster, 1991), pp. 72–73; Jeffrey, *Education for Children of the Poor,* p. 114; Cohen, interview with Mc-Comb, tape 4, pp. 8–11.

40. Cohen to Abraham Holtzman, February 24, 1967, Chron. Files, Box 91, Cohen Papers.

41. Cohen to the secretary, March 21, 1966, Box 87, Cohen Papers.

42. Cohen to the president, March 16, 1966, Box 87, Cohen Papers.

43. Cohen to Charles Schultze and Gardner Ackley, March 17, 1966, Box 87, Cohen Papers.

44. Cohen to the president, March 17, 1966, Box 87, Cohen Papers.

45. Ibid., April 6, 1966, and Cohen to Jack Valenti, April 6, 1966, Box 87, Cohen Papers.

46. Cohen to Ellen Winston, April 28, 1966, Box 87, Cohen Papers.

47. Cohen to the secretary, May 12, 1966, Box 88, Cohen Papers.

48. See Cohen to Douglas Cater, September 9, 1966, September 3, 1966, and September 14, 1966, Box 89, Cohen Papers; Cohen to the secretary, December 7, 1966, and Cohen to Califano, December 15, 1966, Box 90, Cohen Papers.

49. Michael Barone, *Our Country* (New York: Free Press, 1990), p. 414.

50. Max Frankel, "Johnson Proposes Raising Social Security Benefits; Seeks Higher Payroll Tax," *New York Times,* January 24, 1967, p. 1.

51. Cohen to Douglas Cater, January 13, 1967, Chron. Files, Box 91, Cohen Papers.

52. "Planning Set for Welfare Movement," *Washington Post,* February 4, 1967, p. 82, and Frances Fox Piven and Richard A. Cloward, *Poor People's Movements: Why They Succeed, How They Fail* (New York: Random House, 1977), pp. 264–361 (quote on page 276).

53. William Chapman, "Public Welfare System a Failure, Reagan Says," *Washington Post,* September 20, 1967, p. 6.

54. Cohen to Prof. Abraham Holtzman, February 24, 1967, Box 91, Cohen Papers.

55. William Chapman, "White House Opens Fight for Social Security Rise," *Washington Post,* March 2, 1967, p. 2, and Cohen to Charles Schultze, March 23, 1967, Box 91, Cohen Papers.

56. John J. Corson and Don Simpson to the secretary, February 28, 1967, Box 112, Cohen Papers.

57. Confidential memorandums, April 21 and June 17, 1967, Box 112, Cohen Papers.

58. Cohen to Darwin Huxley, May 2, 1967, and Cohen to the secretary, May 5, 1967, Box 92, Cohen Papers.

59. Cohen to the secretary, June 24, 1967, Box 92, and Cohen to the secretary, July 6, 1967, Box 93, Cohen Papers.

60. Cohen to the secretary, June 6, 1967, "Major Points of Emphasis in Redirection of Welfare Programs," Box 92, Cohen Papers.

61. Cohen to John Corson, June 12, 1967, Box 92, Cohen Papers.

62. Cohen to the secretary, July 8 and 14, 1967, Box 137, Cohen Papers.

63. Cohen to the secretary, July 21 and 24, 1967, Box 137, Cohen Papers, and John D. Morris, "House Unit Backs Rise in Tax Rates on Aged Benefits," *New York Times,* July 23, 1987, p. 1.

64. Cohen to the president, July 14, 1967, and Cohen to Wicky, July 15, 1967, Box 93, Cohen Papers.

65. Califano to the president, July 18, 1967, WHCF, EXLE/WE, Box 164, LBJ Library.

66. "House Unit Prepares Welfare Aid Changes Forcing Many Able-Bodied Adults Off Rolls," *Wall Street Journal,* July 27, 1967, p. 9; "Way Sought to Cut Down on Child Relief," *Washington Post,* July 26, 1967, p. 11; Califano, *Triumph and Tragedy of Lyndon Johnson,* 213; Matusow, *Unraveling of America,* p. 363.

67. Cohen to assistant secretaries, August 9, 1967, Box 93, Cohen Papers.

68. "Social Security–Welfare Bill Comes before House Today," *Washington Star,* August 16, 1967, p. 3; William Steif, "7.6 Million on Welfare in U.S.," *Washington Daily News,* August 16, 1967, p. 25; Joseph Loftus, "House GOP Unit Backs Bill Raising Social Security Benefits," *New York Times,* August 17, 1967, p. 21.

69. Cohen to LBJ, August 24 and 28, 1967, Chron. Files, Box 93, Cohen Papers.

70. Betty James, "Welfare Rally Threatens Riots," *Washington Star,* August 29, 1967, p. 1, and Eve Edstrom, "Blistering Attacks on Welfare Curbs Fail to Sway Long," *Washington Post,* September 1, 1967, p. 4.

71. Joseph S. Loftus, "Training of Needy Broadened by U.S.," *New York Times,* August 30, 1967, p. 21.

72. Cohen to secretary, August 31, 1967, Box 93, Cohen Papers.

73. "Notes on Wilbur J. Cohen Trip to Bolivia and Peru, September 2–14, 1967," n.d., Cohen Papers.

74. James F. Clarity, "Lindsay Tells Senators of Peril in Limits on Welfare Assistance," *New York Times,* September 13, 1967, p. 31.

75. Barry Kalb, "Angry Welfare Group Holds Hill Sit-In," *Washington Star,* September 3, 1967, p. 3, and Eve Edstrom, "Irate Welfare Mothers Hold Wait-In," *Washington Post,* September 20, 1967, p. 1.

76. Tom Wicker, "Still No Room at the Inn," *New York Times,* September 24, 1967, E13.

77. "Miss Switzer Is Honored," *Washington Star,* September 20, 1967, C10.

78. Vera Glaser, "Welfare Head Agrees–Nation's Programs *Are* a Disgrace!" *Des Moines Register,* October 11, 1967; Ruth Dean, "Welfare Head Finds Reality in Own Back Yard," *Washington Star,* September 24, 1967, E9; Jo Ann Levine, "Rehabilitation Is Her Specialty," *Christian Science Monitor,* September 18, 1967. On Mary Switzer's career, see Martha Lentz Walker, *Beyond Bureaucracy: Mary Elizabeth Switzer and Rehabilitation* (Lanham, Md.: University Press of America, 1985).

79. Elizabeth Wickenden to Wilbur Cohen, August 21, 1967, and Charles I. Schottland to Cohen, September 19, 1967, Box 137, Cohen Papers.

80. Cohen to Wicky, October 25, 1967, Chron. File, Box 94, Cohen Papers.

81. Cohen to the president, October 17, 1967, Box 94, Cohen Papers.

82. In fact, as Hartke might have known, Social Security taxes had been used for fiscal purposes in 1965. Cohen to Califano, October 26 and 30, 1967, and Cohen to LBJ, November 3, 1967, Box 94, Cohen Papers.

83. Cohen to LBJ, November 3, 1967, Box 94, Cohen Papers.

84. Cohen to Califano, November 4, 1967, Box 94, Cohen Papers.

85. John D. Morris, "Senate Panel Is Expected to Cut 6.1 Billion Dollar Rise in Old Age Tax," *New York Times,* November 8, 1967, p. 18.

86. Cohen to Wickenden, October 25, 1967, Box 94, Cohen Papers.

87. This editorial was clipped by the White House and put in its central files.

88. Cohen to Califano, December 8, 1967, Box 94, Cohen Papers.

89. William Chapman, "Welfare Curb Wouldn't Be Fought," *Washington Post,* December 10, 1967, p. 3.

90. Carol Honsa, "Welfare Chief Defends Controversial Changes," *Washington Post,* December 9, 1967, p. 7.

91. Helen Delich Bentley, "Meany Calls Benefit Bill a Bad One," *Baltimore Sun,* December 11, 1967, p. 1; Cohen to Mills, December 11, 1967, Box 94, Cohen Papers; Califano to the president, December 11, 1967, WHCF, Box 164, LBJ Library.

92. Cohen to the president, December 11, 1967, and Gardner to the president, December 11, 1967, Box 51, Califano Papers, LBJ Library.

93. Mike Manatos to the president, December 13, 1967, WHCF, Box 164, LBJ Library.

94. Material in WHCF, Box 164, LBJ Library.

CHAPTER TWELVE. SECRETARY COHEN

1. See, for example, Dick Kirschten, "Hospitals Told They May Come under Public Utility Law," *Chicago Sun Times,* August 20, 1967. This article and the others cited in this chapter come from the weekly press clippings that the Department of Health, Education, and Welfare compiled and distributed to its employees; I obtained a copy from the Wisconsin State Historical Society. Some of the clippings do not show page numbers.

2. See, for example, Connie V. Reed, "HEW Undersecretary Is Warmhearted Social Expert," *Flint Journal,* September 24, 1967, and "Cohen on Social Security," a letter from Cohen to the editor, *Washington Post,* September 1, 1967, p. 20.

3. "U.S. Officials Get Rockefeller Prizes," *New York Times,* November 13, 1967, p. 31.

4. Cohen, interview with Blanche Coll, Austin, Texas, October 19, 1985, Oral History Collection, LBJ Library.

5. Sid Johnson, interview with author, American Public Welfare Association, Washington, D.C., September 6, 1991.

6. Jonathan Spivak, "Gardner Plans to Reshape Agency to Stress Consumer Needs; Outcry by Lobbies Likely," *Wall Street Journal,* January 11, 1968, p. 30.

7. Cohen to Larry Levinson, December 26, 1967, Box 94, Cohen Papers.

8. Cohen to Califano, January 19, 1968, Box 95, Cohen Papers.

9. Nan Robertson, "Gardner Departs with No Fanfare," *New York Times,* March 2, 1968, p. 26.

10. Cohen, third interview with David McComb, Silver Spring, Maryland, May 10, 1969, Oral History Collection, tape 4, p. 35, LBJ Library.

11. Joseph Califano, *The Triumph and Tragedy of Lyndon Johnson* (New York: Simon and Schuster, 1991), does a good job in capturing the siege mentality in the White House at this time.

12. Cohen, interview with McComb, p. 35; Eve Edstrom, "Gardner Leaving HEW, Chief Aim Not Achieved," *Washington Post,* January 27, 1968, p. 2.

13. Flood had taken over from Congressman John Fogarty, who died in 1967. Statement of Daniel Flood, in *Departments of Labor, and Health, Education, and Welfare Appropriations for 1969, Hearings before a Subcommittee of the Committee on Appropriations, House of Representatives, Ninetieth Congress, Second Session, Part 2, Statement of the Secretary of Health, Education, and Welfare, Overview of 1969 Budget* (Washington, D.C.: Government Printing Office, 1968), p. 1 (hereafter cited as *1969 Appropriations*).

14. *Labor-Health, Education, and Welfare Appropriations for 1962, Hearings before the Subcommittee of the Committee on Appropriations, United States Senate, Eighty-Seventh Congress, First Session on HR 7035, Making Appropriations for the Department of Labor and Health Education and Welfare and Related Agencies, for the Fiscal Year Ending June 30, 1962, and for Other Purposes.* (Washington, D.C.: Government Printing Office, 1961).

15. *1969 Appropriations,* p. 15.

16. Ibid., p. 55.

17. Ibid., pp. 13, 194–195. For Cohen's view of vocational education in the 1930s, see chapter 2.

18. *1969 Appropriations,* p. 76.

19. Cohen to the president, March 9, 12, 14, and 18, 1968, Cohen to Wilbur Mills, March 14, 1968, Cohen to Mrs. Stewart Udall, March 18, 1968, Box 96, Cohen Papers.

20. L. F. Sandars, M.D., to Lyndon Johnson, February 28, 1968, and Macy to the president, March 8, 1968, Macy Files, LBJ Library; Cohen to Dr. Row, president, American Association of Physicians and Surgeons, March 19, 1968, and Cohen to Dr. Castleberry, March 22, 1968, Box 96, Cohen Papers.

21. Norman A. Stoll to John Macy, February 17, 1968, Macy Files, and telegram from Darwin Huxley to the president, February 16, 1968, WHCF, Name Files, LBJ Library.

22. Cohen, interview with McComb, tape 4, p. 36.

23. For press coverage of the Cohens after Wilbur's nomination, see William J. Easton, "LBJ Choice for HEW Post a Man of Practical Vision," *Chicago Daily News,* March 23, 1968; "Cohen A Good Choice," *Milwaukee Journal,* March 23, 1968; Laurence C. Eklund, "Cohen Shaped Important Health, Welfare Laws," *Milwaukee Journal,* March 23, 1968; Marjorie Hunter, "Wilbur Cohen Picked for Gardner's Cabinet Post," *New York Times,* March 23, 1968, p. 1; Jack Miller, "New HEW Chief Knows Ropes Well," *Washington Star,* March 23, 1968, p. 2; "New HEW Boss Old Hand at Agency," *Washington Daily News,* March 23, 1968, p. 6; Jo Ann Levine, "New U.S. Welfare Secretary Helped Shape Office's Goals," *Christian Science Monitor,* March 25, 1968; "Another Presidential Problem," *Chicago's American,* March 26, 1968; Warren Hoge, "The Experts' Expert Is New Chief of HEW," *New York Post,* March 30, 1968;

"Social Welfare Expert," *New York Times,* March 25, 1968, p. 64; "Mountain Project Has Lady Ambassador," *Charleston Gazette,* April 19, 1968; Claudia Baskin, "Mrs. Cohen Pushes Project," *Washington Star,* March 28, 1968, D4; Dorothy McCardle, "HEW Gets Two for One with the Wilbur Cohens," *Washington Post,* March 28, 1968, B1.

24. See Martha Derthick, *Policymaking for Social Security* (Washington, D.C.: Brookings Institution, 1979), p. 26, and "The Salami Slicer," *Time,* April 5, 1968.

25. "Cohen Hits Riot Report 'White Racism' Stress," *Washington Star,* March 26, 1968, p. 2; Eve Edstrom, "Riot Panel's Report Criticized by Cohen," *Washington Post,* March 26, 1968, p. 1; Califano, *Triumph and Tragedy of Lyndon Johnson,* p. 260.

26. Carl T. Rowan, "Gratuitous Attack on Riot Report," *Washington Star,* March 29, 1968, p. 13.

27. Eve Edstrom, "Cohen Reverses Himself, Praises Riot Panel Report," *Washington Post,* April 3, 1968, p. 23, and "Riot Report Now Praised," *Baltimore Sun,* April 3, 1968, p. 7.

28. Ronald H. Spector, *After Tet: The Bloodiest Year in Vietnam* (New York: Free Press), pp. 21–22.

29. Cohen to "Humor in Uniform" editor, December 14, 1968, Cohen Papers; diary backup, March 31, 1968, File 11, Box 94, LBJ Library; Eloise Cohen, interview with author, Austin, Texas, December 8, 1990.

30. Allen Matusow, *The Unraveling of America* (New York: Harper and Row, 1984), p. 396, and Martin Luther King quoted in Califano, *Triumph and Tragedy of Lyndon Johnson,* p. 287.

31. Transcript, "Conference of the Secretary, DHEW, with Representatives of the Poor People's March," April 30, 1968, p. 6, Box 110, Cohen Papers (hereafter cited as Transcript).

32. Ibid., p. 9.

33. Ibid., p. 17.

34. Ibid., p. 20.

35. Ibid., pp. 73–76.

36. Stuart Auerbach, "HEW's Cohen Is Third in Cabinet to Endorse Humphrey," *Washington Post,* April 25, 1968, p. 2, and Ernest B. Furguson, "Cohen Backs Humphrey," *Baltimore Sun,* April 25, 1968, p. 4.

37. For Cohen on Robert Kennedy, see third interview with William W. Moss, Ann Arbor, July 20, 1972, Oral History Collection, p. 103, JFK Library.

38. "Senate Unit Approves Cohen as HEW Chief," *Washington Post,* May 4, 1968, C25, and "Senate Confirms Cohen for HEW," *Washington Post,* May 10, 1968, p. 25.

39. "LBJ Hails Cohen at Swearing In," *Washington Post,* May 17, 1968, p. 11; Cohen, interview with David McComb, March 2, 1969, Oral History Collections, p. 28, LBJ Library; Cohen to the president, May 3, 1968, WHCF, LBJ Library.

40. Pitzele to Cohen, February 19, 1977, Darwin Papers.

41. Cohen to LBJ, May 2, 1968, Box 96, Cohen Papers.

42. Austin C. Wehrwein, "Cohen Suggests Welfare Change," *Christian Science Monitor,* May 24, 1968.

43. See Cohen to the attorney general, May 14, 1968, Box 96, Cohen Papers.

44. Eve Edstrom, "U.S. Takeover of Relief Plans Studied," *Washington Post,* June 13, 1968, p. 39.

45. Jonathan Spivak, "HEW's Cohen and the Bag Lunchers," *Wall Street Journal,* May 24, 1968, p. 24.

46. Johnson, interview with author.

47. Willard Clopton, Jr., "Marchers Caution U.S. on Using Force," *Washington Post,* June 1, 1968, p. 1, and Tom Harney, "30,000 More Marchers?" *Washington Daily News,* June 1, 1968, p. 5.

48. Jonathan Spivak, "Cohen Maps Final Plans to Streamline His Agency's Massive Health Functions," *Wall Street Journal,* June 14, 1968, p. 4, and "U.S. Health Services Are Merged," *Washington Star,* June 16, 1968, p. 1.

49. Altmeyer to Cohen, August 17, 1968, Box 97, Cohen Papers, and Eve Edstrom, "Social Security Is 33 Yrs. Old," *Washington Post,* August 15, 1968, p. 3.

50. Henry Brandon, "Wilbur Cohen Talks About," *New York Times Magazine,* June 23, 1968.

51. Jonathan Spivak, "New Doctor in the Big Research House," *Wall Street Journal,* August 27, 1968, p. 12, and Harold M. Schmeck, Jr., "Health Institutes' Era of Expansion Ends as Leadership Changes," *New York Times,* September 1, 1968, p. 42.

52. Bruce E. Thorp, "Liberal Sociologists Picket Cohen's Talk," *Milwaukee Journal,* August 27, 1968, and Alan Lupo, "Sociologists Find Rebels in Ranks," *Boston Globe,* August 27, 1968.

53. Cohen to Paul Osterman, July 16, 1968, Box 97, Cohen Papers.

54. For a historical exposition of this point of view, see Matusow, *Unraveling of America,* p. 307.

55. Cohen to William Haber, April 29, 1968, Box 96, Cohen Papers.

56. Cohen to the president, September 12, 1968, Box 97, Cohen Papers.

57. Cohen to Dr. James A. Shannon, September 24, 1968, Box 97, Cohen Papers.

58. This section is based on the president's copy of "Off-the-Record Review," September 26, 1968, diary backup, container 111, LBJ Library. One colloquy in this briefing neatly captured Cohen's approach to legislation:

President: Is any part of Medicare going for nursing when I have to have a nurse around the clock?

Secretary Cohen: Not private duty, no. Medicare does not cover private duty.

President: We will go down the road ten years from now and add on a little extra for nursing care?

Secretary Cohen: Yes. I think about ten years from now.

President: If I want to have nurses around the clock for me, then I can pay an extra $20 a month to?

Secretary Cohen: I would say this: the kind of program I would envisage first is that the physician would have to approve that you need it and secondly, probably Medicare would pay half of the costs. So you would have some financial incentive not to just say, "I want a nurse around the clock."

President: Then you would add an extra amount to your contribution to Medicare.

Secretary Cohen: Yes.

President: Are we going to think about submitting something like that?

Secretary Cohen: Yes."

59. Cohen, interview with McComb, March 2, 1969, pp. 29–39, and "Nixon Attacked by Wilbur Cohen on Aid to Elderly," *Washington Star,* October 23, 1968, p. 6.

60. Richard Phalon, "Cost for Welfare Now Top City Bill," *New York Times,* November 1, 1968, p. 1, and Peter Kihss, "City Relief Rolls Pass 900,000 Mark," *New York Times,* October 17, 1968, p. 1.

61. Cohen to Truman, November 6, 1968, Box 98, Cohen Papers.

62. "Cohen Hails HEW Record, Asks Successor to Match It," *Washington Post,* November 9, 1968, p. 4.

63. Marjorie Hunter, "Cohen Holding Cabinet Job till Last Minute," *New York Times,* November 15, 1968, p. 33.

64. Alan Barth, "Wilbur Cohen–Leaving HEW but Not Its Interests," *Washington Post,* January 6, 1969, p. 18.

65. Cohen to Harry McPherson, Jr., December 12, 1968; Cohen to Joseph Califano, December 8, 1968; Cohen to the president, December 9, 1968; Cohen to the president, December 10, 1968, Box 98, Cohen Papers.

66. Cohen to the president, December 17, 1968, Box 98, Cohen Papers.

67. "Cohen Retains Medicare Health Premium at $8," *Washington Star,* January 1, 1969, p. 2.

68. Cohen to the president, December 18, 1968, Cohen to editor, *Wall Street Journal,* December 30, 1968, Cohen to Wicky, January 13, 1969, Cohen to the president, January 16, 1969, Cohen to Dean Coston, January 19, 1969, Cohen to Sid Johnson, January 19, 1969, Cohen to Darwin Huxley, January 20, 1969, Cohen to Aaron Cohen, January 20, 1969, Cohen to Arthur Altmeyer, January 20, 1969, Box 98, Cohen Papers.

69. Cohen to Christopher Cohen, Cohen to Bruce Cohen, Cohen to Eloise Cohen, Cohen to Stuart Cohen, January 20, 1969, Box 98, Cohen Papers.

70. Cohen to the president, January 7, 1969, Box 98, Cohen Papers.

71. Cohen to Morris Abram, January 14, 1969, Box 98, Cohen Papers.

72. Cohen to the president, January 8, 1969, Box 98, Cohen Papers.

CHAPTER THIRTEEN. AFTERMATH

1. Statement by Wilbur J. Cohen to the Board of Regents, May 2, 1969, Box 18, Michigan Papers.

2. Cohen to Mr. and Mrs. Harold Howe, October 31, 1969, Box 15, Michigan Papers.

3. Ibid., and Cohen to J. Douglas Brown, November 13, 1969, Box 240, Cohen Papers.

4. Cohen to Mr. and Mrs. Harold Howe, October 31, 1969, Box 15, Michigan Papers.

5. Cohen to Richard Graham, director of the Teacher Corps, August 21, 1969, Box 15, Michigan Papers; Cohen to Alan Pifer, August 22, 1969, Box 239, Cohen Papers; Cohen to Mr. David Hunter, Stern Family Fund, September 3, 1969, Box 239, Cohen Papers.

6. Cohen, "The State of the School Message, 1970," September 8, 1970, Box 241, Cohen Papers, and John Gardner, *The Recovery of Confidence* (New York: Norton, 1970).

7. Cohen to Robert H. Finch, June 3, 1969, Box 239, Cohen Papers.

8. Cohen to Ribicoff, June 10, 1969, Box 231, Cohen Papers; Cohen to Theodore C. Sorensen, June 9, 1969, Cohen to John Brademas, June 19, 1969, and Cohen to John Gardner, July 1, 1969, Box 240, Cohen Papers.

9. Cohen to Lyndon Johnson, June 25, 1969, Box 217, Cohen Papers.

10. Telegram, Moynihan to Cohen, August 4, 1969, Box 223, Cohen Papers. On FAP, see Edward Berkowitz, *America's Welfare State* (Baltimore: Johns Hopkins Press, 1991), pp. 120–133. Other good overviews of welfare reform in this period include Laurence E. Lynn and David Whitman, *The President as Policymaker: Jimmy Carter and Welfare Reform* (Philadelphia: Temple University Press, 1981); Vincent J. Burke and Vee Burke, *Nixon's Good Deed: The Politics of a Guaranteed Annual Income* (New York: Columbia University Press, 1974); Daniel Patrick Moynihan, *The Politics of a Guaranteed Annual Income: The Nixon Administration and the Family Assistance Plan* (New York: Vintage Books, 1973); Lester M. Salamon, *Welfare: The Elusive Consensus* (New York: Praeger Press, 1978).

11. Cohen to Mills, October 10, 1969, Box 223, Cohen Papers.

12. Moynihan to Cohen, August 10, 1970, and Cohen to Moynihan, August 27, 1970, Box 223, Cohen Papers; Cohen to Moynihan, September 16, 1970, Box 241, Cohen Papers.

13. Mrs. Sheppie Abramowitz (coordinator of Research, Senator Muskie's L Street Office) to Cohen, November 25, 1970, and Cohen to Senator Ribicoff, December 18, 1970, Box 223, Cohen Papers.

14. Cohen to Wilbur Mills, February 11, 1971, Box 223, Cohen Papers.

15. Alice M. Hoffman and Howard S. Hoffman, eds., *The Cruikshank Chronicles* (Hamden, Conn.: Archon Books, 1989), pp. 1–3, and Cohen to Bert Seidman, August 20, 1969, Box 239, Cohen Papers. On the health insurance muddle of the 1970s, see Rashi Fein, *The Search for a Health Insurance Policy* (Cambridge: Harvard University Press, 1986); Paul Starr, *The Social Transformation of American Medicine* (New York: Basic Books, 1982); Daniel Fox, *Health Policies, Health Politics* (Princeton, N.J.: Princeton University Press, 1987).

16. Autobiographical fragment, April 2, 1971, Box 279, Cohen Papers.

17. Cruikshank to Cohen, September 21, 1973, Box 207, Cohen Papers.

18. Cohen to Ribicoff, September 25, 1973, Box 231, Cohen Papers.

19. Cohen to Ball, June 25, 1969, Box 239, Cohen Papers; Altmeyer to Cohen, July 1, 1969, Altmeyer Papers, Wisconsin State Historical Society, Madison; Robert J. Myers, with Richard L. Vernaci, *Within the System: My Half Century in Social Security* (Winsted, Conn.: Actex Publications, 1992), pp. 160–182, letter from Cohen to Myers, p. 166.

20. Cohen to Sen. Edmund Muskie, May 25, 1970, and Cohen to John Gardner, June 12, 1970, Box 240, Cohen Papers.

21. Mills to Cohen, March 8, 1972, and Cohen to Mills, March 13, 1972, Box 223, Cohen Papers.

22. Muskie to Cohen, May 17, 1972, Box 223, Cohen Papers.

23. Cohen to Ribicoff, July 19, 1972, and Cohen to Muskie, July 31, 1972, Box 242, Cohen Papers.

24. Discussions on McGovern presidential campaign, fragment, 1972, Box 478, Cohen Papers, LBJ Library, and Cohen to William Gorham, August 31, 1972, Box 15, Michigan Papers.

25. Cohen to Douglas Brown, August 31, 1972, Box 202, Cohen Papers.

26. Ibid.

27. Brown to Cohen, September 11, 1972, Box 202, Cohen Papers.

28. Cohen to Brown, March 26, 1974, Box 243, Cohen Papers.

29. Cohen to William Haber, August 17, 1972, Box 214, Cohen Papers.

30. Wilbur J. Cohen and Milton Friedman, *Social Security: Universal or Selective* (Washington, D.C.: American Enterprise Institute, 1972), p. 26.

31. Cohen to Robert Ball, December 1, 1970, Box 201, Cohen Papers, and Cohen and Friedman, *Social Security*, p. 2.

32. Cohen and Friedman, *Social Security*, pp. 54, 69.

33. Ball to Cohen, June 1, 1972, Box 201, Cohen Papers, and Altmeyer to Cohen, May 5, 1972, Box 6, Cohen Papers.

34. Cohen to Ball, January 22, 1973, Box 243, Cohen Papers.

35. Telegram from Cohen to Ball, January 31, 1973, Box 243, Cohen Papers, and Ball to Cohen, April 16, 1973, Box 201, Cohen Papers.

36. Daniel Moynihan, the House liberal, was in India, a favored outpost for government officials out of favor. See Cohen to Patrick Moynihan, July 25, 1973, Box 223, Cohen Papers.

37. See, for example, the 1973 proposal by Sen. Lawton Chiles for the Government in the Sunshine Act, Senate bill 260, explained in Ribicoff and Lawton Chiles to Cohen, July 10, 1973, Box 223, Cohen Papers.

38. Mills to Cohen, October 4, 1973, Box 223, Cohen Papers.

39. Cohen to Mills, January 13, 1975, and Cohen to Mills, April 1, 1975, Box 244, Cohen Papers.

40. Cohen to Mills, March 23, 1976, Box 245, Cohen Papers.

41. John P. Young, executive vice-president, Richard D. Irwin Inc., to Haber and Cohen, January 5, 1973, Box 214, Cohen Papers.

42. Cohen to Douglas Brown, January 21, 1974, Box 202, Cohen Papers.

43. Cohen to Ball, Cruikshank, and Bert Seidman, September 19, 1974, Box 244, Cohen Papers, and Robert Ball to Wilbur Cohen, October 9, 1974, Box 201, Cohen Papers. It should be pointed out that Robert Ball later started a somewhat similar organization, the National Academy of Social Insurance; it still exists.

44. Cohen to Abraham Ribicoff, March 27, 1974, Box 243, Cohen Papers.

45. Cohen to John Gardner, August 7, 1974, Box 243, Cohen Papers.

46. Cohen to Mills, November 12, 1974, Box 244, Cohen Papers, and Cohen to Wilbur D. Mills, March 9, 1974, Box 243, Cohen Papers.

47. Cohen to Abe Ribicoff, January 6, 1975, Box 244, Cohen Papers.

48. Haber to Cohen, June 25, 1978, Box 214, Cohen Papers.

49. Cohen to C. Harding Mott, September 5, 1975, Box 244, Cohen Papers.

50. Cohen to Robert Ball, Lucy Benson, Joseph Duffey, Rashi Fein, and Harry McPherson, January 8, 1976, Box 245, Cohen Papers.

51. Wilbur J. Cohen, "A Democratic Party Approach to Improving the Health, Education, and Welfare of All the American People," January 8, 1976, Box 266, Cohen Papers.

52. Cohen to Joseph Califano, July 20, 1976, Box 245, Cohen Papers.

53. Cohen to William Gorham, June 30, 1976, Box 15, Michigan Papers, and Cohen to John Gardner, July 28, 1976, Box 245, Cohen Papers.

54. Carter to Joseph Califano, August 19, 1976, Box 245, Cohen Papers.

55. Robert Ball to Wilbur Cohen, December 6, 1976, Box 201, Cohen Papers.

56. Telegram from Cohen to Califano, December 22, 1976, Box 204, Cohen Papers.

57. Mailgram, Cohen to Califano, January 25, 1977, Box 204, Cohen Papers.

58. Wilbur J. Cohen, "Fathers and Sons," remarks delivered on February 3, 1977 in Milwaukee, Darwin Papers.

59. Cohen to Mrs. Zena Harman, March 31, 1977, Box 246, Cohen Papers.

60. Cohen to Califano, February 21, 1977, February 24, 1977, and February 23, 1977, Box 204, Cohen Papers; Cohen to Daniel Patrick Moynihan, March 25, 1977, Box 223, Cohen Papers; Cohen to Hale Champion, March 30, 1977, Box 246, Cohen Papers.

61. Cohen to J. Douglas Brown, March 15, 1977, Cohen to Califano, March 17, 1977, and Cohen to Ribicoff, March 18, 1977, Box 246, Cohen Papers; Joseph A. Califano, Jr., *Governing America* (New York: Simon and Schuster, 1981), pp. 373–376.

62. Cohen to J. Douglas Brown, April 18, 1977, Box 246, Cohen Papers.

63. Wilbur J. Cohen, "Restoring the Financial Integrity of the Social Security System," testimony delivered on June 16, 1977, before the Senate Committee on Finance, Subcommittee on Social Security, Box 18, Michigan Papers; Cohen to Eileen Shanahan, April 29, 1977, Box 246, Cohen Papers; Califano to Cohen, June 27, 1977, Box 204, Cohen Papers.

64. Morton Gordon, "Notes on the Retirement of Dean Wilbur J. Cohen," October 15, 1977, Box 18, Michigan Papers.

65. Cohen to Califano, October 18, 1977, Box 204, Cohen Papers, and Chris Cohen, interview with author, Glencoe, Illinois, October 20, 1990.

66. Cohen to Califano, October 18, 1977, Box 204, Cohen Papers; Ribicoff to Cohen, February 21, 1978, Box 231, Cohen Papers; Cohen to Califano, January 19, 1978, Box 204, Cohen Papers.

67. "National Commission on Unemployment Compensation," Box 279, Cohen Papers.

68. Cohen to Califano, May 28, 1978, Box 18, Michigan Papers; Cohen, "The White House Conference on Families," Box 279, Cohen Papers; Gilbert Steiner, *The Futility of Family Policy* (Washington, D.C.: Brookings Institution, 1981).

69. Cohen to Ball, February 10, 1978, and Ball to Cohen, March 6, 1978, Box 201, Cohen Papers.

70. Cohen to Bert Seidman, Nelson Cruikshank, Robert Ball, and Elizabeth Wickenden, August 21, 1978, Box 247, Cohen Papers.

71. I base this account on Wilbur J. Cohen, "Some Notes on Social Security Proposals in 1978–1979," Carter Files, Box 204, Cohen Papers, and on Califano, *Governing America,* pp. 386–397.

72. Ball, Cohen, and Cruikshank to the president, December 19, 1978, Box 204, Cohen Papers.

73. Califano, *Governing America,* p. 387.

74. I have written about these amendments at length in *Disabled Policy* (New York: Cambridge University Press, 1987).

75. Cohen to J. J. Pickle, August 22, 1979, Box 230, Cohen Papers.

76. For a good overview of the issues that Social Security faced in the 1970s, see W. Andrew Achenbaum, *Social Security: Visions and Revisions* (New York: Cambridge University Press, 1986), pp. 61–80.

77. For a good, quick introduction to the resurgence of conservatism in American politics in the 1970s and 1980s, see William C. Berman, *America's Right Turn: From Nixon to Bush* (Baltimore: Johns Hopkins University Press, 1994).

78. Autobiographical fragment, Box 279, Cohen Papers.

79. Cohen to Bruce, Rosie, Brian, and Duncan [Cohen], July 10, 1980 (courtesy Bruce Cohen).

80. Paul Light, *Artful Work* (New York: Random House, 1985).

81. Wilbur J. Cohen, "On Becoming 70," autobiographical fragment, Box 278, Cohen Papers.

82. Robert Pear, "Social Security Marking Golden Anniversary," *New York Times,* August 14, 1985, p. 1; I am grateful to Blanche Coll for sharing her file on the fiftieth anniversary of the Social Security Act with me. I have written on these events in the introduction to *Social Security After Fifty* (Westport, Conn.: Greenwood Press, 1987).

83. Circular letter from Eloise Cohen to friends, December 1987, privately obtained.

84. Wolfgang Saxon, "Wilbur Cohen, Leading Architect of Social Legislation, Dies at 73," *New York Times,* May 19, 1987, D30.

85. "Wilbur Cohen's Frontiers, *New York Times,* May 20, 1987, A30.

86. *Congressional Record, House,* May 18, 1987, p. H3633.

87. I am grateful to Darwin Huxley for providing me with a copy of this inscription.

INDEX